CRITICAL ENCOUNTERS

WITH TEXTS

Finding a Place to Stand

SECOND EDITION

Margaret Himley • Anne Fitzsimmons

The Writing Program, Syracuse University

PEARSON

Custom Publishing

Printed in the United States of America

10 9 8 7 6 5 4 3

ISBN 0-536-95428-3

2005240229

KK/KS

Please visit our web site at *www.pearsoncustom.com*

PEARSON CUSTOM PUBLISHING
75 Arlington Street, Suite 300, Boston, MA 02116
A Pearson Education Company

Copyright Acknowledgments

Contents

Finding a Place to Stand

Margaret Himley & Anne Fitzsimmons

April 2005

Entangled with History

> " . . . *never before have individual histories (because of their necessary relations with space, image and consumption) been so deeply entangled with general history"* (Augé 119).

O n August 23, 2003 in Syracuse, NY, Margaret opens up the morning paper, called *The Post-Standard*, and reads the headlines on the front page. "EPA Forced to Call 9/11 Air Safe" is the top story, claiming that the White House directed the Environmental Protection Agency to give New Yorkers "misleading assurances" that the debris-laden air from the collapse of the World Trade Center posed no health risks. She has friends in New York City and worries about what this might mean and what else might have been covered up, if this report turns out to be true.

A story entitled "Israel vows to hunt militants" reports on Israel's promise to kill militant leaders unless the Palestinian authorities rein in these armed groups, as tens of thousands of Hamas supporters mourn the death of one of their leaders.

And she also skims the lead story on the opening of the NY State Fair. The picture of a young woman on the Ultimate Drop ride on the midway is in startling contrast to the stories of death and mourning.

She glances at the news briefs and sees that the Alabama chief justice who has refused to remove his Ten Commandments memorial from the court house has been suspended by a federal court—a story she has been watching casually over the last few weeks, as she's interested in when and how and why church-state relations become 'news.'

She stops to read with care and interest "Liberia's Women Warriors" (A-5) and learns about Black Diamond, 22, a Liberian rebel commander: "Whether blasting mortars at enemy troops or slapping down armed looters, she and her all-female Women's Artillery Commandos fight for revenge, they say, against wrongs by Liberia's brutal government forces" (A-5). Margaret is intrigued, because she's interested in the idea of 'women soldiers' and would like to know more about the role of women and their much-touted "ferocity" in the 14 years of conflict while Charles Taylor was President.

The editorials juxtapose liberal Maureen Dowd's argument that the Bush team has now created the "monster in Iraq" that served as justification for the war, while conservative Jim Hoaglund describes how the "seamy world of international corruption, failing governments and boundless greed" fuels the business of war (A-6).

The business section talks about lawsuits and mergers and new software, while the sports section reports on the U.S. Open, the local soccer team, and the lawsuit by Patrick Dennehy's father against Baylor University. The life and leisure section talks about all the popular golf spots around Central New York (which she doesn't really care about) and her horoscope assures her that "acceptance" will be the key to getting along with others today. She reads *Doonesbury* and *Mallard Fillmore* and *The Boondocks* on the comics page—and chuckles over their takes on the war in Iraq, political correctness, and the governor recall in California.

This is the beginning of a typical reading day. Margaret will follow up on some of these topics by searching online for more information about the women commandos in Liberia, and add Hoaglund's editorial to a folder of articles she's collecting on militarism. She knows she'll see pictures of the U.S. Open when she watches the evening news later that day. These are Margaret's particular efforts to stay aware of world events, to follow up on interests of her own, to gather up the information she needs to analyze events and reach decisions about what she might want to do in response, if anything.

Working with Texts

This is the *work* we all have to do with texts now, because we are living in a world that French sociologist Marc Augé has called the "supermodern" (29). We have nearly instant access to stories and images and events from around the globe, relayed by satellites or transmitted by digital technologies. We grow familiar with references to places and figures from Moscow to Peking, beamed daily into our living rooms, even if we don't really know all that much about them. We live within a density of present events with fewer and fewer traditional frameworks to hold them together. And, a bit unmoored, we ourselves are on the move—in transit, out of place—as students abroad, as tourists, as immigrants, as global nomads or citizens of the world. As a result, we spend more and more of our time in what Augé calls "non-places," or those temporary locations such as airports, malls, throughways, refugee camps, and college dormitories.

In this supermodern world, "The individual production of meaning is thus more necessary than ever" (Augé 37). But it's harder and harder to be a critical reader because there is so much to know and things happen so quickly. It becomes more and more difficult to gain the knowledge, perspective, and depth that we need to move beyond shallow stereotype and glitzy sound bite. At the beginning of the Iraq War in March 2003, for example, many of us in the U.S. didn't know much more about Iraq than phrases about Saddam Hussein being a madman and despot or a vague sense of wars between Iraq and Iran or an awareness that the country has rich oil deposits. If we were to become informed, we had to listen not only to CNN but also to NPR, to read editorials not only in the local paper but also in *The Independent* in Britain, and to study not only history books but also contemporary websites and blogs.

Writing with Purpose and Authority

The scene of writing has been transformed by these rapid shifts produced by globalization, technology, and communication. No longer alone in a garret, drafting with paper and pen, creating text out of her own knowledge or experience, the writer now faces a networked computer screen and has access to text-making possibilities and information-accessing potential undreamed of in the not very distant past. Search engines have dramatically expanded our ability to read, and we have fast, thorough, systematic access to what often seems like unlimited information on endless topics. We can raid a nearly infinite number and variety of texts as we construct our own (Sosnoski). It's remarkably easy to import an image of the Iraq War, or pull up the exact date of Michael Jordan's retirement from the Bulls, or locate a working definition of human cloning, or find out what editorials in Malaysia are saying about the US's role in the global economy.

It is also remarkably challenging to make sense of this superabundance of information, to determine the values and beliefs and investments that inform it, to assess the credibility of sites and sources, and most importantly to locate ourselves in this endlessly expanding network of information, or *Link/Age* (Tornow). As Augé notes in the epigraph, our lives are deeply entangled with others across the globe, because we have nearly instant access to news, because we watch international films, because so many of the goods we use in our daily life are produced in other countries, because we travel more and more, and because an economic problem in Malaysia is likely to affect the US economy (and vice versa).

Think about this: A relatively small, local event, like the discovery of mad cow disease in a herd in Washington state, has far reaching implications for US farmers and consumers, as well as farmers and consumers in Canada and Europe, and around the world, for that matter. In fact, one sick cow impacts global trade, consumer trends, dietary habits, veterinary practices, meat production and costs, and US federal agency policies. One sick cow can also complicate our views of the world, and make our daily decisions as well as our need for information more urgent: Should we continue to eat beef? Can we trust the government's assurances that our meat supply is safe? Why are cows fed the remains of other cows anyway? What is a *prion*? How is the disease transmitted? What kinds of measures are implemented to keep US imports and exports safe? How will a possible decline in the beef industry affect other industries? What is being done to monitor the effects of global trade—its benefits as well as its catastrophes?

How then can a writer identify a purpose, analyze audiences, and achieve power and authority? We argue in this book that writers succeed when they approach topics from multiple perspectives and recognize the complexity, history, and interconnectedness of information, ideas, and texts. Postcolonial writer Amitava Kumar illustrates what it means to put multiple perspectives into dialogue:

> *When Charles Barkley defends his aggressiveness against Angolan players at an Olympic game by saying, 'It's a ghetto thing, you won't understand,' he needs to be heard. At the same time, Barkley needs to understand too that there are ways of broaching historical links with the Angolans that would help explain what put him in the ghetto in the first place. Or, dammit, just help explain why the folks King Charles grew up with remain in the ghetto while he is a star selling his powerful body and a brand of cologne on TV (145).*

From one perspective, anyone not from a U.S. ghetto may not understand Barkley's aggressiveness against the Angolan players, because people's particular experiences are irreducibly different. From another perspective, however, black U.S. ghettos have been produced by the same historical forces, such as slavery and colonization, that have shaped the African country of Angola. That's also true, and produces some common ground. But yet from third perspective, what requires explaining is why we in the U.S. reward athletes in the regal way that we do. This one statement from "King Charles" opens up larger, interconnected topics and perspectives and calls forth different experiences and histories.

Critical Encounters with Texts

Reading—reading widely, reading critically, reading passionately, reading for perspective and purpose, reading as a researcher, reading inventively—is fundamental to writing. In this book we frame this kind of reading as a *critical encounter*. We have borrowed this trope from feminist post-colonial theorist Sara Ahmed (6-9) in order to define reading as a meeting between yourself and other people, other perspectives, other histories, other geographies, even other visions of yourself.

Think about meeting someone new for the first time. We make quick judgments about who they are, where they are from, whether we will like them or not, based on their clothes, their age, their (apparent) ethnicity or sexuality, their way of speaking, their stance and gestures. Sometimes those judgments prove accurate, and sometimes they reveal to us how wrong we are, how limited our knowledge and perspective can be. Sometimes we feel attracted to this new person, eager to get to know them better; sometimes we feel threatened or indifferent. These initial responses have a history and a geography. Produced at a particular moment, they are framed by and within larger times and particular places.

Meeting a text for the first time is a similar encounter with the familiar and the unfamiliar, the known and the unknown, the certain and the uncertain. Sometimes we know exactly what a writer means. At other times, we may not understand a particular word, or we can't seem to get the argument, or we fail to recognize a reference, or we just can't discern the perspective of the author. We hit the limits of our knowledge or experience. We find ourselves a bit lost as we follow the links in a web page or hunt up sources referenced in a bibliography or try to map the history of an idea or claim.

What reading, researching, and writing practices do we deploy to take on purpose, power, and authority within this landscape?

What are the strategies for working with diverse, often challenging texts and using them in our own projects?

How do we understand not just what a text is *saying*, but what it is *doing* in particular contexts—and *why*?

This new and enlarged and ever-changing textual landscape requires a lot of work from us, but happily it also rewards us with expanded, more critical, more productive ways of thinking about the world and our place in it.

Three Reading Practices

[1] Close Reading

Sometimes we have to read *closely* in order to understand, perhaps even memorize the content, as when we are preparing for the CPA exam or mastering the intricacies of cell biology.

For example, the first essay in the reader is a chapter entitled "Recognising Strangers" from *Strange Encounters: Embodied Others in Post-Coloniality* by Sara Ahmed—and it's challenging. A close reading of the first paragraph will get you off to a strong start:

> *How do you recognise a stranger? To ask such a question, is to challenge the assumption that the stranger is the one we simply fail to recognise, that the stranger is simply any-body whom we do not know. It is to suggest that the stranger is some-body whom we have already recognised in the very moment in which they are 'seen' or 'faced' as a stranger. The figure of the stranger is far from simply being strange; it is a figure that is painfully familiar in that very strange/r/ness. The stranger has already come too close; the stranger is 'in my face.' The stranger then is not simply the one whom we have not yet encountered, but the one whom we have already encountered, or already faced. The stranger comes to be faced as a form of recognition: we recognise somebody as a stranger, rather than simply failing to recognise them.*

What a strange text, you might reasonably assert! Ahmed starts with a question that seems almost silly, because it challenges our commonsensical idea that the world is divided into people we know and people we do not know, or 'strangers.' And then she writes a number of variations on this question. She is developing a theoretical or conceptual argument around the key phrase 'strange encounters.' Here are some close reading strategies you might use to trace out this argument:

- <u>Look up key words in the dictionary</u>.

  For example, "recognize" (the U.S. spelling) means "1. To know to be something that has been perceived before: *recognize a face*. 2. To know or identify from past experience or knowledge: *recognize hostility*.

  That helps. If I 'recognize' you as a friend, or a stranger, or an enemy, or an ally, it is because I already know something about friends and strangers and enemies and allies, and I can put you in one of those categories. We recognize by dress, skin color, body posture that which is not of 'us'—but which is still known as 'strange.' So instead of hitting the limits of my knowledge in this encounter, I'm actually using the knowledge I already have.

- <u>Invent an example</u>.

  For example, I might hear a knock at my door, open the door, and worry because the person is a stranger. If I open the door and begin to worry, it might be because the person is not only unknown to me individually, but seems somehow out of place. A woman in an apron who could be a new neighbor is less likely to be recognized as a stranger, perhaps, than a woman poorly dressed and carrying lots of old grocery bags. One seems to belong; one seems to threaten, to be out place, to not belong. Why? Because I have a sense of who belongs in my neighborhood and who doesn't, based on class, maybe, or race, or nationality.

- <u>Look at words in italics or otherwise emphasized</u>.

  Ahmed marks a distinction between '*any-body*' and '*some-body*.' Ask yourself why she has hyphenated the two words? What does that accomplish? It takes two ordinary, everyday pronouns and alters their meaning by separating 'any' and 'some' from 'body.' Hmmm, 'body'—this kind of body versus that kind of body. 'Anybody' as undifferentiated—it could be 'anybody.' 'Somebody' becomes differentiated from all those anybodies.

  That seems important because it takes us back to the idea of recognizing, of seeing patterns or hierarchies in masses.

- <u>Analyze the structure of the paragraph</u>.

  In this case, Ahmed starts with a question and provides an answer in the last sentence.

- <u>Paraphrase</u>.

  Select a sentence or a phrase and try to put it in your own words. For example, "The stranger then is not simply the one whom we have not yet encountered, but the one whom we have already encountered, or already faced" might be paraphrased as "We only label someone a stranger if we already know who strangers are likely to be."

- Summary.

  Here's one way to summarize this paragraph: Ahmed takes a commonsense understanding of who becomes figured as 'the stranger' and asks questions about it in several ways. In this way she comes to argue that 'strangers' are people we already have a category system for placing them in. The figure of the stranger does not take us to the end of our knowledge, but rather makes visible how our knowledge works.

[2] Critical Reading

Sometimes we have to read critically in order to evaluate a methodology or argument, as when we are analyzing the effects of a national tax cut on the poor or arguing for or against Spike Lee as a talented filmmaker.

For example, in a journalistic essay called "The Thin Red Line," Jennifer Egan begins with a story about Jill McArdle, who lives on Chicago's South Side and who as a teenager habitually cut herself to ease her anxiety and emotional distress. Egan then goes on to report that this kind of "moderate self-mutilation" is on the rise and offers a range of analyses as to why and what it means. Here are some critical reading strategies you might use to trace out and evaluate the claims:

- Map out the essay:

  Notice that the essay in divided into sections (with a space separating each section). The essay opens in section one with Egan telling the story of Jill McArdle, from the initial cutting and then burning to a suicide attempt. The second section defines the key clinical or psychological term—self-mutilation—and quotes from experts. The third section returns to Jill and narrates the night she attempted suicide, and then cites figures and offers a few explanations for this behavior (e.g., physical pain to obscure intolerable psychic pain, the addictive quality of cutting, the gendered aspects). And so on . . . .

- Ask questions:

  Mark places in the essay that raise questions for you—for example, is cutting similar or not to tattooing and piercing, and is it one more form of body control or transformation? Why are most cutters white? Why does cutting start at around the age of 14?

- Raise challenges:

  Mark places in the essay that you think are or might be wrong. Are the surveys large enough or recent enough to be useful? Are there other explanations for this behavior that Egan doesn't offer or address? Does Egan rely too heavily on narratives?

- Draw examples or counter-examples:

  Think back to people you know who cut—and test the theories and claims in Egan's essay against your own experiences and knowledges.

- Talk with others:

  Ask your roommate or your friends or your parents or your classmates what they think about cutting. Tell them about Egan's essay and listen to their responses. Figure out what that teaches you.

- Reread the essay:

  Come back to the essay with greater awareness, more knowledge, fuller context, and some questions and ideas of your own.

- Take a stand:

  Imagine that you have been asked to write a review of this essay: How would you summarize it? How would you assess it? What is strong? What is weak or missing? What is your final evaluation of the essay and its argument?

[3] Inventive Reading

And sometimes you have to read *inventively*, looking for the larger frameworks or debates or conversations that a text is embedded in and responding to. An article in the newspaper about the call for a constitutional amendment against 'gay marriage,' for example, raises lots of larger questions—why now? on what basis? for whose benefit? against what counter-arguments? Maybe it would be useful to look historically at how our contemporary definition of marriage emerged, or to look at the legal documents establishing civil unions in Vermont, or to look at LGBT sources for their analysis.

Here's another example. The first chapter from Marjane Satrapi's graphic autobiography *Persepolis: The Story of a Childhood* is called "The Veil." Satrapi is writing about growing up in Iran, and she starts with an account of the veil in Iranian culture. How does a U.S. reader approach this topic? Don't let the cartoon style fool you into thinking this is going to be easy. Here are some inventive reading strategies you might use to understand an idea or reference or history that you know little about:

- Inventory:

  Jot down quickly all that you know about the veil in Islamic culture—from watching the news, seeing images, people you have talked with. This is your starting point—what you know, what you don't know, why you have a particular way of knowing and not knowing.

- A Quick Research Search:

  Go to a search engine or another source of information, and type in *veil* and read around in the first couple of websites that turn up.

- Close Reading:

  Since this is a short chapter, read and reread it several times. Write out the questions it poses for you, such as, Do women still wear the veil? Is it always a sign of oppression? What is the Western view? What do Islamic women themselves say? What does the veil symbolize to various groups of people? Why?

- Authorial Purpose:
  Based on this close reading and perhaps discussion with others, explain as best you can (and you can't ever fully know this) what you think Satrapi is trying to accomplish by writing her life as a cartoon and by starting with the veil.

- Intended Audience(s):
  Based on the text itself, who do you think is her intended audiences? Westerners? Why? What assumptions of Westerners might she be trying to unsettle or challenge or confirm? What in the text suggests that to you?

- Develop a project:
  Decide what you'd like to know about and how you are going to find information so that you can write a 'good enough' essay on this graphic autobiography and on this topic.

- Draft:
  Begin to put your ideas into words or, in this case, drawings.

In sum, even though the three reading practices—*close, critical, inventive*—may appear discrete, they actually overlap, and all are what writing teachers call *recursive*. Readers often read closely, critically, and inventively at the same time. That is, they note details, as they assess rhetorical effect. They evaluate writers and their arguments, as they make connections to the larger issues. They move ahead in the text, drawing their own conclusions, and then circle back to see how a second, third or fourth reading might affect that conclusion.

Reading recursively does not necessarily happen automatically, though; it requires practice, training, and sometimes even permission. If you have been asked to read closely and mostly for content through most your schooling, then it will take guidance and reinforcement for you to attempt different kinds of critical encounters with texts.

Reading, Researching, and Writing Projects

As readers and writers we need to take the long view of our work. What kinds of reading and writing do we like to do? What kinds of interests or values or topics often turn up? What questions compel us? What points do we want to make? Whom are we trying to persuade? Composition theorist Joseph Harris calls these our "projects" (588).

Let's say you want to understand better the phenomenon of body piercing. You have watched your friends get pierced and wondered for a while if you wanted to do it and wondered why it has become so popular for some people. Who gets pierced, and why? Is it safe? What are the health questions? How will it affect job opportunities? Is there a history of piercing here and in other cultures? What will your family say? You hypothesize that it is a form of rebellion.

First you talk with your roommate who has 19 piercings, and learn about the different sites on the body and the different kinds of piercings she has done—and why. You learn, too, how much they cost, if they hurt, what style she prefers, and where near campus she gets them done.

Then you decide to check out some websites, so you start with Google.com and type in body piercings:

Images | Groups | Directory | News

Searched the web for **body piercings**.
Results **1–10** of about **140,000**. Search took **0.07** seconds.
Tip: In most browsers you can just hit the return key instead of clicking on the search button.

body jewelry, belly button rings, tongue rings, piercing ...
... rings. ENTER HERE **body piercings** jewelry, belly button rings, tongue rings, ENTER HERE ... possible! contact@**body-piercings**-jewelry.com. Web Links.
Description: Includes a selection of belly and tongue rings, straight and curved barbells, captive bead rings,...
Category: Shopping > Jewelry > Body > Piercing
www.body-piercings-jewelry.com/—4k—Cached—Similar pages

BME: **Body** Modification Ezine—The biggest and best online bod- ...
... of the shadows: Yakuza Aug 18: IN: Family makes life out of tattoos, **piercings** Aug 18 ... BME GLOSSARY: Blair: well known **body** artist (scarification, piercing, etc). ...
Description: Comprehensive resource on **body** piercing, tattoos, scarification, subincision, castration, **body** art,...
Category: Arts > Bodyart > Magazines and E-zines
www.bmezine.com/ - 16k—Aug 22, 2003—Cached—Similar pages

BME: **Body** Piercing Pictures and Experiences
... and personal experiences about **body** piercing of every imaginable kind. Please understand
that while there are a lot of very well done **piercings** here, and a lot ...
www.bmezine.com/pierce/bme-pirc.html—10k—Cached—Similar pages
[More results from www.bmezine.com]

Tattoos, Piercing and **Body** Art Homepage
... be sure to check out all the site has to offer! Tattoos/**Body Piercings**.
with Karen Hudson Your Guide to one of hundreds of sites. ...
tattoo.about.com/mbody.htm—33k—Aug 22, 2003—Cached—Similar pages

Bodyart/piercing FAQ Index
... bodyart/piercing-faq/jewelry/partD Subject: rec.arts.bodyart: Piercing FAQ 2D—**Body Piercings** & Their Suggested Jewelry Maintainer: Anne Greenblatt Category: Mature Content
www.faqs.org/faqs/bodyart/piercing-faq/—24k—Aug 22, 2003—Cached—Similar pages

National Geographic Photo Gallery: Tattoos, **Body Piercings**
See **body** art via the National Geographic lens: Photographs by Chris Rainier
show tattoos, **piercings,** and scarification in cultures around the world. ...
Description: Bodyart via the National Geographic lens: Photographs by Chris Rainier show
tattoos, **piercings,** and...
Category: Arts > Bodyart > Image Galleries
www.nationalgeographic.com/tattoos/ - 8k—Aug 22, 2003—Cached—Similar pages

Body Piercings
... If we are to glorify God in our bodies, how do **body piercings** glorify Christ? ... One
note of warning to the church on this subject of **body piercings** . ...
Description: [Overcoming Life Digest]
Category: Arts > Bodyart > Piercing > Articles
www.bible.com/answers/apiercin.html—23k—Aug 22, 2003—Cached—Similar pages

Body Jewelry by TongueStud.com
How is your **body** jewelry threaded? ... At TongueStud.com, we have the largest catalog
of 100% Satisfaction Guaranteed **body** piercing jewelry in the world. ...
Description: Features stainless steel and titanium jewelry with a variety of adornments.
Also contains a selection...
Category: Shopping > Jewelry > Body > Piercing
tonguestud.com/ - 21k—Aug 22, 2003—Cached—Similar pages

Indiana Find : Indiana > Personal Care > Tatoos and **Body** ...
... Indiana Find : Indiana > Personal Care > Tatoos and **Body Piercings**. ...
www.indianafind.com/browse.php?cat=214—31k—Aug 22, 2003—Cached—Similar pages

www.dlc.fi/~frog/essay/papers/dresscode.txt
I have had many run-ins with my school administration about ear and
other **body piercings**. Because of my multiple **piercings** in my ...
6k—Cached—Similar pages

If you pursue some of these links, you'll find companies that sell everything from
straight piercings to labrets and plugs. You'll find a religious site that uses the Bible
to argue that piercing is abnormal and unnatural. You'll find a photo gallery from
National Geographic, portraying scarring on West African Men as a sign of bravery and piercings as part of the Modern Primitivism movement in the US and a sign
of beauty among the Mursi women in Ethiopia. You'll also find a site full of pictures and personal experience stories, with piercings and tattoos on all parts of
the body, including genitalia.

You start asking questions. Why is there such a diversity of belief or opinion?
What underlying assumptions about the body and culture and identity inform this
diversity? What are various histories of piercing? Is it becoming more and more
popular with US teens? Why? What does the act of piercing mean to your roommate? How are you reacting to these new ideas and perspectives? Why?

Composition theorist James Sosnoski claims that the kind of reading we've
just been doing is characterized by a high degree of selectivity and a lot of skim-

ming, working more with fragments of texts than whole essays or articles or books, imposing your own context and your own purposes on what you find (163).

Selective reading also leads to more deeply engaged close reading, as you make decisions about your interests and focus, as you think through the assignment or question that triggered your initial searches, as you develop purpose and perspective, and as you work within given time frames.

Because this topic has become significant to you, you may want to explore some scholarly perspectives, too (or perhaps you've decided that you're interested enough in the topic to make it the subject of your next writing assignment). You head for the library's databases, go into the Sociological Abstracts, type in "body piercing" as your keywords, and the following beginning of a list appears:

TI: **Body Piercing** and Discourse Analysis: Exploring the Articulation of Pain among Homeless 'Gutterpunks'
AU: Romanienko, Lisa
SO: Southern sociological society (SSS), 2003

TI: Rebels with a Cause: Group Identification as a Response to Perceived discrimination from the Mainstream
AU: Jetten, Jolanda; Branscomb, Nyla R; Schmitt, Michael T; Spears, Russell
SO: Personality and Social Psychology Bulletin, 2001, 27, 9, Sept, 1204-1213

TI: Marking the **Body**: Identity and Identification in Contemporary **Body** Modification
AU: Sweetman, Paul Jon
SO: Dissertation Abstracts International, C: Worldwide, 2000, 61, 3, fall, 691-C

TI: Tattooing and **Body Piercing**: **Body** Art Practices among College Students
AU: Greif, Judith; Hewitt, Walter; Armstrong, Myrna L
SO: Clinical Nursing Research, 1999, 8, 4, Nov, 368-385

TI: **Body** Modification: An Introduction
AU: Featherstone, Mike
SO: **Body** & Society, 1999, 5, 2-3, June-Sept, 1-13

TI: The Possibility of Primitiveness: Towards a Sociology of **Body** Marks in Cool Societies
AU: Turner, Bryan S
SO: **Body** & Society, 1999, 5, 2-3, June-Sept, 39-50

Even just the first six entries open up even more possibilities for you. You learn that sociologists, psychologists, cultural studies theorists, feminists, anthropologists, and clinical nurses are all interested in this topic from different disciplinary and political angles. You learn that body piercing may be considered art, a kind of rebellion, a form of identity and community, a strategy for dealing with pain, or debated as modern primitivism or cyber technology, or condemned as the self-mutilation of those in despised social groups. You learn that your library has some of these articles, and doesn't have others. You learn that some are abstracts only, others full-text. You learn other descriptors for further searches: youth, subculture, emotions, discourse analysis, body image, sociology of culture, self destructive behavior—and you experiment with some of these keywords.

The database entry for Bryan Turner's article "The Possibility of Primitiveness: Towards a Sociology of Body Marks in Cool Society" includes the following abstract:

> *It is argued that tattooing & body piercing in modern societies cannot be naively innocent acts; such activities cannot recapture primitiveness, because they take place in a social context where social membership is not expressed through hot loyalties & thick commitments. Body marks in primitive society were obligatory signatures of social membership in solidaristic groups, wherein life-cycle changes were necessarily marked by tattooing & scarification. Modern societies are metaphorically like airport departure lounges where passengers are encouraged to be cool & distant, orderly & regulated. Critiqued are recent attempts to discover & unearth Dionysian moments of creative tribalism in modern youth groups or working-class communities. Body marks are commercial objects in a leisure marketplace & have become optional aspects of a body aesthetic, which playfully & ironically indicate social membership. They cannot serve as charismatic entrance points to the primitive.*

And in reading the abstract you might find yourself intrigued (and annoyed) by Turner's argument that tattooing in modern societies (which he describes as airport departure lounges, or what Augé calls non-places) does not reclaim the 'primitive' at all. In fact, Turner says, modern tattooing has less to do with rites of passage or forming communities, and more to do with cultural notions of what is "cool." You locate the full text of the article, and decide that you would like to try to challenge the writer's claims, or at least to develop your own ideas about the significance of tattooing.

You might realize that engaging in such a project might benefit from some field research: visits to local tattoo parlors; observations of and interviews with people with tattoos in your community; visits to chat rooms devoted to body art. Suddenly, a topic that had seemed rather obvious to you, familiar and comfortable and safe, has taken on a scope you never imagined, and challenges you not only to read and investigate but to produce meaning—not pat answers (Tattooing among college students is a way to signal belonging...), not trite conclusions (Teenagers have always felt a need to rebel, and tattooing is the latest form their rebellion takes...), but provocative claims that invite others to deepen their own perceptions and appreciations of the topic.

Reading becomes researching becomes reading, and at different points in the process becomes writing, as you take notes, download material, reassemble ideas, collaborate with other thinkers, draft texts, and take your own stance on it all.

Working with this Book: Challenges and Curveballs

This book offers essays and poems and newspaper articles and visual essays as texts to encounter, as starting points for further reading and exploration. These are print texts that serve as jumping off points to further reading and researching.

Sometimes the readings are challenging because they are academic, and you will encounter disciplinary knowledges and discourses that you, perhaps as a class, will have to take some time to understand.

Sometimes the readings are challenging because they present unconventional perspectives or uncommon topics, which may unsettle your assumptions about the body, about language, about sexuality and gender, about representation. You may find yourself agreeing or disagreeing, and in both cases you'll learn more by looking at the assumptions that drive the argument and claims.

Sometimes the readings are challenging because, at first, they don't seem interesting to you. If you are not intersexed, for example, you might question why you would read Cheryl Chase's essay "Hermaphrodites with Attitude." We'll ask you to find points of entry by analyzing assumptions in the text: what does it say about being male or female? What does it claim about the role of doctors in our society, or the possibilities for medical-scientific intervention that might revolutionize the body? How might this topic relate to cosmetic surgery or designer babies?

Sometimes the readings are *curveballs*—texts that may make you think, get angry, fret, wonder, and, we hope, want to read further. You may need to do some background reading, you may need to pursue references in the bibliography, you may want to look at different perspectives in the library or online, you may want to interview someone on campus or test these ideas out on your housemates or friends, or you may want to do some research of your own by observing a site or constructing a classroom survey or asking your family about their history. Your teacher is likely to provide suggestions and insight and response to help you shape your project.

We encourage you to compare and contrast readings. Say you read bell hooks' essay called "Straightening our Hair," which starts from her account of hair pressing as an intimate ritual in black women's culture and moves into an analysis of 'hair' in terms of dominant, oppressive standards of beauty. You might find hook's argument useful background, as you read the two poems about black bodies by Lucille Clifton. Or you might compare bell hooks' account with Wendy Hesford's description of a family photograph—first prominently displayed on the fireplace mantel, later stored in a box in the basement—which relates her altered understanding of her own family's history to the economic and historical practices of colonialism. Or you might juxtapose all three readings and see what claims or new ideas you come up with.

We encourage you not to worry too much if you don't understand something or if the reference is outside of your experience in some way or you feel overwhelmed at times. That's all part of critical encounters and learning. One scholar, realizing she had neglected to include some important research in her first book, referred to her shame as "fruitful embarrassment" (Cohn and Enloe 1194). We agree. Think of as those moments of surprise ("I *never* thought of it that way before!") or suspicion ("I wonder where *that* fact came from!") or startling real-ization ("I never *knew* that!") as the chance to think twice about something, to learn from others, to reconsider a decision or claim or belief, even to re-examine ideas you have taken for granted all your life.

Of course it is risky to draw attention to what you don't know, especially in an academic environment where passing the test, getting it right, knowing the answer become the markers of success. But if we don't allow for questioning and inquiring, if the answers are always worth more than the questions, then we quickly limit the range of ideas we can work with.

Think about it: the more you read, the more you come in contact with views, language, experiences, and claims that transcend what you already know. Soon, the "embarrassment" of not knowing will be replaced by the confidence of having filled in gaps and understanding something in a new or more complex way. The willingness to address what you don't know can be a most generative and empowering trait.

We offer these readings (only) as starting places for active reading and critical encounters—as challenges to take up, as ideas and claims to make sense of, extend, critique, deepen, contextualize, historicize. We hope you will take the time to work with these readings as means for opening up ideas and debates and bodies of scholarship—and for deciding how you and your classmates will trace out your own critical encounters.

References

Ahmed, Sara. *Strange Encounters: Embodied Others in Post-Coloniality* (NY: Routledge, 2000).

Augé, Marc. *non-places: introduction to an anthropology of supermodernity.* Trans. By John Howe (London: Verso, 1995).

Cohn, Carol and Cynthia Enloe. "A Conversation with Cynthia Enloe: Feminists Look at Masculinity and the Men Who Wage War." *Signs: Journal of Women in Culture and Society*, Vol. 28, No. 4, 2003, 1187-1207.

Harris, Joseph. "Opinion: Revision as a Critical Practice." *College English*, Vol. 65, Number 6, July 2003, 577-592.

Kumar, Amitava. *Passport Photos.* (Berkeley: University of California Press, 2000).

Sosnoski, James. "Hyper-readers and their Reading Engines" in *Passions, Pedagogies, and 21st Century Technologies* edited by Gail E. Hawisher and Cynthia L. Selfe (Logan, Utah: Utah State University Press, 1999) (161-177).

Tornow, Joan. *Link/Age: Composing in the Online Classroom* (Logan, Utah: Utah State University Press, 1997).

1

Recognising Strangers

SARA AHMED

I turn around as you pass me. You are a stranger. I have not seen you before. No, perhaps I have. You are very familiar. You shuffle along the foot path, head down, a grey mac shimmering around your feet. You look dirty. There are scars and marks on your hands. You don't return my stare. I think I can smell you as you pass. I think I can hear you muttering. I know you already. And I hold myself together and breathe a sigh of relief as you turn the corner. I want you not to be in my face. I cast you aside with a triumph of one who knows this street. It is not the street where you live.

How do you recognise a stranger? To ask such a question, is to challenge the assumption that the stranger is the one we simply fail to recognise, that the stranger is simply *any-body* whom we do not know. It is to suggest that the stranger is *some-body* whom we have *already recognised* in the very moment in which they are 'seen' or 'faced' as a stranger. The figure of the stranger is far from simply being strange; it is a figure that is painfully familiar in that very strange(r)ness.[1] The stranger has already come too close; the stranger is 'in my face'. The stranger then is not simply the one whom we have not yet encountered, but the one whom we have already encountered, or already faced. The stranger comes to be faced as a form of recognition: we recognise somebody *as a stranger*, rather than simply failing to recognise them.

How does this recognition take place? How can we tell the difference between strangers and other others? In this chapter, I will argue that there are techniques that allow us to differentiate between those who are strangers and those who belong in a given space (such as neighbours or fellow inhabitants). Such techniques involve ways of reading the bodies of others we come to face. Strangers are not simply those who are not known in this dwelling, but those who are, in their very proximity, *already recognised as not belonging*, as being out of place. Such a recognition of those who are out of place allows both the demarcation and enforcement of the boundaries of 'this place', as where 'we' dwell. The enforcement of boundaries requires that some-body—here locatable in the dirty figure of the stranger—has already crossed the line, has already come too close: in Alfred Schutz's terms, the stranger is always approaching (1944: 499). The recognition of strangers is a means by which inhabitable or bounded spaces are produced ('this street'), not simply as the place or locality of residence, but as the very living form of a community.

In this chapter, I analyse how the discourse of stranger danger produces the stranger as a figure—a shape that appears to have linguistic and bodily integrity—which comes then to embody that which must be expelled from the purified space of the community, the purified life of the good citizen, and the purified body of 'the child'. Such an approach to 'the stranger' considers how encounters between others involve the production and over-representation of the stranger as a figure of the unknowable. That is, such encounters allow the stranger to appear, to take form, *by recuperating all that is unknowable into a figure that we imagine we might face here, now, in the street.*

On Recognition

To recognise means: to know again, to acknowledge and to admit. How do we know the stranger *again*? The recognisability of strangers is determinate in the social demarcation of spaces of belonging: the stranger is 'known again' as that which has already contaminated such spaces as a threat to both property and person: 'many residents are concerned about the strangers with whom they must share the public space, including wandering homeless people, aggressive beggars, muggers, anonymous black youths, and drug addicts' (Anderson 1990: 238). Recognising strangers is here embedded in a discourse of survival: it is a question of how to survive the proximity of strangers who are already figurable, *who have already taken shape*, in the everyday encounters we have with others.

A consideration of the production of the stranger's figure through modes of recognition requires that we begin with an analysis of the function of local encounters in public life. As Erving Goffman suggests, 'public life' refers to the realm of activity generated by face-to-face interactions that are organised by norms of co-mingling (1972: ix). Such an approach does not take for granted the realm of the public as a physical space that is already determined, but considers how 'the public' comes to be lived through local encounters, through the very gestures and habits of meeting up with others. How do such meetings, such face-to-face encounters, involve modes of recognition that produce the stranger as a figure?

Louis Althusser's thesis of subjectivity as determined through acts of misrecognition evokes the function of public life. Althusser writes:

> *ideology 'acts' or 'functions' in such a way that it 'recruits' subjects among the individuals (it recruits them all), or 'transforms' the individuals into subjects (it transforms them all) by that very precise operation which I have called* interpellation *or hailing, and which can be imagined along the lines of the most commonplace everyday police (or other) hailing: 'Hey, you there!'*
>
> *(1971: 162–163)*

All individuals are transformed into subjects through the ideological function of interpellation, which is imagined as a commonplace everyday police (or other) hailing. The recognition of the other as 'you there' is a misrecognition which produces the 'you' as a subject, and as subject to the very law implicated in recognition (the subject is suspect in such encounters). Althusser's thesis is clearly to be understood as a universal theory of how subjects come into being as such. However, we might note the following. First, the constitution of the subject through hailing implies that subjectivity is predicated upon an elided 'inter-subjectivity' (see Ahmed 1998a: 143). Second, the function of the act of hailing an-other, 'hey you', opens out the possibility *that subjects become differentiated at the very same moment that they are constituted as such*. If we think of the constitution of subjects as implicated in the uncertainties of public life, then we could imagine how such differentiation might work: the address of the policeman shifts according to whether individuals are already recognisable as, 'wandering homeless people, aggressive beggars, muggers, anonymous black youths, and drug addicts' (Anderson 1990: 238). Hailing as a form of recognition which constitutes the subject it recognises (= misrecognition) might function to differentiate *between* subjects, for example, by hailing differently those who seem to belong and those who might already be assigned a place—out of place—as 'suspect'.

Such an over-reading of Althusser's dramatisation of interpellation through commonplace hailing suggests that the subject is not simply constituted in the present as such. Rather, inter-subjective encounters in public life continually reinterpellate subjects into differentiated economies of names and signs, where they are assigned different value in social spaces. Noticeably, the use of the narrative of the police hailing associates the constitution of subjects with their subjection to a discourse of criminality, which defines the one who is hailed as a threat to property ('Hey, you there'). If we consider how hailing constitutes the subject, then we can also think about how hailing constitutes the stranger in a relationship precisely to the Law of the subject (the stranger is constituted as the unlawful entry into the nation space, the stranger hence allows Law to mark out its terrain). To this extent, the act of hailing or recognising some-body as a stranger serves to constitute the lawful subject, the one who has the right to dwell, and the stranger at the very same time. It is not that the 'you' is or can be simply a stranger, but that to address some-body as a stranger constitutes the 'you' as the stranger in relation to the one who dwells (the friend and neighbour). In this sense, the (mis)recognition of strangers serves to differentiate between the familiar and the strange, a differentiation that allows the figure of the stranger to appear. The failure embedded in such misrecognition—rather than the failure of recognition—determines the impossibility of reducing the other to the figure of the stranger: as I will argue in Chapter 2, the singularity of the figure conceals the different histories of lived embodiment which mark some bodies as stranger than others.

By analysing recognition in this way, I am suggesting that the (lawful) subject is not simply constituted by being recognised by the other, which is the primary post-Hegelian model of recognition (see Taylor 1994). Rather, I am suggesting that it is the recognition of others that is central to the constitution of the subject. The very act through which the subject differentiates between others is the moment that the subject comes to inhabit or dwell in the world. The subject is not, then, simply differentiated from the (its) other, but comes into being by learning how to differentiate between others. This recognition operates as *a visual economy*: it involves ways of *seeing the difference* between familiar and strange others as they are (re)presented to the subject. As a mode of subject constitution, recognition involves differentiating between others on the basis of how they 'appear'.[2]

Given the way in which the recognition of strangers operates to produce who 'we' are, we can see that strangers already 'fit' within the 'cognitive, moral or aesthetic map of the world', rather than being, as Zygmunt Bauman argues, 'the people who do not fit' (1997: 46). There are established ways of dealing with 'the strangers' who are already encountered and recognised in public life. The recognisability of strangers involves, not only techniques for differentiating strange from familiar (ways of seeing), but also ways of living: there are, in Alfred Schutz's terms, 'standardized situations' in which we might encounter strangers and which allow us to negotiate our way past them (1944: 499). Goffman's work on bodily stigma, for example, attends to how the bodies of others that are marked as different, such as disabled bodies, are read in ways which allow the subject to keep their distance (1984: 12). Social encounters involve rules and procedures for 'dealing with' the bodies that are read as strange (Morris 1996: 72–74).

Encounters between embodied others hence involve *spatial negotiations* with those who are already recognised as either familiar or strange. For Schutz, the stranger is always approaching—coming closer to those who are at home (1944: 499). In the sociological analysis of strangers offered by Simmel, the stranger is understood, paradoxically, as both near and far (1991: 146). In the next section, I consider how the determination of social space and imagined forms of belonging takes place through the differentiation between strangers and neighbours in relationships of proximity and distance.

Neighbourhoods and dwelling

How do you recognise who is a stranger in your neighbourhood? To rephrase my original question in this way is to point to the relation between the recognition of strangers and one's habitat or dwelling: others are recognised as strangers by those who inhabit a given space, who 'make it' their own. As Michael Dillon argues, 'with the delimitation of any place of dwelling, the constitution of a people, a nation, a state, or a democracy necessarily specifies who is *estranged from* that identity, place or regime' (1999: 119; emphasis added). At one level, this seems to suggest the relativisability of the condition of strangers: any-one can be a stranger if they leave home (the house, the neighbourhood, the region, the nation).[3] However, in this section I want to argue that forms of dwelling cannot be equated in order to allow such a relativisation. Some homes and neighbourhoods are privileged such that they define the terrain of the inhabitable world. The recognition of strangers brings into play relations of social and political antagonism that *mark some others as stranger than other others.*

How do neighbourhoods become imagined? In the work of Howard Hallman, neighbourhoods are understood as arising from the 'natural human trait' of being neighbourly, which combines a concern with others and a concern for self (1984: 11). According to Hallman, the neighbourhood is an organic community that grows, 'naturally wherever people live close to one another' (1984: 11). It is both a limited territory—a physical space with clear boundaries—and a social community where 'residents do things together' (1984: 13).The simple fact of living nearby gives neighbours a common social bond. However, according to Hallman, some neighbourhoods are closer and hence better than others. He argues that neighbourhoods are more likely to be successful as communities when people live near 'like people': 'people with similarities tend to achieve closer neighbour relationships' (1984: 24). Hallman defines a close neighbourhood through an analogy with a healthy body, 'with wounds healed, illness cured, and wellness maintained' (1984: 256).

The analogy between the ideal neighbourhood and a healthy body serves to define the ideal neighbourhood as fully integrated, homogeneous, and sealed: it is like a body that is fully contained by the skin (see Chapter 2). This implies that a good or healthy neighbourhood does not leak outside itself, and hence does not let outsiders (or foreign agents/viruses) in. The model of the neighbourhood as an organic community—where a sense of community arises from the simple fact of shared residence—defines social health in terms of the production of purified spaces and the expulsion of difference through ways of living together. Matthew Crenson's consideration of neighbourhood politics hence concludes, 'social homogeneity and solidarity . . . may contribute to the defensive capabilities of neighbourhoods, and in fact it may take an external attack upon some of these homogenous neighbourhoods to activate the latent sense of fellow feeling along local residents' (1983: 257). Likewise, David Morris and Karl Hess describe neighbourhoods as protective and defensive, like 'tiny underdeveloped nations' (1975: 16).

Neighbourhoods become imagined as organic and pure spaces through the social perception of the danger posed by outsiders to moral and social health or well-being. So although neighbourhoods have been represented as organic and pure communities, there is also an assumption that those communities will fail (to be). A failed community is hence one which has weak or negative connections: where neighbours appear as if they are strangers to each other. The neighbour who is also a stranger—who only passes as a neighbour—is hence the danger that may always threaten the community from within. As David Sibley argues, 'the resistance to a different sort of person moving into a neighbourhood stems from feelings of anxiety, nervousness or fear. Who is felt to belong and not to belong contributes to an important way of shaping social space' (1995: 3). However, the failure of the community should not just be understood in terms of failed communities. *It is the very potential of the community to fail which is required for the constitution of the community.* It is the enforcement of the boundaries between those who are already recognised as out of place (even other fellow residents) that allows those boundaries to be established. The 'ideal' community has to be worked towards and that labour requires failure as its moment of constitution (to this extent, then, the organic community is a fantasy that *requires* its own negation).

It is symptomatic then of the very nature of neighbourhood that it enters public discourse as a site of *crisis*: it is only by attending to the trauma of neighbourhoods which fail that the ideal of the healthy neighbourhood can be maintained as a possibility (which is then, endlessly deferred as 'the real', as well as endlessly kept in place as 'the ideal', by that very language of crisis). Such failed communities are the source of fascination: they demonstrate the need to regulate social spaces. On British television in 1998, there were a number of programmes dedicated to 'neighbours from hell', neighbours who are dirty, who make too much noise, who steal, and who are 'at war' with each other. On *Panorama*'s 'Neighbours from Hell' (30 March 1998), urinating in the street becomes the ultimate expression of the antisociability of stranger neighbours. The passing of bodily fluids in public spaces becomes symptomatic of the failure to pass as neighbours. In the United Kingdom, new powers of eviction for local councils give further power to the community to reassert itself against these stranger neighbours. The imaginary community of the neighbourhood hence requires enforcement through Law.

The enforcement of the boundaries which allow neighbourhoods to be imagined as pure and organic spaces can be understood as central to neighbourhood watch schemes. Such schemes began in the United States in the 1970s, and in the United Kingdom in 1982. The National Neighbourhood Watch Association in the United Kingdom (NNWA) describes it as, 'the best known and most effective example of the police and community working together in partnership to prevent crime, build safer communities and improve quality of life'. In the United Kingdom, there are currently over 161,000 schemes and over 10 million people involved. Neighbourhood Watch brings together the creation of an ideal community as one 'which cares' and the production of safer spaces through the discourse of 'crime prevention'. Its main motto is, 'Crime cannot survive in a community that cares—Neighbourhood Watch works'. In other words, crime only exists when communities fail, when communities do not care. Marginalised or under-valued spaces where there is a high rate of crime against property are hence immediately understood in terms of *a failure to care*.

Neighbourhood Watch schemes are more common in middle-class areas, where residents are more likely to want to co-operate with the police, and where there is more 'property' with value to protect (Hill 1994: 150). The value attached to certain spaces of belonging is enforced or 'watched' through schemes that allow middle-class spaces to become valued: the subject who watches out for crime, is also *maintaining the value of her or his neighbourhood*. The link here between value of spaces, the protection of property, and the maintenance of social privilege helps us to theorise how the defence of social boundaries against unwelcome intrusions and intruders produces certain categories of strangers—those who don't belong in the leafy suburbs—that are socially legitimated and enforced. In Elijah Anderson's work, there is a discussion of how the concern with safety amongst residents means that, 'they join their diverse counterparts in local struggles to fight crime and otherwise preserve the ideal character for the neighbourhood, forming town watches and shoring up municipal codes that might discourage undesirables and encourage others more to their liking' (1990: 4). The production of safe spaces that have value or 'ideal character' involves the expulsion of unlike and undesirable 'characters'. In Anderson's work, these characters have *already* materialised or taken the form of, 'wandering homeless people, aggressive beggars, muggers, anonymous black youths, and drug addicts' (1990: 238).

How does neighbourhood watch work to produce such safe spaces? The literature produced on the Neighbourhood Watch schemes by the Home Office in the United Kingdom certainly links the designation of value to social spaces with the detection of strange events, and the expulsion of strangers. There is a double emphasis on the improvement of community living and on security and crime prevention. So Neighbourhood Watch schemes are described as both providing 'the eyes and ears of the police' and as providing, 'the soul and heart of the community' (Home Office 1997). The NWS link the production of safe spaces with the organic growth of a healthy social body: 'Neighbourhood Watch is not just about reducing burglary figures—it's about creating communities who care. It brings local people together and can make a real contribution to improving their lives. The activity of Watch members can foster a new community spirit and a belief in the community's ability to tackle problems. At the same time, you feel secure, knowing your neighbours are keeping an eye on your property' (1997). There is a constant shift between an emphasis on a caring community and a safe one: a safe community moreover is one in which you feel safe as your property is being 'watched' by your neighbours. A link is established here between safety (in which safety is associated with property), a discourse on good neighbourliness (looking out for each other) and the production of community as purified space ('a new community spirit'). Hence, 'it is widely accepted that within every community, there is the potential for crime prevention. Neighbourhood Watch is a way of tapping into this and of drawing a community together'. Neighbourhood Watch hence constitutes the neighbourhood as a community through the protection of the property of nearby others from the threat posed by the very proximity of distant others.

In an earlier Neighbourhood Watch pamphlet (Home Office 1992), the reader is addressed more directly, 'Deciding to join your local group means you have made a positive commitment to act against crime in your community. You have also become one of the largest and most successful grass-roots movements in the country.' Here, the reader is praised for her or his community spirit: not only are you a good neighbour—willing to look out for your neighbours—but you are also a good citizen, who has displayed a positive commitment to 'act against crime in the community'. Neighbourhood watch purifies the space of the community *through purifying the life of the good citizen*, whose life becomes heroic, dedicated to fighting against crime and disorder. Significantly, then, the praise given to the reader/citizen involves a form of reward/recognition: 'You can also get lower insurance premiums from some Insurance companies' (1992). The reward demonstrates the value given to social spaces where subjects watch out for the extraordinary sounds and signs of crime, or the sounds and signs of that which is suspect and suspicious.

But how does Neighbourhood Watch involve techniques of differentiating between the ordinary life of the purified neighbourhood and the extraordinary events that threaten to contaminate that space? The Home Office pamphlet is cautious, 'Sometimes it is hard to tell if you are witnessing a crime or not. You must rely on common sense. . . . You may also become suspicious if you notice something out of the ordinary. Don't be afraid to call your local police station to report the incident' (1992). Here, common sense should tell the good citizen what they are witnessing. Whatever happens, the good citizen must be a witness: a witness to an event that might or might not be a crime, an *event that unfolds before the patient eye and ear*. The last sentence moves from the importance of differentiating between extraordinary events through common sense (is it a crime?), to the differentiation between ordinary and extraordinary. Here, you might be made suspicious by *some-thing* out of the ordinary. The good citizen is a citizen who *suspects rather than is suspect*, who watches out for departures from ordinary life in the imagined space of the neighbourhood. The good citizen hence watches out for the one who loiters, acts suspiciously, looks out of place. As a Chief Inspector explains in a letter to *The Independent*, 'Neighbourhood Watch is about looking after your property and that of your neighbours, taking sensible crime prevention action *and reporting suspicious persons to the police*' (Scougal 1996, emphasis added). According to the leaflet given by the Divisional Commander to Neighbourhood Watch coordinators, Neighbourhood Watch 'rests on the concept of good neighbourliness', which means that, 'Neighbours are encouraged to report suspicious persons and unusual events to the police'. With such an exercise in good neighbourliness and good citizenship, the neighbourhood comes to police itself: not only is it 'the heart and soul of the community', but in being the 'heart and soul of the community', it is also *the ears and eyes of the police*'.

The signifier 'suspicious' does an enormous amount of work in Neighbourhood Watch discourse precisely insofar as it is *empty*. The good citizen is not given any information about how to tell what or who is suspicious in the first place. It is my argument that the very failure to provide us with techniques for telling the difference is itself a technique of knowledge. It is the technique of *common sense* that is produced through Neighbourhood Watch discourse. Common sense not only defines what 'we' should take for granted (that is, what is normalised and already known as 'the given'), but it also involves the normalisation of ways of 'sensing' the difference between common and uncommon. That is, information is not given about how to tell the difference between normal and suspicious, because that difference is already 'sensed' through a prior history of making sense *as* the making of 'the common'. The good citizen knows what they are looking for, because they know what is common, and so what departs from the common: 'You must rely on common sense' (1992). Neighbourhood watch is hence about *making* the common: it makes the community ('the heart and soul of the community') insofar as it looks out for and hears the threat to the common posed by those who are uncommon, or those who are 'out of place' in 'this place' ('the eyes and ears of the police').

In this way, the 'suspicious person' and 'the stranger' are intimately linked: they are both emptied of any content, or any direct relationship to a referent, precisely as they are tied to a (missing) history of seeing and hearing others: *they are both already seen and heard as 'the uncommon' which allows 'the common' to take its shape*. The failure to name those who inhabit the signifier 'suspicious' hence produces the figure of the unspecified stranger, a figure that is required by the making or sensing of 'the common', of what 'we' are, as a form of distinction or value (property). Neighbourhood Watch can be characterised as a form of humanism. Such a humanism—Neighbourhood Watch is 'about creating communities who care' (1992)—conceals the exclusions that operate to allow the definition and policing of the 'we' of the good neighbourhood. The definition and enforcement of the good 'we' operates through the recognition of others as strangers: by seeing those who do not belong simply as 'strangers' (that is, by not naming *who* are the ones who do not belong in the community), forms of social exclusion are both concealed and revealed (what is concealed is the brute fact of the matter—only some others are recognisable as 'the stranger', the one who is out of place). In this sense, the policing of valued spaces allows the legitimation of social exclusion by being tied to a heroic 'we' who takes shape against the figure of the unspecified stranger. The production of the stranger as a figure that has linguistic and bodily integrity conceals how strangers are always already specified or differentiated. Neighbourhood Watch becomes definable as a mechanism for ensuring, not only that certain spaces maintain their (property) value, but that *certain lives become valued over other lives*. The recognition of strangers within the neighbourhood does not mean that anybody can be a stranger, depending on her or his location in the world: rather, some-bodies are more recognisable as strangers than other-bodies precisely because they are already read and valued in the demarcation of social spaces.

What is also significant about the Neighbourhood Watch concern with seeing and hearing the difference (becoming the eyes and ears of the police), is that it involves the production of a model of 'good citizenship'. The discourse on good citizenship involves an individualising of responsibility for crime (Stanko 1997). This model of the good citizen, which Stanko's work suggests is very much gendered as masculine, takes such responsibility in part through a form of self-policing by, in some sense, *becoming the police*. Certainly in post-Foucauldian work on surveillance, the emphasis is on the shift from public forms of monitoring—where the subject is watched by an anonymous and partially unseen and partially seen Other—to self-monitoring, when *the subject adopts the gaze of the other* (Foucault 1975). My analysis of Neighbourhood Watch might complicate this model of displacement from the gaze of the other to the gaze of the self. The 'eye' of the good citizen is certainly the site of labour—it is this 'eye' that is doing the work. However, that 'eye' does not simply return to the body, as that which must be transformed and regulated as 'the seen', but looks elsewhere, to and at others. In other words, 'the good citizen' is one who watches (out for) suspicious persons and strangers, and who in that very act, becomes aligned, not only with the police (and hence the Law), but with the imagined community itself whose boundaries are protected *in the very labour of his look*.

Furthermore, self-policing communities are inscribed as moral communities, those that care. Caring evokes a figure of who must be cared for, who must be protected from the risks of crime and the danger of strangers. So Neighbourhood Watch 'reassures vulnerable members of the community that you are keeping a neighbourly eye on them' (1992). The construction of the figure of the vulnerable member/body alongside the heroic good citizen provides the moral justification for the injunction to watch; it detaches 'watching out for' from 'busybodying' (1992) by redefining it as 'watching out on behalf of'. The discourse of vulnerability allows self-policing to be readable as the protection of others: the risk posed by suspects and strangers is a risk posed to the vulnerable bodies of children, the elderly and women. The figuring of the good citizen is built on the image of the strong citizen: in this sense, the good citizen is figurable primarily as white, masculine and middle-class, the heroic subject who can protect the vulnerable bodies of 'weaker others': 'crime cannot survive in a community that cares—Neighbourhood Watch Works' (NNWA).

The 1997 pamphlet also describes the newer scheme 'Street Watch' (there are currently over 20,000 in operation in the United Kingdom) which, 'covers many different activities, ranging from providing transport or escort services for elderly people, to walking a specific route regularly, keeping an eye out for trouble and reporting it to the police'. Here, the good citizen is valued not only for his heart, eyes and ears, but also his feet.[4] He takes specific routes, but most importantly, according to the Home Secretary responsible for the introduction of the scheme, Michael Howard, he is 'walking with purpose' (Bennetto 1995). Street Watch is described as 'patrolling with a purpose'.

We can consider here Hallman's definition of who and what must be watched in his work on neighbourhoods: 'people who seem to have no purpose in the neighbourhood' (Hallman 1984: 159). Strangers are suspicious because they 'have no purpose', that is, they have no legitimate function within the space which could justify their existence or intrusion. Strangers are hence recognisable precisely insofar as they *do not enter into the exchanges of capital that transforms spaces into places*. Strangers are constructed as an illegitimate presence in the neighbourhood: they have no purpose, and hence they must be suspect. You can recognise the stranger through their loitering gait: strangers loiter, they do not enter the legitimate exchanges of capital that might justify their presence. In contrast, the street watcher is constructed as a heroic figure whose purpose is the very detection of those who are without a legitimate purpose, of those whose purpose can hence only be explained as suspicious, as criminal, as a crime (Young 1996: 5). The stranger's presence on the street is a crime (waiting to happen). The proximity of such loitering strangers in the purified space of the good neighbourhood hence requires that the heroic citizen take a specific route: those who are recognisable as strangers, *whose lack of purpose conceals the purpose of crime*, need to be expelled through purposeful patrolling in order that the value of property can be protected.

Such a construction of the good citizen through the figure of the loitering stranger is clearly subject to forms of social differentiation: in one reading, the good citizen is structured around the body of the dominant (white, middle-class) man, who protects the vulnerable bodies of women and children from the threat of marginalised (black, working-class) men. However, these differences are concealed by the very modes of recognition: the figure of the stranger appears as 'the stranger' precisely by being cut off from these histories of determination (= stranger fetishism). That is, the recognition of strangers involves the differentiation between some others and other others at the same time as it conceals that very act of differentiation. What is significant about Neighbourhood Watch is precisely the way in which it links the formation of community with safety and the detection of crime: such links produce the figure of the stranger as a *visible danger* to the 'we' of the community, and hence as the necessary condition for making what 'we' have in common.

Stranger danger

If the construction and enforcement of purified spaces of belonging takes place through the production of the figures of the good citizen, the vulnerable body and the loitering stranger, then how is this linked to the social perception of danger? In this section, I examine the discourse of stranger danger as a way of analysing how strangers are already recognised as posing danger to property and person, not just in particular valued dwellings and neighbourhoods, but also in public life as such. I want to consider, not only how the construction of stranger danger is tied to valued and devalued spaces, but also how strangers are read as posing danger *wherever* they are: the projection of danger onto the figure of the stranger allows the definition of the subject-at-home, and home as inhabitable space, as inherently safe and valuable. One *knows again* those whom one does not know by assuming they are the *origin* of danger.

Partly, this concern with public life involves a consideration of urban space and cities as 'a world of strangers' (Lofland 1973). Lofland suggests that cities, in particular public spaces within cities (such as streets and leisure spaces), involve perpetual encounters between people who are not personally known to each other, although they may be known through forms of visual identification and recognition (1973: 15–16). As a result, he argues that cities involve particular kinds of social and spatial encounters. I would not want to refute the premise that there are different kinds of spaces that involve different kinds of encounters between others (such as urban and rural spaces, or such as different forms of the public within urban spaces). However, Lofland's account does involve a form of spatial determinism—these spaces determine these encounters between others—which shifts quickly into a form of cultural determinism—cultures have different spaces and therefore involve different encounters between others.[5] What I am interested in is how the very encounters that take place between others involve the forming of both cultural and spatial boundaries: that is, how the (mis)recognition of others as strangers is what allows the demarcation of given spaces within 'the public domain', but also the legitimation of certain forms of mobility or movement within the public, and the delegitimation of others.

I am positing here a relationship between dwelling and movement:[6] spaces' are claimed, or 'owned' not so much by inhabiting what is already there, but by moving within, or passing through, different spaces which are only given value as places (with boundaries) through the movement or 'passing through' itself. The relationship between movement, occupation and ownership is well documented in feminist work: for example, women's restricted movement within public spaces is a result, not only of the fear of crime, but of the regulation of femininity, in which 'being seen' in certain spaces becomes a sign of irresponsibility (Stanko 1997: 489). Women's movements are regulated by a desire for 'safe-keeping': respectability becomes measured by the visible signs of a desire to 'stay safe'. In this sense, movement becomes a form of subject constitution: *where* 'one' goes or does not go determines *what* one 'is', or where one is seen to be, determines what one is seen to be.

Elijah Anderson's work on how communities are established through the concern with safety examines how the fear of crime becomes a fear of strangers. Such a fear produces a way of inhabiting the world, as well as moving through it. He writes, 'Many worry about a figure lurking in the shadows, hiding in a doorway or behind a clump of bushes, ready to pounce on the unsuspecting victim' (Anderson 1990: 5). The danger posed by the stranger is imagined as partly concealed: the stranger always lurks in dark spaces. While the victim is unsuspecting, the safe subject must be suspecting: the safe subject suspects that the suspect is around the corner, always hidden to the gaze, to the watchful eye. The danger of the stranger is hence always there in the imagined future of the subject who is safely at home, the stranger is always lurking as the threat of that-which-might-yet-be. Safety hence requires that the subject must become familiar with the terrain: the safe subject must become 'street wise' and 'alive to dangerous situations' (Anderson 1990: 6). Certain lives become liveable as both safe and valuable insofar as they are *alive to* the danger of strangers.

The discourse of personal safety is not about the production of safe and purified spaces from which strangers are expelled (such as 'the home'), but also defines ways of moving through spaces that are already dangerous given the possibility that strangers are close by, waiting in the shadows of the streets (where good citizens walk only with purpose, living their legitimated lives). The possibility of personal safety for mobile subjects hence requires 'collective definitions' of that which is 'safe, harmless, trustworthy' and that which is 'bad, dangerous and hostile' (Anderson 1990: 216). Such collective definitions provide the subject with the knowledge required to move within the world, allowing the subject to differentiate between familiar and strange, safe and dangerous, as well as to differentiate between different kinds of strangers ('characters').

Clearly, discourses of personal safety involve forms of self-governance that differentiate between subjects. As much feminist research has suggested, safety for women is often constructed in terms of not entering public spaces, or staying within the home (see Stanko 1990). Safety for men also involves forms of self-governance, not in terms of refusing to enter the public space, but in terms of *how* one enters that space. So at one level, the discoruse of personal safety presumes a vulnerable citizen who is gendered as feminine, at another level, it legislates for a form of mobile and masculine subjectivity that is not only a safe form of subjectivity, but also one that is heroic. Such a mobile subject, who can 'avoid' the danger of strangers in public spaces is constructed as 'street wise'. This subject's mobility is legitimated as a form of dwelling: first, in relation to the vulnerable bodies that stay within the home; and second, in relation to the strangers whose passing though public spaces is delegitimated as the 'origin' of danger (the movement of strangers is hence not a form of dwelling: it does not lead to the legitimated occupation of space).

The knowledges embedded in street wisdom are linked by Anderson to a kind of 'field research' (Anderson 1990: 216). The wise subject, the one who knows where and where not to walk, how and how not to move, who and who not to talk to, has an expertise that can be understood as both *bodily and cultural capital*. It is such wise subjects who will prevail in a world of strangers and dangers: 'To prevail means simply to get safely to one's destination, and the ones who are most successful are those who are "streetwise" ' (Anderson 1990: 231). In this sense, the discourse of stranger danger involves techniques of knowledge that allow wise subjects to prevail: to arrive at their destination, to leave and return home and still maintain a safe distance between themselves and dangerous strangers. Community is not just established through the designation of pure and safe spaces, but becomes established *as a way of moving through space*. Becoming street wise defines the subject in terms of the collective: the wise subject has collective knowledge about what is, 'safe, harmless, trustworthy' and what is 'bad, dangerous and hostile' that gives that subject the ability to move safely in a world of strangers and dangers. The stranger is here produced as a figure of danger that grants the wise subject and community, those who already claim both knowledge and capital, the ability to prevail.

The discourse of stranger danger also involves the figuring, not only of the wiser subject who can move through dangerous places (a mobile subject who is racialised, classed and gendered), but also the vulnerable body, the one who is most at risk. Here, 'the child' becomes a figure of vulnerability, the purified body that is most endangered by the contaminating desires of strangers. Indeed, it is the literature on child protection that has familiarised 'stranger danger' as the mechanism for ensuring personal safety. One double page of the Home Office leaflet on crime prevention in the United Kingdom is hence dedicated to 'your family' and, 'to keeping your children safe' (the ideal reader/subject/citizen is always a parent, bound to Law and duty through the demands of parenthood). The pamphlet advises, 'Do not talk to strangers. Most well-meaning adults will not approach a child who is on his own, unless he is obviously distressed or in need. Tell your children never to talk to strangers, and to politely ignore any approach from a stranger. Get them to tell you if a stranger tries to talk to them.' Immediately, strangers are differentiated from 'well-meaning' adults, who would not approach children. Indeed, the child itself must become 'street wise': one colouring-in book produced by the Lancashire Constabulary in the United Kingdom is entitled, 'Operation Streetwise workbook' and aims 'to provide children with an exciting opportunity to learn and practice personal safety skills'. Here, growing up is narrated in terms of acquiring the wisdom to deal with danger that already stalks in the figure of the stranger.[7]

The figure of the child comes to perform a certain role within the narrative of crime prevention and stranger danger: the innocence of the child is what is most at risk from the proximity of strangers. The child comes to embody, in a narrative that is both nostalgic (returning to an imagined past) and fearful (projecting an unimaginable future), all that could be stolen or lost by the proximity of strangers. The child's innocence and purity becomes a matter of social and national responsibility: through figuring the stranger as too close to the child, the stranger becomes recognisable as an attack on the moral purity of nation space itself. It is over the bodies of children that the moral campaign against strangers is waged.

In recent debates in the press, the paedophile is hence represented as the ultimate stranger that communities must have the power to evict. A change in the law in 1997 allowed the British police force to inform members of the community when a paedophile is in their midst, on a 'need to know' basis. Community action groups, as well as some local councils, have redefined the need to know as *a right to know*: arguing that paedophiles should not be allowed into communities as they pose a risk to children, 'Recent moves include attempts by some councils to ban paedophiles from their communities altogether, and campaigns to keep them in prison longer' (Hilpern 1997). The construction of sex offenders against children as monsters who do not belong in a community is clear in the following statement from John O'Sullivan, from the pressure group, *Parents Against Child Abuse*: 'If there is a wild lion loose in the street, the police would tell us. A paedophile in the neighbourhood is the same. They might not rip the flesh, but they are just as damaging to the mind of a child. We need to know who they are.' The number of vigilante attacks on suspected paedophiles in Britain in the 1990s suggests what this knowledge will be used for.

Significantly, then, the paedophile comes to embody the most dangerous stranger as he poses the greatest risk to the vulnerable and pure body of the child. The community comes together through the recognition of such dangerous strangers: they must expel him, he who is the wild animal, the lion, at loose in the street. The monstrosity of such recognisable strangers is figured through the tearing of the skin of the child. The monsters who must be excluded to keep children safe, prey on children: they require the heroic action of the moral community that cares. The imaginary community is constructed as a safe community where children's bodies are not vulnerable: the moral community itself becomes the child, pure, innocent and free. The recognition of dangerous strangers allows the enforcement of the boundaries of such communities: a definition of the purity of the 'we' against the monstrous 'it'.

Sally Engle Merry's *Urban Danger: Life in a Neighbourhood of Strangers*, discusses how the fear of crime 'focuses on the threat of the violent attack by a stranger' (Merry 1981: 6). Such a fear means that the familiar is already designated as safe: one is safe at home, unless there is an intrusion from a stranger. One could comment here how such a reduction of danger to the stranger conceals the danger that may be embedded in the familiar: much feminist work, for example, demonstrates how the perception of the rapist as a stranger conceals how most sexual attacks are committed by friends or family. As Elizabeth Stanko argues, 'Danger many of us believe arises from the random action of strangers who are, we further assume, usually men of colour. Yet according to most people's experiences . . . danger and violence arise within our interpersonal relationships' (1990: 3). The projection of danger onto the figure of the stranger allows violence to be figured as exceptional and extraordinary—as coming from outside the protective walls of the home, family, community or nation. As a result, the discourse of stranger danger involves *a refusal to recognise how violence is structured by, and legitimated through, the formation of home and community as such.*

The stranger is here figured as the violent monster whose elimination would mean safety for women and children. Such a figuration allows the home to be imagined as a safe haven: an imagining that cannot deal with the violence that is instituted through the social relations within the home. As Merry argues, 'Violence at the hand of the stranger is usually perceived as dangerous, but an assault in the context of a fight with a known enemy or neighbour is rarely viewed in this way' (Merry 1981: 14). The notion of violence as domestic, while now recognised through Law as a result of years of feminist campaigning, remains a difficult one for the social imaginary: the violent husband is then read as a monster underneath, as a stranger passing as husband, rather than as a husband exercising the power that is already legitimated through hegemonic forms of masculinity. According to stranger danger discourse, the stranger husband has intruded into the ideal home: he is not understood as an element *in the ordinary production of domestic space*, and in the formation of relations of power and exchange within that space.

The ultimate violent strangers are hence figured as immigrants: they are the outsiders in the nation space whose 'behaviour seems unpredictable and beyond control' (Merry 1981: 125). Cultural difference becomes the text upon which the fear of crime is written: 'cultural difference exacerbates feelings of danger. Encounters with culturally alien people are defined by anxiety and uncertainty, which inhibits social interaction and reinforces social boundaries' (Merry 1981: 125). The projection of danger onto that which is already recognisable as different—as different from the familiar space of home and homeland—hence allows violence to take place: it becomes a mechanism for the enforcement of boundary lines that almost secure the home-nation as safe haven. On the one hand, the fear of crime embedded in the discourse of stranger danger allows the protection of domestic, social and national space from the outsider inside, the stranger neighbour, by projecting danger onto the outsider. On the other hand, the stranger only appears as a figure of danger by coming too close to home: the boundary line is always crossed, both 'justifying' the fear and legitimating the enforcement. In doing so, the discourse of stranger danger, not only allows the abdication of any social and political responsibility for the violence that takes place within legitimated spaces, and which is sanctioned through Law, but also becomes a mechanism for the justification of acts of violence against those who are already recognised as strangers.

In this chapter, I have examined how 'the stranger' is produced as a figure precisely by being associated with a danger to the purified space of the community, the purified life of the good citizen, and the purified body of 'the child'. Rather than assuming that the stranger is any-body we don't recognise, I have argued that strangers are those that are already recognised through techniques for differentiating between the familiar and strange in discourses such as Neighbourhood Watch and crime prevention. The 'knowing again' of strangers defines the stranger as a danger to both moral health and well-being. The knowing again of strangers as the danger of the unknown is a means by which the 'we' of the community is established, enforced and legitimated.

Recognising Strangers

1 To the extent that I am challenging the assumed opposition between strange and familiar (and also in Chapter 4, between home and away), I am following Freud, whose model of the uncanny emphasises how the strange leads back to the familiar. He also suggests that homely (*das Heimliche*) and unhomely (*das Unheimliche*) are intimately linked (Freud 1964: 225–226). However, Freud explains this intimacy of apparent opposites through a model of repression: 'this uncanny is in reality nothing new or alien, but something which is familiar and old established in the mind and which has become alienated from it only through a process of repression' (1964: 241). In contrast, I am seeking to explain the familiarity of the stranger by considering the *production* rather than repression of that which is strange: the stranger is produced as an effect of recognition and as a category

of knowledge (see Chapter 2), and is henceforth familiar in its very stranger-ness. When we look out 'for strangers' we already know what we are looking for.

2 In Chapter 2, I consider how the recognition of strangers involves an economy of touch, as well as a visual economy. We can also note here that recognition has become an important part of political struggle—marginalised groups struggle to be recognised, or *to be seen*, by mainstream politics, which is also a struggle against forms of misrecognition (Taylor 1994; Fraser 1997). A key debate has emerged within feminism on the limits of the politics of recognition (see also Brown 1995; Skeggs 1999). Although I can't enter these debates here, my analysis of how recognition operates as a visual economy in everyday life and social encounters between others might suggest some limits to a politics of recognition, although it might also suggest the difficulties of simply overcoming recognition. In Chapter 6, I complicate this model of recognition as 'seeing the difference' by considering the implications of the structural possibility that the difference might not be seeable as the subject may be passing as it 'passes through' the community.

3 For a discussion of the relationship between migration and strangers see Chapter 4. Here, I argue that migration does not allow us to relativise the condition of strangerness.

4 Alene Branton, secretary to the steering committee of the National Neighbourhood Watch Association in the UK, is reported to have said, 'We were set up to be the eyes and ears of the police. We never expected to be the feet as well' (Bennetto 1995).

5 He contrasts the modern proximity of strangers with 'primitive cultures' where strangers are more at a distance.

6 I also consider the relationship between dwelling and movement in chapters 4 and 8 where I develop the notion of 'global nomadic citizenship'.

7 Importantly, stranger danger discourse attempts to define the stranger as anybody we don't know; it seeks to contest what I have called the recognisability of strangers, and the assumption that 'strangers' only look a certain way. As James Brewer puts it, 'Who are the bad guys? How can you recognise them before its too late? . . . What do the bad guys look like? They look like *YOU*' (1994: 15, 17). What this reveals, despite itself, is precisely the ways in which strangers are already recognised as looking unlike 'YOU': the discourse of stranger danger seeks to contest the very familiarity of strangers, but can only do so, by first confirming that familiarity, and the 'common-sense' assumption that danger is posed only by certain bodies, who are marked by their difference from the everyday of the neighbourhood.

2

Social Class and the Hidden Curriculum of Work

JEAN ANYON

Scholars in political economy and the sociology of knowledge have recently argued that public schools in complex industrial societies like our own make available different types of educational experience and curriculum knowledge to students in different social classes. Bowles and Gintis[1] for example, have argued that students in different social-class backgrounds are rewarded for classroom behaviors that correspond to personality traits allegedly rewarded in the different occupational strata—the working classes for docility and obedience, the managerial classes for initiative and personal assertiveness. Basil Bernstein, Pierre Bourdieu, and Michael W. Apple[2] focusing on school knowledge, have argued that knowledge and skills leading to social power and regard (medical, legal, managerial) are made available to the advantaged social groups but are withheld from the working classes to whom a more "practical" curriculum is offered (manual

---

[1]S. Bowles and H. Gintes, *Schooling in Capitalist America: Educational Reform and the Contradictions of Economic Life* (New York: Basic Books, 1976). [Author's note]

[2]B. Bernstein, *Class, Codes and Control, Vol. 3. Towards a Theory of Educational Transmission*, 2d ed. (London: Routledge & Kegan Paul, 1977); P. Bourdieu and J. Passeron, *Reproduction in Education, Society and Culture* (Beverly Hills, Calif: Sage, 1977); M.W. Apple, *Ideology and Curriculum* (Boston: Routledge Kegan Paul, 1979). [Author's note]

skills, clerical knowledge). While there has been considerable argumentation of these points regarding education in England, France, and North America, there has been little or no attempt to investigate these ideas empirically in elementary or secondary schools and classrooms in this country.[3]

This article offers tentative empirical support (and qualification) of the above arguments by providing illustrative examples of differences in student *work* in classrooms in contrasting social class communities. The examples were gathered *as* part of an ethnographical[4] study of curricular, pedagogical, and pupil evaluation practices in five elementary schools. The article attempts a theoretical contribution as well and assesses student work in the light of a theoretical approach to social-class analysis. . . . It will be suggested that there is a "hidden curriculum" in schoolwork that has profound implications for the theory—and consequence—of everyday activity in education. . . .

The Sample of Schools

. . . The social-class designation of each of the five schools will be identified, and the income, occupation, and other relevant available social characteristics of the students and their parents will be described. The first three schools are in a medium-sized city district in northern New Jersey, and the other two are in a nearby New Jersey suburb.

The first two schools I will call *working class schools*. Most of the parents have blue-collar jobs. Less than a third of the fathers are skilled, while the majority are in unskilled or semiskilled jobs. During the period of the study (1978–1979), approximately 15 percent of the fathers were unemployed. The large majority (85 percent) of the families are white. The following occupations are typical: platform, storeroom, and stockroom workers; foundry-men, pipe welders, and boilermakers; semiskilled and unskilled assembly-line operatives; gas station attendants, auto mechanics, maintenance workers, and security guards. Less than 30 percent of the women work, some part-time and some full-time, on assembly lines, in storerooms and stockrooms, as waitresses, barmaids, or sales clerks. Of the fifth-grade parents, none of the wives of the skilled workers had jobs. Approximately 15 percent of the families in each school are at or below the federal "poverty" level; most of the rest of the family incomes are at or below $12,000, except some of the skilled workers whose incomes are higher.[5] The incomes of the majority of the families in these two schools (at or below $12,000) are typical of 38.6 percent of the families in the United States.[6]

---

[3]But see, in a related vein, M.W. Apple and N. King, "What Do Schools Teach?" *Curriculum Inquiry* 6 (1977); 341–58; R.C. Rist, *The Urban School: A Factory for Failure* (Cambridge, Mass.: MIT Press, 1973). [Author's note]

[4]*ethnographical:* Based on an anthropological study of cultures or subcultures—the "cultures" in this case being the five schools being observed.

[5]The U.S. Bureau of the Census defines *poverty* for a nonfarm family of four as a yearly income of $6,191 a year or less. U.S. Bureau of the Census, *Statistical Abstract of the United States: 1978* (Washington, D.C.: U.S. Government Printing Office, 1978), p. 465, table 754. [Author's note]

[6]U.S. Bureau of the Census, "Money Income in 1977 of Families and Persons in the United States," *Current Population Reports* Series P-60, no. 118 (Washington, D.C.: U.S. Government Printing Office, 1978), p. 2, table A. [Author's note]

The third school is called the *middle-class school*, although because of 5 neighborhood residence patterns, the population is a mixture of several social classes. The parents' occupations can be divided into three groups: a small group of blue-collar "rich," who are skilled, well-paid workers such as printers, carpenters, plumbers, and construction workers. The second group is composed of parents in working-class and middle-class white-collar jobs: women in office jobs, technicians, supervisors in industry, and parents employed by the city (such as firemen, policemen, and several of the school's teachers). The third group is composed of occupations such as personnel directors in local firms, accountants, "middle management," and a few small capitalists (owners of shops in the area). The children of several local doctors attend this school. Most family incomes are between $13,000 and $25,000, with a few higher. This income range is typical of 38.9 percent of the families in the United States.[7]

The fourth school has a parent population that is at the upper income level of the upper middle class and is predominantly professional. This school will be called the *affluent professional school*. Typical jobs are: cardiologist, interior designer, corporate lawyer or engineer, executive in advertising or television. There are some families who are not as affluent as the majority (the family of the superintendent of the district's schools, and the one or two families in which the fathers are skilled workers). In addition, a few of the families are more affluent than the majority and can be classified in the capitalist class (a partner in a prestigious Wall Street stock brokerage firm). Approximately 90 percent of the children in this school are white. Most family incomes are between $40,000 and $80,000. This income span represents approximately 7 percent of the families in the United States.[8]

In the fifth school the majority of the families belong to the capitalist class. This school will be called the *executive elite school* because most of the fathers are top executives (for example, presidents and vice-presidents) in major United States-based multinational corporations—for example, AT&T, RCA, Citibank, American Express, U.S. Steel. A sizable group of fathers are top executives in financial firms in Wall Street. There are also a number of fathers who list their occupations as "general counsel" to a particular corporation, and these corporations are also among the large multi-nationals. Many of the mothers do volunteer work in the Junior League, Junior Fortnightly, or other service groups; some are intricately involved in town politics; and some are themselves in well-paid occupations. There are no minority children in the school. Almost all the family incomes are over $100,000 with some in the $500,000 range. The incomes in this school represent less than 1 percent of the families in the United States.[9]

Since each of the five schools is only one instance of elementary education in a particular social class context, I will not generalize beyond the sample. However,

---

[7]Ibid. [Author's note]

[8]This figure is an estimate. According to the Bureau of the Census, only 2.6 percent of families in the United States have money income of $50,000 or over. U.S. Bureau of the Census, *Current Population Reports* Series P-60. For figures on income at these higher levels, see J.D. Smith and S. Franklin, "The Concentration of Personal Wealth, 1922–1969," *American Economic Review* 64 (1974): 162–67. [Author's note]

[9]Smith and Franklin, "The Concentration of Personal Wealth." [Author's note]

the examples of schoolwork which follow will suggest characteristics of education in each social setting that appear to have theoretical and social significance and to be worth investigation in a larger number of schools.

The Working Class Schools

In the two working-class schools, work is following the steps of a procedure. The procedure is usually mechanical, involving rote behavior and very little decision making or choice. The teachers rarely explain why the work is being assigned, how it might connect to other assignments, or what the idea is that lies behind the procedure or gives it coherence and perhaps meaning or significance. Available textbooks are not always used, and the teachers often prepare their own dittos or put work examples on the board. Most of the rules regarding work are designations of what the children are to do; the rules are steps to follow. These steps are told to the children by the teachers and are often written on the board. The children are usually told to copy the steps as notes. These notes are to be studied. Work is often evaluated not according to whether it is right or wrong but according to whether the children followed the right steps.

The following examples illustrate these points. In math, when two-digit division was introduced, the teacher in one school gave a four-minute lecture on what the terms are called (which number is the divisor, dividend, quotient, and remainder). The children were told to copy these names in their notebooks. Then the teacher told them the steps to follow to do the problems, saying, "This is how you do them." The teacher listed the steps on the board, and they appeared several days later as a chart hung in the middle of the front wall: "Divide, Multiply, Subtract, Bring Down." The children often did examples of two-digit division. When the teacher went over the examples with them, he told them what the procedure was for each problem, rarely asking them to conceptualize or explain it themselves: "Three into twenty-two is seven; do your subtraction and one is left over." During the week that two-digit division was introduced (or at any other time), the investigator did not observe any discussion of the idea of grouping involved in division, any use of manipulables, or any attempt to relate two-digit division to any other mathematical process. Nor was there any attempt to relate the steps to an actual or possible thought process of the children. The observer did not hear the terms *dividend, quotient,* and so on, used again. The math teacher in the other working-class school followed similar procedures regarding two-digit division and at one point her class seemed confused. She said, "You're confusing yourselves. You're tensing up. Remember, when you do this, it's the same steps over and over again—and that's the way division always is." Several weeks later, after a test, a group of her children "still didn't get it," and she made no attempt to explain the concept of dividing things into groups or to give them manipulables for their own investigation. Rather, she went over the steps with them again and told them that they "needed more practice."

In other areas of math, work is also carrying out often unexplained fragmented procedures. For example, one of the teachers led the children through a series of steps to make a 1-inch grid on their paper *without* telling them that they were making a 1-inch grid or that it would be used to study scale. She said, "Take your ruler. Put it across the top. Make a mark at every number. Then move your ruler down to the bottom. No, put it across the bottom. Now make a mark on top of every number. Now draw a line from. . . ." At this point a girl said that she had a faster way to do it and the teacher said, "No, you don't; you don't even know what I'm making yet. Do it this way or it's wrong." After they had made the lines up and down and across, the teacher told them she wanted them to make a figure by connecting some dots and to measure that, using the scale of 1 inch equals 1 mile. Then they were to cut it out. She said, "Don't cut it until I check it."

In both working-class schools, work in language arts is mechanics of punctuation (commas, periods, question marks, exclamation points), capitalization, and the four kinds of sentences. One teacher explained to me, "Simple punctuation is all they'll ever use." Regarding punctuation, either a teacher or a ditto stated the rules for where, for example, to put commas. The investigator heard no classroom discussion of the aural context of punctuation (which, of course, is what gives each mark its meaning). Nor did the investigator hear any statement or inference that placing a punctuation mark could be a decision-making process, depending, for example, on one's intended meaning. Rather, the children were told to follow the rules. Language arts did not involve creative writing. There were several writing assignments throughout the year but in each instance the children were given a ditto, and they wrote answers to questions on the sheet. For example, they wrote their "autobiography" by answering such questions as "Where were you born?" "What is your favorite animal?" on a sheet entitled "All About Me."

In one of the working-class schools, the class had a science period several times a week. On the three occasions observed, the children were not called upon to set up experiments or to give explanations for facts or concepts. Rather, on each occasion the teacher told them in his own words what the book said. The children copied the teacher's sentences from the board. Each day that preceded the day they were to do a science experiment, the teacher told them to copy the directions from the book for the procedure they would carry out the next day and to study the list at home that night. The day after each experiment, the teacher went over what they had "found" (they did the experiments as a class, and each was actually a class demonstration led by the teacher). Then the teacher wrote what they "found" on the board, and the children copied that in their notebooks. Once or twice a year there are science projects. The project is chosen and assigned by the teacher from a box of 3-by-5-inch cards. On the card the teacher has written the question to be answered, the books to use, and how much to write. Explaining the cards to the observer, the teacher said, "It tells them exactly what to do, or they couldn't do it."

Social studies in the working-class schools is also largely mechanical, rote work that was given little explanation or connection to larger contexts. In one school, for example, although there was a book available, social studies work was to copy the teacher's notes from the board. Several times a week for a period of several months the children copied these notes. The fifth grades in the district were to study United States history. The teacher used a booklet she had purchased called "The Fabulous Fifty States." Each day she put information from the booklet in outline form on the board and the children copied it. The type of information did not vary: the name of the state, its abbreviation, state capital, nickname of the state, its main products, main business, and a "Fabulous Fact" ("Idaho grew twenty-seven billion potatoes in one year. That's enough potatoes for each man, woman, and . . .") As the children finished copying the sentences, the teacher erased them and wrote more. Children would occasionally go to the front to pull down the wall map in order to locate the states they were copying, and the teacher did not dissuade them. But the observer never saw her refer to the map; nor did the observer ever hear her make other than perfunctory remarks concerning the information the children were copying. Occasionally the children colored in a ditto and cut it out to make a stand-up figure (representing, for example, a man roping a cow in the Southwest). These were referred to by the teacher as their social studies "projects."

Rote behavior was often called for in classroom work. When going over 15 math and language art skills sheets, for example, as the teacher asked for the answer to each problem, he fired the questions rapidly, staccato, and the scene reminded the observer of a sergeant drilling recruits: above all, the questions demanded that you stay at attention: "The next one? What do I put here? . . . Here? Give us the next." Or "How many commas in this sentence? Where do I put them . . . The next one?"

The four fifth grade teachers observed in the working-class schools attempted to control classroom time and space by making decisions without consulting the children and without explaining the basis for their decisions. The teacher's control thus often seemed capricious. Teachers, for instance, very often ignored the bells to switch classes—deciding among themselves to keep the children after the period was officially over to continue with the work or for disciplinary reasons or so they (the teachers) could stand in the hall and talk. There were no clocks in the rooms in either school, and the children often asked, "What period is this?" "When do we go to gym?" The children had no access to materials. These were handed out by teachers and closely guarded. Things in the room "belonged" to the teacher: "Bob, bring me my garbage can." The teachers continually gave the children orders. Only three times did the investigator hear a teacher in either working-class school preface a directive with an unsarcastic "please," or "let's" or "would you." Instead, the teachers said, "Shut up," "Shut your mouth," "Open your books," "Throw your gum away—if you want to rot your teeth, do it on your own time." Teachers made every effort to control the movement of the children, and often shouted, "'Why are you out of your seat??!!" If the children got permission to leave the room, they had to take a written pass with the date and time. . . .

Middle-Class School

In the middle-class school, work is getting the right answer. If one accumulates enough right answers, one gets a good grade. One must follow the directions in order to get the right answers, but the directions often call for some figuring, some choice, some decision making. For example, the children must often figure out by themselves what the directions ask them to do and how to get the answer: what do you do first, second, and perhaps third? Answers are usually found in books or by listening to the teacher. Answers are usually words, sentences, numbers, or facts and dates; one writes them on paper, and one should be neat. Answers must be given in the right order, and one cannot make them up.

The following activities are illustrative. Math involves some choice: one may do two-digit division the long way or the short way, and there are some math problems that can be done "in your head." When the teacher explains how to do two-digit division, there is recognition that a cognitive process is involved; she gives you several ways and says, "I want to make sure you understand what you're doing—so you get it right"; and, when they go over the homework, she asks the *children* to tell how they did the problem and what answer they got.

In social studies the daily work is to read the assigned pages in the textbook and to answer the teacher's questions. The questions are almost always designed to check on whether the students have read the assignment and understood it: who did so-and-so; what happened after that; when did it happen, where, and sometimes, why did it happen? The answers are in the book and in one's understanding of the book; the teacher's hints when one doesn't know the answers are to "read it again" or to look at the picture or at the rest of the paragraph. One is to search for the answer in the "context," in what is given.

Language arts is "simple grammar, what they need for everyday life." The language arts teacher says, "They should learn to speak properly, to write business letters and thank-you letters, and to understand what nouns and verbs and simple subjects are." Here, as well, actual work is to choose the right answers, to understand what is given. The teacher often says, "Please read the next sentence and then I'll question you about it." One teacher said in some exasperation to a boy who was fooling around in class, "If you don't know the answers to the questions I ask, then you can't stay in this *class!* [pause] You *never* know the answers to the questions I ask, and it's not fair to me—and certainly not to you!"

Most lessons are based on the textbook. This does not involve a critical perspective on what is given there. For example, a critical perspective in social studies is perceived as dangerous by these teachers because it may lead to controversial topics; the parents might complain. The children, however, are often curious especially in social studies. Their questions are tolerated and usually answered perfunctorily. But after a few minutes the teacher will say, "All right, we're not going any farther. Please open your social studies workbook." While the teachers spend a lot of time explaining and expanding on what the textbooks say, there is little attempt to analyze how or why things happen, or to give thought to how pieces of a culture, or, say, a system of numbers or elements of a language fit together or can be analyzed. What has happened in the past and what exists now may not be equitable or fair, but (shrug) that is the way things are and one does not confront such matters in school. For example, in social studies after a child is called on to read a passage about the pilgrims, the teacher summarizes the paragraph and then says, "So you can see how strict they were about everything." A child asks, "Why?" "Well, because they felt that if you weren't busy you'd get into trouble." Another child asks, "Is it true that they burned women at the stake?" The teacher says, "Yes, if a woman did anything strange, they hanged them. [*sic*] What would a woman do, do you think, to make them burn them? [*sic*] See if you can come up with better answers than my other [social studies] class." Several children offer suggestions, to which the teacher nods but does not comment. Then she says, "Okay, good," and calls on the next child to read.

Work tasks do not usually require creativity. Serious attention is rarely given in school work on *how* the children develop or express their own feelings and ideas, either linguistically or in graphic form. On the occasions when creativity or self-expression is requested, it is peripheral to the main activity or it is "enriched" or "for fun." During a lesson on what similes are, for example, the teacher explains what they are, puts several on the board, gives some other examples herself, and then asks the children if they can "make some up." She calls on three children who give similes, two of which are actually in the book they have open before them. The teacher does not comment on this and then asks several others to choose similes from the list of phrases in the book. Several do so correctly, and she says, "Oh good! You're picking them out! See how good we are?" Their homework is to pick out the rest of the similes from the list.

Creativity is not often required in social studies and science projects, either. Social studies projects, for example, are given with directions to "find information on your topic" and write it up. The children are not supposed to copy but to "put it in your own words." Although a number of the projects subsequently went beyond the teacher's direction to find information and had quite expressive covers and inside illustrations, the teacher's evaluative comments had to do with the amount of information, whether they had "copied," and if their work was neat.

The style of control of the three fifth-grade teachers observed in this school varied from somewhat easygoing to strict, but in contrast to the working-class schools, the teachers' decisions were usually based on external rules and regulations—for example, on criteria that were known or available to the children. Thus, the teachers always honor the bells for changing classes, and they usually evaluate children's work by what is in the textbooks and answer booklets.

There is little excitement in schoolwork for the children, and the assignments are perceived as having little to do with their interests and feelings. As one child said, what you do is "store facts up in your head like cold storage—until you need it later for a test or your job." Thus, doing well is important because there are thought to be *other* likely rewards: a good job or college.[10]

Affluent Professional School

In the affluent professional school, work is a creative activity carried out independently. The students are continually asked to express and apply ideas and concepts. Work involves individual thought and expressiveness, expansion and illustration of ideas, and choice of appropriate method and material. (The class is not considered an open classroom, and the principal explained that because of the large number of discipline problems in the fifth grade this year they did not departmentalize. The teacher who agreed to take part in the study said she is "more structured this year" than she usually is.) The products of work in this class are often written stories, editorials and essays, or representations of ideas in mural, graph, or craft form. The products of work should not be like anybody else's and should show individuality. They should exhibit good design, and (this is important) they must also fit empirical reality. The relatively few rules to be followed

---

[10]A dominant feeling expressed directly and indirectly by teachers in this school, was boredom with their work. They did, however, in contrast to the working-class schools, almost always carry out lessons during class times. [Author's note]

regarding work are usually criteria for, or limits on, individual activity. One's product is usually evaluated for the quality of its expression and for the appropriateness of its conception to the task. In many cases, one's own satisfaction with the product is an important criterion for its evaluation. When right answers are called for, as in commercial materials like SRA (Science Research Associates) and math, it is important that the children decide on an answer as a result of thinking about the idea involved in what they're being asked to do. Teacher's hints are to "think about it some more."

The following activities are illustrative. The class takes home a sheet requesting each child's parents to fill in the number of cars they have, the number of television sets, refrigerators, games, or rooms in the house, and so on. Each child is to figure the average number of a type of possession owned by the fifth grade. Each child must compile the "data" from all the sheets. A calculator is available in the classroom to do the mechanics of finding the average. Some children decide to send sheets to the fourth-grade families for comparison. Their work should be "verified" by a classmate before it is handed in.

Each child and his or her family has made a geoboard. The teacher asks the class to get their geoboards from the side cabinet, to take a handful of rubber bands, and then to listen to what she would like them to do. She says, "I would like you to design a figure and then find the perimeter and area. When you have it, check with your neighbor. After you've done that, please transfer it to graph paper and tomorrow I'll ask you to make up a question about it for someone. When you hand it in, please let me know whose it is and who verified it. Then I have something else for you to do that's really fun. [pause] Find the average number of chocolate chips in three cookies. I'll give you three cookies, and you'll have to *eat* your way through, I'm afraid!" Then she goes around the room and gives help, suggestions, praise, and admonitions that they are getting noisy. They work sitting, or standing up at their desks, at benches in the back, or on the floor. A child hands the teacher his paper and she comments, "I'm not accepting this paper. Do a better design." To another child she says, "That's fantastic! But you'll never find the area. Why don't you draw a figure inside [the big one] and subtract to get the area?"

The school district requires the fifth grade to study ancient civilizations (in particular, Egypt, Athens, and Sumer). In this classroom, the emphasis is on illustrating and re-creating the culture of the people of ancient times. The following are typical activities: the children made an 8mm film on Egypt, which one of the parents edited. A girl in the class wrote the script, and the class acted it out. They put the sound on themselves. They read stories of those days. They wrote essays and stories depicting the lives of the people and the societal and occupational divisions. They chose from a list of projects, all of which involved graphical presentations of ideas. For example: "Make a mural depicting the division of labor in Egyptian society."

Each wrote and exchanged a letter in hieroglyphics with a fifth grader in another class, and they also exchanged stories they wrote in cuneiform. They made a scroll and singed the edges so it looked authentic. They each chose an occupation and made an Egyptian plaque representing that occupation, simulating the appropriate Egyptian design. They carved their design on a cylinder of wax, pressed the wax into clay, and then baked the clay. Although one girl did not choose an occupation but carved instead a series of gods and slaves, the teacher said, "That's all right, Amber, it's beautiful." As they were working the teacher said, "Don't cut into your clay until you're satisfied with your design."

Social studies also involves almost daily presentation by the children of some event from the news. The teacher's questions ask the children to expand what they say, to give more details, and to be more specific. Occasionally she adds some remarks to help them see connections between events.

The emphasis on expressing and illustrating ideas in social studies is accompanied in language arts by an emphasis on creative writing. Each child wrote a rebus story for a first grader whom they had interviewed to see what kind of story the child liked best. They wrote editorials on pending decisions by the school board and radio plays, some of which were read over the school intercom from the office and one of which was performed in the auditorium. There is no language arts textbook because, the teacher said, "The principal wants us to be creative." There is not much grammar, but there is punctuation. One morning when the observer arrived, the class was doing a punctuation ditto. The teacher later apologized for using the ditto. "It's just for review," she said. "I don't teach punctuation that way. We use their language." The ditto had three unambiguous rules for where to put commas in a sentence. As the teacher was going around to help the children with the ditto, she repeated several times, "Where you put commas depends on how you say the sentence; it depends on the situation and what you want to say." Several weeks later the observer saw another punctuation activity. The teacher had printed a five-paragraph story on an oak tag and then cut it into phrases. She read the whole story to the class from the book, then passed out the phrases. The group had to decide how the phrases could best be put together again. (They arranged the phrases on the floor.) The point was not to replicate the story, although that was not irrelevant, but to "decide what you think the best way is." Punctuation marks on cardboard pieces were then handed out, and the children discussed and then decided what mark was best at each place they thought one was needed. At the end of each paragraph the teacher asked, "Are you satisfied with the way the paragraphs are now? Read it to yourself and see how it sounds." Then she read the original story again, and they compared the two.

Describing her goals in science to the investigator, the teacher said, "We use ESS (Elementary Science Study). It's very good because it gives a hands-on experience— so they can make *sense* out of it. It doesn't matter whether it [what they find] is right or wrong. I bring them together and there's value in discussing their ideas."

The products of work in this class are often highly valued by the children and the teacher. In fact, this was the only school in which the investigator was not allowed to take original pieces of the children's work for her files. If the work was small enough, however, and was on paper, the investigator could duplicate it on the copying machine in the office.

The teacher's attempt to control the class involves constant negotiation. She does not give direct orders unless she is angry because the children have been too noisy. Normally, she tries to get them to foresee the consequences of their actions and to decide accordingly. For example, lining them up to go see a play written by the sixth graders, she says, "I presume you're lined up by someone with whom you want to sit. I hope you're lined up by someone you won't get in trouble with." . . .

One of the few rules governing the children's movement is that no more than three children may be out of the room at once. There is a school rule that anyone can go to the library at any time to get a book. In the fifth grade I observed, they sign their name on the chalkboard and leave. There are no passes. Finally, the children have a fair amount of officially sanctioned say over what happens in the class. For example, they often negotiate what work is to be done. If the teacher wants to move on to the next subject, but the children say they are not ready, they want to work on their present projects some *more*, she very often lets them do it.

Executive Elite School

In the executive elite school, work is developing one's analytical intellectual powers. Children are continually asked to reason through a problem, to produce intellectual products that are both logically sound and of top academic quality. A primary goal of thought is to conceptualize rules by which elements may fit together in systems and then to apply these rules in solving a problem. Schoolwork helps one to achieve, to excel, to prepare for life.

The following are illustrative. The math teacher teaches area and perimeter by having the children derive formulas for each. First she helps them, through discussion at the board, to arrive at $A = W \times L$ as a formula (not *the* formula) for area. After discussing several, she says, "Can anyone make up a formula for perimeter? Can you figure that out yourselves? [pause] Knowing what we know, can we think of a formula?" She works out three children's suggestions at the board, saying to two, "Yes, that's a good one," and then asks the class if they can think of any more. No one volunteers. To prod them, she says, "If you use rules and good reasoning, you get many ways. Chris, can you think up a formula?"

She discusses two-digit division with the children as a decision-making process. Presenting a new type of problem to them, she asks, "What's the *first* decision you'd make if presented with this kind of example? What is the first thing you'd *think*? Craig?" Craig says, "To find my first partial quotient." She responds, "Yes, that would be your first decision. How would you do that?" Craig explains, and then the teacher says, "OK, we'll see how that works for you." The class tries his way. Subsequently, she comments on the merits and shortcomings of several other children's decisions. Later, she tells the investigator that her goals in math are to develop their reasoning and mathematical thinking and that, unfortunately, "there's no time for manipulables."

While right answers are important in math, they are not "given" by the book or by the teacher but may be challenged by the children. Going over some problems in late September the teacher says, "Raise your hand if you do not agree." A child says, "I don't agree with sixty-four." The teacher responds, "OK, there's a question about sixty-four. [to class] Please check it. Owen, they're disagreeing with you. Kristen, they're checking yours." The teacher emphasized this repeatedly during September and October with statements like "Don't be afraid to say you disagree. In the last [math] class, somebody disagreed, and they were right. Before you disagree, check yours, and if you still think we're wrong, then we'll check it out." By Thanksgiving, the children did not often speak in terms of right and wrong math problems but of whether they agreed with the answer that had been given.

There are complicated math mimeos with many word problems. Whenever they go over the examples, they discuss how each child has set up the problem. The children must explain it precisely. On one occasion the teacher said, "I'm more— just as interested in *how* you set up the problem as in what answer you find. If you set up a problem in a good way, the answer is *easy* to find."

Social studies work is most often reading and discussion of concepts and independent research. There are only occasional artistic, expressive, or illustrative projects. Ancient Athens and Sumer are, rather, societies to analyze. The following questions are typical of those that guide the children's independent research. "What mistakes did Pericles make after the war?" "What mistakes did the citizens of Athens make?" "What are the elements of a civilization?" "How did Greece build an economic empire?" "Compare the way Athens chose its leaders with the way we choose ours." Occasionally the children are asked to make up sample questions for their social studies tests. On an occasion when the investigator was present, the social studies teacher rejected a child's question by saying, "That's just fact. If I asked you that question on a test, you'd complain it was just memory! Good questions ask for concepts."

In social studies—but also in reading, science, and health—the teachers initiate classroom discussions of current social issues and problems. These discussions occurred on every one of the investigator's visits, and a teacher told me, "These children's opinions are important—it's important that they learn to reason things through." The classroom discussions always struck the observer as quite realistic and analytical, dealing with concrete social issues like the following: "Why do workers strike?" "Is that right or wrong?" "Why do we have inflation, and what can be done to stop it?" "Why do companies put chemicals in food when the natural ingredients are available?" and so on. Usually the children did not have to be prodded to give their opinions. In fact, their statements and the interchanges between them struck the observer as quite sophisticated conceptually and verbally, and well-informed. Occasionally the teachers would prod with statements such as, "Even if you don't know [the answers], if you think logically about it, you can figure it out." And "I'm asking you [these] questions to help you think this through."

Language arts emphasizes language as a complex system, one that should be mastered. The children are asked to diagram sentences of complex grammatical construction, to memorize irregular verb conjugations (he lay, he has lain, and so on . . .), and to use the proper participles, conjunctions, and interjections in their speech. The teacher (the same one who teaches social studies) told them, "It is not enough to get these right on tests; you must use what you learn [in grammar classes] in your written and oral work. I will grade you on that."

Most writing assignments are either research reports and essays for social studies or experiment analyses and write-ups for science. There is only an occasional story or other "creative writing" assignment. On the occasion observed by the investigator (the writing of a Halloween story), the points the teacher stressed in preparing the children to write involved the structural aspects of a story rather than the expression of feelings or other ideas. The teacher showed them a filmstrip, "The Seven Parts of a Story," and lectured them on plot development, mood setting, character development, consistency, and the use of a logical or appropriate ending. The stories they subsequently wrote were, in fact, well-structured, but many were also personal and expressive. The teacher's evaluative comments, however, did not refer to the expressiveness or artistry but were all directed toward whether they had "developed" the story well.

Language arts work also involved a large amount of practice in presentation of the self and in managing situations where the child was expected to be in charge. For example, there was a series of assignments in which each child had to be a "student teacher." The child had to plan a lesson in grammar, outlining, punctuation, or other language arts topic and explain the concept to the class. Each child was to prepare a worksheet or game and a homework assignment as well. After each presentation, the teacher and other children gave a critical appraisal of the "student teacher's" performance. Their criteria were: whether the student spoke clearly, whether the lesson was interesting, whether the student made any mistakes, and whether he or she kept control of the class. On an occasion when a child did not maintain control, the teacher said, "When you're up there, you have authority and you have to use it. I'll back you up."

The executive elite school is the only school where bells do not demarcate the periods of time. The two fifth-grade teachers were very strict about changing classes on schedule, however, as specific plans for each session had been made. The teachers attempted to keep tight control over the children during lessons, and the children were sometimes flippant, boisterous, and occasionally rude. However, the children may be brought into line by reminding them that "It is up to you." "You must control yourself," "you are responsible for your work," you must "set your own priorities." One teacher told a child, "You are the only driver of your car and only you can regulate your speed." A new teacher complained to the observer that she had thought "these children" would have more control.

While strict attention to the lesson at hand is required, the teachers make relatively little attempt to regulate the movement of the children at other times. For example, except for the kindergartners the children in this school do not have to wait for the bell to ring in the morning; they may go to their classroom when they arrive at school. Fifth graders often came early to read, to finish work, or to catch up. After the first two months of school, the fifth-grade teachers did not line the children up to change classes or to go to gym, and so on, but, when the children were ready and quiet, they were told they could go—sometimes without the teachers.

In the classroom, the children could get materials when they needed them and took what they needed from closets and from the teacher's desk. They were in charge of the office at lunchtime. During class they did not have to sign out or ask permission to leave the room; they just got up and left. Because of the pressure to get work done, however, they did not leave the room very often. The teachers were very polite to the children, and the investigator heard no sarcasm, no nasty remarks, and few direct orders. The teachers never called the children "honey" or "dear" but always called them by name. The teachers were expected to be available before school, after school, and for part of their lunchtime to provide extra help if needed.

The foregoing analysis of differences in schoolwork in contrasting social class contexts suggests the following conclusion: the "hidden curriculum" of schoolwork is tacit preparation for relating to the process of production in a particular way. Differing curricular, pedagogical, and pupil evaluation practices emphasize different cognitive and behavioral skills in each social setting and thus contribute to the development in the children of certain potential relationships to physical and symbolic capital,[11] to authority, and to the process of work. School experience, in the sample of schools discussed here, differed qualitatively by social class. These differences may not only contribute to the development in the children in each social class of certain types of economically significant relationships and not others, but would thereby help to reproduce this system of relations in society. In the contribution to the reproduction of unequal social relations lies a theoretical meaning and social consequence of classroom practice.

The identification of different emphases in classrooms in a sample of contrasting social class contexts implies that further research should be conducted in a large number of schools to investigate the types of work tasks and interactions in each to see if they differ in the ways discussed here and to see if similar potential relationships are uncovered. Such research could have as a product the further elucidation of complex but not readily apparent connections between everyday activity in schools and classrooms and the unequal structure of economic relationships in which we work and live.

[11]*Physical and symbolic capital:* Elsewhere Anyon defines capital as "property that is used to produce profit, interest, or rent": she defines symbolic capital as the knowledge and skills that "may yield social and cultural power."

3

One History of Disability in America: How Collective Action Became Possible

SHARON BARNARTT AND RICHARD SCOTCH

Many histories have been written about people with impairments. Some consider people with impairments in general; others either consider the history of people with specific types of physical impairments or delve into the history of disability laws and policies.[1] Although these histories are useful, and will be cited here, by themselves they do not help us to understand the central question that this chapter attempts to answer, which is how contentious political action by people with impairments became possible.

The focus of this chapter is on how the history of people with impairments contributed to their readiness to become mobilized to participate in contentious political action.[2] This history prevented substantial mobilization from occurring for many years, but it also set the stage for the mobilizations that began in the 1970s. The answer to the question of why and how social movement activity in the deaf and disability communities occurred cannot be answered simply. We will see that it arose not *only* from the spillover from other social movements of the 1960s, not *only* because there were increasing numbers of people with impairments, and not *only* because Ed Roberts was in Berkeley. Rather, it was the interplay of social, demographic, political, and economic factors that produced a situation conducive to the development of contentious action by people with impairments. Differences in the social histories of people with various types of impairments set the stage for the diversity of issues, tactics, and timing in contentious actions. Communities of people with some types of impairments have developed over the years, in ways that have made cross-disability collective action somewhat difficult to achieve even now.

In this chapter we do not belabor the history of abuses such as the sterilization of retarded people or the fact that institutional settings were predominantly facilities for children from poor or immigrant families (Trent, 1994: 185). The mere presence of inequities or injustices does not explain contentious action. There are many situations in the world that participants or observers may think are abusive, discriminatory, outrageous, immoral, or otherwise inappropriate but which do not lead to collective action. Rather, the social, economic, political, and cultural conditions must support the expression of the grievance in collective action. But since contentious action will also not occur without a grievance, we show how grievances arose, and how social and cultural situations developed that were conducive to the expression of grievances through collective action.

What Facilitates the Emergence of Contentious Action?

One of the questions scholars of social movements have considered is, "What types of social conditions facilitate the growth of contentious actions?" Many answers have been proposed (McAdam, McCarthy, and Zald, 1988). Scholars who focused on social conditions that facilitate the genesis of social movements have included social structural strain (Smelser, 1962),[3] inequities in access to resources (McCarthy and Zald, 1973), the presence of existing social networks (Morris, 1984), the absence of competing solidarities, and the presence of aggrieved and otherwise powerless people (Lipsky, 1968; Piven and Cloward, 1979). Those who have focused on political conditions have included relative deprivation (Davies, 1963), changes in the structure of political opportunities, lack of repressive social control, and the sudden imposition of a grievance. Those who have focused on economic conditions have suggested that economic prosperity is a precondition of social movement activity. Those who have focused on demographic or geographic conditions have suggested that ecological concentrations of homogenous people must exist—and therefore, that numbers of the relevant people must be large enough to make such concentrations feasible, if not also common. Finally, those who focus on cultural characteristics, attitudes, or ideologies (a group that until recently has been rather rare among social movements scholars) have suggested that the "politicization of private life" and the existence of collective action "frames" that fit into existing cultural assumptions are necessary precursors to collective action (Snow et al., 1986; Snow and Benford, 1988, 1992).

Individually, each answer to the question suggests a condition that is necessary, but not sufficient, for such contentious political activity to occur. Taken together, they begin to provide a more complete answer to the question, but it is not clear how many of these necessary conditions must exist in one time period for collective action to become possible.

Several factors seem more important than others. These include ecological concentrations of homogenous people that occur either through voluntary or involuntary groupings; the presence of organizations; the basis for grievances; and the presence of collective action frames. The presence either of formal organizations or informal groups of people within the oppressed (or dominated) community is primary among the necessary conditions. In the absence of indigenous organizational strength, a community would be unable to take advantage of situations— such as a change in the political opportunity structure, a suddenly imposed grievance, or increasing relative deprivation—that would otherwise be conducive to contentious political action. Organizations offer several crucial resources upon which social movements can be built including a membership base, a communication network, and leaders. In addition, groups can provide money, stable and predictable sources of funding, and labor. Such resources are especially crucial at the beginning of a movement, when outside resources are not available or reliable (McAdam, 1982; McAdam, McCarthy, and Zald, 1988; Morris, 1984). What we need to know, then, from the history of people with disabilities is how and when these facilitating conditions came to exist.

The Colonial Era

In the early years of European settlement in North America, disability was well known. People with disabilities either were born with them or their disability was the result of war-related injuries. Few impairments resulting from childhood or even adult illnesses were seen at that time because of the high childhood mortality rate. Almost one out of four children did not survive to age five and less than half survived to adulthood (Winzer, 1997). Adult mortality was also high. Women were perpetually pregnant or nursing, and life expectancy was about thirty-five years. People at that time were more likely to die from conditions that now might produce impairments than they were to survive with an impairment, because medical care was not sufficiently advanced to be able to cure severe acute illnesses.[4]

During colonial times, people who had cognitive or mental impairments, mobility impairments, or were blind or deaf were part of the social landscape (Trent, 1994: 7). For some families, having a member with such an impairment was not catastrophic. At the time of the American Revolution, over 90 percent of Americans were farmers. In that preindustrial economy, many types of impairments were not severe enough to prevent a person from working on the farm or in small-scale production. For example, deafness might not prevent a person from working in the fields, although loss of arm mobility might (Barnartt, 1992). Thus, people with impairments could still be economically productive (Gooding, 1994: 13).[5] In addition, many, if not most, people lived in extended families. If daily care was needed, families with many members could often manage. The downside of family care was that disabled children were expected to remain at home, and education or rehabilitation was unknown (Bowe, 1978: 9).

In the colonial era, the community response to a poor family who had a member with a physical impairment was to try to keep the family intact. This included providing cash or food assistance when possible. Called "outdoor-relief," it was a way to keep people with impairments in their homes and a way to provide some assistance to people who were infirm but not poor enough to need to go into a workhouse.[6] Funded by local governments, it was the most common type of societal response to disability at that time (Stone, 1984).

A few large cities, such as New York, Boston, and Philadelphia, had formal institutions for people with impairments. These workhouses or almshouses were primarily meant for people who were poor, but many of their inhabitants also had physical impairments (Ferguson, 1994: 25–29). Because there were so few institutions, it is likely that only a small proportion of people with impairments were in them. Some people with impairments were auctioned off as indentured servants (Crewe, Zola, and Associates, 1983: 1).

Since most people with impairments lived with their families, if the family was wealthy, having a disabled family member was seen as a private problem (Ferguson, 1994: 28). In Europe disabled children of wealthy or royal families often received services and types of education that disabled children from less wealthy families did not. This was sometimes done in order to permit the children to inherit wealth (Bowe, 1978: 8).[7]

Even in colonial America some wealthy families sent their children with impairments to Europe for "special education." Van Cleve and Crouch note the case of a family that sent its three deaf children to Scotland in the 1770s to receive a type of special education not yet available in the New World. But they also note the case of a family that was neither prominent nor wealthy that also hired a tutor for their deaf son (Van Cleve and Crouch, 1989: 18, 21–24).

For people whose impairments resulted from their service in the military, society took some responsibility. This was true as early as 1636, when the Plymouth Colony decreed that a soldier maimed by war would be "maintained competently by the Collonie during his life" (Liachowitz, 1988: 21). During the 1600s there were also provisions made for disabled seamen, who were the first group to receive federal medical care benefits (Straus, 1965). After the Revolutionary War, a number of laws were passed that indicated the duty of the community (in this case the nation) was to support wounded soldiers under some circumstances and for some, usually limited, periods of time (Liachowitz, 1988: 22–28). Voluntary charitable groups became involved before 1700, beginning a tradition of charity that would continue for about two hundred years (Crewe, Zola, and Associates, 1983).

Although it is clear that during this period the lives of people with impairments were not totally rosy, neither were they likely to be substantially worse than the lives of the majority of those without impairments.[8] The majority of the population of colonial North America lived on farms and were not terribly wealthy. Children with impairments were unlikely to be educated, but they were not unique, because universal public education was not introduced until early in the twentieth century.

There were no communities of people with impairments at that time. Not only that, but it is also unlikely that people with impairments had much contact with one another. They did not meet in schools, in rehabilitation clinics, in work situations, or in residential facilities, because these did not exist. They did not meet in towns because transportation was not readily available. (It must be remembered, however, that most people, with or without impairments, lived somewhat isolated lives during that time.) If there were perceptions of unfairness or inequity among people with impairments, they would have been unlikely to have easily communicated those feelings to others with impairments. However, such perceptions were unlikely to have been characteristic of the times in any case. Thus, there were no conditions during colonial times that would have been conducive to the development of protests or any other form of collective action by people with impairments.

The First Half of the Nineteenth Century

The War of 1812 and the Mexican War of 1846–1848 each produced more ex-soldiers with physical impairments. As had occurred after the Revolutionary War, laws were passed to provide money or grants of land for people with service-connected disabilities, but they still did not provide for medical or rehabilitative care (Albrecht, 1992: 97).

Some very important economic and social changes began at this time, which was the beginning of the Industrial Revolution. The process of industrialization was linked with rapid urbanization, and both had profound implications for the causation of disability, for the recognition and social construction of the notion of disability, and for disability policy.

Industrialization led to an increase in the numbers of people with disabilities. Factories, and the mines that produced raw material for them, were dangerous places to work. Workers in factories had disabling accidents. In addition, workers in mines contracted disabling illnesses such as black lung disease. The increased population density that came with urbanization led to increases in disease transmission and more epidemics. While many diseases were acute, killing large numbers of people, they also left survivors with physical and mental impairments. Thus, although industrialization is associated with increased standards of living and life expectancies, it is also associated with rising rates of chronic illness and physical disability (Albrecht, 1992: 42–43).

Industrialization and urbanization set the stage for changes in how disability was recognized and viewed within American society. As the result of a social structure in which economic success was primarily based upon working at paid jobs, disability came to be defined in economic terms as the inability to work (Berkowitz, 1987; Stone, 1984). Deviant or atypical characteristics that had been accepted in rural settings may have become less acceptable in urban settings, and accepted social roles previously open to people with disabilities who lived on farms or in small villages, such as "beggar" or "village idiot," disappeared (Hahn, 1997; Oliver, 1993: 51). With the advent of industrialization, there was greater emphasis on literacy. People with learning disabilities or mild intellectual or developmental impairments, who would not have stood out in societies in which literacy was poor or nonexistent, began to be recognized as having impairments (Winzer, 1997). Thus, the *recognition* of impairments as being disabling, as well as the numbers of impairments, may have increased as industrialization progressed.

As public education became more widespread, schools were also established for children who were deaf or blind. The first school for deaf children was established in Connecticut in 1817 and in 1832 the first school for blind children opened in Boston. By 1843, six states had state residential schools for deaf children, and, by 1857, there were nineteen such schools (Van Cleve and Crouch, 1989: 43–47, 71). Some of the schools were established by deaf people themselves; the earliest of these was the Indiana School for the Deaf, founded in 1843 (Padden, 1996).

Since deaf people—children and some adults—were isolated together in residential schools and often encouraged to use sign language, conversing in it quickly become a cherished part of their daily lives. Further, because sign language was a modality shared primarily with other deaf people and not the dominant society, this difference naturally drew deaf people closer together. These schools permitted deaf children and some adults to meet and interact, and they set the stage for the development of a deaf community (Jankowski, 1997: 46).

As mentioned previously, the Perkins School for the Blind was established in Boston in 1832 (Bowe, 1978: 11). The philosophy behind the establishment of that and other schools was to help blind people become self sufficient by offering them primarily vocational training. No one realized, however, that the schools had done nothing to "prepare *society* to receive them" (Matson, 1990: 5). As part of the school for blind children, Howe, the founder, began what was in essence the first sheltered workshop. This grew out of the vocational training program that was at the heart of his school; and it became necessary when it became clear that there was societal resistance to hiring blind people, whether they had training or not (Pelka, 1997: 282). However, Howe's school did not encourage the growth of a community in the same way that the deaf schools did. For one thing, communication was not such a large issue for blind children, who could communicate with their families and other children. But probably the more important factor was that Howe specifically tried to prevent community formation by refusing to allow alumni reunions (Van Cleve and Crouch, 1989: 148).

The first school for "idiots" (who we would now call people with developmental delays) was opened in 1848. At least six others were opened over the next twenty years (Trent, 1994: 14–15). However, children and adults with mental impairments and other physical impairments often remained in their communities of origin. For example, in New York state in 1856, only 6 percent (424) of almshouse inmates were labeled as being "idiots," and about 22 percent (1,644) were labeled "lunatics" (Ferguson, 1994: 35). These numbers can be compared to reports that indicated that there were 1,812 "idiots" and 2,742 persons labeled "insane" in the state at that time (Ferguson, 1994: 63). Although these numbers probably substantially underestimate the true prevalence of these conditions, they suggest that the proportions that were institutionalized were small. This is supported by a survey of "idiots" done in upstate New York in 1873, which indicated that 67 percent lived in the homes of family or friends (Ferguson, 1994: 64). Children or adults with impairments who lived with their families were unlikely to interact with any people who had similar impairments.

The period from 1820 to 1850 saw the increasing use of almshouses to warehouse poor people as well as those with physical and mental impairments (Ferguson, 1994: 29–30). Those who were placed in almshouses experienced wretched conditions and physical abuse. Because poor and disabled people were housed together, those with impairments may have interacted with others with similar problems. Although the oppressive nature of the almshouses was recognized by some (e.g., Charles Dickens), collective action against the conditions from within was unlikely to occur because of the variety of social, physical, and mental problems that occurred at the almshouses.

Because schools for children who were deaf, blind, or had developmental delays were being opened, children with similar impairments were beginning to interact with each other on a regular basis as pupils of segregated, usually residential, schools. Some of those who grew up in residential schools began to form communities. This was clearly true for deaf people, many of whom upon graduation secured jobs at the same residential schools they grew up in. In 1851, 36 percent of the teachers at these schools were deaf (Jankowski, 1997: 22).[9] Other former students stayed in areas close to the schools but did not get jobs there. In 1848 the *American Annals of the Deaf*, originally a publication for teachers of deaf students, began to be published (and continues to this day). In 1858 the New England Gallaudet Association of Deaf Mutes, the first organization set up by and for deaf adults, was established.

Thus, during this time period, a difference in social organization that would have a large impact on collective action more than 150 years later began to manifest itself. Although rates of disability probably were increasing, people with physical impairments other than deafness were most likely to remain fairly isolated, except for those children who attended segregated schools for blind or retarded children. It is among deaf people that we see the beginnings of the existence of shared values and interaction, in person or through print media, which are the hallmarks of a community. In the second half of the nineteenth century the deaf community emerged as a stronger force—only to experience several severe attacks against it.

The Second Half of the Nineteenth Century

Major social changes that occurred during the second half of the nineteenth century had an impact on people with disabilities many years later. One of the era's major events was the Civil War. The war provoked changes in how disabled veterans were treated by society. Not only were servicemen with disabilities given cash and other benefits, as had happened after the earlier wars, but, for the first time, medical or rehabilitative care was also provided (Albrecht, 1992: 96). In part, this change recognized that medical or rehabilitation providers had something to offer veterans, which had not previously been the case. But it was not until the very end of the nineteenth century that such practitioners really had much to offer.

Laws relating to blacks' civil rights were also passed as a result of the Civil War. These laws abolished slavery and provided for citizenship and voting rights for blacks, thus introducing the idea of civil rights for persons other than white, nondisabled males. The thirteenth, fourteenth, and fifteenth amendments to the U.S. Constitution abolished slavery, guaranteed due process under the law, and guaranteed the right to vote regardless of race, creed, color, or condition of previous servitude (but not sex), respectively. Civil Rights Acts were passed in 1866 and 1875, although parts of the latter were later overturned by the U.S. Supreme Court. In 1887 the 1866 Civil Rights Act was extended to include ethnic and religious groups (Barnartt and Seelman, 1988).

In the last half of the nineteenth century, the sources of disability that had begun to increase in the early 1800s continued to rise. People other than military servicemen were increasingly exposed to chances of disabling injuries. Workplace injuries were becoming more common in factories and in railroad, mining, and timber industries. Because of this, toward the end of the century, labor unions and reformers would begin to agitate for a system of compensation for workplace injuries similar to that which existed in Germany at that time (Albrecht, 1992: 97–99).

A vibrant deaf community developed toward the end of the nineteenth century. One impetus for that development came from overcoming the isolation that results from deafness, which was doubly distancing when compared to the isolation experienced by people with other types of physical or mental impairments at that time. Not only did deaf people seldom see other deaf people, they could also not communicate easily with the people with whom they did interact. So deaf people began to establish many organized ways in which to meet and interact with each other. An early example of a social club was the Deaf Mutes Union League of New York, founded in 1886 (Van Cleve and Crouch, 1989: 95). Other organizations established around this time included the National Association of the Deaf (NAD), which began in 1880, the American Athletic Association of the Deaf, the National Congress of the Jewish Deaf, and the American Professional Society of the Deaf (Van Cleve and Crouch, 1989: 87). In 1864, Congress passed legislation that called for the creation of Gallaudet University (then called the National Deaf-Mute College, a part of the Columbia Institution for the Deaf and Dumb).[10]

Another reason for the growth of the deaf community was that many deaf men worked as printers. As a result, there were many newspapers for the deaf community (Neisser, 1983: 235). The first, *The Deaf Mute*, began at the North Carolina Institution for the Deaf and Blind in 1849. By the end of the century as many as fifty residential schools published newspapers (Van Cleve and Crouch, 1989: 98), which included information of general interest to deaf people, such as advice and personal news, as well as news about activities specific to that school. But they also included articles aimed at hearing people, which portrayed deaf people's accomplishments and discussed incidents of perceived discrimination against deaf workers. For example, the *Silent Worker* began in 1891 as a school newspaper, but expanded its scope to include coverage of national and even international events within a few years (Buchanan, 1993).[11]

Even as the deaf community became organized for interaction and communication in the late 1800s, it suffered several setbacks. The first occurred in 1880, at an international meeting called the Milan Congress. At this meeting a resolution was passed that supported the teaching of speech to deaf people, rather than signs (Van Cleve and Crouch, 1989: 108–10). As a result, during the last two decades of the nineteenth century and through the first half of the next century, educators and others, including parents, increasingly attempted to wrest control of the schools from educators, many of whom were deaf themselves, who favored the use of sign language (Buchanan, 1993: 182).

The second event with negative consequences for deaf people occurred in 1883. In that year Alexander Graham Bell, who was married to a deaf woman, and whose invention of the telephone was actually an attempt to assist her, wrote an influential paper called the "Memoir upon the Formation of a Deaf Variety of the Human Race." This paper advocated societal opposition to deaf people intermarrying (Van Cleve and Crouch, 1989: 142). The following year, Bell reprinted many copies of this paper and sent it to members of Congress as well as many principals of deaf schools and others involved in deaf education (Van Cleve and Crouch, 1989: 149).[12]

It is actually not clear whether Bell's paper or his invention of the telephone actually had a more negative impact on deaf people. But it is clear that the Milan Congress did have a strong negative impact on deaf people, because it resulted in fewer deaf teachers and superintendents at the state schools as time went on. Ironically, however, it may also have had an energizing and mobilizing effect. Although it did not mobilize the deaf community for disruptive collective action, the National Association of the Deaf (which was then called the National Association of Deaf-Mutes) tried to ward off some of the threats to sign language (Jankowski, 1997: 5). Because groups that experience external threats develop stronger internal bonds, the threats to the deaf community may have had the paradoxical effect of strengthening it.

Some aspects of the deaf community's development began to create a rift between deaf people and those with other types of impairments. In part, the split was occurring simply because the deaf community was growing, and it did not include people with other types of impairments. But there were also intentional efforts to separate deaf people from people with other types of impairments. For example, the *Silent Worker* made explicit attempts to distinguish the situation of deaf people from the situation of people with other types of impairments, if not actually to derogate them. One of these is an editorial that discussed why deaf workers were better earners than were blind people (Buchanan, 1993: 179).

Similar community development did not occur for people with other types of impairments. For people with mild mental retardation, the patterns of segregation and institutionalization that began in the early years of the century continued. In the period from 1850 to 1860 there were some experiments with small, school-like residential facilities for children who were not severely retarded, but almshouses remained the only option for severely retarded people who needed to be institutionalized (Ferguson, 1994: 157–58). The school-based experiments failed, and by the end of the century, asylums took people with both mild and severe retardation. Asylums had few pretensions at education (Ferguson, 1994: 80). They were dependent upon medical practice, and they used medical, rather than educational, paradigms (Trent, 1994: 36). Despite efforts at institutionalization, however, more people with retardation lived in the community than in any type of institutional situation. In 1890, only 5,254 people were counted by the decennial census as being inmates at asylums for "idiots," at a time when the country's population was more than sixty-two million (Ferguson, 1994: 83).

During the late 1800s there were changes in the situation for blind people that were somewhat akin to those occurring in the deaf community. Several Braille systems were invented, and at least one teacher at the Perkins School was blind (Pelka, 1997: 49). Several organizations of and for blind people were begun during this time, including the Friedlander Union (1871) and the New York Blind Aid Association (1887). An alumni group was formed in 1895 at the Missouri School for the Blind. This group was later opened to graduates from other schools, and it changed its name to the American Blind People's Higher Education and General Improvement Association. After gaining support from blind people and groups in more than a dozen states and holding several conventions, the organization was "invaded" by school administrators and in 1905 became the American Association of Workers for the Blind (Matson, 1990: 6). An Alumni Association of California Schools for the Blind was also formed before the turn of the century (Matson, 1990: 8). Thus, situations conducive to the development of a blindness community began to emerge, although it is clear that for blind people that development was not as pervasive as it was for deaf people at that time.

In the area of mental health, the beginnings of an oppositional consciousness (Groch, 1994) emerged. Elizabeth Packard formed a group called the Anti-Insane Asylum Society in the 1860s. She published books and pamphlets that described the commitment of her husband to an insane asylum against her (and presumably also his) will (Pelka, 1997: 252). Later in the 1800s and early in the 1900s Clifford Beers would speak out on issues relating to people with mental disabilities and Helen Keller would do the same for people with multiple sensory impairments.

During the late 1800s, the stage began to be set for the contentious action that emerged later. The passage of civil rights laws for blacks provided the basis for a feeling of relative deprivation among other groups of people. The sheer numbers of people with impairments increased, as did the numbers and types of situations in which people with impairments were grouped or concentrated. A few organizations were established that drew together people with similar types of impairments, although there were not yet any cross-disability organizations. The trends toward legal definition of disabilities, the development of organizations to support persons with disabilities, and the development of communities of persons with various disabilities continued into the twentieth century, along with new trends that were conducive to the development of social movements.

The Early Twentieth Century: 1900–1945

The early twentieth century saw large societal changes as well as changes in the medical and social situation of people with disabilities. Several factors made the situation more conducive to the subsequent development of a social movement for people with impairments. These factors were a large increase in the number of people with physical impairments, increases in places where people with impairments might involuntarily meet, and the growth of situations that could provoke a feeling of relative deprivation.

World War I left between 123,000 and 300,000 American veterans with disabilities (Gritzer and Arluke, 1985: 39; Pelka, 1997: 101; Treanor, 1993: 15). Immediately after the war, the first federal legislation relating to rehabilitation was passed; it focused upon disabled veterans only. Disabled vets are closer to the age when people are likely to protest than are older people whose impairments show up later in life (Straus, 1965). That very few protests occurred at this time was a function of the time period, not the ages of the largest numbers of people with impairments.

Longevity was another factor that increased the numbers of people with impairments. Improvements in hygiene, public health, and nutrition lowered the mortality rate, and people begin to live longer. Prior to the beginning of the twentieth century, relatively few people who became seriously disabled survived (Straus, 1965). Diseases and injuries that formerly would have caused death became curable or treatable by improvements in medical pharmacology and technology—but such treatments often left physical impairments in their wake. In the years from 1900 to 1940, life expectancy increased by twelve years for men and by fourteen years for women, and the proportion who survived to age sixty-five increased by almost 18 percent for men and over 20 percent for women (Albrecht, 1992: 51). While some of the added life expectancy for women can be attributed to the increasing safety of pregnancy and child-bearing, at least part of the increase for both sexes has to be attributed to improvements in physicians' abilities to treat some types of diseases, such as diabetes. As Albrecht (1992: 49) notes, "The impaired population began to increase in number, severity and life expectancy." On the other hand, this increase occurred among people who would be unlikely under any circumstances to join in contentious actions (Abramowitz and Nassi, 1981).

Ironically, some of the factors that increased life expectancy also increased the problem of polio, which began to appear in epidemic proportions in the early years of the century. It is possible that improvements in sewer systems as well as overall hygiene reduced the exposure of very young children to endemic polio viruses and so actually increased the severity of the disease when older children were exposed to it. Whatever the cause, large numbers contracted the disease and survived, but with impairments. In 1916, 27,000 people were left paralyzed. There were epidemics in New York in 1931; in New Jersey, Pennsylvania, and Los Angeles in 1932; in Boston in 1935; and in Chicago in 1936, among other places (see http://www.polio.com).

Perhaps as a result of the increasing numbers of people with impairments, during the first part of the twentieth century there was growth in opportunities to share "common social space." Although people with physical and mental impairments were sometimes isolated, hidden, or otherwise kept from the mainstream of society (Treanor, 1993: 13), it is also true that many new organizations of and for people with impairments were established. These included the National Fraternal Society of the Deaf (1901), the Disabled American Veterans (1920), the League of the Physically Handicapped (1935), the National Federation of the Blind (1940), and the American Federation of the Physically Handicapped (1940). These and similar organizations provided places in which people with impairments might meet. With the establishment of the League of the Physically Handicapped and the American Federation of the Physically Handicapped, there were, for the first time, places where people could interact with people who had impairments different than their own. A pattern of many impairment-specific organizations and a few cross-disability organizations was being established that would continue until the latter part of the century and would affect the types of collective actions occurring decades later.

In addition to organizations and schools, there were increasing numbers of involuntary situations in which people with impairments might meet. Primary among these were rehabilitation facilities and hospitals. The number of sheltered workshops increased because of the passage of the Fair Labor Standards Act of 1938, which gave such workshops exclusive bidding rights on certain types of goods and services for the federal government.[13] All in all, the isolation of people with impairments was beginning to break down.

During the first decades of the twentieth century, several situations developed that fostered a feeling of relative deprivation, or a sense that "my group is even worse off than your group, and that's not fair." One situation derived from the effect of wars on the participation of people with impairments in the labor force. During the first and second world wars, most "able-bodied" men were drafted, but deaf men and people with other types of impairments were considered not able-bodied, so they were not drafted for the military. Ironically, however, men with mental retardation were drafted. During World War I, retarded men were drafted who had previously lived in institutional settings; some of these men did well in the military, but they were still returned to institutional settings after the war ended (Scheerenberger, 1983: 175). During World War II retarded men also served in the military or worked in defense industries. Even some people in institutions helped the war effort by assisting farmers, canning, repairing toys and clothes, participating in air-raid duties, and assisting with scrap salvage (Scheerenberger, 1983: 215).

The wars had a strong impact on workers in the deaf community. Although deaf workers were not drafted into the military, they were "drafted" for civilian war-related industries. During World War I, there were so many deaf men working in the Akron, Ohio, plants of Goodyear and Firestone that Firestone provided sports facilities, a dance hall, and a club room in which they could socialize (Van Cleve and Crouch, 1989: 164). The labor of men with other types of impairments was used during World War II (Hahn, 1997). After the wars ended, the services of many of these workers with impairments were no longer needed, just as women's labor was no longer needed. However, this was not as true for deaf men; after the war, Goodyear and Firestone continued to recruit them because the company experience had been so positive (Van Cleve and Crouch, 1989: 164).

Such experiences in the labor force could have been conducive to feelings of relative deprivation. People with impairments who worked during wartime might feel deprived in a real sense, because they had lost their jobs, but they also might feel deprived compared to other groups, such as blacks and women. During the war years, blacks moved from the South to work in factories in northern industrial cities. Although women who worked during World War II were also fired when the soldiers returned, the baby boom that occurred shortly thereafter fueled a need for labor in traditionally female occupations such as nursing and teaching. The result was increased female participation in the labor force during the 1950s and 1960s for women aged forty-five to sixty-four and in subsequent years for younger women, as changes in the demand structure of the labor force began to pull women back into the labor force (Oppenheimer, 1976). People with impairments, on the other hand, had jobs during the wars, showed that they could do the work, and then lost the jobs again, while other groups still had jobs or were increasingly getting new jobs.

The increased availability of education, especially vocational rehabilitation, for people with impairments may also have added to a feeling of relative deprivation. The 1935 Social Security Act provided for state grants for vocational rehabilitation services, and rehabilitation was increasingly becoming a medical specialty of some standing. Partly because of this, there were increasing numbers of people with impairments who were well educated, despite educational discrimination experienced by some people with impairments. There were even visible role models, although the most visible role model of all, President Franklin Delano Roosevelt, kept his impairment hidden almost all of the time. The increased educational opportunities did not, however, lead to better economic opportunities.

During this time a collective consciousness in several segments of the deaf and disability communities began to develop. In the deaf community, there was resistance to the assault on sign language that had begun at the Milan Congress. Newspapers, such as *The Silent Worker*, "championed the accomplishments of deaf citizens and help define and defend their rights in the United States and abroad" (Buchanan, 1993: 173). In the disability community, the Disabled American Veterans marched on Washington, D.C., in 1921 (Ronald Drach, personal communication, March 26, 1997). Beginning in 1935 and continuing until 1938, the League of the Physically Handicapped conducted sit-ins, strikes, pickets, and other actions in New York City and Washington, D.C. They were protesting work-related policies and discrimination in general, as well as some of the specific policies that governed the Works Progress Administration (WPA) and the Emergency Relief Bureau (ERB), two of President Roosevelt's programs to provide Depression-era relief (Longmore, 1997).

Finally, the 1930s and early 1940s saw the beginnings of an emergence of an important collective consciousness related to disability, although not among the potential beneficiaries. Parents of children with mental retardation began to organize in the 1930s, forming groups such as the Cuyahoga County Council for the Retarded Child (1933), the Washington Association for Retarded Children (1936), and the New York Welfare League for Retarded Children (Dwybad, 1990; Scheerenberger, 1983: 228). Although their activism did not pick up until the late 1940s, and primarily took the form of lawsuits, this was the beginning of an important change. Parents and other family members had always been involved with their family members with impairments, but as a group, they had been as separated and isolated as the people with impairments. The parents' movement would show that "making a fuss" could produce change.[14] As one parent noted, speaking of the (much later) success experienced when the 1975 Education for all Handicapped Children Act was passed: It "brought a profound change in parents, a change that has been internalized and cannot be undone. . . . No longer did they need to be grateful for every crumb; they could actually make demands on behalf of their children and expect reasonable responses to those demands" (Palka, 1997: 240).

These organizational beginnings, and the activism that would come from them, presaged a time when people with impairments could develop a collective consciousness. In this period there was an intensification of several earlier trends. There were increases in numbers of people with impairments, and more common social space was available to them. There were also events that could seem discriminatory, and there were opportunities to work together to develop the sort of collective consciousness necessary in order to foment a social movement. Although several groups did try to do just that, they failed, because conditions were not yet right.

What conditions would have improved the chances that these early disability protests would have succeeded? Protests cannot succeed if society does not legitimize the demands of the protesters. During this period, it is clear that the protests were not perceived as being legitimate because they were not framed in a way that resonated with the society or with the targets of the protests. It was not until the end of the 1960s that there would be an acceptable and accepted frame into which disability protests could be successfully inserted.

Post-War America: 1945–1960

During this period, both the incidence and prevalence rates for impairments continued to increase.[15] Incidence rates increased for several reasons. Wars, again, were one reason. World War II left many disabled veterans. Some of these (approximately 2,500) were men with spinal cord injuries. This type of injury could finally be treated. After World War I, men with similar wounds died because medical rehabilitation techniques were not good enough to save them (Driedger, 1989).[16] Many of the World War II vets with spinal cord injuries were at the same hospital in California and went on to found the Paralyzed Veterans of America (Pelka, 1997: 236, 344). The Korean and Vietnam wars also added to the numbers of people with impairments.

A second cause of the increasing incidence of impairment continued to be polio: There were large epidemics in 1946 (25,000 cases), 1952 (58,000 cases), and 1953 (35,000 cases). These polio outbreaks provided the basis for some close friendships and social networks among those (particularly children) who spent months or years in rehabilitation facilities; the rehab hospitals may unwittingly have provided common social space that would help to develop networks of people with similar impairments and similar concerns.[17] A new source of impairments emerged during this time period because of the use of thalidomide, a drug given to pregnant women for morning sickness that produced impairments in their babies. This was more of a factor in Europe than in the United States, because the use of thalidomide was banned earlier in the United States than it was in Europe.

The prevalence rates for impairments increased because new drugs kept people with impairments alive longer. This was particularly true of antibiotics such as penicillin, which became available publicly after World War II, and streptomycin, which became available in the 1950s. Both played a significant role in increasing the life expectancies of children with retardation who previously had been very susceptible to infections (Scheerenberger, 1983: 222).

During this period the numbers of disability organizations increased nationally and internationally. In the United States, organizations such as the Blinded Veterans Association (1945), the National Mental Health Foundation (1946), the Paralyzed Veterans of America (1947), We Are Not Alone (1949), and the National Wheelchair Basketball Association (1949) emerged during the immediate post-war years. In 1947, the first meeting of the President's Committee on National Employ the Handicapped Week was held. This organization later became the President's Committee on Employment of the Physically Handicapped. On the international level, new organizations included the World Federation of the Deaf (1951) and the International Federation of the Blind (later called the World Blind Union).

Why were these organizations important, since they were not conducting protests? The answer is that these organizations—sports, political, or lobbying—provided opportunities for people with impairments to meet. Along with schools, they provided children and adults with impairments the opportunity to interact and begin to develop a collective consciousness. Judy Heumann, who was one of the early leaders of protests in New York City and elsewhere, described what this interaction meant to her:

> [M]y first real experience meeting other disabled people occurred in the school. I remember the feeling of relief when I was finally able to talk to other disabled people, who confirmed that my experiences as a disabled person were all too real. . . . In school we talked about situations such as, "What would you do if you were going down the street and somebody started staring at you?" We decided that we would turn around and say, "Take a picture, it lasts longer." I remember the first time we said this to somebody. . . . We didn't notice his reaction because we were laughing so hard. It was school experiences like these that made me realize that together with other disabled people we could assume power. (Heumann, 1992: 192–93)

The proliferation of groups during this period meant that there were membership bases, communication networks, and leaders—the components necessary for the infrastructure upon which contentious action could be built.

There were, in addition, some changes that affected the ability of people with impairments to organize for contentious action. One was an increase in the degree of specialization seen within the field of medicine and the degree of differentiation of specialties seen within helping professions that dealt with people with impairments. This led to a situation in which people with different types of impairments tended to be separated by the medical system. Another trend, which began in the post-World War II years, was a more widespread acceptance of the idea that rehabilitation was possible, even for people with severe impairments (Dwybad, 1990: 156).

These trends may have had both positive and negative consequences. They increased contacts among people with similar impairments who had the same or similar practitioners, clinics, or hospitals, and so provided involuntary meeting places. But the consciousness and networks that might arise from such interactions were more likely to have been impairment-specific than to be cross-disability. The impacts of this trend were played out in protests that occurred in subsequent years.

One of the most important changes of the post-World War II period was increased parental and journalistic attention to public institutions for people with mental retardation and other impairments. The numbers of people who lived in institutions for mentally retarded people increased dramatically, from almost 117,000 in 1946 to over 193,000 by 1967 (Trent, 1994: 251). This change was, in part, fueled by advice from medical professionals to parents to "put [your] retarded children away and forget about them" (Trent, 1994: 241). In addition, the population of these institutions changed from being one of primarily juvenile delinquents to one that included younger children, more severely impaired children, and adults (Trent, 1994: 252). The numbers of people in state psychiatric hospitals peaked in 1955, although the numbers of people in state schools did not peak until 1968 (Trent, 1994: 242).

Concomitantly, there were a number of journalistic exposés on conditions in these institutions. Some were done by contentious objectors who worked in the institutions during the war (Trent, 1994: 228, 237). Partially in response, the Cerebral Palsy Society of New York City (later to become a chapter of the United Cerebral Palsy Associations, Inc.) was established in 1946, and what was to become the Association for Retarded Children began with a convention in 1950.

The parents' organizations were concerned about neglect and mishandling of their children in institutions. They demanded that the institutions provide better physical environments, more appropriate medical and dental care, better therapy and training, and show more concern about their children's happiness. They also objected to the ways in which parents of retarded children were portrayed and treated by professionals and service providers—as grief-stricken, having a death wish, rejecting, and being completely ignorant of what was best for their child (Scheerenberger, 1983: 230). These organizations and others would be involved in some of the early lawsuits that were filed in regard to institutional conditions. In addition, the notion of deinstitutionalization began to surface among parents in the 1950s, although it did not become a national goal until the 1970s.

As noted previously, the parents' movement mounted one of the first challenges to the status quo regarding disability. The parents were the first group to exhibit an "oppositional consciousness" on a large scale and sustain it for a number of years. Although their tactics were not, by and large, those of contentious collective action, their examples of a collective consciousness, the demands they made, and their successes could serve as models for groups of potential beneficiaries when they began to mount their own movement in subsequent years.

Other changes occurred during this time. In 1948, the needs of disabled veterans returning to school after World War II led to the establishment of a disabled student services program at the University of Illinois at Champaign (Pelka, 1997: 166). In some ways this was the beginning of the concept of independent living.[18] Veterans also conducted at least one protest during the 1950s (Palmer, 2000). There were also legal and policy changes during this time period, including several expansions of Social Security programs to include more people with impairments, and vocational rehabilitation programs were expanded.

Expressions of an oppositional consciousness began to occur. At its 1948 convention, the president of the National Federation of the Blind presented a document entitled, "A Bill of Rights for the Blind." This document begins with language some would find radical even today: "I have a serious question to ask the sighted persons present—would you swap vision for a good chicken dinner? On the face of it this is an absurd question, for no one who has vision would swap it for anything. But for those of us who are blind, this question is not necessarily absurd. It is not that we prefer to have lost our eyesight, but having been deprived of it, we have discovered that it is dispensable" (Matson, 1990: 36).

At least one struggle occurred at this time between people with impairments and those without (who were usually in control of the situation). This incident, which occurred during the 1950s, was a struggle between the National Federation of the Blind, on the one hand, and both the system of sheltered workshops and those who ran them, on the other. The latter groups, the "blindness system," included employees of state agencies and commissions—some were blind themselves (Matson, 1990: 73). The issues involved who could speak for blind people and who should not, whether blindness was a terrible affliction or one with which someone could live well, and other issues that still resonate today. Although a large amount of anger was expressed in national and other meetings, there was no contentious action at this time.

Several incidents of contentious action by people with impairments had occurred by this time, but they were isolated, unsuccessful, and did not impel subsequent actions. Neither the world nor the disability community was really ready for much more than that. But it was coming. The changes of the post war period set the stage for the emergence of a concerted effort at contentious action. The development of organizational bases, similar to those that had existed in the deaf community for many years, was one crucial factor, but it is unlikely that contentious action would have developed without many of the other changes discussed here. Although we argue later that the social movements of the 1960s were important for the development of contentious action in the disability community, the importance of the changes that took place immediately after World War II cannot be overlooked.

The 1960s and Beyond

The 1960s saw the emergence of the "social movement society" in America (Meyer and Tarrow, 1998). During this period protests intensified in the civil rights movement and early protests began in the women's liberation movement, the first protest for which occurred in 1966 (Minkoff, 1997). The 1960s also sparked the student movement (which began with the free speech movement at the University of California, Berkeley) and the anti-war movement. The turbulent decade had a significant influence on members of the disability and deaf communities.

A number of authors have suggested that the disability rights movement arose from, or because of, the civil rights movement. Treanor (1993: 33) goes so far as to make the somewhat questionable statement that, "You could say that more than any other decade, the sixties sowed the seeds which made possible President Bush's signing of the Americans with Disabilities Act on July 26, 1990." If this is the case, what were the mechanisms by which this might have occurred?

We suggest two such mechanisms. The first is the fact that, for the first time, the civil rights movement provided a way of framing disability protests so that they could resonate in American society. The second is that the social movements of the 1960s contributed, both directly and indirectly, to components of what would become the disability movement.

Frames and Claims

One of the most important tasks that social movements actively engage in is the production of meaning for participants, antagonists, and observers (Snow and Benford, 1988: 198). That is, participants in social movements actively construct a collective consciousness. A central part of any collective consciousness is a frame, or an overall system of interpretation that enables individuals to "locate, perceive, identify, and label occurrences" (Snow et. al., 1986: 464). Collective action frames permit individuals to recognize and diagnose problems and to propose solutions. They help social movements to mobilize potential adherents for action (Snow and Benford, 1988: 199) and they also mobilize "conscience constituents"—those who will not themselves benefit from the movement but who nonetheless support its goals and work to achieve those goals (McCarthy and Zald, 1987). Frames also help to garner bystander support and demobilize antagonists (Klandermans, 1992: 80). Frames provide meaningful reasons, within the context of a culture, for why a demand made by a social movement should be satisfied.

If an appropriate frame exists or can be created, it will make it easier for members of the social movement to recruit participants for contentious action, as well as supporters for that action, than it might otherwise have been. Because they fit within that cultural context, culturally resonant frames increase the likelihood that some or all members of a society will support the social movement's demands— and, therefore, that the movement will succeed. If a culturally appropriate frame does not exist or cannot be created, the social movement is unlikely to succeed in having its demands met.[19] Leaders of social movements are unlikely to invent new frames if they can avoid it. Rather, they are more likely to use already existing, previously successful, frames, which they can modify, if necessary, to fit their movement's issues.

There are four types of processes that can be used in social movements to build upon previously successful frames. These include frame bridging, frame amplification, frame extension, and frame transformation (Snow et al., 1986). It is easier for social movements to use any of these processes than to invent a new frame and then elicit support for it every time a new issue turns up.

For those protesting within the disability community, one of the most important things to come out of the civil rights movement was the "frame" of civil rights. This frame included the notion that places should be accessible to all groups; the notion that all citizens should be able to exercise their political power through the voting booth; the notion that discrimination in hiring, promotion, or firing was not acceptable; and the notion that separate facilities were inherently unequal.

After the successful application of the frame of civil rights to blacks, the women's movement attempted to extend that frame to women. If the recategorization succeeded, the women's movement reasoned, our society would be more likely to recognize that women could legitimately make demands that had previously been seen as appropriate only for blacks to make. However, the frame extension was not easy.

The first extension of any frame is more difficult than successive frame extensions, because the first extension involves two processes. It involves acceptance of the idea of extending the frame at all, and it involves acceptance of the appropriateness of extending that particular frame to that particular group. There had to be acceptance of the idea that women were a minority group, and therefore experienced discrimination, before there could be a perception of women's problems as *group issues*, rather than individual problems, and as *minority group issues* appropriately interpreted through the use of a civil rights frame. Influential in the cam-

Dressed in American Revolutionary garb, protestors outside the U.S. Circuit Court of Appeals in Philadelphia connected the American ideals of freedom and independence to the disability rights movement.

paign to gain acceptance of that frame extension was an article by Helen Hacker (1951) called "Women as a Minority Group." There was resistance to this early frame extension from men in the civil rights movement as well as members of Congress when the 1964 Civil Rights Act was debated (Freeman, 1975). The arguments were not just about the appropriateness of that specific frame extension but also about the appropriateness of frame extension at all.

Frame extensions are more likely to succeed if there has been precedent for extending that frame to other groups or situations. If the *idea* of frame extension has already been accepted by the general population, it will be easier to mobilize support and participants for subsequent frame extensions than if there is no such precedent. If there is precedent, the task of the social movement is merely that of justifying the extension of a particular frame to their group or situation.[20] The success of the extension of the frame of civil rights to women set a precedent for subsequent attempts to extend the frame of civil rights to other groups. The frame of civil rights became a master frame, one that could apply to a number of groups (Snow and Benford, 1992), including people with impairments.

Although successive frame extensions may be easier than the initial one, there is no guarantee that all attempts at frame extension will succeed. Rather, some attempts may fail. An example of such failure (to date) can be seen in attempts by the gay rights movement to extend the frame of civil rights to gay people. During one debate over permitting gays to serve in the military, opponents specifically denied that the frame of civil rights applies to gays in statements such as, "The freedom train to Selma never stopped at Sodom" (Loose, 1993). Thus, even though frame extensions may become easier as time goes on, not all attempts will succeed. Rather, there are cultural limits to the extensibility of any frame. Of course, part of the task of any social movement is to justify the frame extension it wants and to deny that its group is beyond those limits.

The civil rights frame was first applied to people with impairments in the early 1970s. As noted in a report about one of the earliest disability community protests, a march in Washington, D.C., that took place on May 5, 1972: "The civil rights concept has become equated with only racial minorities and for another minority of citizens outside of the defined parameters of the equal rights movement to take hold of this banner was a challenge. . . . Obviously to apply the label of discrimination to the disabled was unheard of" (Thoben, 1972: 25).

Activists within the deaf community and disability communities attempted to extend the civil rights frame to themselves (Fine and Asch, 1988). We will see in subsequent chapters how they did this. For now, suffice it to say that the attempt at frame extension in the disability community did not succeed in the 1930s but did succeed in later decades because, by the late 1970s, precedents for frame extension had already been set. The civil rights and other social movements from the 1960s were not a sufficient condition for the emergence of disability activism, but they probably were a necessary condition.

Other social movements occurred during this time period, which, although not providing frames for contentious political action, did provide fodder for claims

In a rally in Washington, D.C., before the passage of the ADA, demonstrators extend the frame of civil rights by incorporating slogans from the civil rights movement.

made by people with disabilities, especially those claims that criticized medical personnel. One social movement was the patients' rights movement. This movement attempted to challenge the paternalism of doctors and their hegemony over treatment, and it was responsible for the subsequent adoption of informed consent in treatment as well as in research. The other relevant social movement was the women's health movement. As part of the feminist movement of the 1960s, participants in the women's health movement attempted to limit the extent to which the medical establishment controlled women's bodies and lives. In doing so, they challenged medical education as well as popular culture, formed self-help groups, created alternative services, and lobbied for changes in federal, state, and local laws (Rodwin, 1994). One direct effect of that movement can be seen in the writings of Irving Zola, who, as a respected scholar in the area of disability, was married to one of the founders of the Boston Women's Health Collective, a major player in the women's health movement.

Thus other social movements of the 1960s had a profound impact on what was possible for people with impairments. Whereas claims made in the 1930s basically fell on "deaf" ears in a society that could not comprehend them, claims made by the deaf and disability communities in the 1970s and 1980s resonated with frames that had been used by prior social movements and had been accepted by at least some sectors of society.

Social Movement Spillover

The social movements of the 1960s and early 1970s unintentionally helped the disability community in a number of ways. These movements did not simply provide a collective action frame. They also provided other components of social movements, which were taken up by the disability community in a process called spillover (Meyer and Whittier, 1994: 277). Earlier social movements provided tactics, rhetoric, symbols, ideas, personnel, and, in some cases, support for the protests in the disability community. Let us examine these in more detail.

Tactics

Several of the tactics newly used by participants in the civil rights movement in the South included bus boycotts, sit-ins, and freedom rides (McAdam, 1997). Disability and deaf activists linked their issues to those of the civil rights movement by their use of similar strategies of nonviolent resistance and civil disobedience.

Symbols

One of the ways in which participants in social movements manipulate frames is through their use of symbols that link their situation to the desired frame. One of the symbols that is clearly linked to the civil rights movement is the phrase "I Have a Dream." Protestors during the Deaf President Now (DPN) protest at Gallaudet used that symbol when, on a march to the Capitol, they carried a banner that said, "I Have a Dream." The use of this phrase linked their protest symbolically to Dr. Martin Luther King and the civil rights movement. Other symbols taken from the civil rights movement are the songs "We Shall Overcome" and "We Shall Not be

Justin Dart has been called the Martin Luther King, Jr., of the disability rights movement.

Moved," which protesters sang during the 1977 Rehabilitation Act protests (Treanor, 1993: 76).

Activists

Activists who attempt to extend a frame from a prior social movement are often influenced by members of that prior movement. This is most likely to occur if participants from the original social movement carry the frame with them directly to the new movement. This was seen quite clearly in the relationship between the civil rights movement and the women's movement, in which many participants in the former movement went on to foment the latter (McAdam, 1988; Freeman, 1975).

There was a small amount of direct diffusion of personnel from the earlier civil rights and women's movements to the disability community, as, later, there was diffusion of personnel from the early disability protests to the deaf community. Wade Blank, the founder of Americans Disabled for Public Transit (ADAPT) learned political organizing from the civil rights movement, participated in the march to Selma with Martin Luther King, Jr., and worked with draft resisters during the Vietnam War era (Pelka, 1997: 43). Mary Jane Owen, who became a disability activist after she became disabled, had been a member of the Congress of Racial Equality (CORE) in the 1940s and a Vietnam War protester in the 1960s (Pelka, 1977: 232).

But direct diffusion of personnel from one movement to another is not the only way in which activists' thinking may be changed. There can also be diffusion of ideas and frames from one movement to another. The thinking of activists from the earlier movement, either in person or in their writings, may influence the thinking of activists in newer social movements. A number of examples of such influence are often cited by leaders in the disability community, such as Irving Zola (1983b), who was influenced by the civil rights movement and the women's movement. Gunnar Dwybad, a leader of the National Association for Retarded Children, saw the civil rights movement as a model for actions that could be used for issues relating to his cause (Pelka, 1997: 23), although it is not clear that he ever actually used that model to instigate contentious action. Ed Roberts was at the University of California, Berkeley, around the time of the free speech movement, and his fight for independent living was influenced by that and the women's movement (Shapiro, 1993: 47). Justin Dart, another prominent disability rights activist, studied and was influenced by the writings of Martin Luther King, Jr. (Shapiro, 1993: 111). There are many other examples in the disability and deaf communities that make it clear that writings of activists in earlier movements spilled over to the disability community and affected some of its potential leaders, even if there was little actual spillover of personnel.

Support from Other Movements

Earlier movements can be important for subsequent movements if the earlier movement still exists and can provide support to the subsequent movement. This is especially true if an earlier social movement can assist in frame extension to the newer movement by propounding the frame extension itself.[21] Although a coalition with, or support from, one social movement cannot by itself produce a frame extension, it can help. This has happened a number of times in the disability rights movement. Individual civil rights activists and civil rights organizations have supported the movement, and civil rights organizations have been involved in actions by disability rights protestors several times. One instance of this occurred during the 1977 HEW sit-in in San Francisco, when the Black Panthers provided food and endorsed the protestors' goals in their newspaper (Johnson, 1983). Support by civil rights activists was also expressed before DPN, when behind-the-scenes lobbying for a deaf president occurred, as well as during the protest. Civil rights leader Jesse Jackson and Dorothy Gilliam, a respected black columnist for the *Washington Post*, both made their voices heard in favor of DPN (Christiansen and Barnartt, 1995). Finally, during lobbying for the ADA, the executive director of the Leadership Conference on Civil Rights was quoted as saying the ADA "is basically the Civil Rights Act of 1964 with respect to persons with disabilities" (Berkowitz, 1992).

Success

Finally, if an earlier social movement was successful, it can convey the notion that protests *can* succeed. It thus provides a motivation for subsequent groups to engage in that type of nontraditional political action rather than traditional forms of political action in the hopes that their movement, too, can succeed.

Other Changes during the 1960s

The social movements of the 1960s were not the only aspect of that decade that would facilitate subsequent protests in the deaf and disability communities. Other important factors included the Vietnam War, changes in perceptions of mental retardation, legal changes, medical and technological advancements, some obscure publications in the field of linguistics, and changes in the educational attainments and occupational involvement of people with impairments that could heighten feelings of relative deprivation.

The Vietnam War

The Vietnam War had a large impact on society as well as on people with impairments. As in previous wars, the numbers of people with disabilities increased as a result of the conflict. But the Vietnam War also increased the *visibility* of disability through books and movies about disabled veterans. Disabled vets who experienced discrimination were, perhaps, less likely to endure it quietly, because they felt they had sacrificed for their country at a time when others refused to (Gooding, 1994: 2).

Another impact of the war was related to contentious action itself. Protests against the war helped to bring about the routinization of protest, as well as greater acceptance of protest as a method of expressing grievances (Meyer and Tarrow, 1998). Vietnam War protests also contributed tactics, such as university takeovers and teach-ins, which would be emulated by protests in the deaf and disability communities.

Changing Perceptions of Retardation

As noted previously, between 1950 and 1968 institutions for people with mental retardation expanded at a faster rate than at any time in U.S. history. For example, from 1964 to 1965 the numbers of institutionalized people with retardation increased by almost 8,000, the largest single year increase ever (numbers calculated from Trent, 1994: 251). The total number of people living in institutions peaked at about 188,000 in larger institutions and 125,000 in smaller facilities in 1988 (Trent, 1994: 265). In part, the increase in numbers of institutions was due to a massive infusion of cash for construction of facilities for people with retardation that came from the Mental Retardation Facilities and Community Mental Health Centers Construction Act of 1963 (PL 88-164). The truism that says that "a built bed is a filled bed" applies to mental health and mental retardation institutions as well as to the acute care hospitals to which it was originally applied.

At the same time, attitudes toward retardation were changing. The changes began in the early 1960s, due in part to the fact that then-President Kennedy had a retarded sister, and his family was active in promoting improvements for people with retardation. Among other events, Eunice Kennedy Shriver published an article on the topic in the *Saturday Evening Post*; President Kennedy addressed Congress on the subject of mental retardation and mental health; and he appointed a special President's Panel on Mental Retardation (Straus, 1965). One of the recommendations of this panel was that there should be a "new legal, as well as social, concept of the retarded, including protection of their civil rights; life guardianship provisions when needed; an enlightened attitude on the part of the law and the courts" (Scheerenberger, 1983: 248). This recommendation was extremely enlightened for its time—and it was not really accepted for at least another decade, if then.

Ideas such as normalization, deinstitutionalization, and community placement, which had been around since the 1950s, were becoming more accepted because of concerns about civil liberties as well as fiscal conservatism (Trent, 1994: 270). Both ideas supported the notion that the best place for children and adults with retardation (as well as for people with psychiatric illnesses) was not the institution but the community. These notions drove some of the lawsuits instituted by the parents' movement in the early 1970s, which determined that the constitutional rights of people in some institutions were being violated (Scheerenberger, 1983: 252). In addition to winning improved living situations for institutionalized residents, successful lawsuits also conveyed the idea that activism about disability issues can succeed, an important message for potential disability activists.

Legal Changes

Several legal changes during this period had a profound impact on events in the disability community, even though the laws passed did not apply directly to them. The application of the frame of civil rights to blacks occurred primarily through laws and Supreme Court decisions. In addition to the post-Civil War laws and constitutional amendments, important laws and decisions included the 1954 *Brown v. the Board of Education* decision by the Supreme Court, the 1964 Civil Rights Act, Executive Order 11246,[22] the Voting Rights Act of 1965, which has subsequently been renewed, and the Open Housing Act of 1968, which dealt with discrimination in aspects of housing (Barnartt and Seelman, 1988). The application of the frame of civil rights to women also occurred initially through legislation, including the 1963 Equal Pay Act, the 1964 Civil Rights Act (to which the words "and sex" had been added by Southern senators in order to try to kill the bill), Executive Order 11246 and other, subsequent laws. The major federal laws that provided civil rights for women, members of racial and ethnic groups, and members of religious groups were passed in the 1960s.[23]

There were, however, no laws that connected disabilities with civil rights. From 1920 until 1950, disability legislation focused on income support and vocational rehabilitation (Berkowitz, 1979; Stone, 1984), and disability policy before the 1970s was characterized as "benevolent paternalism" (Hull, 1979: 21).

But there was one legal change during the 1960s that did have a direct impact on people with impairments and which began to redirect the focus of disability policy. In 1968, the Architectural Barriers Act was passed. This was the first law that even hinted at civil rights for people with impairments. It would have major implications for the disability community and, to a lesser extent, the deaf community. In this law, for the first time, access as a civil rights issue was raised for disabled people; and, for the first time, it was raised in federal law. The idea of civil rights for people with impairments was more important than the content of the law, at least initially, because there were no enforcement mechanisms built into the Architectural Barriers Act. It was not until the Rehabilitation Act of 1973 was passed (and regulations for it promulgated in 1977) that teeth were given to that law. (That law set up the Architectural and Transportation Barriers Compliance Board to enforce the previously unenforced Architectural Barriers Act.)

Also during this time, decisions from the federal courts declared that the constitutional rights of mentally retarded residents were being violated by inhumane treatment; that rights to due process must be maintained, even for people living in institutions; and that mentally retarded or mentally ill people working in institutions were covered by the Fair Labor Standards Act of 1966 (Scheerenberger, 1983: 251).[24]

Medical Advancements

Medical advancements from the 1960s on affected some people with impairments, as well as having important implications for the composition of the disability community. One advancement is the increased ability of doctors to keep people with spinal cord injuries and polio alive. If one peruses biographies of leaders in the disability movement, (see, e.g., Pelka 1997), the high proportion of those people with spinal cord injuries becomes apparent. (Leaders in the independent living movement appear more likely to have been polio survivors, although it is not possible to say that with any certainty without further empirical verification.) The effects of these and other medical developments were to "create" more people with severe disabilities by keeping people alive. In addition, technological developments such as speech synthesizers and motorized wheel chairs increasingly permit people with severe impairments to function in ways that had not previously been possible.

Technological Changes

In the deaf community, a major technological change occurred in 1964, when Robert Weitbrecht invented an acoustic coupler that made possible the use of the teletype machine to send messages over telephone lines. Called the TTY, it was a large and expensive telephone substitute. More recently, TDDs (Telephone Devices for the Deaf) were invented in the 1970s as smaller, cheaper, and more portable versions of TTYs. For the first time, deaf people could communicate with each other using devices similar to those used by hearing people. TTYs and TDDs did not immediately permit deaf people to communicate with hearing people, however, because the technology required that the hearing person also have a similar device, and few did. It is only since the ADA in 1990 mandated that all states set up relay systems, in which an operator acts as a go-between who can voice what the TTY is typing for a hearing person, and also type what the hearing person is voicing for a deaf person.

The Linguistics of ASL

Another change that had a major impact on the deaf community in subsequent years was the work of William Stokoe at Gallaudet. A professor of English, he published the first books that used linguistics to promote the argument that American Sign Language was linguistically identical to spoken languages, rather than being either a crude system of gestures or a signed dialect of English (Stokoe, 1960; Stokoe, Casterline, and Cronenberg, 1965). This argument began to give American Sign Language a legitimacy that had been taken from it by the Milan Congress in 1880.

Education, Occupation, and Relative Deprivation

One final factor that contributed to disability activism was the continuation of the trend toward some people with impairments getting more education and better jobs. In the deaf community, this was documented in a book by Alan Crammatte published in 1965 called *The Formidable Peak: A Study of Deaf People in Professional Employment*. In that book, he demonstrated that there were deaf professionals and described some of the difficulties they faced in their lives and careers (although he downplayed any notion of discrimination).

By the late 1960s increasing numbers of people with impairments were better educated, due, in part, to the GI bill, which paid for college educations for returning veterans—some of whom had impairments—after World War II, the Korean War, and the Vietnam War. This education, in and of itself, was likely to be a factor in the emergence of protests, because it gave protest leaders some capabilities that less educated people did not have. It also introduced issues of accessibility in colleges that had been unheard of before the late 1940s.

The greater numbers of people with impairments attending college meant that some were also likely to hold better jobs. At the most basic level, this meant that some people would have access to resources that make it easier for social movements to emerge, such as typewriters, copy machines, and office space. Perhaps the more important aspect of increasing education and involvement in the labor force, however, was that more people began to encounter subtle and overt prejudice and discrimination.

It had been clear for many years that deaf people held a lower social status and worked in lower paying jobs than did hearing people (Christiansen and Barnartt, 1987), and the same was true for people with other types of impairments (see, e.g., Kirchner and Peterson, 1985). Not much had been made of that fact until the 1960s. Before that, there was really no way to interpret such information that made sense in any culturally accepted way. People with disabilities had been defined, de facto, as nonworkers by disability policies that paid them for not working and explicitly declared them unable to work. If they did work, and if they encountered prejudice or discrimination in the labor force, this fact did not fit into the culturally accepted view of disabled people.

But discriminatory situations were beginning to attract the attention of people with impairments. Kenneth Jernigan, in a speech that was repeated several times, told the following story:

> *In 1970 Tom Munn (a blind man) took a Michigan State Civil Service examination for the position of mechanic. He passed with a score of 96, and his name was placed on the register. He was not offered employment; others (with lower scores) were hired. In 1972 the Civil Service Commission created a separate list for the handicapped. Munn's name was transferred from the open register to the separate list, and his score was reduced from 96 to 70—which (regardless of performance) was the grade to be given to all so-called "successful" future blind applicants. Munn requested that his performance be evaluated. The request was refused. In 1974 (acting on his own) he secured a work trial evaluation with the Motor Transport Division of the Department of Management and Budget. He did the job without difficulty. The results were ignored. . . . They call it compassion and say we are incompetent. They tell us there is no discrimination—that the blind are not a minority. But we know who we are, and we will never go back. (Matson, 1990: 391)*

In a similar situation, Judy Heumann was denied a teaching job in New York City. Such situations were to have an increasingly profound impact on the deaf and disability communities, as she and others were able to turn their anger into contentious action. As people with impairments were increasingly likely to experience relative deprivation, instead of absolute deprivation, they became aware that other groups had laws protecting them from discrimination but they did not.

This experience of relative deprivation was important to the development of a collective consciousness. Absolute deprivation seldom leads to contentious action, because people who experience it seldom have the resources with which to mount contentious action. Relative deprivation is more likely to lead to such action, however, partly because it involves comparisons to successful groups and partly because it occurs when potential movement activists are beginning to accumulate resources.

There was now a frame into which the experiences of prejudice, discrimination, and relative deprivation could be fitted. In the 1930s, saying that the public works programs of the Depression discriminated against people with impairments did not resonate with cultural notions of disability, and so it was not accepted. Once there was a frame of civil rights, people with disabilities could claim that they deserved to have such rights, and society might begin to listen. We will see in subsequent chapters that members of the deaf and disability communities took this message to society when there was the possibility of frame extension, and when social conditions permitted and facilitated protests.

Notes

1. See, for example, Berkowitz (1987); Bowe (1978); Ferguson (1994); Matson (1990); Pelka (1997); Scheerenberger (1983); Stone (1984); Treanor (1993); Trent (1994); Van Cleve and Crouch (1989).
2. This strategy is similar to that followed by several books about the history of the civil rights movement (McAdam, 1982; Morris, 1984).
3. Because structural strain is ubiquitous, that factor, by itself, cannot easily explain the emergence of contentious political action (McAdam, 1982).
4. Examples are illnesses such as polio and cystic fibrosis—it is unlikely that many people survived those diseases before the early twentieth century.
5. Paradoxically, societies with higher levels of industrialization can be more disabling than less industrialized societies (Oliver, 1993; Gooding, 1994: 10).
6. Workhouses were one of the earliest forms of assistance for poor people; such assistance was sometimes called "indoor relief" (Stone, 1984).
7. This was true in Spain in the mid-1600s, when several deaf sons of noble families were educated to speak and lipread (Van Cleve and Crouch, 1989: 15). We presume that they were educated in other areas as well.
8. This was true of earlier time periods, as well. Blind workers during the Middle Ages enjoyed the same types of protection in guilds that others did (Matson, 1990).
9. This amount peaked at 42.5 percent in 1879 (Jankowski, 1997: 22).
10. In Gallaudet's early years, art and sports were emphasized. The university had a football team as early as 1880 (Neisser, 1983: 241–43).
11. The *Silent Worker* wrote about the situation of deaf women, if they were mentioned at all, in a paternalistic way. It was also silent about issues such as racial segregation within the deaf community (Buchanan, 1993: 178–79).
12. The Eugenics movement in general was beginning to lead to the institutionalization or forced sterilization of people with impairments as well as pressure against immigration of people with impairments and the marriage of people with impairments to one another.
13. The standards were not actually *fair*, since the law waived minimum wages as well as other types of federal workplace regulations for these workshops (Pelka, 1997: 282).
14. The mothers' marches in the early 1950s, which demanded gamma globulin injections for their children as polio preventatives (even though this had not been shown to be effective) are another example of parents making a fuss (Straus, 1965).

15. Incidence rates indicate the number of people newly affected by a condition during a given period of time, while prevalence rates indicate the total number of people with that condition at one point in time.

16. Even as late as the 1950s, however, people with some types of spinal cord injuries, especially higher breaks, did not always survive. With changes in emergency medical techniques as well as in acute care, rates of survival of people with spinal cord or head injuries have increased substantially in the last several decades (Pope and Tarlov, 1991).

17. The evidence on this point is not clear. Zola (1983a) thinks that this did not happen, while other activists, such as Karen Hirsch (personal communication, 1998), think that it did.

18. Beginning in 1962, the independent living concept was expanded by Ed Roberts when he agitated for a similar program at University of California at Berkeley. This program succeeded and later became the Independent Living Center in Berkeley.

19. Snow and Benford (1992: 144) note that, "the failure of mass mobilizations when structural conditions are otherwise ripe may be accounted for in part by the absence of a resonant master frame."

20. Thus, Shapiro (1993: 116) notes that there was less opposition from the business community to extending the frame of civil rights to people with disabilities through the ADA than there had been to extending that frame to blacks (and women) when the 1964 Civil Rights Act was proposed.

21. Conversely, it can detract from the frame extension if it denies that the frame applies. Take, for example, blacks' denial of frame extension to the gay rights movement. The ultimate effect of this denial is yet to be determined (Duke, 1993).

22. Although not a law passed by Congress, an executive order has the force of law. This one strengthened the compliance provisions of the 1964 Civil Rights Act and for the first time required affirmative action by federal contractors.

23. Although the laws that applied to blacks and members of other racial and ethnic groups resulted from contentious action, the laws that applied to women did not. Rather, significant legislation was passed before substantial numbers of contentious actions occurred.

24. However, extension of coverage of the Fair Labor Standards Act to workers in sheltered workshops did not occur until 1987 (Matson, 1990: 781).

4

Prom Promises

Rules and Ruling: Proms as Sites of Social Control

AMY L. BEST

Youth as a self and social construction has become indeterminate, alien and sometimes hazardous in the public eye. A source of repeated moral panics and the object of social regulation, youth cannot be contained and controlled within a limited number of social spheres. Youth cultures are often viewed in the popular press as aberrant, unpredictable and dangerous in terms of the investments they produce, social relations they affirm, and the anti-politics they sometimes legitimate.

—Henry Giroux, *Fugitive Cultures*

The "Prom Promise"

There is tremendous adult concern to prohibit underage drinking and illegal drug use at proms. Each year at assemblies and in school newspapers officials urge students to abstain from drinking at proms, citing a bevy of frightening statistics on alcohol-related injuries and fatalities that occur during prom season. Parent's associations host all-night postprom parties to keep kids off the road on the night of the prom. Prom magazines warn of the sexual dangers of drinking on prom night for girls. The theme of youth drinking frequently presents itself in television sitcoms and dramas, and in films. The message about youth drinking, similar to the message adults promote about youth sex, is to abstain; to "just say no."

In the final episode of the 1999 season of the successful TV drama *E.R.*, a group of four kids are injured in a serious car accident. It is worth noting that they were on the way to their prom. Dressed in prom dresses and tuxedos they are rushed into the emergency room on hospital gurneys, as a din of grisly screams and cries unfolds around them. What we learn is that the driver had been drinking; significantly though, it is never made clear how much. We also learn that of the driver's three friends also in the car one sustains such severe burns that he eventually dies on the operating table, and another is left paralyzed. Admittedly, it is a gripping and horrifying scene. The burn victim, as he lies on the operating table in agonizing pain, must say goodbye to his parents. "This was supposed to be the most memorable night of my life," he utters as he dies before our eyes. Faced with an equally harsh reality, the driver slowly realizes the egregious act he has committed; he must live the rest of his life knowing he has killed his best friend. We are left with a strikingly grim, albeit predictable message: because there was drinking and driving on prom night, three lives have ended before they ever began.

Antidrinking and antidrug campaigns targeting youth have become a national concern meriting nationally organized action. The most widespread crusade in the past decade has been the Prom Promise. Introduced in 1990 by Nationwide Insurance, one of the leading insurance providers in the United States, the Prom Promise is a program created to raise greater awareness among youth about alcohol-related automobile accidents. Modeling standard insurance protocol, the Prom Promise works as a contract between the student and the school whereby the student signing the contract pledges to remain alcohol and drug free during the prom. Though none of the four schools I studied participated in the Prom Promise, a number of schools do yearly. An estimated 3.4 million teens in 4,200 schools were expected to participate in the Prom Promise in 1997, according to one teen publication.[1] To encourage greater participation, Nationwide Insurance moderates a regional competition between participating schools; the school with the most pledges from the student body wins a number of prizes.

Though a nationwide campaign, the relative local success of the Prom Promise often depends on the support of individual communities and schools, and of course, the students. As such, local newspapers typically include a list of those schools participating in the Prom Promise. Florists' shops and tuxedo rental stores often promise discounts on prom sundries if students bring in their signed copy of the Prom Promise. One school principal promised his students that if enough signatures were garnered that he would move his office to the roof of the school on the day of the prom.

The Prom Promise is an attempt to regulate primarily from "below"; to ensure its success, students must consent to their own regulation. Students pledge, "Whether or not I go to the prom, I promise Insurance Prom Promise not to use alcohol or other drugs. This is a promise I take seriously. It's one I intend to keep for my sake and the sake of my friends."[2] In theory, students become the direct instruments of surveillance and discipline.[3] One school in New Jersey, featured on the local evening news, deputized students as "prom cops"; stationed at the entrance to the prom, they helped administer breathalyzer tests and encouraged other students to sign the Promise before the event.

What actually occurs at many schools, however, is that students sign this contract with every intention of violating it. Consider a conversation I had with Scott, a white student from Woodrow, about the Promise, which his school had once tried to implement, unsuccessfully:

SD: The Prom Promise is a thing that is put on by I don't know who, I think it's bullshit. They're [the school administration] not pushing it this year, some years they really push it. You know kids promise and it's a joke. You're signing it in jest. I saw a kid who changed the Prom Promise into the Prom Compromise.

AB: What was his compromise, to not drink?

SD: To drink, to say, "Fuck this. I'm not going to do what they're asking me to do, I'm gonna go and get, you know, hammered."

AB: Who's *they*?

SD: *They* being your safety-minded adult, your adult that feels that you should obey and be boring, basically, and have fun in a very traditional fifties kind of way.

For Scott, the Prom Promise signifies yet another futile exercise in adult control, reflecting nothing more than an attempt by adults to prescribe how students can have "fun."

Other schools adopt different strategies to manage students' alcohol and drug consumption. Most schools invoke a host of rules around the prom, ranging from the simply undemocratic to the truly absurd. One school principal in Pennsylvania prohibited students from renting limousines for the prom, a standard practice at other schools, arguing that this would prevent students from drinking. Unlikely to curtail student drinking, this strategy is additionally ineffective in actually preventing drinking and driving since more students would be forced to drive themselves to and from the prom, whether intoxicated or not. At another school outside Boston, a principal, stationed at the entrance to the prom, required students to breathe in his face so that he might better be able to check for alcohol on their breath. These are extreme examples of the abject control educational "lone rangers" can wield over youth. In most school settings, however, the control teachers exercise is not despotic, reflecting instead the larger institutional constraints and the prevailing organization of schooling that make controlling students virtually obligatory.[4] These controls are generally considered essential to the smooth operation of school.[5]

Suburban Life and the Middle Class at the Rudolph Prom

> *They made a big deal about the drugs and alcohol but that's obvious. You know you can't do that so that wasn't a big deal. And they couldn't do anything about all the kids that wanted to smoke because, they just go outside and smoke. The prom was more relaxed. Nobody was like . . . it wasn't like school at all with the rules and everything. The only rules we had were like the drinking and drugs. If you were caught the same rules applied that were at school. That wasn't a big problem for anyone. (White female student, Rudolph High School)*

All high schools have rules. High schools function as regulated spaces ordered by codes of discipline and norms of conduct.[6] Rules reflect the authorization of schools as legitimate sites of control; they express the practices and values that we expect kids to embrace as their own.[7] The specific context of schooling largely determines the different patterns of rules schools develop around the prom. Most often these rules are expressions of the particular pedagogical and ideological commitments of the school and community, organized not only to manage relations between the school and its students, but to connect students to a series of extended social relations beyond the immediate school setting.[8]

Rudolph, a predominately middle-class, white, suburban high school, subjected its students to a most rigid set of rules. Time was used to control the space of the prom. As this is a normalized dimension of the school experience, students are accustomed to having their actions governed by time; the ringing of the school bell is a regular feature of school life, and students have come to expect that their time will be organized in such a manner. At nine o'clock, one hour after the prom began, all kids attending were required to be present at the Rudolph prom. After students arrived, they could not leave the prom. Two plainclothes policemen waited at the entrance, ensuring no one reentered once they left. Guiding this particular rule was an effort to prevent students from venturing to their cars to drink, to return to the prom later. As Ondre, an African-American student, suggests, rules around drinking and drug consumption were particularly stringent and were managed through the use of time restraints:

> *I know at Rudolph we were supposed to be there by nine o'clock. The doors would be locked at nine so you couldn't come in and especially like the drinking thing was enforced or whatever. Oh, if they smell alcohol, or even suspect you, your parents will be called and you won't be allowed in.*

Direct communication with parents was another strategy the administration at Rudolph deployed. One month before the prom, the principal sent home an open letter to students' parents addressing the issue of drinking and declaring his commitment to making the prom an alcohol-free space. Contained in the letter was a direct plea for parents to join his crusade against youth drinking by urging them not to host any preprom parties. Many students, even their parents, thought this an unreasonable request. Flora, a white student from Rudolph, explained,

> *They sent home a letter that they advised us not to have a pre-prom party because it's a new principal. My mom, like, laughed. And they said, "They shouldn't have even the temptation of alcohol or something. 'Cause they think parents might serve us or something. I don't know, but we are [having a party]. My friend right around the block is having it. The parents go and the kids go and take pictures and stuff like that. There's tons of parties.*

The assumption here is that when youth drink, they drink excessively and are unable to monitor or restrict their own consumption. The other assumption made by the principal is that students' parents would ally themselves with him and his antidrinking agenda. To the contrary, parents, having their own agenda, allied themselves with their own kids against the school. Indeed, it is not uncommon for parents to loosen strict curfews, or to allow their children to enjoy a celebratory glass of champagne on what many consider the "eve" of their children's adulthood.

Students were required to submit a permission slip with parental approval to attend the prom. The name of their date was noted on the form and any changes in dates had to be approved by the administration before kids could attend. School announcements warned in advance that students would be removed from the premises if approval by the administration had not been granted. Fiona described how this worked at the prom:

> *At about nine o'clock I guess it was, everybody goes upstairs and you have to find your table and sit at it and the teachers go around and check at the tables to make sure, like they have a card, each teacher gets a set of note cards and you go look for them and make sure they are sitting there. 'Cause if you aren't sitting, if Mike is with some girl, somebody else, then she has to leave. Because you have to have a signed permission slip saying that you can go.*

Knowing who is going to the prom with whom enabled the administration to anticipate and ultimately forestall any unexpected surprises. In fact, all students were required to go to the prom with a date, though one exception was made in the case of a developmentally disabled student who was eventually permitted to go to the prom by himself only after his parents contacted the school. Students were also prohibited from going to the prom in same-sex groups or as same-sex couples. (Other schools placed no restrictions on persons with whom kids came to their prom; kids were "officially" free to either go by themselves, with a group, or accompanied by a same-sex partner.) As inferred by several Rudolph students, exceptions to this rule would be honored only if the same-sex couple could demonstrate to the school that they were "truly" lesbian or gay. Consider the following discussion I had with two students from Rudolph about two young woman who wanted to attend the prom together last year, but were prevented from doing so by the school administration:

ML: I think they [the school administration] thought it was just so they could go. They didn't really think they wanted to go together.

AB: Oh, so did they try?

FJ: They tried to go together but they didn't want two girls going together, I guess.

ML: They allowed it this year, but they [the students] have to prove that they are really [lesbians].

AB: So is there anyone at your school like that's, that's out?

FJ: What about Jane?

ML: Is she going with a girl?

FJ: I think.

ML: Is she really?

FJ: I don't know, maybe. I don't think she's going actually, maybe she's not going.

AB: So how did this come about, was there a discussion around this?

FJ: With the school? No! Tanya came up to me in school one day and was just like, "They won't let me go," because she just wanted to go with a girl. Because she's not really into [being gay], she doesn't go out with lots of boys or anything like that. She doesn't have many boyfriends or anything like that. It's really hard for her. I think it's hard for those people who don't have like a boyfriend. I feel bad, she's just like one example. Like she's not going this year because she doesn't have a boyfriend or anything. All their guys friends are really already going with someone. There is just people who have to go with someone just because.

AB: Is anyone allowed to go by themselves? Do you have to bring a date?

ML: You have to bring a date.

Whether intentional or not, this rule imposed by the Rudolph administration made it virtually impossible for a lesbian or gay student to bring a same-sex partner to the prom.[9] When I asked another student why Rudolph enforced this rule, she said that the school had adopted this rule to prevent any conflicts between student cliques.

Though not explicitly coded in a discourse of compulsory heterosexuality, this practice secured the prom as a heterosexual space. Even gender-specific dress codes were enforced. One student told me that the school required boys to wear tuxedos, and among students, it generally was understood that girls were not allowed to wear tuxedos. However, it is not simply that the school administration sought to uphold heterosexuality as the norm, though that was the effect. This decision has as much to do with regulating youth more generally as it does with specifically regulating their sexuality. This unofficial policy reflects at its core an unwillingness by adults to take seriously the idea that kids *could* be gay, lesbian, bisexual, or transgendered; kids could not decide to take up a position that consciously locates themselves this way "at such a young age."

Aside from a few dissenting voices, by a large measure, students consented to the normative order of heterosexuality. Asking Ondre, a young African-American student, if anyone had challenged the hegemony of these school rules, she responded,

OF: No.

AB: They wouldn't do that?

OF: No, that's not politically correct at Rudolph. You can't say you're gay.

AB: Because they wouldn't allow it?

OF: No, like the administration *might* allow it, it's just like the . . . I don't think the students. They would get so ripped on and talked about. They wouldn't do that, just for reputation, for all the big popularity contest and everything. No one would admit to being gay. Not at this age, especially . . . at Rudolph.

AB: Why?

OF: Money, wealth, it's one big popularity contest.

AB: Does money play into that?

OF: Well, first of all they assume you're rich because you go to Rudolph or [are] living in the area. The township and everything is just like politically correct. I really don't know how to explain it but, it's like, we call it the Rudolph bubble and nothing goes wrong. Everybody lives in their little perfect world. Nobody has, like, family problems. I mean everybody has family problems but they're not heard of at Rudolph. Everybody perfectly has the mother, father, sister, brother. Everybody goes to college, has college funds. It's just the Rudolph bubble. It's just perfect—a perfect world.

Her use of a "bubble" as a metaphor for white suburban life provides a cogent image of how middle-class suburban communities work to insulate and protect themselves and their kids from forces that are designated as disruptive or corrupting.[10] In this instance, students are safeguarded from the threat of transgressive sexualities. To a young African-American woman originally from an "inner-city" community, the school's attempt to contain and segregate the students (whether enforced by the administration or the students themselves) is especially meaningful. In many ways, her blackness and her black boyfriend from the "inner city" whom she brought to the prom signify the very sort of "difference" that communities like Rudolph seek to exclude.[11]

Ondre, one of the few African-American students attending Rudolph, was able to offer this salient critique of the practices deployed by the school to maintain "suburban security," particularly as it took shape within her own community, in a way that the white students could not.[12] These practices were a part of a normative and naturalized order of school at Rudolph, and were largely accepted by the students and teachers. Talking about life at Rudolph, Chip, a white middle-class student, provided the following:

You don't have to worry about anything, like, bad happening. It's a small school. The kids are really nice. It's really like, cliquey. There is definitely distinctive groups between kids, but, I mean I enjoy it, you know? It's a small school which makes it a little tough. Like everybody knows each other. I mean, everybody has their own reputation in the school. That's about it. It gets kind of old after four years, seeing the same exact people everyday. I pretty much enjoy it, you know, what I mean? It wasn't anything bad. It wasn't like torture. Some of the rules were a little too strict. Like, um, you're not allowed to go outside the building like at all or else you'll get a two-day suspension or something like that. If you have a book in your car you can't even go out to the parking lot without asking permission. I personally think that's a little bit too strict; other than that it's not that bad.

Embedded within Chip's discussion of school life is a tone of resignation. Chip accepts the school rules; they are strict, but such is the trade-off to secure safety in a small town.

I came to view the prom at Rudolph as a "metaphor to separate and sanitize," a phrase developed by Michelle Fine for understanding the ongoing operation of whiteness within institutional settings.[13] The question, of course, is to separate and sanitize from what? Being queer? Listening to rap, wearing hip-hop clothes? Being pregnant? Being a high school flunky? Being in a gang? Not being white, not being middle-class? Hadn't the students suggested earlier that the school administration had wanted to prevent student cliques from forming at the prom? Are students' cliques just a suburban precursor to gang affiliations? Perhaps these rules were an attempt to guard youth from themselves. The school implicitly assumed that these kids, left to their own devices, would veer off track and be headed for trouble.[14]

What are the material forces behind the development of such unyielding rules, and what is at stake? In addition to securing heterosexual and gender uniformity, these rules, ostensibly, are linked to class security, upward mobility, and white privilege. Rudolph High School is an academically driven school, expressed not only in its curriculum but in its culture.[15] Similar to other upper-middle-class suburban public schools, life at Rudolph is structured to secure and ensure the future success of these students. Like other suburban schools, parental and community involvement in kids' school lives is considerable; parents and teachers are enlisted to make sure these kids, most of whom are white and middle class, excel.[16] The rules at the prom, though imposed directly by school officials, are an expression of the larger community's vision of school as an essential stepping stone to secure and sustain a middle class, and their children's location within it.[17] The fact that this is a community comprised of mostly professionals contributes to this being a setting in which the future academic success of its students supplants the immediate need for greater freedom. Students' agency is bartered, bargained, and exchanged for their easy entry into the ranks of the professional middle class. Given the imperative to maintain the school's smooth (re)production of a middle class, it is not surprising that the Rudolph High School prom would be tightly organized.

Educating "The Best and The Brightest": Reading Privilege at the Stylone Prom

In contrast to the students at Rudolph, where countless rules infringed upon the experience of the prom, students at Stylone, an elite public school for "the talented and gifted," enjoyed considerable freedom at their high school prom. Relative to Rudolph's, their prom appeared to be an unregulated school space. In fact, when I asked the senior faculty advisor at Stylone, Mrs. Stark, a middle-aged white woman, about some of the rules that were enforced at the other schools, she expressed surprise at their policies. As I learned more about Stylone, I realized the aims and objectives of the school were entirely different from those at Rudolph. First, Stylone High School is one of the four most academically rigorous public high schools in its city's public school system, resembling more a private school than a public one. Second, its students possess tremendous cultural and intellectual capital relative to the students at the other three schools I studied. These two factors played a significant role in how Stylone's prom was organized and managed.

When I first met Mrs. Stark at the prom, she invited me to sit down beside her and we started talking about the kids. She began pointing out different kids and telling me about them. "That tall boy over there," she said, "is going to Princeton this fall; he is ranked number one in the state for tennis." Pointing to a young Asian woman she said, "There is a Westinghouse winner" (taking for granted that I was familiar with the Westinghouse Science Awards). Pointing to a young white woman, she said, "And over there is a Westinghouse finalist; she is going to MIT this fall." Nodding her head in the direction of another young Asian woman, she said, "And she played the cello at my son's wedding ceremony last year." This sort of boasting struck me as strangely interesting; I had not experienced anything like it when I spoke with the faculty advisors or teachers from other schools. Mrs. Stark was actively working to construct my interpretation of the school as an exclusive one and in so doing was trying to distinguish between Stylone and the other public schools in the city. This was expressed in countless ways, as my fieldnotes suggest:

> *I asked Mrs. Stark if all the kids were college bound and with a dismissive nod she said, "Oh yes," as though it should be obvious. She told me that some prom magazine had contacted her to ask if they could come to the prom, proudly declaring to me she had said "No." With a distinctive tone of arrogance, she added that their school was the first to decline the magazine and that she didn't care. It was "too disruptive and the kids didn't need that." She told me that* Seventeen *magazine had also contacted them to see if they could come. As I chatted with Mrs. Stark, I watched the kids move about, greeting each other and commenting on the dresses. I noticed it was about 8:15 and a significant group of kids had already arrived, which was different from the other schools. Boys came in their tuxedos and the girls came in evening gowns and cocktail dresses. It was clear to me that most of these kids had spent a lot of money on their clothes. Leaning her head toward me, Mrs. Stark told me there was a 500-person wedding downstairs and she bet none of the guests were as well dressed as these kids! Many of the dresses were elegant. She added that these kids all looked so "beautiful, individual and soooo tasteful." She had yet to see two dresses alike, nor had I seen two of the same. I could tell that many of the dresses had been bought in boutiques and women's sections of upscale department stores, like Bloomingdale's and Saks Fifth Avenue. Few of the girls' dresses looked as though they had been found in the teen section of Macy's or JC Penney's. (May 1997)*

It became even more apparent to me that coded in her bragging was an attempt to distinguish these kids from not only other city public high school kids, but from public school kids in general. Maybe she was trying to prove to me that this was not another inner-city high school, though I needed little convincing. Her attempts were deeply coded in class discourse, operating not only through a rhetoric of academic achievement but through a rhetoric of cultural style. Her comments about the tastefulness of students' dress styles signified her attempt to place these kids above other public high school students. Amira Proweller, in discussing the social organization of a private girls' school, provides insight into how the operation of schooling works at elite institutions, saying, "As students receive valuable instruction in academic skills, they are also the focus of a larger educational project to socialize a gendered elite.

The emphasis here is on the production of a class elite where students receive daily lessons in class appropriate norms, values and dispositions. Acquired resources then translate into upper-middle class cultural capital that benefit them now in school and hold out promises for educational and occupational attainments in the future."[18]

This understanding of Stylone as an elite school is so pervasive that it was embedded in most teachers' talk about the school, its students, and other schools. Quoting again from my fieldnotes:

> *One of the white chaperones, a teacher named Jack, approached me. After chit-chatting for a minute he asked if I would be studying a high school in the Bronx, where he had worked before coming to Stylone. I said no and he said that I would see some interesting differences. He said that the clothes are very "different" and that the kids' expressions in the Bronx were much more "provincial," in short, less informed by current fashion. The exclusion and insularity of Bronx high schools came as little surprise to me. The Bronx is an isolated community, forcibly segregated from the rest of the city, though his comment seemed conspicuously condescending. (May 1997)*

Students also helped to construct their school as an exclusive one. Consider the following conversation I had with one young white male student. His story is one of educational privilege serving "the best and the brightest":

RT: It's unlike any other school. This school is like no other in the United States. I'll tell you a story. We went on a ski trip once and almost everybody [Stylone students] on the ski trip was white. We went to a McDonald's or like, a Denny's and this student, he went to the counter and ordered, and the guy [behind the counter] was like, "Wow, you speak English *good*," and the guy just stares at him [he pauses] and he's like [sarcastically], "So do you." It's a school unlike any other school.

AB: What do you mean?

RT: It's a totally free environment. Anything goes. It's also very politically aware. One time we had a substitute teacher and we were doing the *New York Times* crossword puzzle. And she was like, "Students at Stylone are doing the New York Times crossword puzzle?" People think of Stylone as sort of a nerdy school. That you have to be oriented toward math and science. It really wasn't. Although we had a handful of Westinghouse finalists, science competitions, math competitions, and chess competitions, but yet, it was a cool school. It facilitated whatever work you wanted to do. You were encouraged to do everything. We had trophies. The theater was amazing, so high tech. There are always four or five plays going on throughout the school year.

The first portion of this student's story alludes to how language operates as cultural capital; students at Stylone are well-spoken. His narrative also makes visible that the copious resources available to these students, combined with a progressive pedagogy that encourages students' critical engagement, are what make this school unlike other public schools.[19]

Among their teachers and parents, as well as the larger society, these kids are identified as "the best and the brightest," and therefore it is assumed they are more deserving of the resources that are often absent at other public schools. As Mara Sapon-Shevin has argued, gifted education programs like those at Stylone produce and maintain enormous social and economic inequalities in education that correspond to histories and relations of race and class by providing students with a vastly different and an almost always superior education.[20]

This explains why the kids at Stylone, as one chaperone had commented, were kids who with few exceptions "have a stake in society."[21] These kids largely consent to the organization of their academic, social, and school life, primarily, of course, because they benefit directly from its organization. Accordingly, these kids willingly manage themselves. Their consent, though apparent in the student's talk above, was most clearly displayed through the way they related to their teachers. While the prom, a nonacademic space, may have required less rigid forms of surveillance of students by teachers, I witnessed a camaraderie between the teachers and their students at the prom that was noticeably absent at other schools. Stylone was the only school in my research where the kids selected and invited their chaperones. One white student talked about this within a larger context of how the school was organized:

RT: Sometimes teachers get offended when they are not chosen. You have the teachers who are teaching the most talented kids in the country . . . we choose everything. Our speaker at graduation we chose.

AB: So, how come the kids decide?

RT: Well, I think it is because you are dealing with gifted children. I mean, I don't necessarily agree that they are dealing with gifted children so that you have to treat them with a certain dignity or a certain respect that the other schools or the other students don't get. I think it's important that the administration allow students to make more decisions. Even important decisions, like with school policy. We have a parent-teacher-student administration. Like, once a month we have a big meeting, five students, five teachers. There is some stabbornness with the old-school teachers, you tell the student what to do and he follows. But the principal is different. She is fair and she loves the students . . . they really do push the students to behave how they expect them too. And it's one thing to expect them to behave and then you don't give them the freedom to express themselves. So, if you expect them to behave in an adult way, but you don't really give them the choice. They have to give us the opportunity to go both paths.

Although consenting to supervision, these kids (because they were identified as "gifted") were able to define the terms of their supervision by selecting certain teachers as supervisors. One of the chaperones boasted to me that it is quite an honor to be invited as a chaperone to the prom. Viewing this as an honor instead of as a faculty responsibility radically reframes teacher-student relations as less antagonistic or hierarchical because teachers are unable to categorize this as burdensome work.[22]

The differences between the way Rudolph kids and Stylone kids related to their teachers at the prom were striking. At Rudolph's prom, in the beginning of the evening I watched the kids walk to the very back of the cocktail room, the farthest possible distance from where the chaperones stood at the entrance, while kids at Stylone lingered by the chaperones' table; they hugged and kissed each other "hello" and extended these courtesies to the teachers until Mrs. Stark had to ask them to move inside because lines were beginning to form behind them. I came to see this spatial ordering as a reinscription of symbolic divisions between the teachers and the students, divisions that operate as fundamental features of the everyday ruling in schools. The tension between how teachers relate to school as a work space and how students relate to school as a supervised space often generates antagonism between teachers and students.

These tensions, typically easy to see in most schools, were virtually absent at Stylone. While many students at Stylone cheered and hollered when two chaperones came onto the dance floor to dance, the chaperones at Rudolph (or at Hudson) did not venture to the dance floor. Instead, I watched two female chaperones at Rudolph dance together on the rug lining the perimeter of the dance floor. The dance floor at Rudolph's prom was a space designated for students alone—suggestive, I would argue, of the way kids understand school and school-related sites as spaces of control.

The absence of direct control of the students by the school and its teachers at Stylone, although reflective of a progressive pedagogy of "openness" for these kids, is ultimately about securing their class privilege by allowing these kids to exercise decision-making control (though this is only meaningful as a form of privilege insofar as other students at other public schools are denied it).[23] The prom space was structured for kids to practice privilege, a privilege heavily coded in and ordered around relations of class and rase.[24] At Stylone, one student told me that the prom is completely organized by the students. A small committee appoints a larger group of students to various subcommittees. Each committee is responsible for planning a different aspect of the prom. One committee is solely responsible for administering surveys to the student body. In the spirit of democracy, the polls are designed to determine what the entire student body wants at its prom. A range of detailed questions are asked, such as, "Would you be willing to pay five more dollars for an ice cream bar?" Throughout the development of the prom, decisions are routinely evaluated by the student body. The teachers and administration, while watching over the progression of the prom's organization, rarely intervene in its development. Organizing and experiencing the prom at Stylone provided an opportunity for the school to hook these kids, as members of the cultural and intellectual elite, in relations of ruling by allowing them to actively participate in the "management" of this space. While it is difficult to argue that these relations form a stable and homogeneous class culture at this school, what can be argued is that these relations embed meanings of class in school. Through the distinct activities that define the Stylone prom, students come to understand their experiences and their identities in terms of class and class categories. Many of these students know that their educational experience at Stylone is one of privilege that students at most public schools do not share. Both teachers and students use this class lens to narrate and make sense of this event, and in so doing, reconstitute class relations.

Responding to the Rules

At a school like Rudolph, where rules pervade all spaces and shape all social relations, how did the kids respond? To assume that kids simply accept the ruled would cast students as docile recipients of their control. Of course, kids rarely accept fully the terms of their own governance. How do they navigate what seems to be an endless stream of control?

Spaces of Trickery

All four high schools had some sort of method to check the kids into the prom. At Stylone, upon entry kids picked up their table cards. Because kids at Woodrow and Hudson were not assigned to tables, they signed their names in a guest book greeting their teachers as they came into the building. The strategy for "checking kids in" at Rudolph was arguably the most formalized. At the beginning of the prom, the chaperones at Rudolph formed a receiving line in the entry way. Each student was required to greet each chaperone in the receiving line before they could gain entry to the grand ballroom. One of the chaperones told me, as she found her station within the line, that they had had a receiving line at the prom for years, it was a "nice" way to "check in" the kids and also ensure that kids were not under the influence of drugs or alcohol. I stood back and watched as kids were received by their teachers. That the teachers "received" the kids contributed to the sense that the prom belonged to the teachers and not the kids. It seemed emblematic of the direct control the school itself exercised over these kids' lives.

However, many students interpreted the receiving line in a way that radically departed from how the teachers understood it. One young white male student, Chip, provided a creative reinterpretation of the receiving line that developed from his "experience" as a student within a hierarchical school organization. Rather than accept the hegemonic meaning of the receiving line, Chip offered another reading:

AB: Did you guys go through the receiving line?

CP: Yeah.

AB: What did you think about that? I'd never seen that at a prom before.

CP: You never saw that? You see, I don't know why, because for some reason I liked that so much. Like, I loved doing that. I don't know why, I guess because, um, teachers always expect, like, kids to be, like, drunk or stoned or something but, I mean, like, you're totally not. It's kind of like making them feel stupid. I think just because they think you're gonna be, like, drunk or something or doing something bad but, you're totally not. You're totally sober. They're totally looking to catch somebody and they're just not going to, so it's kind of funny the way you laugh at them a little bit.

Although Chip also perceives the receiving line as an instrument of surveillance and control, the receiving line symbolizes a space in which he can contest this school rule through an inverted reading. Chip's reading challenges the way teachers define students "as always in trouble" and resists the hegemony of particular school practices. Michael De Certeau's work on the culture of everyday life provides theoretical insight into this process. As he explains, "Innumerable ways of playing and foiling the other's game . . . characterize the subtle and stubborn resistant activity of groups which, since they lack their own space, have to get along within a network of already established forces and representations. People have to make do with what they have. In these combatant stratagems, there is a certain art in placing one's blows, a pleasure in getting around the rules of a constraining space . . . even in the field of manipulation and enjoyment."[25] The receiving line emerged as a space of trickery for many kids. Little acts, like jumping on the end of the receiving line and mimicking the chaperones as they greeted the students, represented momentary disruptions of the school's power to manage and regulate the activities of youth. The receiving line, while an expression of power, also signifies a space in which this power is refuted. Destabilizing the ongoing operation of power in schools in this way enables kids to carve out spaces of their own and to make the prom theirs.

The Dance Floor

> *After the prom there was no party so we went from one spot in the woods to another and the cops found us all three times. Finally [we] gave up at around 4 a.m. and came home. A few guys were arrested for being intoxicated but no girls were. (White female student)*

Securing privacy and autonomy in school or even outside school can be an enormously difficult task for kids. As the young woman above suggests, students are often required to go to great lengths to find unsupervised leisure spaces, and even then these spaces are never fully secured from adults. At each prom I attended, I watched kids search for and attempt to create makeshift private spaces for themselves within this highly public space. I saw several couples escape off to darkened corners of the room or venture to less traveled areas of the building outside the ballroom to create momentary sites of intimacy in a highly supervised space. Literally ignoring their surroundings, these couples sat close together and kissed and talked. Scores of students at Rudolph's prom, many of them smokers, escaped outside to an adjoining veranda, a significantly less supervised area than inside the ballroom. Whether they smoked or not, many students spent a considerable portion of their prom outside.

Attempts by students to create an unsupervised space can influence the organization of the dance floor; an excerpt from my fieldnotes provides another example of how the dance floor at Rudolph's prom was shaped by kids' struggle to claim a space for themselves:

> *When I walked into the grand ballroom where Rudolph's prom was held, many kids had already found their way to the dance floor. Upon first glance, it appeared that they were all dancing. However, on second glance, I noticed several kids standing and talking to one another, rather than dancing. These students came together in small shifting groups, moving their bodies to the music as if they were actually dancing. Off to the side of the dance floor, on the rug, I spotted two older*

> *women teachers line dancing in unison. Not once in the evening did*
> *I see any teacher dance on the dance floor. (May 1997)*

The teachers danced, but not on the dance floor, and the students occupied the dance floor but many of them did not dance. The spatial organization of students' bodies and teachers' bodies seemed to suggest an order to the dance floor, through which it came to be defined as a space for and of youth.

After the Prom

At times kids upset the power of schools in more concerted ways. Most of the kids I spoke with had made postprom plans. Agreeing not to drink at the prom, many of the kids at Rudolph postponed drinking until later in the evening. "Nobody I was with drank before the prom but I know after the prom, like, down the shore it was just drinking . . . all weekend," one student reported. For many, drinking at the prom simply was not worth potential suspension, or worse. "It's so enforced and so restricted that like everybody is so worked up and really nobody does it [drinking] before prom," another student offered. Consider this conversation I shared with Chip:

AB: What about the rules for the prom? I understand there were . . .

CP: Drinking rules, you mean? The thing they emphasized most is like no drinking, drugs, or anything like that beforehand. Everybody obeyed that one.

AB: Oh really?

CP: Yeah, pretty much. At prom, definitely.

At Rudolph, a large group of the kids headed to the beach after the prom for a weekend of freedom and independence from adult supervision. One Rudolph student described the weekend as "a big alcoholic weekend, like for days after, you'd taste beer. It was just awful, I mean, it was a lot of fun and no one got too out of control. No one got sick, no one got alcohol poisoning, thank god." Discussing the politics around drinking, the prom, and the weekend "down the shore," Mitch and Fiona, two white students at Rudolph elaborate:

ML: People don't really drink that night anyway.

FJ: The next day is a drinking day.

ML: Next three days.

AB: Oh really?

FJ: Yeah, like everybody. Last year we went, people go down the shore after the prom or they go the next morning. Saturday morning, you still have Sunday night for juniors and then seniors usually have the next day off for senior cut day so they stay down three days. Last year we stayed down Sunday. We had Saturday night so we did. My friends, we stayed at a hotel. All the senior guys, they all stayed at this other hotel. There had to be like forty people there. I remember running into them a couple times; they were down the block and they were like always drinking. All day, all night down the shore and stuff like that.

ML: Everybody goes down the shore, but not in the same place. Everybody goes down the shore, Wildwood, Long Beach Island.

FJ: Everybody goes down the shore, it's kind of known.

At Woodrow High School, as at Rudolph, an entire set of extended activities were organized by the students independent of school. In the students' constant pursuit of unsupervised space, an event once lasting a few hours has been transformed into a series of activities occurring over several days. While the prom itself is identified by students as a school event, the activities to follow exist outside school, beyond the reaches of the school's control. Elise, a biracial student at Woodrow, talks about plans for after the prom:

> *Like, a lot of people are going camping, a lot are going to rent a hotel room. And then, like, the people who are doing the hotel thing, like, that's Friday night but Saturday night. You see the prom weekend is like the whole, it's gonna be the whole weekend, so Saturday night we're going camping and Friday night we're doing the hotel thing. They're supposedly renting like a whole—they're going to the Holiday Inn and getting one whole floor, like sixteen rooms.*

Some kids who did not go to the prom at Rudolph still participated in the activities after the prom. Sandy, a Rudolph student, told me, "My friends went [down the shore] at like 4:00. A couple of my friends who didn't go to the prom went down and they just started . . ." Another white student at Rudolph related,

> *My friend Bren didn't go and Katie didn't go [to the prom]. They are like best friends. They decided they were too cool for the prom this year. They were a bit obnoxious about it. They were like, "Oh you guys are so dumb why are you going to the prom, it's stupid, last year was awful." I was like, "Okay whatever: you guys go to the shore and get started, we're going to the prom." They were too cool this year.*

Chip added,

CP: A few of my friends just didn't go [to the prom]. Like they went to the shore right after school on Friday.

AB: Why didn't they go?

CP: Why didn't they? I guess for a couple of them it was like an issue of money to get all the money together for a tuxedo and for the prom bid they'd just rather spend that money on the shore and their hotel and stuff and they'd have a good time that way. I guess just some of them like didn't want to go through the trouble of finding a date and doing all that kind of stuff. So they just didn't go, they didn't bother with it.

As I spoke with kids at Rudolph, I began to see the redefinition of spaces of importance emerging within their talk:

AB: So could you tell me a little bit what school was like on Wednesday after the prom? Was there talk about the prom?

CP: There wasn't really talk about the prom, it was more like, talk about the shore and everything that happened, you know what I mean?

The prom, for many kids at Rudolph, especially, became secondary in importance to the activities that followed the prom. Chip elaborated further:

AB: The shore, I heard that for a lot of people it was a big drinking thing.

CP: Yeah, it was awesome. We had so much fun because like, it was kind of like the cliques in my group like really don't hang out, you know what I mean. But like Monday, yeah because Tuesday we had was senior cut day. So, Monday night it was basically just like the senior grade, it was cool because a lot of us haven't just hung out in like two years, you know what I mean? In high school all the girls in our grade go with the older guys and by the time senior year none of us like them. So we really don't hang out so like we finally got a chance to all hang out and have fun together for the first time in a while so that was really fun. I like that a lot. I had a good time.

The idea that the events that followed the prom were somehow better or more important than the prom itself was a theme expressed by students who attended other schools. One student wrote about what she did after her prom:

> *All the pressure was finally over. Afterwards the group split up and half of the group was driven back in the limo. We all changed at my house and piled into cars. My friend had a cottage on the lake a couple hours away . . . so eight of us drove there. We had driven down a couple weeks earlier and decorated with lights and had prepared food and snacks. Basically we talked all night and watched movies. At 5 in the morning I convinced some of my friends to go row boating with me. We didn't sleep all night and the next day went sailing and ate lunch, played cards and had a great time. Overall I think the prom is over-rated. It was too much stress and pressure. Once we got out of our formal wear and hung out, we felt better. I'm glad we went but the after prom was definitely better.*

Responding to the students' postprom events, a number of schools have tried to usurp the power kids can assert by providing a supervised postprom party. The organizing committee at Woodrow High School said that their postprom party was intended to provide kids with a fun and safe space to go after the prom. While their concern for students' safety seems genuine, this is also an attempt to manage how kids can experience the entire prom night. Similarly, another school in New Jersey scheduled graduation the day directly following the prom to prevent students from having these several-day "freedom" excursions where reckless drinking and sex were assumed to ensue.

Many students refuse to go to the school-organized postprom events, deciding instead to organize their own activities, while some only go in the absence of available alternatives. "I suspect everybody goes for a little while, or most everyone anyway, those that can walk," one student said about the postprom party at Woodrow. One young man wrote about the postprom party at his school,

> *After the prom was really boring. We went to a school sponsored event, but most of us really wanted to go to a party. Nobody was having one.*

To enlist kids to attend the Woodrow postprom party, the organizing committee, comprised mostly of parents, promised gifts like microwaves, stereos, and CDs to be raffled, tying kids in direct ways to a culture of consumption. Matt, an African-American student from Woodrow, though originally willing to go to the postprom party because of the possibility of winning some prizes found upon arriving that he could have more fun someplace else outside school:

> *After the prom everybody planned to go to the after party but the after party wasn't like everybody thought it would be, like fun. So everybody stayed there for an hour or two and we considered going to breakfast, so we went to breakfast. . . . Everybody was going to Denny's. After that we like just rode around. Some of my friends went to New York City.*

The fact that this student preferred "just riding around" to being at the postprom party is suggestive of how kids define this space and its connection to school. Like the prom, this postprom party was a regulated space, governed by rules reflecting the ideologies and authority of the school. Once they entered, kids could not leave and return later. At the entrance stood the principal beside a long table at which several chaperones sat. Each student was required to check in and was warned that if they left they would not be readmitted.

Though many students did attend the postprom party, kids creatively worked this space to their own ends and refused to enter it except on their own terms. One strategy kids deployed to upset the ongoing surveillance by schools was the manipulation of time between leaving the prom and arriving at the postprom party. Students were expected to go directly from the prom to the postprom party, stopping briefly to change out of their prom clothes into more comfortable clothing. Instead, many kids prolonged the time between the prom and the postprom party by stopping at a community diner or college coffeehouse for something to eat.

Additionally significant is the fact that high school students are usually prohibited from entering public settings. Strict rules around loitering at such places as McDonald's and public parks set limits on how kids are able to interact in public settings; the possibility of their being removed from these spaces is always imminent. On the night of the prom, these kids occupied these public spaces without risk of their removal. As teenagers, they challenged how they came to these spaces. For any onlooker, it was obvious that these kids were coming from their prom; many were still dressed in their prom attire. This is a radical departure from the way kids are typically allowed to enter and occupy public spaces. Samuel, a student from Hudson, reflected on how he spent his time after the prom:

AB: What was that like, going out to other places?

S: It was funny, because in the middle of the night everybody was like, "Okay we're hungry let's go out to eat," and then one of the other girl's prom dates, Alex, right, he was like, "Oh, we're going to McDonald's." And he was like, "What will we look like going in there with prom suits into McDonald's, like, let me have a number two" [laughs]. You know, you all dressed up and you're supposed to go to a nice place and Alex was like, "Who told you that lie?" He was joking around, though. And so we was going to go to this diner, we was going to go to the one right here, the one on Second Avenue, Cosmos and then the limo driver said he knew a nice place in Queens that was real fancy and nice and everything and we was like, "Is it expensive?" and he was like "Naw, it's just food." And then, so, we went there and it wasn't that bad. You know, we had fun.

AB: What kind of restaurant was it?

S: It was a nice fancy restaurant. It had everything. It had [something] like this high, it had shrimp, hamburgers, cheeseburgers, club sandwiches. It's like a diner, but it had everything in it. Ice creams and everything. So, we sat there and we had fun and we started bugging out and we started talking about the prom, and pictures, and then we went to South Street Seaport and took some more pictures and that was basically it. I liked the diner, it was real nice and relaxing.

Prom night offers itself as a time when kids are allowed to venture to spaces from which they are typically excluded, like upscale restaurants or hotels. They negotiate the meanings of these spaces, redefining them on prom night as spaces of freedom, often finding themselves with more bargaining power in these settings because of the way they are dressed and because they have gathered enough money to buy their entry into these spaces. On prom night they are able to enjoy a type of independence, free of supervision, that they are denied on a day-to-day basis.

Reconsidering Rules

Rules both naturalize and normalize the operation of power in schools in that they are visible but largely taken-for-granted features of life in school. Attending a suburban high school like Rudolph, I often felt overwhelmed by the ongoing sense of being controlled, of being ruled. Like many of the kids at Rudolph, I remember that my days in school were filled with finding more inventive ways to navigate a constellation of rules framing school life and shaping my relationship to a broader project of schooling. A rich layering of disciplinary forms appears in virtually all aspects of schooling. The regulation and management of social spaces outside of the classroom are significant sites in which the social forms authorized by schools are extended, legitimated, and re-created, enabling schools to control in more encompassing ways how kids engage, negotiate, and contest power inside and outside school. In light of the fact that students often feel constrained by school itself, not only inside the classroom but outside it, we should not take lightly the weight of this control.

In an immediate sense, rules as a text tell us little about the complexities of schooling as a social practice, or about the primary actors involved. But if we look at rules as coming into being through the local, ongoing negotiations of them by students, then we can get at how rules secure and (re)produce specific forms of domination, as well as how kids work within and around them. There is always more to rules than immediately appears; rules around drugs and alcohol regulate the direct action they promise to deter as well as serving to manage an entire terrain of social and sexual relations, as was clearly the case at Rudolph High School.

In addition to exploring the ways rules and ruling shape how youth come to and organize themselves around the prom, this chapter has also concerned itself with how rules and ruling are organized in connection with the (re)production of class and race privilege. An investigation of the underlying ideological workings that give rules shape within specific school sites reveals not only a relationship between youth and school, but makes visible a more complex set of ties that are being shaped and formed between youth and a larger organization of external social relations *through* school. What are the relationships being forged? Both Rudolph and Stylone High Schools are schools that educate upper-middle-class youth; yet, the way each school organized its prom varied in remarkable ways. Expressing a suburban ideology of "safety," Rudolph High School organized its prom to secure heterosexual, class, race, and gender uniformity among its students, thus sacrificing their agency and freedom. To the contrary, Stylone students enjoyed considerable freedom and autonomy. Given that Stylone's curriculum is designed to serve the "the best and the brightest," it is not surprising that students were able to express their agency in myriad ways. What should not be overlooked is that the agency Stylone students were granted resecures their class and race privilege. The organization of the prom in regard to rules at both schools reveals a curriculum embedded in a set of social relations organized to uphold class and race inequalities between schools. In addition to expressing upper-middle-class agendas, the relations organizing these proms embed and reconstitute class and class relations as a meaningful feature of school culture and students' school identities.

5

Introduction: In Search of Freaks

ROBERT BOGDAN

OTIS JORDAN, a man with poorly functioning and underformed limbs who is better known in the carnival world as "Otis the Frog Man," was banned in 1984 from appearing as part of the Sutton Side-show at the New York State Fair. A vocal citizen had objected, calling the exhibition of people with deformities an "intolerable anachronism." The protester contended that handicapped people were being exploited and that the state's fair funds could be put to better use by helping people with disabilities instead of making them freaks.

As a result of the complaint, and in spite of Jordan's objections, Sutton's "Incredible Wonders of the World" was moved from the heart of the midway, where business and visibility were best, to the back of the fair. The showmen were asked not to use the term *freak* or allow performances of people like Otis Jordan, people the public would consider disabled (Kaleina 1984).[1]

On September 8, 1984, the Associated Press released a story ("City to Cite" 1984) about a committee formed in Alton, Illinois, to erect a statue in honor of Robert Wadlow, a local boy who had reached the height of eight feet eleven inches before his death in 1940 at the age of twenty-two. Wadlow had appeared in the circus in the 1930s and, using the novelty of his height, had gotten a job promoting shoes at stores throughout the United States (Fadner 1944). But a committee spokesperson wanted to clarify: "He was not a circus freak as a lot of people might think. He was an intelligent, caring man."

During the past twenty years numerous intellectuals and artists have confronted us with freaks.[2] Yet the frequent mention and coffee-table display of art-photography books, which include pictures taken at freak shows, are no indication that freak shows are now accepted. Rather, as the work of Diane Arbus personifies, "freak" has become a metaphor for estrangement, alienation, marginality, the dark side of the human experience (Arbus 1972; Sontag 1977). Indeed, Arbus's biographer suggests that her flirtation with freaks was but one dimension of her odyssey through the bowels of society—her suicide being the last stop on the trip (Bosworth 1984).

Otis Jordan and the spokesperson for Robert Wadlow's statue committee remind us of what we all sense when we hear the word *freak* and think of "freak shows." Seen by many as crude, rude, and exploitive, the freak show is despicable, a practice on the margin, limited to a class with poor taste, representing, as one disability rights activist put it, the "pornography of disability."[3]

Although freak shows are now on the contemptible fringe, from approximately 1840 through 1940 the formally organized exhibition for amusement and profit of people with physical, mental, or behavioral anomalies, both alleged and real, was an accepted part of American life. Hundreds of freak shows traversed America in the last quarter of the nineteenth and first quarter of the twentieth centuries. Yet only five exist today,[4] and their continued existence is precarious. Personnel, plagued by low-priced admissions, poor attendance, and attacks from indignant activists, cannot tell from week to week whether they can last the season. Barely alive, the freak show is approaching its finale.

Given the tradition of the study of deviance and abnormality, one would expect a large body of social scientific literature on freak shows. There is none.[5] The low status of the convention, combined with the decline in the number of such businesses, may explain this lack in part. In addition, until the relatively recent interest in the natural history of social problems (Conrad and Schneider 1980; Spector and Kitsuse 1977), social scientists interested in deviance seldom turned to the past for their data (see Erikson 1966 and Mizruchi 1983 for exceptions). Thus freak shows have remained in the hands of circus buffs and a few nonconformists in the humanities. I believe, however, that these displays of human beings present an exciting opportunity to develop understanding of past practices and changing conceptions of abnormality, as well as the beginnings of a grounded theory in the management of human differences.

The Social Construction of Freaks

In the mid 1920s, Jack Earle, a very tall University of Texas student, visited the Ringling Brothers circus sideshow.[6] Clyde Ingalls, the show's famous manager, spotted Earle in the audience; after the show he approached the young man to ask, "How would you like to be a giant?" (Fig. 1, see p. 85).

While it is uncertain how much of this story changed on becoming incorporated into circus lore, it clarifies a point that freak show personnel understood but outside observers neglect: being extremely tall is a matter of physiology—being a giant involves something more. Similarly, being a freak is not a personal matter, a physical condition that some people have (Goffman 1963; Becker 1963). The onstage freak is something else off stage. "Freak" is a frame of mind, a set of practices, a way of thinking about and presenting people.[7] It is the enactment of a tradition, the performance of a stylized presentation.

While people called "freaks" will be included in this discussion, the people themselves are not of primary concern. Rather, the focus is on the social arrangements in which they found themselves, the place and meaning of the freak show in the world of which they were a part, and the way the resulting exhibits were presented to the public. The social construction—the manufacture of freaks—is the main attraction.

But don't leave! There will be exhibits (and it will be okay to look!). For we need examples—flesh on the bones of institutional analysis. We need to understand what it was like to participate in the freak show and what meanings emerged to make the enterprise coherent to the exhibits, the promoters, and the audience alike.

Vocabulary

Many terms have been used to refer to the practice of exhibiting people for money and to the various forms that such exhibits took. "Raree Show" and "Hall of Human Curiosities" were early-nineteenth-century terms. "Sideshow," "Ten in One," "Kid Show," "Pitshow," "Odditorium," "Congress of Oddities," "Congress of Human Wonders," "Museum of Nature's Mistakes," "Freak Show," and a host of variations on these titles were late-nineteenth- and twentieth-century designations.

A broad range of terms were applied to the people exhibited, the freaks. Because natural scientists and physicians were interested in many exhibits, and because showmen exploited scientific interest in constructing freaks, the lexicon is a complex hodgepodge of medical terminology and show-world hype. The more recent proliferation of euphemisms generated by the freak show's decline in popularity and the moral indignation surrounding the exhibition of human anomalies creates a long list of imprecise terms.[8] "Curiosities," "lusus naturae," "freaks of nature," "rarities," "oddities," "eccentrics," "wonders," "marvels," "nature's mistakes," "strange people," "prodigies," "monsters,"[9] "very special people," and "freaks" form a partial list. The exact use and definition of these words varies from user to user and from time to time. They do not, however, all mean the same thing; indeed, some have very exact meanings when used by particular people. The terminology will be clarified as this discussion proceeds.

Types of Freaks

What were the various kinds of human freaks? In discussions of human oddities in the eighteenth and nineteenth centuries, there developed an important and revealing, albeit blurry and noninclusive, distinction between two types of exhibits. The distinction is revealing because it illustrates the connection between science and freak shows, a connection that showmen profited by and tried to maintain well into the twentieth century. The distinction was between so-called examples of new and unknown "races" and "lusus naturae" or nature's jokes or mistakes.

The first type is related to the exploration of the non-Western world then in progress. As explorers and natural scientists traversed the world, they brought back not only tales of unfamiliar cultures but also specimens of the distant won-

Fig. 1. Jack Earle in the Ringling Brothers, Barnum and Bailey Sideshow. Earle is in the top row, third from the right, wearing a tall hat and military outfit. Other well-known exhibits in the picture include the Doll Family, Koo-Koo the Bird Girl, Clicko the Bushman, and Iko and Eko. Photo by Century, c. 1934. (Hertzberg Coll., San Antonio Public Library.)

ders. Tribal people, brought to the United States with all the accoutrements of their culture out of context, stimulated the popular imagination and kindled belief in races of tailed people, dwarfs, giants, and even people with double heads (Clair 1968) that paralleled creatures of ancient mythology (Thompson 1968). The interest thus spawned was an opportunity, a platform, and a backdrop for showmen's creations. Promoters quickly began to exhibit what they claimed were examples of previously undiscovered types of humans: not only non-Western people but also, fraudulently, as a promotional strategy, Americans with physical anomalies.

The second major category of exhibit consisted of "monsters," the medical term for people born with a demonstrable difference. Lusus naturae, or "freaks of

nature," were of interest to physicians for whom the field of teratology, the study of these so-called monsters, had become a fad. To the joy (and often at the instigation) of showmen, debates raged among scientists and laypersons alike as to whether a particular exhibit actually represented a new species or was simply a lusus naturae.

In the last quarter of the nineteenth century the blurred distinction between species and freaks of nature became moot; all human exhibits, including tribal people of normal stature and body configuration, as well as people who performed unusual feats such as swallowing swords, fell under the generic term *freak*.

Those twentieth-century authors who have written about the sideshow, mainly popular historians and humanities scholars, address the question "What were the various kinds of human freaks?" by concentrating on the physical characteristics of exhibits with anomalies (Drimmer 1973; Durant and Durant 1957; Fiedler 1978; Howard 1977). Their books and articles are organized like medical or special education textbooks, with headings covering such topics as little people (dwarfs and midgets), giants, hairy people, human skeletons, armless and legless wonders, wild men, fat people, albinos, Siamese twins, people with extra limbs, half men/half women, people with skin disorders, and anatomical wonders. They are eager to provide readers a quick course in genetics, endocrinology, and embryology. One of the most widely read, Drimmer's *Very Special People*, romanticizes exhibits by casting them as courageous warriors battling the disadvantage they received at birth. These writings, however, ignore exhibits *without* blatant physical anomalies, not to mention the social constuction of freaks.

The humanities scholar Leslie Fiedler, in his popular book *Freaks* (1978), still concentrates on exhibits with physical anomalies, but he breaks the mold of writers who focus on "freak" as a physiological condition. Rather, his mythological, psychoanalytic approach posits that human beings have a deep, psychic fear of people with specific abnormalities. Dwarfs, for example, confront us with our phobia that we will never grow up. Yet although Fiedler's study of "human curiosities" shifts the focus from "them" to "us," it also reifies "freak" by taking "it" as a constant and inevitable outpouring of basic human nature. Moreover, in his writing he slips back to treating the person exhibited as the subject of the study. His typology of human oddities does not stray from the traditional view of "freak" as a physiological condition, and it excludes exhibits with no physical anomalies. Thus, rather than penetrating the socially constructed dimension of the freak show, he merely mystifies it.

In answer to the question "What were the various kinds of freaks?" people who have been inside the exhibiting business use the physiological categories as well, but they also use the distinctions *born freaks, made freaks,* and *novelty acts* (Gresham 1948; Kelly 1950). According to this classification, "born freaks" are people with real physical anomalies who came by their condition naturally. While this category includes people who developed their uniqueness later in life, central are people who had an abnormality at birth: Siamese twins and armless and legless people are examples. "Made freaks" do something to themselves that make them unusual enough for exhibit, such as getting adorned with tattoos or growing their beards or hair exceptionally long. The "novelty act" (or "working act") does not rely on any physical characteristic but rather boasts an unusual performance or ability such as sword swallowing (the more contemporary versions used neon tubes) or snake charming.

In addition to these three main "types," sideshow people refer to "gaffed freaks": the fakes, the phonies—the armless wonder whose arms are tucked under a tight fitting shirt, the four-legged woman whose extra legs really belong to a person hidden from the audience,[10] or the Siamese twins who were in fact two (Fig. 2). When in public freak show personnel showed disdain for the gaff; their

Fig. 2. Phony Siamese twins. Adolph-Rudolph were gaffs: joined twins are always identical. Note the dissimilar facial features. Photo by Frank Wendt, c. 1899. (Becker Coll., Syracuse University.)

competitors might try to get away with it, but they would not. The "born freak" was publicly acknowledged as having esteem.

This is the standard typology as those in the business present it, and it has not changed over the last hundred and twenty years. More inclusive than other schemes, it is a good starting point for approaching the subject of freaks. Yet even though the "insiders'" way of categorizing differentiates freak show exhibits in the abstract, even they had difficulty applying the distinctions. Non-Western people, for example, were exhibited in freak shows on the basis of their cultural differences. Although showmen called them "freaks" and displayed them on the same platform as people with physiological and mental disabilities, their place in the commonsense typology is unclear. The categories did not, moreover, acknowledge the pervasive hype, fraud, and deception that was characteristic of the whole freak show enterprise. If taken at face value, the insiders' typology veils more than it reveals. It interests us not because it clarifies the freak show or the exhibits, but because it enlarges the subject and grounds us in the commonsense notions of the amusement world.

Exhibiting people, although often treated as an educational and scientific pursuit, was always first and foremost a for-profit activity. Presentors learned from the medicine shows that packaging of the product was as important as what was inside. Thus, using information from science, exploration, medicine, and current events, and appealing to popular images and symbols, promoters created a public conception of the exhibit that would have the widest appeal, attract the most people, and collect the most dimes. Every exhibit was, in the strict use of the word, a fraud. This is not to say that many freaks did not have profound physical, mental, and behavioral differences, for as we will see, many did; but, with very few exceptions, every person exhibited was misrepresented to the public. The gaff was only the extreme of this misrepresentation.

The major lesson to be learned from a study of the exhibition of people as freaks is not about the cruelty of the exhibitors or the naïveté of the audience. How we view people who are different has less to do with what they are physiologically than with who we are culturally (Sarason and Doris 1979). As with the tall Jack Earle, having a disability or another difference did not make the people discussed in this book freaks. "Freak" is a way of thinking, of presenting, a set of practices, an institution—not a characteristic of an individual. Freak shows can teach us not to confuse the role a person plays with who that person really is.

Why 1840?

By "freak show" I mean the formally organized exhibition of people with alleged and real physical, mental, or behavioral anomalies for amusement and profit. The "formally organized" part of the definition is important, for it distinguishes freak shows from early exhibitions of single attractions that were not attached to organizations such as circuses and carnivals.[11]

In the nineteenth century the United States was moving from an agrarian, family- and community-based society to one in which formal organizations like schools, factories, businesses, hospitals, and government agencies would dominate. During this time the organizations that would eventually house freak shows developed. It would be a distortion to state that in 1840 human exhibits changed all at once from unattached attractions to freak shows, for the process was slow and had been under way for half a century. But 1840 is significant because by that time the transition had progressed significantly and because, close to that date, P. T. Barnum became the proprietor of an organization in New York City, the American Museum, that looms large in the history of the American freak show. It was this establishment that brought the freak show to prominence as a central part of what would soon constitute the popular amusement industry.

Significantly, once human exhibits became attached to organizations, distinct patterns of constructing and presenting freaks could be institutionalized, conventions that endure to this day. The freak show thus joined the burgeoning popular amusement industry, and the organizations that made up that industry, housing as they did an occupation with a special approach to the world, developed a particular way of life. That culture is crucial to an understanding of the manufacture of freaks.

In Search of Freaks!

How does one go about studying freak shows? What types of material are available? Although many of the standard historical sources are useful (Flint 1972),[12] certain unusual sources deserve attention here because they help to introduce the concoction of freaks and the place of freak shows in American life.

One kind of information is found in abundance: the materials that were used to publicize the exhibits—handbills, newspaper advertisements, canvas bannerline posters, and the promotional photographs and advertising booklets that exhibited people sold as a way of supplementing their incomes.[13] At first glance these materials appear useless. They are so contrived, so obviously produced merely to win customers' attention that they can be easily dismissed as lies. But fraud is central to the freak show, and lies make good data—that is, if one knows that they are lies and if deception is the subject of investigation. After all, misrepresentation is integral to the manufacture of freaks.

Freak Portrait Photographs

If you visited a proper American household of the 1860s to early 1900s, you would wind up sitting in an ornately decorated parlor (Seale 1981). There, often supported by their own stands, would be thick, elaborately crafted and lavishly decorated photograph albums containing formally posed, studio portraits (M. Mitchell 1979; Taft 1938). Pictures of family members filled most albums, but Victorian and post-Victorian Americans collected pictures of other people as well: statesmen, generals, performers, and, interestingly, freaks.

Nineteenth-century Americans suffered from "cartomania" (Bassham 1978, 3; Darrah 1981; McCullock 1981)—a compulsion to collect photographs. They bought pictures to fill their albums, which they spent hours looking over and showing to friends. The photo album was the television of Victorian homes: what Victorians viewed, what they collected, reflected their interests and tastes. Judging by the number of freak images produced, it is safe to say that human oddities were not only fascinating but quite acceptable as Victorian houseguests—as long as they stayed in their albums.

Prior to 1850, technology limited imagery production to two basic processes: one resulted in an image similar to the daguerreotype, the other rendered the calotype. Because glass negatives were not employed (daguerreotypes used no negative and calotypes employed paper), the production of high-quality multiple copies, and thus wide-spread marketing of photographs, was impossible. In 1851, however, the development of the collodion process, or "set-plate" technique, enabled photographers for the first time to make many prints from one exposure, and by the early 1860s the carte de visite (hence the word *cartomania*) was all the rage (Darrah 1981), with annual sales of 400 million in the peak years of their production (Mitchell 1979, 15).

Drawings and prints provide the earliest visual record of human oddities. Some daguerreotype images of freaks have survived the years—including Tom Thumb and the "Aztec children" (Harvard Coll.)—but it was not until the mass-produced carte de visite that a comprehensive record of human exhibits could be assembled. Popular freak show attractions of the 1860s posed for photographers and sold their carte de visite likenesses to Victorian Americans. Mathew Brady (Meredity 1970), premier early photographer, famous for his Lincoln portraits and his striking visual chronicle of the Civil War, made cartes de visite of Barnum's American Museum freak attractions (Kunhardt and Kunhardt 1977).[14] In his studio on Broadway, across from Barnum's landmark, he took pictures of popular authors, statesmen, dignitaries, and such freak show notables as Henry Johnson (What Is It? or Zip); Captain Bates and his wife Anna Swan, the married giants; Major Newell, the midget; Charles Tripp, the armless wonder; Admiral Dot; General Tom Thumb and his wife; Lavinia Warren; Chang and Eng, the original Siamese twins; Annie Jones, the bearded lady; the Lucasie albino family; and the Fiji cannibals. The Barnum freaks that Brady captured on film went on to be the prototypes of later freak exhibits.

By the late 1860s larger and clearer cabinet photographs were being produced, which reignited the collecting craze. Although the cabinet photo eventually replaced the carte de visite, enough of the smaller images remained in circulation in the 1880s to warrant at least a few pages for them in contemporary photograph albums.

In the last three decades of the nineteenth century, freak shows and photographers flourished (M. Mitchell 1979). Particular photographers took up freak portraits as a specialty. Human oddities would regularly climb the stairs to their top-floor studios (lighting was provided by skylights), carefully pose, and then they or their manager would pick the images to be duplicated.[15] In some cases thousands of reproductions would be ordered at one time.

They posed in front of one of various painted backdrops depicting scenes that ranged from jungle terrain to Victorian parlors. Props were selected, costumes worn, and the pose struck—all to reflect the image that the manager and the subject wanted to promote. Some exhibits were presented in an exotic mode, others in a way that aggrandized their status. Dwarfs were photographed in oversized chairs to appear smaller than life, and giants were shot in scaled-down chairs to appear larger. Fat people's garments were stuffed with rags to add to their size. In addition, negatives were doctored, with, for example, additional hair added to exhibits whose abundance of hair was their oddity (Figs. 3 and 4).[16]

Exhibits and managers would carefully review the proofs and give printing instructions that would enhance the image, perhaps to emphasize the oddity or to promote a particular presentation. On photographs in the Harvard Theater Collection, some of the cabinet pictures still bear the photographers' notes. On one photo of an albino woman, the instructions read: "Make half length and have the hair show as white as possible." On the back of an 1880s picture of R. J. James,

Figs. 3 and 4. Two versions of a hairy man. In producing the photo on the right extra hair was added to the exhibit. Photos by Charles Eisenmann, c. 1884. (Becker Coll., Syracuse University.)

"The Ohio Fat Boy," the instructions call for a retake with looser clothing to make him look larger.

In some photos, the freaks' managers posed with their exhibits. In others, the exhibit's family was included. Exhibited children often sat with their parents, and older exhibits appeared with spouse and children. In the 1880s and 1890s major cities had photography studios that catered to freak show clienteles. Because studios branded their photocards with their logo, it is relatively easy to compile a list of studios—from Lonma in Eastport, Maine, to Rulofon in San Francisco.[17]

In post–Civil War America, New York City was the freak show capital of the country, and the Bowery was its center. Photographers had to work hard to keep up with the demand for freak portraits. With thousands being sold, more New York photographers entered into the freak portrait business.[18] Yet one person stands out, in both the quality and the extent of his effort (Roth and Cromie 1980, 79; M. Mitchell 1979): Charles Eisenmann, whose photographic legacy is truly amazing.[19] Every major freak show attraction sat for his Bowery studio camera during the 1880s and 1890s, and many made repeated appearances. More photos by Eisenmann are available for study than by any other photographer, and major circus and theater libraries are rich with his images.

Showmen and exhibits cashed in on America's photo-collecting craze. Freaks placed photocards on the platform in front of them for sale, which, if a patron requested, could be signed, dated, and even inscribed with a personal message. The "armless wonder's" "footwritten" messages were in high demand. Ann Leak

Thompson, the "armless lady," was famous for her catchy phrases: "I write poetry and prose holding my pen between my toes" (Harvard Coll.), or "Hands deprived, toes derived" (Becker Coll.).

Freaks sold thousands of these pictures, and because the markup was good, profits were high. The income was usually split between the show's management and the attraction, although the most popular exhibits negotiated to keep a higher percentage of the cash. The photos provided benefits to the show besides the direct flow of cash, however. Not only were they good publicity, but selling them also provided the attractions with a diversion from the tedious routine of sitting on the stage. Photograph sales were also a tangible measure of the exhibits' popularity relative to others on the platform.

The great bulk of sales of freak portraits occurred at the exhibition proper. In the nineteenth century, however, pictures of particularly popular exhibits, such as Tom Thumb, could also be bought from the photographers and their agents (Kunhardt and Kunhardt 1977). Lavinia Warren, Tom Thumb's wife, was referred to as the most photographed woman in the world. She ordered fifty thousand pictures of herself at a time (Desmond 1954, 222) and these were widely available from photography vendors.

In some cases these freak portraits with their occasional handwritten messages are all that remains, the only communication left. The only evidence of Ella Harper, for example, is an Eisenmann cabinet portrait of a pretty thirteen-year-old with severe orthopedic problems, on all fours (Fig. 5). On the back of the picture is written: "I am called the camel girl because my knees turn backward. I can walk best on my hands and feet as you see me in the picture. I have traveled considerably in the show business for the past four years and now, this is 1886, I now

Fig. 5. Ella Harper, "the Camel Girl." Photo by Charles Eisenmann, 1886. (Becker Coll., Syracuse University.)

Fig. 6. The Jones Siamese twins. Family portrait, with the twins in the foreground. Photographer unknown, 1889. (Becker Coll., Syracuse University.)

intend to quit the show business and go to school and fit myself for another occupation" (Becker Coll.).

During the nineteenth century and into the twentieth, freak show patrons took their treasured photo souvenirs home and placed them in their albums. Often they wrote information on the back—the name of the attraction, his or her age or birthdate, where and when the exhibit was seen—as a reminder. While the reliability of this information is never certain, notated pictures can be helpful in tracing exhibits' stories. This misspelled note for example, was written on the back of a cabinet photo showing a young family consisting of mother, father, a five-year-old, and infant Siamese twins (Fig. 6): "The Jones twins. Born in Russianville, Ind June 25, 1889. Joined at buttock, had there own normal lags, they had but one rectum. They died while on tour with a carnival show when about 15 months old" (Becker Coll.). By means of the photo and notation, the twins could be identified as those described in an 1880s medical journal (Huff 1889).

Eisenmann and the other Victorian photographers left a rich collection of clear and elegant images that help us to understand freak shows and their place in nineteenth-century America. After the turn of the century, although the collecting craze declined, a market for freak photos persisted. The Barnum and Bailey Circus sideshow attractions, for instance, continued to sell cabinet-style photocards until at least 1916. With the invention of cheap, lower-quality processes to reprint pictures in a postcard format, however, and with the decline of the studio photographer, freak portraits began to figure less importantly in sideshow life. Nonetheless, well into the 1940s freak postcard portraits were regularly sold to promote the show and to supplement income—and Otis Jordan, "The Frog Man," was selling portraits at the New York State Fair in the 1980s.

Of course, most of the millions of freak portraits that were created have been destroyed (some probably by appalled spring cleaners), but they occasionally turn up still in attics and old trunks. They can be purchased at antique shops, estate sales, and through antique photographic dealers. For the student of freak shows these are an important resource, our most complete record of the one hundred years of freak show popularity.

"True Life" Pamphlets

Although freak portraits capture the visual dimension of presentation, they cannot convey the details of the stories constructed to explain the exhibits to the audience. Luckily, in addition to photos, exhibits sold biographical pamphlets from their platforms (Fig. 7). These pamphlets are not, however, as plentiful as the portraits, for two reasons. First, they were not as popular; while virtually every exhibit sold pictures, the sale of pamphlets was less pervasive. Second, unlike the photos, which were printed and mounted on enduring materials, the booklets were printed on inexpensive paper that disintegrated over the years. Nonetheless, extensive collections of these booklets exist, covering the period of our concern.[20]

The titles of these pamphlets reveal their content: "Biography, Medical Description and Songs of Miss Millie/Christine, the Two Headed Nightingale" (1883); "Sketch of the Life of General Decker, the Smallest Man in the World" 1874); "Life and History of Alfonso, the Human Ostrich" (c. 1903); "Life and Adventures of the Burdett Twins" (1881); "Interesting Facts and Illustrations of the Royal Padaung Giraffe-Neck Women" (1933); "Sketch of the Life, Personal Appearance, Character and Manners of Tom Thumb" (1854); "History and Description of Abomah, the African Amazon Giantess" (c. 1900); "Personal Facts Regarding Percilla the Monkey Girl" (c. 1940); and "What We Know About Waino and Plutano, the Wild Men of Borneo" (c. 1878).

With minor variations, by 1860 a pattern in contents had been established. First, a short biography of the subjects was presented: where they were born, what their early life was like, how they were discovered, and what the condition of other family members was. This part concluded with a description of the exhibit's recent history—where they had been shown, who had seen them, and how patrons had reacted to them. Second, a description of physical condition was given, commonly written by or quoted from a medical doctor or a person affiliated with the natural

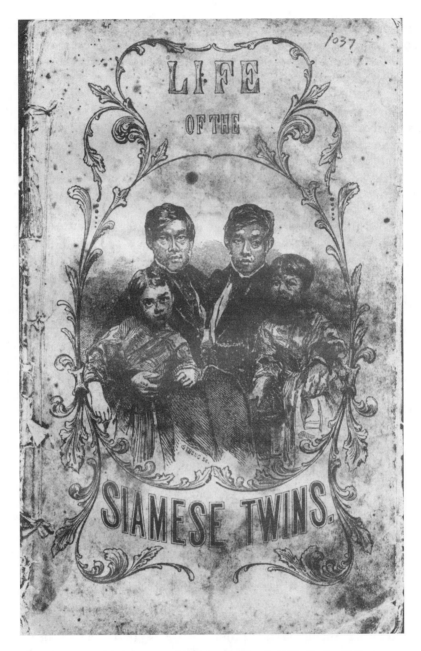

Fig. 7. Cover of Siamese twins' "true life" pamphlet. C. 1855. (Becker Coll., Syracuse University.)

sciences. Third, the pamphlets contained endorsements from people—elected officials, newspaper editors, royalty, and clergy—who had seen the exhibit and vouched for its authenticity, interest, and propriety for public viewing. Medical personnel and scientists commented on the authenticity and scientific relevance of the curiosity. Fourth, if the exhibit was said to come from some exotic land, a brief history of its exploration and a short description of the geography, plants, animals, and native people would be included. In addition, most pamphlets contained drawings or photographs and, occasionally, songs or poems, either written by the freak or in celebration of the exhibit.

These "true life" pamphlets were filled with exaggeration, fabrication, and out-and-out lies. Their purpose was to promote the exhibit, to present the details of the story that had been created to draw potential patrons in. Like the freak photos, the stories were part and parcel of the freak image which the managers, promoters, and freaks themselves wanted to promulgate. Some pamphlets were forty and more pages long, going on in elaborate, fraudulent detail about the trek through the jungle that resulted in finding the lost tribe of which the exhibit was a member—when in fact the person was born and raised in New Jersey.

The "true life" pamphlets, like the freak portraits, changed over the years. Their length, the detail, the endorsements were greatest and grandest in the nineteenth and early twentieth centuries. After 1920 they went the way of the photograph, and the quality and elaborate detail of the prose was curtailed. Pamphlets that would once have been several dozen pages were reduced to sometimes only one folded page. In some cases the portrait and the "true life" pamphlet merged into a postcard format, with a picture of the freak on one side and a few paragraphs of biography and description on the other. The decline in the quality and detail of both photo and booklets parallels the decline of the freak show itself.

I have drawn extensively on the freak portraits and "true life" stories in the pages that follow. When juxtaposed with candid memoirs, interviews, letters, newspaper reports, and medical and scientific articles, the modes of presentation discussed in this book emerge.

Notes

1. The controversy occurred in August 1984. The next year the restrictions were dropped. Although the word *freak* did not appear on the advertisement banners, a banner depicting Otis Jordan as "The Frog Man" was displayed in a prominent place, and Jordan was the leading attraction. In 1986 there was no human freak show at the fair. Rather than being dropped because of official action, however, it was discontinued primarily because it was not profitable.

   Barbara Baskin was the disability rights activist who led the fight to ban the sideshow. She wanted "this anachronism permanently abolished" (personal correspondence, 1983). For court rulings regarding the right of people with disabilities to display themselves for profit, see Lewis (1970, chap. 21); *Gaylon v. Municipal Court of San Bernardino* (1964); *World Fair Freaks and Attractions, Inc. v. Hodges* (1972); and Shipley (n.d.).

2. Most notable is Diane Arbus (Arbus 1972; Bosworth 1984). See also Levenson and Gray (1982); Fiedler (1978); Price and Price (1981); and Steinbrunner and Goldblatt (1972).

3. This phrase was used by Douglas Biklen of the Center on Human Policy, Syracuse University, Syracuse, New York.

4. Five were estimated to be still in operation during the 1985 season (Ward Hall, personal correspondence, 1985).

5. The only sociologists who have dealt with circuses, carnivals, and sideshows are Truzzi (1968a, 1968b, 1973, 1979) and Easto (Easto and Truzzi 1972, 1974).

6. Earle's real name was Jacob Ehrlich. Prior to joining the circus he had a number of minor film roles. He was actually seven feet seven inches tall, but was promoted as being eight feet seven inches—"the tallest man in the world." See Johnston (1934c, 72–73) and Lee (1970).

7. I approach the subject relying on the theoretical assumptions of the sociological theory of symbolic interaction (Blumer 1969). Also see Berger and Luckmann (1967); Spector and Kitsuse (1977); and Conrad and Schneider (1980). To the extent I am also interested in the taken-for-granted aspects of the freak show world and the structure of that world, I draw on ethnomethodology (Garfinkel 1967). In my emphasis on "presentation" I draw from Goffman (1959). With regard to the social context of freak shows, their rise and fall, some ideas of structural functionist analysis are employed. My analysis has been inductive (Bogdan and Taylor 1982; Glaser and Strauss 1967).

8. For a discussion, see Drimmer (1973), and Fiedler (1978). Later in the book I will discuss the controversy surrounding the "Revolt of the Freaks," which was supposedly precipitated by Barnum and Bailey exhibits not wanting the word *freak* used to refer to them. As we shall see, this was a publicity stunt, not an issue or an action initiated by those on display (Lentz 1977; Latzke 1903).

9. The word *monster* derives either from *moneo*, meaning to warn, or *monstro*, meaning to show forth. In both cases the origin reveals ancient beliefs that abnormal births were an evil sign. See Fiedler (1978).

10. See Ringling Collection for a photo of a phony four-legged girl.

11. I use the work *organization* here in the sociological sense of the "formal organization."

12. Memoirs reviewed include Barnum (1855, 1872); Bradna and Hartzell (1952); Coup (1901); Dadswell (1946); Dufour and Kirby (1977); Fadner (1944); Fellows and Freeman (1936); Hall (1981); Holtman (1968); Kelly (1982); Robinson (1925); and Middleton (1913).

13. In the big circuses the profit was split between exhibit and management. The details of the arrangements can be found in contracts between attractions and owners (Pfening Coll.).

14. The original glass negatives are in the Meserve Collection.

15. In some cases the photos were supplied, and thereby were chosen by the owner of the establishment that the exhibit worked for. This was most often the case when exhibits worked for organizations such as the circus, where they signed up for the season. (See contracts in Pfening Coll.).

16. Ron Becker pointed this out to me when I was reviewing his extensive collection of freak portraits.

17. The list includes Harrie Rose Studio in Indianapolis; Sword Brothers in York, Pennsylvania; Burrell in Providence, Rhode Island; Star Photo Gallery in Detroit; Johnson's in Kansas City; Grier Brothers in Philadelphia; Pugg Studio in Minneapolis; Hall Studio in Lowell, Massachusetts; Stuart in Buffalo; Gardner in Atlanta; Potter and Roberts in Cleveland; Wilker in Baltimore; Landi in Cincinnati; Herschel in Chicago; Baker in Columbus, Ohio; Hughes in St. Louis; Lonma in

Eastport, Maine; Chickerney in Boston; Morris in Pittsburgh; and Rulofon in San Francisco—to name only a few.

18. Kern, Wood, Obermuller, Mora, Wendt, Chapman, Bogardus, O'Brien, Edward, Pachmann, Feinberg, Oliver, Sherman, McHugh, and Falk are but a few of the names that appear in decorative letters on the bottom or back of 1880, 1890, and 1900 cabinet photos taken in New York. See "Artists of the Bowery" (1885) for a description of the Bowery photographic scene.

19. Eisenmann was born in Germany in 1850 and immigrated to the United States in his teens. He went into business as a photographer in 1876, moving to his shop at 229 Bowery in about 1879. The two-story building, which remains intact today, served as both his business and his home. He, his wife, who assisted him in his work, and their daughter lived in these cramped quarters for seven years. The business prospered, and by 1884 he had opened a branch studio on 14th Street and moved his family to a house in the northern suburbs of Manhattan.

For fifteen years, Eisenmann was the most popular and prolific photographer in the freak show world. He produced thousands of negatives and countless prints. Most freaks passed through the Bowery during their careers, and the best came to him for their pictures. Even the aging Barnum sat for Eisenmann in 1885. Frank Wendt was his partner and eventually took over the business.

20. Booklets go back as far as 1834. The largest collection of these booklets is in the Hertzberg Collection, San Antonio Public Library, San Antonio, Texas.

6

Whether their perpetrators realize it or not,
Disability Awareness Days send

The Wrong Message

VALERIE BREW-PARRISH

Hey, Hey, Hey, it's Disability Awareness Day! Everyone gets a chance to see what it's really like to have a disability! Yank out those blindfolds, grab cotton to stuff in your ears, and plop yourself in a wheelchair to navigate around an obstacle course! To get the most out of Disability Awareness Day, it is important to try almost all the disabilities on for size.

Now it is time to tie one of your arms behind you so you can fully appreciate a paralyzed limb.

No doubt about it, life with a disability is a tragedy! Why these poor gimps, blinks, and others would be better off dead! They are so courageous and yet pitiful as they go about their daily routines. Yep, I'm so glad it is their fate and not mine . . .

Sadly, these are the misconceptions that the public holds about those of us who live with disabilities. Disability simulations do nothing but reinforce these negative stereotypes about persons with disabilities.

Like the Jerry Lewis Telethon, disability simulations should be abolished. The disability community should be as outraged by disability simulations as they are over the negative implications of telethons. Overwhelming feelings of pity well up in those who simulate a disability — and pity does not equate with dignity. Disability simulations rob persons with disabilities of their dignity and self respect.

Simulations are phony. To "simulate" means to assume the mere appearance of — without the reality. The reality is this: nondisabled persons can never understand what it is like to have a disability. Jumping in a wheelchair for a few minutes, wearing a blindfold, and stuffing cotton in one's ears does not make a person understand life with a disability.

People who have never been disabled who simulate a disability are often terrified. Many of the "simulators" even cheat a little. Haven't we all observed a person standing up in their wheelchair in order to lift the chair over a curb? They breathe a collective sigh of relief knowing full well that their charade will soon come to an end and their momentary disability will gratefully vanish.

Agencies purportedly serving disabled clients frequently advocate disability simulations, with fancy brochures encouraging the public to assume a disability with blindfolds and wheelchairs. The pamphlets gleefully expound the theory that disability simulations are useful for teaching family members and others what the person with a disability is really experiencing.

What these rehab professionals fail to realize is that the public does not have the coping skills or strategies developed by people who actually have disabilities.

This point was clearly illustrated a few years ago when airline personnel decided to blindfold themselves to test evacuation procedures in case of an airline crash. The results were disastrous. Naturally. The airline staff had no training in mobility or orientation. Therefore, they erroneously concluded that blind persons could never safely evacuate a plane. Nothing could be further from the truth.

When I'm disoriented in a dark place, I let my blind husband lead the way! The National Federation of the Blind has long argued that disability simulations are destructive. Other disability groups should follow their lead and speak out against these sordid attempts to empathize with us by becoming a gimp for a day.

For several years, I was employed at a large university that sponsored an annual "Disability Awareness Day." Despite protests from students and staff with disabilities, the nondisabled sponsors of the event continued the spectacle.

I was told by participants that I was an inspiration because I coped so well with my disability. Others told me they would rather be dead than live with a disabling condition. The participants of the simulation debacle now looked at me with pity. In their eyes, I was no longer on an equal basis with them; they felt superior because all of their limbs were in proper working condition.

Regrettably, it seems every annual celebration of the passage of the Americans with Disabilities Act, every disability awareness event, is combined with a tasteless display of disability simulations. In many instances, persons with disabilities are actually participating in and perpetuating these contemptible attempts to make the public aware.

Awareness Days can be beneficial if it they are done properly; it is important for the public to meet with persons with disabilities and to interact with us. Why not have people who use wheelchairs discuss obstacles and the need for accessibility? Deaf persons can demonstrate sign language skills, and blind persons can show proper travel techniques. The public needs to know we exist; that we are professionals, parents and homeowners just like them.

But disability simulations need to die a quick death. There are more effective and positive ways to educate the public. Come on folks, we can do a better job getting our messages across. We do not need people to pretend they have disabilities and simulate our disabilities to understand us. All of us need to demand to be treated with dignity. When disability simulations become extinct, perhaps the flood of pity will dry up and be replaced with respect.

7

Streetwork—an Encounter with Place

Jacquelin Burgess & Peter Jackson

ABSTRACT   *The* Streetwork *project is a practical exercise in carrying out a qualitative study of people-in-place. It forms the core of our teaching in cultural geography at University College London (UCL). Forming part of a second year course, the project develops the initial exposure to qualitative fieldwork experienced during a first year field course. The nature and implementation of the project is described and the skills training involved in the course is outlined. The project has been taught in a number of different settings and student reaction indicates that it is a valuable exercise. However, a variety of problems have been raised in the course of teaching the project and the paper concludes with a discussion of these issues.*

Context

We are fortunate to be working in a department that actively encourages innovation in teaching, both in terms of developing new courses and novel approaches in field research. The *Streetwork* project has evolved over the last 15 years, benefiting greatly from the tolerant, if occasionally bemused, support of our colleagues—and from generations of students, enthusiastic enough to try anything once! For students, the process begins on the first year field trip during the Easter vacation. We offer a variety of field projects to groups of up to 30 students. Since 1975, Jacquie has encouraged students to try out Mass Observation, working from the original guidelines of Tom Harrisson and the archive at the University of Sussex; qualitative and quantitative approaches to landscape appreciation in the Forest of Dean; and in-depth interviewing of elderly people in the small mining village of Sacriston in County Durham. Peter has experimented with different methods of recording people's social networks (in Gloucester, Cwmbran and Durham) and with oral histories in Cardiff's Tiger Bay (Butetown).

The Sacriston project was particularly successful, running for six years from 1981 and providing a strong foundation for qualitative work in the second year. For the majority of our students, it was the first time they realised that geographical research could also involve genuine encounters with people-in-place—that it was possible to undertake research which did not depend on wheedling their way into people's houses with spurious claims about the value of their questionnaire survey; filling in forms with answers that meant very little either to the respondent or the student; producing bland and boring "Thus, it can be seen that. . ." reports of their results.

Based on these experiences in the first year, we have been able to develop a variety of second year courses, in each of which qualitative methods have occupied a central place. Since 1980 (when Peter joined the department), our collaborative teaching has evolved from courses on environmental perception, behavioural and humanistic geography, to the cultural and historical geography course which we now teach jointly with Hugh Prince and Nuala Johnson. Peter brought an expertise in participant observation and a training in urban ethnography which complemented Jacquie's experience with interviews and techniques of environmental interpretation.

If they wish, students may now follow courses with a significant element of qualitative research through the three years of their undergraduate education. When students register for our second year course, they not only have practical experience in qualitative methods (from the Easter field class), they will also have carried out a first year project in the 'Ideas in Geography' course which is based on readings and a semi-structured interview with a member of staff (as originally described by Cosgrove, 1981). Our first year 'Geographical Enquiry' course also has a module of three lectures devoted to principles of qualitative research. The second year 'Cultural and Historical Geography' course may be followed by four specialist third year courses: 'Methods in Historical Geography' (text-based); 'Urban Historical Geography' (text and field-based); 'Urban Ethnography' (text and practical-based); and 'Environmental Interpretation' (a course on media studies which is examined by 5000-word course paper requiring original empirical research).

The Streetwork Project

We regard the second year course as the core of our teaching in cultural geography, and the *Streetwork* project as the core of that course. The project takes place approximately half-way through the course which is divided into four modules (on Cultural Landscapes, Senses of Place, Cultural Politics, and Postmodernism).

We introduce the project with a discussion of different 'ways of knowing', using extracts from Jane Jacobs' *The Death and Life of Great American Cities* (1961) and Paul Harrison's *Inside the Inner City* (1983). The extracts are intended to serve as models of the kind of interpretative essay that students will be asked to produce and as illustrations of different 'subject positions' (an 'insider' writing about the stretch of Hudson Street where she lives in New York and an 'outsider's' journalistic account of poverty in the inner London borough of Hackney). Through this exercise and previous classroom discussions, students become accustomed to working in groups, learn to value their own experience and begin to 'find a voice'—skills that are all put into practice in their *Streetwork* projects.

The best way to describe the project is to reproduce the handout we give to students (Fig. 1). The name of the project is borrowed from Colin Ward (Ward & Fyson, 1973) where it clearly has radical associations. Some element of this may carry over into our own use of the term which cannot entirely escape such political connotations. The aims of the project highlight some of the transformations that have occurred in human geography over the last 15 years. It draws on some of the methods of environmental perception and humanistic geography—with an emphasis on developing the students' powers of observation and sensitivity to both their own and others' environmental experience; the exploration of those environmental, historical, social and cultural characteristics which contribute to a sense of place; and the appreciation of difference, one of the hallmarks of contemporary cultural geography.

Streetwork: an exercise in urban interpretation

The objective of this project is to *encounter a place* with which you are currently unfamiliar; to open yourself up to the urban experience; and to describe and interpret the symbols and meanings that are conveyed through that experience. As cultural geographers, you will need to question the extent to which "people and place' are indivisible. To begin with, you will be an "outsider', open to features that may have become commonplace or routine for local people. Your perceptions may be more acute that an insider's less focused curiosity, dulled by routine observation and habitual experience. But you may be unaware of the subtle nuances of meaning that structure and hold communities together in place. Take your time to get used to the area and don't make hasty judgements.

The aim is to produce an *interpretive account* of your chosen place, conveying your experiences as a traveller and explorer. Think carefully about the language you will use, the analysis you will make. (Remember the examples from Jane Jacobs and Paul Harrison.)

Where? Choose somewhere you don't know well. Spend time walking around until somewhere "feels' interesting. Exercise your intuition and empathy (you've all go it!). The place could be a nineteenth-century High Street, an Edwardian suburb, a 1930s shopping centre, an industrial backstreet, a tenement block, a market, a modern housing estate, a major development (like

---

Barbican), a gentrifying neighbourhood, or an "ethnic' enclave (like Brick Lane).

How? Become *aware* of your environment: watch, look and listen more acutely than normal. Concentrate on specific features of the environment (colours, sounds, faces, architectural styles, graffiti, street furniture, clothes. . .): whatever makes the area feel different or distinctive.

- talk to people, on buses, buy things, or ask directions.
- contact someone who is knowledgeable about the area and who can give you an introduction (a community worker, a residents' association, a local teacher).
- take photographs, make sketches, draw maps and keep a diary.
- collect information about the area, read the local paper, use the library, visit the parks.
- find out about the area's history, about important local buildings or famous residents.
- for the times beyond living memory, examine the character of the built environment, historic institutions.
- find out what issues concern people today.

You will be working in *groups of four people*, so you should try to work out a convenient division of labour. But, at least for the first few times, visit the area as a group. Compare your impressions of the neighbourhood and decide who will follow up which leads. Each group will be asked to make a *progress report* to the rest of class. By then you should have chosen an area, begun the research and thought about a possible theme. The *end product* will be an interpretive essay of 2500 words with appropriate illustrations.

Fig. 1. Streetwork: student handout.

Students are asked to form small groups (of typically between three and five) and to choose an area that they wish to study. There is some fluidity in the composition of groups over the initial few weeks of the project as students find a group and an area in which they feel comfortable. We try to interfere as little as possible in this process but we do not allow students to work on their own or in excessively large groups, on the basis that they will learn most from each other in relatively small groups as well as being safer than working individually. Each group is encouraged to choose a street, a market, an estate or neighourhood which they do not know well. On the rare occasions when more than one group has chosen the same area, we have not prevented this and allowed them to compare notes as their projects begin to take shape. Over the years, we have had groups working in places ranging from suburban Richmond, Barnes, Dulwich and High Barnet to inner-city Poplar, Brick Lane, Waterloo and Peckham. The handout and training sessions give students initial guidance on how to make contacts with different groups in their area, and how to begin to explore their area's sense of place. One of the hardest and most challenging elements of the project is for students to determine what will form the 'story' of their street—finding the interpretive thread which binds the field experiences and research materials together. We return to this issue below.

As the project has evolved, we have incorporated a substantial element of skills training into the project. These are devoted, first, to the acquisition and appraisal of particular field research skills; and, second, to the development of personal skills required for working collaboratively in small groups, planning a research programme and making presentations to an audience. During the first term, students are introduced to a variety of field research methods. These begin with techniques through which they can open themselves up to the environment and become more aware. We use a variety of gaming exercises to get students outside the lecture theatre, drawing on the literature developed by the urban education and environmental education movements (e.g. Farbstein & Kantrowitz, 1978; Goodey, 1982). As students continue with the course, we discuss and appraise their experiences and consider ways in which such techniques might be incorporated in their *Streetwork* projects. This is followed about three weeks later by an introduction to participant observation techniques. Students are encouraged to visit their project area for a day and to practice some of these skills. They are asked to keep a field diary of the day, recording their observations, experiences, feelings and hunches about the street. Each group makes a short presentation to the class about their field day and the group as a whole then spends time evaluating these experiences. This is followed by a third workshop in which we introduce students to the practice of formal and semi-structured interviews. We focus on how to ask questions, body language, establishing rapport, covering the agenda, recording and interpreting responses. These sessions build on and reinforce experiences already gained in the first year.

The field training sessions are all carried out in first term, equipping students for a more intensive period of field research over the winter months. Students know that they will be required to make a formal presentation of their research to the class in late February. To prepare them for this, we show a Video-Arts programme *Making your Case* (1986) and discuss the skills/tricks-of-the trade needed to make an effective presentation in public. All teachers have problems with students not attending classes, especially when they comprise seminars by their peers. In our experience, we get the highest attendance at these presentations and a tremendous amount of peer group support takes place during and after them. Once students have acquired the skills which give them confidence in their personal and academic capabilities, there really isn't any holding them!

Problems and Issues

Having used the *Streetwork* project for several years in a number of different settings (London, Minneapolis-St Paul and Montreal), we are convinced that it is a valuable exercise which can be successfully adapted to different kinds of urban environment. (Though it does require an urban setting with different kinds of neighbourhood and a reasonably active street culture, the shopping mall may be an alternative 'winter city' location.) Rather than singing the praises of the project, however, we would like to conclude with a discussion of some of the problems and issues that have been raised in the course of teaching the *Streetwork* project over the years.

As with any group project, there is a problem of student assessment. Students work in groups of four or five and there have been occasional instances of the 'free-loader' problem where students feel justifiably resentful of colleagues who are not pulling their weight. Learning to negotiate an equitable division of labour is, of course, a useful skill but one that is hard to build into the assessment of the project. The problem is partially resolved by giving students an individual mark for their reports, although it is not always easy to distinguish which students contributed most to the project if they have pooled their findings. (Students have even used each other's photographs without acknowledgement, raising thorny issues of plagiarism and attribution.)

Students have also had difficulty writing up the project, searching for a theme that will distinguish their project from the others in their group (though this is not a requirement). Some have found it hard to break with the tradition of writing in the third-person and to find an appropriate voice in which to convey their interpretation. Others have relied so heavily on quotation and interview that they have neglected to describe the area adequately, devaluing their own observations and interpretations. Almost all students have experienced difficulty in striking the right balance between offering their own interpretation and acknowledging their sources, including the methodological literature on which they may have drawn. The overriding problem is to convince students that we really do want something *different* in this project—an interpretive essay, written from their own point of view—as opposed to the standard research papers that are required in other courses.

This may be one reason why, despite the commitment and enthusiasm of the teachers, this course remains under-subscribed in relation to some of the larger second-year courses at UCL. More traditional (regionally-based) courses and courses on 'Third World' issues continue to attract the largest student numbers. The numbers taking the course have fluctuated over the years, from 20 to 50, apparently depending on the visibility and success of qualitative teaching in the first year. The variation in numbers has caused few problems, though it would be increasingly difficult to accommodate all the students' presentations of their projects if the class size were much bigger. It is never easy to gauge the reasons for the popularity of different courses but we would suggest a number of possible reasons. The *Streetwork* exercise is perceived to be more time-consuming than standard library-based projects. It is a more risky undertaking than standard course-papers, so students feel less certain of achieving a reasonable grade (although the project only counts for 40% of the final mark). These problems are exacerbated by the fact that the entire course (aside from the project) is perceived to deal with 'difficult' issues—gender and sexuality, social constructions of space and place, intersubjectivity, postmodernism and other relatively sophisticated ideas. Despite our best efforts to convey this jargon-laden material in an accessible way, the perception remains that the course is hard work: which, in the best sense of the term, it certainly is!

One final problem concerns the ethical issues that have arisen in relation to the project. For example, students have often encountered blatant forms of overt racism or more subtle kinds of sexual harassment as they conduct interviews in inner city pubs and clubs. They may never have experienced this before and need careful advice on how to handle such situations. Should they react passively in order to generate data that is relatively untainted by their own liberal interventions? Or should they voice their own opinions and run the risk of alienating their informants? Aside from such stark choices, fieldwork regularly involves a host of smaller judgements which call upon relatively inexperienced students to make difficult ethical decisions. As teachers, we feel it is our job to recognise this and to provide a supportive environment in which students can express their reactions and ideas, learning from us and from each other. We provide a forum for this by encouraging student discussions throughout the course, making a particular point to raise these issues as students present their progress reports towards the end of the course.

Despite these difficulties, we are convinced (not least by the students' comments on their course evaluations) [1] that the *Streetwork* project is a useful exercise from which they learn a tremendous amount. Students say they have enjoyed the opportunity to put theory into practice, to gain exposure to 'real world' situations, to appreciate the depth of other people's experiences and to undertake a piece of creative writing. By working on this project, students come to value their own experience, learn to work effectively in small groups, experiment with different writing styles and forms of visual presentation and gain practical experience of the theoretical issues raised elsewhere in the course. If students forget everything else about the course, their experience of the *Streetwork* project is generally one that lives with them and on which they can continue to draw even after they have left college

Correspondence: Jacquelin Burgess and Peter Jackson, Department of Geography, University College London, 26 Bedford Way, London WC1H 0AP, United Kingdom.

Editor's Note

[1] *A version of the Streetwork project has recently been tried at the University of Reading and generated similarly favourable reactions from students (see the commentaries by Lowe & Sidaway, this symposium).*

References

Cosgrove, D. (1981) Teaching geographical thought through student interviews, *Journal of Geography in Higher Education*, 5, 19–22.

Farbstein, J. & Kantrowitz, M. (1978) *People in Places: experiencing, using and changing the built environment* (New York, Prentice-Hall).

Goodey, B. (1982) Values in place: interpretations and implications from Bedford, in: J. Gold & J. Burgess (Eds) *Valued Environments*, pp. 10–34 (London, Allen & Unwin).

Harrison, P. (1983) *Inside the Inner City* (Harmondsworth, Penguin).

Jacobs, J. (1961) *The Death and Life of Great American Cities*, 1965 edn (Harmondsworth, Penguin).

Video Arts (1986) *Making Your Case* (London, Video Arts Ltd).

Ward, C. & Fyson, A. (1973) *Streetwork: the exploding school* (London, Routledge & Kegan Paul).

8

Hermaphrodities with Attitude: Mapping the Emergence of Intersex Political Activism

CHERYL CHASE

The insistence on two clearly distinguished sexes has calamitous personal consequences for the many individuals who arrive in the world with sexual anatomy that fails to be easily distinguished as male or female. Such individuals are labeled "intersexuals" or "hermaphrodites" by modern medical discourse.[1] About one in a hundred births exhibits some anomaly in sex differentiation,[2] and about one in two thousand is different enough to render problematic the question "Is it a boy or a girl?"[3] Since the early 1960s, nearly every

---

[1]Claude J. Migeon, Gary D. Berkovitz, and Terry R. Brown, "Sexual Differentiation and Ambiguity," in *Wilkins: The Diagnosis and Treatment of Endocrine Disorders in Childhood and Adolescence*, ed. Michael S. Kappy, Robert M. Blizzard, and Claude J. Migeon (Springfield, Ill.: Charles C. Thomas, 1994), 573–715.
[2]Lalitha Raman-Wilms et al., "Fetal Genital Effects of First-Trimester Sex Hormone Exposure: A Meta-Analysis," *Obstetrics and Gynecology* 85 (1995): 141-48.
[3]Anne Fausto-Sterling, *Body Building: How Biologists Construct Sexuality* (New York: Basic Books, forthcoming).

major city in the United States has had a hospital with a standing team of medical experts who intervene in these cases to assign—through drastic surgical means—a male or female status to intersex infants. The fact that this system for preserving the boundaries of the categories male and female has existed for so long without drawing criticism or scrutiny from any quarter indicates the extreme discomfort that sexual ambiguity excites in our culture. Pediatric genital surgeries literalize what might otherwise be considered a theoretical operation: the attempted production of normatively sexed bodies and gendered subjects through constitutive acts of violence. Over the last few years, however, intersex people have begun to politicize intersex identities, thus transforming intensely personal experiences of violation into collective opposition to the medical regulation of bodies that queer the foundations of heteronormative identification and desires.

Hermaphrodites: Medical Authority and Cultural Invisibility

Many people familiar with the ideas that gender is a phenomenon not adequately described by male/female dimorphism and that the interpretation of physical sex differences is culturally constructed remain surprised to learn just how variable sexual anatomy is.[4] Though the male/female binary is constructed as natural and presumed to be immutable, the phenomenon of intersexuality offers clear evidence to the contrary and furnishes an opportunity to deploy "nature" strategically to disrupt heteronormative systems of sex, gender, and sexuality. The concept of bodily sex, in popular usage, refers to multiple components including karyotype (organization of sex chromosomes), gonadal differentiation (e.g., ovarian or testicular), genital morphology, configuration of internal reproductive organs, and pubertal sex characteristics such as breasts and facial hair. Because these characteristics are expected to be concordant in each individual—either all male or all female—an observer, once having attributed male or female sex to a particular individual, assumes the values of other unobserved characteristics.[5]

Because medicine intervenes quickly in intersex births to change the infant's body, the phenomenon of intersexuality is today largely unknown outside specialized medical practices. General public awareness of intersex bodies slowly vanished in modern Western European societies as medicine gradually appropriated to itself the authority to interpret—and eventually manage—the category which had previously been widely known as "hermaphroditism." Victorian medical taxonomy began to efface hermaphroditism as a legitimated status by establishing mixed gonadal histology as a necessary criterion for "true" hermaphroditism. By this criterion, both ovarian and testicular tissue types had to be present. Given the limitations of Victorian surgery and anesthesia, such confirmation was impossible in

---

[4]Judith Butler, *Gender Trouble: Feminism and the Subversion of Identity* (New York: Routledge, 1990); Thomas Laqueur, *Making Sex: Body and Gender from the Greeks to Freud* (Cambridge, Mass.: Harvard University Press, 1990).

[5]Suzanne Kessler and Wendy McKenna, *Gender: An Ethnomethodological Approach* (New York: John Wiley and Sons, 1978).

a living patient. All other anomalies were reclassified as "pseudohermaphroditisms" masking a "true sex" determined by the gonads.[6]

With advances in anesthesia, surgery, embryology, and endocrinology, however, twentieth-century medicine moved from merely labeling intersexed bodies to the far more invasive practice of "fixing" them to conform with a diagnosed true sex. The techniques and protocols for physically transforming intersexed bodies were developed primarily at Johns Hopkins University in Baltimore during the 1920s and 1930s under the guidance of urologist Hugh Hampton Young. "Only during the last few years," Young enthused in the preface to his pioneering textbook, *Genital Abnormalities*, "have we begun to get somewhere near the explanation of the marvels of anatomic abnormality that may be portrayed by these amazing individuals. But the surgery of the hermaphrodite has remained a terra incognita." The "sad state of these unfortunates" prompted Young to devise "a great variety of surgical procedures" by which he attempted to normalize their bodily appearances to the greatest extents possible.[7]

Quite a few of Young's patients resisted his efforts. One, a "snappy' young negro woman with a good figure" and a large clitoris, had married a man but found her passion only with women. She refused "to be made into a man" because removal of her vagina would mean the loss of her "meal ticket," namely, her husband.[8] By the 1950s, the principle of rapid postnatal detection and intervention for intersex infants had been developed at John Hopkins with the stated goal of completing surgery early enough so that the child would have no memory of it.[9] One wonders whether the insistence on early intervention was not at least partly motivated by the resistance offered by adult intersexuals to normalization through surgery. Frightened parents of ambiguously sexed infants were much more open to suggestions of normalizing surgery, while the infants themselves could of course offer no resistance whatever. Most of the theoretical foundations justifying these interventions are attributable to psychologist John Money, a sex researcher invited to Johns Hopkins by Lawson Wilkins, the founder of pediatric endocrinology.[10] Wilkins's numerous students subsequently carried these protocols to hospitals throughout the United States and abroad.[11] Suzanne Kessler notes that today

---

[6]Alice Domurat Dreger, "Doubtful Sex: Cases and Concepts of Hermaphroditism in France and Britain, 1868–1915," (Ph.D. diss., Indiana University, 1995); Alice Domurat Dreger, "Doubtful Sex: The Fate of the Hermaphrodite in Victorian Medicine," *Victorian Studies* (spring 1995): 336–70; Alice Domurat Dreger, "Hermaphrodites in Love: The Truth of the Gonads," *Science and Homosexualities*, ed. Vernon Rosario (New York: Routledge, 1997), 46–66; Alice Domurat Dreger, "Doctors Containing Hermaphrodites: The Victorian Legacy," *Chrysalis: The Journal of Transgressive Gender Identities* (fall 1997): 15–22.

[7]Hugh Hampton Young, *Genital Abnormalities, Hermaphroditism, and Related Adrenal Diseases* (Baltimore: Williams and Wilkins, 1937), xxxix–xl.

[8]Ibid., 139–42.

[9]Howard W. Jones: Jr. and William Wallace Scott, *Hermaphroditism, Genital Anomalies, and Related Endocrine Disorders* (Baltimore: Williams and Wilkins, 1958), 269.

[10]John Money, Joan G. Hampson, and John L. Hampson, "An Examination of Some Basic Sexual Concepts: The Evidence of Human Hermaphroditism," *Bulletin of the Johns Hopkins Hospital* 97 (1955): 301–19; John Money, Joan G. Hampson, and John L. Hampson, "Hermaphroditism: Recommendations Concerning Assignment of Sex, Change of Sex, and Psychologic Management," *Bulletin of Johns Hopkins Hospital* 97 (1955): 284–300; John Money, *Venuses Penuses* (Buffalo: Prometheus, 1986).

[11]Robert M. Blizzard, "Lawson Wilkins," in Kappy et al. *Wilkins*, xi–xiv.

Wilkins and Money's protocols enjoy a "consensus of approval rarely encountered in science."[12]

In keeping with the Johns Hopkins model, the birth of an intersex infant today is deemed a "psychosocial emergency" that propels a multidisciplinary team of intersex specialists into action. Significantly, they are surgeons and endocrinologists rather than psychologists, bioethicists, representatives from intersex peer support organizations, or parents of intersex children. The team examines the infant and chooses either male or female as a "sex of assignment," then informs the parents that this is the child's "true sex." Medical technology, including surgery and hormones, is then used to make the child's body conform as closely as possible to that sex.

The sort of deviation from sex norms exhibited by intersexuals is so highly stigmatized that the likely prospect of emotional harm due to social rejection of the intersexual provides physicians with their most compelling argument to justify medically unnecessary surgical interventions. Intersex status is considered to be so incompatible with emotional health that misrepresentation, concealment of facts, and outright lying (both to parents and later to the intersex person) are unabashedly advocated in professional medical literature.[13] Rather, the systematic hushing up of the fact of intersex births and the use of violent techniques to normalize intersex bodies have caused profound emotional and physical harm to intersexuals and their families. The harm begins when the birth is treated as a medical crisis, and the consequences of that initial treatment ripple out ever afterward. The impact of this treatment is so devastating that until just a few years ago, people whose lives have been touched by intersexuality maintained silence about their ordeal. As recently as 1993, no one publicly disputed surgeon Milton Edgerton when he wrote that in forty years of clitoral surgery on intersexuals, "not one has complained of loss of sensation, *even when the entire clitoris was removed.*"[14]

The tragic irony is that, while intersexual anatomy occasionally indicates an underlying medical problem such as adrenal malfunction, ambiguous genitals are in and of themselves neither painful nor harmful to health. Surgery is essentially a destructive process. It can remove and to a limited extent relocate tissue, but it cannot create new structures. This technical limitation, taken together with the framing of the feminine as a condition of lack, leads physicians to assign 90 percent of anatomically ambiguous infants as female by excising genital tissue. Members of the Johns Hopkins intersex team have justified female assignment by saying, "You can make a hole, but you can't build a pole."[15] Positively heroic

---

[12]Suzanne Kessler. "The Medical Construction of Gender: Case Management of Intersexual Infants," *Signs: Journal of Women in Culture and Society* 16 (1990): 3–26.

[13]J. Dewhurst and D. B. Grant. "Intersex Problems," *Archives of Disease in Childhood* 59 (1984): 1191–94: Anita Natarajan, "Medical Ethics and Truth-Telling in the Case of Androgen Insensitivity Syndrome," *Canadian Medical Association Journal* 154 (1996): 568–70; Tom Mazur, "Ambiguous Genitalia: Detection and Counseling." *Pediatric Nursing* (1983): 417–22; E. M. E. Slijper et al., "Neonates with Abnormal Genital Development Assigned the Female Sex: Parent Counseling," *Journal of Sex Education and Therapy* 20 (1994): 9–17.

[14]Milton T. Edgerton. "Discussion: Clitoroplasty for Clitoromegaly due to Adrenogenital Syndrome without Loss of Sensitivity (by Nobuyuki Sagehashi)," *Plastic and Reconstructive Surgery* 91 (1993): 956.

[15]Melissa Hendricks, "Is It a Boy or a Girl?" *Johns Hopkins Magazine*, November, 1993, 10–16.

efforts shore up a tenuous masculine status for the remaining 10 percent assigned male, who are subjected to multiple operations—twenty-two in one case[16] —with the goal of straightening the penis and constructing a urethra to enable standing urinary posture. For some, the surgeries end only when the child grows old enough to resist.[17]

Children assigned to the female sex are subjected to surgery that removes the troubling hypertrophic clitoris (the same tissue that would have been a troubling micropenis if the child had been assigned male). Through the 1960s, feminizing pediatric genital surgery was openly labeled "clitorectomy" and was compared favorably to the African practices that have been the recent focus of such intense scrutiny. As three Harvard surgeons noted, "Evidence that the clitoris is not essential for normal coitus may be gained from certain sociological data. For instance, it is the custom of a number of African tribes to excise the clitoris and other parts of the external genitals. Yet normal sexual function is observed in these females."[18] A modified operation that removes most of the clitoris and relocates a bit of the tip is variously (and euphemistically) called clitoroplasty, clitoral reduction, or clitoral recession and is described as a "simple cosmetic procedure" to differentiate it from the now infamous clitorectomy. However, the operation is far from benign. Here is a slightly simplified summary (in my own words) of the surgical technique—recommended by Johns Hopkins Surgeons Oesterling, Gearhart, and Jeffs—that is representative of the operation:

> *They make an incision around the phallus, at the corona, then dissect the skin away from its underside. Next they dissect the skin away from the dorsal side and remove as much of the corpora, or erectile bodies, as necessary to create an "appropriate size clitoris." Next, stitches are placed from the pubic area along both sides of the entire length of what remains of the phallus; when these stitches are tightened, it folds up like pleats in a skirt, and recesses into a concealed position behind the mons pubis. If the result is still "too large," the glans is further reduced by cutting away a pie-shaped wedge.* [19]

For most intersexuals, this sort of arcane, dehumanized medical description, illustrated with close-ups of genital surgery and naked children with blacked-out eyes, is the only available version of *Our Bodies, Ourselves*. We as a culture have relinquished to medicine the authority to police the boundaries of male and female, leaving intersexuals to recover as best they can, alone and silent, from violent normalization.

---

[16]John E Stecker et al., "Hypospadias Cripples," *Urologic Clinics of North America: Symposium on Hypospadias* 8 (1981): 539–44.

[17]Jeff McClintock, "Growing Up in the Surgical Maelstrom," *Chrysalis: The Journal of Transgressive Gender Identities* (fall 1997): 53–54.

[18]Robert E. Gross. Judson Randolph, and John F. Crigler, "Clitorectomy for Sexual Abnormalities: Indications and Technique," *Surgery* 59 (1966): 300–308.

[19]Joseph E. Oesterling, John P. Gearhart, and Robert D. Jeffs, "A Unified Approach to Early Reconstructive Surgery of the Child with Ambiguous Genitalia," *Journal of Urology* 138 (1987): 1079–84.

My Career as a Hermaphrodite: Renegotiating Cultural Meanings

I was born with ambiguous genitals. A doctor specializing in intersexuality deliberated for three days—sedating my mother each time she asked what was wrong with her baby—before concluding that I was male, with a micropenis, complete hypospadias, undescended testes, and a strange extra opening behind the urethra. A male birth certificate was completed for me, and my parents began raising me as a boy. When I was a year and a half old my parents consulted a different set of experts, who admitted me to a hospital for "sex determination." "Determine" is a remarkably apt word in this context, meaning both "to ascertain by investigation" and "to cause to come to a resolution." It perfectly describes the two-stage process whereby science produces through a series of masked operations what it claims merely to observe. Doctors told my parents that a thorough medical investigation would be necessary to determine (in the first sense of that word) what my "true sex" was. They judged my genital appendage to be inadequate as a penis, too short to mark masculine status effectively or to penetrate females. As a female, however, I would be penetrable and potentially fertile. My anatomy having been relabeled as vagina, urethra, labia, and outsized clitoris, my sex was determined (in the second sense) by amputating my genital appendage. Following doctors' orders, my parents then changed my name, combed their house to eliminate all traces of my existence as a boy (photographs, birthday cards, etc.), changed my birth certificate, moved to a different town, instructed extended family members no longer to refer to me as a boy, and never told anyone else—including me—just what had happened. My intersexuality and change of sex were the family's dirty little secrets.

At age eight, I was returned to the hospital for abdominal surgery that trimmed away the testicular portion of my gonads, each of which was partly ovarian and partly testicular in character. No explanation was given to me then for the long hospital stay or the abdominal surgery, nor for the regular hospital visits afterward, in which doctors photographed my genitals and inserted fingers and instruments into my vagina and anus. These visits ceased as soon as I began to menstruate. At the time of the sex change, doctors had assured my parents that their once son/now daughter would grow into a woman who could have a normal sex life and babies. With the confirmation of menstruation, my parents apparently concluded that that prediction had been borne out and their ordeal was behind them. For me, the worst part of the nightmare was just beginning.

As an adolescent, I became aware that I had no clitoris or inner labia and was unable to orgasm. By the end of my teens, I began to do research in medical libraries, trying to discover what might have happened to me. When I finally determined to obtain my medical records, it took me three years to overcome the obstruction of the doctors whom I asked for help. When I did obtain them, a scant three pages, I first learned that I was a "true hermaphrodite" who had been my parents' son for a year and a half and who bore a name unfamiliar to me. The records also documented my clitorectomy. This was the middle 1970s, when I was in my early twenties. I had come to identify myself as lesbian, at a time when lesbianism and a biologically based gender essentialism were virtually synonymous: men were rapists who caused war and environmental destruction; women were good and would heal the earth; lesbians were a superior form of being uncontaminated by "men's energy." In such a world, how could I tell anyone that I had actually possessed the dreaded "phallus"? I was no longer a woman in my own eyes but rather a monstrous and mythical creature. Because my hermaphroditism and long-buried boyhood were the history behind the clitorectomy, I could never speak openly about that or my consequent inability to orgasm. I was so traumatized by discovering the circumstances that produced my embodiment that I could not speak of these matters with anyone.

Nearly fifteen years later, I suffered an emotional meltdown. In the eyes of the world, I was a highly successful businesswoman, a principal in an international high tech company. To myself, I was a freak, incapable of loving or being loved, filled with shame about my status as a hermaphrodite and about my sexual dysfunction. Unable to make peace with myself, I finally sought help from a psychotherapist, who reacted to each revelation about my history and predicament with some version of "no, it's not" or "so what?" I would say, "I'm not really a woman," and she would say, "Of course you are. You look female." I would say, "My complete withdrawal from sexuality has destroyed every relationship I've ever entered." She would say, "Everybody has their ups and downs," I tried another therapist and met with a similar response. Increasingly desperate, I confided my story to several friends, who shrank away in embarrassed silence. I was in emotional agony, feeling utterly alone, seeing no possible way out. I decided to kill myself.

Confronting suicide as a real possibility proved to be my personal epiphany. I fantasized killing myself quite messily and dramatically in the office of the surgeon who had cut off my clitoris, forcibly confronting him with the horror he had imposed on my life. But in acknowledging the desire to put my pain to some use, not to utterly waste my life, I turned a crucial corner, finding a way to direct my rage productively out into the world rather than destructively at myself. I had no conceptual framework for developing a more positive self-consciousness. I knew only that I felt mutilated, not fully human, but that I was determined to heal. I struggled for weeks in emotional chaos, unable to eat or sleep or work. I could not accept my image of a hermaphroditic body any more than I could accept the butchered one the surgeons left me with. Thoughts of myself as a Frankenstein's monster patchwork alternated with longings for escape by death, only to be followed by outrage, anger, and a determination to survive. I could not accept that it was just or right or good to treat any person as I had been treated—my sex changed, my genitals cut up, my experience silenced and rendered invisible. I bore a private hell within me, wretchedly alone in my condition without even my tormentors for company. Finally, I began to envision myself standing in a driving storm but with clear skies and a rainbow visible in the distance. I was still in agony, but I was beginning to see the painful process in which I was caught up in terms of revitalization and re-birth, a means of investing my life with a new sense of authenticity that possessed vast potentials for further transformation. Since then, I have seen this experience of movement through pain to personal empowerment described by other intersex and transsexual activists.[20]

---

[20]Kira Triea, "The Awakening," *Hermaphrodites with Attitude* (winter 1994): 1; Susan Stryker, "My Words to Victor Frankenstein above the Village of Chamounix: Performing Transgender Rage," *GLQ* I (1994): 237–54.

I slowly developed a newly politicized and critically aware form of self-understanding. I had been the kind of lesbian who at times had a girlfriend but who had never really participated in the life of a lesbian community. I felt almost completely isolated from gay politics, feminism, and queer and gender theory. I did possess the rudimentary knowledge that the gay rights movement had gathered momentum only when it could effectively deny that homosexuality was sick or inferior and assert to the contrary that "gay is good." As impossible as it then seemed, I pledged similarly to affirm that "intersex is good," that the body I was born with was not diseased, only different. I vowed to embrace the sense of being "not a woman" that I initially had been so terrified to discover.

I began searching for community and consequently moved to San Francisco in the fall of 1992, based entirely on my vague notion that people living in the "queer mecca" would have the most conceptually sophisticated, socially tolerant, and politically astute analysis of sexed and gendered embodiment. I found what I was looking for in part because my arrival in the Bay Area corresponded with the rather sudden emergence of an energetic transgender political movement. Transgender Nation (TN) had developed out of Queer Nation, a post-gay/lesbian group that sought to transcend identity politics. TN's actions garnered media attention—especially when members were arrested during a "zap" of the American Psychiatric Association's annual convention when they protested the psychiatric labeling of transsexuality as mental illness. Transsexual performance artist Kate Bornstein was introducing transgender issues in an entertaining way to the San Francisco gay/lesbian community and beyond. Female-to-male issues had achieved a new level of visibility due in large part to efforts made by Lou Sullivan, a gay FTM activist who had died an untimely death from HIV-related illnesses in 1991. And in the wake of her underground best-selling novel, *Stone Butch Blues*, Leslie Feinberg's manifesto *Transgender Liberation: A Movement Whose Time Has Come* was finding a substantial audience, linking transgender social justice to a broader progressive political agenda for the first time.[21] At the same time, a vigorous new wave of gender scholarship had emerged in the academy.[22] In this context; intersex activist and theoretician Morgan Holmes could analyze her own clitorectomy for her master's thesis and have it taken seriously as academic work.[23] Openly transsexual scholars, including Susan Stryker and Sandy Stone, were visible in responsible academic positions at major universities. Stone's "*Empire* Strikes Back: A Posttranssexual Manifesto" refigured open, visible transsexuals not as gender conformists propping up a system of rigid, binary sex but as "a set of embodied texts whose potential for productive disruption of structured sexualities and spectra of desire has yet to be explored."[24]

[21]Leslie Feinberg, *Stone Butch Blues* (Ithaca, N.Y.: Firebrand, 1993); Leslie Feinberg, *Transgender Liberation: A Movement Whose Time Has Come* (New York: World View Forum, 1992).
[22]See, for example, Judith Butler, *Bodies That Matter: On the Discursive Limits of "Sex"* (New York: Routledge, 1993); Butler, *Gender Trouble*; Laqueur, *Making Sex;* and Julia Epstein and Kristina Straub, eds., *Body Guards: The Cultural Politics of Gender Ambiguity* (New York: Routledge, 1991).
[23]Morgan Holmes, "Medical Politics and Cultural Imperatives: Intersexuality Beyond Pathology and Erasure" (master's thesis, York University, Toronto, 1994).
[24]Sandy Stone, "The *Empire* Strikes Back: A Posttranssexual Manifesto," in Epstein and Straub, *Body Guards*, 280-304, quotation on 296.

Into this heady atmosphere, I brought my own experience. Introduced by Bornstein to other gender activists, I explored with them the cultural politics of intersexuality, which to me represented yet another new configuration of bodies, identities, desires, and sexualities from which to confront the violently normativizing aspects of the dominant sex/gender system. In the fall of 1993, TN pioneer Anne Ogborn invited me to participate in a weekend retreat called the New Woman Conference, where postoperative transsexual women shared their stories, their griefs and joys, and enjoyed the freedom to swim or sunbathe in the nude with others who had surgically changed genitals. I saw that participants returned home in a state of euphoria, and I determined to bring that same sort of healing experience to intersex people.

Birth of an Intersex Movement: Opposition and Allies

Upon moving to San Francisco, I started telling my story indiscriminately to everyone I met. Over the course of a year, simply by speaking openly within my own social circles, I learned of six other intersexuals—including two who had been fortunate enough to escape medical attention. I realized that intersexuality, rather than being extremely rare, must be relatively common. I decided to create a support network. In the summer of 1993, I produced some pamphlets, obtained a post office box, and began to publicize the Intersex Society of North America (ISNA) through small notices in the media. Before long, I was receiving several letters per week from intersexuals throughout the United States and Canada and occasionally some from Europe. While the details varied, the letters gave a remarkably coherent picture of the emotional consequences of medical intervention. Morgan Holmes: "All the things my body might have grown to do, all the possibilities, went down the hall with my amputated clitoris to the pathology department. The rest of me went to the recovery room—I'm still recovering." Angela Moreno: "I am horrified by what has been done to me and by the conspiracy of silence and lies. I am filled with grief and rage, but also relief finally to believe that maybe I am not the only one." Thomas: "I pray that I will have the means to repay, in some measure, the American Urological Association for all that it has done for my benefit. I am having some trouble, though, in connecting the timing mechanism to the fuse."

ISNA's most immediate goal has been to create community of intersex people who could provide peer support to deal with shame, stigma, grief, and rage as well as with practical issues such as how to obtain old medical records or locate a sympathetic psychotherapist or endocrinologist. To that end, I cooperated with journalists whom I judged capable of reporting widely and responsibly on our efforts, listed ISNA with self-help and referral clearinghouses, and established a presence on the Internet (http://www.isna.org). ISNA now connects hundreds of intersexuals across North America, Europe, Australia, and New Zealand. It has also begun sponsoring an annual intersex retreat, the first of which took place in 1996 and which moved participants every bit as profoundly as the New Woman Conference had moved me in 1993.

ISNA's longer-term and more fundamental goal, however, is to change the way intersex infants are treated. We advocate that surgery not be performed on ambiguous genitals unless there is medical reason (such as blocked or painful urination), and that parents be given the conceptual tools and emotional support to accept their children's physical differences. While it is fascinating to think about the potential development of new genders or subject positions grounded in forms of embodiment that fall outside the familiar male/female dichotomy, we recognize that the two-sex/gender model is currently hegemonic and therefore advocate that children be raised either as boys or girls, according to which designation seems most likely to offer the child the greatest future sense of comfort. Advocating gender assignment without resorting to normalizing surgery is a radical position given that it requires the willful disruption of the assumed concordance between body shape and gender category. However, this is the only position that prevents irreversible physical damage to the intersex person's body, that respects the intersex person's agency regarding his/her own flesh, and that recognizes genital sensation and erotic functioning to be at least as important as reproductive capacity. If an intersex child or adult decides to change gender or to undergo surgical or hormonal alteration of his/her body, that decision should also be fully respected and facilitated. The key point is that intersex subjects should not be violated for the comfort and convenience of others.

One part of reaching ISNA's long-term goal has been to document the emotional and physical carnage resulting from medical interventions. As a rapidly growing literature makes abundantly clear (see the bibliography on our website, http://www.isna.org/bigbib.html), the medical management of intersexuality has changed little in the forty years since my first surgery. Kessler expresses surprise that "in spite of the thousands of genital operations performed every year, there are no meta-analyses from within the medical community on levels of success."[25] They do not know whether postsurgical intersexuals are "silent and happy or silent and unhappy."[26] There is no research effort to improve erotic functioning for adult intersexuals whose genitals have been altered, nor are there psychotherapists specializing in working with adult intersex clients trying to heal from the trauma of medical intervention. To provide a counterpoint to the mountains of medical literature that neglect intersex experience and to begin compiling an ethnographic account of that experience, *ISNA's Hermaphrodites with Attitude* newsletter has developed into a forum for intersexuals to tell their own stories. We have sent complimentary copies of the newsletter filled with searing personal narratives to academics, writers, journalists, minority rights organizations, and medical practitioners—to anybody we thought might make a difference in our campaign to change the way intersex bodies are managed.

ISNA's presence has begun to generate effects. It has helped politicize the growing number of intersex organizations, as well as intersex identities themselves. When I first began organizing ISNA, I met leaders of the Turner's Syndrome Society, the oldest known support group focusing on atypical sexual differentiation, founded in 1987. Turner's Syndrome is defined by an XO genetic

---

[25]Suzanne Kessler, *Lessons from the Intersexed* (New Brunswick, N.J.: Rutgers University Press, forthcoming).

[26]Robert Jeffs, quoted in Ellen Barry, "United States of Ambiguity," Boston *Phoenix*, 22 November 1996, 6–8, quotation on 6.

karyotype that results in a female body morphology with nonfunctioning ovaries, extremely short stature, and a variety of other physical differences described in the medical literature with such stigmatizing labels as "web-necked" and "fish-mouthed." Each of these women told me what a profound, life-changing experience it had been simply to meet another person like herself. I was inspired by their accomplishments (they are a national organization serving thousands of members), but I wanted ISNA to have a different focus. I was less willing to think of intersexuality as a pathology or disability, more interested in challenging its medicalization entirely, and more interested still in politicizing a pan-intersexual identity across the divisions of particular etiologies in order to destabilize more effectively the heteronormative assumptions underlying the violence directed at our bodies.

When I established ISNA in 1993, no such politicized groups existed. In the United Kingdom in 1988, the mother of a girl with androgen-insensitivity syndrome (AIS, which produces genetic males with female genital morphologies) formed the AIS Support Group. The group, which initially lobbied for increased medical attention (better surgical techniques for producing greater vaginal depth, more research into the osteoporosis that often attends AIS), now has chapters in five countries. Another group, K. S. and Associates, was formed in 1989 by the mother of a boy with Klinefelter's Syndrome and today serves over one thousand families. Klinefelter's is characterized by the presence of one or more additional X chromosomes, which produce bodies with fairly masculine external genitals. Above-average height, and somewhat gangly limbs. At puberty, people with K. S. often experience pelvic broadening and the development of breasts. K. S. and Associates continues to be dominated by parents, is highly medical in orientation, and has resisted attempts by adult Klinefelter's Syndrome men to discuss gender identity or sexual orientation issues related to their intersex condition.

Since ISNA has been on the scene, other groups with a more resistant stance vis-à-vis the medical establishment have begun to appear. In 1995, a mother who refused medical pressure for female assignment for her intersex child formed the Ambiguous Genitalia Support Network, which introduces parents of intersexuals to each other and encourages the development of pen-pal support relationships. In 1996, another mother who had rejected medical pressure to assign her intersex infant as a female by removing his penis formed the Hermaphrodite Education and Listening Post (HELP) to provide peer support and medical information. Neither of these parent-oriented groups, however, frames its work in overtly political terms. Still, political analysis and action of the sort advocated by ISNA has not been without effect on the more narrowly defined service-oriented or parent-dominated groups. The AIS Support Group, now more representative of both adults and parents, noted in a recent newsletter,

> *Our first impression of ISNA was that they were perhaps a bit too angry and militant to gain the support of the medical profession. However, we have to say that, having read [political analyses of intersexuality by ISNA, Kessler, Fausto-Sterling, and Holmes], we feel that the feminist concepts relating to the patriarchal treatment of*

intersexuality are extremely interesting and do make a lot of sense. After all, the lives of intersexed people are stigmatized by the cultural disapproval of their genital appearance, [which need not] affect their experience as sexual human beings.[27]

Other more militant groups have now begun to pop up. In 1994, German intersexuals formed both the Workgroup on Violence in Pediatrics and Gynecology and the Genital Mutilation Survivors' Support Network, and Hijra Nippon now represents activist intersexuals in Japan.

Outside the rather small community of intersex organizations, ISNA's work has generated a complex patchwork of alliances and oppositions. Queer activists, especially transgender activists, have provided encouragement, advice, and logistical support to the intersex movement. The direct action group Transsexual Menace helped an ad hoc group of militant intersexuals calling themselves Hermaphrodites with Attitude plan and carry out a picket of the 1996 annual meeting of the American Academy of Pediatrics in Boston—the first recorded instance of intersex public protest in modern history.[28] ISNA was also invited to join GenderPAC, a recently formed national consortium of transgender organizations that lobbies against discrimination based on atypical expressions of gender or embodiment. More mainstream gay and lesbian political organizations such as the National Gay and Lesbian Task Force have also been willing to include intersex concerns as part of their political agendas. Transgender and lesbian/gay groups have been supportive of intersex political activism largely because they see similarities in the medicalization of these various identities as a form of social control and (especially for transsexuals) empathize with our struggle to assert agency within a medical discourse that works to efface the ability to exercise informed consent about what happens to one's own body.

Gay/lesbian caucuses and special interest groups within professional medical associations have been especially receptive to ISNA's agenda. One physician on the Internet discussion group glb-medical wrote:

The effect of Cheryl Chase's postings—admittedly, after the shock wore off—was to make me realize that THOSE WHO HAVE BEEN TREATED might very well think [they had not been well served by medical intervention]. This matters a lot. As a gay man, and simply as a person, I have struggled for much of my adult life to find my own natural self, to disentangle the confusions caused by others' presumptions about how I am/should be. But, thankfully, their decisions were not surgically imposed on me!

Queer psychiatrists, starting with Bill Byne at New York's Mount Sinai Hospital, have been quick to support ISNA, in part because the psychological principles underlying the current intersex treatment protocols are manifestly unsound. They seem almost willfully designed to exacerbate rather than ameliorate already difficult emotional issues arising from sexual difference. Some of these psychiatrists

[27]AIS Support Group, "Letter to America," *ALIAS* (spring 1996): 3–4.
[28]Barry, "United States of Ambiguity," 7.

see the surgical and endocrinological domination of a problem that even surgeons and endocrinologists acknowledge to be psychosocial rather than biomedical as an unjustified invasion of their area of professional competence.

ISNA has deliberately cultivated a network of nonintersexed advocates who command a measure of social legitimacy and can speak in contexts where uninterpreted intersex voices will not be heard. Because there is a strong impulse to discount what intersexuals have to say about intersexuality, sympathetic representation has been welcome—especially in helping intersexuals reframe intersexuality in nonmedical terms. Some gender theory scholars, feminist critics of science, medical historians, and anthropologists have been quick to understand and support intersex activism. Years before ISNA came into existence, feminist biologist and science studies scholar Anne Fausto-Sterling had written about intersexuality in relation to intellectually suspect scientific practices that perpetuate masculinist constructs of gender, and she became an early ISNA ally.[29] Likewise, social psychologist Suzanne Kessler had written a brilliant ethnography of surgeons who specialize in treating intersexuals. After speaking with several "products" of their practice, she, too, became a strong supporter of intersex activism.[30] Historian of science Alice Dreger, whose work focuses not only on hermaphroditism but on other forms of potentially benign atypical embodiment that become subject to destructively normalizing medical interventions (conjoined twins. for example), has been especially supportive. Fausto-Sterling, Kessler, and Dreger will each shortly publish works that analyze the medical treatment of intersexuality as being culturally motivated and criticize it as harmful to its ostensible patients.[31]

Allies who help contest the medicalization of intersexuality are especially important because ISNA has found it almost entirely fruitless to attempt direct, nonconfrontational interactions with the medical specialists who themselves determine policy on the treatment of intersex infants and who actually carry out the surgeries. Joycelyn Elders, the Clinton administration's first surgeon general, is a pediatric endocrinologist with many years of experience managing intersex infants but, in spite of a generally feminist approach to health care and frequent overtures from ISNA, she has been dismissive of the concerns of intersexuals themselves.[32] Another pediatrician remarked in an Internet discussion on intersexuality: "I think this whole issue is preposterous. . . . To suggest that [medical decisions about the treatment of intersex conditions] are somehow cruel or arbitrary is insulting, ignorant and misguided. . . . To spread the claims that [ISNA] is making is just plain wrong, and I hope that this

---

[29]Anne Fausto-Sterling, "The Five Sexes: Why Male and Female Are Not Enough," *The Sciences* 33, no. 2 (March/April 1993): 20–25; Anne Fausto-Sterling, *Myths of Gender: Biological Theories about Women and Men,* 2d ed. (New York: Basic Books, 1985), 134–41.

[30]Kessler, "The Medical Construction of Gender"; Suzanne Kessler, "Meanings of Genital Variability," *Chrysalis: The Journal of Transgressive Gender Identities* (fall 1997): 33–38.

[31]Anne Fausto-Sterling, *Building Bodies: Biology and the Social Construction of Sexuality* (New York: Basic Books, forthcoming); Kessler, "Meanings of Genital Variability"; Alice Domurat Dreger, *Hermaphrodites and the Medical Invention of Sex* (Cambridge, Mass.: Harvard University Press, forthcoming).

[32]"Dr. Elders' Medical History," *New Yorker,* 26 September 1994: 45–46; Joycelyn Elders and David Chanoff, *From Sharecropper's Daughter to Surgeon General of the United States of America* (New York: William Morrow, 1996).

[on-line group of doctors and scientists] will not blindly accept them." Yet another participant in that same chat asked what was for him obviously a rhetorical question: "Who is the enemy? I really don't think it's the medical establishment. Since when did we establish the male/female hegemony?" While a surgeon quoted in a *New York Times* article on ISNA summarily dismissed us as "zealots,"[33] there is considerable anecdotal information supplied by ISNA sympathizers that professional meetings in the fields of pediatrics, urology, genital plastic surgery, and endocrinology are buzzing with anxious and defensive discussions of intersex activism. In response to the Hermaphrodites with Attitude protests at the American Academy of Pediatrics meeting, that organization felt compelled to issue the following statement to the press: "The Academy is deeply concerned about the emotional, cognitive, and body image development of intersexuals, and believes that successful early genital surgery minimizes these issues." Further protests were planned for 1997.

The roots of resistance to the truth claims of intersexuals run deep in the medical establishment. Not only does ISNA critique the normativist biases couched within most scientific practice, it advocates a treatment protocol for intersex infants that disrupts conventional understandings of the relationship between bodies and genders. But on a level more personally threatening to medical practitioners, ISNA's position implies that they have—unwittingly at best, through willful denial at worst—spent their careers inflicting a profound harm from which their patients will never fully recover. ISNA's position threatens to destroy the assumptions motivating an entire medical subspecialty, thus jeopardizing the ability to perform what many surgeons find to be technically difficult and fascinating work. Melissa Hendricks notes that Dr. Gearhart is known to colleagues as a surgical "artist" who can "carve a large phallus down into a clitoris" with consummate skill.[34] More than one ISNA member has discovered that surgeons actually operated on their genitals at no charge. The medical establishment's fascination with its own power to change sex and its drive to rescue parents from their intersex children are so strong that heroic interventions are delivered without regard to the capitalist model that ordinarily governs medical services.

Given such deep and mutually reinforcing reasons for opposing ISNA's position, it is hardly surprising that medical intersex specialists have, for the most part, turned a deaf ear toward us. The lone exception as of April 1997 is urologist Justine Schober. After watching a videotape of the 1996 ISNA retreat and receiving other input from HELP and the AIS Support Group, she suggests in a new textbook on pediatric surgery that while technology has advanced to the point that "our needs [as surgeons] and the needs of parents to have a presentable child can be satisfied," it is time to acknowledge that problems exist that "we as surgeons . . . cannot address. Success in psychosocial adjustment is the true goal of sexual assignment and genitoplasty. . . . Surgery makes parents and doctors comfortable, but counseling makes people comfortable too, and is not irreversible.[35]

---

[33]Natalie Angier, "Intersexual Healing: An Anomaly Finds a Group," *New York Times*, 4 February 1996, E14.

[34]Hendricks, "Is It a Boy or a Girl?" 10.

[35]Justine M. Schober, "Long Term Outcomes of Feminizing Genitoplasty for Intersex," in *Pediatric Surgery and Urology: Long Term Outcomes*, ed. Pierre Mouriquant (Philadelphia: W. B. Saunders, forthcoming)

While ISNA will continue to approach the medical establishment for dialogue (and continue supporting protests outside the closed doors when doctors refuse to talk), perhaps the most important aspect of our current activities is the struggle to change public perceptions. By using the mass media, the Internet, and our growing network of allies and sympathizers to make the general public aware of the frequency of intersexuality and of the intense suffering that medical treatment has caused, we seek to create an environment in which many parents of intersex children will have already heard about the intersex movement when their child is born. Such informed parents we hope will be better able to resist medical pressure for unnecessary genital surgery and secrecy and to find their way to a peer-support group and counseling rather than to a surgical theater.

9

Homage to My Hair

LUCILLE CLIFTON

When i feel her jump up and dance
i hear the music! my God
i'm talking about my nappy hair!
she is a challenge to your hand
black man,
she is as tasty on your tongue as good greens
black man,
she can touch your mind
with her electric fingers and
the grayer she do get, good God,
the blacker she do be!

10

Homage to My Hips

LUCILLE CLIFTON

These hips are big hips
they need space to
move around in.
they don't fit into little
petty places, these hips
are free hips.
they don't like to be held back.
these hips have never been enslaved,
they go where they want to go
they do what they want to do.
these hips are mighty hips.
these hips are magic hips.
i have known them
to put a spell on a man and
spin him like a top!

11

Marginalia

BILLY COLLINS

Sometimes the notes are ferocious,
skirmishes against the author
raging along the borders of every page
in tiny black script.
If I could just get my hands on you,
Kierkegaard, or Conor Cruise O'Brien,
they seem to say,
I would bolt the door and beat some logic into your head.

Other comments are more offhand, dismissive -
"Nonsense." "Please!" "HA!!" -
that kind of thing.
I remember once looking up from my reading,
my thumb as a bookmark,
trying to imagine what the person must look like
why wrote "Don't be a ninny"
alongside a paragraph in The Life of Emily Dickinson.

Students are more modest
needing to leave only their splayed footprints
along the shore of the page.

One scrawls "Metaphor" next to a stanza of Eliot's.
Another notes the presence of "Irony"
fifty times outside the paragraphs of A Modest Proposal.

Or they are fans who cheer from the empty bleachers,
Hands cupped around their mouths.
"Absolutely," they shout
to Duns Scotus and James Baldwin.
"Yes." "Bull's-eye." My man!"
Check marks, asterisks, and exclamation points
rain down along the sidelines.

And if you have managed to graduate from college
without ever having written "Man vs. Nature"
in a margin, perhaps now
is the time to take one step forward.

We have all seized the white perimeter as our own
and reached for a pen if only to show
we did not just laze in an armchair turning pages;
we pressed a thought into the wayside,
planted an impression along the verge.

Even Irish monks in their cold scriptoria
jotted along the borders of the Gospels
brief asides about the pains of copying,
a bird signing near their window,
or the sunlight that illuminated their page-
anonymous men catching a ride into the future
on a vessel more lasting than themselves.

And you have not read Joshua Reynolds,
they say, until you have read him
enwreathed with Blake's furious scribbling.

Yet the one I think of most often,
the one that dangles from me like a locket,
was written in the copy of Catcher in the Rye
I borrowed from the local library
one slow, hot summer.
I was just beginning high school then,
reading books on a davenport in my parents' living room,
and I cannot tell you
how vastly my loneliness was deepened,
how poignant and amplified the world before me seemed,
when I found on one page

A few greasy looking smears
and next to them, written in soft pencil—
by a beautiful girl, I could tell,
whom I would never meet—
"Pardon the egg salad stains, but I'm in love."

12

The Zoot-Suit and Style Warfare

BY STUART COSGROVE

Introduction: The Silent Noise of Sinister Clowns

> What about those fellows waiting still and silent there on the platform,
> so still and silent they clash with the crowd in their very immobility,
> standing noisy in their very silence; harsh as a cry of terror in their
> quietness? What about these three boys, coming now along the plat-
> form, tall and slender, walking with swinging shoulders in their well-
> pressed, too-hot-for-summer suits, their collars high and tight about
> their necks, their identical hats of black cheap felt set upon the crowns
> of their heads with a severe formality above their conked hair? It was
> as though I'd never seen their like before: walking slowly, their shoul-
> ders swaying, their legs swinging from their hips in trousers that bal-
> looned upward from cuffs fitting snug about their ankles; their coats
> long and hip-tight with shoulders far too broad to be those of natural
> western men. These fellows whose bodies seemed - what had one of my
> teachers said of me? - 'You're like one of those African sculptures, dis-
> torted in the interest of design.' Well, what design and whose?[1]

The zoot-suit is more than an exaggerated costume, more than a sartorial statement, it is the bearer of a complex and contradictory history. When the nameless

From History Workshop Journal. Vol. 18 (Autumn 1984) pp. 77-91.
by permission of Oxford University Press

narrator of Ellison's Invisible Man confronted the subversive sight of three young and extravagantly dressed blacks, his reaction was one of fascination not of fear. These youths were not simply grotesque dandies parading the city's secret underworld, they were "the stewards of something uncomfortable"[2], a spectacular reminder that the social order had failed to contain their energy and difference. The zoot-suit was more than the drape-shape of 1940s fashion, more than a colourful stage-prop hanging from the shoulders of Cab Calloway, it was, in the most direct and obvious ways, an emblem of ethnicity and a way of negotiating an identiy. The zoot-suit was a refusal: a subcultural gesture that refused to concede to the manners of subservience. By the late 1930s, the term "zoot" was in common circulation within urban jazz culture. Zoot meant something worn or performed in an extravagant style, and since many young blacks wore suits with outrageously padded shoulders and trousers that were fiercely tapered at the ankles, the term zoot-suit passed into everyday usage. In the sub-cultural world of Harlem's nightlife, the language of rhyming slang succinctly described the zoot-suit's unmistakable style: 'a killer-diller coat with a drapeshape, real-pleats and shoulders padded like a lunatic's cell'. The study of the relationship between fashion and social action is notoriously underdeveloped, but there is every indication that the zoot-suit riots that erupted in the United States in the summer of 1943 had a profound effect on a whole generation of socially disadvantaged youths. It was during his period as a young zoot-suiter that the Chicano union activist Cesar Chavez first came into contact with community politics, and it was through the experiences of participating in zoot-suit riots in Harlem that the young pimp 'Detroit Red' began a political education that transformed him into the Black radical leader Malcolm X. Although the zoot-suit occupies an almost mythical place within the history of jazz music, its social and political importance has been virtually ignored. There can be no certainty about when, where or why the zoot-suit came into existence, but what is certain is that during the summer months of 1943 "the killer-diller coat" was the uniform of young rioters and the symbol of a moral panic about juvenile delinquency that was to intensify in the post-war period.

At the height of the Los Angeles riots of June 1943, the New York Times carried a front page article which claimed without reservation that the first zoot-suit had been purchased by a black bus worker, Clyde Duncan, from a tailor's shop in Gainesville, Georgia.[3] Allegedly, Duncan had been inspired by the film "Gone with the Wind" and had set out to look like Rhett Butler. This explanation clearly found favour throughout the USA. The national press forwarded countless others. Some reports claimed that the zoot-suit was an invention of Harlem nigh' life, others suggested it grew out of jazz culture and the exhibitionist stage costumes of the band leaders, and some argued that the zoot-suit was derived from military uniforms and imported from Britain. The alternative and independent press, particularly Crisis and Negro Quarterly, more convincingly argued that the zoot-suit was the product of a particular social context.[4] They emphasized the importance of Mexican-American youths, or pachucos, in the emergence of zoot-suit style and, in tentative ways, tried to relate their appearance on the streets to the concept of pachuquismo.

In his pioneering book, *The Labyrinth of Solitude,* the Mexican poet and social commentator Octavio Paz throws imaginative light on pachuco style and indirectly establishes a framework within which the zoot-suit can be understood. Paz's study of the Mexican national consciousness examines the changes brought about by the movement of labour, particularly the generations of Mexicans who migrated northwards to the USA. This movement, and the new economic and social patterns it implies, has, according to Paz, forced young Mexican-Americans into an ambivalent experience between two cultures.

> *What distinguishes them, I think, is their furtive, restless air: they act like persons who are wearing disguises, who are afraid of a stranger's look because it could strip them and leave them stark naked.... This spiritual condition or lack of a spirit, has given birth to a type known as the pachuco. The pachucos are youths, for the most part of Mexican origin, who form gangs in southern cities; they can be identified by their language and behaviour as well as by the clothing they affect. They are instinctive rebels, and North American racism has vented its wrath on them more than once. But the pachucos do not attempt to vindicate their race or the nationality of their forebears. Their attitude reveals an obstinate, almost fanatical will-to-be, but this will affirms nothing specific except their determination . . . not to be like those around them.*[5]

Pachuco youth embodied all the characteristics of second generation working-class immigrants. In the most obvious ways they had been stripped of their customs, beliefs and language. The pachucos were a disinherited generation within a disadvantaged sector of North American society; and predictably their experiences in education, welfare and employment alienated them from the aspirations of their parents and the dominant assumptions of the society in which they lived. The pachuco subculture was defined not only by ostentatious fashion, but by petty crime, delinquency and drug-taking. Rather than disguise their alienation or efface their hostility to the dominant society, the pachucos adopted an arrogant posture. They flaunted their difference, and the zoot-suit became the means by which that difference was announced. Those "impassive and sinister clowns" whose purpose was 'to cause terror instead of laughter,'[6] invited the kind of attention that led to both prestige and persecution. For Octavio Paz the pachuco's appropriation of the zoot-suit was an admission of the ambivalent place he occupied. It is the only way he can establish a more vital relationship with the society he is antagonizing. As a victim he can occupy a place in the world that previously ignored him; as a delinquent, he can become one of its wicked heroes.'[7] The Zoot-Suit Riots of 1943 encapsulated this paradox. They emerged out of the dialectics of delinquency and persecution, during a period in which American society was undergoing profound structural change.

The major social change brought about by the United States' involvement in the war was the recruitment to the armed forces of over four million civilians and the entrance of over five million women into the war-time labour force. The rapid increase in military recruitment and the radical shift in the composition of the labour force led in turn to changes in family life, particularly the erosion of parental control and authority. The large scale and prolonged separation of millions of families precipitated an unprecedented increase in the rate of juvenile crime and delinquency. By the summer of 1943 it was commonplace for teenagers to be left to their own initiatives whilst their parents were either on active military service or involved in war work. The increase in night work compounded the problem. With their parents or guardians working unsocial hours, it became possible for many more young people to gather late into the night at major urban centers or simply on the street corners. The rate of social mobility intensified during the period of the Zoot-Suit Riots. With over 15 million civilians and 12 million military personnel on the move throughout the country, there was a corresponding increase in vagrancy. Petty crimes became more difficult to detect and control, itinerants became increasingly common, and social transience put unforeseen pressure on housing and welfare. The new patterns of social mobility also led to congestion in military and industrial areas. Significantly, it was the overcrowded military towns along the Pacific coast and the industrial towns of Detroit, Pittsburgh and Los Angeles that witnessed the most violent outbreaks of Zoot-Suit Rioting.[8]

"Delinquency" emerged from the dictionary of new sociology to become an everyday term, as wartime statistics revealed these new patterns of adolescent behaviour. The pachucos of the Los Angeles area were particularly vulnerable to the effects of war. Being neither Mexican nor American, the pachucos, like the black youths with whom they shared the zoot-suit style, simply did not fit. In their own terms they were "24-hour orphans", having rejected the ideologies of their migrant parents. As the war furthered the dislocation of family relationships, the pachucos gravitated away from the home to the only place where their status was visible, the streets and bars of the towns and cities. But if the pachucos laid themselves open to a life of delinquency and detention, they also asserted their distinct identity, with their own style of dress, their own way of life and a shared set of experiences.

The Zoot-Suit Riots: Liberty, Disorder, and the Forbidden

The Zoot-Suit Riots sharply revealed a polarization between two youth groups within wartime society: the gangs of predominantly black and Mexican youths who were at the forefront of the zoot-suit subculture, and the predominantly white American servicemen stationed along the Pacific coast. The riots invariably had racial and social resonances but the primary issue seems to have been patriotism and attitudes to the war. With the entry of the United States into the war in December 1941, the nation had to come to terms with the restrictions of rationing and the prospects of conscription. In March 1942, the War Production Board's first rationing act had a direct effect on the manufacture of suits and all clothing containing wool. In an attempt to institute a 26% cut-back in the use of fabrics. the War Production Board drew up regulations for the wartime manufacture of what Esquire magazine called, "streamlined suits by Uncle Sam."[9] The regulations effectively forbade the manufacture of zoot-suits and most legitimate tailoring companies ceased to manufacture or advertise any suits that fell outside the War Production Board's guide lines. However, the demand for zoot-suits did not decline and a network of bootleg tailors based in Los Angeles and New York continued to manufacture the garments. Thus the polarization between servicemen and pachucos was immediately visible: the chino shirt and battledress were evidently uniforms of patriotism, whereas wearing a zoot-suit was a deliberate and public way of flouting the regulations of rationing. The zoot-suit was a moral and social scandal in the eyes of the authorities, not simply because it was associated with petty crime and violence, but because it openly snubbed the laws of rationing. In the fragile harmony of wartime society, the zoo-suiters were, according to Octavio Paz, "a symbol of love and joy or of horror and loathing, an embodiment of liberty, of disorder, of the forbidden."[10]

The Zoot-Suit Riots, which were initially confined to Los Angeles, began in the first few days of June 1943. During the first weekend of the month, over 60 zoot-suiters were arrested and charged at Los Angeles County jail, after violent and well publicized fights between servicemen on shore leave and gangs of Mexican-American youths. In order to prevent further outbreaks of fighting, the police patrolled the eastern sections of the city, as rumours spread from the military bases that servicemen were intending to form vigilante groups. The Washington Post's report of the incidents, on the morning of Wednesday 9 June 1943, clearly saw the events from the point of view of the servicemen.

> *Disgusted with being robbed and beaten with tire irons, weighted ropes, belts and fists employed by overwhelming numbers of the youthful hoodlums, the uniformed men passed the word quietly among themselves and opened their campaign in force on Friday night.*

> *At central jail, where spectators jammed the sidewalks and police made no efforts to halt auto loads of servicemen openly cruising in search of zoot-suiters, the youths streamed gladly into the sanctity of the cells after being snatched from bar rooms, pool halls and theaters and stripped of their attire.*[11]

Courtesy of the Library of Congress.

During the ensuing weeks of rioting, the ritualistic stripping of zoot-suiters became the major means by which the servicemen" re-established their status over the pachuco's. It became commonplace for gangs of marines to ambush zoot-suiters, strip them down to their underwear and leave them helpless in the streets. In one particularly vicious incident, a gang of drunken sailors rampaged through a cinema after discovering two zoot-suiters. They dragged the pachuco's onto the stage as the film was being screened, stripped them in front of the audience and as a final insult, urinated on the suits.

The press coverage of these incidents ranged from the careful and cautionary liberalism of The Los Angeles Times to the more hysterical hate-mongering of William Randolph Hearst's west coast papers. Although the practice of stripping and publicly humiliating the zoot-suiters was not prompted by the press, several reports did little to discourage the attacks:

> ...*zoot-suits smouldered in the ashes of street bonfires where they had been tossed by grimly methodical tank forces of service men.... The zooters, who earlier in the day had spread boasts that they were organized to 'kill every cop' they could find, showed no inclination to try to make good their boasts.... Searching parties of soldiers, sailors and Marines hunted them out and drove them out into the open like bird dogs flushing quail. Procedure was standard: grab a zooter. Take off his pants and frock coat and tear them up or burn them. Trim the 'Argentine Ducktail' haircut that goes with the screwy costume.*[12]

The second week of June witnessed the worst incidents of rioting and public disorder. A sailor was slashed and disfigured by a pachuco gang; a policeman was run down when he tried to question a car load of zoot-suiters; a young Mexican was stabbed at a party by drunken Marines; a trainload of sailors were stoned by pachuco's as their train approached Long Beach; streetfights broke out daily in San Bernardino; over 400 vigilantes toured the streets of San Diego looking for zoot-suiters, and many individuals from both factions were arrested.[13] On 9 June, the Los Angeles Times published the first in a series of editorials designed to reduce the level of violence, but which also tried to allay the growing concern about the racial character of the riots.

> *To preserve the peace and good name of the Los Angeles area, the strongest measures must be taken jointly by the police, the Sheriff's office and Army and Navy authorities, to prevent any further outbreaks of 'zoot suit' rioting. While members of the armed forces received considerable provocation at the hands of the unidentified miscreants, such a situation cannot be cured by indiscriminate assault on every youth wearing a particular type of costume. It would not do, for a large number of reasons, to let the impression circulate in South America that persons of Spanish-American ancestry were being singled out for mistreatment in Southern California. And the incidents here were capable of being exaggerated to give that impression.*[14]

The Chief, The Black Widows and The Tomahawk Kid

The pleas for tolerance from civic authorities and representatives of the church and state had no immediate effect, and the riots became more frequent and more violent. A zoot-suited youth was shot by a special police officer in Azusa, a gang of pachucos were arrested for rioting and carrying weapons in the Lincoln Heights area; 25 black zoot-suiters were arrested for wrecking an electric railway train in Watts, and 1000 additional police were drafted into East Los Angeles. The press coverage increasingly focused on the most "spectacular" incidents and began to identify leaders of zoot-suit style. On the morning of Thursday 10 June 1943, most newspapers carried photographs and reports on three 'notorious' zoot-suit gang leaders. Of the thousands of pachucos that allegedly belonged to the hundreds of zoot-suit gangs in Los Angeles, the press singled out the arrests of Lewis D English, a 23-yearold-black, charged with felony and carrying a "16-inch razor sharp butcher knife;" Frank H. Tellez, a 22-year-old Mexican held on vagrancy charges, and another Mexican, Luis 'The Chief' Verdusco (27 years of age), allegedly the leader of the Los Angeles pachuco's.[15]

The arrests of English, Tellez and Verdusco seemed to confirm popular perceptions of the zoot-suiters widely expressed for weeks prior to the riots. Firstly, that the zoot-suit gangs were predominantly, but not exclusively, comprised of black and Mexican youths. Secondly, that many of the zoot-suiters were old enough to be in the armed forces but were either avoiding conscription or had been exempted on medical grounds. Finally, in the case of Frank Tellez, who was photographed wearing a pancake hat with a rear feather, that zoot-suit style was an expensive fashion often funded by theft and petty extortion. Tellez allegedly wore a colourful long drape coat that was "part of a $75 suit" and a pair of pegged trousers "very full at the knees and narrow at the cuffs" which were allegedly part of another suit. The caption of the Associated Press photograph indignantly added that "Tellez holds a medical discharge from the Army".[16] What newspaper reports tended to suppress was information on the Marines who were arrested for inciting riots, the existence of gangs of white American zoot-suiters, and the opinions of Mexican-American servicemen stationed in California, who were part of the war effort but who refused to take part in vigilante raids on pachuco hangouts.

As the Zoot-Suit Riots spread throughout California to cities in Texas and Arizona, a new dimension began to influence press coverage of the riots in Los Angeles. On a day when 125 zoot-suited youths clashed with Marines in Watts and armed police had to quell riots in Boyle Heights, the Los Angeles press concentrated on a razor attack on a local mother, Betty Morgan. What distinguished this incident from hundreds of comparable attacks was that the assailants were girls. The press related the incident to the arrest of Amelia Venegas, a woman zoot-suiter who was charged with carrying, and threatening to use, a brass knuckleduster. The revelation that girls were active within pachuco subculture led to consistent press coverage of the activities of two female gangs: the Slick Chicks and the Black Widows.[17] The latter gang took its name from the members' distinctive dress, black zoot-suit jackets, short black skirts and black fish-net stockings. In retrospect the Black Widows, and their active part in the subcultural violence of the Zoot-Suit Riots, disturb conventional understandings of the concept of pachuquismo.

As Joan W. Moore implies in *Homeboys,* her definitive study of Los Angeles youth gangs, the concept of pachuquismo is too readily and unproblematically equated with the better known concept of machismo[18]. Undoubtedly, they share certain ideological traits, not least a swaggering and at times aggressive sense of power and bravado, but the two concepts derive from different sets of social definitions. Whereas machismo can be defined in terms of male power and sexuality, pachuquismo predominantly derives from ethnic, generational and classbased aspirations, and is less evidently a question of gender. What the Zoot-Suit Riots brought to the surface was the complexity of pachuco style. The Black Widows and their aggressive image confounded the pachuco stereotype of the lazy male delinquent who avoided conscription for a life of dandyism and petty crime, and reinforced radical readings of pachuco subculture. The Black Widows were a reminder that ethnic and generational alienation was a pressing social problem and an indication of the tensions that existed in minority, low-income communities.

Although detailed information on the role of girls within zoot-suit sub-culture is limited to very brief press reports, the appearance of female pachucos coincided with a dramatic rise in the delinquency rates among girls aged between 12 and 20 years old. The disintegration of traditional family relationships and the entry of young women into the labour force undoubtedly had an effect on the social roles and responsibilities of female adolescents, but it is difficult to be precise about the relationships between changed patterns of social experience and the rise in delinquency. However, war-time society brought about an increase in unprepared and irregular sexual intercourse, which in turn led to significant increases in the rates of abortion, illegitimate births and venereal diseases. Although statistics are difficult to trace, there are many indications that the war years saw a remarkable increase in the numbers of young women who were taken into social care or referred to penal institutions, as a result of the specific social problems they had to encounter.

Later studies provide evidence that young women and girls were also heavily involved in the traffic and transaction of soft drugs. The pachuco sub-culture within the Los Angeles metropolitan area was directly associated with a widespread growth in the use of marijuana. It has been suggested that female zoot-suiters concealed quantities of drugs on their bodies, since they were less likely to be closely searched by male members of the law enforcement agencies. Unfortunately the absence of consistent or reliable information on the female gangs makes it particularly difficult to be certain about their status within the riots, or their place within traditions of feminine resistance. The Black Widows and Slick Chicks were spectacular in a sub-cultural sense, but their black drape jackets, tight skirts, fish net stockings and heavily emphasized make-up, were ridiculed in the press. The Black Widows clearly existed outside the orthodoxies of war-time society playing no part in the industrial war effort, and openly challenging conventional notions of feminine beauty and sexuality.

Towards the end of the second week of June, the riots in Los Angeles were dying out. Sporadic incidents broke out in other cities, particularly Detroit, New York and Philadelphia, where two members of Gene Krupa's dance band were beaten up in a station for wearing the band's zoot-suit costumes; but these, like the residual events in Los Angeles, were not taken seriously. The authorities failed to read the inarticulate warning signs proffered in two separate incidents in California: in one a zoot-suiter was arrested for throwing gasoline flares at a theatre; and in the second another was arrested for carrying a silver tomahawk. The Zoot-Suit Riots had become a public and spectacular enactment of social disaffection. The authorities in Detroit chose to dismiss a Zoot-Suit Riot at the city's Cooley High School as an adolescent imitation of the Los Angeles disturbances.[19] Within three weeks Detroit was in the midst of the worst race riot in its history.[20] The United States was still involved in the war abroad when violent events on the home front signaled the beginnings of a new era in racial politics.

Official Fears of Fifth Column Fashion

Official reactions to the Zoot-Suit Riots varied enormously. The most urgent problem that concerned California's State Senators was the adverse effect that the events might have on the relationship between the United States and Mexico. This concern stemmed partly from the wish to preserve good international relations, but rather more from the significance of relations with Mexico for the economy of Southern California, as an item in the Los Angeles Times made clear. 'In San Francisco Senator Downey declared that the riots may have 'extremely grave consequences' in impairing relations between the United States and Mexico and may endanger the program of importing Mexican labor to aid in harvesting California crops.[21] These fears were compounded when the Mexican Embassy formally drew the Zoot-Suit Riots to the attention of the State Department. It was the fear of an international incident[22] that could only have an adverse effect on California's economy, rather than any real concern for the social conditions of the MexicanAmerican community, that motivated Governor Warren of California to order a public investigation into the causes of the riots. In an ambiguous press statement, the Governor hinted that the riots may have been instigated by outside or even foreign agitators:

> *As we love our country and the boys we are sending overseas to defend it, we are all duty bound to suppress every discordant activity which is designed to stir up international strife or adversely affect our relationships with our allies in the United Nations.*[23]

The Zoot-Suit Riots provoked two related investigations; a fact finding investigative committee headed by Attorney General Robert Kenny and an un-American activities investigation presided over by State Senator Jack B Tenney. The un-American activities investigation was ordered "to determine whether the present Zoot-Suit Riots were sponsored by Nazi agencies attempting to spread disunity between the United States and Latin-American countries."[24] Senator Tenney, a member of the un-American Activities committee for Los Angeles County, claimed he had evidence that the Zoot-Suit Riots were "axis-sponsored" but the evidence was never presented.[25] However, the notion that the riots might have been initiated by outside agitators persisted throughout the month of June, and was fueled by Japanese propaganda broadcasts accusing the North American government of ignoring the brutality of US marines. The arguments of the un-American activities investigation were given a certain amount of credibility by a Mexican pastor based in Watts, who according to the press had been "a pretty rough customer himself, serving as a captain in Pancho Villa's revolutionary army."[26] Reverend Francisco Quintanilla, the pastor of the Mexican Methodist church, was convinced the riots were the result of fifth columnists. "When boys start attacking servicemen it means the enemy is right at home. It means they are being fed vicious propaganda by enemy agents who wish to stir up all the racial and class hatreds they can put their evil fingers on."[27]

The attention given to the dubious claims of nazi-instigation tended to obfuscate other more credible opinions. Examination of the social conditions of pachuco youths tended to be marginalized in favour of other more "newsworthy" angles. At no stage in the press coverage were the opinions of community workers or youth leaders sought, and so, ironically, the most progressive opinion to appear in the major newspapers was offered by the Deputy Chief of Police, E.W. Lester. In press releases and on radio he provided a short history of gang subcultures in the Los Angeles area and then tried, albeit briefly, to place the riots in a social context.

> *The Deputy Chief said most of the youths came from overcrowded colorless homes that offered no opportunities for leisure-time activities. He said it is wrong to blame law enforcement agencies for the present situation, but that society as a whole must be charged with mishandling the problems.*[28]

On the morning of Friday, 11 June 1943, The Los Angeles Times broke with its regular practices and printed an editorial appeal, "Time For Sanity" on its front page. The main purpose of the editorial was to dispel suggestions that the riots were racially motivated, and to challenge the growing opinion that white servicemen from the Southern States had actively colluded with the police in their vigilante campaign against the zoot-suiters.

> *There seems to be no simple or complete explanation for the growth of the grotesque gangs. Many reasons have been offered, some apparently valid, some farfetched. But it does appear to be definitely established that any attempts at curbing the movement have had nothing whatever to do with race persecution, although some elements have loudly raised the cry of this very thing.*[29]

A month later, the editorial of July's issue of Crisis presented a diametrically opposed point of view:

> *These riots would not occur - no matter what the instant provocation - if the vast majority of the population, including more often than not the law enforcement officers and machinery, did not share in varying degrees the belief that Negroes are and must be kept second-class citizens.*[30]

But this view got short shrift, particularly from the authorities, whose initial response to the riots was largely retributive. Emphasis was placed on arrest and punishment. The Los Angeles City Council considered a proposal from Councillor Norris Nelson, that "it be made a jail offense to wear zoot-suits with reat pleats within the city limits of LA"[31], and a discussion ensued for over an hour before it was resolved that the laws pertaining to rioting and disorderly conduct were sufficient to contain the zoot-suit threat. However, the council did encourage the War Production Board (WPB) to reiterate its regulations on the manufacture of suits. The regional office of the WPB based in San Francisco investigated tailors manufacturing in the area of men's fashion and took steps "to curb illegal production of men's clothing in violation of WPB limitation orders."[32] Only when Governor Warren's fact-finding commission made its public recommendations did the political analysis of the riots go beyond the first principles of punishment and proscription. The recommendations called for a more responsible co-operation from the press; a program of special training for police officers working in multi-racial communities; additional detention centres; a juvenile forestry camp for youth under the age of 16; an increase in military and shore police; an increase in the youth facilities provided by the church; an increase in neighbourhood recreation facilities and an end to discrimination in the use of public facilities. In addition to these measures, the commission urged that arrests should be made without undue emphasis on members of minority groups and encouraged lawyers to protect the rights of youths arrested for participation in gang activity. The findings were a delicate balance of punishment and palliative; it made no significant mention of the social conditions of Mexican labourers and no recommendation about the kind of public spending that would be needed to alter the social experiences of pachuco youth. The outcome of the Zoot-Suit Riots was an inadequate. highly localized and relatively ineffective body of short term public policies that provided no guidelines for the more serious riots in Detroit and Harlem later in the same summer.

The Mystery of The Signifying Monkey

The pachuco is the prey of society, but instead of hiding he adorns himself to attract the hunter's attention. Persecution redeems him and breaks his solitude: his salvation depends on him becoming part of the very society he appears to deny.[33]

The zoot-suit was associated with a multiplicity of different traits and conditions. It was simultaneously the garb of the victim and the attacker, the persecutor and the persecuted, the "sinister clown" and the grotesque dandy. But the central opposition was between the style of the delinquent and that of the disinherited. To wear a zoot-suit was to risk the repressive intolerance of wartime society and to invite the attention of the police, the parent generation and the uniformed members of the armed forces. For many pachucos the Zoot-Suit Riots were simply high times in Los Angeles when momentarily they had control of the streets; for others it was a realization that they were outcasts in a society that was not of their making. For the black radical writer, Chester Himes, the riots in his neighbourhood were unambiguous: Zoot Riots are Race Riots."[34] For other contemporary commentators the wearing of the zoot-suit could be anything from unconscious dandyism to a conscious "political" engagement. The Zoot-Suit Riots were not political riots in the strictest sense, but for many participants they were an entry into the language of politics, an inarticulate rejection of the "straight world" and its organization.

It is remarkable how many post-war activists were inspired by the zoot-suit disturbances. Luis Valdez of the radical theatre company, El Teatro Campesino allegedly learned the "chicano" from his cousin the zoot-suiter Billy Miranda.[35] The novelists Ralph Ellison and Richard Wright both conveyed a literary and political fascination with the power and potential of the zoot-suit. One of Ellison's editorials for the journal Negro Quarterly expressed his own sense of frustration at the enigmatic attraction of zoot-suit style.

A third major problem, and one that is indispensable to the centralization and direction of power is that of learning the meaning of myths and symbols which abound among the Negro masses. For without this knowledge, leadership, no matter how correct its program, will fail. Much in Negro life remains a mystery; perhaps the zoot-suit conceals profound political meaning; perhaps the symmetrical frenzy of the Lindy-hop conceals clues to great potential powers, if only leaders could solve this riddle.[36]

Although Ellison's remarks are undoubtedly compromised by their own mysterious idealism, he touches on the zoot-suit's major source of interest. It is in everyday rituals that resistance can find natural and unconscious expression. In retrospect, the zoot-suit's history can be seen as a point of intersection, between the related potential of ethnicity and politics on the one hand, and the pleasures of identity and difference on the other. It is the zoot-suit's political and ethnic associations that have made it such a rich reference point for subsequent generations. From the music of Thelonious Monk and Kid Creole to the jazz-poetry of Larry Neal, the zoot-suit has inherited new meanings and new mysteries. In his book Hoodoo Hollerin' Bebop Ghosts, Neal uses the image of the zoot-suit as the symbol of Black America's cultural resistance. For Neal, the zoot-suit ceased to be a costume and became a tapestry of meaning, where music. politics and social action merged. The zoot-suit became a symbol for the enigmas of Black culture and the mystery of the signifying monkey:

> *But there is rhythm here*
> *Its own special substance.*
> *I hear Billie sing, no Good Man, and dig Prez, wearing the Zoot suit*
> *of life, the Porkpie hat tilted at the correct angle; through the Harlem*
> *smoke of beer and whisky, I understand the mystery of the Signifying*
> *Monkey.*[37]

The author wishes to acknowledge the support of the British Academy for the research for this article.

Notes

1. Ralph Ellison Invisible Man New York 1947 p 380
2. Invisible Man p 381
3. 'Zoot Suit Originated in Georgia' New York Times 11 June 1943 p 21
4. For the most extensive sociological study of the zoot-suit riots of 1943 see Ralph H Turner and Samuel J Surace 'zoot Suiters and Mexicans: Symbols in Crowd Behaviour' American Journal of Sociology 62 1956 pp 14-20

5. Octavio Paz The Labyrinth of Solitude London 1967 pp 5-6
6. Labyrinth of Solitude p 8
7. As note 6
8. See KL Nelson (ed) The Impact of War on Amencan Life New York 1971
9. OE Schoeffler and W Gale Esquire's Encyclopedia of Twentieth-Century Men's Fashion New York 1973 p 24
10. As note 6
11. 'Zoot-suiters Again on the Prowl as Navy Holds Back Sailors' Washington Post 9 June 1943 p 1
12. Quoted in S Menefee Assignment USA New York 1943 p 189
13. Details of the riots are taken from newspaper reports and press releases for the weeks in question, particularly from the Los Angeles Times, New York Times, Washington Post, Washington Star and Time Magazine
14. 'Strong Measures Must be Taken Against Rioting' Los Angeles Times 9 June 1943 p 4
15. 'Zoot-Suit Fighting Spreads On the Coast' New York Times 10 June 1943 p 23
16. As note 15
17. 'Zoot-Girls Use Knife in Attack' Los Angeles Times 11 June 1943 p 1
18. Joan W Moore Homeboys: Gangs, Drugs and Prison in the Barrios of Los Angeles Philadelphia 1978
19. 'Zoot Suit Warfare Spreads to Pupils of Detroit Area' Washington Star 11 June 1943 p 1
20. Although the Detroit Race Riots of 1943 were not zoot-suit riots, nor evidently about 'youth' or 'delinquency', the social context in which they took place was obviously comparable. For a lengthy study of the Detroit riots see R Shogun and T Craig The Detroit Race Riot: a study in violence Philadelphia and New York 1964
21. 'zoot Suit War Inquiry Ordered by Governor' Los Angeles Times 9 June 1943 p A
22. 'Warren Orders Zoot Suit Quiz; Quiet Reigns After Rioting' Los Angeles Times 10 June 1943 p 1
23. As note 22
24. 'Tenney Feels Riots Caused by Nazi Move for Disunity' Los Angeles Times 9 Junc 1943 p A
25. As note 24
26. 'Watts Pastor Blames Riots on Fifth Column' Los Angeles Times 11 June 1943 p A
27. As note 26
28. 'California Governor Appeals for Quelling of Zoot Suit Riots' Washington Star 1 June 1943 pA3
29. 'Time for Sanity' Los Angeles Times 11 June 1943 p 1
30. 'The Riots' The Crisis July 1943 p 199
31. 'Ban on Freak Suits Studied by Councilmen' Los Angeles Times 9 June 1943 p A3
33. Labyrinth of Solitude p 9

34. Chester Himes 'Zoot Riots are Race Riots' The Crisis July 1943; reprinted in Himes Black on Black: Baby Sister and Selected Writings London 1975

35. El Teatro Campesino presented the first Chicano play to achieve full commercial Broadway production. The play, written by Luis Valdez and entitled 'Zoot Suit' was a drama documentary on the Sleepy Lagoon murder and the events leading to the Los Angeles riots. (The Sleepy Lagoon murder of August 1942 resulted in 24 pachucos being indicted for conspiracy to murder.)

36. Quoted in Larry Neal 'Ellison's Zoot Suit' in J Hersey (ed) Ralph Ellison: A Collection of Critical Essays New Jersey 1974 p 67

37. From Larry Neal's poem 'Malcolm X: an Autobiography' in L Neal Hoodoo Hollerin' Bebop Chosts Washington DC 1974 p 9

13

Holy Matrimony!

LISA DUGGAN

*AS POLITICIANS SQUARE OFF ON GAY MARRIAGE, PRO-
GRESSIVES MUST ENTER THE DEBATE*

The political storm over marriage is now intensifying as gay couples wed in
San Francisco and President Bush vows to stop them with a constitutional
amendment. Gay marriage threatens to wreak havoc as a "wedge issue" in
the November elections, but it isn't entirely clear which party's prospects will be
promoted, and which damaged, through marriage politics this year. Progressives
certainly haven't figured out how best to enter the contentious and confusing public debate. Widespread anxiety over changing demographics and contested social
norms is producing the background noise for a relatively volatile political calcu-
lus on all sides.

If Britney Spears's high-speed annulment and the competitive gold-digging with
a sucker punch on TV's *Joe Millionaire* are any indication, concern over the state
of the marital union is justified. Statistics confirm what entertainment culture spec-
tacularizes—marriage is less stable and central to the organization of American
life than ever. There are now more unmarried households than married ones, and

Lisa Duggan is the author of The Twilight of Equality? Neoliberalism, Cultural Politics and the Attack on
Democracy *(Beacon). She teaches queer studies in the American studies program and the Center for the
Study of Gender and Sexuality at NYU.*

a variety of formal and informal, permanent and transient, solemn and casual partnership and kinship arrangements have displaced any singular, static model of domestic life. Political responses to these changes have long been polarized between those who want to bring back Ozzie and Harriet and those who are fighting for the democratization of state recognition of households, along with equitable distribution of services and benefits to Americans, based on how we actually live rather than on some imagined, lost ideal. But today, in part because of the public's own ambivalence, the major political parties have been reluctant to come down firmly on either side of this divide.

What is most vexing the political parties right now is same-sex marriage. The Republican electoral alliance is split on this issue. On the one hand, hard-line religious and moral conservatives have been working to rigidify the boundaries of "traditional" marriage and to shore up its privileged status. These groups are now pushing to pass a constitutional amendment defining marriage as between "a man and a woman." On the other hand, libertarians, states' rights advocates and social moderates prefer to retain conventional gendered marriage but support allowing some diversification of forms of partnership and household recognition at the state level. They oppose a constitutional amendment as a federal imposition on the states, or as just too mean to help Republicans during an election year. The religious and moral right appears to be winning out in the wake of the Massachusetts Supreme Judicial Court's decision that the state must extend civil marriage to same-sex couples. Bush, however grudgingly, fulfilled his promise to the Christian right when he announced on February 24 that he will support a federal marriage amendment.

With their convention in Boston, and Massachusetts Senator John Kerry the likely presidential nominee, Democrats will be fighting any "too liberal" charge associated with gay weddings by noting their opposition to same-sex marriage (the only remaining candidates who support it are Al Sharpton and Dennis Kucinich), while opposing a federal marriage amendment and emphasizing support for civil unions and domestic partnerships. Their carefully calibrated rhetoric will urge tolerance without questioning the supremacy of married, two-parent families. Indeed, the Bush Administration's recent proposal to spend $1.5 billion promoting marriage, "especially" among low-income populations, has not encountered energetic opposition from many Democrats, who have supported like-minded efforts in the past. Progressives, meanwhile, are struggling to articulate a small-d democratic politics of marriage that demands full equality for lesbians and gays without accepting the logic of the "family values" crowd.

It may be tempting to see this squabble as an example of symbolic politics, with the debate over the future of marriage potentially displacing bigger and more significant battles over war and peace, taxes and fairness, corporate greed and good government. But state regulation of households and partnerships does in fact affect the basic safety, prosperity, equality and welfare of all Americans—it determines who will make medical decisions for us in emergencies, who may share our pensions or Social Security benefits, who may legally co-parent our children and much more. It's just hard to sort out the real issues from the smokescreens as the rhetoric heats up this election year.

Moral conservatives have so far taken the lead in the struggle to frame the meaning of the "marriage crisis." In their apocalyptic imagination, the stability of heterosexual unions and the social order they insure are threatened on all sides—by the specter of gay marriage, by women's independent choices within and outside marriage, and by government neutrality, toleration or support of single-parent and unmarried households, especially among the poor. But wait! It gets worse: As Stanley Kurtz argued in *The Weekly Standard* last August, "Among the likeliest effects of gay marriage is to take us down a slippery slope to legalized polygamy and 'polyamory' (group marriage). Marriage will be transformed into a variety of relationship contracts, linking two, three, or more individuals (however weakly and temporarily) in every conceivable combination of male and female."

I'm not sure, given the rise of transgender activism, just how many combinations there are of male and female. But the dystopic vision is clear. Moral conservatives want to prevent courts and legislatures from opening a Pandora's box of legal options—a flexible menu of choices for forms of household and partnership recognition open to all citizens, depending on specific and varying needs. Such a menu would threaten the normative status of the nuclear family, undermining state endorsement of heterosexual privilege, the male "headed" household and "family values" moralism as social welfare policy.

The problem is not that any such flexible menu is currently available anywhere at present. What has emerged over decades of political wrangling at the municipal and state level is a hodgepodge of legal categories—civil marriage, civil union (with the same state-level benefits as civil marriage but without the portability from state to state, or federal recognition), domestic partnership (with fewer benefits than civil marriage) and reciprocal beneficiaries (which carries the fewest benefits). The categories are neither equivalent nor open to all. Civil marriage, thus far (and until May in Massachusetts) open only to one man and one woman who are not close blood relatives, carries the most specific benefits and mutual responsibilities (more than 1,049 automatic federal and additional state protections, benefits and responsibilities, according to the federal government's General Accounting Office). It endows couples and their children with both real and symbolic citizenship rights at the highest level. Civil union (in Vermont) or domestic partnership (in five states and over sixty municipalities) has been made available to gay and lesbian couples and sometimes to heterosexual couples who choose not to marry (or not to have to divorce) as well. Only the reciprocal beneficiaries status has been available (in different versions in Hawaii and Vermont) to close relatives, or those with no proclaimed conjugal bond. It has so far provided the most limited benefits, but it is in some senses the most radical innovation. It potentially separates state recognition of households or partnerships from the business of sexual regulation altogether.

The right wing's fear of a "slippery slope" suggests some ways that this eclectic array of statuses might move us in a progressive direction. Kurtz himself, citing Brigham Young University professor Alan Hawkins, sketches out what is to him a distasteful scenario:

> *Consider the plight of an underemployed and uninsured single mother in her early 30s who sees little real prospect of marriage (to a man) in her future. Suppose she has a good friend, also female and heterosexual, who is single and childless but employed with good spousal*

benefits. Sooner or later, friends like this are going to start contracting same-sex marriages of convenience. The single mom will get medical and governmental benefits, will share her friend's paycheck, and will gain an additional caretaker for the kids besides. Her friend will gain companionship and a family life. The marriage would obviously be sexually open. And if lightning struck and the right man came along for one of the women, they could always divorce and marry heterosexually.

In a narrow sense, the women and children in this arrangement would be better off. Yet the larger effects of such unions on the institution of marriage would be devastating. At a stroke, marriage would be severed not only from the complementarity of the sexes but also from its connection to romance and sexual exclusivity—and even from the hope of permanence.

Gee. Sounds good. Then consider how such arrangements might benefit women, children and others even more substantially. What if there were a way to separate the tax advantages joint household recognition, or the responsibilities of joint parenting, from the next-of-kin recognition so that such rights might go to a non-co-resident relative, a friend or a lover? And what if many benefits, such as health insurance, could be available to all without regard for household or partnership status? The moral conservative's nightmare vision of a flexible menu of options might become a route to progressive equality! That could happen—*if* all statuses could be opened to all without exclusions, allowing different kinds of households to fit state benefits to their changing needs; *if* no status conferred any invidious privilidge or advantage over any other, or over none at all; and *if* material benefits such as health insurance were detached from partnership or household form altogether (federally guaranteed universal healthcare, for instance, would be far more democratic and egalitarian than health insurance as a partnership benefit). Meanwhile, the "sanctity" of traditional marriages could be retained and honored by religious groups and families, according to their own values and definitions.

Efforts to stop any such democratization of households have escalated steadily ever since a Hawaii state court decision conjured up visions of legitimate gay weddings in 1993. Thirty-eight states have passed legislation or constitutional amendments restricting marriage to heterosexual couples. In 1996 Bill Clinton signed the federal Defense of Marriage Act, designed to prevent any future state-level same-sex marriages from carrying the federal recognition and portability that civil marriage has so far guaranteed (though many believe DOMA is vulnerable to constitutional challenge). The proposed federal marriage amendment with more than a hundred sponsors in the House and a handful of supporters in the Senate so far, would go much further than DOMA to write marriage restriction into the Constitution. Depending on the final wording, and the results of inevitable litigation over its interpretation, the amendment might also put a stop not solely to gay marriage but to all diversification of partnership and household recognition. In one stroke all the hard-won civil union, domestic partnership and reciprocal beneficiary statuses could be wiped off the books, leaving civil marriage. restricted to heterosexual couples, as the sole form of recognition available at the federal, state or municipal level (and possibly at private businesses and organizations as well) throughout the country.

Fortunately for advocates of partnership and household diversity, a marriage amendment faces a long, steep uphill battle as supporters struggle to pass it, first in Congress and then in three-fourths of the state legislatures, before it can become law. Many conservatives are clearly leery of the expensive, acrimonious battle ahead. George W. Bush withheld his own endorsement of the amendment until after his State of the Union address, in which he chose to emphasize his plan to promote conventional marriage instead.

To many, this looked like election-year strategy—an effort to pander to moral conservatives without giving them the explicit approval they craved. And surely such tactical concerns are shaping every word uttered by Bush on this issue. But it would be a mistake to attribute this Administration's interest in marriage promotion solely to such motives. There is a deeper commitment to preserving gendered marriage, on economic as well as moral grounds.

Bush's marriage-promotion initiative isn't new; it first appeared in the welfare reauthorization legislation passed by the House two years ago, which is now before the Senate and may come up for a vote as soon as this spring. Bush's $1.5 billion package, to be used to hire counselors and offer classes in marital harmony, extends the commitment contained in the 1996 welfare "reform" bill, passed under Clinton, to "end the dependence of needy parents on government benefits by promoting . . . marriage." Women and children, in other words, should depend on men for basic economic support, while women care for dependents—children, elderly parents, disabled family members, etc. Under such a model, married-couple households might "relieve" the state of the expense of helping to support single-parent households, and of the cost of a wide range of social services childcare and disability services to home nursing. Marriage thus becomes a privatization scheme: Individual married-couple-led households give women and children access to higher wages, and also "privately" provide many services once offered through social welfare agencies. More specifically, the unpaid labor of married women fills the gap created by government service cuts.

Besides being sexist and outdated, this model of marriage is not exactly realistic. Relatively few men today earn a "family wage," and employed married women are not able to care fully for dependents by themselves. Marriage promotion, moreover, has not proven an effective means of alleviating poverty and reducing the need for government benefits. But even without any measurable economic impact, the effort to promote marriage among low-income populations works at the rhetorical level to shift blame for economic hardship onto the marital practices of the poor rather than on the loss of jobs, employment benefits or government services.

Republicans and Democrats are by and large in agreement that as social programs are whittled away gender-differentiated marriage (heterosexual, with different expectations for women and men) should take up the slack. Clinton's marriage-promoting welfare law embodied this principle, which also helps to explain the ambivalence of conservative and centrist Democrats toward genuine gender equality in marriage (illustrated in the retro discussion of the proper role of political wives in the current presidential campaign) and their opposition to gay marriage. So there is an economic agenda, as well as surface moralism, attached to calls for the preservation of traditional marriage. The campaign to save gendered marriage has some rational basis, for neoliberals in both parties, as a politics of privatization.

Unwilling to support gay marriage, defend Judith Steinberg's remote relation to her husband's now-defunct presidential campaign (though Laura Bush did so) or openly attack marriage promotion as public policy, the Democrats are left with lame advocacy of second-class status for gays, mandatory secondary supportive roles for political wives and public silence about welfare policy. No viable Democratic candidate has yet been able to shift the frame of reference to escape a weakly defensive posture on these issues. So it's left to progressives, both within the Democratic Party and outside it, to formulate a clear, positive vision of how best to address the needs of real households for state recognition and social support.

But progressives are divided, too, in their approach to marriage politics. The hateful campaign to exclude same-sex couples from full marriage rights creates tremendous pressure on gay-rights advocates and supporters to emphasize access to civil marriage as a core right of citizenship. A few marriage-equality advocates have continued to call for the multiplication of democratically accessible forms of state recognition for households and partnerships, and for the dethronement of sanctified marriage as privileged civic status, but many have couched their advocacy in language that glorifies marital bliss, sometimes echoing the "family values" rhetoric of their opponents. The "Roadmap to Equality: A Freedom to Marry Educational Guide," published by Lambda Legal Defense and Education Fund and Marriage Equality California, begins with the kind of banal American Dream rhetoric that appeals to some gay people, but misdescribes, annoys and even stigmatizes many others:

> *Gay people are very much like everyone else. They grow up, fall in love, form families and have children. They mow their lawns, shop for groceries and worry about making ends meet. They want good schools for their children, and security for their families as a whole.*

The guide goes on to recycle some of the more noxious views routinely spouted by conservative moralists:

> *Denying marriage rights to lesbian and gay couples keeps them in a state of permanent adolescence. . . . Both legally and socially, married couples are held in greater esteem than unmarried couples because of the commitment they have made in a serious, public, legally enforceable manner. For lesbian and gay couples who wish to make that very same commitment, the very same option must be available. There is no other way for gay people to be fully equal to non-gay people.*

No other way? How about abolishing state endorsement of the sanctified religious wedding or ending the use of the term "marriage" altogether (as lesbian and gay progressives and queer leftists have advocated for decades)? In a bid for equality, some gay groups are producing rhetoric that insults and marginalizes unmarried people, while promoting marriage in much the same terms as the welfare reformers use to stigmatize single-parent households, divorce and "out of wedlock" births. If pursued in this way, the drive for gay-marriage equality can undermine rather than support the broader movement for social justice and democratic diversity.

Meanwhile, critics of marriage promotion, located primarily in feminist policy and research organizations, are working to counter rosy views of the institution of marriage. The National Organization for Women's Legal Defense and Education Fund has documented the planned flow of money and services away from poor women and children and toward conservative organizations, contained in the proposed welfare reauthorization bill (see www.nowldef.org). A group of academic researchers and professors organized by Anna Marie Smith of Cornell University, Martha Albertson Fineman of Emory University and Gwendolyn Mink of Smith College have created a website to circulate critiques of marriage promotion as a substitute for effective social welfare programs (http://falcon.arts.cornell.edu/ams3/npmbasis.html). As they point out, "While marriage has provided some women the cushion of emotional and economic security, it also has locked many women in unsatisfying, exploitative, abusive and even violent relationships." Their research findings and legislative analysis demonstrate that "federal and state governments are transforming the burden of caring for our needy sisters and brothers into a private obligation."

The agendas of lesbian and gay marriage—equality advocates and progressive feminist critics of marriage promotion don't necessarily or inevitably conflict, though their efforts are currently running on separate political and rhetorical tracks. Given the rising political stakes. and the narrow horizons of political possibility, it seems imperative now that progressives find ways to make room for a more integrated, broadly democratic marriage politics. To respond to widespread changes in household organization and incipient dissatisfaction with the marital status quo, progressives could begin to disentangle the religious, symbolic, kinship and economic functions of marriage, making a case for both civil equality and the separation of church and state. They could argue that civil marriage (perhaps renamed or reconfigured), like any other household status, should be open to all who are willing to make the trek to city hall, whether or not they also choose to seek a church's blessing. Beginning with the imperfect menu of household and partnership statuses now unevenly available from state to state, it might not be such an impossibly utopian leap to suggest that we should expand and democratize what we've already got, rather than contract our options.

Such a vision, long advocated by feminist and queer progressives, may now be finding some broader support. Kay Whitlock, the national representative for LGBT issues for the American Friends Service Committee, circulated a statement at the National Religious Leadership Roundtable last fall that argued, "We cannot speak about equal civil marriage rights and the discrimination that currently exists without also speaking of the twin evil of coercive marriage policies promoted with federal dollars. . . . For us, it is critical that the LGBT movement work for equal civil marriage rights in ways that do not further reinforce the idea that if a couple is married, they are more worthy of rights and recognition than people involved in intimate relationships who are not married." The statement continued, "We do not want to convey the message that marriage is what all queer people should aspire to. We also do not want the discussion of marriage to overwhelm and suppress discussion about a broader definition of human rights and basic benefits that ought to accompany those rights."

This seems like a good place to start. The question is, How can arguments like this be heard in the midst of the clamor against gay marriage on the right, when Democrats are reduced to a timid whisper and gay groups are too often sounding like the American Family Association? Might it be possible to tap into an undercurrent of dissatisfaction with the current state of the marital union—and appeal to the public's understanding of the enormous distance between rhetoric and reality on this subject? Politicians pay lip service to conservative family values, but voters do not always bolt when their actual lives fail to conform to the prescriptions—as Bill Clinton's enduring popularity despite repeated sex scandals demonstrated. Polls show widely contradictory public views on the subjects of marriage and divorce, adultery and gay rights. Questions with only slight wording changes can yield widely differing results. Why not muster the courage to lead the public a little on this issue? Civil unions, considered beyond the pale only a few years ago, are now supported by many conservatives. The political center can and does shift—and right now, it is particularly fluid and volatile in this area.

In the current climate, progressives might profit by pointing out the multiple ways that conservative marriage politics aim to limit freedom in the most intimate aspects of our lives—through banning gay marriage as well as promoting traditional marriage. Given current demographic trends, it couldn't hurt to ask: Why do Republicans want to turn back the clock, rather than accept reality? And why can't Democrats find some way to support law and policy that advances the goals of intimate freedom and political equality, even during an election year?

14

The Book Vendor

MITCHELL DUNEIER

It is not hard to understand why Hakim Hasan came to see himself as a public character. Early one July morning, a deliveryman pulled his truck up to the curb behind Hakim's vending table on Greenwich Avenue off the corner of Sixth Avenue and carried a large box of flowers over to him.

"Can you hold these until the flower shop opens up?" the deliveryman asked.

"No problem," responded Hakim as he continued to set up the books on his table. "Put them right under there."

When the store opened for business, he brought them inside and gave them to the owner.

"Why did that man trust you with the flowers?" I later asked.

"People like me are the eyes and ears of this street," he explained, echoing Jane Jacobs again. "Yes, I could take those flowers and sell them for a few hundred dollars. But that deliveryman sees me here every day. I'm as dependable as any store-owner."

A few days later, an elderly black man on his afternoon walk came up to the table. "Can I sit down?" he asked Hakim, who gave him a chair.

The man was panting and sweating, so Hakim went to the telephone on the corner and called 911.

As they waited for the paramedics to arrive, the man said he was going into the subway.

From *Sidewalk* by Mitchell Duncir Farrar, Straus, Giroux, NY: 1999

"It's too hot for you down there," Hakim replied. "You wait right here for the ambulance!"

Soon an ambulance arrived, and the crew carried away the old man. It turned out he had suffered an asthma attack.

Another day, I was present at the table when a traffic officer walked by to give out parking tickets.

"Are any of these your cars?" she asked Hakim.

"Yes, that one, and that one," said Hakim, pointing.

"What is that all about?" I asked.

"The day I met her, we got into an argument," he explained. "She was getting ready to give the guy across the street a ticket. I say, "You can't do this!' She said, "Why not?' I say, " 'Cause I'm getting ready to put a quarter in.' She said, "You can't do that.' I guess that, because of the way I made my argument, she didn't give out the ticket, and from that point onward we became friends. And when she comes on the block, she asks me, for every car on the block that has a violation sign, "Is that your car?' Meaning, "Is it someone you know?' And depending on whether I say yes or no, that's it—they get a ticket."

Once, a group of German tourists wearing Nikon cameras passed the table. Though the information booth run by the Village Alliance Business Improvement District was open on a little island across the street, they walked up to Hakim instead.

"How do we get to Greenwich Village?" one man asked.

"This *is* Greenwich Village," Hakim explained.

"Are these things part of your job description as a vendor?" I asked him once.

"Let me put it to you this way, Mitch," he replied. "I kind of see what I loosely call my work on the sidewalk as going far, far beyond just trying to make a living selling books. That sometimes even seems secondary. Over time, when people see you on the sidewalk, there is a kind of trust that starts. They've seen you so long that they walk up to you. There have been occasions when I've had to have directions translated out of Spanish into French to get somebody to go someplace!"

It is not only directions and assistance that I have seen Hakim give out. He also tells people a great deal about books—so much so that he once told me he was thinking of charging tuition to the people who stand in his space on the sidewalk.

I think he was only half joking. Indeed, Hakim seems to consider himself a person of some consequence out on the street, not merely a public character but a street intellectual of sorts as well. His self-image is sometimes reinforced by his customers. On a September afternoon, a middle-aged man walked up to his table. "Do you got the book *The Middle Passage*?"

"By Charles Johnson?" asked Hakim. "Is it a novel?"

"No. It's by Tom Feelings."

"Oh, it's a big, oversized black book with beautiful pictures! No, I do not have that. Yeah, I know the book. It's forty bucks."

"I know that if anyone knows, you know."

"Well, I'm one of the few who may know. There's a lot of people out here who know. I try to do my homework. I stay up late at night going through periodicals, newspapers, all kinds of stuff, to try to figure out what's published."

Hakim is one of many street book vendors throughout Greenwich Village and New York City generally. Most of these vendors specialize in one or more of the following: expensive art and photography books; dictionaries; *New York Times* best-sellers; "black books"; new quality mass-market and trade paperbacks of all varieties; used and out-of-print books; comic books; pornography; and discarded magazines.

On Sixth Avenue alone, among the vendors of new books, a passerby may encounter Muhammad and his family, who sell "black books" and an incense known as "the Sweet Smell of Success" at the corner of Sixth Avenue and Eighth Street. Down the block, an elderly white man sells best-sellers and high-quality hardcovers on the weekends. At Sixth and Greenwich (across the street), one encounters Howard, a comics vendor, also white, and Alice, a Filipina woman (Hakim's sometime business partner), who sells used paperbacks and current best-sellers.

These vendors take in anywhere from fifty to a couple of hundred dollars a day. By selling discounted books on the street (and I will discuss how these books get to the street in a later chapter), they serve an important function in the lives of their customers. Indeed, if all they did was to sell books at prices lower than those of the bookstores, this would be enough to explain why they are able to sustain themselves on the street. But to understand *how* Hakim functions as a public character, I thought it would be helpful to look more closely at the meaning the book table has in the minds of both the vendor and the customer who patronizes it.

It goes without saying, perhaps, that one good way to find out more about people is to get to know them at first hand, but this is more easily said than done. When I began, I knew that if I was to find out what was taking place on the sidewalk, I would have to bridge many gaps between myself and the people I hoped to understand. This involved thinking carefully about who they are and who I am.

I was uneasy.

One of the most notorious gaps in American society is the difference between people related to race and the discourse revolving around this volatile issue. Though there were also differences between our social classes (I was raised in a middle-class suburb, whereas most of them grew up in lower- and working-class urban neighborhoods), religions (I am Jewish and most of them are Muslim or Christian), levels of education (I hold a Ph.D. in sociology and attended two years of law school, whereas some of them did not graduate from high school), and occupations (I am a college professor of sociology and they are street vendors), none of these differences seemed to be as significant as that of race. Actually, the interaction between race and class differences very likely made me uneasy, though I was unaware of that at the time.

When I stood at Hakim's table, I felt that, as a white male, I stood out. In my mind, I had no place at his table, because he was selling so-called black books. I thought that his product formed the boundary of a sort of exclusionary black zone where African Americans were welcome but whites were not.

It is interesting that I felt this way. African Americans buy products every day from stores owned by whites, often having to travel to other neighborhoods to acquire the goods they need. They must shop among whites, and often speak of enduring slights and insults from the proprietors of these businesses.[1] I myself rarely have to go to neighborhoods not dominated by whites in search of goods or services. None of the book vendors ever insulted, offended, or threatened me. None of them told me I was not welcome at his table. None of them ever made anti-white or anti-Semitic remarks. Yet I felt unwelcome in ways I had not felt during previous studies that had brought me into contact with African Americans. This was because many of the conversations I heard were about so-called black books and because the people participating in them seemed to be defining themselves as a people. (Actually, there were also white customers at Hakim's table, though I didn't know it at the time.) I felt out of place. Also, I wanted the trust that would be necessary to write about the life of the street, and race differences seem a great obstacle to such trust.

One day, before I knew Hakim and after I had concluded that these tables were not an appropriate place for me to hang out, I walked by his book table on my way to an appointment. I was surprised to see for sale a copy of *Slim's Table*, my own first book.

"Where did you get this from?" I asked, wondering if it had been stolen.

"I have my sources," Hakim responded. "Do you have some interest in this book?"

"Well, I wrote it," I responded.

"Really? Do you live around here?"

"Yes. I live around the corner, on Mercer Street."

"Why don't you give me your address and telephone number for my Rolodex."

His Rolodex? I wondered. This unhoused man has a Rolodex? Why I assumed that Hakim was unhoused is difficult to know for certain. In part, it was due to the context in which he was working: many of the African-American men selling things on the block lived right there on the sidewalk. There was no way for me to distinguish easily between those vendors who were unhoused and those who were not, and I had never taken the time to think much about it. I gave him my telephone number and walked off to my appointment.

A few weeks later, I ran into an African-American man who had been in my first-year class at the New York University School of Law. Purely by coincidence, he told me that he was on his way to see a book vendor from whom he had been getting some of his reading material during the past year. It was Hakim.

I told my classmate about my interest in getting to know Hakim, and explained my reservations. He told me that he didn't think it would be as hard as I thought. Hakim had apparently gone through spells of sleeping in the parks during his time as a vendor, and sometimes stayed at my classmate's home with his wife and children.

A few days later my classmate brought him to meet me in the law-school lounge. When I told Hakim that I wanted to get to know him and the people at his vending table, he was circumspect, saying only that he would think about it. A few days later, he dropped off a brief but eloquent note at my apartment, explaining that he didn't think it was a good idea. "My suspicion is couched in the collective memory of a people who have been academically slandered for generations," he wrote. "African Americans are at a point where we have to be suspicious of people who want to tell stories about us."

During the next couple of months, Hakim and I saw each other about once a week or so on our own. On a few occasions we met and talked at the Cozy Soup & Burger on Broadway. It seemed that we had decided to get to know each other better.

Early one morning a few months later, I approached his table as he was setting up and asked, What are you doing working on Sixth Avenue in the first place?

I think there are a number of black folks in these corporate environments that have to make this decision, he replied. Some are not as extreme as I am. Some take it out on themselves in other ways.

It had not occurred to me that Hakim had come to work on the street from a corporate environment. Learning this about him has been significant as I have worked to understand his life on the street. In the universities where I teach, I meet many African-American students who believe that it will be very difficult for them to maintain their integrity while working in corporate life. Many of them have come to this conclusion by hearing of the experiences of relatives and friends who have already had problems; others have themselves sensed racial intolerance on campus.[2] Yet, in choosing to work on the street, Hakim had clearly made what would be a radical, if not entirely incomprehensible, decision by the standards of my African-American students. Once we had discussed some of these issues in depth over the subsequent weeks, Hakim volunteered that he felt comfortable letting me observe his table with the purpose of writing about it, and I began to do so.

He told me he was born Anthony E. Francis in Brooklyn, New York, in 1957. His parents, Harriet E. and Ansley J. Francis, had come to Brooklyn from the U.S. Virgin Islands; they separated when he was in grade school. He joined the Nation of Islam as a high-school student. Later, he attended Rutgers University, his tuition paid by grants and loans for disadvantaged youth. He told me he had completed his coursework but never received a diploma, because at the end of his senior year he owed about five hundred dollars to the school.

During college, he wrote articles for *The Black Voice*, a school newspaper, as well as for a national magazine called *The Black Collegian*.[3] Hakim said that, two years after finishing at Rutgers, he ended his affiliation with the American Muslim Mission, although he retained his adopted Muslim name. In his own words, "I could no longer walk in lockstep. I needed my longitude and latitude." Even though he is no longer a practicing Muslim, he often says he still feels a special respect for people who have chosen that path.

After college, he told me, he aspired to enter publishing, but was turned down for every position for which he applied. He then began a series of jobs as a proofreader in law, accounting, and investment-banking firms, including Peat Marwick, Drexel Burnham Lambert, and Robinson, Silverman. During this period, he says, he read hundreds of books and magazines and spent most of his free time in bookstores throughout the city, including the Liberation Bookstore, the well-known African-American bookstore in Harlem. He told me he was dismissed from Robinson, Silverman in 1991, during an employee review, for alleged incompetence according to some unnamed attorney at the firm.[4]

He had observed the sidewalk book vendors in Greenwich Village and believed that they had discovered a way to subsist in New York without buying into the "corporate-employee mind-set." As a vendor of black books, he decided, he would have work that was meaningful—that sustained him economically and intellectually. He began by working for one of the other vendors for a few days, and then borrowed money from a former roommate to start his own table.

When Hakim and his customers use the term "black books," he says, they are using a kind of shorthand for works on a constellation of related subjects and issues. These books may be geared toward helping people of African descent understand where they fit in; codifying the achievements of people of African descent; uncovering the history of African Americans, and of white racism; or helping African Americans develop the knowledge and pride necessary to participate in the wider society.

The publishers of such books often signal their prospective readers by printing the label "African-American Studies" or "Black Studies" on the upper left-hand corner of the back cover. These labels refer to an academic discipline that began to be codified only as recently as the 1960s.[5] Responding to pressure from the first significant population of blacks to be admitted to college, around the time of the Vietnam War, a handful of universities began to offer instruction in the history, literature, and sociology of Americans of African origin. Though there was some debate about the ultimate purpose of this intellectual endeavor, it developed in response to a real demand for deeper understanding of African and African-American history and culture. Courses appropriate to enhancing such understanding came to be recognized as an academic discipline. Though African-American studies reached African-American college students through academic channels, the emerging discipline also had—and continues to have—a secondary impact among African Americans outside the universities, through the influence of alternative distributive networks among the greater African-American population.

As Hakim and I got to know each other over the course of many months, he often greeted me warmly when I came to his table. Standing by, I would note the great range in the educational backgrounds of customers who come to his table to talk about books, and the way this range testifies to this secondary impact of African-American studies. It also illustrates how the very presence of books on the street tends to prompt discussions about moral and intellectual issues. Of course, one might find such discussions taking place in churches, mosques, chess clubs, coffeehouses, reading groups, and colleges, though I don't know if the range in education among the participants is as great in any of those places. On any given day at Hakim's table, one might encounter a high-school dropout, a blue-collar worker, a film student, a law professor, a jazz critic, or a teacher in a Muslim high school. (The last of these figures, Shair Abdul-Mani, has studied and mastered over five languages.) I also discovered that I was wrong in my initial impression that this was an exclusively "black zone." A wide range of whites often stopped at the table to talk about books, including—among many other—a psychologist, a retired shoemaker, and a graduate student in English at Columbia. I think this variety gives a good sense of the wide-reaching impact a book vendor can have on the lives of many people on the street.

Over four years, I witnessed hundreds of these conversations, and Hakim suggested that if I was going to write accurately about them I might put a tape recorder in the milk crate underneath his vending table for a few weeks.

One such conversation took place on a Saturday morning in July, when a young African-American man came up to the table. Jerome Miller, who was twenty-two years old (as he told me later), was on a break from his job at the corner Vitamin Shoppe, where he earned $6.50 per hour as a part-time stock clerk. Approximately five feet eight inches tall, with a goatee and sideburns, he generally wears a pair of Italian-leather hightop shoes, black slacks, and a blue button-down shirt with a T-shirt underneath. I had seen him on previous occasions but was not present for this discussion. It represents a kind of relationship I have observed many times, perhaps once every few weeks over my years on the block.

"How you doing?" Hakim asked. "You off today?"

"No, I'm working," responded Jerome.

"So some Saturdays you on and some Saturdays you off," declared Hakim.

"Yeah. Like not last week, but the week before I worked on Saturday."

There was silence for a few seconds as a siren blared on Sixth Avenue.

"The next book I think you should read is this—*Makes Me Wanna Holler,* by Nathan McCall," Hakim told Jerome. "And one of these days this week I got to get you more information, because, like we were talking about the other day, I want to see if I can get you into that GED program to finish your high-school education. I'm more than certain you can do it. There's a man I know in the neighborhood, I mentioned it to him, and he's willing to help. He's a teacher, and he knows a lot about the examination. So we got to get some more information and see how we can fit it in. Once you pass that GED exam, then you on the way."

"That's what I'd like to do," Jerome responded.

"There's an article in yesterday's *New York Times,*" Hakim continued. "Did you see the *Times* yesterday?"

"No," said Jerome.

"Well, the *Times* is something you need to read, and the Sunday *Times* has a wealth of information. It's thick and costs you about $2.50. In fact, what time you leave here on Saturday?"

"About 6:00 p.m."

"You can get it right here at the corner newsstand before you go home the night before. Because they have the bulldog edition the night before. They had an article in the business section about jobs, and the different kinds of preparation you need for these jobs. I think if you get the right kind of training you can do a lot better for yourself. You got to make that effort now to get that GED, and then probably get yourself into a junior college."

"The problem is that I used to go to this trade school in high school, but I didn't learn anything. It was bullshit. So I dropped out in ninth grade."

"How did your parents react?"

"It didn't matter. Nobody could tell me anything back then. I just got a job selling drugs for a while. Then I decided to get out of that."

"How old are you now?"

"Twenty-two."

"So how far do you think you can go, unless you plan on opening up a business of your own from scratch, with a ninth-grade education?"

Jerome stood silently.

"It's not that you dumb or anything," Hakim continued. "If you can read that book that I gave you last week, *Blacks in the White Establishment,*[6] and you did read it, and you did comprehend it, then you are clearly smart enough to do serious schoolwork. I think the problem before was that you might not have felt motivated due to the kind of classes you were taking."

"I need to have someone teach me something that I want to know about," responded Jerome.

"What is it that you want to know?" Hakim asked.

"Teach something that is interesting. I mean, I always say I'm gonna do it, but I end up straying away from it, you know what I mean?"

"Well, you didn't finish school, but you have managed to work and to read books on your own. How do you explain that?"

"I read books all the time, because they are interesting."

"What I'm trying to say is, you found school so nonmotivating when you were fourteen or fifteen years old, but you still managed to read. A lot of guys come down here who dropped out of high school in ninth grade but don't have a functional vocabulary like you definitely do have. Or their reading comprehension does not enable them to read the kind of books that I assign to you. I cannot assign these books to them."

"I just find myself wanting to know about things, and what goes on around me," said Jerome.

"So why don't you start thinking about converting wanting to know things into being able to sit in a class and get that work done?" Hakim asked.

"I can do that. And now I'm pretty sure it wouldn't be a problem. Another reason is that I got a little young one growing up."

"You got a little child? How old?"

"Two. A girl named Geneva. You want to give your kids the things you never had before."

"Are you still involved with the mother?"

"She's not up here right now."

"Where's she at?"

"Florida."

"So, obviously, your daughter is with her. So you don't see her that often."

"At first, you know what I'm saying, it was kind of hard. But I still didn't run away, 'cause I know I have to take care of my own. So I work and I send the money."

"What does your father do?"

"He used to be a carpenter the last time I talked to him, a year or two ago. He used to take care of us when we was younger, but everything changes. My parents haven't been together from when I was born. And my mother and I don't have a deep relationship. I mean, we talk, and I know she's my mother. I'm fortunate to just be alive, because she left me when I was a day old. And my father, I just don't know about it. We need to have a father-and-son discussion. I'm trying to have me and my daughter be close, so we can have discussions, because I don't want it to be like me and my father."

"Are your mom and dad still living here?"

"No. My father moved back to Jamaica, where he's from, and my mother moved down to Florida."

"Oh, she's in Florida as well? So how did you wind up staying up here by yourself? You got other relatives here?"

"You know how black families is. They don't really stick together."

"You think so?"

"Yeah. I mean, my family, they don't really stick together. If they would stick together they could have anything they want. But if they don't stick together there's nothing they could accomplish like that. My mom's got four of us, two boys and two girls. Put it like this—they claims I'm the bad one, or whatever."

"Well, are you?"

"I used to be. I mean, I don't think I'm a bad one. I didn't really follow the way, like natural, like everybody else. I've always been the rebellious type. Even when I was younger, I've been on my own. Even when my mom was there or whatever, I always depend on myself, buy my own self my clothes or whatever."

"You pay your own rent?"

"Yeah. I do."

"So, even though you didn't finish school, you still, to a large extent, responsible. What do you ultimately want to do?"

"I'd like to go into my own business."

"What kind of business?"

"I want to have a club and a restaurant. A place for recreation, where people can hang out."

"Yeah. As far as I'm concerned, you twenty-two years old. And what I'm advising you to do right now is think about trying to get yourself into a state of mind where you can divide your time in such a way that you have time to eat, work, and study for this GED exam. There's other men in this neighborhood who have repeatedly asked me about this, and I have helped them pass this exam. And I will continue to assign you books from my table that will help you bring your level of comprehension to another level."

"I'll get back with you. I have to go back to work," said Jerome.

"All right," Hakim responded.

A few weeks after this conversation, I saw Jerome through the window of The Vitamin Shoppe wiping down some shelves. It occurred to me that I might try to find out what he thought of his interactions with Hakim, and what role he thought books and reading played in his life. A couple of days later, when he was wandering through Greenwich Village on a day off from work, I introduced myself to him, and he said that he recognized me from the neighborhood. I explained my work and asked if we could sit down and talk. We went to the C3 Restaurant.

"I used to watch him through the window of The Vitamin Shoppe when I was working," he began. "A few times it was him and these people across the street having a conversation, and I knew I should be a part of the conversation, but I'm working. I know it's a deep conversation, because the people have been there for twenty or thirty minutes, so they have to be discussing something that's really deep. One day I was passing by and he was having a conversation with this older black guy who was saying that all black kids were bad, and I was trying to tell him that it ain't all of us that is the same way—that maybe you have two out of ten that was bad. Hakim didn't want to get into it, because he knew the guy was kind of ignorant. And I recognized that Hakim was selling black books, and I was very interested in black books, and I saw a book that I liked, so I picked it up. That's when we got started talking about how black youth was growing up today, and basically that's how it got started."

"What are black books?"

"Well, it teaches you about yourself and how white people look at you. It teaches you stuff that white people don't teach you. I didn't really know anything about myself, because they basically don't teach nothing like that in school. You know what I'm saying? Hakim doesn't only sell black books. He also sells white fictions or whatever. He gotta do what he gotta do to pay the bills."

"What books on his table were of interest to you?"

"The book by Haki Mahdabuti called *Black Men: Young, Dangerous, and Obsolete,* or something like that. I just liked the title and the picture on the cover, of a face of a man and a little girl. So I picked it up and I asked him what he thought about the book. I decided to get the book because of what he thought about it. 'Cause Hakim be about consciousness, and at this point in time you gotta be about consciousness. Then I brought it home and started reading it. And a lot of the stuff in there I could relate to. And it gives you reference to other books."

"Had you been reading a lot before you went to his table?"

"Not really. I think that was maybe the first book I started reading. I could talk to Hakim about the books. Because in the bookstore they have a lot of arrogance. They have their Ph.D. or whatever their title may be, and they arrogant in a certain way. But at his table we could talk about the books."

"You feel more comfortable with a street vendor than in a bookstore?"

"You can talk to the vendor, because he sits there and he sees what goes on. He sees all that. And people talk to him more and relate. A lot of people, they don't want to stop in no bookstore, because it's easier for them to conversate with a guy on the street and to see what he thinks about the book. That's why I would rather buy books from the guys on the street than in the stores."

"How many books have you read in your life?"

"I've only read the books I read since I met Hakim. He had a little influence on me. He told me to go back to school. He knows what he's talking about. He's been there. So I can relate to him, 'cause he's been through a lot of stuff. The way I see it is, a lot of the younger generation been through the same stuff like the older generation. That's the way you learn from them, because they've been there before."

"Is it hard for you to afford to buy books?"

"No. I would rather buy a book than buy clothes. Because I'm getting knowledge. I have this yearning for reading. I never really had it before. It's just something that came over me when I saw those books on the street. Because I know myself, but I don't really know much about myself. Reading a book, I could see what other people are talking about."

"When do you read?"

"I read on the train. Because I don't do anything else really than go to work and come home. So I read on the train."

"Do you talk to any other book vendors in the city?"

"There's this Muslim guy who sets up near my subway station in the Bronx, by the Number 5, Dyre Avenue stop. Yeah, we talked once. I got a book called *Malcolm Speaks* from him."

"What book did you buy next from Hakim?"

"He assigned me another book from his table called *Blacks in the White Establishment.* It's about inner-city kids going to prep schools and graduating. Tell you the truth, a lot of the kids in my neighborhood, even though they bad, if you give them a way to go forth, they will go forth. So that's what me and Hakim a lot of times talk about. He sees what goes on just like I see what goes on. That's why I try to listen to whatever he tells me. My parents would try to tell me what to do, but I never listen, so I end up in the predicament that I'm in. So I try to listen to what he has to say."

"What did you read next?"

"I read *Stolen Legacy*. It goes back to Aristotle and all these other people from back then. 'Cause it's, like—it's funny that a lot of the things that black people do never show up. It's like we never brought anything to the table. And that's not right. Because we brought as much as anybody else ever brought to the table. We've been in America before a lot of people, and the way we get treated in America is not right. And it teaches you how Egypt got stolen from a part of Africa. 'Cause they consider Egypt not a part of Africa now. Which it *is* a part of Africa. It's like you taking a seed from an orange and you saying it's not a part of the orange. So that's a part of Africa.

"It teaches you about yourself. Like where you come from, way back. And it lets you know you have a self-worth in yourself. Once you start reading black books, you learn about yourself more. And not just following what everybody else thinks. Because, if you read what society says, then being black is like the sin of the earth, man."

"Who do you talk about books with, other than Hakim?"

"I have a roommate named Troy. Me and him live in a basement of this house in the Bronx. He works at Woolworth's. I bring books to him and I tell him to read them and he says he's gonna read them. I don't know, maybe he's not interested. But I have another friend who just got out of prison, and we talk a lot about books. He told me he was reading this book to his son. So then we got into a discussion about books. When I went to his house, I brought all my books with me. Then he said he got a lot of books, too. Because when he was in jail there was nothing better to do than read books. So he went up into his closet and was showing me his books. And I got this one from him, *From Superman to Man,* by J. A. Rogers.[7] And he had this other book I took from him called *Catch a Fire,* about Bob Marley and reggae music.[8] So after that we was talking about books. Because he was saying he has to teach his son about himself. Because a lot of our kids know nothing about themselves."

After my conversation with Jerome, I left New York for a few months. On my next trip back to the city, I asked Hakim how Jerome was doing, and used the conversation as an opportunity to find out how he saw his relationship with the young man.

"Jerome was here today. He stopped by during his brief break from The Vitamin Shoppe. From the very moment that we had our initial conversations, there was this level of trust being developed. And this is how relationships develop with many young black men. I started asking him questions about his life, what he hoped to accomplish in life, and he started to reflect on these things and open up and tell me a lot more about himself. I think what made him important to me was that I saw a significant level of genuineness in his discussion about himself that made me respect him. Furthermore, he seemed to be willing to work. He wasn't necessarily even saying to me, as some of these young kids say, that racism is the complete and total barrier, and that he therefore can't make progress. And furthermore, he was willing to listen to what I had to say."

"Were your discussions mainly about the books he bought?"

"No. After talking to him for a while, I came to the conclusion that I would help him in any way I could. On Friday, he and I were talking about what he should do if he encounters the police. And I was explaining to him that even in situations when you know you're right, you try to be respectful to these people and as calm as possible. That there's times when you realize that the reason you have to go through all of this is because you are a black man. But I told him that petitions and slogans will not bring you back to life. There's levels of common sense that I have to teach sometimes."

"What are black books, and how important are they to the intellectual development of men like Jerome?"

"They are books that emanate out of what is considered the black experience. With Jerome, I suspect they are very important. The other day he had a book called *Up from Slavery.*[9] For Jerome, what these books represent is a kind of history of navigation through the society. That's how I see these books. What went on and how did said person confront said situation, and in effect who were the victims and who were vanquished. No matter what these books really are, what they talk about, basically that is what these books for a lot of these guys represent, a point of black social navigation in the white society, be it history or economics or whatever the case may be. The first book Jerome bought was *Black Men,* by Haki Mahdabuti. That is what I think it means to him: How do I wake up in the morning and try to make progress, and how did other people do this? I think that's what they represent for a lot of these young guys that come here."

"Do you think that these books are in any sense counterproductive or dangerous for a kid that doesn't have a good grasp of history?"

"It's complicated, depending on how the individual chooses to reconcile what I consider to be a rather epic racial history in this country. There are a lot of black folk who come to these books hoping to find the kind of affirmative and in many cases mythic black self. I believe that, if the serious reading moves one to a point where he or she is able to make determinations of the difference between fact and propaganda, that's another thing. Jerome is not yet at that point. He is at the fundamental level, where he is trying to find out something about himself. It is very clear from my conversations with Jerome that he has not yet read a lot of what is considered to be the classic work in African-American literature or African-American thought. But that's okay. Because people gotta start where they are.

"Where I come in at is the ability to say, 'Okay, listen, that's fine, but now you gotta look at this and this and this.' That's why you got to be very careful and responsible about how you deal with people, particularly in this realm that I'm in. I could come down here and rant and rave and carry on and say, 'Well, listen, these books are just the greatest thing going on since people put pen to paper.' Like, some of these people might pick up some of these books and say, 'We're descendants of kings and queens.' And I might interject and say, 'Does that mean all of us were? Or maybe some of us? A few of us?' What this does is, it brings to bear a level of critical thinking, of critical evolution, so that we don't create a kind of mythic black history to act as a countervailing thrust to a white history that has basically made black folks into caricatures or a form of scholastic-appendix matter.

"People like Jerome come here and they're looking to find something that affirms what they perceive 'themselves' to be, or what they once were. So you got to work with them. But that is why I say to Jerome, 'You have to read as widely as possible, and, most importantly, you need to learn how to think and raise questions and ask yourself critical questions in order to arrive at conclusions about information and what you are reading and not to accept stuff.' There's so much I do not know. The reason that I know what I know is because there were folks up the road who were very patient and said, "You need to read this book,' or "You need to take a peek at this,' or "You need to examine or re-examine this book.' "

"Whatever happened with the GED? Did he ever follow up on your suggestion that he get his high-school-equivalency degree?"

"On Saturday, we talked about the GED thing again. I said, 'I don't want to seem like I'm bugging you about this, but I have a [telephone] number here for a guy who teaches these classes to prepare you for the test.' I think that, when Jerome wants to take that step, he'll take it. I think it becomes a little counterproductive to proselytize. So I talk to him and prod him. And I also told him that I know it's tough. You not getting paid a lot of money. But if you can get in the program and if you have to buy books and stuff, I'll help you buy the books."

"He seems a little reluctant to do it."

"Very often people find themselves at a certain place in life and they figure there's no hope. There's nothing else out here you can do. Maybe nobody ever told him that 'Yes, you twenty-two years old, but you still *can* do this, and there's still light at the end of the tunnel.' I said, 'Listen, I know there's things that you going through with you family, things have been rough, but you still have time to do a lot of things. You a young man. You a lot younger than I am. And quite frankly, I think you have the intelligence to undertake this and do this. And if so, you can finish this GED thing and find yourself in a junior college, and who knows where you can go from there.' But from my end, I'm also mindful of not trying to push him. Because I don't want him to think that every time I come here that this guy's telling me what to do."

"How do you get young men to open up to you?"

"Well, you know, some days it is more easy than others. It could be by a smile or an inflection in your voice. Or the way in which you answer a question. Or, quite frankly, the way in which you induce conversation. As I have developed a relationship with men like Jerome, they start to talk to me about their father and mother and the chasm between them. And I identify with that, because, when I was growing up, my father and mother didn't make it, and it was my mother who raised all of us. So I can identify very, very deeply with him."

When Hakim tries to let Jerome know, "You twenty-two years old, but you still *can* do this," he is providing a level of personal support and encouragement at present found in few or none of the family relations and institutions in Jerome's life. At the same time, it is possible that, by defying certain social norms and working outside the institutions of the formal economy, Hakim affects young black men like Jerome less significantly than he otherwise might: if he took a job as a schoolteacher, he might be able to affect the lives of many more children. But Hakim believes that he cannot work within those institutions. In any case, he contributes to social cohesion by giving needed support to men like Jerome.

Jerome is an "at-risk youth," facing substantial needs that are not being met by the institutions of American society. For young black men who have not completed high school, the prospects are especially bleak (less than 60 percent are employed in the formal economy),[10] and the numbers in prison, on parole, or on probation are high (higher than 40 percent for males between 18 and 24 years old).[11]

The extent to which young people who grow up in single-parent families are particularly at risk is a politically charged issue, because many scholars are uncomfortable with the idea that men are necessary to raise healthy children.[12] Sara McLanahan and Gary Sandefur indicate in *Growing Up with a Single Parent* that low income is the most important factor in the problems of children who grow up without a father, giving some support to these feminist scholars.[13] They also report that the remainder of the disadvantage from such an upbringing stems from "inadequate parental guidance and attention."[14] This may simply be a matter of having less parenting (another finding not necessarily in conflict with those who wish to rethink the family). Much of the effect they note comes from the fact that having one parent "reduce[s] a child's access to social capital outside the family by weakening connections to other adults and institutions in the community that would have been available to the child had the relationship with the father remained intact.'[15]

Such developmental risks are not new, and as a result informal relationships between older men and children and young adults have traditionally been important in African-American communities, where formal ties between fathers and their children have historically been weak. Though this is not necessarily a uniquely African-American tradition, in African-American communities such informal mentors are known as "old heads." In his firsthand study of the Philadelphia African-American residential areas, *Streetwise,* Elijah Anderson explains, "The male old head's role is to teach, support, encourage, and in effect, socialize young men to meet their responsibilities with regard to the work ethic, family life, the law, and decency," and this can also apply to the socialization of young women.[16] Here on the sidewalk of Greenwich Village, Hakim was assuming the recognizable old-head role by telling Jerome not to give up.

Though sociologists have long referred to role models, old heads, and mentoring, they have always provided evidence for these relationships with nostalgic stories and reminiscences. Through this present-day documentary account, we can better understand the nature of the old-head/young-man relationship. It is not necessarily one of authority or domination: commands are not given, and obedience is not expected. The special nature of this relationship is better understood as an example of what the German sociologist Max Weber called "the exercise of 'influence' over other persons."[17] If the young boy complies with the old head's suggestions, he does so voluntarily. His decision to do so may be based on a rational calculation of the advantage to his own life, but not on a calculation related to the power of the old head to make him suffer in any way if he does not comply. In his old-head role, Hakim is not shy about reprimanding a younger person for failing to live up to high standards; he is not afraid to give advice based on the wisdom of experience or learning. For Jerome, Hakim is a symbol of precisely those values necessary to live in accordance with ideals of self-worth.

One aspect of such "influence" as it is developed on the sidewalk is that specific advice need not be followed for the relationship to maintain itself through repeated visits to the table. The continuing discussion between Hakim and Jerome regarding the GED has not led Jerome to take a GED course. The old head's specific advice may be less important to the young man than the very fact that he has a conversation about his life with an older man who is willing to listen. Likewise, though Hakim would like to see Jerome take the test and improve the material circumstances of his life, he also feels satisfied that Jerome wants to listen and talk. The relationship serves an important purpose in a world where, according to Hakim's testimony, many young persons do not want to listen to him.

In fact, the expectation of continued discussion, rather than compliance with authoritative commands, seems to be the marker of many stable relationships between Hakim and young persons on the sidewalk. Advice is usually easier to give than to take; in order for such relationships to be stable, it may be necessary for Hakim to demonstrate a certain tolerance when his advice goes untaken. Besides, even if Jerome does ultimately follow Hakim's advice, it is likely that a long period of apparent inactivity would precede any visible action. For Jerome to accept Hakim's advice on the GED, he would have to change his work schedule in a manner that might not be acceptable to his bosses. And even if Hakim helps him with some of his expenses, the GED course would likely result in other costs.

What is the basis of Hakim's influence? The old head has knowledge deriving from experience—i.e., wisdom. Jerome says about Hakim, "He knows what he's talking about. He's been there," indicating that he is willing to listen to the older man because of some fundamental experience Hakim can draw upon in legitimating his worldview. But this experience does not always, in and of itself, serve as the final source of legitimacy. Rather, in many cases, the old head makes arguments that can be legitimized by rational means. When Hakim tells Jerome to read the *Times,* for example, he is not doing so merely out of a general claim based on his experience. He goes on to legitimize the claim by explaining how a particular article provides information about the job market that is relevant to the young man's life. In fact, such advice demonstrates that Hakim is not simply relying on his own experience in the job market, or that of his generation, but is giving advice based on some of the best data about the structure of contemporary American society.

Finally, Hakim's influence seems also to derive from the fact that, to use Jerome's words, he is "about consciousness." The young man's statement derives from inferences he makes about Hakim based on conversations about "black books." He believes that Hakim is a man who sees the advancement of African Americans as a value *per se.*

In writing *Streetwise,* Anderson discovered that, "as economic and social circumstances of the urban ghetto have changed, the traditional old head has been losing prestige and credibility as a role model." This is because it is difficult for old heads who learned their lessons about life in a manufacturing economy to legitimize their claims to authority when the street economy poses a more attractive alternative, given the decline in manufacturing jobs: Young men do not possess the alternatives they once did. And it is difficult for young men to believe in the lessons of the old head when the institutional paths to fulfill those lessons have been eroded. As one young man quoted by Anderson says of the old heads, "They don't understand the way the world really is."

In recent years, other analysts have described in detail the decline of community institutions like churches and YMCAs within high-poverty areas as the working- and middle-class old heads described by Anderson have moved out of these districts. In his influential study *When Work Disappears,* the sociologist William Julius Wilson describes the devastation of those institutional infrastructures that he and his staff found in the highest-poverty neighborhoods, such as the Bronx area Jerome comes from. When those institutions go, the developmental hazards associated with the absence of relations between fathers and children are certainly exacerbated. Wilson emphasizes that major structural transformations in the economic and political order will be required if these problems are to be solved.

Anderson reports that one place young people do turn within the context of the current vacuum is what he calls the "new old head"—a person who derives his legitimacy from the "influx of the drug culture. . . . The emerging old head is younger and may be the product of a street gang, making money fast and scorning the law and traditional values."[18]

The image of urban social change as a movement from the old head of the formal economy to the old head of the underground economy leaves open the question of what other kinds of mentoring relationships between older and younger men have emerged in the face of the decline of the industrial economy and the rise of the "new urban poor." In his contribution to the life of the sidewalk, Hakim is an old head who is located squarely in the new urban economy, imparting lessons about life that seem to have direct meaning and application for a young man from a high-poverty area. Though the exact meaning of Hakim's life is not necessarily clear, his presence emphasizes that gang leaders and drug dealers are not the only alternatives to the traditional old head. With that in mind, I asked Hakim what lessons he thinks his life as a street vendor can teach to a young man like Jerome who is working in the formal economy.

"I don't necessarily know if my life is a model for him, depending on what it is he thinks he has to do. I came to this sidewalk by choice, not by force. If I was walking up the street nonchalantly, and let's say I was a black lawyer at one of these high-priced law firms in New York City, the same question could be posed: how is the existence of that lawyer a model for Jerome? He might not be able to relate to the lawyer. So I think that the fact that I'm on the sidewalk may not be the model. What is the model is what I try to explain to him. There were times when people who worked for GM, in the factory, might have been good models. But those factory jobs are gone. So what you have to impart to a young guy is that they have to have diverse skills and flexibility. My own experience is that I had to confront a very painful need to figure out how to exist economically without having to go and apply for what is considered a 'job.' And I think part of the answer for these young people lies there. They have to muster up creative ideas and find ways to finance these ideas to create small little entrepreneurial enclaves so that they can have some kind of economic futures."

"But how can Jerome have faith in what you are telling him to do? Even if he never took any of your advice about finishing high school, he could still do what you do—work on the sidewalk."

"I've had the luxury—if you want to call it the luxury—of working in the formal economy, and of working at certain companies that required a certain level of training, however rudimentary, and a certain level of education. And if I decided right now to leave these sidewalks, throw on a suit, and have to go and talk to people at one of these office buildings in the formal economy, I'm capable of doing that. What I'm trying to explain to Jerome is, you make choices in life, but at the same time what you try to do in spite of certain setbacks is prepare yourself for the next step, no matter how arduous it might seem. I'm telling him that, even if I was a crack addict sitting on the sidewalk, there are possibilities for you. I'm not necessarily the barometer for your possibilities, but the fact is that you have a certain level of potential if you go and use it.

"When I think about very successful black folk, some of these people are very important academics, bankers, lawyers, and journalists. In many cases these persons are so busy just trying to sustain themselves and do what they have to do, they don't have time for people like me, and forget about a guy like Jerome. I have problems with this idea of a role model, because 'role model' generally has meant, at least by the media's definition, some of these very high-profile people, but the truth of the matter is that the little people who really have proved catalytic to a lot of very successful people hardly ever get talked about, or even make it into the sweep of history."

Hakim could not have been unaware of his own importance to young men like Jerome when he made reference to the influence of those "little people." He also knows that sidewalk contacts of the kind depicted here cannot substitute for the larger transformations and rebuilding of family, institutions, and neighborhoods.[19] But just as there is no substitute for wholesome institutional structures, so there is no substitute for the power of the informal social relations that constitute a wholesome sidewalk life and society. Indeed, it is important to recognize the importance of the informal activity of public characters like Hakim. As Jane Jacobs wrote in *The Death and Life of Great American Cities,* the "first fundamental lesson of successful city life . . . [is] that people must take a modicum of public responsibility for each other even if they have no ties to each other. . . . The essence of this responsibility is that you do it without being hired."

Notes

1. See Patricia Williams, *The Alchemy of Race and Rights* (Cambridge, Mass.: Harvard University Press, 1991); Regina Austin, "Social Inequality, Physical Restraints on Mobility, and the Black Public Sphere," a paper presented at "*An American Dilemma* Revisited: Fiftieth Anniversary Conference," Harvard University, September 29, 1995; Regina Austin, "An Honest Living: Street Vendors, Municipal Regulation, and the Black Public Sphere," *Yale Law Journal* 10, no. 8 (June 1994).

2. See Joe R. Feagin, Hernan Vera, and Nikitah Imani, *The Agony of Education: Black Students at White Colleges and Universities* (New York: Routledge, 1996); Walter R. Allen, Edgar Epps, and Nesha Z. Haniff, *College in Black and White* (Albany: SUNY Press, 1991), p. 12. For some of the most influential popular books about the variety of experiences of African Americans in the workplace, see Jill Nelson, *Volunteer Slavery: My Authentic Negro Experience* (Chicago: Noble Press, 1993); Nathan McCall, *Makes Me Wanna Holler* (New York: Simon & Schuster, 1993); Sara Lawrence Lightfoot, *I've Known Rivers* (New York: Addison Wesley, 1994); Brent Staples, *Parallel Time* (New York: Pantheon, 1994).

3. I have looked up his article in that magazine, "None Dare Call It Treason: Black Greeks," which won a 1982 Unity Award in Media, an award given annually by Lincoln University. The article argued that African Americans must cease their membership in all Greek-lettered fraternities and sororities.

4. Although I have never doubted any of the things Hakim told me about his life, in conducting this study I have looked upon it as my responsibility to check salient things people tell me about themselves before reporting them. (Usually my need to check things that I regarded as salient, of course, said something more about me than about them.) I wanted to make sure that he had attended Rutgers and worked for all those years in the formal economy. He thought this was reasonable in light of my project and agreed to request his college records as well as official employment information from the last firm he worked at. Everything checked out. I have seen Hakim's final transcript from Rutgers University, indicating that he completed his B.A. According to an official letter on firm stationery, he worked at Robinson, Silverman as a proofreader on the latenight shift, from 9:00 p.m. to 4:00 a.m., from April 25, 1988, through January 18, 1991. This letter to Hakim from the director of administrative services states that the firm will provide no information beyond verifying the dates and times of his employment.

5. See Houston Baker, *Rap, Black Studies, and the Academy* (Chicago: University of Chicago Press, 1993).

6. G. William Domhoff, *Blacks in the White Establishment: A Study of Race and Class in America* (New Haven: Yale University Press, 1991).

7. J. A. Rogers, *From Superman to Man* (Freeport, N.Y.: Books for Libraries Press, 1972).

8. Timothy Holt, *Catch a Fire: The Life of Bob Marley* (New York: Holt, Rinehart and Winston, 1983).

9. Booker T. Washington, *Up from Slavery* (New York: Dover Publications, 1995).

10. Ronald B. Mincy, *Nurturing Young Black Males: Challenges to Agencies, Programs, and Social Policy* (Washington, D.C.: Urban Institute, 1994), p. 12.

11. Ibid.

12. Judith Stacey, *In the Name of the Family: Rethinking Family Values in the Postmodern Age* (Boston: Beacon Press, 1996).

13. Sara McLanahan and Gary Sandefur, *Growing Up with a Single Parent* (Cambridge, Mass.: Harvard University Press, 1994).
14. Ibid., p. 3.
15. Ibid., p. 5.
16. Elijah Anderson, *Streetwise* (Chicago: University of Chicago Press, 1990), p. 69.
17. Max Weber, *Economy and Society,* Vol. 1 (Berkeley: University of California Press, 1978), p. 212.
18. Anderson, *Streetwise,* p. 72.
19. See William Julius Wilson, *When Work Disappears* (New York: Alfred A. Knopf, 1997).

15

The Thin Red Line

JENNIFER EGAN

One Saturday night in January, Jill McArdle went to a party some distance from her home in West Beverly, a fiercely Irish enclave on Chicago's South Side. She was anxious before setting out; she'd been having a hard time in social situations—parties, especially. At 5 feet 10 inches with long blond hair, green eyes and an underbite that often makes her look as if she's half-smiling, Jill cuts an imposing figure for 16; she is the sort of girl boys notice instantly and are sometimes afraid of. And the fear is mutual, despite her air of confidence.

Jill's troubles begin with her own desire to make everyone happy, a guiding principle that yields mixed results in the flirtatious, beer-swilling atmosphere of teenage parties. "I feel I have to be all cute and sexy for these boys," she says. "And the next morning when I realize what a fool I looked like, it's the worst feeling ever. . . . 'Oh God, what did I do? Was I flirting with that boy? Is his girlfriend in school tomorrow going to give me a hard time? Are they all going to hate me?'"

Watching Jill in action, you would never guess she was prone to this sort of self-scrutiny. Winner of her cheerleading squad's coveted Spirit Award last year, she is part of a Catholic-school crowd consisting mostly of fellow cheerleaders and the male athletes they cheer for, clean-cut kids who congregate in basement rec rooms of spare, working-class houses where hockey sticks hang on the walls and a fish tank sometimes bubbles in one corner. Jill is a popular, even dominating presence at these parties; once she introduced a series of guys to me with the phrase, "This is my boy," her arm slung across the shoulders of some shy youth in a baseball cap, usually shorter than she, whose name invariably seemed to be Kevin or Patrick.

But in truth, the pressures of adolescence have wreaked extraordinary havoc in Jill's life. "Around my house there's this park, and there used to be like a hundred kids hanging out up there," she says, recalling her first year in high school, two years ago. "And the boys would say stuff to me that was so disgusting . . . perverted stuff, and I'd just be so embarrassed. But the older girls assumed that I was a slut. . . . They'd give me dirty looks in school." Blaming herself for having somehow provoked these reactions, Jill began to feel ashamed and isolated. Her unease spiraled into panic in the spring of that year, when a boy she'd trusted began spreading lies about her. "He goes and tells all of his friends that I did all this sexual stuff with him, and I was just blown away. It made me feel dirty, like I was absolutely nothing."

Jill, then 14, found herself moved to do something she had never done before. "I was in the bathroom going completely crazy, just bawling my eyes out, and I think my mom was wallpapering—there was a wallpaper cutter there. I had so much anxiety, I couldn't concentrate on anything until I somehow let that out, and not being able to let it out in words, I took the razor and started cutting my leg and I got excited about seeing my blood. It felt good to see the blood coming out, like that was my other pain leaving, too. It felt right and it felt good for me to let it out that way."

Jill had made a galvanizing discovery: cutting herself could temporarily ease her emotional distress. It became a habit. Once, she left school early, sat in an alley and carved "Life Sucks" into her leg with the point of a compass. Eventually, her friends got wind of her behavior and told her parents, who were frightened and mystified. They took Jill to Children's Memorial Hospital, where she was treated for depression and put on Prozac, which she took for a few months until she felt better. By last summer she was cutting again in secret and also burning—mostly her upper thighs, where her mother, who by now was anxiously monitoring Jill's behavior, wouldn't see the cuts if she emerged from the family bathroom in a towel. Last summer, Jill wore boxers over her bathing suit even to swim. By January, her state was so precarious that one bad night would have the power to devastate her.

No one recognized Jill's behavior as self-mutilation, as it is clinically known (other names include self-injury, self-harm, self-abuse and the misnomer delicate self-cutting), a disorder that is not new but, because it is finally being properly identified and better understood, is suddenly getting attention. Princess Diana shocked people by admitting that she cut herself during her unhappy marriage. Johnny Depp has publicly revealed that his arms bear scars from self-inflicted wounds. The plot of "Female Perversions," a recent movie that fictionalized the book of the same name by Louise Kaplan, a psychiatrist, hinges on the discovery of a young girl cutting herself. And Steven Levenkron, a psychotherapist who wrote a best-selling novel in the 1970's about an anorexic, recently published "The Luckiest Girl in the World," about a teen-age self-injurer.

"I'm afraid, here we go again," Levenkron says, likening the prevalence of self-injury to that of anorexia. "Self-injury is probably a bit epidemic." Dr. Armando Favazza, a professor of psychiatry at the University of Missouri-Columbia medical school, estimates the number of sufferers at 750 per 100,000 Americans, or close to two million, but suggests that the actual figure may be higher.

Long dismissed by the psychiatric community as merely a symptom of other disorders—notably borderline personality disorder—self-mutilation is generating new interest as a subject of study. Dr. Barbara Stanley of the New York State Psychiatric Institute explains: "Some of us said, maybe we shouldn't be focusing so much on diagnostic studies. . . . Maybe this behavior means something unto itself."

Indeed it does. Favazza, whose book "Bodies Under Siege" was the first to comprehensively explore self-mutilation, defines it as "the direct, deliberate destruction or alteration of one's own body tissue without conscious suicidal intent." His numbers apply to what he calls "moderate/ superficial self-mutilation" like Jill's, rather than involuntary acts like the head banging of autistic or retarded people, or "coarse" self-mutilations like the eye enucleations and self-castrations that are occasionally performed by psychotics. Moderate self-mutilation can include cutting, burning, plucking hairs from the head and body (known as trichotillomania), bone breaking, head banging, needle poking, skin scratching or rubbing glass into the skin.

The fact that awareness of self-mutilation is growing at a time when tattooing, piercing, scarification and branding are on the rise has not been lost on researchers. While experts disagree on the relationship between the behaviors, the increasing popularity of body modification among teenagers, coupled with the two million people injuring in secret, begins to make us look like a nation obsessed with cutting. Marilee Strong, who interviewed nearly 100 injurers for her book, "A Bright Red Scream," to be published in 1998, calls it "the addiction of the 90's."

On that Saturday night in January, despite Jill's anxious resolutions, things at the party ultimately went awry. "It was really late," she says, "and I was supposed to stay at my best friend's house, but she left and I didn't go with her. I was drunk, and it was me down there in the basement with all these boys. . . . I'd walk by and they'd grab my butt or something, so I sat on a chair in the corner. And they tipped the chair over and made me fall off of it."

Realizing she was in a situation she would punish herself for later, Jill went upstairs and tried in vain to get a friend to leave the party with her. She had nowhere to stay—no way to get home without calling her parents—so she ended up at the home of her friend's brother, who was in his 20's and lived near the party. This proved to be another mistake. "I wake up there the next morning, and these guys were basically dirty 20-year-olds," she says, "and they tell me: 'You want a job living here with us? We'll pay you a hundred bucks if you strip for us once a week.' . . . I was just like: 'I have to go home! I have to go home!'"

But by now, a cycle of shame and self-blame was already in motion. On finally arriving at the two-story brick house where she lives with her parents and brothers (one older, one younger), Jill learned that she was being grounded for not having called home the night before. Her bedroom, right off the kitchen, is a small, makeshift room with accordion doors that do not seal off the noise from the rest of the house. "All Sunday I just slept and slept, and I was just so depressed, so disgusted with myself. . . . I felt like the dirtiest thing ever because of everything that had happened the night before."

For all her popularity, Jill felt too fragile that morning to ask her friends for reassurance. "I feel really inferior to them, like they're so much better at everything than me," she says of the other cheerleaders. "I feel like I have to be the pleaser, and I can never do anything wrong. When I fail to make other people happy, I get so angry with myself."

That Sunday, no one was happy with Jill: her parents, the friend whose house she hadn't slept at and, in her fearful imagination, countless older girls who by now had heard of her sloppy conduct at the party and were waiting to pounce. "Monday morning came and I was scared to death to have to go to school and see people," she says. "I started cutting myself. First I used a knife—I was in the bathroom doing it and then I told my mom because I was scared. She was like, 'Why the hell are you doing this? You're going to give me and your father a heart attack: . . . She took the knife away. So then I took a candle holder and went outside and cracked it against the ground and took a piece of glass and started cutting myself with that, and then I took fingernail clippers and was trying to dig at my skin and like pull it off, but it didn't help anymore, it wasn't working. . . . That night, I was like, 'My mom is so mad at me, she doesn't even care that I was doing this,' so that's when I took all the aspirin."

Jill isn't sure how many aspirin she took, but estimates it was around 30. "That night was like the scariest night in my life," she says. "I was puking and sweating and had ringing in my ears and I couldn't focus on anything." Still, she slept through a second day before telling her parents what was really ailing her. They rushed her to a hospital, where she wound up in intensive care for three days with arrhythmia while IV's flushed out her system, and she was lucky not to have permanently damaged her liver.

"That was very shocking, to think that she was going through so much pain without us being aware of it," says her father, Jim McArdle, a ruddy-faced police lieutenant with a soft voice, who chooses his words carefully. "There's a ton of denial," he admits. "It's like: 'It happened once, it's never going to happen again. It happened twice, it's not going to happen three times.' The third time you're like. . . ." He trails off helplessly.

Self-injury rarely stops after two or three incidents. According to the only large-scale survey ever taken of self-injurers (240 American females), in 1989, the average practitioner begins at 14—as Jill did—and continues injuring, often with increasing severity into her late 20's. Generally white, she is also likely to suffer from other compulsive disorders like bulimia or alcoholism. Dr. Jan Hart, who surveyed 87 high-functioning self-injurers for her 1996 doctoral dissertation at U.C.L.A., found their most common professions to be teacher and nurse, followed by manager.

The notion of teachers, nurses and high-school students like Jill seeking out ways to hurt themselves in a culture where the avoidance of pain and discomfort is a virtual obsession may seem paradoxical. But it isn't. People harm themselves because it makes them feel better; they use physical pain to obfuscate a deeper, more intolerable psychic pain associated with feelings of anger, sadness or abandonment. Often, the injury is used to relieve the pressure or hysteria these emotions can cause, as it did for Jill; it can also jolt people out of states of numbness and emptiness—it can make them feel alive.

These mood-regulating effects, along with a certain addictive quality (over time, the injurer usually must hurt herself more frequently and more violently to achieve the same degree of relief) have prompted many clinicians to speculate that cutting, for example, releases the body's own opiates, known as betaendorphins. According to Lisa Cross, a New Haven psychotherapist who has treated self-injurers, patients have for centuries described the sensation of being bled in the same terms of relief and release as she hears from self-injurers. And people who have been professionally scarred or pierced sometimes describe feeling high from the experience.

Women seeking treatment for self-injury far outnumber men. There are many speculations as to why this might be, the most common of which is that women are more likely to turn their anger inward. Dusty Miller, author of "Women Who Hurt Themselves," believes that self-injury reflects a culturally sanctioned antagonism between women and their bodies: "Our bodies are always too fat, our breasts are too small. . . . The body becomes the object of our own violence."

But the fact that few men are treated for self-injury doesn't mean they aren't hurting themselves, too. Among adolescent injurers, the ratio of boys to girls is near equal, and cutting is rampant among both male and female prisoners. Self-Mutilators Anonymous, a New York support group, was initiated 11 years ago by two men, one of whom, Sheldon Goldberg, 59, gouged his face with cuticle scissors, "deep digging" to remove ingrown hairs. "I would have so many bandages on my face from cutting that I would sit on the subway all dressed up to go to work," says Goldberg, a former advertising art director, "and people would look at me and I would realize a wound had opened up and I was bleeding all over my shirt." Now, five reconstructive operations later, the lower half of Goldberg's face is solid scar tissue. "But men can get away with it," he says. "When people ask me what happened, I say: 'I was in the war. I was in a fire.' Men can use all the macho stuff."

It's February, and a frigid midwestern wind thumps at the windows of Keepataw Lodge at the Rock Creek Center, a general psychiatric institution in Lemont, Ill. It is the home of the SAFE (Self-Abuse Finally Ends) Alternatives Program, the nation's only in-patient treatment center for self-injurers, started in 1985. Jill, in jeans, hiking boots and a Pucci-style shirt, lounges on an upholstered banquette in the lodge's skylighted atrium. She has been here 10 days, spending her mornings in the hospital's adolescent program completing assignments her school has faxed in, dividing her afternoons between individual and group therapy.

She's ebullient—partly from sheer relief at being surrounded by people with her same problem. "It's really weird how many people in the group have my same kind of thinking," she says, repeatedly removing and replacing a pen cap with hands scarred by cigarette-lighter burns. "How they grew up feeling like they didn't deserve to feel their feelings, like they had to keep people happy. . . . I don't even know who I am anymore, because everything I do depends on what other people want."

Her cheerleading friends have visited, bearing get-well cards and magazines, but Jill finds playing hostess on the grounds of a mental hospital a tall order. "I'd make up things like, 'Oh, I have a group in 10 minutes, so you guys better leave,' because I couldn't take it to have them sitting there and me not knowing how to make them happy in such a weird environment," she says.

Her parents arrive to meet with her doctor and then take Jill home after her group therapy; for insurance reasons, she must continue the 30-day SAFE program from home as an outpatient. (Blue Cross refused to cover her hospitalization costs before SAFE because her problem was "self-inflicted"; the family is appealing.) Jim and Nancy McArdle are warm, open people who seem a little shell-shocked by their sudden immersion in the mental-health system. Jim, who in happier times likes to kid and joke, sits tentatively at a table with his hands folded. Jill is the most animated of the three. "I'll just turn it off, like I never even knew what that was," she says of the behavior that landed her in the hospital only three weeks ago. An anxious glance from her mother, an attractive woman with reddish brown hair who works as a respiratory therapist, gives Jill pause. "Last time we thought it was going to be fine too," she reflects. "But then eventually it just all fell back even worse than it was before. It's scary to think about. I don't want to spend my life in hospitals."

This is a reasonable fear. Most of Jill's fellow patients at SAFE are women in their late 20's and early 30's, many of whom have been hospitalized repeatedly since their teen-age years, some of whom have children. (SAFE accepts men, but its clientele is 99 percent female.) In free moments during the program's highly structured day, many of these patients can be found on the outdoor smoking deck, perched on white lawn chairs under an overhead heating lamp beside a thicket of spiky trees. (Unlike many psychiatric wards, SAFE does not lock its doors.) The deck's cynosure is a white plastic bucket clogged with what look to be thousands of cigarette butts; even when the deck is empty of smokers, the air reeks.

"Hi! What's your diagnosis?" Jane C., a Southerner in her early 30's, cheerfully queries a patient who has just arrived. "Bipolar? Me, too! Although that can mean a lot of different things. What're your symptoms?" Jane, who insisted her last name not be used, is one of those people who can't bear to see anyone left out. She has olive skin, an animated, birdlike face and wide, dark eyes like those in Byzantine paintings. She smiles even while she's talking.

The patient bums a cigarette from her, and Jane lights it. "Cheers," she says, and the two women touch cigarettes as if they were wine glasses.

Jane once made a list called Reasons for Cutting, and the reasons numbered more than 30. But the word she uses most often is power. Like many self-injurers (65 percent according to the 1989 survey; some believe it is much higher), Jane reports a history of sexual abuse that began when she was 7. Shortly thereafter, she raked a hairbrush across her face. By age 10, she was in her parents' bathroom making her own discovery of the razor blade. "I cut right in the fold of a finger," she says. "It was so sharp and so smooth and so well hidden, and yet there was some sense of empowerment. If somebody else is hurting me or making me bleed, then I take that instrument away and 1 make me bleed. It says: 'You can't hurt me anymore. I'm in charge of that.'"

Sometimes Jane pounds her head repeatedly against a wall. "When my head's spinning, when I'm near hysteria, it's like a slap in the face," she says. "I've had multitudes of concussions—it's amazing I have any sense at all." It is virtually impossible to imagine this polished, friendly young woman doing any of these things. Much like Jill, Jane, herself a former cheerleader, masks her vulnerabilities with an assertive and jovial persona. "She's created this face to the world that's totally in control when there's really chaos going on underneath," says Dr. Wendy Friedman Lader, SAFE's clinical director. "There's something very adaptive about that, but it's a surreal kind of existence." Even Jane's many scars are well hidden, thanks to what she calls her "scar-erasing technique," which sounds something like dermabrasion.

Like many victims of early trauma, Jane is plagued by episodes of dissociation, when she feels numb or dead or separate from her body. Cross, the New Haven psychotherapist, explains the genesis of dissociation this way: "When you are abused, the natural thing to do is to take yourself out of your body. Your body becomes the bad part of you that's being punished, and you, the intact, positive part, are far away." But what begins as a crucial self-protective device can become an inadvertent response to any kind of stress or fear. "There have been times when I don't even feel like I'm alive," Jane says. "I'll do something to feel—anything. And that's usually cutting. Just seeing blood. . . . I don't know why."

At SAFE, Jane C. is often in the company of Jamie Matthews, 20, a quiet, watchful young woman with pale skin and long brown hair who seems to bask in her friend's overabundant energy. Cutting herself, Jamie says, is a way of coping with her rage. "I would get so angry and upset so tense, so all I could think about was the physical pain, doing it harder and doing it more. And then afterwards it was a relief . . . sometimes I would sleep."

As a student at a small college in upstate New York, Jamie lived in a dormitory, so privacy was a major preoccupation. "I would lie in bed at school—that was the best place for me to do it because if my roommate walked in, she would think I was sleeping—and I would lay on my back with the knife underneath me, and then pull it out the side, across my back." Jamie already completed the SAFE program once, last summer, but relapsed back at school. The last time she injured herself, she says, was when it felt best. "It was actually pleasureful. It gave me chills; it was that kind of feeling. I sat there smiling, watching myself bleed." Descriptions like these, along with the intimate rituals that accompany some people's injuring—candles, incense, special instruments—have led some clinicians to compare self-injury to masturbation.

Jamie's self-injury has caused her a multitude of problems, yet there is almost a tenderness in her voice when she speaks of her self-harming acts. "It's all mine," she says. "It's nothing that anybody can experience with me or take from me. I guess it's like my little secret. I've got physical scars. . . . It shows that my life isn't easy. I can look at different scars and think, yeah, I know when that happened, so it tells a story. I'm afraid of them fading."

Self-injury can appear, at first, to be a viable coping mechanism; the wounds are superficial, no one else is getting hurt and the injurer feels in control of her life. But what begins as an occasional shallow cut can progress to sliced veins and repeated visits to the emergency room. As with any compulsion, the struggle to resist one's urges can eclipse all other thoughts and interests, and despair over the inability to control the behavior can even lead to suicide attempts. "It's like a cancer," says Cross. "It just seems to start eating into more and more of your life."

Jane C. managed to hide her problems for many years. She was married and had a successful career as a sales executive at a medical-supply company, whose wares she frequently used to suture and bandage her self-inflicted wounds. Eventually, despite her vigilant secrecy, Jane got caught—her mother appeared at her house unexpectedly and found her in the bathroom, drenched in blood. Weakened by her emotional turmoil and a severe eating disorder, Jane ultimately almost passed out on the highway while driving home from a sales call, and finally left her job three and a half years ago. "I went on disability, which was really hard on my pride," she says. "I've never not worked in my whole life."

Jane C.'s discovery by her mother is a fairly routine step in the life cycle of self-injury—for all the secrecy surrounding it, it is finally a graphic nonverbal message. "I think that there's a wish implicit in the injury that someone else will notice and ask about it," says Christine Sterkel, a psychologist with SAFE. This was clearly true in Jill's case; after burning her hands, she covered the wounds with band-aids until Christmas morning, then appeared before her family without them. "In the park, she cracked a bottle and cut both her wrists," a friend of Jill's told me. "Everyone gathered around her, and I think that's what she wanted. She was crying and I'd be hugging her and stuff and then she'd raise her head and be laughing."

Later in the afternoon, Jill, Jane C., Jamie and the other SAFE patients settle on couches and chairs for one of the many focused group therapy sessions they participate in throughout the week. Patients must sign a "no-harm contract" before entering the program; group therapy is a forum for grappling with the flood of feelings they would normally be numbing through self-injury. It is not, as I had envisioned, an occasion for trading gruesome tales of the injuring itself. Karen Conterio, SAFE's founder, has treated thousands of patients and rejects the public confessional that is a staple of 12-step programs. "Self-mutilation is a behavior, it's not an identity," she says, and encourages patients to save their war stories for individual therapy.

Beyond that caveat, Conterio, 39, a lithe, athletic woman with short blond hair, lets her patients set the agenda. Today, Jill and the others discuss their feelings of shame—shame they repressed by injuring, shame over the injuring itself. At emergency rooms, their wounds were often mistaken for suicide attempts, which in most states requires that a patient be locked up in a psychiatric ward, often in physical restraints.

Later, in a small office adorned with mementos given to her by former patients—a knit blanket, a papier-mâché mask—Conterio tells me that she's less concerned with guiding patients toward a specific cause for their self-injury than with helping them learn to tolerate their feelings and express them verbally—in other words, begin functioning as adults. Still, revisiting one's past is a key step in this process. As Maureen Ford, a psychologist at SAFE, puts it: "Self-injury is a kind of violence. So how is it that violence has entered their life in some way previously?"

In Jill McArdle's case, the answer isn't obvious. She is part of an intact, supportive family; as far as she knows, she has never been sexually abused. But there were problems. Jill's brother, a year older than she, was born with health troubles that cost him one kidney and left him only partial use of the other. Today he is well, but, Nancy McArdle says: "It was three, four years of just not knowing from one day to the next how he was going to do, in the hospital all the time. . . . Jill picked up on it right away and tried to make everything easy on us where she was concerned." (Jamie Matthews also grew up with a chronically ill sibling.) Beyond worrying constantly about her ill son, Nancy McArdle, whose own childhood was marked by alcoholism in her family, admits to feeling a general sense of impending catastrophe while her children were young. "I wouldn't drive on expressways—I'd take a different route," she says. "If I saw a storm coming, I'd think it was a tornado." Giggling at the memory, Jill says: "She'd make us all go into the basement with pillows and blankets. I've been petrified of storms ever since then."

Nancy McArdle has since been given a diagnosis of obsessive-compulsive disorder and is on Prozac, and she and Jill can now laugh about those old fears. But it's easy to see how Jill, as a child with a terrified mother, a chronically ill sibling and a father who kept a certain distance from the emotional upheavals in the household, might have felt isolated and imperiled. She quickly developed an unusual tolerance for pain. "I'd fall and I'd never cry. . . . I never felt any pain, really. It was there, but I pushed it back." Triumphing over physical pain was something she could excel at—distinguishing herself from her physically weak older brother, while at the same time reassuring her mother that she, anyway, would always be strong.

This mix of toughness and a hypervigilant desire to please is still the engine of Jill's social persona, which mingles easy affection with an opacity that seals off her real thoughts. "She never tells anybody how she feels—ever," Nancy McArdle says. Jill agrees: "I turn it all inside. I just think I have to help myself, it all has to be up to me."

But paradoxically, the child who feels that she must be completely self-sufficient, that no one can help her or that she doesn't deserve help is uniquely ill equipped for the independence she seeks. Terrified to express emotions like sadness or rage for fear of driving everyone away from her, such a person becomes more easily overwhelmed by those feelings and turns them on herself. "I and my razors and my pieces of glass and the pins and the needles are the only things I can trust to bring relief," paraphrases Dr. Kaplan, author of "Female Perversions." "These are their care givers. These have the power to soothe and bring relief of the tension building up inside. . . . They don't expect the environment to hold them." Tending to their own wounds, which many injurers do solicitously, is the final part of the experience. In a sense, self-injury becomes a perverse ritual of self-caretaking in which the injurer assumes all roles of an abusive relationship: the abuser, the victim and the comforting presence who soothes her afterward.

In someone like Jane C., whose childhood was severely traumatic, physiology may be partly to blame; trauma can cause lasting neurological changes, especially if it occurs while the central nervous system is still developing. Dr. Bessel van der Kolk, a professor of psychiatry at Boston University who specializes in trauma, explains: "The shock absorbers of the brain are shot. If everything is running smoothly, if it crawls along just fine—as it does in nobody's life—you're fine. But the moment you get hurt, jealous, upset, fall in love, fall out of love, your reaction becomes much stronger."

It is for this reason, many people believe, that self-injury begins during adolescence. "They go through early childhood developing very poor capacities to deal with states of internal disruption," says Dr. Karen Latza, a Chicago psychologist who does diagnostic work for SAFE. "I can't think of a single thing that involves more internal upheaval than the adolescent years. The changes that come with their menstrual cycles or with sexual arousal engender panic in the young self-injurer."

Jill fits such a model: for all her popularity, she steers clear of romance out of an apprehension she attributes to the friend who lied about her. "I just think that every boy would be like that, just make up stuff," she says. But there is a second danger for Jill: her irrepressible impulse to please, which could make her vulnerable to unwanted sexual attention. As if sensing this, Jill tends to develop a distaste for boys who take an interest in her.

The next time I see Jill at SAFE, the weather is warmer, the ice on the ponds at Rock Creek is melting, and she seems antsy to resume her old life. "I'm just sick of having to wake up every morning and go to therapy, therapy, therapy," she says. Cheerleading tryouts are that night; the following week, she will begin easing back into school. The thought of facing her peers en masse fills her with anxiety. "Last Thursday I went to a hockey game and I saw all these boys, and seriously, my skin was crawling. . . . They'd give me looks, and I couldn't even look at them."

After the SAFE group, Jill and I drive to Mt. Carmel High School, in a run-down neighborhood on Chicago's South Side, for her tryouts. Her fellow cheerleaders greet her enthusiastically; Jill brings one of them a birthday present. Another girl fawns over Jill in a fanged display of unctuous sweetness. "That's the bitch I hate," Jill says matter-of-factly. The girl, still within earshot, shoots her a look. "She thinks I'm kidding, but I'm not," Jill says.

With glitter over their eyes and tiny mirrored hearts pasted to their cheeks, these incumbent cheerleaders huddle in a stairwell outside the gymnasium, awaiting the chance to defend their positions on the squad. Their coach, Suzy Davy, assures me privately that Jill will be chosen. "She was just so cute and energetic," Davy says of Jill's performance last year, which earned her the Spirit Award during the same period when she was cutting and burning herself in secret. "She wasn't fake. She was just out there and she said, 'This is me!'"

Finally the girls file into the gym, shoes squeaking on the varnished wood, and spread out on the floor to stretch. Some of them seem to be vying for Jill's attention; others keep a respectful distance. And it strikes me that by cutting herself—by getting caught and hospitalized Jill has freed herself from her own tough persona, at least for a time. Everyone knows that something is wrong, that no matter how happy and confident she may seem, there is unhappiness, too, and a need to be cared for. She has revealed herself in the only way she was able.

There is nothing new about self-injury. As Favazza documents in "Bodies Under Siege," from the Christian flagellant cults of the 13th and 14th centuries to male Australian Aborigines who undergo subcision, or the slicing open of the penis along the urethra, as a rite of passage, the equation of bodily mortification with transcendence and healing is repeated across cultures. Many such rituals occur in the context of adolescent initiation rites—ceremonies involving youths about the same age as most boys and girls who begin cutting themselves. "We've done away with rites of passage, but the pattern can still exist," says Favazza. "And the younger teenagers who are seeking to become adults, the ones who can't make it the ordinary way, somehow tap into that."

One group that consciously seeks to tap into primitive rituals and vanished rites of passage are practitioners of what is called new tribalism or extreme body arts, who embrace such forms of body modification as tattooing, piercing and, more recently, scarification and branding. Some of these practices are performed as public rituals of a sort, particularly in gay S & M culture, where they are known as blood-sports. Ron Athey, an H.I.V-positive performance artist, cuts and pierces himself before audiences while reading aloud from autobiographical texts. An entirely different sort of performance is practiced by Orlan, a French woman who has undergone repeated facial plastic surgeries on video.

More often, body modification takes place in private studios like Modern American Bodyarts in Bay Ridge, Brooklyn, a small, scrupulously clean storefront bedecked with African masks. Here, a multiply pierced and heavily tattooed artist, Keith Alexander, pierces clients, cuts designs into them using scalpels and brands them with sheet metal bent into designs, heated up to 1,800 degrees and "pressed firmly and quickly into the flesh."

Partly, the purpose of these practices is to create a decorative scar. Raelyn Gallina, a body artist in San Francisco, takes impressions of her blood designs with Bounty paper towels and has a portfolio of hundreds. But the experience and the scar itself are also symbolic. Gallina says: "You know that you're going to endure some pain, you're going to shed your blood. . . . That act, once it happens and you come out victorious, makes you go through a transformation. We have so little control over what goes on around us. . . . It comes down to you and your body."

Of course "control," or the illusion of control, is perhaps the primary motivation behind self-injury too. And the parallels don't end there. Gallina, like many body modifiers, says that a high proportion of her female clients report having been sexually abused. Rebecca Blackmon, 35, a slim, fair-haired woman with a gentle voice, was such a person. "I wanted to heal all the sexual parts of my body," she says. She began in 1989 by having her clitoral hood pierced; now, her pubic bone and stomach are branded, her nipples, tongue and belly button are pierced and a crescent moon of thick scar tissue from repeated cuttings encircles the lower half of both her breasts. "It's made me a lot more aware of my body; it's made me a lot more sexual," Blackmon says. Her feelings about her abuse have changed, too. "It's not so present in my mind all the time."

Clearly, body modifiers like Blackmon share the urge of many self-injurers to return to the site of their abuse—the body—and alter it in a manner that feels symbolically curative. And as with self-injury, "after-care," or tending to one's wounds, is an important part of the process. "The ritual part to me is the daily taking care of it," says Blackmon. "The daily cleansing it, pampering it, putting heat packs on it." Among body modifiers who cut, there is great concern over scar enhancement, or thwarting the body's healing process. Common scarring techniques include dousing the freshly cut skin in rubbing alcohol and setting it afire; rubbing cigar ash or ink into the open wounds and advising clients to pick off their newly formed scabs each day.

But the many resonances of motive and procedure between self-injurers and body modifiers can obscure a crucial difference: control. Getting an occasional brand or cut design in the course of a functional life is not the same as slashing at one's flesh—or fighting the urge to do so—on a daily basis. One is a shared act of pride; the other a secretive act steeped in shame. And many body modifiers—perhaps the majority, now that piercing and tattooing have become so commonplace—are motivated not by the process at all but by the simple desire to belong to a group that is visibly outside the mainstream.

One of the most famous body modifiers is Fakir Musafar, 66, who spent much of his early life secretly indulging his own urges to do such things as bind his waist to 19 inches and sew together parts of himself with needle and thread. As a teenager in South Dakota, he assembled a photography dark room in his mother's fruit cellar so that "if she knocked and I was in there putting needles in myself or ripping flesh, I'd say, 'Sorry, I'm developing film and I can't open the door now.'" Now a certified director of a state-licensed school for branding and body piercing in San Francisco, Fakir, as he is known, has seen his secret practices embraced by a growing population of young people. He performs rituals around the world, including the O-Kee-Pa, in which he hangs suspended from two giant hooks that penetrate permanent holes near his pectorals.

Favazza asked Fakir to contribute an epilogue to the second edition of "Bodies Under Siege," published recently. In it, Fakir suggests that self-mutilation and body modification share a common root in a collective human unconscious. "There's an undercurrent in everybody that's quite universal," Fakir says, "to experience in the body self-initiation or healing. If there is some way socially that these urges can be faced, they don't overpower people and get them into mental hospitals." The argument makes a kind of sense, but there is a lot it doesn't explain: if these longings are so universal, why are those cutting themselves, and being cut, so often the victims of trauma and neglect? And using Fakir's logic, couldn't one argue that anorexics and bulimics are merely performing their own symbolic body manipulations? Surely the coexistence of urges, symbolism and a sense of meaning or empowerment is not enough to make a practice healthy.

But Fakir has led a long, rich life, and Blackmon feels she has reclaimed her body, so perhaps there may be a context in which "self-injury" controlled and guided along safe paths, could serve as part of a healing process. Favazza seems to think so." "If it can be controlled and relabeled and not get out of hand, everybody would be better off," he says. "There's less shame associated with it, there's less possibility for bad accidents to occur. . . . But we're dealing with a lot of ifs, ands and buts here."

It's a sunny, springlike St. Patrick's Day, and the McArdle household is teeming with relatives and small children eating corned beef and green-frosted cupcakes from a generous spread on the dining-room table. Jill's bedroom smells of styling gel and electric curlers, and her cheerleading outfit is heaped in one corner. Her hair, which spirals in curls down her back, is crowned with a ring of metallic green and silver shamrocks. With a friend at her side, she works the family phone, trying to figure out where the best parties will take place during the South Side Irish parade.

Soon we're wandering through a neighborhood awash in Irish pride. Jill and her friend sneak cans of beer from the pockets of their windbreakers and guzzle them as we walk. "I love this day," Jill says. She finished the SAFE program two weeks ago but returns twice each week to see her therapist. "I'm feeling so much better," she says, smoking a cigarette as we pass Monroe Park, where the boys used to tease her. "Usually I'd be afraid to go somewhere because maybe somebody wouldn't want me. Now I don't care. Now it's like I'm O.K. with myself. It's their own problem."

We begin a desultory journey from party to party that leads from a cramped back porch beside a half-frozen portable swimming pool to a basement rec room with a hanging wicker chair and a bubble-hockey set. Jill cheerfully explains my presence to anyone with an interest: "She's writing an article on self-mutilation. That's what I was in the hospital for," seeming mildly amused by the double takes this bombshell induces. An old friend of hers, a boy, informs me that Jill is "a nice, friendly person who likes to talk."

She waits for him to say more. "Remember in eighth grade when you used to say to me, 'You have a thousand faces'?" she prompts. "Remember that?"

The boy looks puzzled. "Eighth grade was a long time ago," he says.

Finally we head to Western Avenue for a glimpse of the parade. As we walk in the bright sunlight, I notice that Jill's friend has fresh scars covering her forearms. She tells me rather proudly that she went on a recent binge of cutting herself, but insists she did not get the idea from Jill. Jill tells me privately that she thinks her friend did it to get attention, because the day after, she wore a short-sleeved shirt in the dead of winter, and everyone saw. Jill has been urging her friend to seek help.

The riotous spectators seem almost to drown out the tail end of the parade. Jill plunges into the drunken crowd, tripping over her untied shoelace, her friend straining to keep up with her. Men gape at her under her crown of shamrocks; she cheerily bellows hello at them and then swirls out of sight. We turn onto an alley, and in the sudden quiet, Jill stops a group of strangers and lights her cigarette off one of theirs. Her friend seizes this moment to kneel down and carefully tie Jill's shoelace.

Outside Jill's house, the girls hide their beers and cigarette butts in the bushes, then go inside to exchange a few pleasantries with Jill's family. The openness Jill showed toward her parents at SAFE has vanished behind a sheen of wary cheerfulness. Watching her, I find myself wondering whether self-injury will wind up as a mere footnote to her adolescence or become a problem that will consume her adulthood, as it has Jane C.'s. Often, particularly in someone with an intact family and friends, the behavior will simply fade away. "This disorder does rend to burn out, for some reason," says Cross. "Life takes over." And Jill knows where to get treatment, should she need it again. Jamie Matthews felt like a failure when she relapsed, until she talked to a friend who has repeatedly sought help with her eating disorder. "She said it's like a spiral staircase," Jamie says. "You keep going around in circles, but each time you're at a different level."

As for Jane C., she returned home shortly after Jill left SAFE and reports that the azaleas are blooming. It's hard, she says, returning to a place where she has always felt she was wearing a mask. "One night I was incredibly close," she says. "I mean, I had the blade to the skin. I sat there and I thought, It doesn't matter to anybody else. And I was just about hysterical, but I stopped myself. I thought, This isn't the only way that works."

Jill, too, seems to be making a kind of staggered progress. "I know I have to take care of myself more instead of other people," she says. "I'm at peace with myself." Since leaving the program, she says, she has had no impulses to hurt herself. "Part of me always used to want to do it, but that part of me dissolved."

Her mother, admittedly a worrier by nature, is less sure, and says she has resorted to sneaking into Jill's room in the wee hours with a penlight, lifting the covers while her daughter sleeps to check for new cuts or burns. So far, she's pleased to say, there has been nothing to report. As Jill and her friend finally burst from the house and clamber arm in arm down the block into the late afternoon, Nancy McArdle watches them from the living-room window and says, "You can't ever relax."

16

Entering Adolescence: Literacy and Allegiance in Junior High

MARGARET J. FINDERS

I turn now to the end of a story: The last weeks in May at a junior high school. I begin here because I believe that an examination of one culminating event reveals the themes and tensions that permeated my year at Northern Hills Junior High School. The distribution of the junior high yearbook serves as a window onto the complex processes that create and constrain, within the school context, social roles that are informed by socioeconomic status, gender, and social-group allegiances. As school years draw to a close, students across the nation anticipate the biggest school-sanctioned literacy event of the year: the sale and distribution of the school yearbook. Like students elsewhere, Northern Hills Junior High students anxiously awaited its arrival.

"A Sense of Belonging": Social Roles and the Yearbook "Event"

At Northern Hills, seventh grade marked the year in which students first produced and published a school yearbook, providing, it seems, a signpost of students' entrance into the adolescent arena. Many of these seventh graders bought their first yearbook, a symbol of distinction that separated them from elementary students. As elementary students, they had heard from older siblings and friends about *the junior high yearbook*, and its significance had been made clear since early October, when they were warned by way of intercom announcements to "Order now. Don't wait. Yearbooks will sell out fast."

With yearbook photographers occasionally popping into classrooms and disruptions from the intercom regularly announcing that band members or the volleyball team or the drama club should report to the gym for yearbook photographs, the presence of the yearbook was felt not just in May but throughout the year.

Produced by 65 students working together with the help of two staff advisors, the yearbook, a 48-page soft-bound document, captured the year through photographs, student-produced artwork, and captions. Sports held a prominent place in the pages of the yearbook: Photos of football, track, basketball, and wrestling events for the boys and track, tennis, volleyball, and basketball for the girls filled the pages. The book also contained photos of Soda—a drug and alcohol awareness club—and drama club.

I believe that most teachers would agree with one of the yearbook's faculty advisors, the media specialist, who described the importance of the yearbook this way:

> *If you can find your mug in here [yearbook], it gives you a tremendous sense of belonging. We tried to cover all of the major events, and it's important to find yourself. We took a lot of pictures. If you and your mom can find yourself in here, then everything is just A-OK.*

Here, the media specialist pointed out the importance of belonging, describing how belonging is documented by a photo in the yearbook. Similarly, Smith (1986) describes the necessity of belonging in regard to literacy learning. Using the metaphor of a "literacy club," he writes:

> *And once again, membership in the literacy club adds to the individual's sense of personal identity, of who he or she is. "Hi, kid, you're one of us," say the members of the literacy club. (p. 38)*

Borrowing Smith's metaphor, Meyers (1992) examines how students' social relations and thinking processes impinge on each other by categorizing students' uses of literacy within different social contexts as follows: to share membership, to contest membership, to fake membership, and to maintain membership. At Northern Hills, the junior high yearbook served similar functions, documenting membership in what might be considered an adolescent club. I use the term "club" to describe a set of discursive practices that shape and create social roles. As it is used here, a club provides an opportunity to examine the institutional conception of membership, of belonging. Giroux (1992) argues that "student experience will have to be analyzed as part of a wider relationship between culture and power" (p. 16). What implicit cultural attributes encompass becoming "one of us"? What is valued? What roles are made available? How is the organization structured? What privileges and rewards are conferred by such a membership? What are the duties and obligations?

Photographs of after-school club and team activities dominated the book, revealing implicit values: Clearly, high value was placed on extracurricular participation, team membership, and competition.

Teachers, administrators, and many parents perceived extracurricular involvement as the key to both enjoyment and academic success. The faculty and student handbooks referred to sports, drama, and club activities as "cocurricular" rather than as "extracurricular." While carried on outside the designated school day, these activities were perceived by teachers, administrators, and many parents as central to the school's academic program. When asked what was most beneficial for her daughter during the school year, one mother explained, "After-school sports. I really like them. They keep her involved." This parent, like many others, believed that involvement in after-school activities would have a positive academic impact.

I contend that an examination of the school as a club makes visible disparate positions of status and power. Infused with the discourse of adolescence, the junior high school filters attention toward one particular group of students and, as you will see, renders others invisible.

Social Boundaries: The Queens and the Cookies

Just a few days before the sale of yearbooks, intercom announcements and rumors of the exact date of arrival revved students up. During second period, Mr. Anson, the building principal, announced, "The yearbooks are not here yet, but we will let you know the moment they get here." "The moment" was enunciated with such clarity that students in Mrs. Zmoleck's language arts class began buzzing with excitement. Mrs. Zmoleck attempted to distract them from the coming attraction. "Okay, it's free-reading time," she announced to counterbalance Mr. Anson on the intercom. For several days, Mr. Anson's morning announcements continued to remind students of the sale of yearbooks—as if any of them could not be keenly aware of the impending arrival.

Teachers' conversations, too, were laced with references to the arrival of the yearbook as they planned for the event. At Northern Hills Junior High, the yearbook had become a central part of the end-of-the-year curriculum. The distribution date seemed to be the only negative concern mentioned by teachers, who feared that an early release date might sabotage their scheduled plans for "signing time" in class during the last week of school. They talked to each other about the need to save the yearbook for the last week so it would fit within their curricular calendar. For the most part, teachers described the yearbook as a celebration and a well-earned reward for a year of hard work. They allocated class time for signing and sharing yearbooks. Perceived as a way to control the behavior of the 531 seventh and eighth graders who in late May might not be eager to participate in discussions or complete end-of-semester projects, signing time was a tool for negotiating with students, often appearing as a bribe. Teachers told students: "If we get all our work done . . . ," "If you are all good . . . ," "If you cooperate, and we can hurry through this . . ." The following teacher comment received several nods and "me toos" from staff in the teacher's lounge: "I give them the last five to ten minutes to write depending on how the class goes. It's a reward. It's a privilege. It's their reward for good behavior."

When the book was sold one full week before the last day of the school year, several teachers expressed frustration: "What are we going to do with them the last week? Students won't have anything to do"; "It gives them something to do at the end of school." Teachers explained that all the students looked forward to receiving the book, and that this sense of urgency might have forced the early sales.

The yearbook played such a large part in the end-of-school activities because the teachers and administrators all believed, as the media specialist articulated, that it gave a tremendous sense of belonging. The discourse of adolescence that privileges peer-group allegiances constructed filters, it seems, that prevented school personnel from seeing the yearbook as exclusionary. Although the yearbook was viewed as a symbol of solidarity for all students, only a particular population of students was made to feel as if they belonged to this club. Other students remained outsiders.

Having provided insight into the role of the yearbook from the institutional perspective, I turn now to the focal students themselves, describing the day of arrival of the yearbook from their perspective.

The Arrival of the Yearbook: Tiffany's Scene

It was lunch time, but students crowded the hallway outside the cafeteria. Crouched down in bunches, girls giggled, shrieked, and tipped one another over as they huddled together to sign each other's books. Boys and girls leaned against lockers or used a friend's back to steady a book for signing. Yearbooks flew across the corridor with a verbal "Hey, sign mine," tagged onto them.

It was easy to hear Tiffany's voice above the loud chatter. She leaped up from a crowd of girls, her long red hair flying back as she cackled loudly and ran full speed to the end of the hall, sloshing small amounts of her chocolate malt across the tan carpet as she went. She slammed into a group of friends and yanked a yearbook from one boy's hand, screaming, "Whose's this? You want me to sign it, don't you?" She looked over her shoulder at me, shouting, "I just have to keep writing until they'll let me stop. Everybody wants me to sign their book." She grinned and plopped herself down in the middle of the group. Like a pile of puppies, her friends pushed up against each other as she elbowed them over and wriggled her way in.

The Arrival of the Yearbook: Cleo's Scene

Inside, the cafeteria was much less crowded on that day. The large room was nearly empty and particularly quiet. I scanned the room and found Cleo and her friends in their usual seats in the middle of the front section, "the woof-woof tables," as Tiffany's friends described the area. Without difficulty, because there were so few students in the area, I made my way to them and stuffed my backpack under the table. Beth, Pat, Cleo, and Dottie were eating in silence. Not one yearbook was visible at their table. Sensing the awkwardness of the silence, I did not ask about it. Instead, I mentioned the rainy weather, and Dottie complained that she and her mother had worked late the night before, trimming all the tall, wet grass from around their trailer so they wouldn't be charged a penalty fee by the trailer-park management. Lunch continued with talk about rain, cookies, and favorite flavors of malts.

After lunch, I asked Cleo privately about the yearbooks. "Oh, I'm not very interested in them," she reported. When I reminded her that she had told me a week before that she thought she'd get one, she just shrugged her shoulders and repeated that she wasn't interested: "I don't know why I would want one. None of my friends are in there anyway."

The literacy event surrounding the arrival of the yearbook appears very different when one looks through the eyes of Tiffany and Cleo. These two scenes illustrate sharp contrasts between the two groups of girlfriends.

The yearbook was one mechanism that created tangible boundaries between groups. Students used photos and messages to assess status and document allegiances. One powerful position within the school was that of yearbook staff member. Many considered it an honor to be a member of the yearbook staff and especially to be one of the eighth-grade photographers, who were allowed to leave study halls throughout the year to snap candid shots of the student body. This position held power because it carried the privilege of added mobility around the school and access to other classrooms. Most important, individuals who held this position acted as gatekeepers, controlling who populated the pages of the yearbook.

The queens literally counted the number of photos each had in the yearbook, using the number as a measurement of popularity. When the yearbook arrived, these girls quickly flipped through the pages looking for themselves and their friends as proof of their belonging. On the other hand, Cleo's remark, "None of my friends are in there anyway," makes it clear that the cookies were aware of their absence.

Tiffany's and Cleo's networks of friends seemed to have very little in common. Tiffany loved to socialize. Her friends were active in athletic events, attended school activities and dances, and spent much of their leisure time together with same-age peers. In contrast, Cleo, like her friends, spent most of her leisure time with her family. She did not participate in any extracurricular activities and preferred to spend her time at home.

Constant comments from Northern Hills staff that "Everybody gets one" and "Everyone loves them" reveal that Cleo and Dottie and many others were invisible to school personnel. Current enrollment was 531; 425 books were ordered. Eight were sold to adults, 10 were distributed as complimentary copies, 10 were mailed to students who no longer lived in the district, and 5 remained unsold. In all, 397 copies were sold to students, which left 134 students without yearbooks. That figure represents 25% of the total student population. While students may not have purchased a yearbook for a variety of reasons, the socioeconomic status of families may have been a critical issue. For whatever reason, when teachers rewarded students with "signing time," one out of four students was not able to participate.

Economic constraints prevented some students from fully participating in the culture of the school and from participating in the biggest school-sanctioned literacy event of the year. This lack of a sense of belonging, of shared culture, was a constant tension in the conversations of Cleo, her family, and her friends. Cleo and Dottie lived in trailer parks, which in the Midwest carries a stigma that spills over into the school context, where some teachers and some administrators perceive that such living arrangements lead to school problems.

At times, it was not simply a matter of economics that interfered with the institution's construction of full participation in school activities, but the perceptions of economic status that others brought to the school context. This attitude was more fully illustrated by the principal's comments about students who come from trailer parks, which he described as "places that are too closely knit. They live too closely together. They know each other's problems and that causes problems at school." Likewise, constructions of the social dimension of schooling created obstacles for some students. At Northern Hills, I often heard the category "trailer-park kids" used to connote a lack of appropriate social skills in particular students. Some teachers described their class makeup in terms of numbers of students from trailer parks. A teacher's comment such as "I've got seven trailer-park kids" conveyed to other teachers the implicit yet clearly understood assumption of impending trouble for that teacher.

While economic resources played a major part in determining who would participate more fully in ways that the school had constructed participation, there was much evidence to suggest that an equal if not greater factor was the circulation of what Bourdieu (1977) calls cultural capital: the attitudes, beliefs, cultural background, knowledge, and skills that are passed from one generation to the next. In order to understand the cultural capital that each girl carried to school, I turn now to their homes.

Perspectives from the Homes of the Social Queens

Tiffany and Angie were prominent members of this school's "club," clearly evidenced by the fact that each had four pictures in the yearbook. Besides her "mug shot," Tiffany appeared in team pictures with the volleyball team and the basketball team. She also appeared on the collage pages with her arms thrown around Lauren at the fall school dance. All of her best friends appeared throughout the book in candid shots and in volleyball, basketball, and track pictures.

While Tiffany's parents were concerned when her social life interfered with academics, they both explained that it was the cocurricular activities, especially sports, that were helping to shape her in a positive way. They attributed Tiffany's success in school to a great extent to her participation in extracurricular activities, and they encouraged her to undertake every opportunity that was available to her. "She's a very social person. With sports and friends and all," her mother told me. Later in the year, her father attributed her school-year success to this fact:

> I think overall it's been successful because of participating in extracurricular activities. That's been good for her, not only physically but mentally. But I personally didn't think I'd survive this year with her, from the standpoint of the constantly, about every other week, getting a letter from the school about this or that, incomplete assignments or whatever just due to her social butterfly attitude she had throughout the year, you know.

Notice the values placed on the benefits of extracurricular activities, "not only physically but mentally." While her father acknowledged that her "social butterfly attitude" caused some difficulties at home due to the demands it entailed (making driving arrangements, attending sporting events and social functions, and occasionally dealing with incomplete assignments), he accepted them as healthy signs of this developmental period. The discourse of adolescence reverberates in Tiffany's father's words. Letters from school, incomplete assignments, along with the social butterfly attitude, signaled to him that Tiffany was a normal adolescent.

Like Tiffany, Angie was actively involved in the school's social life. She participated in volleyball, basketball, and track as well as chorus and weight-lifting. Angie's mother described her, too, as social:

> *A big part of her life's her social life. She's involved in a lot of things. It's an important part of school, in terms of learning because if you've got a happy child, all around happy child, she's going to do better at everything. Probably doesn't need to be quite as involved as she is, but she needs it. I think it's important to have extracurricular activities to keep her happy.*

Parents of the queens expressed concern that there simply wasn't as much time for reading or family now that they were in junior high, but they strongly supported the importance of extracurricular activities as a direct route to school success: physically, socially, and academically.

Perspectives from the Homes of the Tough Cookies

Missing from the yearbook were any pictures other than the official "mug shots" of Cleo, Dottie, or their friends. Tough cookies did not participate in any extracurricular activities and were invisible to the eighth-grade photographers who were busy throughout the year taking candid shots around school.

Even purchasing a yearbook created tension. Consider Cleo's mother's frustration with her inability to send $8.00 to school so her daughter could have a yearbook to sign like all the other girls. Torn between the pressures of stretching a tight budget and wanting her daughter to belong, she said:

> *I do not understand. I do not understand why they assume that everybody has tons of money, and every time I turn around it's more money for this and more money for that. Where do they get the idea that we've got all this money?*

Like Cleo, Dottie had a picture only in the mug-shot section. Like Cleo's mother, Dottie's mother did not have the economic resources to allow Dottie to participate fully in school in ways the school might have envisioned. For instance, after Dottie's language arts teacher encouraged her to try out for the fall play, her mother explained to me why she did not "choose" to participate: "I think Dottie told you that we don't have a car right now. She's embarrassed and doesn't want her teachers to know."

Understanding the social dimensions of this condition go far beyond any economic factors. While Cleo's mother may have regretted that Cleo did not get a yearbook and Dottie's mother might have liked Dottie to try out for the play, both women regularly expressed values that conflicted with the sense of belonging that permeated the messages surrounding the sale of the yearbook. Cleo's mother explained her anxiety and worries in the move to junior high:

> *The biggest thing for me is the social stuff. I'm not ready for her to move outside the family, and it's hard for me to say, "yeah, you can do it," because I don't feel comfortable yet.*

Later in the same interview, she told me that she planned for her daughter to attend a nearby college so she can remain at home. She explained the importance of family in this way:

> *Like the Orientals and even the Indian people, [I think] families are most important. And everybody works together to get wherever they're going. And I really don't think that us, as White people or whatever, I don't think we do that. I think we just start cutting off, saying you're on your own, you know. And I really do think that families should always stick together as long as possible. I mean you give them a boost up. I don't like that boot-out stuff.*

In opposition to the discourse of adolescence, which privileges allegiance with same-age peers, this quote reveals a continued emphasis on close ties with significant adults. Unlike parents of the social queens, who regarded severing ties with adults as a sign of normal progression into adolescence, the parents of the cookies regarded maintaining allegiances with family as central. Emphasis on maintaining family ties in working-class families during adolescence is documented elsewhere (Schlegel & Barry, 1991; Weiss, 1993). McRobbie's (1978) study documents the centrality of home and family life for working-class girls. I argue that one must account for marked differential role constructions that accompany the move into adolescence. In the school setting, it seems that adolescence as a life stage may have constructed filters that deny diversity.

Cleo's mother regularly made sharp contrasts between academic and social aspects of schooling. She explained, "I want Cleo to be educated. I don't want her to be social." Like Cleo's mother, Dottie's mother discouraged her daughter from participating in any cocurricular activities: "Maybe when she is in high school, 16 or 17, then she can do track or something. *Not now!*"

Both women expressed a strong distrust of the social side of schooling and presented a set of values that conflicted with Northern Hills teachers' thinking about appropriate pedagogy for the language arts classroom. (Note the importance of peer response and collaborative groups in reading and writing workshops in the work of Atwell, 1987, and Graves, 1983.) Both women deemphasized the importance of peer groups. Both mothers strongly resisted the notion that social activities were a part of the educational process or a sign of progression into the developmental stage of adolescence.

"Sign Mine": Constructing Identity and Claiming Allegiance

Time to write in the school yearbook was perceived as a reward by teachers, and students often announced that this sanctioned writing time was their right, demanding time to scrawl their messages across the face of another student.

Literacies—both sanctioned literacies and literate underlife—served to maintain particular social roles and document particular allegiances. At Northern Hills, writing in the yearbook provides a unique opportunity to examine the dimensions of sanctioned literacies (those that are recognized and circulated by adults in authority) and literate underlife (those literate practices that are out of sight and out of control of those in authority, practices in opposition to the institution). Within the pages of the yearbook, literate practices marked membership and measured status within social groups. Messages were borrowed, erased, and scribbled over to present a particular kind of self as well as to document and deny allegiances. Six pages were included at the back for just such writing practices. Clearly, writing in the yearbook privileged those who matched the dominant image of the adolescent, both economically and culturally. The cookies are absent from the remaining discussion.

Presenting a particular self through their literate choices, boys' inscriptions centered on action while girls' messages focused on relationships. Messages such as "Your [*sic*] a total babe," "Yo, The spirit 40 lives on," and "Stay sweet and sexy, NOT" found their way onto these pages. Just as the sixth-grade girls in Cherland's (1994) study used dress, demeanor, and leisure-time activities (including reading) as a way to "do gender," signing the yearbook was a means of marking gender. Drawing on West and Zimmerman (1987), Cherland writes that "doing gender involves a complex of socially guided perceptual, interactional, and micro-political activities that cast particular pursuits as expressions of masculine and feminine 'natures' " (p. 12). Of the messages printed above, "Your [*sic*] a total babe" and "Yo, The spirit 40 lives on" were written by males, while "Stay sweet and sexy, NOT" was written by seventh-grade girls. The boys often inscribed their basketball jersey number into their messages: "The spirit 40 lives on." Although many girls participated in basketball, no reference to sports was evident in their yearbook inscriptions.

Both boys and girls sought to affix a kind of permanence to their messages. Yearbook inscriptions served, it seems, to secure one's role and relationships in print. "Forever" and "lives on" appeared in an overwhelming majority of messages. Girls most often signed their inscriptions with B.F.F. (Best Friends Forever) while boys secured their social position by such comments as "Yo, #15 Forever" and "We're #1 forever." In these attempts to attach permanence to a presentation of self, such signatures were clearly declarations of cultural masculine and feminine identification: Boys sought to present a competitive self while girls sought attachment with others.

Romance marked the signatures of the seventh-grade girls. They often searched for red and pink pens with which to write and dotted their I's with hearts. The girls often drew hearts around boys' pictures and wrote "Love," carefully turning the letter O into a small red heart near a particular boy's picture.

Boys' inscriptions focused on action and on power, presenting the male self as a powerful competitor at the top of the social hierarchy. Girls, in contrast, presented the self through the male gaze, finding a place in the social order through one's ability to attract male attention: "Stay sweet and sexy" was the most common inscription for girls.

Some yearbooks were considered to be "ruined" by boys who wrote comments that girls feared would result in punishment at home. Comments such as "Hey, Boobs, I hope I see ALOT of you this summer" created bursts of muffled anger in groups of girls, yet the girls refused to tell adults about such practices and quickly hushed each other up so a teacher would not approach them. Similar to the Oak

Town girls in Cherland's 1994 study, the Northern Hills girls never reported such acts. Cherland writes of similar acts of sexual harassment:

> *Instead of telling the child what she must do, the culture tells her what she is (Bourdieu, 1991). MTV, the television news, novels, fashion advertisements, older relatives and the boys at school all told Oak Town girls what they were: powerless people whose bodies were "naturally" the object of others' desires. It is not surprising, therefore, that most accepted the practice of sexual harassment. Bourdieu suggests that people come to accept these violent suggestions inscribed in the practices of everyday life, no matter what their status or class, and no matter what the effect on them, because cultural discourses position them as people who must accept the warning, while they in turn come to interpret themselves as those who must submit. In this way, domination is sustained through interpersonal relations, and symbolic violence is accepted as legitimate. (p. 42)*

While Northern Hills girls expressed outrage about certain boys' writing practices, they continued to ask Stevie, "the one who ruined that yearbook," to "sign mine" and granted status to the girl who was the victim of the message. Clearly, this comment can be read as a way boys exert control over girls. But trained by the larger culture, the Northern Hills girls received it as a mark of distinction, accepting their position as powerless people defined through their body images.

Gossip about the comment carried much currency for several days. While the Northern Hills male presented the self as a powerful actor, he represented the female as object of desire. The early adolescent girl accepts his representation of her as an object, more specifically as an anatomical commodity.

Although this particular comment was made invisible, by blocking it out with a thick black marker, the seventh graders continued to regard its presence. Under the black ink was the secret sexual message that was revealed to those deemed an appropriate audience. Girls led each other by the hand to the yearbook, "See, this is where it is." The phrase was repeated in present tense: "where it is," not "where it was." The sexual message remained present under the black marker. As children, these girls accepted sexuality as taboo; yet, as early adolescents, they sought to enact a sexual self through their literate practices. Although hidden from adults, the message was not erased. It was not erased from the yearbook or from the construction of identity that these girls were internalizing.

Patrolling the Borders: Literacy as Ritual of Exclusion

KATIE: Can I sign your yearbook?

BARB: No.

A quick glance at the yearbook shows row after row of white faces ordered by alphabetical arrangement. The seeming homogeneity conceals diversity: Invisible barriers such as attitudes, beliefs, economics, and experiences separate these young people into at least two camps. The girls created markers to maintain the borders between them. Allegiances became visible in both the act of writing and in the messages themselves. What is written and to whom is controlled by one's social status. Yearbooks circulated across social boundaries, yet those with the greatest social status stood in judgment of those less powerful. Students carefully monitored who could sign their yearbooks. To allow one of lesser status to mark one's book appeared to lower the status of the book owner. Students often asked for and were denied signing privileges. The cookies did not participate in signing, and within the queens' friendship network, a hierarchy was clearly visible. Some students were in fact told "No," after asking, "Can I sign your yearbook?" In the same way, some students refused to sign yearbooks of those perceived to be outside the circle of significance. Who had the right to write was clearly an issue of entitlement defined by Shuman (1986) as "the rights of both addressors and addressees, as well as to the onlookers, witnesses, eavesdroppers and third-party listeners to a message, as well as the characters in the message" (p. 18). If one was perceived as an outsider, then one was not entitled to write. Likewise, one might or might not be entitled to even view the message. Students guarded their written texts and controlled who had the right to see them.

The issue of entitlement, according to Shuman (1993), concerns one's rights to "appropriate another's voice as a means of borrowing authority, whether in an act of complicity or resistance to that authority" (p. 136). Messages inscribed in the yearbook illustrate positions of both compliance and resistance—most often compliance to peers deemed higher in social status and resistance to adults. Layers of authority become visible when one examines these written texts. For example, as an act of resistance, one student parodied Mr. Tibidioux, her language arts teacher, taking that teacher's own words to mock his authority: "It is clear that . . ." Borrowing these words from his recurring instruction for writing appropriate responses, she wrote them in a yearbook and then, to claim publicly that she knew that he was leaving the school system at the close of the year, she added, "It is clear that Scooby-doo [rhymes with Tibidioux] is leaving," spoofing his name and his practice. Standing in judgment, the queens erased some teachers' pictures altogether. To exercise their authority over others, they drew over and scribbled on teachers' images and those of other students.

Students with the greatest status were freed from judgment, and their written comments became models for others to copy. As I watched, one student carefully moved her finger across the page, working cautiously to transfer a phrase exactly from one yearbook to another. Because a particular phrase was perceived as carrying more currency in this arena, this teen appropriated the words of another student as her own in order for her own voice to contain that power. Students shared texts and at times took another person's message for their own, copying the same phrase from one yearbook to the next to the next. In such borrowing of texts, one, in a sense, borrowed the social status of another. In taking another's message as her own, each girl had to be careful not to overstep her boundaries, and, as Shuman (1986) suggests, write what she was not entitled to write.

In the act of writing, students inadvertently may mark themselves as outsiders by writing a message judged inappropriate by others. If one was not savvy enough to create an appropriate text or powerful enough to forgo judgment, often, out of fear of marking oneself as outsider, one just scribbled safe messages such as "Have a good summer" or "See ya next year."

Some students, in order to preserve their social position, asked a friend, "What should I write? What do you want me to say?" Students took this opportunity to exert their position of authority and made such playful comments as "Say I'm 'just too cool' " or "Say 'she's always got a taco' " (a current description for shorts or jeans that were considered too tight across the seat of the pants) or "Write, 'BFF ASS' " (a code for best friends forever and always stay sweet or sexy). Many comments were so highly coded that only those few insiders could translate them.

In order for students to demonstrate that they were with it, comments carrying the current pop jargon taken from movies, television, or local sources become etched into this school-sanctioned document, creating an unusual juxtaposition of sanctioned and out-of-bounds literacies. Dark, graffiti-like messages boldly cut across the white-bordered layout and quite literally "defaced" students and teachers alike. With big pink erasers, students rubbed out the faces of outsiders.

Constructing a dual set of standards as a way to separate themselves from adults and from children, the queens at times judged their yearbook writing as appropriate for their friends but too obscene to share with parents, teachers, or those outside their social network. Adhering to the adolescent code, the queens sought to present a sexual self, lacing romance and sexual innuendo into their messages. They reported to me that such topics were appropriate for them as teenagers and continued to hide them from parents and teachers.

In all of this writing, the queens demonstrated a tremendous sense of play. Signing yearbooks had the feeling of recess, providing playtime away from the institutional demands of schooling, away from adult supervision. Similar to the playground, who could play was controlled by the peer dynamic. The yearbook was used to stake out territory and control social interactions. Yearbook messages regulated relationships and interests. In these ways, yearbook writing served two purposes: to construct a border around particular adolescents and to measure growth into adulthood.

Embracing Adolescence: The Yearbook as Process and Object

The yearbook provided a pictorial history, freezing moments of friendship, of athletic prowess, of academic endeavors. It provided, too, a unique opportunity to blur the boundaries between school-sanctioned literacies and literate underlife: sanctioned time in the school context given over to leisure, words written publicly yet secretly and quite literally written across the faces of authority while under the watchful gaze of those in authority. For seventh graders here, it was their first yearbook, a symbol of membership in the junior high school and entry into an adolescent arena: photos published as proof of sanctioned membership in the junior high, words scribbled across those pages as proof of the unsanctioned resistance that marks one as adolescent.

As a member of any club, one accepts the rules and obligations of the organization in order to enjoy the rights and benefits that accompany such a membership. Membership in the junior high "club" carried dues; competition and cocurricular participation were a central part of such obligations. In other words, one must embrace or at least comply with the roles that such a membership enlists.

Belonging to the Northern Hills district is a privilege that few parents or teachers would refute. With top standardized test scores and a near zero dropout rate, Northern Hills is looked on as a highly successful, fully functioning district. A full array of cocurricular opportunities, well-kept grounds and facilities, abundant instructional materials, and low student-teacher ratios serve as markers of school success that carry across state lines and distinguish the Northern Hills Community School District as one of the finest in the nation. Northern Hills, fully entitled to call itself a place of pride, closely matches an idealized school. Yet, do we fully understand the implications of this match? Terry Eagleton (1991) writes:

> *In the field of education, for example, symbolic violence operates not so much by the teacher speaking "ideologically" to the students, but by the teacher being perceived as in possession of an amount of "cultural capital" which the student needs to acquire. The educational system thus contributes to reproducing the dominant social order not so much by the viewpoint it fosters, but by this regulated distribution of cultural capital . . . those who lack the "correct" taste are unobtrusively excluded, relegated to shame and silence. (pp. 157–58)*

I contend that it is not the teacher alone but the entire institution and larger community that distribute a pervasive cultural capital. As a "Place of Pride," Northern Hills articulates a progressivism that characterizes its curriculum; yet such an insistent argument masks the traditional remnants that persist under the surface. When we examine school as a symbol of membership in a larger culture, we uncover a powerful ideology that continues to privilege the dominant class and insists on maintaining the status quo. The junior high comes equipped with one way of being in the world. The junior high school arena requires the strong sense of competition and team membership that permeated the pages of the yearbook. To resist the demands of this adolescent organization marks one as less than a fully functioning member.

I would argue that the characteristics of adolescence as a developmental stage are not so much a part of this stage because they are biologically wired or psychologically triggered. They emerge because they are ideological constructs that are fostered by the schedule and structure of the junior high school. Beyond economics, the emphasis at Northern Hills on cocurricular activities that fill up afterschool, evening, and weekend hours requires children to realign their positions within their family structure. A focus on winning both in the classroom and on the athletic field nurtured a keen focus on the self. Thus, to fully participate in this club, earning the privileges that it entails, demanded strong same-age social networks, severing or at least distancing from parental ties, and placing emphasis on a competitive self, all highly prized by Northern Hills standards. Members in good standing met such demands. Anyone who was unwilling or unable to meet them was marginalized.

The junior high yearbook packed the ideology of the school district and the larger culture into its 48 pages, translating a set of values into images and texts that were carried through the halls and through the community. Looking back at the yearbook as literacy event, looking through the eyes of Cleo and Tiffany, the yearbook takes on significance both as process (ideological inculcation) and object (cultural capital).

Throughout this examination of the yearbook as event, it becomes clear that while the discourse of adolescence denies diversity, those complexities, however subtle, do exist, creating invisible obstacles. A vast tangle of competing expectations and allegiances shapes the school context, which in turn shapes social roles. As an actual event and as a larger symbol, the school yearbook illustrates how one's membership constricts and enables particular literate practices that in turn constrict and enable particular roles available to group members.

Conceived of as an opportunity for all to celebrate the completion of another successful academic year, the yearbook provided much more. It served as a marker. For Tiffany and the other social queens it reaffirmed thier position in the school arena and in the larger community. They measured their status by the number and size of their pictures and by the number of requests to sign books: "Everybody wants me to sign their book." For Cleo and her friends, it also reaffirmed their position: "None of my friends are in there anyway."

The role of the yearbook within the institutional context remains central to the closing of the school year. The yearbook stands as an icon. Unknowingly, some are allowed to speak while others are silenced, some to write while others are written upon.

References for "Entering Adolescence" by Margaret J. Finders

Atwell, N. (1987). *In the middle: Writing, reading and learning with adolescents.* Portsmouth, NH: Boynton/Cook.

Bourdieu, P. (1977). *Outline of a theory of practice.* Cambridge, UK: Cambridge University Press.

Cherland, M. (1994). *Private practices: Girls reading fiction and constructing identity.* London: Taylor and Francis.

Eaagleton, T. (1991). *Ideology: An introduction.* New York: Verso.

Giroux, H, (1992). Critical literacy and student experience: Donald Graves' approach to literacy. In Patrick Shannon (Ed.), *Becoming political: Reading and writing in the politics of literacy education* (pp. 15-20). Portsmouth, NH: Heinemann.

Graves, D. (1983). *Writing: Teachers and children at work.* Portsmouth, NH: Heinemann.

McRobbie, A. (1978). Working class girls and the culture of feminity. In Women's Studies Group (Eds.), *Women take issue: Aspects of women's subordination* (pp. 96-108). London: Hutchinson.

Meyers, J. (1992). The social contexts of school and personal literacy. *Reading Research Quarterly, 27,* 297-333.

Schlegel, A. and BARRY, H. III. (1991). *Adolescence: An anthropological inquiry.* New York: The Free Press.

Shuman, A. (1986). *Storytelling rights: The uses of oral and written texts by urban adolescents.* Cambridge, UK: Cambridge University Press.

Shuman, A. (1993). "Get outa my face": Entitlement and authoritative discourse. In S. Hill & J. Irvien (Eds.), *Responsibility and evidence in oral discourse* (pp. 135-160). New York: Cambridge University Press.

Smith, F. (1986). *Insult to intelligence: The bureacratic invasion of our classrooms.* Portsmouth, NH: Heinemann.

Weiss, L. (1993). Disempowering white working-class females: The role of the high school. In L. Weiss & M. Fine (Eds.), *Beyond silenced voices: Class, race, and gender in the United States schools* (pp. 95-121). Albany: SUNY Press.

West, C. and Zimmerman, D. H. (1987). Doing gender. *Gender and Society*, 1, 2, pp. 125-151.

17

Witnessing Whiteness

MICHELLE FINE

Michelle Fine is Professor of Psychology at the City University of New York Graduate Center and the Senior Consultant at the Philadelphia Schools Collaborative. Her recent publications include Chartering Urban School Reform: Reflections on Public High Schools in the Midst of Change *(1994)*, Beyond Silenced Voices: Class, Race and Gender in American Schools *(with Lois Weis, 1992)*, Disruptive Voices: The Transgressive Possibilities of Feminist Research *(1992)*, and Framing Dropouts: Notes on the Politics of an Urban High School *(1991). She has provided courtroom expert testimony for cases including the Anthony T. Lee, et al. and the United States of America vs Macon County Board of Education; Shannon Richey Faulkner and the United States of America vs James E. Jones, et al. for The Citadel, The Military College of South Carolina; Ulcena vs Babylon School District, High School and Babylon School Board; and the Board of Education of the Borough of Englewood Cliffs vs Board of Education of the City of Englewood vs Board of Education of the Borough of Tenafly. In addition, she works nationally as a consultant to parents' groups, community groups, and teacher unions on issues of school reform. She was recently awarded the Janet Helms Distinguished Scholar Award 1994.*

What if we took the position that racial inequities were not primarily attributable to individual acts of discrimination targeted against persons of color, but increasingly to acts of cumulative privileging quietly loaded up

223

on whites? That is, what if by keeping our eyes on those who gather disadvantage, we have not noticed white folks, varied by class and gender, nevertheless stuffing their academic and social pickup trucks with goodies otherwise not as readily available to people of color?

It is to this question of "witnessing whiteness" that I chose to turn in this essay. With the raw nerve of reflection and the need for better racial thinking, I avert my gaze from the "inequities" produced through "colors" (where my work has lingered for so long) and turn, instead, to the "merit" that accumulates within the hue of "whiteness." While Toni Morrison (1992), Ruth Frankenburg (1993), Christine Sleeter (1993), Michael Novick (1995), and many others have argued that whiteness and "other colors" must be recognized in their rainbowed interdependence, if not in their parasitic webbing, I find myself trying to understand how whiteness accrues privilege and status; gets itself surrounded by protective pillows of resources and/or benefits of the doubt; how whiteness repels gossip and voyeurism and instead demands dignity.[1]

This essay focuses on three sites of research in which I have had the opportunity to witness not only the ways in which "people of color" accumulate "deficits," but the ways in which white adolescents and adults accumulate "benefits." My work has moved toward institutional analyses because I worry that those of us interested in qualitative inquiry and critical "race" theory have focused fetishistically on those who endure discrimination. By so doing we have been unable/unwilling to analyze how those who inherit privilege do so. As such, we have camouflaged the intricate institutional webbing that connects "whiteness" and "other colors."

So, this essay tries to chart a theoretical argument about the institutional processes by which "whiteness" is today produced as advantage through schools and the economy. Historically, in both psychology and education, whiteness has remained both unmarked and unstudied. More recently, by some scholars, it has been elevated to the status of "independent variable," one that scientists use to predict other outcomes. In this essay I want to reverse conceptually this notion by asserting that institutions work by producing "whiteness" as merit/advantage within elites and, more elusively, within the working class/poor. Four theoretical assumptions arrange my thinking.

First, as I've said, whiteness, like all "colors," is being manufactured, in part, through institutional arrangements. This is particularly the case in institutions designed "as if" hierarchy, stratification, and scarcity were inevitable. Schools and work, for example, do not merely *manage* race; they *create* and *enforce* racial meanings. Second, in such institutions, whiteness is actually *coproduced* with other colors, usually alongside blackness, in symbiotic relation. Where whiteness grows as a seemingly "natural" proxy for quality, merit, and advantage, "color" disintegrates to embody deficit or "lack." Third, whiteness and "color" are therefore not merely created in parallel, but are fundamentally relational and need to be studied as a system; they might, in statistical terms, be considered "nested" rather than coherent or independent variables. Fourth, the institutional design of whiteness, like the production of all colors, creates an organizational *discourse* of race and a personal *embodiment* of race, affecting perceptions of Self and Others, producing both individuals' sense of racial "identities" and collective experiences of racial "tensions," even coalitions. Once this process is sufficiently institutionalized and embodied, the observer, that is, the scholar, can easily miss the institutional choreography which has produced a stratified rainbow of colors. What remains visible are the miraculous ways in which quality seems to rise to the glistening white top.

To understand this production, I import Pierre Bourdieu's (1991) writings, in which he invokes the word *institution*:

> *The act of institution is an act of magic (p. 119). . . . An act of communication, but of a particular kind: it signifies to someone what his identity is, but in a way that both expresses it to him and imposes it on him by expressing it in front of everyone and thus informing him in an authoritative manner of what he is and what he must be (p. 121). This is also one of the functions of the act of institution: to discourage permanently any attempt to cross the line, to transgress, desert, or quit. (p. 336)*

This essay is a plea to re-search institutions: to notice, to remove the white glaucoma that has ruined scholarly vision, as we lift up the school and work-related dynamics that make whites and other racial groups seem so separable, and so relentlessly rank ordered.

Scene One, "White Lies"

The scene is Wedowee, Alabama, the site where the principal, Hulond Humphries, was charged in 1994 with racial harassment. My involvement emerges because I am among those representing the United States Justice Department; I am meeting with students at Randolph County High School (RCHS). Callie is a young white woman. She's a junior at RCHS: "My mother asked for someone, you know, the principal, to watch me and find out if I'm dating a black boy. So Mr. Humphries called me in and he told me if I kept on dating John I wouldn't be able to get any white boys. No one else would go out with me. We could have a child who's not very smart. And if I go to a family reunion, I may be the only white woman there and no one's going to even talk to me. Then I'd be an outcast." Trina, an African American eleventh grader jumps in. "He called us all into the auditorium after their talk and asked how many of us are going to the prom with someone of the other race. Lots of us raised our hands. Then he asked Rovanda [a biracial student at the school], 'Rovanda, who you taking to the prom?' And Rovanda said, 'I'm taking Chris,' her white boyfriend. And he just looked up in the bleachers, and he said, 'I won't have it. No interracial dating in my school.' And Rovanda said, 'Who would you like me to take to the prom?' He said, 'You were a mistake, and we don't want other mistakes like you.' " Tasha joined in, "He said he was canceling the prom." King said, "When he called Rovanda a mistake, it was like he took an axe and cut through the heart of a tree. The heart of our school."

I opened with questions about tracking at the high school. This high school has an "advanced" and a "standard" track. Knowing something about the (unfortunately predictable) racial splitting by track, I asked the students in the group—white students and African American students—what track are you in? The white kids raised their hand when I said "advanced"; then the African American kids raised their hands when I said "standard." I later learned how profoundly the aggregate numbers, over time, bore out that simple hand-raising exercise.

It's important to know that at this school, like at many schools, students have what is considered a race-neutral "choice" about which track they opt into. And they "chose" by race. White racism here—and elsewhere—is so thoroughly institutionalized and embodied that young people, when given an opportunity, "choose" their "place," and seemingly with little protest. I asked "Why did you choose the standard track? The standard track doesn't allow you to attend a four-year college like University of Alabama. You don't take enough math or science to make it into a four-year college." African American students offered a litany of painful, if predictable, responses. "Because I was scared." "Because we thought it [advanced] was too hard." "Because my friends were in the standard track." When Tigray mumbled, "Because maybe they are smarter than we are," Callie, the young white woman who opened the scene, responded, "That's the scam they pull on you. There are plenty of dumb white kids in my classes, but they would never go to the standard track." I pressed Callie, "What would happen if you told your guidance counselor you wanted to be in a standard track?" She laughed, "She'd say, 'Callie, what are you talking about? You're not going into the standard track, you're going to college.' " Indeed in this "integrated" school the advanced track is almost all white; no varsity cheerleader has ever been Black; an African American boy who ran for President of the Student Council talks of harassment from the principal; almost all the faculty were white. Every strata of school life—academics, social relations, postsecondary opportunities, and sexuality—layered by race. Visually apparent, and vigilantly enforced (see Oakes, 1980; Rosenbaum, 1976).

Wanting to understand the principal's motive for his public performance of racializing, I met with Hulond Humphries. We met in the basement of the school district building. Clear that I represented the team for the Justice Department, I probed with pen in hand, "Why did you say what you said about the prom? You must have known it would cause the kind of hysteria that it did." To which he said, "It's not that I have anything against interracial dating. . . . It's just that those black boys really want our white girls." He continued, "Now with that feminism, Black girls are wanting our white boys." Clear lines. Blacks as sexual predators. Whites as prey. Bourdieu's verb spreads to sexuality.

The night before I went to the school, I had the privilege of visiting the African Zion Church just outside of town. I sat, stood, sang for hours, ecstatic and anxious to be part of chanting, singing, praying, preaching, and testifying about what it was like to be a student, a parent, a community member, Black, within reach of those schools. Then the most elder Reverend booms, "Every ten years or so God tests the racial waters of the United States. We are privileged that this year He chose Wedowee for His test. And what is our job? To *love* those people to death."

That was the racial tapestry of schooling in Wedowee, Alabama; the fabric in which young whites and African American children's lives were intimately interwoven. What is striking is how much the students, white and black, knew their place and rarely dared to protest aloud. White students' place was just "north" of black students'. Black students' place was just below white students'. In this small working-class town, southern affect and congeniality allowed little anger to seep explicitly into cross-racial interactions. The Black church was the "safe space," the emotional safety valve, the place to put and contain anger, the "sanity check" on Sunday evening which would allow all to return to the perverse, hostile, if sometimes congenial stratification that many explained constitutes community life Monday through Friday.

Discursively and materially whiteness is here produced and maintained through the withholding of opportunity from, and the denigration of that which is Black. The prom was simply a metaphor for all the attempts to separate and sanitize white from black, to insure privilege. But being *white*, in and of itself, in troubled economic times, today guarantees little in Alabama. At least for these poor and working-class families. Unemployment and poverty rates run high across racial groups. Therefore—and this is my major point—this racial formation was filled with parasitic interdependence such that *whites needed Blacks in order to become privileged*. African American students *were* getting less than white students. However, as true, *nobody* was getting a very rigorous academic education. No one was taking math courses more difficult than Advanced Algebra, and still none of the African American students had been enrolled even at this level. One might cynically argue that the white students were "lucky" to have the Black students so they could imagine themselves enjoying any "privilege." The cleansing of whiteness—in class tracks, dating, cheerleading, and college opportunities—was the job of the institution.

Two theoretical insights warrant attention. One is that these poor and working-class racial identities and concomitant "racial tensions," perhaps even "desires," were invented and sustained through privilege and power defined and insured by withholding. Whiteness was produced *through* the exclusion and denial of opportunity of people to color. In other words, giving Blacks access to white opportunities would threaten to stain, indeed blacken, that which is white. Access is a threat to whiteness when whiteness requires the exportation (and denigration) of color.

Second, this case points up evidence of how institutional leadership and seemingly race-neutral policies/practices work to insure white privilege. The leader of this institution, Hulond Humphries, articulated publicly what he fundamentally believed about race, capacity, sexuality, and who deserves to be educated. In a racially hostile environment, it's not only very hard for biracial and African Americans to participate with full heart and mind. As devastating, in such environments, *white students* develop a profoundly false sense of superiority premised almost entirely on denigration which requires opposition to sustain the racial hierarchy. Opposition and denigration became a fix, a steroid to white identity. This public school, in its leadership, policies, and daily practices, did little to interrupt—and much to produce—this steroid. All in the name of creating and maintaining merit and "quality." As the work of Sam Gaertner et al. (1995) reveals, we may be witnessing today a reassertion of prowhite policies and practices rather than (or in addition to) actively hostile discrimination targeted at people of color. If this is the case, that whiteness is "catching" privilege, then where we look for evidence of discrimination and prejudice will have to move to the cumulative benefits of being white, rather than the (exclusive) tracking of blatant racism against, in this case, Blacks. Documenting racism *against*, as if separable from racism *for*, may be a diversionary strategy by which our eyes have been averted from the real prize.

Scene Two: Whiting Out Social Critique

In Wedowee, denigration by race among the poor and working class was publicly institutionalized and personally internalized. And critique was hard to find. For Scene Two we head North to track an institution in which race and gender critique was once voiced vociferously, among the privileged, but it "disappeared" over time. This is a story of the University of Pennsylvania's Law School in which we (Lani Guinier, Michelle Fine, Jane Balin, Ann Bartow, and Deborah Satchel, 1994) studied the gender and race dynamics percolating within an elite law school. Again we witness how white rises to the top through seemingly neutral policies and practices.

A first-year black woman law student offers: "I think it is still that people don't understand why African Americans are still struggling, or why we're struggling. To me it's incredible! It's like a blindness! And I listen to some of the comments in class, and I realize that I'm just coming from an entirely different world. From the perspective of most people, I'm just more aware of my history and law and things as it relates to black people. And I think that part of it has to do to with the fact that white students think they're going to be a lawyer. They don't have to think about who they're going to represent, or that they have to represent all black people."

This is a study in which we surveyed first, second, and third year law students' attitudes, beliefs, and experiences, and then we examined three cohorts of academic performance in a school in which dropouts are remarkably rare. We conducted individual and group interviews with students across the law school, men and women, and students of all colors. In the condensed version of the findings, the attitudinal data reveal vast initial differences in political perspective, levels of alienation, and visions for the future both by race and gender. But as bold as they were, these statistically significant initial differences disappeared over time. They were barely discernable by graduation year. By year three, most law students saw the school, social justice, and the world as white males did in year one.

The sad tale is that social critique by race/gender doesn't age very well within educational institutions. It gets snuffed out so that over time such concerns either turn inward or they get muffled. Through the process of what might be called "professional socialization," the young adults we studied grew anesthetized to things that they once, in the beginnings of their school career, considered outrageous (e.g., generic "he," adversarial method, differential participation by gender, inaccessible faculty, sexist jokes). Among first-year women, for instance, 25 percent were interested in Public Interest Law compared to 7 percent of the men. Yet by year three only 8 percent of women and 7 percent of men expressed an interest in Public Interest law. First-year women reported concerns with the issues of social justice and social problems, and even dismay at the use of the generic "he." By year three their political attitudes were akin to the white men's. Not that the men got more progressive. The women had "become gentlemen," as one professor encouraged them to do.

Unlike Wedowee, where critique was ghettoized on Sunday and stratification embodied Monday through Friday, here critique saw light of day for year one of law school and then it turned inward, against self, obvious in lowered grades, worsened mental health, and conservatized politics for white women, and women and men of color.

First-year black female: "I don't know, maybe I'm just paranoid or something. And I wonder how people are perceiving that, [they must be] thinking about it all the time. I get the sense that maybe people won't listen to me as much as if I were a white person saying it. And then people, when they do listen to me, they say, 'well of course she's going to say that, because she's thinking of her own self-interest.' " White people speak for the common good, and people of color speak for self-interest.

First-year Latino male: "It's one of the pressures, the initial pressures of being in a very social environment, like in law school. Feeling that what you contribute is not being weighed as much as everybody else's contribution because someone is attaching something else to what you're saying. It's very disconcerting for me, and it makes me kind of zone out of the whole process." Remember that, zoning out when you feel like no one's paying attention to what you're saying.

First-year black male: "Whenever a minority issue comes up I feel like I'm expected to say something. If I don't say something I'm shunning my race, and if I do say something nobody listens. So you're battling with both sides of the coin. And then if you come forth and you say something, people think they're complimenting you and they say, 'Wow! That's really a . . . statement!' 'That was really awesome!' 'That was really intelligent!' [laughter] As if I was the first person to have ever spoken in the place. And they had no idea that I had an education. I find it very disturbing, and you have to deal with it and get along with the rest of the class."

At Penn, like in Wedowee, institution-based racial/gendered sedimentation grew into "merit" over time. What began in year one as prominent race/gender differences in critical perspective grew silenced, converted into an institutional story of gendered/racial success and failure. By year three, these differences just looked like "merit" and its absence, not gender or race. Thus, when we study school-based "success" and "failure" as though they were *inherently individualistic* and therefore only *coincidentally* white (or not) and male (or not), we *deinstitutionalize* pathways toward success and failure, and we deny the racial and gendered scaffolding of academic hierarchies.

By the end of the law school experience, year three students of color and white women at Penn feel and look inadequate (see Guinier et al. for detailed analysis of the data). With their critique whited out and their progressive politics forced underground, their mental health falters and their achievement torpedoes. Over time, it seemed as though race and gender were simply (naturally?) the best "predictors" of performance. Few wanted to talk about this. It was considered heretic (if obvious) to conclude, as we did, that race and gender stratifications were instead products of institutional hierarchy, alienation, and stratification.

Liberal notions of *legal access* to historically white male institutions grow suspect under the scrutiny of these data. Institutional transformation is as necessary as it is feared. Without it, institutions (and equity advocates) may be inviting white women and men and women of color into institutions that are ultimately damaging (if credentialing), while these institutions remain unchanged.

Scene Three: "Those Angry White Men"

With the generosity of a Spencer Foundation grant, Lois Weis and I, with our graduate students, have been conducting interviews in Jersey City and Buffalo with white, African American, Latino, and Asian young adults—age twenty-one to twenty-nine—poor and working class. In one slice of this project we have collected oral histories from white working-class men, narrating, in part, their current economic plight. By listening to these "angry white men" one can hear how global flight of capital and the consequential labor-market scarcity has sharpened and prolonged racial identities, tensions, and sedimentation. While relative to their fathers these white working-class men have taken a disproportional hit under the macroeconomic policies of Reagan and Bush, the flight of capital out of the Northeast and out of the country, and the dismantling of blue collar unions, these men, when interviewed, lay blame for their economic woes squarely at the feet of African American males. Not Republicans, not global capitalists, not elites. African American men—as in Wedowee—are discursively imported to buffer the pain, protest the loss, and still secure the artificial privilege of whiteness (see Aronowitz and DeFazio, 1993; Harrison, 1982; Reich, 1991). Occluded are the macrostructures that have forced white working-class men out of the labor market and into an obsession with Black men, affirmative action, and welfare. The fetish of Wedowee returns.

"What's your experience been like here as a white male?" Jim reports: "For the most part I haven't noticed. I think more or less the white male has become the new minority. At this point blacks, Hispanics, or women, it's just that with all these quotas, instead of hiring who's best for the job, you have to hire according to your quota system. Which is very wrong." "Do you have any sense of, like, social movements, like civil rights?" "Civil rights, as far as I'm concerned, is way out of proportion." "Talk to me more about that." "Well, granted, the African Americans were slaves. But that was over two hundred years ago. They were given their freedom. And as a country, I guess you could say, you know, we tried. Well, I think that all of us try. But most of us really tried to make things a little more equal. We tried to smooth over the rough spots. And you get some of those other ones, some of those militants who are now claiming that after all this time they're still not treated equal.

"This takes me to another subject where," states Paul, "where blacks, I don't have anything against blacks, whether you're white or black or yellow, whatever. I mean I have black friends. I talk to them and they agree, you know. They consider themselves, well, let me give you an example. Like there's white trash and there's good white people. Right? And so there's black trash and there's good black people. And it's the same way with any race. But then, as soon as they don't get the job, right away they yell, 'discrimination.' "

Mark is a white fireman who paints the Jersey City firehouse as a historically reliable site for civil service work. A noninvaded space, once secure for, and exclusive to, working-class white males. "It's just right now with these minority quotas . . . Affirmative Action is about to blow us all apart." This Fire Department, as is true for many fire departments, has been a significant venue for not-very-well-educated, working-class white males to secure job security and benefits. Mark is as certain that minorities have gained access to the fire department unfairly as he is sure that white men have gained access through merit.

What we hear from these young white males across Buffalo and Jersey City are innocent identities carved in opposition to people of color. In our interviews, you can't go for more than fifteen, twenty minutes with a white man before affirmative action put-downs or quotes about "welfare cheats" are inserted into the conversation. We hear whiteness, again, being produced and narrated in contrast to Blackness and in response to an alleged "scarcity of opportunities." This rhetoric relies upon fetishistic opposition and denigration. These men, indeed powerfully assaulted by economic shifts, systematically refuse to examine the large structural conditions that have betrayed them. Instead of looking critically up and out, and organizing along class lines, they focus narrowly and virulently on men (and women) of color. Despite the evidence of class-based politics, they adhere to whiteness as their badge of deservingness.

Conclusions

Psychologists and educators have contributed mightily to the resurrection and reification of racial stratification. I want to suggest that we turn a corner and move ourselves into the role of what Gramsci (1971) has called public intellectuals; engaged in raising up a set of questions about racial formation that haven't been raised, certainly not within these two fields. In times and sites of constructed "scarcity" such as schools and labor in current times, whiteness is being reconstituted as quality, deservingness, and merit. We have a social science that colludes in this fantasy when we need one that dismantles.

All of these scenes raise up important questions about the theories, methods, and ethics by which we study what Winant and Omi call racial formation; the relation of whiteness and other racial/ethnic groups. If we—that is, psychologists and educators—persist in our analyses "as if" races/ethnicities were distinct, separable, and independent rather than produced, coupled, and ranked, then we will continue to "discover" that white kids (or adults) "have it" (whatever it is) and students/workers of color don't. Or we will continue to agitate for everyone to have access to inhospitable institutions—when in fact many forms of institutional life are fundamentally constituted through racial, class, and gender sedimentation and exclusion.

I don't mean to be cynical at the end of this essay, only to agitate for social scientists to understand that *we* collude in the seeming mystery of (non) "mobility" and (un) "equal opportunity" when we presume that we can disaggregate quantitatively and qualitatively in our studies what "whites" have and what "people of color" don't, and then—as liberals— "pump into those students/workers of color" the characteristics we think that white students/workers have, and others need. If institutions refuse to dismantle the filters which limit opportunities for intellectual and economic work, such analyses (and interventions) may ultimately boomerang and punish victims.

Those of us engaged in qualitative work in schooling and the economy have important decisions to make. We have documented well inequities in academic outcomes, and the disparate treatment of students by race (Banks and Banks, 1989;

Delpit, 1993; Schofield, 1989), class (Fine, 1991; Weis, 1990) and gender (Bilkin and Pollard, 1993). We have advocated interventions "for" those historically at the short end of the proverbial stick. We have argued for access to historically hostile institutions for students and workers long denied such promising opportunities.

The work reported in this chapter cautions, however, that we may have reached a moment in which theoretically, empirically, and strategically it's time to shift gears (or multiply). If institutions are organized such that being white (or male, or elite) buys protection and if this protection necessitates the institutional subversion of opportunities for persons of color in policies/practices that appear race-neutral, then liberal strategies for access are limited. By that I mean that those who have been historically excluded may disproportionately "fail" to perform "to standard." Some will drop out. A few will go nuts. A handful will survive as "the good ones." The institutional mantra of deficit and merit will triumph.

Today the cultural gaze of surveillance—whether it be a gaze of pity, blame, or liberal hope—falls on persons of color. Whether we consider the school in Wedowee or the students at Penn or listen to white working-class men angry about affirmative action, social surveillance, as Foucault foretold, falls squarely on those who are marked: Colored. In this paper I have argued that social scientists too have colluded in this myopia, legitimizing the fetish, turning away from opportunities to surveil "white," refusing, therefore, to notice the institutional choreography that renders whiteness meritocratic and other colors deficient.

With this paper I invite colleagues to consider not only the unfair disadvantages that accrue institutionally to darker hues, but the institutionalized pillows and profit that surround and grow embodied, by "white." Social scientists need to interrupt the cultural gaze, not make a science of it.

References

Aronowitz, S., and Difazio, W. (1995). *The Jobless Future*. Minneapolis: University of Minnesota Press.

Banks, J. A., and Banks, C. M. (1989). *Multicultural Education: Issues and Perspectives*. Boston: Allyn.

Biklin, S. K., and Pollard, D. (1993). *Gender and Education*. Chicago, IL: National Society for the Study of Education.

Bluestone, B., and Harrison, B. (1982). *The Deindustrialization of America*. New York, NY: Basic Books.

Bourdieu, P. (1991). *Language and Symbolic Power*. Cambridge, MA: Howard.

Delpit, L. (1993). "The Silenced Dialogue." In L. Weis and M. Fine (eds.) *Beyond Silenced Voices*. Albany, NY: SUNY Press.

Fine, M. (1991). *Framing Dropouts*. Albany, NY: SUNY Press.

Foucault, M. (1978). *Discipline and Punish*. New York, NY: Vintage.

Frankenberg, R. (1993). *White Women, Race Matters*. Minneapolis: University of Minnesota Press.

Gaertner, S. L., Davidio, J. F., Banker, B. S., Rust, M. C., Nier, J. A., Mottola, G. R., and Ward, C. M. (in press). "Does White Racism Necessarily Mean Anti-Blackness? Aversive Racism and Pro-Whiteness." In this volume.

Gramsci, A. (1971). *Selections from Prison Notebooks*. New York, NY: International.

Guinier, L., Fine, M., Balin, J., with Bartow, A., and Stachel, L. "Becoming Gentlemen: Women's Experiences at One Ivy League Law School." *University of Pennsylvania Law Review*, 143(4), 1–110.

Morrison, T. (1992). *Playing in the Dark*. New York, NY: Harvard.

Novick, M. (1995). *White Lies, White Power*. Monroe, ME: Common Courage Press.

Oakes, J. (1988, January). "Tracking: Can Schools Take a Different Route?" *National Education Association*, 41–47.

Reich, R. (1991). *The Work of Nations: Preparing Ourselves for 21st-Century Capitalism*. New York, NY: Alfred Knopf.

Rosenbaum, J. (1976). *Making Inequality*. New York, NY: John Wiley and Sons.

Schofield, J. W. (1989). *Black and White in School*. New York, NY: Teachers College Press.

Sleeter, C. E. (1993). "How White Teachers Construct Race." In C. McCarthy and W. Crichlow (eds.) *Race, Identity and Representation in Education*. New York, NY: Routledge.

Weis, L., Proweller, A., and Contri, C. (in press). "Re-examining a 'Moment in History': Loss of Privilege inside White, Working Class Masculinity in the 1990s." In this volume.

WEIS, L. (1990). *Working Class without Work*. New York, NY: Routledge.

Note

1. We need only note who among so many prominent adult males recently accused of violence against women have drawn and fixated our (whose "our" white woman) attention—and who appear too pudgy or dull or sleepy to watch. Need I note that we have not been obsessed with Senator Packwood's (non)hearings, the Joel Rifkin serial killings of prostitutes, esteemed Judge Sol Wachtler's masquerading as a cowboy and posing death threats to his former lover and her daughter anywhere near as passionately as "we" (there she goes again) have been obsessed by the O.J. hearings (which eventually wore off—but are still being telecast), Senator Mel Reynold's telephone sex, Colin Ferguson's masquerade as a lawyer, or Clarence Thomas.

   This is not an invitation to "not look" at men of color who have committed, or been accused of committing, horrendous acts of violence against women, it is simply to notice that when white men do the same our cultural instinct is to resist voyeurism. Elite white men at least enjoy the dignity of "privacy." Not quite as vulnerable to gossip, they are rejected culturally as the site for social surveillance.

18

Changing the
Face of Poverty

Nonprofits and the Problem of Representation

Diana George

Constructively changing the ways the poor are represented in every aspect of life is one progressive intervention that can challenge everyone to look at the face of poverty and not turn away.

—BELL HOOKS, Outlaw Culture.

ENCLOSED: No Address Labels to Use Up.
No Calendars to Look At.
No Petitions to Sign.

And No Pictures of Starving Children.

Fig. 1 Text from the outer envelope of a 1998 Oxfam appeal

As I write this, Thanksgiving is near. I am about to go out and fill a box with nonperishables for the annual St. Vincent De Paul food drive. Christmas lights already outline some porches. Each day my mailbox is stuffed with catalogs and bills and with appeals from the Native American Scholarship Fund, the Salvation Army, WOJB—Voice of the Anishinabe, the Navaho Health Foundation, the Barbara Kettle Gundlach Shelter Home for Abused Women, Little Brothers Friends of the Elderly, Habitat for Humanity, and more. One *New Yorker ad for Children, Inc.* reads, "You don't have to leave your own country to find third-world poverty." Alongside the ad copy, from a black-and-white full-page photo, a young girl in torn and ill-fitting clothes looks directly at the viewer. The copy continues. "Just travel along the hillsides and down through the valleys where the Appalachian coal mines have been shut down. Sad, hungry faces of little children. like Amy's, will haunt you."

The Oxfam promise that I quote above—to use no pictures of starving children—is surely an attempt to avoid the emotional overload of such images as the one *Children. Inc.* offers (fig 2). Still, those pictures—those representations of poverty—have typically been one way nonprofits have kept the poor before us. In a culture saturated by the image, how else do we convince Americans that—despite the prosperity they see all around them—there is real need out there? The solution for most nonprofits has been to show the despair. To do that they must represent poverty as something that can be seen and easily recognized: fallen down shacks and trashed out public housing, broken windows, dilapidated porches, barefoot kids with stringy hair, emaciated old women and men staring out at the camera with empty eyes. In such images, poverty is dirt and rags and helplessness. In mail, in magazines, and in newspapers, ads echoing these appeals must vie for our time, attention, and dollars with Eddie Bauer, Nordstrom's, the Gap, and others like them whose polished and attractive images fill our days.

In the pages that follow, I offer one way of understanding how the images nonprofits must rely on may, as Stanley Aronowitz has noted about so many public appeals, result in charity but not activism—not in real structural change or an understanding of the systems that remain in place to keep many in poverty even while the culture at large is a prosperous one.[1] I begin with a discussion of what it means to rely on an image to represent an argument about something as complex as poverty and social responsibility—and how nonprofits must convince potential benefactors that they are dealing with the *most* needy, with the "deserving" and not the "undeserving" poor. In the second part of this essay. I examine a particular representation of poverty—publicity videos produced by Habitat for Humanity—in order to suggest that reliance on stereotypes of poverty can, in fact, work against the aims of the organization producing them. Finally, I look at alternate representations of poverty, especially those offered by the poor themselves and by men and women who work among the poor in this country. If it is possible, as bell hooks suggests above, to constructively change the ways the poor are represented, then such a change must begin with those whose lives are defined by need.

"We Must See Them": The Problems of Representation

Consumer's Union Executive Director Rhoda H. Karpatkin explains her motive for commissioning Eugene Richards's 1985 photo documentary *Below the Line: Living Poor in America* with a workplace anecdote: "In the Consumers Union lunchroom one day, I asked several of my suburban coworkers if they see people who

Fig. 2

are hungry or homeless. Many do not. Yet we must *see* them before we can care about them. And we must care about them before we are moved to end the intolerable conditions that mark their lives."[2] That motive—to *show* the reality of hard lives in order to move others to act or, at least, react—is an old one.

We might reach back to the paintings of eighteenth-century French moralist Jean-Baptist Grueze, who equated much poverty with moral decay, or to similar representations by Greuze's English contemporary William Hogarth, whose paintings and engravings of English street life linked abject poverty to an unholy and unrepentant lifestyle, one that might lead to the horrors of *Gin Lane*, or the dismal life and ultimate execution of the Idle Apprentice. Or, better yet, we could look to Sir William Beechey's 1793 portrait of the Ford children giving alms to a ragged boy they have encountered in the lane on the edge of their estate.[3] Painted in the manner of Gainsborough, these pretty, delicate upper-class children lean forward to place a coin in the hand of a young beggar—his rags barely covering him, his chest curved inward against hunger and cold.

Paintings, however, are easily understood as interpretations, even fictions—in the case of Grueze and Hogarth, they are eighteenth-century morality tales intended to uplift the monied class at the same time that they reconfirm old prejudices and fears. As industrialization concentrated more poverty and crime in the cities, nineteenth-century journalists and reformers turned to other ways of uncovering the truth and despair of urban poverty, once again, in order to move others to action or at least to sympathy.

Whatever his methods—and they are contested—moving readers to sympathy, if not reform, was certainly a motive for Henry Mayhew when in 1850–1851 he published the first of four volumes of interviews, stories, and firsthand descriptions detailing the lives of London's poor and working poor.[4] In his introduction to the final volume *Those That Will Not Work*, Mayhew writes of beginning with the aim of not simply contributing new facts or with only the hope of making "the solution of the social problem more easy to us, but, setting more plainly before us some of its latent causes, [to] make us look with more pity and less anger on those who want the fortitude to resist their influence."[5] Mayhew reveals with this short statement, and even with the title of this volume, the ambivalence with which even reformers or journalists sympathetic to the plight of the poor approached their subject. "Those that will not work": are they victims to be pitied, or are they simply a drain on resources, a site of criminal behavior, or worse? What Mayhew asks is that his readers, in the least, temper their anger.

At the turn of this century, American novelist and journalist Jack London traveled to England to look again at London street life, to do more than Mayhew and actually *become* one of the London homeless. His accounts, as well, provide almost too vivid moments of the actuality of living in destitution. At one point as London walks beside two men who keep picking things up from the side-walk, he is so taken aback when he understands what they are doing that he pauses in shock and, for his reader, puts his revelation into italics: "*They picked up stray crumbs of bread the size of peas, apple cores so black and dirty one would not take them to be apple cores, and these things these two men took into their mouths, and chewed them, and swallowed them; and this, between six and seven o-clock in the evening of August 20, year of our Lord 1902, in the heart of the greatest, wealth-*

iest, and most powerful empire the world has ever seen."[6] For London, in contrast to Mayhew, there was little question of who or what was to blame. Writing in a moment of social realism with such contemporaries as Theodore Dreiser and Frank Norris, whose short stories and novels placed the individual at the mercy of an American capitalist machine out of control, London collects the stories of England's street people, thrown out to hunger and cold when industry has no more use for them: "The unfit and the unneeded! Industry does not clamor for them. There are no jobs going begging through lack of men and women. . . . Women and plenty to spare, are found to toil under the sweat-shop masters for tenpence a day of fourteen hours. Alfred Freeman crawls to muddy death because he loses his job. Ellen Hughes Hun prefers Regent's Canal to Islington Workhouse. Frank Cavilla cuts the throats of his wife and children because he cannot find work enough to give them food and shelter."[7] It is a bleak world made all the more bleak by the assuredness with which London offers his readers little hope.

For reformers, the firsthand account has perennially been the most compelling, for it is through such stark representations that writers and, even more so, photographers challenge their audiences to dare deny the truth before them. Photojournalist Jacob A. Riis's 1890 publication *How the Other Half Lives*, the first thoroughgoing attempt at documenting poverty using photography, certainly marked a turning point for social reform. Using his camera as a way to capture New York tenement life, Riis showed the filth, decay, chaos, and dangerous crowding of which most Americans knew nothing. For Riis, the tenements were "the nurseries of pauperism and crime that fill our jails and police courts; that throw off a scum of forty thousand human wrecks to the island asylums and workhouses year by year; that turned out in the last eight years a round half million beggars to prey upon our charities; that maintain a standing army of ten thousand tramps with all that that implies; because, above all, they touch the family life with deadly moral contagion." Quite bluntly, Riis challenged his readers: "What are you going to do about it?"[8] Riis's photographs are such unflinching documents that they are often credited with forcing housing reform in New York's tenement district.

It was that bluntness, the promise of photography to show what we might not otherwise see, that gave the publisher of Helen Campbell's *Darkness and Daylight: or Lights and Shadows of New York Life* the courage to boast that here we have a volume of uncommon faithfulness to the harsh face of street life in 1892 New York, brought even more vividly into view by "recent developments in photography [which] have rendered it possible to catch instantaneously all the details of a scene with the utmost fidelity." "It is said," writes this publisher, "that figures do not lie. Neither does the camera. In looking on these pages, the reader is brought face to face with real life as it is in New York; *not* AS IT WAS, but AS IT IS TO-DAY. Exactly as the reader sees these pictures, just so were the scenes presented to the camera's merciless and unfailing eye at the moment when the action depicted took place. Nothing is lacking but the actual *movement* of the persons represented."[9] Despite the publisher's assurance that we have before us what was captured by the untainted lens of the camera, the illustrations for *Darkness and Daylight are*, in fact, engravings made from the photos of Bellevue Hospital photographer O. G. Mason, photojournalist Riis, and others. Still, the claim is crucial to the book's argument that we must be able to *see* the poverty (and depravity) that fills the streets of New York in order to truly understand it and, ultimately, to be moved to end it. The motive is a humanistic one—the belief that seeing is not only believing but understanding as well. Furthermore, such a belief constitutes a faith that, once understood, the problem can—indeed will—be solved.

In depicting the poor, whether in literature, journalism, painting, or photography, representations swing between imaging the impoverished as dangerous, intemperate, low-life street thugs, or as helpless victims. Often, the two representations are somehow set together, as in Mayhew's depiction of those who *will not* work but whose lives must still be looked on with pity. Helen Campbell's volume—while it has much in common with *Riis's How the Other Half Lives* and even takes some of its engravings from those and similar photographs—actually is the story of a Christian temperance mission, suggesting that the true horror of New York Street life begins and ends in the bottle. The pages of this dense book are headed with such running titles as "Human Beasts in Filthy Dens."[10] Of the reformers I mention above, it is only London who rarely strays from the insistence that the impoverished he sees are victims of a larger system. His refrain, "Then the thing happens," is London's way of reminding his readers that the homeless wanderers he spends his days with are only an unfortunate incident away from having been self-supporting working-class or middle-class men and women.

For Hogarth and Grueze, the connection was clear: an immoral life led inevitably to a degraded condition. A return to morality was a return to prosperity and the warmth of hearth and home. Such stories of Penitent Magdalenes and Prodigal Sons might well seem appropriate moralistic tales for eighteenth-century class-conscious English society, and not at all related to what we understand of poverty in the United States today. And yet, the Appalachian child posing for *Children, Inc.* and the unwashed, unshaven, homeless man cautiously leaning into his coffee in a Milwaukee Rescue Mission photo[11] are likely to evoke much the same response as those eighteenth-century images: pity and alms-giving mixed with slight disapproval (fig. 3).

The issue at hand and the difficulty for nonprofits, then, is how to make real the dimensions of poverty and evoke the desire to give or to act without turning benefactors away. The question of seeing remains at the heart of problems of representation. What exactly is it that we see? Here I find Henry Mayhew's words once again useful for understanding what it is we might see. As he introduces that final volume devoted to "those that will not work," Mayhew tells his readers,

> *The attainment of the truth, then, will be my primary aim; but by the truth, I wish it to be understood, I mean something more than the bare facts. Facts, according to my ideas, are merely the elements of truths, and not the truths themselves; of all matters there are none so utterly useless by themselves as your mere matters of fact. A fact, so long as it remains an isolated fact, is a dull, dead, uninformed thing; no object nor event by itself can possibly give us any knowledge, we must compare it with some other, even to distinguish it; and it is the distinctive quality thus developed that constitutes the essence of a thing.*[12]

Help Feed The Homeless This Thanksgiving

For 105 years, the Milwaukee Rescue Mission has been providing food, shelter and compassionate care to Milwaukee's homeless. This season we expect hundreds of homeless men, women, and children to come to our door seeking help. For only $1.56 the Mission can provide a hungry, homeless person with a hot meal. Your gift can make a real difference in someone's life.

Yes, I want to help the homeless this Thanksgiving.

Name _____

Address _____

City _____ State _____

Zip _____ Phone _____

☐ $15.60 to provide food and shelter this Thanksgiving season
☐ $31.20 to provide food and shelter this Thanksgiving season
☐ $156.00 to provide food and shelter this Thanksgiving season
☐ $___ to provide food and shelter this Thanksgiving season

M R M
Milwaukee Rescue Mission

Your tax-deductible gift can be made payable to:
Milwaukee Rescue Mission • Dept. 1114
830 N. 19th Street • Milwaukee, WI 53233 • (414) 344-2211

Fig. 3

If we think, then, of representation in the way cultural theorist Stuart Hall has explained it—as constitutive of reality or meaning rather than as an attempt to replicate a "fact" already there—easy to see and understand—then Mayhew's remarks must lead us to ask what it is we are representing in the images of poverty most in use by today's nonprofits. What, then, is the essence of this thing poverty as it takes form in the popular imagination?

Certainly this century's most extensive and thoroughgoing attempt to represent poverty in the United States has been the Farm Security Administration's vast photo project documenting the face of rural poverty throughout the Depression and Dust Bowl years. Following the tradition of earlier documentarists like Riis and Lewis Hine, photographers including Walker Evans, Dorothea Lange, Arthur Rothstein, and others of the FSA created some of the most recognized images we have of America in hardship. These images continue, I would argue, to set the limits for representations of poverty today. Yet, even those images, as historian James Curtis notes in his full-length study of FSA photography, are not mere "facts" recorded with the unflinching eye of the camera lens. The clientele for these images—like the clientele for today's nonprofits—was primarily urban and middle class, and these images, "and entire photographic series," Curtis writes, were manipulated "to conform to the dominant cultural values" of this clientele.[13]

In his analysis of Dorothea Lange's photograph of Florence Thompson, generally known as *Migrant Mother or Migrant Madonna*, Curtis points particularly to the photographic choices Lange made that were "undoubtedly influenced by prevailing cultural biases."[14] The FSA documentary project portrayed the human spirit, the indomitable will of individuals who refused to yield to troubles they could not control, and *Migrant Mother* was certainly that. Florence Thompson, Curtis tells us, was traveling with her husband and seven children in the migrant work camps of California when Lange encountered her, and the choices Lange made in coming to that final shot that is now so recognizable were crucial for the way the image has been read over the years. The series of shots Lange took leading up to the final image indicates, for example, that she made the decision to leave a teenage daughter out, to compose the final group in a classic Madonna and child manner, to eliminate the clutter of the makeshift shelter and more—decisions that, in essence, placed Florence Thompson and her children clearly into the class of *deserving* over undeserving, or shiftless, or any other less acceptable representation that might have been made from the same family. This is an image that America not only accepted but embraced as emblematic of human courage and strength. In fact, this image remains so familiar that in 1998 the United States Postal Service chose it as one of several that would represent the thirties in a run of stamps commemorating each decade of the twentieth century.

In any number of nonprofit appeals, we can see versions of *Migrant Mother*, or of the shacks and bare dirt yards and delicate children in tattered clothing so familiar in Walker Evans's FSA photos. The issue is not that such conditions did not exist then. They did. They do today as well. And yet to rely primarily on these kinds of images while the country, the economy, the conditions, and the dimensions of poverty and need have changed considerably is to limit the ways nonprofits might respond to the need that is there.

Habitat for Humanity: A Case in Point

I have chosen Habitat for Humanity publicity videos for my focus because Habitat is a popular and far-reaching nonprofit with affiliates not only in the United States but throughout the world. Its goal is not a modest one: Habitat for Humanity aims to eliminate poverty housing from the globe. More than that, Habitat puts housing into the hands of the people who will be housed—into the hands of the homeowners and their neighbors. This is not another program aimed at keeping people in what has become known as the poverty or welfare cycle.

To be very clear, then, I am not criticizing the work of Habitat for Humanity. It is an organization that has done an amazing job of addressing what is, as cofounder Millard Fuller tells us again and again, a worldwide problem. What I would draw attention to, however, is how that problem of inadequate housing and its solution are represented, especially in publicity material produced and distributed by the organization, and how those representations can feed into the troubles that Habitat continues to have as it attempts to change the ways Americans think of helping others. What's more, the kinds of visual arguments Habitat and other nonprofits use to advocate for action or change have become increasingly common tools for getting the message to the public, and yet, I would argue, these messages too often fail to overturn cultural commonplaces that represent poverty as an individual problem that can be addressed on an individual basis. Habitat's catch phrase—A Hand Up, Not a Hand-Out—appeals to a nation that believes anyone can achieve economic security with just the right attitude and set of circumstances.

Habitat's basic program has a kind of elegance. Applicants who are chosen as homeowners put in sweat equity hours to build their home and to help build the homes of others chosen by Habitat. The organization then sells the home to the applicant at cost (that cost held down through Habitat's ability to provide volunteer labor and donated materials) and charges a small monthly mortgage that includes no interest. Unlike public assistance, which is raised or lowered depending on the recipient's circumstances, most Habitat affiliates do not raise mortgage payments when homeowners get better jobs or find themselves in better financial shape. And once the house is paid for, it belongs to the home-owner.

Obviously, in order to run a program like this one, Habitat must produce publicity appeals aimed at convincing potential donors to give time, money, and material. Print ads, public service television and radio spots, commercial appeals linked to products like Maxwell House coffee, and publicity videos meant to be played for churches, volunteer organizations, and even in-flight video appeals on certain airlines are common media for Habitat.

Habitat publicity videos are typically configured as problem-solution arguments. The problem is that too many people have inadequate shelter. The solution is community involvement in a program like Habitat for Humanity. The most common setup for these productions is an opening sequence of images—a visual montage—in which we see black-and-white shots of rural shacks, of men and women clearly in despair, and of thin children in ragged clothing. The voice-over narrative of one such montage tells us the story:

> *Poverty condemns millions of people throughout the world to live in deplorable and inhuman conditions. These people are trapped in a cycle of poverty, living in places offering little protection from the rain, wind, and cold. Terrible sanitary conditions make each day a battle with disease and death. And, for this, they often pay over half their income in rent because, for the poor, there are no other choices. Daily, these families are denied a most basic human need: a decent place to live. The reasons for this worldwide tragedy are many. They vary from city to city, country to country, but the result is painfully the same whether the families are in New York or New Delhi.*[15]

It is a compelling dilemma.

Organizations like Habitat for Humanity, in order to convey the seriousness of this struggle and, of course, to raise funds and volunteer support for their efforts in addressing it, must produce all sorts of publicity. And in that publicity they must tell us quickly what the problem is and what we can do to help. To do that, Habitat gives us a visual representation of poverty, a representation that mirrors the most common understandings of poverty in America.

Now, there is nothing inherently wrong with that representation unless, of course, what you want to do (as Habitat does) is convince the American people to believe in the radical idea that those who have must care for the needs of others, not just by writing a check, but by enabling an entirely different life-style. For Americans, it is truly radical to think that our poorer neighbors might actually be allowed to buy a home at no interest and with the donated time and materials of others. It is a radical notion that such a program means that these neighbors then own that house and aren't obliged to do more than keep up with payments in order to continue owning it. And it is a radical idea that Habitat does this work not only in our neighborhoods (not isolated in low-income housing developments) but throughout the world. Habitat International truly believes that we are all responsible for partnering with our neighbors throughout the world so that every-one might eventually have, at least, a simple decent place to live. Like the philos-ophy behind many nonprofits, Habitat's is not a mainstream notion.

Still, that representation of poverty—clinging as it does to commonplaces drawn from FSA photographs in this century, from Jacob Riis's nineteenth-cen-tury photos of urban poverty, and from documentaries of Third World hunger—has serious limitations, which must be obvious to those who remember the moment that the Bush administration confidently announced that, after looking everywhere, they had discovered no real hunger in the United States. And that myth that poverty cannot/does not actually exist in the heart of capitalism has once again been rein-forced in the 1998 Heritage Foundation report in which Robert Rector echoed the perennial argument that there is little true poverty in this country ("Myth").[16] Her-itage Foundation's finding comes despite figures from the National Coalition for the Homeless ("Myths and Facts About Homelessness"), which tell us that in 1997 nearly one in five homeless people in twenty-nine cities across the United States was employed in a full- or part-time job.[17]

In her call for a changed representation of poverty in America, bell hooks argues that in this culture poverty "is seen as synonymous with depravity, lack and worthlessness." She continues, "I talked with young black women receiving state aid, who have not worked in years, about the issue of representation. They all agree that they do not want to be identified as poor. In their apartments they have the material possessions that indicate success (a VCR, a color television), even if it means that they do without necessities and plunge into debt to buy these items."[18] Hers is hardly a noble image of poverty, but it is a true one and one that complicates the job of an organization like Habitat that must identify "worthy" applicants. This phenomenon of poverty in the center of wealth, in a country with its national mythology of hearty individuals facing the hardness of the Depression with dignity and pride, is certainly a part of what Manning Marable challenges when he asks readers not to judge poverty in the United States by the standards of other countries. Writing of poverty among black Americans, Marable reminds us that "the process of impoverishment is profoundly national and regional."[19] It does little good to compare the impoverished of this country with Third World poverty or, for that matter, with Depression Era poverty.

The solution in these Habitat videos is just as visible and compelling a repre-sentation as is the problem. The solution, it seems, is a modern-day barn raising. In clip after clip, Habitat volunteers are shown lined up to raise walls, to hammer nails, to cut boards, to offer each other the "hand up not a hand out," as these pub-licity messages tell us again and again. Like the barn- raising scene from Peter Weir's *Witness*, framed walls come together against blue skies. People who would normally live in very different worlds come together to help a neighbor. It is all finished in record time: a week, even a day. Volunteers can come together quickly. Do something. Get out just as quickly.

The real trouble with Habitat's representation, then, is twofold: it tells us that the signs of poverty are visible and easily recognized. And it suggests that one of the most serious results of poverty (inadequate shelter) can be addressed quickly with volunteer efforts to bring individuals up and out of the poverty cycle.

Of course, if Habitat works, what could be wrong with the representation? It is an organization so popular that it receives support from diametrically opposed camps. Newt Gingrich and Jesse Jackson have both pounded nails and raised funds for Habitat. This is what Millard Fuller calls the "theology of the hammer." People might not agree on political parties and they might not agree on how to worship or even what to worship, Fuller says, but they can all agree on a hammer. All can come together to build houses. Or, can they?

As successful as Habitat has been, it is an organization that continues to struggle with such issues as who to choose for housing, how to support potential homeowners, and how to convince affiliates in the United States to tithe a portion of their funds to the real effort of Habitat: eliminating poverty housing throughout the world, not just in the United States. And, even in the United States, affiliates often have trouble identifying "deserving" applicants or convincing local residents to allow Habitat homes to be built in their neighborhoods. There are certainly many cultural and political reasons for these problems, but I would suggest that the way poverty continues to be represented in this country and on tapes like those videos limits our understanding of what poverty is and how we might address it.

That limitation holds true for those caught in poverty as well as those wanting to help. What if, as a potential Habitat applicant, you don't recognize yourself or you refuse to recognize yourself in those representations? As Stanley Aronowitz points out in *The Politics of Identity*, that can happen very easily as class identities, in particular, have become much more difficult to pin down since World War II, especially with an expansion of consumer credit that allowed class and social status to be linked to consumption rather than to professions or even wages. In his discussion of how electronic media construct the *social imaginary*, Aronowitz talks of the working class with few media representations available to them as having fallen into a kind of "cultural homelessness."[20] How much more true is that of the impoverished in this country who may be neither homeless nor ragged, but are certainly struggling every day to feed their families, pay rent, and find jobs that pay more than what it costs for daycare?

I have been particularly interested in this last question because of a difficulty I mentioned earlier, that of identifying appropriate applicants for Habitat homes or even getting some of the most needy families of a given affiliate to apply for Habitat homes. When I showed the video *Building New Lives* to Kim Puuri, a Copper Country Habitat for Humanity homeowner and now member of the affiliate's Homeowner Selection Committee, and asked her to respond, she was very clear in what she saw as the problem:

> When I see those pictures I usually think of Africa or a third world country and NOT the U.S. It's not that they can't be found here, it's

just that you don't publicly see people that bad off other than street people. If they could gear the publicity more to the geographical areas, it may make more of an impact or get a better response from people. It would mean making several videos. It may not be so much of a stereotype, but an association between Habitat and the people they help. People viewing the videos and pictures see the conditions of the people and feel that their own condition may not be that bad and feel they probably wouldn't qualify.[21]

What this Habitat homeowner has noticed is very close to what Hall describes. That is, the problem with this image, this representation, is not that it is not real enough. The problem has nothing to do with whether or not these are images of poverty as it exists in the world. There is no doubt that this level of poverty does exist in this country and elsewhere despite the Heritage Foundation's attempts to demonstrate otherwise. The problem is that this representation of poverty is a narrow one and functions to narrow the ways we might respond to the poor who do not fit this representation.

The representation I have been discussing is one that insists on constructing poverty as an individual problem that can be dealt with by volunteers on an individual basis. That is the sort of representation common in this country, the sort of representation Paul Wellstone objects to in a recent call to action when he says "We can offer no single description of American poverty." What it takes to break through such a representation is first, as Stuart Hall suggests, to understand it as a representation, to understand it as a way of imparting meaning. And the only way to contest that representation, to allow for other meanings, other descriptions, is to know more about the many dimensions of poverty in America. "More than 35 million Americans—one out of every seven of our fellow citizens—are officially poor. More than one in five American children are poor. And the poor are getting poorer," Wellstone writes.[22] But we can be certain that much of that poverty is not the sort pictured in those black-and-white images. And if it doesn't *look* like poverty, then how do we address it? How do we identify those "deserving" our help?

Indeed, as Herbert Gans has suggested, the labels we have chosen to place on the poor in this country often reveal more than anything "an ideology of undeservingness," by which we have often elided poverty and immorality or laziness or criminality. "By making scapegoats of the poor for fundamental problems they have not caused nor can change," Gans argues, "Americans can also postpone politically difficult and divisive solutions to the country's economic ills and the need to prepare the economy and polity for the challenges of the twenty-first century."[23] These are tough issues to confront and certainly to argue in a twenty-minute video presentation aimed at raising funds and volunteer support, especially when every piece of publicity must make a complex argument visible.

On the Way to Changing the Face of Poverty

Reflecting on more than thirty years of working among the poor, Dorothy Day once wrote, "Poverty is a strange and elusive thing. . . . We need always to be thinking and writing about it, for if we are not among its victims its reality fades from us."[24] Of course, that impulse—to keep the poor before us—is precisely what has led to the many firsthand accounts and documentary photographs and sociological studies and publicity videos like those I have mentioned above. But Day, who devoted her entire life to working with the poor, continues on in a passage quoted here at length for its directness and clear-headed understanding of what it means now, and has meant in the past, to be truly in need:

> *So many good souls who visit us tell us how they were brought up in poverty, but how, through hard work and cooperation, their parents managed to educate all the children—even raise up priests and nuns for the Church. They content that healthful habits and a stable family situation enable people to escape from the poverty class, no matter how mean the slum they may once have been forced to live in. The argument runs, so why can't everybody do it? No, these people don't know about the poor. Their concept of poverty is of something as near and well ordered as a nun's cell.*
>
> *Poverty has many faces. People can, for example, be poor in space alone. . . . Then there are those who live under outwardly decent economic circumstances but are forever on the fearful brink of financial disaster. . . . No matter how high wages go, a sudden illness and an accumulation of doctor and hospital bills, for example, may mean a sudden plunge into destitution.*[25]

What Day tells us here recalls Jack London's warning: "Then the thing happens." It is a reminder that the poor are not only always among us, but at any time might *be* us. At any time so many Americans living on the very edge of financial health might be plunged into destitution.

I suspect some readers wonder why I continue to emphasize the very ordinary nature of those who live in poverty and why I not only consider it so important that nonprofits work to break older stereotypes, but that recipients of those nonprofit appeals learn to read the images of poverty with the knowledge that they are stereotypes and do limit out understanding of need. More than one of the many colleagues and friends I have besieged with my talk of poverty and nonprofit appeals has asked an important question: If nonprofits don't use images that show hunger and need, then how are they to get across the urgency of their message? How do they raise money or awareness? It is a question I have not always answered well or completely. I do believe, however, that an answer might lie in two areas: first, in a knowledge of the actual consequences of relying on those stereotypes to carry a message of need; and second, in an understanding of what we have sometimes called the "visual imperative" of the electronic media.

Once again, as long as people give to nonprofits to support poverty programs, what does the image matter? Does "the vocabulary of poverty," as Michael B. Katz claims, really impoverish the political imagination?[26] I offer one very quick example of how that vocabulary, that stereotype, does indeed impoverish the political imagination. Early in 1999, the Michigan legislature put on fast-track Governor John Engler's most recent plan to cut back the assistance rolls in his state. Engler proposed drug testing for all welfare recipients. Those tested positive would be sent to rehabilitation programs. If they fail to attend those programs or if they are found to continue drug use, they will be dropped from welfare rolls. Despite federal studies that indicate that only about 5 percent of welfare recipients are serious drug and alcohol abusers ("Welfare Drug Test"),[27] this legislation feeds into the notion that if someone is on assistance, there must be something wrong with that person, something that once fixed will make each individual a contributing, self-supporting member of the community.

Democrats' proposed amendments to the Engler bill weren't much better. Amendments asked that only those applicants who have not found a job after participating in Michigan's Work First program be screened "for potential drug and alcohol abuse, learning disabilities, illiteracy, domestic violence, actual or imminent homelessness and mental illness."[28] Clearly, the operative notion here is that only the most deviant, disabled, or disinclined to learn make up the ranks of those who cannot find work.

Although many would argue that such legislation is unconstitutional, it was no idle threat. By July 1999, the legislature has passed Engler's bill and drug testing had begun. Readers might well recall that John Engler's name came to national prominence during his first term in office when he began what has continued to be a deep slashing of public assistance and welfare rolls. His back-to-work or workfare programs have caught on throughout this country, and Engler has been heralded as a governor who takes people off welfare and puts them back into the workplace.

Barbara Ehrenreich's most recent experiment in which she became—Jack London-like—a low-wage employee, not to find out "how the other half lives" but to test out policies like Engler's that claim that "work will lift poor women out of poverty while simultaneously inflating their self-esteem and hence their future value in the labor market," vividly illustrates how impoverished this particular political imaginary actually is. Not only do most jobs held by low-wage employees offer no security and few or no benefits; they are simply not jobs that will provide a living wage. Ehrenreich explains, "According to the National Coalition for the Homeless, for example, in 1998 it took, on average nationwide, an hourly wage of $8.89 to afford a one-bedroom apartment, and the Preamble Center for Public Policy estimates that the odds against a typical welfare recipient's landing a job at such a 'living wage' are about 97 to 1."[29] These are not good odds, and they point again to the reality Dorothy Day wrote of so many years ago: it is important to help individuals, and individuals can certainly raise themselves up out of poverty, but helping the individual without addressing larger structural problems will do little more than help the individual.

The second concern I point to—understanding the role of the media in communicating need—may be even more crucial in changing the face of poverty, for it points directly to how the media work within certain "givens." Speaking on the difficulties of getting United States news media to carry the 1983 story of the Ethiopian famine, communication scholar Brian Winston addresses one of those givens—what he calls the media myth of being in the "grip of the visual imperative."[30] Winston argues that, if we closely analyze the news media, we will discover that it is only such stories as Third World hunger that are caught in the grip of this visual imperative. Many other kinds of stories get long play with stock—

even dull—footage. He names political election stories or stories of economics for which the media will find a number of images that we could not call compelling— the President getting off a plane, for example, or oil wells in a Kansas field. According to Winston, if we were instead to tell the story of hunger as a real story of problems of wealth and distribution and the like, then there would be all kinds of images that would work: wheat fields, graphs, ships moving grain, and more. Instead, however, the story of hunger and poverty exists on the level of crisis reportage so that, according to Winston, this kind of story is *located* in the image.

"Famine," Winston argues, "is a biblical word. We don't have famines in the West. Famines can only come into our collective consciousness . . . if it's in biblical terms." As if to reinforce Winston's point, Michael Buerke, whose BBC report did finally break the Ethiopian famine story in 1984, says much the same: "The curious thing—it came out in the first film we did—is that biblical business. People looked like those depicted in the color illustrations in my old school Bible. Sort of sackcloth color and a certain nobility of features."[31] Winston is much harsher in his assessment. He calls many of these images "masturbatory" images of hunger—a pornography of starvation.

If not those images, then what? Well, I would return to Habitat home-owner Kim Puuri's suggestion that Habitat might have to start making different videos or publicity pieces for different areas/different audiences. In that suggestion, Puuri is actually calling our attention to the most serious problem of such broad representations: they depict poverty as a crisis that we can recognize and address now with just a call, a contribution, a few hours of our time. In addition, these images depict poverty as something that happens to others, people outside the ordinary. As the Michigan legislation suggests, these people are addicts, illiterates and, worse yet, potentially *violent* addicts and illiterates.

Since I have focused many of my comments on Habitat for Humanity publicity, I feel compelled to turn first to Habitat for alternate representations of the people who apply for and get Habitat homes. My own local affiliate published the following fund-raising Christmas card for the 1997 Christmas season (fig. 4). The images of these families are remarkable only for the fact that they are our neighbors. This area, known as the Copper Country, is small enough that families receiving this appeal would recognize some or all of the families pictured on the card. They would have worked with them; many would even be related to them. They are people we know whose financial circumstances are not unlike that of many of their neighbors. What Copper Country Habitat is doing with a card like this one is, in some ways, risky. It is, after all, much easier to imagine need that is far away and desperate in ways that can be seen. Instead this affiliate is counting on the community to know that need looks a lot like the every day. It looks a lot like the people they live with and work with. In fact, it is the people they live and work with.

Other local affiliates do much the same. I have been especially impressed by the work of Chicago's Uptown affiliate. Uptown renovates old apartment houses and turns them into condos. In forming its homeowner's association, Uptown Habitat homeowners have written their own newsletters, written rules for the condo group, advocated for police attention to the crime outside their doorways, and more. The newsletter *HabiChat* published by Uptown Habitat looks much

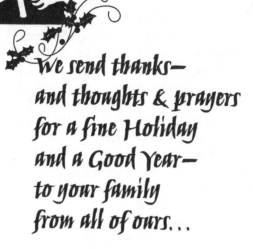

We send thanks—
and thoughts & prayers
for a fine Holiday
and a Good Year—
to your family
from all of ours...

Fig. 4

the Kangas family   the Deforge-Harma family

like many of the newsletters of neighborhood associations throughout suburban America. It includes announcements for Spring Clean-up, marriage and birth announcements, resources for parenting troubles, and more. Such newsletters, sent out as they are to the entire affiliate and not kept isolated within the homeowners association, work to remind Habitat volunteers and donors that Habitat's best work is fundamental to the lives of ordinary people working at one or more low-wage jobs and just trying to get by in safe, inexpensive, decent housing.

Of course, that is Habitat. Despite its goal to eliminate poverty housing on the globe, Habitat can rarely address the needs of the most impoverished. After all, a Habitat homeowner must come up with even a little money for a mortgage, and there are millions of Americans who cannot do that. What of those others? What about that man in the Milwaukee Rescue Mission ad I mentioned earlier? This is clearly a man with little enough to eat much less the resources for a house payment or even the energy for "sweat equity." Perhaps he is a part of those "undeserving" poor, the drunks and addicts Engler would like to push off Michigan's assistance rolls.

Again, I would call attention to how the homeless depict themselves. I offer one last, true story: Outside the San Francisco Hilton just after Christmas a year ago, I bought my third copy of *Streetwise: A Publication of the Coalition on Homelessness San Francisco*. It is not unlike papers sold by homeless men and women in several cities throughout this country. As I tucked the paper into my books, a short, well-dressed woman waiting for a cab turned to ask me if someone was handing out free things. "No. It's a paper. It costs a dollar." In anger, she came closer to me and yelled, "You *paid money* for that trash?"

Stunned both by the suddenness and the volume of her anger, I neglected to ask if she'd read the article on prisons and shelters signed by "Art B, One Homeless Guy, one of the 14,000 in San Francisco living in a shelter or under the freeways." It was pretty good, I wanted to tell her, but she was already off in her cab.

In these street papers, written as this one is by "the homeless and formerly homeless," we are presented with yet another image of desperate poverty. Perhaps because the homeless themselves write articles seeking to uncover the very structures that keep homelessness and poverty alive and well in our cities, some potential readers are driven to the kind of anger I witnessed. More likely, it is that the very sight of a homeless person, so very obviously in need of food, shelter, a recovery program, or more, is enough to frighten away the lady in the cab.

In Tucson during the past year, the City Council threatened to clear the medians of homeless people selling papers. The Council claimed these men and women represented a safety threat. In response Casa Maria, Tucson's Catholic Worker House, distributed a flyer calling for action to block the Council order. In it, Casa Maria accused the Council of acting on the basis of "aesthetics" rather than from any real concern over safety and pointed to the fact that many of the people who sell those papers have actually been able to pay rent and provide themselves with basic necessities just by being allowed to stand on those medians and sell newspapers. Brian Flagg, a worker from Casa Maria, wrote recently "We won this one! It was cool—We filled their meeting with church people & uppity tramps!"[32]

It might indeed take uppity tramps, local newsletters, and committed activists like Brian to change constructively the ways the poor are represented, as bell hooks asks that we do. As well, however, it will take a clear understanding of need in its many forms, and for this the image of Amy standing in a deserted mining town and looking out from a black-and-white photo does not altogether tell *New Yorker* readers what they need to know.

19

Family Album

JOY HARJO

JOY HARJO lives in Albuquerque, where she is a professor of English at the University of New Mexico. Born in Tulsa, Oklahoma, in 1951, she is a member of the Creek (also known as Muscogee) tribe. She is a poet, an editor, an essayist, an author of works for children, and a saxophonist who leads her own band called Poetic Justice. As a poet she received a fellowship from the National Endowment for the Arts. Her books of poems include The Last Song *(1973),* What Moon Drove Me to This *(1980),* She Had Some Horses *(1983), and* In Mad Love and War *(1990).*

FOR MY COUSIN JOHN JACOBS, 1918–1991,
WHO WILL ALWAYS BE WITH ME.

I felt as if I had prepared for the green corn ceremony my whole life. It's nothing I can explain in print; besides, no explanation would fit in the English language. All I can say is that it is central to the mythic construct of the Muscogee people (otherwise known as "Creek"), a rite of resonant renewal, of forgiveness.

The drive to Tallahassee grounds in northeastern Oklahoma with my friends Helen and Jim Burgess and Susan Williams was filled with stories. Stories here are as thick as the insects singing. We were part of the ongoing story of the people. Helen and I had made a promise to take part together in a ceremony that ensures that survival of the people, a link in the epic story of grace. The trees and tall reedlike grasses resounded with singing.

There's nothing quite like it anywhere else I've been, and I've traveled widely. The most similar landscape is in Miskito country in northeastern Nicaragua. I thought I was home once again as I walked with the Miskito people who had suffered terrible destruction of their homeland from both sides of the war. The insects singing provided a matrix of complex harmonies which shift cells in the body that shape imagination. I imagine a similar insect language in a place I've dreamed in west Africa. In summer in Oklahoma it's as if insects shape the world by songs. Their collective punctuation helps the growing corn remember the climb to the sun.

Our first stop on the way to the grounds was Holdenville to visit one of my favorite older cousins and his wife, John and Carol Jacobs. They would meet us later at the grounds. We traded gifts and stories, ate a perfectly fried meal at the Dairy Queen, one of the few restaurants open in a town hit hard by economic depression. I always enjoy visiting and feasting with these, my favorite relatives, and I feel at home in their house, a refuge surrounded with peacocks, dogs, and well-loved cats, guarded by giant beneficent spirits disguised as trees.

Across the road an oil well pumps relentlessly. When I was a child in Oklahoma, the monster insect bodies of the pumping wells terrified me. I would duck down in the car until we passed. Everyone thought it was funny. I was called high-strung and imaginative. I imagined the collapse of the world, as if the wells were giant insects without songs, pumping blood from the body of Earth. I wasn't far off from the truth.

My cousin John, who was more like a beloved uncle, gave me two photographs he had culled for me from family albums. I had never before seen my great-grand-parents on my father's side in photographs; this was the first time. I held them in my hand as reverberations of memory astounded me beyond language. I believe stories are encoded in the DNA spiral and call each cell into perfect position. Sound tempered with emotion and meaning propels the spiral beyond three dimensions.

I recognized myself in this photograph. I saw my sister, my brothers, my son and daughter. My father lived once again at the wheel of a car, my father who favored Cadillacs and Lincolns, cars he was not always able to afford but sacrificed to own because he was compelled by the luxury of well-made vehicles, sung to by the hum of a finely constructed motor. He made sure his cars were well-greased and perfectly tuned. That was his favorite music.

I was not surprised, yet I was shocked, to recognize something I always knew. The images of my great-grandmother Katie Menawe, my great-grandfather Marsie Harjo, my grandmother Naomi, my aunts Lois and Mary, and my uncle Joe were always inside me, as if I were a soul catcher made of a crystal formed from blood. I had heard the names, the stories, and perhaps it was because of the truth of those stories and what the names conveyed that the images had formed, had propelled me into the world. My grandchildren and great-grandchildren will see a magnification of themselves in their grandparents. It's implicit in the way we continue, the same as corn plants, the same as stars or the cascades of insects singing in summer. The old mystery of division and multiplication will always lead us to the root.

I think of my Aunt Lois's admonishments about photographs. She said a photograph can steal your soul. I believe it's true, for an imprint remains behind, forever locked in paper and chemicals. Perhaps the family will always be touring somewhere close to the border, dressed in their Sunday best, acutely aware of the soul stealer that Marsie Harjo hired to photograph them, steadying his tripod to the right of the road. Who's to say they didn't want something left to mark time in that intimate space, a place they could be in forever as a family, the world drenched in sienna?

Nothing would ever be the same again. The family is ever present, as is the photographer, unnamed except for his visual arrangement. I wonder whether he was surprised to see rich Indians.

Both of my great-grandparents' parents were part of the terrible walk of the Muscogee Nation from Alabama to Indian territory, where they were settled on land bordered by what is now Tulsa on the north, the place where my brothers, sister, and I were born. The people were promised that if they made this move they would be left alone by the U.S. Government, which claimed it needed the tribal homelands for expansion. But within a few years white settlers were once again crowding Indian lands, and in 1887 the Dawes Act, sometimes better known as the Allotment Act, was made law.

This act undermined one of the principles that had always kept the people together: that land was communal property which could not be owned. With the Dawes Act, private ownership of land was forced on the people. Land that supposedly belonged in perpetuity to the tribe was divided into plots, allotted to individuals. What was "left over" was opened for white settlement. But this did not content the settlers who proceeded by new laws, other kinds of trickery, and raw force to take over allotments belonging to the Muscogee and other tribes.

On December 1, 1905, oil was struck in Glenpool, Oklahoma. This was one of the richest pools of oil discovered in Oklahoma, which at its height produced

forty million barrels annually. Marsie Harjo's allotted land was here. He was soon a rich man, as were many other Indian people whose allotted land lay over lakes of oil. This intensified the land grab. Many tribal members were swindled of their land, killed for money. It's a struggle that is still played out in the late twentieth century.

Oil money explains the long elegant car Marsie Harjo poses in with his family. In the stories I've been told, he always loved Hudsons. This may or may not be a Hudson. The family was raised in luxury. My grandmother Naomi and my aunt Lois both received their B.F.A. degrees in art and were able to take expensive vacations at a time when many people in this country were suffering economic deprivation. They also had an African-American maid, whose name was Susie. I've tried to find out more about her. I do know she lived with the family for many years and made the best ice cream.

There is an irony here because Marsie Harjo was also half or nearly half African-American. Another irony is the racism directed toward African Americans and African blood in recent years by a tribe whose members originally accepted Africans and often welcomed them as relatives. Humanity was respected above color or ownership. The acceptance of African-American slavery came with the embrace of European-American cultural values. It was then we also began to hate ourselves for our darkness. It's all connected; this attitude towards ownership of land has everything to do with how human beings are treated, with the attitude toward all living things.

There are many ironies in this vision of the family of my great-grandparents, which is my family — a vision that explodes the myth of being Indian in this country for non-Indian and Indian alike. I wonder at the interpretation of the image of this Muscogee family in a car only the wealthy could own by another Muscogee person, or by another tribal person, or by a non-Indian anywhere in this land. This image challenges the popular culture's image of "Indian," an image that fits no tribe or person. I mean to question those accepted images, images that have limited us to cardboard cutout figures, without blood, tears, or laughter.

There were many photographs of this family. I recently sent my cousin Donna Jo Harjo a photograph of her father Joe as a child of about five. He was dressed in a finely made suit and driving a child's-size scale model of a car. She's never lived in this kind of elegance. She lives on her salary as a sorter for a conglomerate nut-and-dried-fruit company in northern California. She has a love for animals, especially cats. Our clan is the Tiger Clan. She also is a great lover of horses. I wonder at this proliferation of photographs and think of the diminishment of the family in numbers to this present generation.

One of the photographs is a straight-on shot of my great-grandparents and two Seminole men dressed traditionally. The Seminoles in their turbans are in stark contrast to my grandparents, especially to Marsie Harjo, who is stately and somewhat stiff with the fear of god in his elegant white-man's clothes, his Homburg hat.

He was quite an advanced thinker and I imagine he repressed what he foresaw for the Muscogee people. I don't think anyone would have believed him. He was a preacher, a Creek Baptist minister. He represents a counter-force to traditional Muscogee culture and embodies a side of the split in our tribe since Christianity, since the people were influenced by the values of European culture. The dividing lines are the same several hundred years later.

My great-grandfather was in Stuart, Florida, to "save" the Seminole people, as he did every winter. He bought a plantation there and, because he hated pineapples, he had every one of the plants dug up and destroyed. Another story I've often heard says he also owned an alligator fram. I went to Stuart last spring on my way to Miami and could find no trace of the mission or the plantation anywhere in the suburban mix of concrete, glass, and advertisements. I had only memories that are easier to reach in a dimension that is as alive and living as the three dimensions we know with our five senses.

My great-grandmother Katie Menawe is much more hidden in this photograph. She is not in the driver's seat, and not next to the driver but in the very back of the car, behind her four children. Yet she quietly presides over everything as she guards her soul from the intrusive camera. I have the sense that Marsie boldly entered the twentieth century ahead of everyone else, while Katie reluctantly followed. I doubt she ever resolved the split in her heart. I don't know too much about her. She and her siblings were orphaned. They were schooled and boarded for some time at Eufaula Indian School. I don't know how old she was when she married Marsie Harjo. Her sister Ella, a noted beauty queen, was my cousin John's mother.

The name "Menawe" is one of those names in the Muscogee tribe that is charged with memory of rebellion, with strength in the face of terrible destruction. Tecumseh came looking for Menawe when he was building his great alliance of nations in the 1800s. Menawe was one of the leaders of the Red Stick War, an armed struggle against the U.S. Government and Andrew Jackson's demand for western settlement of the Muscogee tribes. The fighting forces were made up of Creeks, Seminoles, and Africans. Not many survived the struggle.

The Seminoles successfully resisted colonization by hiding in the Floridian swamps. They beat the United States forces who were aided by other tribes, including other Creeks who were promised land and homes for their help. The promises were like other promises from the U.S. government. For their assistance, the Indian troops were forced to walk to Indian Territory like everyone else, to what later became the state of Oklahoma.

Menawe stayed in Alabama. He was soon forced west, but not before he joined with Jackson's forces to round up Seminoles for the move to Oklahoma. My cousin John said Menawe died on the trail. I know that he died of a broken heart. I have a McKenney Hall print of Menawe, an original hand-colored lithograph dated 1848. Katie has the eyes and composure of this man who was her father.

By going to Tallahassee grounds to join in traditional tribal ceremony, I was taking my place in the circle of relatives. I was one more link in the concatenation of ancestors. Close behind me are my son and daughter, behind them my granddaughter. Next to me, interlocking the pattern, are my cousins, my aunts and uncles. We dance together in this place of knowing beyond the physical dimensions of space, much denser than the chemicals and paper of photographs. It is larger than mere human memory, than any destruction we have walked through to come to this ground of memory. Time can never be stopped; rather, it is poised to make a leap into knowing or a field of questions. I understood this as we stompdanced in the middle of the night, as the stars whirred in the same pattern overhead, as they had been when Katie, Marsie, and the children lived beneath them. I heard time resume as the insects took up their singing once more to guide us through memory. The old Hudson heads to the east of the border of the photograph. For the Muscogee, East is the place of origins, the place the People emerged from so many hundreds of years ago. It is also a place of return.

20

From Poster Child to Protester

LAURA HERSHEY

The following article appeared in the Spring/Summer 1997 issue of *Spectacle*, published by Pachanga Press, Burlington MA.

Orange, pink, and lavender flyers fluttered in the breeze as we handed them to any passer-by willing to take one. "Tune Out Jerry!" the flyers urged. "Boycott the Telethon!" Some two dozen of us lined up in front of the hotel shouting chants, distributing leaflets, and answering questions from the media, while the local segment of the Jerry Lewis Labor Day Telethon broadcast from a ballroom two floors above. Though I would stay outside all afternoon, I remembered all too well the scene that was taking place inside.

The singers croon. The eyelids droop. The money pours in. The firefighters, the Boy Scouts, the business executives, the neighborhood kids, all tiredly smiling proud smiles, carry in their collected funds, in jars, in boots, in oversized checks. The camera rolls. The host smiles. The money pours in. The Poster Child gives awkward answers to inane questions. The host smiles. The Poster Child smiles. The host cries. The money pours in.

You have to keep thinking about the money, because as everyone freely admits, that's what this is all about. The money raised represents hope—year after year, promises of a miracle, the great cure that waits just around the corner. The money manifests faith—faith in the noble research scientists working desperately to identify, and eliminate, flawed genes. The money testifies to human love and compassion, ruthlessly sentimentalized in songs like "They'll Never Walk Alone" which punctuate the twenty or so hours of the telethon.

The money is what justifies, even sanctifies, this annual ritual of tears and guilt. In 1996 the telethon raised over $49 million. That massive amount of money that people—young and old, rich and poor—feel compelled to donate, giving "till it hurts," as Jerry Lewis insists—that money makes it very hard to challenge what is actually going on.

But there we were, back in September 1991, on Denver's busy 16th Street Mall, challenging the Jerry Lewis Labor Day Muscular Dystrophy Telethon. Along with activists in cities around the country, including Chicago, Los Angeles, and Las Vegas, we were protesting the telethon's portrayal of people with disabilities as helpless and pathetic. We were asserting publicly that this colossal begging festival, supposedly carried out on our behalf, is offensive to us and damaging to our efforts to become first-class citizens. Our protests were small, but they would become an annual tradition—much to the annoyance of Jerry Lewis and MDA.

For years we had been protesting against the barriers which keep people with disabilities from using buses, public buildings, and other facilities. Now we were taking on one of the biggest barriers of all: the paternalistic attitudes which prevail in our society, and which are reflected so dramatically in the annual telethon.

It is difficult to raise objections to something like the telethon; people are reluctant to disparage, or even entertain questions about, an effort which they perceive as fundamentally good, or at least well-meaning. That is understandable. It is an uncomfortable truth, in social work, in government activity, and in charitable endeavors, that actions which are intended to help a certain group of people *may actually harm* them. By harm, I mean—among other things—that these actions may reinforce the already devalued status of people with disabilities in this society. Looking closely and critically at the telethon, as some of us have started to do, brings up a number of issues which I feel are essential to understanding the status of people with disabilities as an oppressed minority group in America. These issues include: charity versus civil rights; cure versus accommodation; self-expression and self-determination; and the relationship between pity and bigotry.

The telethon has one goal—to raise as much money as possible for the Muscular Dystrophy Association, or MDA. Conventional wisdom says that the most effective way to do this is to appeal directly to the emotions of viewers—to move people so strongly, with stories of tragic suffering, that they will want to help "save Jerry's kids." Money is tight these days; charitable solicitation is a competitive business. Invoking sympathy sufficient to pry open wallets is not an easy task. But those orchestrating the telethon have a foolproof, not-so-secret weapon: children. Never mind that two-thirds of MDA's 1 million clients are adults—the telethon is not in the business of trying to represent the real lives of people with muscular dystrophy. That's not the point. The point is to paint a picture of a victim so tragic, and at the same time so cute and appealing, that viewers will be compelled to call in a pledge. This victim must also appear helpless, utterly unable to help him/herself, so that the giver can gain a personal sense of virtue and superiority from the act of giving. Finally, the victim must display something called "courage," which does not resemble the bold, active kind of courage most people aspire to or at least fantasize about, in which one takes one's destiny into one's own hands and, by exercising will and choice, affirms oneself and/or one's place in the universe. No, the "courage" demanded in this instance is the willingness to deprecate oneself; to accept other people's versions of one's own reality; to reject one's own identity in favor of an eagerly anticipated cure (this is also called "hope"); to tolerate and even encourage the assumption that life with a disability is a life scarcely worth carrying on with, except for the generosity of Jerry Lewis and everyone involved in the telethon.

At the age of eleven, I was enlisted into this role of cheerful victim. I was a Poster Child. In 1973-74, I became a mini-celebrity, appearing at fundraisers throughout Colorado. I learned to smile whenever a camera appeared, and to say "thank you"—in other words, I learned to look, sound, and act cute and grateful. And on Labor Day, I became a prop in the TV studio where the local portion of the telethon was broadcast. To whole families, driving by to drop their contributions in a giant fishbowl outside the studio; to the camera's blinking red light; to the anchorman who squatted next to me, holding a huge microphone in my face; to everyone, I gave the same cute-and-grateful act, because that's what they wanted.

So I am no stranger to the telethon. And in the two decades since then, the telethon doesn't seem to have changed much. I watch it every year, just to make sure. It's still chillingly familiar. The sappy music, the camera close-ups of wistful faces, the voice-overs telling us about that person's dream to walk someday, the tearful stories told by parents "devastated" by their children's disability, and the contributors coming forward in droves—it was all just the same as I remember it.

But some things **have** changed; I have changed. I don't know what my politics were as an eleven-year-old, if I had any. But my politics now—which are not merely political but also personal, spiritual, and practical—have led me to question and ultimately reject most of the values which the telethon represents.

Let's start with the money. Does **it** help? Doesn't it make the stereotypes, the appeals to pity, the obnoxious on-air begging worth putting up with?

Yes, the money does help—*some* people, with *some* things. We are talking about a lot of money here. MDA Executive Director Robert Ross asserts that during its 26-year history, the telethon has raised over $600 million. In 1996, the telethon raised $49.1 million.

With all this money coming in, I would expect the direct services provided to people with neuromuscular diseases to be much more extensive, and more relevant, than they actually are. I would expect, for example, that when a person develops a condition which begins to limit his or her mobility, that MDA might come through with some money for access modifications to the home, so that the family wouldn't have to choose between moving to an accessible house (which are hard to find), or hauling the person up and down stairs all day. I would expect some support services for independent living—someone to assist with personal and household needs, training in things like cooking and cleaning from a wheelchair, and help with transportation. I would expect MDA to provide a motorized wheelchair for anyone who wants one. Such a chair can boost a disabled person's quality of life enormously. Instead, MDA has very restrictive criteria for determining who receives a motorized wheelchair.

Far be it from me to advise a multimillion-dollar agency on how to spend its money. But when the telethon tells viewers that by donating money to MDA, they are answering the prayers of people with MD—offering them a friend to turn to in times of need—it exaggerates.

Okay, say the defenders of the telethon, so maybe the money doesn't help people **now** as much as it should. Isn't it still laudable that the telethon raises so much money to help find a cure?

Ah, *the cure* . That's the promise that keeps people sending in those checks. That's what keeps this humiliation going year after year. We're getting closer all the time! Jerry Lewis assures us frenetically. He's been saying it for four decades.

Shortly after my stint as Poster Child was over, I remember meeting a stranger in a store who recognized me from the telethon. He said to me, "I bet you really hope they find a cure soon!" When he said this, I realized that by this time, I almost never even contemplated that possibility anymore, let alone hoped for it. I told him that. I don't think he believed me. I find the same reaction now, when I criticize the telethon for implying that people with disabilities sit around hoping and praying for a cure. I've encountered people who, never having tried it, think that living life with a disability is an endless hardship. For many of us, it's actually quite interesting, though not without its problems. And the majority of those problems result from the barriers, both physical and attitudinal, which surround us, or from the lack of decent support services. These are things that can be changed, but only if we as a society recognize them for what they are. We'll never recognize them if we stay so focused on curing individuals of disability, rather than making changes to accommodate disability into our culture.

Now, I'm not arguing that medical research should halt entirely—I'm just weighing the cost-benefit value, in my life and in the lives of my friends with disabilities, of the millions of dollars spent on the search for a cure, a search that will take decades, versus the things we really need now, on which society spends far less. We will probably never benefit from *the cure*. We will benefit from accessible buildings and transportation systems, job opportunities, and attendant services to provide us personal assistance. So will future generations.

We have begun making progress in those areas. In 1990, for example, the Americans with Disabilities Act became law, putting some legal teeth into our fight for civil rights and access.

But for all our progress in the areas of legal protection and accessibility, there's still this lingering attitude that what people with disabilities **really** need is to be cured. Society wants the problem to go away, so it won't have to accommodate people with long-term disabling conditions. It wants **us** to go away, or at least to "get better." One of my major objections to the telethon is the way it reinforces that attitude.

Sure, some people with muscular dystrophy **do** hope and dream of that day when the cure is finally found. As people with disabilities, we're conditioned just like everyone else to believe that disability is our problem. We've been told over and over that our need for accessibility to buses and buildings, and our need for health services, are too expensive, too unreasonable. Our culture considers it shameful to be physically unable to dress oneself, or to need assistance in going to the bathroom. Rather than demanding that the government provide such helping services, many people with disabilities end up hidden in nursing homes or in our own homes, where personal assistance remains the private "burden" of individuals and families. Rather than insisting on having our personal needs and our access needs met, many prefer to keep quiet about these needs, fearful to show ourselves lacking. The telethon itself encourages such self-defeating thinking. We are primed to regard ourselves as substandard. We therefore hesitate to assert our right to have that which, because of our disabilities, we need. The telethon teaches us to think that others will provide for us because they are kind and generous, not because we are a strong and vocal community. When so many of us feel so negative about our disabilities and our needs, it's difficult to develop a political agenda to get our basic needs met. The **cure** is a simple, magical, non-political solution to all the problems in a disabled person's life. That's why it's so appealing, and so disempowering. The other solutions we have to work for, even fight for; we only have to dream about the cure.

The idea of a cure is at least in part an effort to homogenize, to make everyone the same. To draw a parallel, when I was a child and first learned about racial discrimination, I thought it would be great if people could all be one color so we wouldn't have problems like prejudice. What color did I envision for this one-color world? White, of course, because I'm white. I didn't bear black people any malice. I just thought they'd be happier, would suffer less, if they were more like me.

We all have our own ideas about which human condition is best, based on our own assumptions about other people's lives. These assumptions don't always jibe with reality. People who assume that I live for the day when a cure is found, when I (or future generations) can live disability-free, simply don't understand my reality. It's a question of priorities. On the list of things I want, a cure for my disability is pretty low. Higher up on the list would be achievement of my personal, professional, and social goals, and these are not in any way dependent on a cure.

Besides, there's an issue of pride involved. Disability is a part of my whole identity, one I'm not eager to change. Especially not at the cost of my dignity and personhood, as the telethon implicitly demands.

This gets to another important issue the telethon raises in relation to the oppression of people with disabilities: Whose job is it to tell the story, or stories, of a group of people? The telethon is full of "profiles" of people with various forms of muscular dystrophy and their families. Yet these stories are packaged as products, not told as truth. Favorite subjects are children, for reasons discussed earlier—children can be made to appear more helpless, more pathetic, more dependent on the public's generosity. Children are also cute; therefore they seem more deserving of help.

In comparison with my telethon years, recent telethons do profile more adults with muscular dystrophy. Some are successful, competent adults. Yet somehow, even these individuals were made to look desperate and pitiable.

On any given telethon—both on the national broadcast from Las Vegas, and during the cut-aways to local segments—you will see profiles of children and adults with muscular dystrophy. These spots are all fairly similar in tone and emphasis. As if by a prescribed formula, each one contains several key ingredients. In each, the parents speak about their reactions upon hearing their child's diagnosis—even if, as in most cases, this has occurred years, or even decades, before. Naturally, these reactions include disbelief and grief. Yet there is rarely any discussion of how (or whether) the family has since come to accept the knowledge of their child's condition, to find resources (other than those offered by MDA), to plan for the child's future, or to promote the child's self-esteem. The situation is presented as an unmitigated tragedy.

I'm suspicious of this presentation. I'm not trying to minimize the pain a parent might feel upon learning that a child has a disabling, potentially even fatal, diagnosis. There is a very natural grieving process that goes along with disability at any stage. But when I see those emotions exploited so crassly, I can't help wincing. For most of us, our losses, gains, sorrows and joys are simply part of a rich human life. The telethon works very hard to convince people that our suffering is extraordinary. This produces pity, confusion and misunderstanding.

Another common element in these pieces is the emphasis on "what Johnny can't do." A child, usually a boy, is shown sitting at the edge of a playground. The narrator talks about the games the child can't play, and how he has to watch other children running and jumping. He can only dream, the narrator tells us sadly.

Never mind that the kid might be adept at playing Nintendo, or making rude noises with his mouth. In the real world of children, these skills are valued at least as much as running and jumping. The truth is, all children play at different levels of skill; most can't run as they would like, or jump as high, or play as well. Children in wheelchairs **do** play with other kids on the playground—I did. A child in a motorized wheelchair can be mobile, active—and popular, if willing to give rides now and then. But instead of acknowledging any of this, the telethon encourages viewers to project their own worst fears onto people with muscular dystrophy: "Just imagine what it would be like if **your child** couldn't play baseball."

Finally, each piece puts forward an archaic and gloomy picture of the disabled family member's role, and of the role of the family in a disabled person's life. All the families are described as "courageous"; and they all seem to bear total responsibility for the care and support of the person with MD. Spouses and parents alike are shown carrying the person with MD up and down stairs, pushing their wheelchair, and so on. Rarely if ever is the disabled family member shown making any positive contribution. In these stories, the disabled person's status is clearly (even if the word was never used) that of "burden."

I am all for supportive families. My own parents and brother have stood by me throughout my life, backing me with assistance and encouragement. But I have also built a life apart from them. Many people with disabilities do so, getting educated, working, and having families of our own. I am able to live independently, working toward the goals I choose, as long as I have access to the support services I need—primarily attendant services. I am lucky that the state of Colorado pays someone to come to my home and help me get up in the morning and get to bed at night. Most states do not offer this service, forcing people with disabilities to remain in the care of their families, or to enter nursing homes. Indeed, attendant services is the number one disability rights issue of the 1990's. Activists are demanding that the federal government divert a part of the huge budget which currently subsidizes the nursing home industry, and create a national system of attendant services, available to anyone who needs them.

On the telethon, of course, this is a non-issue. Disability is a private problem, demanding faith and fortitude from families, demanding generosity from viewers, demanding nothing from the government, or from society as a whole. If the need for personal assistance is mentioned at all, it is only to highlight, once again, the purported helplessness of people with MD, as in phrases such as "totally dependent on others for the most basic activities the rest of us take for granted." In fact, the opposite is true: With decent attendant services at my disposal, I become more **independent**, not more dependent. But to present that truth might undermine that vision of the long-suffering, burden-bearing family.

The unvarying tone **and** content of the pieces made it difficult to distinguish one "patient" from another. The profiles put forward a stereotyped view of what it means to have a disability, rather than any genuine stories of real people. We are all individuals, and families are all different. Not on the telethon, though. There we are made to fit the mold. Even the language used on the telethon distorts our reality and thereby dehumanizes us: We are "victims," we "suffer" from our conditions, we are "desperate."

I have firsthand experience of this distortion effect. Six or seven years after my Poster Childhood was over, just before my second year of college, I was asked to be interviewed for a local pre-telethon TV special. At first I said no. I was by now quite leery of the telethon mentality. I had also started becoming politicized, and was now more interested in civil rights than in charity. And I couldn't see any reason to participate once again in the simple-minded propaganda I remembered from my on-camera appearances as Poster Child. Back then, I had been asked questions like, "What would you like to say to all those nice people who are calling in their pledges, Laura?" to which the obvious reply was, "Thank you." Such questions left little room for honest expression.

But the local MDA office promised that the interview would be handled differently in this program: The plan was to take a positive, realistic approach and portray the real lives of three real people. So I agreed.

A TV news reporter conducted the interview in my parents' home. She asked good questions and allowed me to give complete, intelligent answers. It was certainly a different process from my earlier experiences. Afterward, I felt good about the upcoming show. I had been able to discuss issues, describe my life as a college student, and project a strong, positive personality.

Or so I thought. When the program aired, I was horrified. Through careful editing, it had turned into a sob story entitled "Waiting For A Miracle." From that point on, I vowed to have nothing to do with the telethon.

Until 1991, that is. I learned that two Chicago activists, Chris Matthews and Mike Ervin, were interested in coordinating actions against the Jerry Lewis telethon. Like me, they were both former poster children. I urged people from Denver's community to join the campaign. My decision to organize a protest did not come without some thought. In fact, I had for years contemplated doing something like this, but had not. I knew that our message would not be an easy one to convey to the public. Many people are involved with the telethon, either as volunteers or as contributors. I knew that openly criticizing it would cause confusion and anger. The telethon enjoys widespread acceptance, even acclaim.

But that is exactly why it's so important, I feel, to raise our voices against it. Because it is accepted *as our reality*. This is my biggest gripe against Jerry Lewis, and against the telethon: the extent to which they claim to tell my story, our stories, without any legitimate authority to do so.

The telethon's hegemony over the image of disability is quite staggering. A 1996 press release issued by MDA states, "According to A.C. Nielsen, last year's Telethon was watched by some 70 million Americans or 27 million households. The MDA Telethon—considered the granddaddy of all Telethons—ranks in viewership with the World Series and the Academy Awards." Those 70 million people are absorbing a message shaped by greed, deception, and bigotry.

The bigotry of Jerry Lewis is worth discussing. I don't necessarily enjoy attacking another person's motives, but I hear defenders saying, "Jerry Lewis is trying to help so many people. How dare you criticize his methods?" This means-justifies-the-ends argument has a long and despicable history, which I don't need to go into here. Even more dangerous is the attitude that people who are "being helped" have no right to say how they want to be helped, or treated, or thought of. This is paternalism at its worst. By being the object of charitable efforts, do we thereby waive our right to respect, and to free speech? If people are really interested in helping me, wouldn't they want to hear me tell my own story, rather than hearing a distorted version of it from someone who not only doesn't share my experience, but who doesn't even seem to want to listen to me? With the stated goal of "helping" his "kids," Jerry Lewis is helping to keep alive the most pernicious myths about people who have disabilities. He ignores our truth, substituting his own distorted assumptions.

If our protest did nothing else, it allowed some of us the opportunity to say, "No, this is not our reality. If you want to know what our lives are like, listen to us. If you want to know what we need, ask us. If you truly want to help us, let us tell you how. And if you pity and fear us, please own that; then let us work together at changing the world so that disability will not be something to fear, but something to try to understand."

The response to our protest has been interesting. Many people seem to resent our daring to object to these distortions, half-truths, and stereotypes. I have been called "ungrateful," "cruel," and "insensitive"—simply for trying to counter all this with the truth, with my truth. At the very least, I feel that the protest has enabled me and others to begin getting on record our own stories, in contrast to the misleading accounts that come from the telethon.

Media is a powerful thing. It can deceive, or it can enlighten. About a week after that 1991 telethon, a publication arrived in my mailbox called <u>MDA News Magazine</u>, put out by the national Muscular Dystrophy Association office. I started to leaf through it, expecting to find the same kinds of negative stereotypes that permeate the hours of the telethon. Instead, I found articles about job-seeking strategies; profiles of successful individuals who have neuromuscular diseases; honest and thoughtful pieces about families of children with neuromuscular diseases; lists of useful resources; and clinical updates. All of it was written in a positive, realistic tone, using respectful and appropriate language. The phrase "people with disabilities" was used at all times—never "victims," or "sufferers," and certainly not "cripples."

One article, written by Marie Hite, whose son has muscular dystrophy, stood out. Its basic theme was very similar to some of the telethon spots I had viewed: the difficulties a child has in coping with a progressively disabling condition. But Hite's treatment of the subject couldn't have been more different from that presented on the telethon. In her article, her son confided that he could no longer climb a neighbor's tree; he asked his mother for an explanation. She replied that his muscles didn't work the same as other children's.

Whereas the telethon would have used this situation to create pity, this article used it to tell a touching, upbeat story. In it, the focus was not so much on how the boy differs from other children, but on how the author helped her son understand his disability, and on his own resourcefulness in adapting to it. The grief was not denied, but neither was it overdone.

Tears instantly flowed down Petey's cheeks. 'But, Mom, I want to climb trees, too,' his voice pleaded.

Silence. . . .

What to say? . . .

I let him know that it was OK to feel sad, and I stayed with him.

Five minutes later, he was OK again.

'Petey, I'm going to help you climb Mrs. Kurly's tree when I get home from work,' I said. His face lit up. . . .

Her conclusion emphasized the boy's fundamental similarity to other children in struggling to understand and come to terms with himself and his world:

He had accepted his limitation as only a 6-year-old can, with childish grace and fantasy.

There are limits—and tree trunks—that love, with a little ingenuity, can rise above. Like other 6-year-olds, Petey just wanted to play in the tree.

In Hite's piece, Petey got what he wanted, with some assistance and adaptation; in fact, this describes fairly well how most people with severe disabilities live—with assistance and adaptation. Petey was portrayed as a real child, full of humanity. What a different view from that to which telethon viewers are exposed annually!

I was impressed by the sophistication and sensitivity of the writing in this magazine—but also a little baffled. How could the same organization that edits this publication, with its realism and insight, also produce the Jerry Lewis telethon? *They know better!* I thought.

Then I realized the reason for the apparent split personality within MDA. I was seeing two very different presentation, intended for two very different audiences. The magazine is aimed at people with neuromuscular diseases and their families. I commend MDA for offering their clients such a high-quality forum for education, information, and the sharing of experiences.

However, I am dismayed that when it comes to informing the general public, MDA chooses to take the opposite approach. Does the organization fear exposing potential donors to the truths revealed so eloquently in its magazine? Does it foresee a decline in contributions if nondisabled people start to see people with disabilities as we really are? Is respect and awareness bad for the bottom line? Is raising consciousness incompatible with raising money?

Images of people with disabilities sink into the public mind every Labor Day, images of helplessness and eternal childhood. We see children frolicking at summer camp, while an announcer tells us how miserable those children are the rest of the year. We hear tear-jerking stories from parents lamenting their child's condition. Pity is the name of the game in telethonland. Pity brings in big bucks.

So what's wrong with that?

Pity is a complex and deceptive emotion. It pretends to care, to have an interest in another human being. It seems to want to take away pain and suffering. But if you look at pity up close, you notice that it also wants to distance itself from its object. A woman calls in a pledge and boasts, "My two children are perfectly healthy, thank God!" Pity does not share another's reality, only remark upon it.

Pity can be very hostile to the achievement of equality and respect. If you feel sorry for someone, you might pledge a donation, but you are not likely to offer them a good job, or approve of them dating your sister or brother. If emotions were to be grouped into families, pity has some rather unsavory kin. On this emotional family tree, pity is very close to—sometimes indistinguishable from—contempt and fear, which are uncomfortably near to hatred.

That might sound like a strong statement. But I would argue that any reaction which creates separation and inequality between people—which pity certainly does, however benevolent it might appear—is destructive. People cannot live together in community, recognizing and respecting each other as human beings, if one group feels superior to the other for any reason.

Pity paves the way for paternalism, for the attempt to control people on the basis of disability. I have lived with the implications of this reaction, this assumption that I am less able to, have less of a right to, run my own life. I saw it in the eyes of the high school journalism teacher who didn't want me in her class. I see it on the faces of people who pass me on the street, and wonder (perhaps) what I am doing out in public.

Of course, many experiences and many emotions go into the formation of bigotry. I cannot blame all discrimination on pity. Nor can I blame all tendencies toward pity on the Jerry Lewis Telethon. But we need to analyze the way this annual event capitalizes on, and feeds, those tendencies. We need to ask ourselves whether all that money, tracked exuberantly on those giant tally boards, is worth it.

I say it's not.

The effects of our protests on the Jerry Lewis Labor Day Telethon have been mixed. It has become a TV show with a split personality.

Beginning with the 1992 telethon, we began to see some changes from previous years. We saw lawyers, accountants, teachers and journalists with muscular dystrophy, receiving recognition as winners of Personal Achievement Awards. We heard the words "dignity" and "self-respect" used over and over, sometimes in strange contexts—as in "Please call in your pledge to help us save these kids' dignity and self-respect." We heard talk about the Americans with Disabilities Act and the need for a personal assistance program.

But we also saw the old familiar scenes: tuxedo-clad local hosts sweating and beaming, well-groomed two-parent families poised to look brave and desperate, Jerry Lewis mugging and weeping.

The Muscular Dystrophy Association has consistently, obstinately refused to acknowledge the validity of our concerns. Marshalling all its defenses, MDA feverishly protects the decades-old tradition. Those of us identified as the telethon's chief critics continue to be told how ungrateful, unreasonable, vicious, and emotionally disturbed we are.

Yet we'll continue to critique this twenty-plus-hour-long epic. It's a microcosm of so many of our society's attitudes towards disability. It's the details which, for me, sum up the telethon perfectly—both its attempts to change and its intrinsic flaws.

A few examples:

The telethon has often featured a Florida woman named Shelley, an obviously intelligent person with a graduate degree and a professional career. In one typical segment, Shelley and her mother were both interviewed about their hope for a cure for muscular dystrophy. Her mother raised one hand a few inches and, near tears, said something like, "If only she could do this, that would be all I would ask for her." While other mothers wish for their grown children to have personal happiness, professional success, and a family, the telethon encourages the belief that the mother of a disabled adult can only hope for one thing—either total or partial cure.

The mother also stated that she is afraid to leave Shelley at home alone, because she can't use the telephone, or answer the doorbell, by herself. I had to wonder why Shelley did not have access to the relatively simple and inexpensive devices now available, such as hands-free telephones, and doorbell intercoms.

This scene was typical of several telethon segments: In presenting an individual with a neuromuscular disorder, the focus would be on functions the person couldn't do. When I see a story like that, I start this mental process of problem-solving—thinking about adaptive equipment, attendant services, access modifications, etc.—things which could help the person function more independently.

But apparently, the general public takes these things at face value: If Shelley can't answer her own telephone, the only possible solution is to cure her disability.

The telethon certainly doesn't encourage viewers to think of other options. If the person can use equipment and personal assistance to live more independently, then viewers may not feel as sorry for her.

There was another vignette about a family with two sons, one of whom has MD. In focusing on the younger, non-disabled son, the narrator made a statement to the effect that he doesn't have a big brother who can take him places and teach him things—he has a brother he has to take care of.

This statement implies that people with disabilities are incapable of giving to <u>any</u> kind of relationship, that we are undesirable even as siblings. (The telethon also promotes the idea that people with disabilities are miserable parents: Fathers and mothers are shown passively watching as their kids run and play, as if someone in a wheelchair could never provide children with affection, discipline, or moral or financial support. And forget any notion that people with MD can be sexual. The telethon presents even spouses as caretakers, not lovers. The denigration of our potential for relationships is perhaps one of the most dehumanizing and negative aspects of the telethon.

The next day, a different family appeared on the local segment of the telethon. Like the first family, there were two teenage boys, one, named Paul, with MD. The brothers were obviously very close. Again, the host made a major point of talking about how the non-disabled boy "takes care of" and assists his brother Paul. At this statement, the father leaned over to the microphone and said pointedly, "Paul helps him a lot too."

The host ignored this attempt to set the record straight, but I was very moved by it. I feel real compassion for people like that family, who participate in the telethon, yet try (usually in vain) to preserve their own dignity and truth.

MDA representatives have stated again and again that pity works, it makes people give money. They might be willing to change a few things, add some references to the ADA here and there, recognize some "achievers" with MD. But they are not about to tone down, in any significant way, their appeals to pity.

We can take credit, though MDA would never acknowledge it, for the changes that have occurred—they are certainly a direct result of our criticism and protests. But we have to increase the pressure, keep raising awareness, and stop this annual insult once and for all.

21

Memory Work

WENDY S. HESFORD

To remember in a critical mode . . . means, in Freirean terms, to con-
front the social amnesia of generations in flight from their own col-
lective histories. (McLaren and Tadeu da Silva, 73–74)

In the basement of my parents' home is a photograph that was once prominently displayed on the fire-place mantel in the family room with other representations of such rites of passage as weddings and school graduations. The
photograph stood beside the sacred family heirloom, a large, black, leather-bound
Holy Bible, with pressed birth announcements, engagements, and obituaries crum-
bling between the pages. It is a "portrait" of my maternal great-grandfather, Edward
William Trevenan, who left his wife, Amelia, and their five children in Cornwall,
England, in 1910 to work as a supervisor of operations at one of the gold mines
in Johannesburg, South Africa [see figure, page 245]. Edward, in his midthirties,
is seated in a small room on a simple wooden chair. The other furnishings are well-
worn and merely functional: two low cots, a small wooden table, two battered
steamer trunks. The floorboards are rough and paint is peeling off the walls. Edward
wears black leather shoes, dark cuffed pants, a button-down shirt (without a collar), and what he would have called "braces" to hold his pants up. He has rolled
his shirt-sleeves up to his elbows, which are placed casually on the chair back and
tabletop. His legs are comfortably crossed, and his shoes shine in the camera's
light. His appearance suggests a sense of control over his modest domain.

On the table are what appear to be the deliberately chosen necessities of an English workingman's life at the turn of the century: two tobacco pipes, two brushes (one for shoes, one for hair), a pot of ink containing a pen, a tin canister and several bottles, some papers (letters home?). The walls, too, are covered with "civilizing" touches: a pocket watch and chain hanging where a clock might be kept at home, a felt pincushion (identifiable as such only because my grandmother, Edward's daughter, still has the memento). Most prominent, however, are what appear to be pages torn from newspapers or magazines of British popular culture, which are tacked up in rather random fashion on the wall behind the beds. For example, one of the images seems to be a cover from *The Graphic*, a popular magazine of the British middle-class in the early twentieth century, the contemporary equivalent of our *Life* and *People* magazines. In addition, there is a page of nine portraits of formally dressed white men and women, each accompanied by a printed caption, illegible at this distance; a full-page photograph of a woman, perhaps a popular actress or singer in costume for some role; and two indistinct images, one of which appears to be men on horseback, some with arms in slings and others with guns. Finally, behind Edward's right arm is an image of two smiling women leaning coyly toward each other.

Before Edward, perched on the edge of a steamer trunk beside the cot on the left, sits a young black man in his mid-teens. My great-grandfather looks neither at the camera nor at anything within the frame of the picture, but gazes out, over, and beyond the visual field; the black youth, on the other hand, looks directly into the camera. He is dressed in baggy plaid pants that end above the knee and a plain long-sleeved shirt. His clothes do not fit well: the pants are clearly too large, gathered at the waist by a thick black belt, and his shirt is too small and rises up his back. Upon his head sits a misshapen felt slouch hat turned up in the front, and on his feet are scuffed and poorly soled white boots.

This description of the photograph may appear fairly straightforward and objective. But, in truth, it is far from neutral, because I have highlighted certain details and rejected or ignored others. In fact, one could argue that my description, like the photograph, reinvents the all-powerful gaze of the white European patriarch, because it does not question or reveal the logic of representation or the moral economy of the photograph and its relation to material realities. For instance, the description does not mention that there are no pictures of my great-grandmother or their children, nor does it shed any light on other social systems or relations that are not in the immediate field of vision. What exists on the other side of the interior walls is not known. Neither the photograph nor the description depicts the struggles that my great-grandmother Amelia must have faced in raising five children on her own or what must have conflicting emotions over her husband's absence, which lasted more than eighteen months. Through omission, the description, like the photograph itself, also ignores the dangerous working conditions in the mines and the black workers' resistance to these conditions, as expressed in riots, strikes, and work stoppages, as well as the brutal suppression of such acts by those in power. The opening description and its focus on what can be seen could be interpreted as a controlling act that reinforces the domestic order of the room—a kind of cartography of the privileged—to see only what we want to see. Yet what is *not* seen is as much a part of the context of the photograph as what *is* seen. And in that

Edward William Trevenan with young man, Johannesburg, South Africa.

respect, the opening description mirrors the patterns of detachment common to the Western ethnographic and autobiographic gaze of which the photograph is emblematic. . . .

Let us turn, then, to the logic of representation and its relationship to material and economic realities, which are no less constructed than the stories we tell about them. Consider, for example, how my description of the photograph simultaneously reinforces and lessens my great-grandfather's position of privilege. First, I call the image a "portrait" of my great-grandfather, which highlights his presence and awards him ownership of the image. Second, I suggest that his self-assured posture conveys a "sense of control over his modest domain" (referring to the actual space, although surely both the space and the black youth were considered part of his "domain"). Third, my use of the term "modest"—a minimizing phrase—places limits on my great-grandfather's power and suggests he was not the "grand colonizer" (a descriptor that is informed by the knowledge that my great-grandfather was in a lower-management position in the mining company).

Hygiene is another cultural concept that seeps into the description by separating order from disorder and distinguishing the powerful from the powerless. My great-grandfather's well-fitted clothing and shoes—shined, I suspect, by the black youth—contrast with the black youth's ill-fitted clothing and worn-out boots. The white male body is presented as neat and controlled, whereas the black male body appears ill-kempt. In other words, the clothing and descriptions of the subjects indicate social boundaries of race and class. Whether the photograph was commissioned by the mining company as a promotional piece or taken at the request of my great-grandfather, the construction of the room—namely, the parallel alignment of beds and trunks—conveys an ideal of domestic order. Interestingly, this image of domesticity lacks women, although the black youth is effeminized in the colonial, homosocial domestic relationship. In this instance *domesticate* is akin to *dominate*. The pocket watch, caught by the camera at 10:35, is an emblem of mechanical time and, along with the light bulb, reflects industrial progress, scientific advance, and the functionalism of male colonialists. By visually reproducing an image of imperial aggression and capitalist civilization, the photograph is a vivid reminder of the privileged group's anxiety and discomfort over changing social boundaries and its need to create a "home" far from home.

This photograph of my great-grandfather recalls nineteenth-century portraiture and foregrounds the paradoxical status of photography in bourgeois culture. In the early 1800s, within the developing context of global economy and a professionalized penal climate in Britain, photography was used as a technology of surveillance that "fixed" an image of the "other" through the photographic regulation of the subproletariat in police procedures and anthropological records. Paradoxically, photography both promised the "mastery of nature" and threatened to level the existing cultural order—that is, it represented the "triumph of a mass culture" (Sekula, 4). Photography, as a technology of representation and power, thus was used both to repress and signify the "other" through the imperatives of medical and anatomical illustration and of criminal documentation (which was informed by constructs of deviance and social pathology) and to celebrate the bourgeois tradition through the honorific portrait tradition (Sekula, 7). As Allan Sekula points out, in the nineteenth century, photography "introduce[d] the panoptic principle into daily life" (10). For example, criminal identification photographs were used to "facilitate the *arrest* of their referent" (7) and, presumably, to "unmask the disguises, the alibis, the excuses, and multiple biographies of those who find or place themselves on the wrong side of the law" (Sekula, 6). However, the moral economy of the photographic image served socially cohesive functions, particularly in the United States, where "family photographs sustained sentimental ties in a nation of migrants" and articulated a "nineteenth-century familialism that would survive and become an essential ideological feature of American mass culture" (8–9).

As the photograph of my great-grandfather and his black servant vividly illustrates, "photography welded the honorific and repressive functions together" (Sekula, 10). The family photograph of my great-grandfather and the black youth placed on the mantelpiece—the family shrine—"took its place within a social and moral hierarchy" (10); it monumentalized, commemorated, and reproduced an idealized image of the family and its value—that is, its accomplishment of social conventionality and status. The seemingly private moment of sentimentality and individualization was shadowed by the two other, more public looks: the averted gaze of my great-grandfather and the black youth's arrested gaze at the camera (Sekula, 10). As the family narratives that accompany this photograph suggest, photography asserts its instrumental power by "naturalizing cultural practices" (M. Hirsch, 7). Presumably, the photograph unveils, captures, and *arrests* the truth. But, we must ask, whose truth does the photograph of my great-grandfather and his black servant capture? Who is looking? Who is being seen? To whom does the terrain of representation belong? Is the black youth's look back at the camera an oppositional gaze?

Historically, in the visual structure of representation, black slaves were punished by white slave owners for looking back; as hooks puts it, "The politics of slavery, of racialized power relations were such that the slaves were denied their right to gaze" (1992, 115). Ironically, the black youth's gaze at the camera is not an unequivocally insurgent act of looking back, but rather his visibility produces a kind of public invisibility. Within the framework of late-nineteenth and early-twentieth-century photographic conventions, he is positioned as an object to be surveyed and regulated. He is caught in the exploiters' (both my great-grandfather and the photographer) production of him as "other." As a colonized subject, he is also positioned as a feminized object, capable only of offering himself up to the gaze of the paternal state (Tagg, 11–12). His gaze at the camera is not, then, an act of resistance. As David Spurr points out in *The Rhetoric of Empire*, "For the observer, sight confers power; for the observed, visibility is a trap" (16). The black youth's gaze at the camera contrasts with my great-grandfather's posture, which intentionally refuses the camera's probe and expresses the omniscience of Western European male culture. His commanding view suggests the colonialist surveying his dominion; it is a statement of control. From this perspective, one could look at the "portrait" of my great-grandfather as a use of visualizing technology for the self-authorization of the proto-typical Western white male, what Mary Louise Pratt calls "the monarch of all I survey" (quoted in Shohat and Stam, 156).

One challenge of reading this photograph is recognizing how it situates me, heir to my great-grandfather, as if I too were looking through the eyes of the colonizer. Here, we see how the context of imperial power shaped the uses of visual technology and how the I/Eye of empire traveled around the globe (156). Reading this photograph is like entering an autobiographical contact zone, a space where the narratives of my great-grandfather's generation and my own connect. More particularly, it is a space where the narratives that shape our lives collide. This is not to suggest that I'm caught in the grip of my great-grandfather's historical consciousness or that my gaze simply replicates his, but rather that I face the challenge of unsettling the historic and familial impulse to position myself at the center and of turning the "othering" gaze back on itself (Ellsworth, 9). In order to expose and transform the family narrative, I must resist the historical impulse to construct myself as a neutral cartographer recharting the circumspective force of the colonial gaze and must, instead, move beyond self-centering ethnocentrism. Moreover, I must avoid inscribing the same privileged mobility that my great-grandfather brought to his supervision of South African gold mines. Mary Louise Pratt claims that the representational phenomena of contact zones produce texts that are heterogeneous in their production as well as their reception. Reading a visual text, which to a certain degree circumvents narrative, nevertheless reinforces a kind of discursive mobility and academic literacy that casts an illusionary meta-narrative of control and coherence. My challenge is to inflect heterogeneity in my re-creation and to simulate it in narrative form by constantly unsettling the narratives themselves by showing how they are transformed as they move from one historical, cultural, and familial space to another. In this chapter, I appropriate Pratt's spatial metaphor in order to examine the production and reception of the family photograph and the clashing and collision of family identities, narratives, and networks of looking.

Despite the temporal, spatial, and cultural distance that separates me from the historical location of this photograph, the passage of the unframed "portrait" from one generation in my family to the next (it has traveled from my great-grandmother to my grandmother in Cornwall, England, to my mother in Essex County, New Jersey, to me in Oberlin, Ohio) indicates a lingering commitment to a sense of public history and the power of self-representation. This photograph can be described in Pratt's terms as an "ethnographic text" that captures my family's privilege and historical role in the objectification of the "other." My goal in this chapter is not to re-create yet another dominant ethnographic reading but to reach beyond a historical dominating sensibility to a reading that does not reproduce a colonial encounter. But in writing my first description of the photograph, I learned I cannot interpret it within the culture I live "without also apprehending the imperial contest itself" (Said, 217). "And," as Edward Said rightfully points out, "This . . . is a cultural fact of extraordinary political as well as interpretive importance" (217). In other words, "representations bear as much on the representer's world as on who or what is represented" (224). Spurr elaborates on the metaphorical relation between the writer and the colonizer":

> *The problem of the colonizer is in some sense the problem of the writer: in the face of what may appear as a vast cultural and geographical blankness, colonization is a form of self-inscription onto the lives of people who are conceived of as an extension of the landscape. For the colonizer as for the writer, it becomes a question of establishing authority through the demarcation of identity and difference. (7)*

While my opening description of the photograph illustrates the power of self-representation and my own role in the reconstruction of my family's history, it also suggests, as revealed through my analysis, that points of contact and collision lie within the "social moment of making memory" (Kuhn, 13). The challenge of reading this photograph is recognizing that the contact zone is *within* my gaze. Indeed, my goal in this chapter is to articulate the dominant narratives that define the historical moments of the photograph's production and reception and to consider how these narratives are now shaped by and mediated through my gaze.

Having presented some of the basic tenets of Pratt's concept of the contact zone in the Introduction and how it shapes my approach to autobiography— namely, my focus on the production and reception of autobiographical acts—I will now consider the particular narratives that shaped my reading of this family photograph as a young girl. This photograph has always fascinated and, at times, embarrassed me. My fascination sprang originally from wanting to know about the lives of my ancestors: where they lived, what they did, whom they knew. My sense of embarrassment is less readily identifiable, although I suspect it stems in part from guilt. When I asked members of my family about the relationship of the young black man to my great-grandfather, I was told that he was one of my great-grandfather's friends. Although I wanted to believe this interpretation, something about the image told me otherwise. Even at age ten, I knew the world was not that simple: a fairly well-dressed white man in South Africa was not likely to be "friends" with a black youth dressed in rags. My lingering sense of guilt arose from the nagging fear that the young black man seated across from my great-grandfather was actually some kind of indentured servant, or worse.

Perhaps it *is* possible that my great-grandfather Edward and the black youth were friends, although the fact that the latter was never named in this narrative of friendship is telling and perhaps another sign of colonial rule. As Spurr points out, "The very process by which one culture subordinates another begins in the act of naming and leaving unnamed, of marking on an unknown territory the lines of division and uniformity, of boundary and continuity" (4). Indeed, as Edward's only living son told me, the youth was referred to as my great-grandfather's "valet," a title that simultaneously suggests the imposition of British social norms onto the South African life and efforts to legitimize the relationship between the two: a personal valet is, after all, no mere servant. Not only is the young man's name unknown, but there is no definitive way to identify his language or place of origin. The colonial government recruited white miners from overseas, but most of its labor came from the indigenous black populations in southern and northern parts of Africa. Perhaps my great-grandfather's servant was initially recruited to work in the mines, but after a cursory medical examination revealed he was unfit or underage, he was relegated to employment outside the mines.[1]

This narrative of friendship may provide a paradigm for the rhetoric of colonial rule, because it allowed certain members of my family to deny their historical position of privilege and, at the same time, reinforced it. But because this narrative emerged in the contact zone of colonial relations, it rewrites the colonial situation in curious and complex ways. For example, reading their relationship as one of friendship or camaraderie rewrites the national colonial narrative at a time when colonial discourse constructed native black South Africans as savages. In other words, the South African youth gets reclassified from the "primitive savage" class into a Europeanized South African—a valet, part of an "advanced" community within the national and local hierarchy. Even if they did share the same living space, which is unlikely (the black youth probably lived with other black workers in overcrowded and unsanitary barracks), this imagined fraternity nonetheless speaks to the economic dependency of British imperialism on black African men's labor.

This narrative of friendship is also complicated by and intertwined with national narratives of immigration. In fact, the very multiplicity of the friendship narrative lies in its capacity to absorb distinct cultural and national narratives together (Jameson, 142). For instance, the constructed parallelism and imagined fraternity between my maternal great-grandfather and the South African youth, a reading that was formed well after my great-grandfather and his family had immigrated to America, rewrites my great grandfather's privileged status as colonizer, replacing it with a narrative about his subordinate status as an immigrant "other" in the United States. By immigrating to this country, Edward became the "other" when his position relative to the culture in which he worked changed: in South Africa, he was situated as the foreigner as colonizer, yet in the United States, he was reconstituted as the foreigner as immigrant (a position of considerably less power).

---

[1]See Jeeves for a discussion of the history of labor and mining in South Africa.

These positions of "otherness" are not historical equivalents. In fact, the allegory of alliance and projected fraternity actually disguises neocolonial relationships between First and Third World powers. I suspect, however, that my great-grand-father regarded immigration as an abandonment of the colonial system. Thus, in this friendship narrative, we see both anxiety and hope—a kind of double-sided consciousness.

Like most European immigrants in the late nineteenth and early twentieth century, my great-grandfather sought a better life for his family. For example, he was adamant about living where his sons would not have to work in the mines. As it was, they lived in New Jersey and worked for Du Pont, a plastics company. Although the friendship narrative may reflect the family's anxiety over its own differences in America, as white Anglo-Saxons they were less subordinate than other immigrants. They did not have to learn another language or a new economic system. Nevertheless, we may read into the family's interpretation of this photograph the double-sidedness of my great-grandfather's movements between England and South Africa and, later, the family's immigration to America. More particularly, the narrative of friendship between my great-grandfather and the South African distances my great-grandfather from the British social system of which he was originally a part, and contributes to the process by which he and his family were to invent and assimilate themselves as Americans. Reading this photograph at the moments of its production and reception involves reading into it the colonial relationship and expansion of Western interests, as well as the family's reconception of itself as Americans. When taken together, the friendship and immigration narratives challenge understandings of power relations that are constructed as fixed binaries (white/other, colonized/colonizer), and call for an understanding of the contradictory nature of subject positions, different national and cultural systems of stratification, and the historically situated nature of power (Friedman, 7).

The anxiety over the unsettling of cultural and geographical boundaries between the "First" and "Third" Worlds created narratives that constructed South Africa as a place where England (and Europe more generally) "projected its forbidden sexual desires and fears" (McClintock, 22). Similar narratives of sexual desire shaped my family's reading of this photograph and its understanding of my great-grandfather's movement abroad. For instance, when I visited Cornwall, England, in the mid-1980s on a foreign-exchange program in my senior year of college, I was told surreptitiously of Edward's lust for the bottle and women. This family secret—perhaps better termed a cultural myth—reflects a national narrative that eroticizes the land as well as the women of South Africa. The image of South Africa as seductive temptress is based on the notion that the land has qualities associated with the female body. As Spurr points out, however, what we see in such narratives is how "the traditions of colonialist and phallocentric discourses coincide" (Spurr, 170). This narrative of sexual desire is also about colonial conquest and imperial aggression. The family's construction of this "secret" mirrors a national sexual anxiety and the eroticization of the colonized, and invokes larger cultural anxieties and fantasies of seduction. That this narrative is framed as a secret or myth and my retelling as a betrayal of family privacy is an example of the cultural coding of disloyalty. Annette Kuhn puts it this way: "Secrets haunt our memory-stories, giving them pattern and shape. Family secrets are the other side of the family's public face, of the stories families tell themselves, and the world, about themselves" (2).

The photograph not only represents a discourse on the imperial "progress" of a nation but it also situates the white male as the father at the head of the "global family." The photograph was taken at a time when social crises were reverberating throughout Britain and its colonies. For instance, Britain experienced crises in gender and race relations on both domestic and international fronts. White masculinity was being contested. Middle-class women were seeking better educations and the right for paid work, and working-class women were fighting for fair employment rights and conditions. In contrast to these social challenges and the weakening of gender, race, and class boundaries, the photograph suggests that history and "progress" belong to white European men. This rendition of *his*-story is also shaped by the way science constructed race, which the medium of photography captured; more particularly, by the discourses of evolution and Social Darwinism, wherein racial ranking was prolific and black people were deemed genetically inferior (see Harding, Stepan and Gilman). Interestingly, these visual and verbal narratives of biological and social superiority and competition parallel those that characterize the rise of autobiography as a genre, which is deeply connected to the historical evolution of Western male self-consciousness and the capitalist ideology of possessive individualism. For instance, early critics of the genre claimed that peoples of the "Third World" were "primitive," that they lacked autobiography and feared their images in the mirror. Gusdorf, for one, argued that "primitives" "lag[ged] behind the Western 'child of civilization' and . . . that they have not emerged from 'the mythic framework of traditional teachings . . . into the perilous domain of history' " (Gusdorf quoted in McClintock, 313). These patterns of objectification continue through Western mappings of the "other" and the consumption of testimonial literature of Third World women in the First World marketplace (see Grewal and Kaplan).

How Far Have We Come?

The movement of the photograph from its prominent location in the family room to the basement of my parents' house is yet another rewriting of the progress narrative. The fact that this photograph of my great-grandfather was displayed in the family room of our newly purchased colonial home in a white, upper-middle-class New England suburb in the late 1970s confirms the family's status and upward mobility. The placement of the photograph carries an implicit message: "Look how far we've come from our humble beginnings."

The landscapes of my childhood and my family's geographical movement prompt questions about how I "encountered the other," how I did or did not acknowledge the presence of certain groups, and how what I experience as home, my safe space, was secured on the basis of historical exclusions, violence, and omissions. I spent my childhood and early adolescence in a segregated suburb of Newark, New Jersey. Class and racial differences were geographically demarcated: the white working class and people of color, mostly African-American families, lived on the west banks of the Passaic River. Unlike the white residents on the Hill, who enjoyed a commanding view, people of color lived in a part of town known as the Valley. People on the Hill projected themselves onto people in the Valley: geo-graphically, "whiteness" rose above and projected itself onto "blackness," or, as Ruth Frankenberg puts it, "Whiteness . . . comes to self-name, invents itself, by means of its declaration that it is *not* that which it projects as Other" (1996, 7). White middle-class families in my hometown were in a position of visual advan-tage, a location that presumably spared them from dealing with problems of race or class. We lived in a three-bedroom, stone-faced colonial house about midway up the Hill. Like most residents on the Hill, we defined ourselves by what we were not. Whiteness was "the invisible norm, the standard against which the dominant culture measures its own worth" constructed as both "everything and nothing" (McLaren 1995, 133). This monolithic construction of whiteness not only obscures ethnic and class differences among whites but also reinscribes the self-other binary; that is, we needed the "other" in order to see ourselves as unified subjects at the center. Like the gaze of my great-grandfather in the photograph, the spectatorial view from the hill functioned like a long chain of signifiers; the projection of black-ness was construed as the necessary construct and counterpart for the establishment of whiteness. A social pecking order also existed among whites, particularly between first- and second-generation immigrants. Italian-American families lived along the crowded maple-lined streets, and a few Jewish families, mostly households headed by doctors and lawyers, dotted the larger lots on the corners. I grew up in a climate of anti-Semitism, which essentialized Jews as part of the white power structure, masked class differences among Jewish families in town, and erased historical memories of struggle.

Washington Street marked the racial boundary between the Valley and the Hill. Most small businesses were located here: an Italian grocer, a Jewish bakery. The border was not a place we inhabited, but a place we traveled through. Like clockwork, my father pulled into Meyer's Bakery after he picked my brother and me up from the Methodist Sunday school on the other side of the Passaic river; crumb buns and donuts would sweeten our return from what always struck me as an alienating experience. Although members of my extended family ran the church, as Sunday-school teachers and treasurer, and sang in the choir, I always felt as if I was just passing through; my presence was a symbolic way for me and my family to uphold an image of goodness. The only other time we stopped on Washington Street—the border—was for my mother to buy fruit and vegetables from an old Ital-ian man, who ran his business from the back of a dilapidated truck. Our experi-ences of the border were our purchasing power, consumption of ethnicity, and commodification of the "other."

Meanwhile, across the railroad tracks on the south border of town, racial uprisings devastated whole neighborhoods. If I had known that more than fifteen hundred people were injured during the 1967 racial uprisings in Newark, that there were more than three hundred fires, and that the town was under military occupation, I may have been frightened and certainly confused. But I felt nothing. My daily life went on as usual. The only time we went into Newark was to pick my father up at the trolley station on the edge of town. Unlike my friends' fathers, who were policemen, firemen, or truck drivers, my father was a white-collar suit-and-tie man who commuted into Manhattan daily. My little brother and I were proud of our father, and we waited anxiously in the backseat of the family car, eager to see his face appear in the cable-car window. If my childhood years can be defined through narratives of protection and control, my adolescent years revealed the paradoxes of these narratives. For example, the ethic of control and anxieties about dating and relationships led me to excessive concern over body image and dieting—an embodiment of this trope of control.

My family left our house on the Hill in New Jersey when my father's company transferred him from New York to Connecticut. At first, we all seemed happy to move to another state and buy a bigger house, which was our chance to differentiate ourselves from most of the working- and lower-middle-class residents in our New Jersey hometown. My English immigrant grandparents had to work hard to assimilate, whereas my family, born in America, displayed our class difference, as our crossing the border zones suggests, through our consumerism—our construction of market identities—and our mobility. There are compelling parallels between my family's economic and geographic mobility and my own mobility, represented by the position I held while gathering research for this book. For six years after completing graduate school, I was a visiting assistant professor of writing at a college far removed from the blue-collar destiny of many of my childhood friends. Working at an elite college meant learning to deal with the privileges and paradoxes of my position, this movement, and its pedagogical implications. Although I grew up in a privileged white, middle-class environment, at Oberlin I struggled with the sense of entitlement shared by many upper-class students. At this time, the continuation of my family's progress narrative was defined not so much by my economic stability as by my cultural and intellectual status as a college professor, albeit in a visiting position. My authority was tied to my advanced academic literacy, which continues to distance me from my family. I am the first woman in my immediate family to go to college and the only person in my family to obtain a doctorate. Now, as an assistant professor at Indiana University with the privilege of being a new homeowner and adoptive parent, I'm rewriting this personal and professional narrative yet again.

The theme of upward mobility was entangled with another cultural narrative about a presumed lack of what might be called "ethnicity." As English immigrants, my family was not visibly or, because they quickly lost their accents, audibly "other." One might think, as I did as a child, that Anglo-British customs were not alive in America—except for certain foods, like the Cornish pasties and saffron buns my grandmother made. To me, these customs, class, and patterns of communication were invisible, naturalized. My family members had the privilege of situating themselves beyond forms of ethnic signification. As the photograph of my maternal great-grandfather suggests, we occupied the position of the privileging signifier. For instance, Italian-American life was "other" to us, as were the lives of Latinos, Jewish-Americans, South Asians, and African-Americans. But because as an adolescent most of my friends were Italian-Americans, I was comfortable with the Italian-American culture. I craved what seemed like exotic foods: chicken savoy (marinated in vinegar, olive oil, and oregano), cavatelli with ricotta, tiramisu, and red table wine. I yearned for animated conversations at dinnertime and elaborate Catholic rituals and ceremonies, for incense and ornate altars. I always wanted to escape what I saw as the "sterility" of my own family heritage. My desire for the "other"—Argerio, Basto, de Angelo, de Giordano, Donatello, Esposito, Giovanni,

Santantonio, Rizzo, Zanfini—was defined by the privilege of not being "other," of knowing the likeness would never be complete. Perhaps in my desire for the "other," the legacy of my great-grandfather's privilege and the self-other binary of imperial subjectivity played out most vividly. As Fredric Jameson puts it, this desire for and impulse to impersonate the "other" are inextricably bound with the historical treatment of ethnic groups as objects of prejudice (146). In fact, these two impulses reinforce each other; a single and centered subject (image of my great-grandfather) needs the self-other, subject-object binary for its formation (Grewal, 234). Reading this photograph and my family's reception of it involves not only the historical contextualization of the colonial gaze and photographic conventions but also a recognition of the cultural narratives of immigration, ethnicity, and upward mobility and of how the material history and shifting categories of the "other" are subsumed within these narratives. My yearning for the Italian-American "other" was, in some sense, a continuation of the historical impulse to impersonate the "other" and construct friendship narratives that erase privilege.

Throughout the 1980s, the photograph, part of a collection of portraits on the mantel, was an accepted part of the family history. But in the early 1990s, when attention to race relations in the United States increased, the photograph disappeared to the basement, where things go if they're out of style or on their way to the Salvation Army or a rummage sale. The deauthorization of the photograph as a family heirloom is telling. It suggests a growing awareness about the historical context of our privilege, albeit an awareness manifested by rendering invisible our most visible yet unspoken secret—our white privilege. Paradoxically, the removal of the photograph to the basement at once represents an awareness of our privilege yet constitutes that privilege as an absence: the family can't bear to witness itself as a negative presence. This denial is tinged, of course, with white guilt about our role within the colonial situation and the historical process of othering. It is also a narrative, like the friendship narrative, that seeks to avoid the problems of white privilege by foregrounding other things—for example, that we can put such experiences aside. The movement of the photograph to the basement, one might argue, is a way of maintaining order and of not "losing face." My adolescent yearning for the Italian-American "other" was also a narrative with whiteness at the center, as the defining core. My reach toward the "other" could thus be interpreted as a reinscription of the white Anglo-American identity that it set out to displace.

The process of reframing these stories imposes new narrative trajectories and autobiographical scripts onto the photograph. Two implied narrative lines in my reconstruction include a redemptive narrative that emphasizes the recuperation of lost memories and the transformation of personal consciousness. The transformation narrative is embedded in a larger narrative about the academy as a radicalizing agent. Although neither narrative is about a triumph over adversity per se, each refers to an increased level of critical consciousness. My reframing of the family photograph and its narratives might be read as emblematic of the movement through Freirean levels of consciousness—that is, the move from "intransitive thought" (where the individual experiences a lack of agency) to "semi-transitive" (a state wherein one claims a sense of agency yet continues to isolate and individualize social problems) to "critical transitivity" (a stage wherein one thinks about one's condition holistically and critically) (Shor 1993, 32). One could argue, for instance, that my reading of the family photograph reflects a certain level of critical transitivity; the constructed analytical narratives go beneath the impressions of the photographic surface to challenge the consequences of representation. However, as the storyteller, I cannot escape the contours of the framing apparatuses or their historical impulses.

Freirean principles encourage critical educators to create pedagogical narratives and forums for sharing and engaging stories of struggle and hope with an awareness of "how, as subjects, we have become disproportionately constituted within dominative regimes of discourses and social practices through race, class, and gender identities" (McLaren and Tadeu da Silva, 68). However, in our creation of these public narratives and spaces we must be careful not to position ourselves as saviors (enlightened beings) and students as mere victims to be saved; not only does this pedagogical narrative uncritically project a state of false consciousness onto our students, but it also fails to acknowledge the "invisible" or masked literacies and levels of critical consciousness that students readily practice and claim both inside and outside the classroom.

This brings me to the second implied narrative trajectory of the academy as a radicalizing agent. It was within the academy, a site of relative privilege and entitlement that sanctions and legitimates middle-class values, that I was first exposed to Freire.[2] That the process of re-education has taken place, and continues to take place, within the structures of the academy suggests that the academy is a place conducive to such growth and transformation. This narrative, of course, is idealistic. But it is a pedagogical narrative of *hope* that I refuse to resign, a narrative that nonetheless must account for the fact that the academy is not an equally accessible or safe place for everyone to articulate social struggles or social dreaming. Thus, we must constantly work to comprehend our own and our students' social and political locations and how institutional relations are shaped by historical understandings and personal and generational biographies.

References

Bloom, Lynn. 1996. "Freshman Composition as a Middle-Class Enterprise." *College English* 58 (6): 654-75.

Ellsworth, Elizabeth. 1992. "Teaching to Support Unassimilated Difference." *Radical Teacher* 42: 4-9.

Frankenberg, Ruth. 1996. "When We Are Capable of Stopping, We Begin to See: Being White, Seeing Whiteness." In *Names We Call Home*, ed. By Becky Thompson and Sangeetz Tyagi, 3-18. New York: Routlege.

Friedman, Diane P. 1992. *An Alchemy of Genres: Cross-Genre Writing by American Feminist Poet-Critics.* Charlottesville: University Press of Virginia.

Grewal, Inderpal. 1994. "Autobiographic Subjects and Diasporic Locations: *Meatless Days* and *Borderlands*." In *Scattered Hegemonies: Postmodernity and Transnational Feminist Practices*, eds. Inderpal Grewal and Caren Kaplan, 231-54. Minneapolis: University of Minnesota Press.

---

[2]See L. Bloom for a discussion of the midlle-class values in relation to the field of composition.

Grewal, Inderpal and Caren Kaplan. 1994. *Scattered Hegemonies: Postmodernity and Transnational Feminist Practices*. Minneapolis: University of Minnesota Press.

Harding, Sandra. 1993. "Eurocentric Scientific Illiteracy—A Challenge for the World Community." In *The "Racial" Economy of Science: Toward a Democratic Future*, ed. Sandra Harding, 1-29. Bloomington: Indiana University Press.

Hirsch, Marianne. 1997. *Family Frames: Photography, Narrative, and Postmemory*. Cambridge: Harvard University Press.

Jameson, Fredric. 1979. "Reification and Utopia in Mass Culture." *Social Text* 1:130-48.

Tagg, John. 1988. *The Burden of Representation*. Amherst: University of Massachusetts Press.

22

Selling Hot Pussy

Representations of Black Female Sexuality in the Cultural Marketplace

BELL HOOKS

Friday night in a small midwestern town—I go with a group of artists and professors to a late night dessert place. As we walk past a group of white men standing in the entry way to the place, we overhear them talking about us, saying that my companions, who are all white, must be liberals from the college, not regular "townies," to be hanging out with a "nigger." Everyone in my group acts as though they did not hear a word of this conversation. Even when I call attention to the comments, no one responds. It's like I am not only not talking, but suddenly, to them, I am not there. I am invisible. For my colleagues, racism expressed in everyday encounters—this is our second such experience together—is only an unpleasantness to be avoided, not something to be confronted or challenged. It is just something negative disrupting the good time, better to not notice and pretend it's not there.

As we enter the dessert place they all burst into laughter and point to a row of gigantic chocolate breasts complete with nipples—huge edible tits. They think this is a delicious idea—seeing no connection between this racialized image and the racism expressed in the entry way. Living in a world where white folks are no longer nursed and nurtured primarily by black female caretakers, they do not look at these symbolic breasts and consciously think about "mammies." They do not see this representation of chocolate breasts as a sign of displaced longing for a racist past when the bodies of black women were commodity, available to anyone white who could pay the price. I look at these dark breasts and think about the representation of black female bodies in popular culture. Seeing them, I think about the connection between contemporary representations and the types of images popularized from slavery on. I remember Harriet Jacobs's powerful exposé of the psychosexual dynamics of slavery in *Incidents in the Life of a Slave Girl.* I remember the way she described that "peculiar" institution of domination and the white people who constructed it as "a cage of obscene birds."

Representations of black female bodies in contemporary popular culture rarely subvert or critique images of black female sexuality which were part of the cultural apparatus of nineteenth-century racism and which still shape perceptions today. Sander Gilman's essay "Black Bodies, White Bodies: Toward an Iconography of Female Sexuality in Late Nineteenth-Century Art, Medicine, and Literature" calls attention to the way black presence in early North American society allowed whites to sexualize their world by projecting onto black bodies a narrative of sexualization disassociated from whiteness. Gilman documents the development of this image, commenting that "by the eighteenth century, the sexuality of the black, male and female, becomes an icon for deviant sexuality." He emphasizes that it is the black female body that is forced to serve as "an icon for black sexuality in general."

Most often attention was not focused on the complete black female on display at a fancy ball in the "civilized" heart of European culture, Paris. She is there to entertain guests with the naked image of Otherness. They are not to look at her as a whole human being. They are to notice only certain parts. Objectified in a manner similar to that of black female slaves who stood on auction blocks while owners and overseers described their important, salable parts, the black women whose naked bodies were displayed for whites at social functions had no presence. They were reduced to mere spectacle. Little is known of their lives, their motivations. Their body parts were offered as evidence to support racist notions that black people were more akin to animals than other humans. When Sarah Bartmann's body was exhibited in 1810, she was ironically and perversely dubbed "the Hottentot Venus." Her naked body was displayed on numerous occasions for five years. When she died, the mutilated parts were still subject to scrutiny. Gilman stressed that: "The audience which had paid to see her buttocks and had fantasized about the uniqueness of her genitalia when she was alive could, after her death and dissection, examine both." Much of the racialized fascination with Bartmann's body concentrated attention on her buttocks.

A similar white European fascination with the bodies of black people, particularly black female bodies, was manifest during the career of Josephine Baker. Content to "exploit" white eroticization of black bodies, Baker called attention to the "butt" in her dance routines. Phyllis Rose, though often condescending in her recent biography, *Jazz Cleopatra: Josephine Baker In Her Time,* perceptively explores Baker's concentration on her ass:

She handled it as though it were an instrument, a rattle, something apart from herself that she could shake. One can hardly overemphasize the importance of the rear end. Baker herself declared that people had been hiding their asses too long. "The rear end exists. I see no reason to be ashamed of it. It's true there are rear ends so stupid, so pretentious, so insignificant that they're good only for sitting on." With Baker's triumph, the erotic gaze of a nation moved downward: she had uncovered a new region for desire.

Many of Baker's dance moves highlighting the "butt" prefigure movements popular in contemporary black dance.

Although contemporary thinking about black female bodies does not attempt to read the body as a sign of "natural" racial inferiority, the fascination with black "butts" continues. In the sexual iconography of the traditional black pornographic imagination, the protruding butt is seen as an indication of a heightened sexuality. Contemporary popular music is one of the primary cultural locations for discussions of black sexuality. In song lyrics, "the butt" is talked about in ways that attempt to challenge racist assumptions that suggest it is an ugly sign of inferiority, even as it remains a sexualized sign. The popular song "Doin' the Butt" fostered the promotion of a hot new dance favoring those who could most protrude their buttocks with pride and glee. A scene in Spike Lee's film *School Daze* depicts an all black party where everyone is attired in swimsuits dancing—doing the butt. It is one of the most compelling moments in the film. The black "butts" on display are unruly and outrageous. They are not the still bodies of the female slave made to appear as mannequin. They are not a silenced body. Displayed as playful cultural nationalist resistance, they challenge assumptions that the black body, its skin color and shape, is a mark of shame. Undoubtedly the most transgressive and provocative moment in *School Daze,* this celebration of buttocks either initiated or coincided with an emphasis on butts, especially the buttocks of women, in fashion magazines. Its potential to disrupt and challenge notions of black bodies, specifically female bodies, was undercut by the overall sexual humiliation and abuse of black females in the film. Many people did not see the film so it was really the song "Doin' the Butt" that challenged dominant ways of thinking about the body which encourage us to ignore asses because they are associated with undesirable and unclean acts. Unmasked, the "butt" could be once again worshiped as an erotic seat of pleasure and excitement.

When calling attention to the body in a manner inviting the gaze to mutilate black female bodies yet again, to focus solely on the "butt," contemporary celebrations of this part of the anatomy do not successfully subvert sexist/racist representations. Just as nineteenth-century representations of black female bodies were constructed to emphasize that these bodies were expendable, contemporary images (even those created in black cultural production) give a similar message. When Richard Wright's protest novel *Native Son* was made into a film in the 1980s, the film did not show the murder of Bigger's black girlfriend Bessie. This was doubly ironic. She is murdered in the novel and then systematically eliminated in the film. Painters exploring race as artistic subject matter in the nineteenth century often created images contrasting white female bodies with black ones in ways that reinforced the greater value of the white female icon. Gilman's essay colludes in this critical project: he is really most concerned with exploring white female sexuality.

A similar strategy is employed in the Wright novel and in the film version. In the novel, Bessie is expendable because Bigger has already committed the more heinous crime of killing a white woman. The first and more important murder subsumes the second. Everyone cares about the fate of Mary Dalton, the ruling-class white female daughter; no one cares about the fate of Bessie. Ironically, just at the moment when Bigger decides that Bessie's body is expendable, that he will kill her, he continues to demand that she help him, that she "do the right thing." Bigger intends to use her then throw her away, a gesture reinforcing that hers is an expendable body. While he must transgress dangerous boundaries to destroy the body of a white female, he can invade and violate a black female body with no fear of retribution and retaliation.

Black and female, sexual outside the context of marriage, Bessie represents "fallen womanhood." She has no protectors, no legal system will defend her rights. Pleading her cause to Bigger, she asks for recognition and compassion for her specific condition.

> *Bigger, please! Don't do this to me! Please! All I do is work, work like a dog! From morning till night. I ain't got no happiness. I ain't never had none. I ain't got nothing and you do this to me . . .*

Poignantly describing the lot of working-class poor black women in the 1940s, her words echo those of poet Nikki Giovanni describing the status of black women in the late 1960s. The opening line to "Woman Poem" reads: "You see my whole life is tied up to unhappiness." There is a radical difference, however. In the 1960s, the black female is naming her unhappiness to demand a hearing, an acknowledgment of her reality, and change her status. This poem speaks to the desire of black women to construct a sexuality apart from that imposed upon us by a racist/sexist culture, calling attention to the ways we are trapped by conventional notions of sexuality and desirability:

> *It's a sex object if you're pretty and no love or love and no sex if you're fat get back fat black woman be a mother grandmother strong thing but not woman gameswoman romantic woman love needer man seeker dick eater sweat getter fuck needing love seeking woman.*

"Woman Poem" is a cry of resistance urging those who exploit and oppress black women, who objectify and dehumanize, to confront the consequences of their actions. Facing herself, the black female realizes all that she must struggle against to achieve self-actualization. She must counter the representation of herself, her body, her being as expendable.

Bombarded with images representing black female bodies as expendable, black women have either passively absorbed this thinking or vehemently resisted it. Popular culture provides countless examples of black female appropriation and exploitation of "negative stereotypes" to either assert control over the representation or at least reap the benefits of it. Since black female sexuality has been represented in racist/sexist iconography as more free and liberated, many black women singers, irrespective of the quality of their voices, have cultivated an image which suggests they are sexually available and licentious. Undesirable in the conventional sense, which defines beauty and sexuality as desirable only to the extent that it is idealized and unattainable, the black female body gains attention only when it is synonymous with accessibility, availability, when it is sexually deviant.

Tina Turner's construction of a public sexual persona most conforms to this idea of black female sexuality. In her recent autobiography, *I, Tina*, she presents a sexualized portrait of herself—providing a narrative that is centrally "sexual confession." Even though she begins by calling attention to the fact that she was raised with puritanical notions of innocence and virtuous womanhood which made her reticent and fearful of sexual experience, all that follows contradicts this portrait. Since the image that has been cultivated and commodified in popular culture is of her as "hot" and highly sexed—the sexually ready and free black woman—a tension exists in the autobiography between the reality she presents and the image she must uphold. Describing her first sexual experience, Turner recalls:

> *Naturally, I lost my virginity in the backseat of a car. This was the fifties, right? I think he had planned it, the little devil—he knew by then that he could get into my pants, because there's already been a lot of kissing and touching inside the blouse, and then under the skirt and so forth. The next step was obvious. And me, as brazen as I was, when it came down to finally doing the real thing, it was like: "Uh-oh, it's time." I mean, I was scared. And then it happened.*
>
> *Well, it hurt so bad—I think my earlobes were hurting. I was just dying, God. And he wanted to do it two or three times! It was like poking an open wound. I could hardly walk afterwards.*
>
> *But I did it for love. The pain was excruciating; but I loved him and he loved me, and that made the pain less—Everything was right. So it was beautiful.*

Only there is nothing beautiful about the scenario Turner describes. A tension exists between the "cool" way she describes this experience, playing it off to suggest she was in control of the situation, and the reality she recounts where she succumbs to male lust and suffers sex. After describing a painful rite of sexual initiation, Turner undermines the confession by telling the reader that she felt good. Through retrospective memory, Turner is able to retell this experience in a manner that suggests she was comfortable with sexual experience at an early age, yet cavalier language does not completely mask the suffering evoked by the details she gives. However, this cavalier attitude accords best with how her fans "see" her. Throughout the biography she will describe situations of extreme sexual victimization and then undermine the impact of her words by evoking the image of herself and other black women as sexually free, suggesting that we assert sexual agency in ways that are never confirmed by the evidence she provides.

Tina Turner's singing career has been based on the construction of an image of black female sexuality that is made synonymous with wild animalistic lust. Raped and exploited by Ike Turner, the man who made this image and imposed it on her, Turner describes the way her public persona as singer was shaped by his pornographic misogynist imagination:

Ike explained: As a kid back in Clarksdale, he'd become fixated on the white jungle goddess who romped through Saturday matinee movie serials—revealing rag-clad women with long flowing hair and names like Sheena, Queen of the Jungle, and Nyoka—particularly Nyoka. He still remembered The Perils of Nyoka, *a fifteen-part Republic Picture serial from 1941, starring Kay Alridge in the title role and featuring a villainess named Vultura, an ape named Satan, and Clayton Moore (later to be TV's Lone Ranger) as love interest. Nyoka, Sheena—Tina! Tina Turner—Ike's own personal Wild Woman. He loved it.*

Turner makes no comment about her thoughts about this image. How can she? It is part of the representation which makes and maintains her stardom.

Ike's pornographic fantasy of the black female as wild sexual savage emerged from the impact of a white patriarchal controlled media shaping his perceptions of reality. His decision to create the wild black woman was perfectly compatible with prevailing representations of black female sexuality in a white supremacist society. Of course the Tina Turner story reveals that she was anything but a wild woman; she was fearful of sexuality, abused, humiliated, fucked, and fucked over. Turner's friends and colleagues document the myriad ways she suffered about the experience of being brutally physically beaten prior to appearing on stage to perform, yet there is no account of how she coped with the contradiction (this story is told by witnesses in *I, Tina*). She was on one hand in excruciating pain inflicted by a misogynist man who dominated her life and her sexuality, and on the other hand projecting in every performance the image of a wild tough sexually liberated woman. Not unlike the lead character in the novel *Story of O* by Pauline Reage, Turner must act as though she glories in her submission, that she delights in being a slave of love. Leaving Ike, after many years of forced marital rape and physical abuse, because his violence is utterly uncontrollable, Turner takes with her the "image" he created.

Despite her experience of abuse rooted in sexist and racist objectification, Turner appropriated the "wild woman" image, using it for career advancement. Always fascinated with wigs and long hair, she created the blonde lioness mane to appear all the more savage and animalistic. Blondeness links her to jungle imagery even as it serves as an endorsement of a racist aesthetics which sees blonde hair as the epitome of beauty. Without Ike, Turner's career has soared to new heights, particularly as she works harder to exploit the visual representation of woman (and particularly black woman) as sexual savage. No longer caught in the sadomasochistic sexual iconography of black female in erotic war with her mate that was the subtext of the Ike and Tina Turner show, she is now portrayed as the autonomous black woman whose sexuality is solely a way to exert power. Inverting old imagery, she places herself in the role of dominator.

Playing the role of Aunty Entity in the film *Mad Max: Beyond the Thunderdome,* released in 1985, Turner's character evokes two racist/sexist stereotypes, that of the black "mammy" turned power hungry and the sexual savage who uses her body to seduce and conquer men. Portrayed as lusting after the white male hero who will both conquer and reject her, Aunty Entity is the contemporary reenactment of that mythic black female in slavery who supposedly "vamped" and seduced virtuous white male slave owners. Of course the contemporary white male hero of *Mad Max* is stronger than his colonial forefathers. He does not succumb to the dangerous lure of the deadly black seductress who rules over a mini-nation whose power is based on the use of shit. Turner is the bad black woman in this film, an image she will continue to exploit.

Turner's video "What's Love Got to Do with It" also highlights the convergence of sexuality and power. Here, the black woman's body is represented as potential weapon. In the video, she walks down rough city streets, strutting her stuff, in a way that declares desirability, allure, while denying access. It is not that she is no longer represented as available; she is "open" only to those whom she chooses. Assuming the role of hunter, she is the sexualized woman who makes men and women her prey (in the alluring gaze of the video, the body moves in the direction of both sexes). This tough black woman has no time for woman bonding, she is out to "catch." Turner's fictive model of black female sexual agency remains rooted in misogynist notions. Rather than being a pleasure-based eroticism, it is ruthless, violent; it is about women using sexual power to do violence to the male Other.

Appropriating the wild woman pornographic myth of black female sexuality created by men in a white supremacist patriarchy, Turner exploits it for her own ends to achieve economic self-sufficiency. When she left Ike, she was broke and in serious debt. The new Turner image conveys the message that happiness and power come to women who learn to beat men at their own game, to throw off any investment in romance and get down to the real dog-eat-dog thing. "What's Love Got to Do with It" sung by Turner evokes images of the strong bitchified black woman who is on the make. Subordinating the idea of romantic love and praising the use of sex for pleasure as commodity to exchange, the song had great appeal for contemporary postmodern culture. It equates pleasure with materiality, making it an object to be sought after, taken, acquired by any means necessary. When sung by black women singers, "What's Love Got to Do with It" called to mind old stereotypes which make the assertion of black female sexuality and prostitution synonymous. Just as black female prostitutes in the 1940s and 1950s actively sought clients in the streets to make money to survive, thereby publicly linking prostitution with black female sexuality, contemporary black female sexuality is fictively constructed in popular rap and R&B songs solely as commodity—sexual service for money and power, pleasure is secondary.

Contrasted with the representation of wild animalistic sexuality, black female singers like Aretha Franklin and younger contemporaries like Anita Baker fundamentally link romance and sexual pleasure. Aretha, though seen as a victim of no-good men, the classic "woman who loves too much" and leaves the lyrics to prove it, also sang songs of resistance. "Respect" was heard by many black folks, especially black women, as a song challenging black male sexism and female victimization while evoking notions of mutual care and support. In a recent pbs special highlighting individual musicians, Aretha Franklin was featured. Much space was given in the documentary to white male producers who shaped her public image. In the documentary, she describes the fun of adding the words "sock it to me" to "Respect" as a powerful refrain. One of the white male producers, Jerry Wexler, offers his interpretation of its meaning, claiming that it was a call for "sexual attention of the highest order." His sexualized interpretations of the song seemed far removed from the way it was heard and celebrated in black communities. Looking at this documentary, which was supposedly a tribute to Aretha Franklin's power, it was impossible not to have one's attention deflected away from the music by the subtext of the film, which can be seen as a visual narrative documenting her obsessive concern with the body and achieving a look suggesting desirability. To achieve this end, Franklin constantly struggles with her weight, and the images in the film chronicle her various shifts in body size and shape. As though mocking this concern with her body, throughout most of the documentary Aretha appears in what seems to be a household setting, a living room maybe, wearing a strapless evening dress, much too small for her breast size, so her breasts appear like two balloons filled with water about to burst. With no idea who shaped and controlled this image, I can only reiterate that it undermined the insistence in the film that she has overcome sexual victimization and remained a powerful singer; the latter seemed more likely than the former.

Black female singers who project a sexualized persona are as obsessed with hair as they are with body size and body parts. As with nineteenth-century sexual iconography, specific parts of the anatomy are designated more sexual and worthy of attention than others. Today much of the sexualized imagery for black female stars seems to be fixated on hair; it and not buttocks signifies animalistic sexuality. This is quintessentially so for Tina Turner and Diana Ross. It is ironically appropriate that much of this hair is synthetic and man-made, artificially constructed as is the sexualized image it is meant to evoke. Within a patriarchal culture where women over forty are not represented as sexually desirable, it is understandable that singers exploiting sexualized representations who are near the age of fifty place less emphasis on body parts that may reflect aging while focusing on hair.

In a course I teach on "The Politics of Sexuality," where we often examine connections between race and sex, we once critically analyzed a *Vanity Fair* cover depicting Diana Ross. Posed on a white background, apparently naked with the exception of white cloth draped loosely around her body, the most striking element in the portrait was the long mane of jet black hair cascading down. There was so much hair that it seemed to be consuming her body (which looked frail and anorexic), negating the possibility that this naked flesh could represent active female sexual agency. The white diaper-like cloth reinforced the idea that this was a portrait of an adult female who wanted to be seen as childlike and innocent. Symbolically, the hair that is almost a covering hearkens back to early pictorial images of Eve in the garden. It evokes wildness, a sense of the "natural" world, even as it shrouds the body, repressing it, keeping it from the gaze of a culture that does not invite women to be sexual subjects. Concurrently, this cover contrasts whiteness and blackness. Whiteness dominates the page, obscuring and erasing the possibility of any assertion of black power. The longing that is most visible in this cover is that of the black woman to embody and be encircled by whiteness, personified by the possession of long straight hair. Since the hair is produced as commodity and purchased, it affirms contemporary notions of female beauty and desirability as that which can be acquired.

According to postmodern analyses of fashion, this is a time when commodities produce bodies, as this image of Ross suggests. In her essay "Fashion and the Cultural Logic of Postmodernity," Gail Faurshou explains that beauty is no longer seen as a sustained "category of precapitalist culture." Instead, "the colonization and the appropriation of the body as its own production/consumption machine in late capitalism is a fundamental theme of contemporary socialization." This cultural shift enables the bodies of black women to be represented in certain domains of the "beautiful" where they were once denied entry, i.e., high fashion magazines. Reinscribed as spectacle, once again on display, the bodies of black women appearing in these magazines are not there to document the beauty of black skin, of black bodies, but rather to call attention to other concerns. They are represented so readers will notice that the magazine is racially inclusive even though their features are often distorted, their bodies contorted into strange and bizarre postures that make the images appear monstrous or grotesque. They seem to represent an anti-aesthetic, one that mocks the very notion of beauty.

Often black female models appear in portraits that make them look less like humans and more like mannequins or robots. Currently, black models whose hair is not straightened are often photographed wearing straight wigs; this seems to be especially the case if the models' features are unconventional, i.e., if she has large lips or particularly dark skin, which is not often featured in the magazine. The October 1989 issue of *Elle* presented a short profile of designer Azzedine Alaia. He stands at a distance from a black female body holding the sleeves of her dress. Wearing a ridiculous straight hair-do, she appears naked holding the dress in front of her body. The caption reads, "they are beautiful aren't they!" His critical gaze is on the model and not the dress. As commentary it suggests that even black women can look beautiful in the right outfit. Of course when you read the piece, this statement is not referring to the model, but is a statement Alaia makes about his clothes. In contemporary post-modern fashion sense, the black female is the best medium for the showing of clothes because her image does not detract from the outfit; it is subordinated.

Years ago, when much fuss was made about the reluctance of fashion magazines to include images of black women, it was assumed that the presence of such representations would in and of themselves challenge racist stereotypes that imply black women are not beautiful. Nowadays, black women are included in magazines in a manner that tends to reinscribe prevailing stereotypes. Darker-skinned models are most likely to appear in photographs where their features are distorted. Biracial women tend to appear in sexualized images. Trendy catalogues like *Tweeds* and *J. Crew* make use of a racialized subtext in their layout and advertisements. Usually they are emphasizing the connection between a white European and American style. When they began to include darker-skinned models, they chose biracial or fair-skinned black women, particularly with blonde or light brown long hair. The nonwhite models appearing in these catalogues must resemble as closely as possible their white counterparts so as not to detract from the racialized subtext. A recent cover of *Tweeds* carried this statement:

> *Color is, perhaps, one of the most important barometers of character and self-assurance. It is as much a part of the international language of clothes as silhouette. The message colors convey, however, should never overwhelm. They should speak as eloquently and intelligently as the wearer. Whenever colors have that intelligence, subtlety, and nuance we tend to call them European.*

Given the racialized terminology evoked in this copy, it follows that when flesh is exposed in attire that is meant to evoke sexual desirability it is worn by a non-white model. As sexist/racist sexual mythology would have it, she is the embodiment of the best of the black female savage tempered by those elements of whiteness that soften this image, giving it an aura of virtue and innocence. In the racialized pornographic imagination, she is the perfect combination of virgin and whore, the ultimate vamp. The impact of this image is so intense that Iman, a highly paid black fashion model who once received worldwide acclaim because she was the perfect black clone of a white ice goddess beauty, has had to change. Postmodern notions that black female beauty is constructed, not innate or inherent, are personified by the career of Iman. Noted in the past for features this culture sees as "Caucasian"[—]thin nose, lips, and limbs—Iman appears in the October 1989 issue of *Vogue* "made over." Her lips and breasts are suddenly full. Having once had her "look" destroyed by a car accident and then remade, Iman now goes a step further. Displayed as the embodiment of a heightened sexuality, she now looks like the racial/sexual stereotype. In one full-page shot, she is naked, wearing only a pair of brocade boots, looking as though she is ready to stand on any street corner and turn a trick, or worse yet, as though she just walked off one of the pages of *Players* (a porn magazine for blacks). Iman's new image appeals to a culture that is eager to reinscribe the image of black woman as sexual primitive. This new representation is a response to contemporary fascination with an ethnic look, with the exotic Other who promises to fulfill racial and sexual stereotypes, to satisfy longings. This image is but an extension of the edible black tit.

Currently, in the fashion world the new black female icon who is also gaining greater notoriety, as she assumes both the persona of sexually hot "savage" and white-identified black girl, is the Caribbean-born model Naomi Campbell. Imported beauty, she, like Iman, is almost constantly visually portrayed nearly nude against a sexualized background. Abandoning her "natural" hair for blonde wigs or ever-lengthening weaves, she has great crossover appeal. Labeled by fashion critics as the black Briget Bardot, she embodies an aesthetic that suggests black women, while appealingly "different," must resemble white women to be considered really beautiful.

Within literature and early film, this sanitized ethnic image was defined as that of the "tragic mulatto." Appearing in film, she was the vamp that white men feared. As Julie Burchill puts it outrageously in *Girls On Film:*

> *In the mature Forties, Hollywood decided to get to grips with the meaty and messy topic of multiracial romance, but it was a morbid business. Even when the girls were gorgeous white girls—multiracial romance brought tears, traumas, and suicide. The message was clear: you intelligent white men suffer enough guilt because of what your grandaddy did—you want to suffer some more! Keep away from those girls.*

Contemporary films portraying biracial stars convey this same message. The warning for women is different from that given men—we are given messages about the danger of asserting sexual desire. Clearly the message from *Imitation of Life* was that attempting to define oneself as sexual subject would lead to rejection and abandonment. In the film *Choose Me,* Rae Dawn Chong plays the role of the highly sexual black woman chasing and seducing the white man who does not desire her (as was first implied in *Imitation of Life*) but instead uses her sexually, beats her, then discards her. The biracial black woman is constantly "gaslighted" in contemporary film. The message her sexualized image conveys does not change even as she continues to chase the white man as if only he had the power to affirm that she is truly desirable.

European films like *Mephisto* and the more recent *Mona Lisa* also portray the almost white, black woman as tragically sexual. The women in the films can only respond to constructions of their reality created by the more powerful. They are trapped. Mona Lisa's struggle to be sexually self-defining leads her to choose lesbianism, even though she is desired by the white male hero. Yet her choice of a female partner does not mean sexual fulfillment as the object of her lust is a drug-addicted young white woman who is always too messed up to be sexual. Mona Lisa nurses and protects her. Rather than asserting sexual agency, she is once again in the role of mammy.

In a more recent film, *The Virgin Machine,* a white German woman obsessed by the longing to understand desire goes to California where she hopes to find a "paradise of black Amazons." However, when she arrives and checks out the lesbian scene, the black women she encounters are portrayed as mean fat grotesques, lewd and licentious. Contemporary films continue to place black women in two categories, mammy or slut, and occasionally a combination of the two. In *Mona Lisa,* one scene serves as powerful commentary on the way black sexuality is perceived in a racist and imperialist social context. The white male who desires the black prostitute Mona Lisa is depicted as a victim of romantic love who wishes to rescue her from a life of ruin. Yet he is also the conqueror, the colonizer, and this is most evident in the scene where he watches a video wherein she engages in fellatio with the black male pimp who torments her. Both the black man and the black woman are presented as available for the white male's sexual consumption. In the context of postmodern sexual practice, the masturbatory voyeuristic technologically based fulfillment of desire is more exciting than actually possessing any real Other.

There are few films or television shows that attempt to challenge assumptions that sexual relationships between black women and white men are not based solely on power relationships which mirror master/slave paradigms. Years ago, when soap operas first tried to portray romantic/sexual involvement between a black woman and a white man, the station received so many letters of protest from outraged viewers that they dropped this plot. Today many viewers are glued to the television screen watching the soap opera *All My Children* primarily to see if the black woman played by Debbie Morgan will win the white man she so desperately loves. These two lovers are never portrayed in bedroom scenes so common now in daytime soaps. Morgan's character is competing not just with an old white woman flame to get her white man, she is competing with a notion of family. And the story poses the question of whether white male desire for black flesh will prevail over commitments to blood and family loyalty.

Despite this plot of interracial sexual romance on the soaps, there is little public discussion of the connections between race and sexuality. In real life, it was the

Miss America pageant where a black woman was chosen to represent beauty and therefore desirability which forced a public discussion of race and sex. When it was revealed that Vanessa Williams, the fair-skinned straightened-hair "beauty," had violated the representation of the Miss America girl as pure and virtuous by having posed nude in a series of photographs showing her engaged in sexual play with a white woman, she lost her crown but gained a different status. After her public "disgrace," she was able to remain in the limelight by appropriating the image of sexualized vamp and playing sexy roles in films. Unmasked by a virtuous white public, she assumed (according to their standards) the rightful erotic place set aside for black women in the popular imagination. The American public that had so brutally critiqued Williams and rejected her had no difficulty accepting and applauding her when she accepted the image of fallen woman. Again, as in the case of Tina Turner, Williams's bid for continued success necessitated her acceptance of conventional racist/sexist representations of black female sexuality.

The contemporary film that has most attempted to address the issue of black female sexual agency is Spike Lee's *She's Gotta Have It*. Sad to say, the black woman does not get "it." By the end of the film, she is still unable to answer the critical question, posed by one of her lovers as he rapes her, "whose pussy is this?" Reworded the question might be: How and when will black females assert sexual agency in ways that liberate us from the confines of colonized desire, of racist/sexist imagery and practice? Had Nola Darling been able to claim her sexuality and name its power, the film would have had a very different impact.

There are few films that explore issues of black female sexuality in ways that intervene and disrupt conventional representations. The short film *Dreaming Rivers,* by the British black film collective Sankofa, juxtaposes the idealized representation of black woman as mother with that of sexual subject, showing adult children facing their narrow notions of black female identity. The film highlights the autonomous sexual identity of a mature black woman which exists apart from her role as mother and caregiver. *Passion of Remembrance,* another film by Sankofa, offers exciting new representations of the black female body and black female sexuality. In one playfully erotic scene, two young black women, a lesbian couple, get dressed to go out. As part of their celebratory preparations they dance together, painting their lips, looking at their images in the mirror, exulting in their black female bodies. They shake to a song that repeats the refrain "let's get loose" without conjuring images of a rotgut colonized sexuality on display for the racist/sexist imagination. Their pleasure, the film suggests, emerges in a decolonized erotic context rooted in commitments to feminist and antiracist politics. When they look in the mirror and focus on specific body parts (their full thick lips and buttocks), the gaze is one of recognition. We see their pleasure and delight in themselves.

Films by African American women filmmakers also offer the most oppositional images of black female sexuality. Seeing for a second time Kathleen Collin's film *Losing Ground,* I was impressed by her daring, the way she portrays black female sexuality in a way that is fresh and exciting. Like *Passion of Remembrance* it is in a domestic setting, where black women face one another (in Collin's film—as mother and daughter), that erotic images of black female sexuality surface outside a context of domination and exploitation. When daughter and mother share a meal, the audience watches as a radical sexual aesthetics emerges as the camera moves from woman to woman, focusing on the shades and textures of their skin, the shapes of their bodies, and the way their delight and pleasure in themselves is evident in their environment. Both black women discreetly flaunt a rich sensual erotic energy that is not directed outward, it is not there to allure or entrap; it is a powerful declaration of black female sexual subjectivity.

When black women relate to our bodies, our sexuality, in ways that place erotic recognition, desire, pleasure, and fulfillment at the center of our efforts to create radical black female subjectivity, we can make new and different representations of ourselves as sexual subjects. To do so we must be willing to transgress traditional boundaries. We must no longer shy away from the critical project of openly interrogating and exploring representations of black female sexuality as they appear everywhere, especially in popular culture. In *The Power of the Image: Essays on Representation and Sexuality,* Annette Kuhn offers a critical manifesto for feminist thinkers who long to explore gender and representation:

> *In order to challenge dominant representations, it is necessary first of all to understand how they work, and thus where to seek points of possible productive transformation. From such understanding flow various politics and practices of oppositional cultural production, among which may be counted feminist interventions . . . there is another justification for a feminist analysis of mainstream images of women: may it not teach us to recognize inconsistencies and contradictions within dominant traditions of representation, to identify points of leverage for our own intervention: cracks and fissures through which may be captured glimpses of what in other circumstance might be possible, visions of "a world outside the order not normally seen or thought about?"*

This is certainly the challenge facing black women, who must confront the old painful representations of our sexuality as a burden we must suffer, representations still haunting the present. We must make the oppositional space where our sexuality can be named and represented, where we are sexual subjects—no longer bound and trapped.

23

Straightening Our Hair

BELL HOOKS

On Saturday mornings we would gather in the kitchen to get our hair fixed, that is straightened. Smells of burning grease and hair, mingled with the scent of our freshly washed bodies, with collard greens cooking on the stove, with fried fish. We did not go to the hairdresser. Mama fixed our hair. Six daughters—there was no way we could have afforded hairdressers. In those days, this process of straightening black women's hair with a hot comb (invented by Madame C. J. Waler) was not connected in my mind with the effort to look white, to live out standards of beauty set by white supremacy. It was connected solely with rites of initiation into womanhood. To arrive at that point where one's hair could be straightened was to move from being perceived as child (whose hair could be neatly combed and braided) to being almost a woman. It was this moment of transition my sisters and I longed for.

Hair pressing was a ritual of black women's culture—of intimacy. It was an exclusive moment when black women (even those who did not know one another well) might meet at home or in the beauty parlor to talk with one another, to listen to the talk. It was as important a world as that of the male barber shop—mysterious, secret. It was a world where the images constructed as barriers between one's self and the world were briefly let go, before they were made again. It was a moment of creativity, a moment of change.

I wanted this change even though I had been told all my life that I was one of the "lucky" ones because I had been born with "good hair"—hair that was fine, almost straight—not good enough but still good. Hair that had no nappy edges, no "kitchen," that area close to the neck that the hot comb could not reach. This "good hair" meant nothing to me when it stood as a barrier to my entering this secret black woman world. I was overjoyed when mama finally agreed that I could join the Saturday ritual, no longer looking on but patiently waiting my turn. I have written of this ritual: "For each of us getting our hair pressed is an important ritual. It is not a sign of our longing to be white. There are no white people in our intimate world. It is a sign of our desire to be women. It is a gesture that says we are approaching womanhood . . . Before we reach the appropriate age we wear braids, plaits that are symbols of our innocence, our youth, our childhood. Then, we are comforted by the parting hands that comb and braid, comforted by the intimacy and bliss. There is a deeper intimacy in the kitchen on Saturdays when hair is pressed, when fish is fried, when sodas are passed around, when soul music drifts over the talk. It is a time without men. It is a time when we work as women to meet each other's needs, to make each other feel good inside, a time of laughter and outrageous talk."

Since the world we lived in was racially segregated, it was easy to overlook the relationship between white supremacy and our obsession with hair. Even though black women with straight hair were perceived to be more beautiful than those with thick, frizzy hair, it was not overtly related to a notion that white women were a more appealing female group or that their straight hair set a beauty standard black women were struggling to live out. While this was probably the ideological framework from which the process of straightening black women's hair emerged, it was expanded so that it became a real space of black woman bonding through ritualized, shared experience. The beauty parlor was a space of consciousness raising, a space where black women shared life stories—hardship, trials, gossip; a place where one could be comforted and one's spirit renewed. It was for some women a place of rest where one did not need to meet the demands of children or men. It was the one hour some folk would spend "off their feet," a soothing, restful time of meditation and silence. These positive empowering implications of the ritual of hair pressing mediate but do not change negative implications. They exist alongside all that is negative.

Within white supremacist capitalist patriarchy, the social and political context in which the custom of black folks straightening our hair emerges, it represents an imitation of the dominant white group's appearance and often indicates internalized racism, self-hatred, and/or low self-esteem. During the 1960s black people who actively worked to critique, challenge, and change white racism pointed to the way in which black people's obsession with straight hair reflected a colonized mentality. It was at this time that the natural hairdo, the "afro," became fashionable as a sign of cultural resistance to racist oppression and as a celebration of blackness. Naturals were equated with political militancy. Many young black folks found just how much political value was placed on straightened hair as a sign of respectability and conformity to societal expectations when they ceased to straighten their hair. When black liberation struggles did not lead to revolutionary change in society the focus on the political relationship between appearance and complicity with white racism ceased and folks who had once sported afros began to straighten their hair.

In keeping with the move to suppress black consciousness and efforts to be self-defining, white corporations began to acknowledge black people and most especially black women as potential consumers of products they could provide, including hair-care products. Permanents specially designed for black women eliminated the need for hair pressing and the hot comb. They not only cost more but they also took much of the economy and profit out of black communities, out of the pockets of black women who had previously reaped the material benefits (see Manning Marable's *How Capitalism Underdeveloped Black America*, South End Press). Gone was the context of ritual, of black women bonding. Seated under noisy hair dryers black women lost a space for dialogue, for creative talk.

Stripped of the positive binding rituals that traditionally surrounded the experience, black women straightening our hair seemed more and more to be exclusively a signifier of white supremacist oppression and exploitation. It was clearly a process that was about black women changing their appearance to imitate white people's looks. This need to look as much like white people as possible, to look safe, is related to a desire to succeed in the white world. Before desegregation black people could worry less about what white folks thought about their hair. In a discussion with black women about beauty at Spelman College, students talked about the importance of wearing straight hair when seeking jobs. They were convinced and probably rightly so that their chances of finding good jobs would be enhanced if they had straight hair. When asked to elaborate they focused on the connection between radical politics and natural hairdos, whether natural or braided. One woman wearing a short natural told of purchasing a straight wig for her job search. No one in the discussion felt black women were free to wear our hair in natural styles without reflecting on the possible negative consequences. Often older black adults, especially parents, respond quite negatively to natural hairdos. I shared with the group that when I arrived home with my hair in braids shortly after accepting my job at Yale my parents told me I looked disgusting.

Despite many changes in racial politics, black women continue to obsess about their hair, and straightening hair continues to be serious business. It continues to tap into the insecurity black women feel about our value in this white supremacist society. Talking with groups of women at various college campuses and with black women in our communities there seems to be general consensus that our obsession with hair in general reflects continued struggles with self-esteem and self-actualization. We talk about the extent to which black women perceive our hair as the enemy, as a problem we must solve, a territory we must conquer. Above all it is a part of our black female body that must be controlled. Most of us were not raised in environments where we learned to regard our hair as sensual or beautiful in an unprocessed state. Many of us talk about situations where white people ask to touch our hair when it is unprocessed then show surprise that the texture is soft or feels good. In the eyes of many white folks and other non-black folks, the natural afro looks like steel wool or a helmet. Responses to natural hairstyles worn by black women usually reveal the extent to which our natural hair is perceived in white supremacist culture as not only ugly but frightening. We also internalize that fear. The extent to which we are comfortable with our hair usually reflects on our overall feelings about our bodies. In our black women's support group, *Sisters of the Yam*, we talk about the ways we don't like our bodies, especially our hair. I suggested to the group that we regard our hair as though it is not part of our body but something quite separate—again a territory to be controlled. To me it was important for us to link this need to control with sexuality, with sexual repression. Curious about what black women who had hot-combed or had permanents felt about the relationship between straightened hair and sexual practice I asked whether people worried about their hairdo, whether they feared partners touching their hair. Straightened hair has always seemed to me to call attention to the desire for hair to stay in place. Not surprisingly many black women responded that they felt uncomfortable if too much attention was focused on their hair, if it seemed to be too messy. Those of us who have liberated our hair and let it go in whatever direction it seems fit often receive negative comments.

Looking at photographs of myself and my sisters when we had straightened hair in high school I noticed how much older we looked than when our hair was not processed. It is ironic that we live in a culture that places so much emphasis on women looking young, yet black women are encouraged to change our hair in ways that make us appear older. This past semester we read Toni Morrison's *The Bluest Eye* in a black women's fiction class. I ask students to write autobiographical statements which reflect their thoughts about the connection between race and physical beauty. A vast majority of black women wrote about their hair. When I asked individual women outside class why they continued to straighten their hair, many asserted that naturals don't look good on them, or that they required too much work. Emily, a favorite student with very short hair, always straightened it and I would tease and challenge her. She explained to me convincingly that a natural hairdo would look horrible with her face, that she did not have the appropriate forehead or bone structure. Later she shared that during spring break she had gone to the beauty parlor to have her perm and as she sat there waiting, thinking about class reading and discussion, it came to her that she was really frightened that no one else would think she was attractive if she did not straighten her hair. She acknowledged that this fear was rooted in feelings of low self-esteem. She decided to make a change. Her new look surprised her because it was so appealing. We talked afterwards about her earlier denial and justification for wearing straightened hair. We talked about the way it hurts to realize connection between racist oppression and the arguments we use to convince ourselves and others that we are not beautiful or acceptable as we are.

In numerous discussions with black women about hair one of the strongest factors that prevent black women from wearing unprocessed hairstyles is the fear of losing other people's approval and regard. Heterosexual black women talked about the extent to which black men respond more favorably to women with straight or straightened hair. Lesbian women point to the fact that many of them do not straighten their hair, raising the question of whether or not this gesture is fundamentally linked to heterosexism and a longing for male approval. I recall visiting a woman friend and her black male companion in New York years ago and having an intense discussion about hair. He took it upon himself to share with me that I could be a fine sister if I would do something about my hair (secretly I thought mama must have hired him). What I remember is his shock when I calmly and happily asserted that I like the touch and feel of unprocessed hair.

When students read about race and physical beauty, several black women describe periods of childhood when they were overcome with longing for straight hair as it was so associated with desirability, with being loved. Few women had received affirmation from family, friends, or lovers when choosing not to straighten their hair and we have many stories to tell about advice we receive from everyone, including total strangers, urging to understand how much more attractive we would be if we would fix (straighten) our hair. When I interviewed for my job at Yale, white female advisers who had never before commented on my hair encouraged me not to wear braids or a large natural to the interview. Although they did not say straighten your hair, they were suggesting that I change my hairstyle so that it would most resemble theirs, so that it would indicate a certain conformity. I wore braids and no one seemed to notice. When I was offered the job I did not ask if it mattered whether or not I wore braids. I tell this story to my students so that they will know by this one experience that we do not always need to surrender our power to be self-defining to succeed in an endeavor. Yet I have found the issue of hairstyle comes up again and again with students when I give lectures. At one conference on black women and leadership I walked into a packed auditorium, my hair unprocessed wild and all over the place. The vast majority of black women seated there had straightened hair. Many of them looked at me with hostile contemptuous stares. I felt as though I was being judged on the spot as someone out on the fringe, an undesirable. Such judgments are made particularly about black women in the United States who choose to wear dreadlocks. They are seen and rightly so as the total antithesis of straightening one's hair, as a political statement. Often black women express contempt for those of us who choose this look.

Ironically, just as the natural unprocessed hair of black women is the subject of disregard and disdain we are witnessing return of the long dyed, blonde look. In their writing my black women students described wearing yellow mops on their heads as children to pretend they had long blonde hair. Recently black women singers who are working to appeal to white audiences, to be seen as crossovers, use hair implanting and hair weaving to have long straight hair. There seems to be a definite connection between a black female entertainer's popularity with white audiences and the degree to which she works to appear white, or to embody aspects of white style. Tina Turner and Aretha Franklin were trend setters; both dyed their hair blonde. In everyday life we see more and more black women using chemicals to be blonde. At one of my talks focusing on the social construction of black female identity within a sexist and racist society, a black woman came to me at the end of the discussion and shared that her seven-year-old daughter was obsessed with blonde hair, so much so that she had made a wig to imitate long blonde curls. This mother wanted to know what she was doing wrong in her parenting. She asserted that their home was a place where blackness was affirmed and celebrated. Yet she had not considered that her processed straightened hair was a message to her daughter that black women are not acceptable unless we alter our appearance or hair texture. Recently I talked with one of my younger sisters about her hair. She uses bright colored dyes, various shades of red. Her skin is very dark. She has a broad nose and short hair. For her these choices of straightened dyed hair were directly related to feelings of low self-esteem. She does not like her features and feels that the hairstyle transforms her. My perception was that her choice of red straightened hair actually called attention to the features she was trying to mask. When she commented that this look receives more attention and compliments, I suggested that the positive feedback might be a direct response to her own projection of a higher level of self-satisfaction. Folk may be responding to that and not her altered looks. We talked about the messages she is sending her dark-skinned daughters—that they will be most attractive if they straighten their hair.

A number of black women have argued that straightened hair is not necessarily a signifier of low self-esteem. They argue that it is a survival strategy; it is easier to function in this society with straightened hair. There are fewer hassles. Or as some folk stated, straightened hair is easier to manage, takes less time. I responded to this argument in our discussion at Spelman by suggesting that perhaps the unwillingness to spend time on ourselves, caring for our bodies, is also a reflection of a sense that this is not important or that we do not deserve such care. In this group and others, black women talked about being raised in households where spending too much time on appearance was ridiculed or considered vanity. Irrespective of the way individual black women choose to do their hair, it is evident that the extent to which we suffer from racist and sexist oppression and exploitation affects the degree to which we feel capable of both selflove and asserting an autonomous presence that is acceptable and pleasing to ourselves. Individual preferences (whether rooted in self-hate or not) cannot negate the reality that our collective obsession with straightening black hair reflects the psychology of oppression and the impact of racist colonization. Together racism and sexism daily reinforce to all black females via the media, advertising, etc. that we will not be considered beautiful or desirable if we do not change ourselves, especially our hair. We cannot resist this socialization if we deny that white supremacy informs our efforts to construct self and identity.

Without organized struggles like the ones that happened in the 1960s and early 1970s, individual black women must struggle alone to acquire the critical consciousness that would enable us to examine issues of race and beauty, our personal choices, from a political standpoint. There are times when I think of straightening my hair just to change my style, just for fun. Then I remind myself that even though such a gesture could be simply playful on my part, an individual expression of desire, I know that such a gesture would carry other implications beyond my control. The reality is: straightened hair is linked historically and currently to a system of racial domination that impresses upon black people, and especially black women, that we are not acceptable as we are, that we are not beautiful. To make such a gesture as an expression of individual freedom and choice would make me complicit with a politic of domination that hurts us. It is easy to surrender this freedom. It is more important that black women resist racism and sexism in every way; that every aspect of our self-representation be a fierce resistance, a radical celebration of our care and respect for ourselves.

Even though I have not had straightened hair for a long time, this did not mean that I am able to really enjoy or appreciate my hair in its natural state. For years I still considered it a problem. (It wasn't naturally nappy enough to make a decent interesting afro. It was too thin.) These complaints expressed my continued dissatisfaction. True liberation of my hair came when I stopped trying to control it in any state and just accepted it as it is. It has been only in recent years that I have ceased to worry about what other people would say about my hair. It has been only in recent years that I could feel consistent pleasure washing, combing, and caring for my hair. These feelings remind me of the pleasure and comfort I felt as a child sitting between my mother's legs feeling the warmth of her body and being as she combed and braided my hair. In a culture of domination, one that is essentially anti-intimacy, we must struggle daily to remain in touch with ourselves and our bodies, with one another. Especially black women and men, as it is our bodies that have been so often devalued, burdened, wounded in alienated labor. Celebrating our bodies, we participate in a liberatory struggle that frees mind and heart.

24

Plagiarisms, Authorships, and the Academic Death Penalty

REBECCA MOORE HOWARD

In composition studies, most published discussions of student plagiarism proceed from the assumption that plagiarism occurs as a result of one of two possible motivations: an absence of ethics or an ignorance of citation conventions. Some students don't appreciate academic textual values and therefore deliberately submit work that is not their own; others don't understand academic citation conventions and therefore plagiarize inadvertently. Both of these are negative interpretations, postulating an absence—of either ethics or knowledge—in the plagiarist. A few recent studies, though, identify positive motivations for *patchwriting*, a textual strategy that has traditionally been classified as plagiarism. Patchwriting involves "copying from a source text and then deleting some words,

Rebecca Moore Howard, an assistant professor in the Department of Interdisciplinary Writing at Colgate University, teaches composition, rhetoric, and linguistics. She is at work on *Standing in the Shadow of Giants*, an extended reflection on the applications of authorship theory to composition pedagogy, to be published by Ablex. With Sandra Jamieson, she is author of *The Bedford Guide to Teaching Writing in the Disciplines: An Instructor's Desk Reference* (1995).

altering grammatical structures, or plugging in one-for-one synonym-substitutes" (Howard 233). Describing the textual strategies of Tanya, a student who in traditional pedagogy might be labeled "remedial," Glynda Hull and Mike Rose celebrate her patchwriting as a valuable stage toward becoming an authoritative academic writer: "we depend upon membership in a community for our language, our voices, our very arguments. We forget that we, like Tanya, continually appropriate each other's language to establish group membership, to grow, and to define ourselves in new ways, and that such appropriation is a fundamental part of language use, even as the appearance of our texts belies it" (152).

These and other studies describe patchwriting as a pedagogical opportunity, not a juridical problem. They recommend that teachers treat it as an important transitional strategy in the student's progress toward membership in a discourse community. To treat it negatively, as a "problem" to be "cured" or punished, would be to undermine its positive intellectual value, thereby obstructing rather than facilitating the learning process.

If teachers are to adopt a positive approach, they must be able to do so within the strictures of their universities' regulations on plagiarism. Those regulations, however, typically describe plagiarism in all its forms as a problem for adjudication, and this generalization leaves teachers little space for pedagogical alternatives. In typical college regulations on plagiarism (which are often grouped under headings wherein *plagiarism* serves as either a synonym for or a subset of "academic dishonesty"), all forms of plagiarism, including patchwriting, are located on a juridical continuum on which expulsion from college—the academic death penalty—sits at the extreme end as a potential punishment.

It is the object of this essay to suggest a plagiarism policy that would respect the textual values expressed in existing policies but that would also revise policy to allow for alternative approaches—and specifically to enable pedagogy that is responsive to contemporary theory. This new policy does not endorse a "more lenient attitude" toward plagiarism; rather, it suggests an enlarged range of definitions and motivations for plagiarism, which in turn enlarges the range of acceptable responses. Such a policy is of necessity a compromise; traditional textual values attribute proprietorship, autonomy, originality, and a corollary morality to "true" authorship, whereas a substantial sector of contemporary theory denies the very possibility of associating any of these qualities with authorship.

Authorships

It has become commonplace to assert that prior to the modern era, mimesis was the means whereby Western writers established their authority, and textual collaboration was their method of composition. The pre-modern writer did not need to cite his sources. (The masculine pronoun is well established as the only appropriate one for discussions of medieval and early modern authorship. Though women did write at that time, the male writer was plainly normative.) Robert Burton in his seventeenth-century *Anatomy of Melancholy* attributes to the Roman writer Lucan the now-familiar metaphorical expression of the mimetic textual economy: "A dwarf standing on the shoulders of a giant may see farther than a giant himself." Implicit in this aphorism is an emphasis on accumulated knowledge. The notion of reverence for the giants, the source, the Authority, is also explicit in the metaphor of standing on the shoulders of giants, as is an endorsement of the practice of imitating the source.

Historian Giles Constable goes so far as to declare, "The term plagiarism should indeed probably be dropped in reference to the Middle Ages, since it expresses a concept of literary individualism and property that is distinctively modern" (39). Martha Woodmansee concurs: the notion of the author as an individual creator of original works is a "relatively recent invention" ("Author Effect" 15). According to Mark Rose, the shift from mimetic to individualistic authorship took place in response to the technological innovation of the printing press. Widespread dissemination of texts gave rise to the possibility of making a living as a writer, unfettered by patrons. From these economic conditions arose copyright laws, beginning in England with the 1710 Statute of Anne and in the U.S. with Congressional legislation in 1790. Amplifying Rose's account of the availability and commodification of texts associated with the emergence of the individual author, Woodmansee emphasizes a third essential element: the appearance of the reader. The eighteenth century saw a dramatic increase in mass literacy in England and most of Western Europe, a commensurately greater demand for texts, and hence enhanced possibilities for the profession of writing.

That this account of authorships in the West is described in historical sequence does not amount to an antipodal chronology of authorship in which mimesis characterizes antiquity and the Middle Ages, displaced by individual, originary authorship in the modern period. Though commonly associated with the modern era, the notion of plagiarism and the concomitant possibility of individual authorship can be traced back to the ancient world. The very etymology of the word *plagiarism* demonstrates the antiquity of the concept: the Roman poet Martial extended the meaning of the Latin *plagiarius* (kidnapper) to indicate the theft of words as well as of slaves. Indeed, the history of Western letters from antiquity through the Middle Ages is punctuated by writers' complaints about their plagiarists. Significantly, the well-worn aphorism concerning giants and dwarfs or pygmies not only valorizes the source and the accumulation of knowledge but also accords to the latest writer the greatest knowledge. In what Robert Merton regards as the earliest verifiable statement of the aphorism, medieval theologian Bernard of Chartres's version, quoted in Jean Gimpel's *The Cathedral Builders*, includes all three elements:

> *We are as dwarfs mounted on the shoulders of giants, so that although we perceive many more things than they, it is not because our vision is more piercing or our stature higher, but because we are carried and elevated higher thanks to their gigantic size. (165)*

The "we" of Bernard's aphorism—the most recent writer—is in possession of something new, a range of vision inaccessible to those giant sources. Embedded in the medieval mimetic economy of authorship, in other words, are essential components of the modern individual economy: the notion of the individual and the notion that he might seize something new. The author, in fact, may *not* be a recent invention. What Mark Rose's and Martha Woodmansee's work does establish, though, is that in the modern era a shift in emphasis has taken place. A chain of causes attendant upon the Gutenberg revolution has produced a textual economy in which the source must be resisted (consider the anxieties of influence described by Harold Bloom and Françoise Meltzer) or bracketed (in scholarly citation, which Constable and many others regard as legitimate plagiarism) and in which mimesis is clearly inferior to the originary compositions of the Romantic genius (Woodmansee, "Author Effect" 18). The individual author defines the post-Gutenberg playing field, and that author is credited with the attributes of proprietorship, autonomy, originality, and morality. Although three centuries after the inception of the modern author these attributes have come to be regarded as "facts" about authorship, their historical emergence demonstrates them to be cultural arbitraries, textual corollaries to the technological and economic conditions of the society that instated them.

Today the technological innovation of the computer is precipitating and accompanying shifts in textual values that may be as profound as the modern emergence of the normative autonomous, individual author. In this new textual economy, Woodmansee says that the computer is "dissolving the boundaries essential to the survival of our modern fiction of the author as the sole creator of unique, original works" ("Author Effect" 25). Peter Holland points to hypertext as one of the ways in which digitized technology destabilizes the normative individual author. In hypertext, readers make additions and changes without necessarily leaving any trace of who contributed what, and a text is never "finished." "Hypertext," Holland says, "enables us to reconsider the whole notion of the intellectual status authorship confers, not least since it creates two types of authors/editors, refusing to distinguish between the two: those who write sentences and those who restructure materials" (21). No longer do we have originators and plagiarists—or giants and pygmies—but the collective, always unfinished text. To debate whether this most recent shift—or indeed, any shift in the representation of authorship—is a "good thing" would be to postulate some sort of pre-discursive reality to textuality. It is sufficient, at least for the moment, to observe that this shift, like its predecessors, reflects and reproduces the social conditions that produced it.

Plagiarisms

Hypertext makes visible what literary critics have theorized: the cumulative, interactive nature of writing that makes impossible the representation of a stable category of authorship and hence a stable category of plagiarism. Susan Stewart brands current legal definitions of literary property as "naive materialism" (15–16). Another critic, Françoise Meltzer, explains Descartes's and Freud's anxieties about originality: writers who want recognition must assert priority; to assert priority is to assert originality; and to assert originality engenders a fear of being robbed. Behind that fear of being robbed is "the larger fear that there is no such thing as originality" (40–41).

If there is no originality, there is no basis for literary property. If there is no originality and no literary property, there is no basis for the notion of plagiarism. Ellen McCracken finds in a short story by Ricardo Piglia a "metaplagiarism" that she celebrates for its challenge to literary property. And Woodmansee questions whether solitary, originary authorship has ever described how any writer composes; instead, she characterizes it as an ideal constructed and promulgated for economic purposes ("Author Effect" 15).

These scholars are working in the tradition of Roland Barthes and Michel Foucault, who describe the author as a cultural arbitrary. Pierre Bourdieu and Jean-Claude Passeron offer a useful explanation of the sense in which "arbitrary" is here used:

> *The selection of meanings which objectively defines a group's or a class's culture as a symbolic system is* arbitrary *insofar as the structure and functions of that culture cannot be deduced from any universal principle, whether physical, biological or spiritual, not being linked by any sort of internal relation to "the nature of things" or any "human nature." (8)*

But again, it is important to acknowledge the synchronic and diachronic complexities of representations of authorship. Mark Rose notes that it is not just post-structuralists who reject a foundational role for the autonomous author: Northrop Frye observed in 1957 that copyright obscures the conventionality of literature, the mimetic nature of composition (Rose 2). Though the individual author, promoted from pygmy to giant, took center stage in the modern textual economy, the giant sources and the accumulation of knowledge were not banished from the drama of authorship.

Keith D. Miller's scholarship, moreover, reveals that the collaborative author is the normative model in at least one contemporary American culture. In various articles and in *Voice of Deliverance*, Miller argues that Martin Luther King, Jr., was engaged in "voice merging"—the African-American folk preaching tradition of patching together unattributed words, phrases, and even extended passages from theological sources, the Bible, and other preachers' sermons. He attributes King's "plagiarism" (a word which, significantly, Miller himself seldom applies to King's textual strategies) to the oral traditions of King's primary community. King's composing practices originate in the oral traditions of the African-American church, where discourse is "communal wealth"; "By enlarging the pool of discourse and the size of audiences, print altered King's rhetorical universe without disturbing its premise that words are shared assets, not personal belongings" ("Composing" 79). To academic and political discourse Martin Luther King, Jr., brought textual values from the discourse of African-American folk preaching. Regardless of what he may have known about the textual values of the academy (and David J. Garrow, among others, argues energetically that King was well aware of and therefore should have adhered to academic injunctions against plagiarism), in his dissertation and speeches he engaged in what Miller describes as "voice merging." He applied the textual practices of one community to his writing in another.

King's textual strategies reveal the multiple communities in which writers work and the resulting complexities of community allegiances. The King case illustrates Joseph Harris's assertion that no one is ever a member of just one community at a time. Perhaps none of us makes neat switches between mutually exclusive communities; instead, our communities and our allegiances to them compete with and overlap each other. We carry the practices and conventions of one community into another, as King did by engaging in African-American voice merging when composing his academic and political prose.

Neither diachronically nor synchronically, then, can authorship be bounded into stable, antipodal categories of mimetic, autonomous, or collaborative authorship. The heterogeneity of theories of authorship, the contradictory definitions that exist simultaneously, render impossible any sort of unitary representation. Yet both pedagogy and institutional policies on student authorship—and specifically, student plagiarism—attempt just that. Representations of student plagiarism seldom acknowledge the heterogeneous definitions of authorship in contemporary letters. Instead, these representations simplify student authorship, depicting it as a unified, stable field. The principle used for the task of unifying and stabilizing student plagiarism is the putative morality of the "true" (autonomous) author. Immorality in these representations is not attributed just to some plagiarists, such as those who purchase term papers. Rather, immorality attaches to the practitioners of all textual practices, including patchwriting, that are classified as plagiarism.

Such moral criteria for plagiarism seem natural and necessary, drawing as they do upon widely held assumptions. Former editor of the *New York Times Magazine* James Atlas attributes flagging "moral character" to those who succumb to the temptation to plagiarize, and so does Chris Raymond in his *Chronicle of Higher Education* reports on Martin Luther King, Jr. In composition studies, too, plagiarism is not infrequently described as immoral. Frank J. McCormick in the *Journal of Teaching Writing* talks about crime and honor; Augustus Kolich in *College English* about moral standards and citizenship; Elaine E. Whitaker in *College Composition and Communication* about academic integrity; Edward M. White in the *Chronicle of Higher Education* about theft and "dirty secrets"; and Edith Skom in the *AAHE Bulletin* about crime, theft, and the plagiarist as "less of a person."

Indeed, punishing plagiarists is not infrequently described as an essential academic obligation. Drummond Rennie, an editor of the *Journal of the American Medical Association*, articulates an attitude familiar in the academy: "The bottom line is, if we don't take a stand on plagiarism, what the hell *do* we take a stand on?" (qtd. in Mooney A13). The prosecution of plagiarism, in his description, is the last line of defense for academic standards.

Informing composition studies are the textual values of individualistic authorship, which culminate in a juridical stance toward all the textual strategies that have come to be labeled as plagiarism. A wide range of composition pedagogy, notably that aligned with expressivism, describes writing as a way to discover and develop one's immanent beliefs. Composition instruction therefore aims to teach writing as discovery and to help writers express themselves in their own authentic language. The binary opposite of this notion—necessary, it would seem, for the notion to have meaning—is plagiarism and writers who purloin the thoughts and expressions of others.

In fact, pedagogy and scholarship that might appear to offer alternatives to individualistic notions of authorship may in fact be based on those very notions. Dramatic examples are provided by Andrea A. Lunsford and Lisa Ede, who detail the ways in which prominent scholars of collaborative learning—not only Peter Elbow but also Kenneth Bruffee—endorse the autonomous author. Lunsford and Ede charge that models for collaboration have "failed to challenge traditional concepts of radical individualism and ownership of ideas and [have] operated primarily in a traditional and largely hierarchical way" (431). Lester Faigley, though warning against "dichotomous categories" of modernism and postmodernism in composition studies, is able to say,

> *Where composition studies has proven least receptive to postmodern theory is in surrendering its belief in the writer as an autonomous self, even at a time when extensive group collaboration is practiced in many writing classrooms. Since the beginning of composition teaching in the late nineteenth century, college writing teachers have been heavily invested in the stability of the self and the attendant beliefs that writing can be a means of self-discovery and intellectual self-realization. (15)*

It is this notion of the "autonomous self" that renders representations of student plagiarism univocal endorsements of the Romantic genius—as evidenced in Edward M. White's statement:

> *Plagiarism is outrageous, because it undermines the whole purpose of education itself: Instead of becoming more of an individual thinker, the plagiarist denies the self and the possibility of learning. Someone who will not, or cannot, distinguish his or her ideas from those of others offends the most basic principles of learning.*

A substantial contingent of composition scholars has, nevertheless, joined the interrogation of the autonomous author. David R. Russell's notion of learning as a collaborative rather than solitary phenomenon contrasts significantly with White's:

> *Learning is at bottom acquiring habits from other people, habits of activity, including communicating and thinking, which are, in the deepest sense, kinds of activity, since there is no real division between mind and body, thinking and doing. (183)*

And Kathryn T. Flannery recapitulates Susan Miller:

> *Students are always caught "intertextually"—they are never inventing a new language out of nothing, but patch together fragments of the multiple texts, the multiple voices (as Bakhtin would put it) that are already available to them. (Flannery 707)*

Composition scholars' representations of the writer are characteristically more fissured. Kurt Spellmeyer, for example, invokes both mimetic and originary composition:

> *Ordinarily we refer to prose that merely restates the language of previous writers as "quotation," "paraphrase," "summary," or "plagiarism." Every writer, of course, borrows something from past achievements and must work within the historical limitations of a genre, but sheer replication is never apropos because writing addresses itself primarily to the not yet written. (18)*

These statements demonstrate that composition studies, like contemporary criticism, presents anything but a unified front on issues of plagiarism and authorship. Susan Miller, Andrea Lunsford, and Lisa Ede question the autonomous author, but Thomas Mallon's trade book, *Stolen Words*, assumes a normative autonomous author. Although Susan Stewart's genealogy of authorship rejects it as a simplistic account of plagiarism that suffers from a lack of historical aware-ness of the relationship between law and literature (Stewart 30 n. 44), *Stolen Words* is a popular and oft-cited source among compositionists. Martha Wood-mansee's and Mark Rose's work in the history and theory of authorship challenges the necessity and even the possibility of the autonomous author, but David Saun-ders, also working in copyright theory, dismisses Woodmansee and Rose as per-petrators of postmodern ephemera. Even collaborative composition theorists, in Lunsford and Ede's account, endorse autonomous authorship. What is happening in textual studies is not the overthrow of a post-Gutenberg paradigm by a post-Internet norm, but a shift of emphases, a shift in perspectives. These perspectives, moreover, may be mutually incompatible but may nevertheless inhabit the same space at the same time.

The dialectic of these simultaneous perspectives constitutes sufficient disci-pline-internal pressure upon the very notion of plagiarism to prompt its redefini-tion in the policies that govern student authorship—institutional policies against plagiarism. Given the contested notions of authorship in the academy today, the Romantic originator can no longer be the sole model of the author on which col-leges' plagiarism policies draw. Nor, in the wake of the postmodern death of the author, can a revised (or discarded) policy declare the student writer a casualty caught in the crossfire. We must redefine institutional policies to account for the dialectic. In that dialectic we may discover phenomena of authorship that were obscured by overdetermined definitions of and legislation against plagiarism.

Redefinition is already underway not only in the realm of theory but also in commentators' fresh advice for teachers' and administrators' pedagogical responses to plagiarism. Although Margaret Kantz assumes that student papers strive to pre-sent "original arguments" (75), she believes that student plagiarism results from teachers' poor task representations (84), rather than from either of the two causes to which plagiarism is traditionally ascribed—a lack of morality or an ignorance of citation conventions (see McLeod 11). Alice Drum, too, postulates the possibility of students' original contributions to their essays, but at the same time she argues that the response to plagiarism should be as much pedagogical as juridical (242–43)—a sentiment apparently shared by Frank McCormick (143).

Lunsford and Ede go a bit further when they challenge the "obsession" with plagiarism engendered by "the institutional reliance on testing 'norms' and the ideology it reflects." Questioning the "formalist, positivist, and individualist ide-ological assumptions on which common notions of plagiarism rest," they advocate that teachers adopt a "rhetorically situated view of plagiarism, one that acknowl-edges that all writing is in an important sense collaborative and that 'common knowledge' varies from community to community and is collaboratively shared" (436–37).

Still other composition scholars have focused specifically on the composing practice of patchwriting. Pedagogical recommendations for preventing, respond-ing to, or curing plagiarism typically recommend instruction in source attribution, but I have argued (as have Glynda Hull and Mike Rose, as well as Elaine Whitaker) that patchwriting may have quite a different genesis. Most writers engage in patch-writing when they are working in unfamiliar discourse, when they must work monologically with the words and ideas of a source text. As a way of helping patchwriters find a voice and gain a sense of community membership, Hull and Rose advocate a provisional "free-wheeling pedagogy of imitation" (151); and I have recommended structured collaborative summary-writing (240–43). Both their recommendations and mine are made not in order to "prevent" or "cure" patchwriting but to help students make maximum intellectual use of it and then move beyond it. These recommendations attribute positive pedagogical value to a composing strategy that has traditionally been labeled "plagiarism" and classified as academic dishonesty—a classification which would ascribe criminality to an important stage in students' learning processes, thereby thwarting learning.

The idea of positive plagiarism is hardly new; T. S. Eliot's "Philip Massinger" articulates what was then and is now a widely shared sentiment: "Immature poets imitate; mature poets steal; bad poets deface what they take, and good poets make it into something better, or at least something different" (143). What revised definitions of plagiarism acknowledge is the possibility that intentions of writers other than poets and writers of fiction might justify practices that have traditionally been classified as plagiarism and that have too readily been excoriated as a sign of the writer's immorality. Student writing must be accorded the same respect as professional writing: it must be treated as subject rather than object formation:

> *The concepts of author and authorship, so radically destabilized in contemporary literary theory—and in current discursive practice in fields as far removed as engineering and law—have also been problematized in the field of rhetoric and composition studies, where scholars have challenged the traditional exclusion of student writing from claims to "real writing" and "authorship," explored the ways in which authority is experienced by student writers, and increasingly sought to map various models of composing processes. (Lunsford and Ede 417)*

Formulating Institutional Policy

By imagining positive, non-juridical definitions of and responses to textual strategies that have long been depicted in the criminal terms of plagiarism, the reports and recommendations of Drum, Howard, Hull and Rose, Kantz, McCormick, and Whitaker render impossible a unitary representation of student authorship. These challenges are, however, insufficient. The regulatory fiction of the autonomous author continues to prevail in academic prohibitions of plagiarism. Institutions' uniformly juridical policies against plagiarism restrict the extent to which pedagogy can respond to revised cultural representations of authorship. Teachers who follow the advice of Drum, Howard, Hull and Rose, Kantz, McCormick, and Whitaker might find themselves professionally compromised if their institutions' regulations provided only for juridical responses. Teachers may therefore be forced into counter-pedagogical responses; as Peter Jaszi and Martha Woodmansee point out, it is students who suffer and pay for intractable policies that are at variance with widely endorsed theories of authorship (9).

Universities' policies describe plagiarism in moral terms when they classify it as a form of "academic dishonesty." At the same time, though, these policies often define plagiarism in formalist terms, as features of texts. Plagiarism policies may even specifically exclude the writer's intentions, stipulating that plagiarism is plagiarism even if the writer is ignorant of its prohibition.

Certainly, morality is the major factor in the purchase of term papers described by Gary M. Galles, Michael Pemberton, and Edward White; and it may apply to other types of plagiarism, as well, *depending upon the writer's intentions*. But morality is not a necessary component of plagiarism, and ignorance of citation conventions is not its sole alternative. A third possibility, too seldom recognized, is that students may have *commendable* reasons for engaging in patchwriting, a textual strategy that is commonly classified as plagiarism.

A college's policy on plagiarism needs to ask the same questions about students' motivations that Stewart, Meltzer, McCracken, and Eliot ask of their professional writers. In reading students' prose, we need first to know whether the writer intended to plagiarize. If the plagiarism was intentional, we then need to know motivations: Was it for personal gain at the expense of others? In order to challenge the concept of plagiarism itself? To weave new patterns from the fabrics of others? And if the plagiarism was not intentional, we still need to know motivations: Was it engendered by an ignorance of citation conventions? By a monologic encounter with unfamiliar words and concepts?

Similarly, we must engage questions of context. Is the student experienced in the discourse of the discipline in which he or she is writing? Has the student been introduced to the textual conventions of the discipline? (Some disciplines, for example, have a considerably higher tolerance for and expectation of students' recapitulating their sources—whether in paraphrase, summary, quotation, or patch-writing—than do others.) Is the student working from sources assigned by the instructor? (In such cases it is unlikely that he or she intended to deceive.) Different answers to these questions should elicit different responses from the questioner. And this raises another inescapable component of plagiarism: the reader. The meaning of a text does not, in fact, reside in the text, but in the interplay of text, intertext(s), writer, social context—and reader. Linda Hutcheon asserts that plagiarism occurs only in the reader's interpretation, when "visible sources become signs of plagiarism, and influences yield to 'intertextual' echoes" (230).

Without specifying how they might be made, Lunsford and Ede (436–37) and Keith Miller ("Redefining") recommend changes in colleges' plagiarism policies. Building upon their work, the next section of this essay drafts a comprehensive institutional policy on plagiarism, a policy consonant with the conditions of contemporary intellectual life, including electronic media, an awareness of historical contingency and cultural diversity, and an attention to the social dynamics of composing.

Given the range of contemporary theories of authorship, a postmodern dismissal of all academic plagiarism policies would be unreasonable; the academy's stance on plagiarism must represent (insofar as it is possible) the dialectic, not just one voice in it. Nor is it likely that many theorists would actually want to abolish all policy on plagiarism, for very few find the purchase of term papers acceptable. It is, however, reasonable to revise definitions of plagiarism to account for the contingent nature of authorship and its constituent discourses; to account for the collaborative nature of writing; to allow authorial intention as a factor in the adjudication of student plagiarism; and to postulate positive value for patchwriting, a textual strategy that is too often classified as plagiarism, regarded as immoral, and punished by "Fs" and even expulsion.

The following plagiarism policy is institution-specific. As will be obvious, a number of changes would have to be made if it were adopted at other colleges—reference to the handbook used at the institution, for example, or to the resources available at the writing center. The defining categories into which it analyzes plagiarism—the categories of cheating, non-attribution, and patchwriting—are overlapping rather than mutually exclusive; this policy does not resolve all ambiguities involved with plagiarism. Instead, it acknowledges the complexities of the issue and offers guidelines for negotiating what will continue to be contested terrain. The policy acknowledges the terms of that contest and urges all participants—writers and readers—to engage it as openly as possible.

A Proposed Policy on Plagiarism

> *It is perhaps never the case that a writer composes "original" material, free of any influence. It might be more accurate to think of creativity, of fresh combinations made from existing sources, or fresh implications for existing materials.*

An important requirement of most academic writing is acknowledging one's sources. We all work from sources, even when we are being creative. American academic culture demands that writers who use the exact words of a source supply quotation marks at the beginning and end of the quotation, so that the reader can know where the voice of the source begins and ends. In addition, the writer must use footnotes, parenthetical notes, or endnotes to cite the source, so that the reader can consult that source if he or she chooses. Writers must also acknowledge the sources not only of words but also of ideas, insofar as is possible, even when they are not quoting word for word. Moreover, in final-draft writing, academic writers may not paraphrase a source by using its phrases and sentences, with a few changes in grammar or word choice—even when the source is cited.

Plagiarism is the representation of a source's words or ideas as one's own. Plagiarism occurs when a writer fails to supply quotation marks for exact quotations; fails to cite the sources of his or her ideas; or adopts the phrasing of his or her sources, with changes in grammar or word choice.

Plagiarism takes three different forms—cheating, non-attribution of sources, and patchwriting:

1. **Cheating** Borrowing, purchasing, or otherwise obtaining work composed by someone else and submitting it under one's own name. The minimum penalty is an "F" in the course; the maximum penalty, suspension from the university.
2. **Non-attribution** Writing one's own paper but including passages copied exactly from the work of another (regardless of whether that work is published or unpublished or whether it comes from a printed or electronic source) without providing (a) footnotes, endnotes, or parenthetical notes that cite the source *and* (b) quotation marks or block indentation to indicate precisely what has been copied from the source. Because non-attribution is sometimes the result of a student's inexperience with conventions of academic writing, instruction in

source attribution and subsequent revision of the paper may be the instructor's most appropriate response. Non-attribution can alternatively be the result of a student's intent to deceive, in which case the minimum penalty is an "F" in the course and the maximum penalty, suspension from the university.

3. **Patchwriting** Writing passages that are not copied exactly but that have nevertheless been borrowed from another source, with some changes—a practice which *The Bedford Handbook for Writers* calls "paraphrasing the source's language too closely" (477). This "patchwriting" is plagiarism *regardless of whether one supplies footnotes, endnotes, or parenthetical notes that acknowledge the source.* However, patchwriting is not always a form of academic dishonesty; it is not always committed by immoral writers. Often it is a form of writing that learners employ when they are unfamiliar with the words and ideas about which they are writing. In this situation, patchwriting can actually help the learner begin to understand the unfamiliar material. Yet it is a transitional writing form; it is never acceptable for final-draft academic writing, for it demonstrates that the writer does not fully understand the source from which he or she is patchwriting. Because patchwriting can result from a student's inexperience with conventions of academic writing, instruction in quotation and source attribution and a request for subsequent revision of the paper may be an appropriate response for the instructor. But because patchwriting often results from a student's unfamiliarity with the words and ideas of a source text, instruction in the material discussed in the source and a request for subsequent revision of the paper is even more frequently the appropriate response. Patchwriting can also be the result of a student's intent to deceive, in which case the minimum penalty is an "F" in the course and the maximum penalty, suspension from the university.

Additional advice for students:

Both citation (footnotes, parenthetical notes, or endnotes) *and* quotation marks are required whenever you copy exact words and phrases from a source. When you paraphrase or summarize but do not copy exactly, citation is still required. When in doubt, cite; over-citation is an error, but under-citation is plagiarism. Your citations should follow a recognized style sheet; you should not make up your own system. If your instructor does not specify a style sheet, you may want to adopt the MLA style, which is described in *The Bedford Handbook for Writers*, §50, or the APA system, §51. For advice about when to quote sources, see §49d; and for detailed explanation of how to quote, §37 and 49e.

The sources you should cite include not only printed materials but also electronic sources. Most style sheets are currently publishing new editions that provide advice for citing sources obtained by computer—materials from the Internet or CD Rom disks, for example.

The sources you should cite also include contributions that others may make to your drafts in progress—friends, family, classmates, and tutors who gave you ideas for your essay or who made suggestions for its improvement. Writers customarily provide a single discursive footnote to acknowledge such contributions. Often the footnote appears at the end of the title or the first paragraph of the essay. Usually one to three sentences, naming the contributors to the paper and sketching the nature and extent of their contributions, suffice.

Patchwriting, the third type of plagiarism listed above, is an issue somewhat more complicated than that of citation. For example, a student who had never before studied theories of mythology read the following passage:

> *The world of the Ancient Near East, however, was familiar with myth of a rather different kind, myth as the spoken word which accompanied the performance of certain all-important religious rituals. (Davidson 11)*

The student then wrote a paper that included this patchwriting:

> *Davidson explains ritual myths as concepts that are illustrated through spoken words but are also accompanied by the performance of religious ceremonies. (Qtd. in Howard 237)*

The student deleted many phrases from the original (such as "The world of the Ancient Near East") and substituted synonyms ("ceremonies" for "rituals," for example). But the structure of the student's prose is that of Davidson, following exactly the latter half of Davidson's sentence. The student obviously did not write this passage with the intention of deceiving, for he acknowledges that these are Davidson's ideas ("Davidson explains"). The student's motivation sprang from neither a lack of morality nor an ignorance of footnoting procedures, but rather from a difficulty in understanding Davidson's text.

Patchwriting in such a situation can be an effective means of helping the writer understand difficult material; blending the words and phrasing of the source with one's own words and phrasing may have helped the student comprehend the source. But it is not an acceptable practice for public writing—for the papers that one hands in. Patchwriting can help the student *toward* comprehending the source; but patchwriting itself demonstrates that the student does not yet understand that source.

The next step beyond patchwriting—a step whereby you can come to understand the text—is effective summary: Read the source through quickly to get its general ideas, perhaps reading only the first sentence of each paragraph. Then re-read, more slowly. Go through it a third time and take notes. Then let some time elapse—a half hour should be enough—and *with the book closed, write your own summary of it.* (Never try to summarize or paraphrase a source while looking at that source.) With the book closed, what you write will be in your own words and sentences. Once you have drafted your summary, go back to the book and check to see if any of your phrasing resembles that of the source; if so, quote it exactly. Provide page citations for both your paraphrases and for quotations. Also, check your version to see what you forgot; what you forgot is usually what you didn't understand. Now it is time to visit your instructor for additional help in understanding the material. But you must never let yourself fall into patchwriting as a substitute for understanding the material.

Additional advice for faculty:
An instructor who suspects that a student has committed plagiarism should inform the Dean of Students. But faculty must be attentive to the complexities of plagiarism, for often a pedagogical rather than judicial response is appropriate. Patchwriting, for example, though unacceptable for final-draft academic writing, is a

technique that learners typically employ in their early encounters with unfamiliar discourse. Because patchwriting represents a blend of the learner's words and phrases with those of the source, it is a valuable strategy for helping the learner appropriate and learn to understand unfamiliar words and ideas. Most patch-writers, far from being immoral members of the academic community, are instead people working their way through cognitive difficulties. The instructor can help in this process by making clear that patchwriting will not suffice for finished academic prose. Even more importantly, the instructor can aid the student in understanding the materials that are presenting such challenges. Once the student feels comfortable with those materials, he or she will probably be able to write about them with greater ease.

Most importantly, the instructor can help the student learn methods for reading and writing about difficult texts. Summarizing texts without simultaneously looking at those texts is an invaluable academic skill. Students should learn that the *wrong* question to ask is "How else can I say this?" Instead, they should learn to read until they understand; then write without looking at the source; and then return to the source to check accuracy and comprehensiveness and to see if any passages are sufficiently similar that they should quote them exactly.

The Writing Center can support this instructional endeavor by conducting workshops on reading and writing from sources; by supplying instructors with handouts on summary-writing; and by providing tutoring for individuals or small groups of students. Instructors can call the director of the center to arrange for workshops, ask for handouts, or refer students for appropriate tutoring.

Finally, faculty should be alert to the possibility that students may not be attributing sources or may be patchwriting because of their own cultural traditions. Students from some non-Western societies, for example—as well as those from some Western subcultures—may have been taught to adopt the voice of an authoritative source or to blend the voice of that source with their own, without citing it. The instructor can help students realize that expectations of attribution—and non-attribution—are culture-specific. The instructor can also assist students not only in learning the "rules" of Western academic culture but also in engaging the often slow process of becoming experienced in writing according to Western academic conventions.

The Constituencies of the Academy

Institutional policies must be centrist; they must describe the multiplicity of beliefs in the community which they purport to represent and protect. We must revise universities' plagiarism policies because at present they describe only one notion of authorship, the unified, autonomous subject whose textual manifestation derives from his or her moral turpitude. But we must not simply replace one prescriptive meta-narrative with another, the individual with the collaborative. Rather, we must articulate policy that acknowledges both; for both prevail in the contemporary academy. The policy offered in the preceding section of this essay does not prescribe a subject—or an absence of one—but instead describes a variety of his or her possible textual locations. It affirms the possibility of individual authorship and hence of plagiarism, but it does not characterize plagiarism as the binary opposite of originality nor as a transgression against textual virtue. Rather, it defines plagiarism in both positive and negative terms. The negative terms are couched not in the language of morality but instead speak of a failure to recognize and acknowledge the collaborative nature of one's writing. The positive terms—heretofore absent from institutions' policies—would enhance colleges' and universities' educational agendas by sanctioning rather than criminalizing an important stage of students' learning processes.

Consonant with traditional plagiarism policies, this one resorts to features of text to differentiate its categories of plagiarism. But, consonant with contemporary theory, it adds the variables of writer, context, and reader to differentiate the two major categories of plagiarism: that which should be treated as an offense and that which should be regarded as a valuable transitional composing strategy.

Such a policy, institutionalized in its entirety—including the sections of advice to students and teachers (though these passages might best be presented in student handbooks and faculty guides, rather than in the college's canon of juridical regulations)—does not work against but enables the transformations in pedagogy that are already underway in the classrooms of practitioners like Hull and Rose. It acknowledges plagiarism as a cultural arbitrary and urges faculty not to be overly zealous in their response to the manifestation of alternative textual values in the work of students from non-Western or non-mainstream cultures.

What this policy does not and cannot do is provide for the future effects of electronic composition. The policy is itself provisional, and it will need to be revised again in a very few years. The free-form collaborations that are already occurring on the Internet have caused a considerable stir. Participants in discussion groups complain about their remarks' being cited without their permission, and the net proposes that participants respect their colleagues by obtaining such permissions. Reaching an impasse while writing a book, essay, or paper, a discussion group participant poses the problem on the net and receives a variety of responses, some from anonymous members; and these responses, impossible to trace, become part of the writer's thinking. Recommendations are being formulated for revising copyright law to account for electronic media. Richard Lanham's book on authorship in cyberspace is published simultaneously in hard copy and on computer disk. University publishers anticipate offering all their books in electronic media. Academic journals are published in cyberspace, and discussion about them proliferates in the same medium. The Internet user surfs through a universe of information, stumbling quite by accident upon all sorts of materials without knowing quite how he or she got there or how to get home again. Citing data from such sources can pose near-impossible challenges for the writer. And when any of these phenomena occur in hypertext, with its multiple authors whose contributions are untraceable, the matter becomes hopelessly entangled.

These and many other aspects of electronic composition (not least of which are the questions of censoring the net and ensuring that writers of electronic texts will be able to reap monetary profits from their endeavors) promise to transform the nature of authorship in the twenty-first century. Because we are at present riding the early wave of this change, we cannot yet describe what authorship will look like in fifty years, much less account for it in present-day policy regarding student plagiarism.

We can, however, address the issues that are already established regarding student writing and focus on the task of enabling the innovative pedagogical approaches already suggested by composition scholars, while recognizing that whatever determinations we reach are necessarily provisional. Jaszi and Woodmansee say that the pressures on the economy of authorship have not yet caused revision of juridical installations regarding copyright and plagiarism; if anything, these have become even more strident in defense of textual purity (8–9). Observing the chasm between theory and the law, we must recognize that pedagogical applications of contemporary theory have gone as far as they can within the limits of now-outdated law. It is time, therefore, to undertake gradual revisions of the law, so that it will reflect rather than obscure the complexities of student authorship.

Works Cited

Atlas, James. "When an Original Idea Sounds Really Familiar." *New York Times*. 28 July 1991: 4:2.

Barthes, Roland. "The Death of the Author." *Image, Music, Text*. Ed. and trans. Stephen Heath. New York: Hill and Wang, 1977.

Bloom, Harold. *The Anxiety of Influence: A Theory of Poetry*. New York: Oxford UP, 1973.

Bourdieu, Pierre, and Jean-Claude Passeron. *Reproduction in Education, Society and Culture*. Trans. Richard Nice. 1977. Newbury Park, CA: Sage, 1990.

Constable, Giles. "Forgery and Plagiarism in the Middle Ages." *Archiv für Diplomatik, Schriftgeschichte, Siegel- und Wappenkunde* 29 (1983): 1–41.

Davidson, Robert. *Genesis 1–11*. Cambridge: Cambridge UP, 1973.

Drum, Alice. "Responding to Plagiarism." *College Composition and Communication* 37 (May 1986): 241–43.

Eliot, T. S. "Philip Massinger." *Essays on Elizabethan Drama*. New York: Harcourt, Brace, & World, 1932. 141–61.

Faigley, Lester. *Fragments of Rationality: Postmodernity and the Subject of Composition*. Pittsburgh: U of Pittsburgh P, 1992.

Flannery, Kathryn T. "Composing and the Question of Agency." *College English* 53.6 (October 1991): 701–13.

Foucault, Michel. *The Order of Things: An Archeology of the Human Sciences*. New York: Vintage, 1973.

———."What Is an Author?" *Language, Countermemory, Practice: Selected Essays and Interviews*. Ed. Donald F. Bouchard. Trans. Donald F. Bouchard and Sherry Simon. Ithaca: Cornell UP, 1977. 113–38.

Galles, Gary M. "Professors Are Woefully Ignorant of a Well-Organized Market Inimical to Learning: The Big Business in Research Papers." *Chronicle of Higher Education* 28 October 1987: B1, B3.

Garrow, David J. "King's Plagiarism: Imitation, Insecurity, and Transformation." *Journal of American History* 78 (June 1991): 86–92.

Gimpel, Jean. *The Cathedral Builders*. Trans. Carl F. Barnes, Jr. New York: Grove, 1961.

Hacker, Diana. *The Bedford Handbook for Writers*. 4th ed. Boston: Bedford, 1994.

Harris, Joseph. "The Idea of Community in the Study of Writing." *College Composition and Communication* 40 (1989): 11–22.

Holland, Peter. "Authorship and Collaboration: The Problem of Editing Shakespeare." *The Politics of the Electronic Text*. Ed. Warren Chernaik et al. Oxford: Office for Humanities Communication, 1993. 17–24.

Howard, Rebecca Moore. "A Plagiarism *Pentimento*." *Journal of Teaching Writing* 11.3 (Summer 1993): 233–46.

Hull, Glynda, and Mike Rose. "Rethinking Remediation: Toward a Social-Cognitive Understanding of Problematic Reading and Writing." *Written Communication* 6.2 (1989): 139–54.

Hutcheon, Linda. "Literary Borrowing . . . and Stealing: Plagiarism, Sources, Influences, and Intertexts." *English Studies in Canada* 12 (1986): 229–39.

Jaszi, Peter, and Martha Woodmansee. Introduction. Woodmansee and Jaszi 1–13.

Kantz, Margaret. "Helping Students Use Textual Sources Persuasively." *College English* 52 (January 1990): 74–91.

Kolich, Augustus M. "Plagiarism: The Worm of Reason." *College English* 45 (February 1983): 141–48.

Lanham, Richard. *The Electronic Word: Democracy, Technology, and the Arts*. Chicago: U of Chicago P, 1994.

Lunsford, Andrea A., and Lisa Ede. "Collaborative Authorship and the Teaching of Writing." Woodmansee and Jaszi 417–38.

Mallon, Thomas. *Stolen Words: Forays into the Origins and Ravages of Plagiarism*. New York: Ticknor and Fields, 1989.

McCormick, Frank. "The Plagiario and the Professor in Our Peculiar Institution." *Journal of Teaching Writing* 8 (Fall/Winter 1989): 133–45.

McCracken, Ellen. "Metaplagiarism and the Critic's Role as Detective: Ricardo Piglia's Reinvention of Roberto Arlt." *PMLA* 106.5 (October 1991): 1071–82.

McLeod, Susan H. "Responding to Plagiarism: The Role of the WPA." *WPA: Writing Program Administration* 15.3 (Spring 1992): 7–16.

Meltzer, Françoise. *Hot Property: The Stakes and Claims of Literary Originality*. Chicago: U of Chicago P, 1994.

Merton, Robert K. *On the Shoulders of Giants: A Shandean Postscript*. New York: Free P, 1965.

Miller, Keith D. "Composing Martin Luther King, Jr." *PMLA* 105.1 (January 1990): 70–82.

———. "Redefining Plagiarism: Martin Luther King's Use of an Oral Tradition." *Chronicle of Higher Education* 20 January 1993: A60.

———. *Voice of Deliverance: The Language of Martin Luther King, Jr. and Its Sources*. New York: Free P, 1992.

Miller, Susan. *Rescuing the Subject: A Critical Introduction to Rhetoric and the Writer*. Carbondale: Southern Illinois UP, 1989.

Mooney, Carolyn J. "Critics Question Higher Education's Commitment and Effectiveness in Dealing with Plagiarism." *Chronicle of Higher Education* 12 February 1992: A13, A16.

Pemberton, Michael. "Threshold of Desperation: Winning the Fight Against Term Paper Mills." *The Writing Instructor* 11.3 (Spring/Summer 1992): 143–52.

Raymond, Chris. "Allegations of Plagiarism Alter Historians' Views of Civil-Rights Leader." *Chronicle of Higher Education* 10 July 1991: A5, A9.

———. "Discovery of Early Plagiarism by Martin Luther King Raises Troubling Questions for Scholars and Admirers." *Chronicle of Higher Education* 21 November 1990: A1, A8.

Rose, Mark. *Authors and Owners: The Invention of Copyright*. Cambridge: Harvard UP, 1993.

Russell, David R. "Vygotsky, Dewey, and Externalism: Beyond the Student/Discipline Dichotomy." *Journal of Advanced Composition* 13.1 (Winter 1993): 173–98.

Saunders, David. *Authorship and Copyright*. New York: Routledge, 1992.

Skom, Edith. "Plagiarism: Quite a Rather Bad Little Crime." *AAHE Bulletin* October 1986: 3–7.

Spellmeyer, Kurt. "Being Philosophical about Composition: Hermeneutics and the Teaching of Writing." *Into the Field: Sites of Composition Studies*. Ed. Anne Ruggles Gere. New York: Modern Language Association, 1993. 9–29.

Stewart, Susan. *Crimes of Writing: Problems in the Containment of Representation*. New York: Oxford UP, 1991.

Whitaker, Elaine E. "A Pedagogy to Address Plagiarism." *College Composition and Communication* 44.4 (December 1993): 509–14.

White, Edward M. "Too Many Campuses Want to Sweep Student Plagiarism Under the Rug." *Chronicle of Higher Education* 24 February 1993: A44.

Woodmansee, Martha. *The Author, Art, and the Market: Rereading the History of Aesthetics*. New York: Columbia UP, 1994.

———. "On the Author Effect: Recovering Collectivity." Woodmansee and Jaszi 15–28.

Woodmansee, Martha, and Peter Jaszi, eds. *The Construction of Authorship: Textual Appropriation in Law and Literature*. Durham: Duke UP, 1994.

25

Deferred

Langston Hughes

This year, maybe, do you think I can graduate?
I'm already two years late.
Dropped out six months when I was seven,
a year when I was eleven,
then got put back when we come North.
To get through high at twenty's kind of late—
But maybe this year I can graduate.

Maybe now I can have that white enamel stove
I dreamed about when we first fell in love
eighteen years ago.
But you know,
rooming and everything
then kids,
cold-water flat and all that.
But now my daughter's married
And my boy's most grown—
quit school to work—
and where we're moving
there ain't no stove—
Maybe I can buy that white enamel stove!

Me, I always did want to study French.
It don't make sense—
I'll never go to France,
but night schools teach French.
Now at last I've got a job
where I get off at five,
in time to wash and dress,
so, s'il-vous plait, I'll study French!

Someday,
I'm gonna buy two new suits
at once!

All I want is
one more bottle of gin.

All I want is to see
my furniture paid for.

All I want is a wife who will
work with me and not against me. Say,
baby, could you see your way clear?

Heaven, heaven, is my home!
This world I'll leave behind
When I set my feet in glory
I'll have a throne for mine!

I want to pass the civil service.

I want a television set.

You know, as old as I am,
I ain't never
owned a decent radio yet?

I'd like to take up Bach.

   Montage
   of a dream
   deferred.

Buddy, have you heard?

                    –1951

26

In Praise of the Humble Comma

PICO IYER

The gods, they say, give breath, and they take it away. But the same could be said — could it not? — of the humble comma. Add it to the present clause, and, of a sudden, the mind is, quite literally, given pause to think; take it out if you wish or forget it and the mind is deprived of a resting place. Yet still the comma gets no respect. It seems just a slip of a thing, a pedant's tick, a blip on the edge of our consciousness, a kind of printer's smudge almost. Small, we claim, is beautiful (especially in the age of the microchip). Yet what is so often used, and so rarely recalled, as the comma — unless it be breath itself?

Punctuation, one is taught, has a point: to keep up law and order. Punctuation marks are the road signs placed along the highway of our communications — to control speeds, provide directions and prevent head-on collisions. A period has the unblinking finality of a red light; the comma is a flashing yellow light that asks us only to slow down; and the semicolon is a stop sign that tells us to ease gradually to a halt, before gradually starting up again. By establishing the relations between words, punctuation establishes the relations between the people using words. That may be one reason why schoolteachers exalt it and lovers defy it ("We love each other and belong to each other let's don't ever hurt each other Nicole let's

329

don't ever hurt each other," wrote Gary Gilmore[1] to his girlfriend). A comma, he must have known, "separates inseparables," in the clinching words of H. W. Fowler, King of English Usage.

Punctuation, then, is a civic prop, a pillar that holds society upright. (A run-on sentence, its phrases piling up without division, is as unsightly as a sink piled high with dirty dishes.) Small wonder, then, that punctuation was one of the first proprieties of the Victorian age, the age of the corset, that the modernists threw off: the sexual revolution might be said to have begun when Joyce's Molly Bloom spilled out all her private thoughts in thirty-six pages of unbridled, almost unperioded and officially censored prose; and another rebellion was surely marked when E. E. Cummings first felt free to commit "God" to the lower case.

Punctuation thus becomes the signature of cultures. The hot-blooded Spaniard seems to be revealed in the passion and urgency of his doubled exclamation points and question marks ("*¡Caramba! ¿Quien sabe?*"), while the impassive Chinese traditionally added to his so-called inscrutability by omitting directions from his ideograms. The anarchy and commotion of the '60s were given voice in the exploding exclamation marks, riotous capital letters and Day-Glo italics of Tom Wolfe's spray-paint prose; and in Communist societies, where the State is absolute, the dignity — and divinity — of capital letters is reserved for Ministries, Sub-Committees and Secretariats.

Yet punctuation is something more than a culture's birthmark; it scores the music in our minds, gets our thoughts moving to the rhythm of our hearts. Punctuation is the notation in the sheet music of our words, telling us where to rest, or when to raise our voices; it acknowledges that the meaning of our discourse, as of any symphonic composition, lies not in the units but in the pauses, the pacing and the phrasing. Punctuation is the way one bats one's eyes, lowers one's voice or blushes demurely. Punctuation adjusts the tone and color and volume till the feeling comes into perfect focus, not disgust exactly, but distaste; not lust, or like, but love.

Punctuation, in short, gives us the human voice, and all the meanings that lie between the words. "You aren't young, are you?" loses its innocence when it loses the question mark. Every child knows the menace of a dropped apostrophe (the parent's "Don't do that" shifting into the more slowly enunciated "Do not do that"), and every believer, the ignominy of having his faith reduced to "faith." Add an exclamation point to "To be or not to be . . ." and the gloomy Dane has all the resolve he needs; add a comma, and the noble sobriety of "God save the Queen" becomes a cry of desperation bordering on double sacrilege.

Sometimes, of course, our markings may be simply a matter of aesthetics. Popping in a comma can be like slipping on the necklace that gives an outfit quiet elegance, or like catching the sound of running water that complements, as it completes, the silence of a Japanese landscape. When V. S. Naipaul, in his latest novel, writes, "He was a middle-aged man, with glasses," the first comma can seem a little precious. Yet it gives the description a spin, as well as a subtlety,

---

[1]*Gary Gilmore* A serial killer executed in 1977. [Editor's note.]

that it otherwise lacks, and it shows that the glasses are not part of the middle-agedness, but something else.

Thus all these tiny scratches give us breadth and heft and depth. A world that has only periods is a world without inflections. It is a world without shade. It has a music without sharps and flats. It is a martial music. It has a jackboot rhythm. Words cannot bend and curve. A comma, by comparison, catches the gentle drift of the mind in thought, turning in on itself and back on itself, reversing, redoubling and returning along the course of its own sweet river music; while the semicolon brings clauses and thoughts together with all the silent discretion of a hostess arranging guests around her dinner table.

Punctuation, then, is a matter of care. Care for words, yes, but also, and more important, for what the words imply. Only a lover notices the small things: the way the afternoon light catches the nape of a neck, or how a strand of hair slips out from behind an ear, or the way a finger curls around a cup. And no one scans a letter so closely as a lover, searching for its small print, straining to hear its nuances, its gasps, its sighs and hesitations, poring over the secret messages that lie in every cadence. The difference between "Jane (whom I adore)" and "Jane, whom I adore," and the difference between them both and "Jane — whom I adore —" marks all the distance between ecstasy and heartache. "No iron can pierce the heart with such force as a period put at just the right place," in Isaac Babel's lovely words: a comma can let us hear a voice break, or a heart. Punctuation, in fact, is a labor of love. Which brings us back, in a way, to gods.

27

Nobody Mean More to Me Than You and the Future Life of Willie Jordan

Black English is not exactly a linguistic buffalo; as children, most of the thirty-five million Afro-Americans living here depend on this language for our discovery of the world. But then we approach our maturity inside a larger social body that will not support our efforts to become anything other than the clones of those who are neither our mothers nor our fathers. We begin to grow up in a house where every true mirror shows us the face of somebody who does not belong there, whose walk and whose talk will never look or sound "right," because that house was meant to shelter a family that is alien and hostile to us. As we learn our way around this environment, either we hide our original word habits, or we completely surrender our own voice, hoping to please those who will never respect anyone different from themselves: Black English is not exactly a linguistic buffalo, but we should understand its status as an endangered species, as a perishing, irreplaceable system of community intelligence, or we should expect its extinction, and, along with that, the extinguishing of much that constitutes our own proud, and singular identity.

333

What we casually call "English" less and less defers to England and its "gentlemen." "English" is no longer a specific matter of geography or an element of class privilege; more than thirty-three countries use this tool as a means of "intranational communication." Countries as disparate as Zimbabwe and Malaysia, or Israel and Uganda, use it as their non-native currency of convenience. Obviously, this tool, this "English," cannot function inside thirty-three discrete societies on the basis of rules and values absolutely determined somewhere else, in a thirty-fourth other country, for example.

In addition to that staggering congeries of non-native users of English, there are five countries, or 333,746,000 people, for whom this thing called "English" serves as a native tongue. Approximately 10% of these native speakers of "English" are Afro-American citizens of the U.S.A. I cite these numbers and varieties of human beings dependent on "English" in order, quickly, to suggest how strange and how tenuous is any concept of "Standard English." Obviously, numerous forms of English now operate inside a natural, an uncontrollable, continuum of development. I would suppose "the standard" for English in Malaysia is not the same as "the standard" in Zimbabwe. I know that standard forms of English for Black people in this country do not copy those of whites. And, in fact, the structural differences between these two kinds of English have intensified, becoming more Black, or less white, despite the expected homogenizing effects of television and other mass media.

Nonetheless, white standards of English persist, supreme and unquestioned, in these United States. Despite our multi-lingual population, and despite the deepening Black and white cleavage within that conglomerate, white standards control our official and popular judgements of verbal proficiency and correct, or incorrect, language skills, including speech. In contrast to India, where at least fourteen languages co-exist as legitimate Indian languages, in contrast to Nicaragua, where all citizens are legally entitled to formal school instruction in their regional or tribal languages, compulsory education in America compels accommodation to exclusively white forms of "English." White English, in America, is "Standard English."

This story begins two years ago. I was teaching a new course, "In Search of the Invisible Black Woman," and my rather large class seemed evenly divided between young Black women and men. Five or six white students also sat in attendance. With unexpected speed and enthusiasm we had moved through historical narratives of the 19th century to literature by and about Black women, in the 20th. I had assigned the first forty pages of Alice Walker's *The Color Purple*, and I came, eagerly, to class that morning:

"So!" I exclaimed, aloud. "What did you think? How did you like it?"

The students studied their hands, or the floor. There was no response. The tense, resistant feeling in the room fairly astounded me.

At last, one student, a young woman still not meeting my eyes, muttered something in my direction:

"What did you say?" I prompted her.

"Why she have them talk so funny. It don't sound right."

"You mean the language?"

Another student lifted his head: "It don't look right, neither. I couldn't hardly read it."

At this, several students dumped on the book. Just about unanimously, their criticisms targeted the language. I listened to what they wanted to say and silently marvelled at the similarities between their casual speech patterns and Alice Walker's written version of Black English.

But I decided against pointing to these identical traits of syntax; I wanted not to make them self-conscious about their own spoken language—not while they clearly felt it was "wrong." Instead I decided to swallow my astonishment. Here was a negative Black reaction to a prize-winning accomplishment of Black literature that white readers across the country had selected as a best seller. Black rejection was aimed at the one irreducibly Black element of Walker's work: the language—Celie's Black English. I wrote the opening lines of *The Color Purple* on the blackboard and asked the students to help me translate these sentences into Standard English:

> *You better not never tell nobody but God. It'd kill your mammy.*
>
> *Dear God,*
>
> *I am fourteen years old. I have always been a good girl. Maybe you can give me a sign letting me know what is happening to me.*
>
> *Last spring after Little Lucious come I heard them fussing. He was pulling on her arm. She say it too soon, Fonso. I ain't well. Finally he leave her alone. A week go by, he pulling on her arm again. She say, Naw, I ain't gonna. Can't you see I'm already half dead, an all of the children.*

Our process of translation exploded with hilarity and even hysterical, shocked laughter: The Black writer, Alice Walker, knew what she was doing! If rudimentary criteria for good fiction includes the manipulation of language so that the syntax and diction of sentences will tell you the identity of speakers, the probable age and sex and class of speakers, and even the locale—urban/rural/southern/western— then Walker had written, perfectly. This is the translation into Standard English that our class produced:

> *Absolutely, one should never confide in anybody besides God. Your secrets could prove devastating to your mother.*
>
> *Dear God,*
>
> *I am fourteen years old. I have always been good. But now, could you help me to understand what is happening to me?*
>
> *Last spring, after my little brother, Lucious, was born, I heard my parents fighting. My father kept pulling at my mother's arm. But she told him, "It's too soon for sex, Alfonso. I am still not feeling well." Finally, my father left her alone. A week went by, and then he began bothering my mother again: pulling her arm. She told him, "No, I won't! Can't you see I'm already exhausted from all of these children?"*

(Our favorite line was "It's too soon for sex, Alphonso.")

Once we could stop laughing, once we could stop our exponentially wild improvisations on the theme of Translated Black English, the students pushed me to explain their own negative first reactions to their spoken language on the printed page. I thought it was probably akin to the shock of seeing yourself in a photograph for the first time. Most of the students had never before seen a written facsimile of the way they talk. None of the students had ever learned how to read and write their own verbal system of communication: Black English. Alternatively, this fact began to baffle or else bemuse and then infuriate my students. Why not? Was it too late? Could they learn how to do it, now? And, ultimately, the final test question, the one testing my sincerity: Could I teach them? Because I had never taught anyone Black English and, as far as I knew, no one, anywhere in the United States, had ever offered such a course, the best I could say was "I'll try."

He looked like a wrestler.

He sat dead center in the packed room and, every time our eyes met, he quickly nodded his head as though anxious to reassure and encourage me.

Short, with strikingly broad shoulders and long arms, he spoke with a surprisingly high, soft voice that matched the soft bright movement of his eyes. His name was Willie Jordan. He would have seemed even more unlikely in the context of Contemporary Women's Poetry, except that ten or twelve other Black men were taking the course, as well. Still, Willie was conspicuous. His extreme fitness, the muscular density of his presence underscored the riveted, gentle attention that he gave to anything anyone said. Generally, he did not join the loud and rowdy dialogue flying back and forth, but there could be no doubt about his interest in our discussions. And, when he stood to present an argument he'd prepared, overnight, that nervous smile of his vanished and an irregular stammering replaced it, as he spoke with visceral sincerity, word by word.

That was how I met Willie Jordan. It was in between "In Search of the Invisible Black Woman" and "The Art of Black English." I was waiting for Departmental approval and I supposed that Willie might be, so to speak, killing time until he, too, could study Black English. But Willie really did want to explore Contemporary Women's Poetry and, to that end, volunteered for extra research and never missed a class.

Towards the end of that semester, Willie approached me for an independent study project on South Africa. It would commence the next semester. I thought Willie's writing needed the kind of improvement only intense practice will yield. I knew his intelligence was outstanding. But he'd wholeheartedly opted for "Standard English" at a rather late age, and the results were stilted and frequently polysyllabic, simply for the sake of having more syllables. Willie's unnatural formality of language seemed to me consistent with the formality of his research into South African apartheid. As he projected his studies, he would have little time, indeed, for newspapers. Instead, more than 90% of his research would mean saturation in strictly historical, if not archival, material. I was certainly interested. It would be tricky to guide him into a more confident and spontaneous relationship with both language and apartheid. It was going to be wonderful to see what happened when he could catch up with himself, entirely, and talk back to the world.

September, 1984: Breezy fall weather and much excitement! My class, "The Art of Black English," was full to the limit of the fire laws. And, in Independent Study,

Willie Jordan showed up, weekly, fifteen minutes early for each of our sessions. I was pretty happy to be teaching, altogether!

I remember an early class when a young brother, replete with his ever-present pork-pie hat, raised his hand and then told us that most of what he'd heard was "all right" except it was "too clean." "The brothers on the street," he continued, "they mix it up more. Like 'fuck' and 'motherfuck.' Or like 'shit.' " He waited. I waited. Then all of us laughed a good while, and we got into a brawl about "correct" and "realistic" Black English that led to Rule 1.

Rule 1: *Black English is about a whole lot more than mothafuckin.*

As a criterion, we decided, "realistic" could take you anywhere you want to go. Artful places. Angry places. Eloquent and sweetalkin places. Polemical places. Church. And the local Bar & Grill. We were checking out a language, not a mood or a scene or one guy's forgettable mouthing off.

It was hard. For most of the students, learning Black English required a fallback to patterns and rhythms of speech that many of their parents had beaten out of them. I mean *beaten*. And, in a majority of cases, correct Black English could be achieved only by striving for *incorrect* Standard English, something they were still pushing at, quite uncertainly. This state of affairs led to Rule 2.

Rule 2: *If it's wrong in Standard English it's probably right in Black English, or, at least, you're hot.*

It was hard. Roommates and family members ridiculed their studies, or remained incredulous. "You *studying* that shit? At school?" But we were beginning to feel the companionship of pioneers. And we decided that we needed another rule that would establish each one of us as equally important to our success. This was Rule 3.

Rule 3: *If it don't sound like something that come out somebody mouth then it don't sound right. If it don't sound right then it ain't hardly right. Period.*

This rule produced two weeks of compositions in which the students agonizingly tried to spell the sound of the Black English sentence they wanted to convey. But Black English is preeminently, an oral/spoken means of communication. *And spelling don't talk.* So we needed Rule 4.

Rule 4: *Forget about the spelling. Let the syntax carry you.*

Once we arrived at Rule 4 we started to fly because syntax, the structure of an idea, leads you to the world view of the speaker and reveals her values. The syntax of a sentence equals the structure of your consciousness. If we insisted that the language of Black English adheres to a distinctive Black syntax, then we were postulating a profound difference between white and Black people, *per se*. Was it a difference to prize or to obliterate?

There are three qualities of Black English—the presence of life, voice, and clarity—that testify to a distinctive Black value system that we became excited about and self-consciously tried to maintain.

1. Black English has been produced by a pre-technocratic, if not anti-technological, culture. More, our culture has been constantly threatened by annihilation or, at least, the swallowed blurring of assimilation. Therefore, our language is a system constructed by people constantly needing to insist that we exist, that we are present. Our language devolves from a culture that abhors all abstraction, or anything tending to obscure or delete the fact of the human being who is here

and now/the truth of the person who is speaking or listening. Consequently, *there is no passive voice construction possible in Black English*. For example, you cannot say, "Black English is being eliminated." You must say, instead, "White people eliminating Black English." The assumption of the presence of life governs all of Black English. Therefore, overwhelmingly, *all action takes place in the language of the present indicative*. And every sentence assumes the living and active participation of at least two human beings, the speaker and the listener.

2. A primary consequence of the person-centered values of Black English is the delivery of voice. If you speak or write Black English, your ideas will necessarily possess that otherwise elusive attribute, *voice*.

3. One main benefit following from the person-centered values of Black English is that of *clarity*. If your idea, your sentence, assumes the presence of at least two living and active people, you will make it understandable because the motivation behind every sentence is the wish to say something real to somebody real.

As the weeks piled up, translation from Standard English into Black English or vice versa occupied a hefty part of our course work.

> *Standard English (hereafter S.E.): "In considering the idea of studying Black English those questioned suggested—"*
>
> *(What's the subject? Where's the person? Is anybody alive in there, in that idea?)*
>
> *Black English (hereafter B.E.): "I been asking people what you think about somebody studying Black English and they answer me like this:"*

But there were interesting limits. You cannot "translate" instances of Standard English preoccupied with abstraction or with nothing/nobody evidently alive, into Black English. That would warp the language into uses antithetical to the guiding perspective of its community of users. Rather you must first change those Standard English sentences, themselves, into ideas consistent with the person-centered assumptions of Black English.

Guidelines for Black English

1. Minimal number of words for every idea: This is the source for the aphoristic and/or poetic force of the language; eliminate every possible word.

2. Clarity: If the sentence is not clear it's not Black English.

3. Eliminate use of the verb *to be* whenever possible. This leads to the deployment of more descriptive and therefore more precise verbs.

4. Use *be* or *been* only when you want to describe a chronic, ongoing state of things.
   He *be* at the office, by 9. (He is always at the office by 9.)
   He *been* with her since forever.

5. Zero copula: Always eliminate the verb *to be* whenever it would combine with another verb, in Standard English.

> S.E.: She is going out with him.
> B.E.: She going out with him.

6. Eliminate *do* as in:
   S.E.: What do you think? What do you want?
   B.E.: What you think? What you want?

Rules number 3, 4, 5, and 6 provide for the use of the minimal number of verbs per idea and, therefore, greater accuracy in the choice of verb.

7. In general, if you wish to say something really positive, try to formulate the idea using emphatic negative structure.
   S.E.: He's fabulous.
   B.E.: He bad.

8. Use double or triple negatives for dramatic emphasis.
   S.E.: Tina Turner sings out of this world.
   B.E.: Ain nobody sing like Tina.

9. Never use the *-ed* suffix to indicate the past tense of a verb.
   S.E.: She closed the door.
   B.E.: She close the door. Or, she have close the door.

10. Regardless of intentional verb time, only use the third person singular, present indicative, for use of the verb to *have*, as an auxiliary.
    S.E.: He had his wallet then he lost it.
    B.E.: He have him wallet then he lose it.
    S.E.: We had seen that movie.
    B.E.: We seen that movie. Or, we have see that movie.

11. Observe a minimal inflection of verbs. Particularly, never change from the first person singular forms to the third person singular.
    S.E.: Present Tense Forms: He goes to the store.
    B.E.: He go to the store.
    S.E.: Past Tense Forms: He went to the store.
    B.E.: He go to the store. Or, he gone to the store. Or, he been to the store.

12. The possessive case scarcely ever appears in Black English. Never use an apostrophe ('s) construction. If you wander into a possessive case component of an idea, then keep logically consistent: *ours, his, theirs, mines*. But, most likely, if you bump into such a component, you have wandered outside the underlying worldview of Black English.
    S.E.: He will take their car tomorrow.
    B.E.: He taking they car tomorrow.

13. Plurality: Logical consistency, continued: If the modifier indicates plurality, then the noun remains in the singular case.
    S.E.: He ate twelve doughnuts.
    B.E.: He eat twelve doughnut.
    S.E.: She has many books.
    B.E.: She have many book.

14. Listen for, or invent, special Black English forms of the past tense, such as: "He losted it. That what she felted." If they are clear and readily understood, then use them.

Do not hesitate to play with words, sometimes inventing them; e.g., "astropotomous" means huge like a hippo plus astronomical and, therefore, signifies real big.

15. In Black English, unless you keenly want to underscore the past tense nature of an action, stay in the present tense and rely on the overall context of your ideas for the conveyance of time and sequence.

16. Never use the suffix *-ly* form of an adverb in Black English.
    S.E.: The rain came down rather quickly.
    B.E.: The rain come down pretty quick.

17. Never use the indefinite article *an* in Black English.
    S.E.: He wanted to ride an elephant.
    B.E.: He want to ride him a elephant.

18. In variant syntax: In correct Black English it is possible to formulate an imperative, an interrogative, and a simple declarative idea with the same syntax:
    B.E.: You going to the store?
        You going to the store.
        You going to the store!

Where was Willie Jordan? We'd reached the mid-term of the semester. Students had formulated Black English guidelines, by consensus, and they were now writing with remarkable beauty, purpose, and enjoyment:

> *I ain hardly speakin for everybody but myself so understan that.*
>
> —KIM PARKS

Samples from Student Writings:

"Janie have a great big ole hole inside her. Tea Cake the only thing that fit that hole. . . .

"That pear tree beautiful to Janie, especial when bees fiddlin with the blossomin pear there growin large and lovely. But personal speakin, the love she get from starin at that tree ain the love what starin back at her in them relationship." (Monica Morris)

"Love is a big theme in *They Eye Was Watching God*. Love show people new corners inside theyself. It pull out good stuff and stuff back bad stuff. . . . Joe worship the doing uh his own hand and need other people to worship him too. But he ain't think about Janie that she a person and ought to live like anybody common do. Queen life not for Janie." (Monica Morris)

"In both life and writin, Black womens have varietous experience of love that be cold like a iceberg or fiery like a inferno. Passion got for the other partner involve, man or woman, seem as shallow, ankledeep water or the most profoundest abyss." (Constance Evans)

"Family love another bond that ain't never break under no pressure." (Constance Evans)

"You know it really cold/When the friend you/Always get out the fire/Act like they don't know you/When you in the heat." (Constance Evans)

"Big classroom discussion bout love at this time. I never take no class where us have any long arguin for and against for two or three day. New to me and great. I find the class time talkin a million time more interestin than detail bout the book." (Kathy Esseks)

As these examples suggest, Black English no longer limited the students, in any way. In fact, one of them, Philip Garfield, would shortly "translate" a pivotal scene from Ibsen's *Doll House*, as his final term paper:

NORA:	I didn't gived no shit. I thinked you a asshole back then, too, you make it so hard for me save mines husband life.
KROGSTAD:	Girl, it clear you ain't any idea what you done. You done exact what once done, and I losed my reputation over it.
NORA:	You asks me believe you once act brave save you wife life?
KROGSTAD:	Law care less why you done it.
NORA:	Law must suck.
KROGSTAD:	Suck or no, if I wants, judge screw you wid dis paper.
NORA:	No way, man. (Philip Garfield)

But where was Willie? Compulsively punctual, and always thoroughly prepared with neatly typed compositions, he had disappeared. He failed to show up for our regularly scheduled conference, and I received neither a note nor a phone call of explanation. A whole week went by. I wondered if Willie had finally been captured by the extremely current happenings in South Africa: passage of a new constitution that did not enfranchise the Black majority, and militant Black South African reaction to that affront. I wondered if he'd been hurt, somewhere. I wondered if the serious workload of weekly readings and writings had overwhelmed him and changed his mind about independent study. Where was Willie Jordan?

One week after the first conference that Willie missed, he called: "Hello, Professor Jordan? This is Willie. I'm sorry I wasn't there last week. But something has come up and I'm pretty upset. I'm sorry but I really can't deal right now."

I asked Willie to drop by my office and just let me see that he was okay: He agreed to do that. When I saw him I knew something hideous had happened. Something had hurt him and scared him to the marrow. He was all agitated and stammering and terse and incoherent. At last, his sadly jumbled account let me surmise as follows: Brooklyn police had murdered his unarmed, twenty-five-year-old brother, Reggie Jordan. Neither Willie nor his elderly parents knew what to do about it. Nobody from the press was interested. His folks had no money. Police ran his family around and around, to no point. And Reggie was really dead. And Willie wanted to fight, but he felt helpless.

With Willie's permission I began to try to secure legal counsel for the Jordan family. Unfortunately Black victims of police violence are truly numerous while the resources available to prosecute their killers are truly scarce. A friend of mine at the Center for Constitutional Rights estimated that just the preparatory costs for bringing the cops into court normally approaches $180,000. Unless the execution of Reggie Jordan became a major community cause for organizing and protest, his murder would simply become a statistical item.

Again with Willie's permission, I contacted every newspaper and media person I could think of. But the William Bastone feature article in *The Village Voice* was the only result from that canvassing.

Again with Willie's permission, I presented the case to my class in Black English. We had talked about the politics of language. We had talked about love and sex and child abuse and men and women. But the murder of Reggie Jordan broke like a hurricane across the room.

There are few "issues" as endemic to Black life as police violence. Most of the students knew and respected and liked Jordan. Many of them came from the very neighborhood where the murder had occurred. All of the students had known somebody close to them who had been killed by police, or had known frightening moments of gratuitous confrontation with the cops. They wanted to do everything at once to avenge death. Number One: They decided to compose personal statements of condolence to Willie Jordan and his family, written in Black English. Number Two: They decided to compose individual messages to the police, in Black English. These should be prefaced by an explanatory paragraph composed by the entire group. Number Three: These individual messages, with their lead paragraph, should be sent to *Newsday*.

The morning after we agreed on these objectives, one of the young women students appeared with an unidentified visitor, who sat through the class, smiling in a peculiar, comfortable way.

Now we had to make more tactical decisions. Because we wanted the messages published, and because we thought it imperative that our outrage be known by the police, the tactical question was this: Should the opening, group paragraph be written in Black English or Standard English?

I have seldom been privy to a discussion with so much heart at the dead heat of it. I will never forget the eloquence, the sudden haltings of speech, the fierce struggle against tears, the furious throwaways and useless explosions that this question elicited.

That one question contained several others, each of them extraordinarily painful to even contemplate. How best to serve the memory of Reggie Jordan? Should we use the language of the killers—Standard English—in order to make our ideas acceptable to those controlling the killers? But wouldn't what we had to say be rejected, summarily, if we said it in our own language, the language of the victim, Reggie Jordan? But if we sought to express ourselves by abandoning our language, wouldn't that mean our suicide on top of Reggie's murder? But if we expressed ourselves in our own language, wouldn't that be suicidal to the wish to communicate with those who, evidently, did not give a damn about us/Reggie/police violence in the Black community?

At the end of one of the longest, most difficult hours of my own life, the students voted, unanimously, to preface their individual messages with a paragraph composed in the language of Reggie Jordan. *"At least we don't give up nothing else. At least we stick to the truth: Be who we been. And stay all the way with Reggie."*

It was heartbreaking to proceed, from that point. Everyone in the room realized that our decision in favor of Black English had doomed our writings, even as the distinctive reality of our Black lives always has doomed our efforts to "be who we been" in this country.

I went to the blackboard and took down this paragraph, dictated by the class:

> *. . . You Cops!*
> *We the brother and sister of Willie Jordan, a fellow stony brook student who the brother of the dead Reggie Jordan. Reggie, like many brother and sister, he a victim of brutal racist police, October 25, 1984. Us ap pall, fed up, because that another senseless death what occur in our community. This what we feel, this, from our heart, for we ain't stayin' silent no more.*

With the completion of this introduction, nobody said anything. I asked for comments. At this invitation, the unidentified visitor, a young Black man, ceaselessly smiling, raised his hand. He was, it so happens, a rookie cop. He had just joined the force in September and, he said, he thought he should clarify a few things. So he came forward and sprawled easily into a posture of barroom, or fireside, nostalgia:

"See," Officer Charles enlightened us, "most times when you out on the street and something come down you do one of two things. Over-react or under-react. Now, if you under-react then you can get yourself kilt. And if you over-react then maybe you kill somebody. Fortunately it's about nine times out of ten and you will over-react. So the brother got kilt. And I'm sorry about that, believe me. But what you have to understand is what kilt him: over-reaction. That's all. Now you talk about Black people and white police but see, now, I'm a cop myself. And [big smile] I'm Black. And just a couple months ago I was on the other side. But see it's the same for me. You a cop, you the ultimate authority: the Ultimate Authority. And you on the street, most of the time you can only do one of two things: over-react or under-react. That's all it is with the brother. Over-reaction. Didn't have nothing to do with race."

That morning Officer Charles had the good fortune to escape without being boiled alive. But barely. And I remember the pride of his smile when I read about the fate of Black policemen and other collaborators in South Africa. I remember him, and I remember the shock and palpable feeling of shame that filled the room. It was as though that foolish, and deadly, young man had just relieved himself of his foolish, and deadly, explanation, face to face with the grief of Reggie Jordan's father and Reggie Jordan's mother. Class ended quietly. I copied the paragraph from the blackboard, collected the individual messages, and left to type them up.

Newsday rejected the piece.

The Village Voice could not find room in their "Letters" section to print the individual messages from the students to the police.

None of the tv news reporters picked up the story.

Nobody raised $180,000 to prosecute the murder of Reggie Jordan.

Reggie Jordan is really dead.

I asked Willie Jordan to write an essay pulling together everything important to him from that semester. He was still deeply beside himself with frustration and amazement and loss. This is what he wrote, un-edited, and in its entirety:

Throughout the course of this semester I have been researching the effects of oppression and exploitation along racial lines in South Africa and its neighboring countries. I have become aware of South African police brutalization of native Africans beyond the extent of the law, even though the laws themselves are catalyst affliction upon Black men, women and children. Many Africans die each year as a result of the deliberate use of police force to protect the white power structure.

Social control agents in South Africa, such as policemen, are also used to force compliance among citizens through both overt and covert tactics. It is not uncommon to find bold-faced coercion and cold-blooded killings of Blacks by South African police for undetermined and/or inadequate reasons. Perhaps the truth is that the only reason for this heinous treatment of Blacks rests in racial differences. We should also understand that what is conveyed through the media is not always accurate and may sometimes be construed as the tip of the iceberg at best.

I recently received a painful reminder that racism, poverty, and the abuse of power are global problems which are by no means unique to South Africa. On October 25, 1984 at approximately 3:00 p.m. my brother, Mr. Reginald Jordan, was shot and killed by two New York City policemen from the 75th precinct in the East New York section of Brooklyn. His life ended at the age of twenty-five. Even up to this current point in time the Police Department has failed to provide my family, which consists of five brothers, eight sisters, and two parents, with a plausible reason for Reggie's death. Out of the many stories that were given to my family by the Police Department, not one of them seems to hold water. In fact, I honestly believe that the Police Department's assessment of my brother's murder is nothing short of absolute bullshit, and thus far no evidence had been produced to alter this perception of the situation.

Furthermore, I believe that one of three cases may have occurred in this incident. First, Reggie's death may have been the desired outcome of the police officer's action, in which case the killing was premeditated. Or, it was a case of mistaken identity, which clarifies the fact that the two officers who killed my brother and their commanding parties are all grossly incompetent. Or, both of the above cases are correct, i.e., Reggie's murderers intended to kill him and the Police Department behaved insubordinately.

Part of the argument of the officers who shot Reggie was that he had attacked one of them and took his gun. This was their major claim. They also said that only one of them had actually shot Reggie. The facts, however, speak for themselves. According to the Death Certifi-

cate and autopsy report, Reggie was shot eight times from point-blank range. The Doctor who performed the autopsy told me himself that two bullets entered the side of my brother's head, four bullets were sprayed into his back, and two bullets struck him in the back of his legs. It is obvious that unnecessary force was used by the police and that it is extremely difficult to shoot someone in his back when he is attacking or approaching you.

After experiencing a situation like this and researching South Africa I believe that to a large degree, justice may only exist as rhetoric. I find it difficult to talk of true justice when the oppression of my people both at home and abroad attests to the fact that inequality and injustice are serious problems whereby Blacks and Third World people are perpetually short-changed by society. Something has to be done about the way in which this world is set up. Although it is a difficult task, we do have the power to make a change.

WILLIE J. JORDAN JR.
EGL 487, SECTION 58, NOVEMBER 14, 1984

It is my privilege to dedicate this book to the future life of Willie J. Jordan Jr.

August 8, 1985

28

Helping Students Use Textual Sources Persuasively

Margaret Kantz

lthough the researched essay as a topic has been much written about, it has been little studied. In the introduction to their bibliography, Ford, Rees, and Ward point out that most of the over 200 articles about researched essays published in professional journals in the last half century describe classroom methods. "Few," they say, "are of a theoretical nature or based on research, and almost none cites even one other work on the subject" (2). Given Ford and Perry's finding that 84% of freshman composition programs and 40% of advanced composition programs included instruction in writing research papers, more theoretical work seems needed. We need a theory-based explanation, one grounded in the findings of the published research on the nature and reasons for our students' problems with writing persuasive researched papers. To understand how to teach students to write such papers, we also need a better understanding of the demands of synthesis tasks.

College English, Volume 52, Number 1, January 1990

As an example for discussing this complex topic, I have used a typical college sophomore. This student is a composite derived from published research, from my own memories of being a student, and from students whom I have taught at an open admissions community college and at both public and private universities. I have also used a few examples taken from my own students, all of whom share many of Shirley's traits. Shirley, first of all, is intelligent and well-motivated. She is a native speaker of English. She has no extraordinary knowledge deficits or emotional problems. She comes from a home where education is valued, and her parents do reading and writing tasks at home and at their jobs. Shirley has certain skills. When she entered first grade, she knew how to listen to and tell stories, and she soon became proficient at reading stories and at writing narratives. During her academic life, Shirley has learned such studying skills as finding the main idea and remembering facts. In terms of the relevant research, Shirley can read and summarize source texts accurately (cf. Spivey; Winograd). She can select material that is relevant for her purpose in writing (Hayes, Waterman, and Robinson; Langer). She can make connections between the available information and her purpose for writing, including the needs of her readers when the audience is specified (Atlas). She can make original connections among ideas (Brown and Day; Langer). She can create an appropriate, audience-based structure for her paper (Spivey), take notes and use them effectively while composing her paper (Kennedy), and she can present information clearly and smoothly (Spivey), without relying on the phrasing of the original sources (Atlas; Winograd). Shirley is, in my experience, a typical college student with an average academic preparation.

Although Shirley seems to have everything going for her, she experiences difficulty with assignments that require her to write original papers based on textual sources. In particular, Shirley is having difficulty in her sophomore-level writing class. Shirley, who likes English history, decided to write about the Battle of Agincourt (this part of Shirley's story is biographical). She found half a dozen histories that described the circumstances of the battle in a few pages each. Although the topic was unfamiliar, the sources agreed on many of the facts. Shirley collated these facts into her own version, noting but not discussing discrepant details, borrowing what she assumed to be her sources' purpose of retelling the story, and modelling the narrative structure of her paper on that of her sources. Since the only comments Shirley could think of would be to agree or disagree with her sources, who had told her everything she knew about the Battle of Agincourt, she did not comment on the material; instead, she concentrated on telling the story clearly and more completely than her sources had done. She was surprised when her paper received a grade of C-. (Page 1 of Shirley's paper is given as Appendix A.)

Although Shirley is a hypothetical student whose case is based on a real event, her difficulties are typical of undergraduates at both private and public colleges and universities. In a recent class of Intermediate Composition in which the students were instructed to create an argument using at least four textual sources that took differing points of view, one student, who analyzed the coverage of a recent championship football game, ranked her source articles in order from those whose approach she most approved to those she least approved. Another student analyzed various approaches taken by the media to the Kent State shootings in 1970, and was surprised and disappointed to find that all of the sources seemed slanted, either by the perspective of the reporter or by that of the people interviewed. Both students did not understand why their instructor said that their papers lacked a genuine argument.

The task of writing researched papers that express original arguments presents many difficulties. Besides the obvious problems of citation format and coordination of source materials with the emerging written product, writing a synthesis can vary in difficulty according to the number and length of the sources, the abstractness or familiarity of the topic, the uses that the writer must make of the material, the degree and quality of original thought required, and the extent to which the sources will supply the structure and purpose of the new paper. It is usually easier to write a paper that uses all of only one short source on a familiar topic than to write a paper that selects material from many long sources on a topic that one must learn as one reads and writes. It is easier to quote than to paraphrase, and it is easier to build the paraphrases, without comment or with random comments, into a description of what one found than it is to use them as evidence in an original argument. It is easier to use whatever one likes, or everything one finds, than to formally select, evaluate, and interpret material. It is easier to use the structure and purpose of a source as the basis for one's paper than it is to create a structure or an original purpose. A writing-from-sources task can be as simple as collating a body of facts from a few short texts on a familiar topic into a new text that reproduces the structure, tone, and purpose of the originals, but it can also involve applying abstract concepts from one area to an original problem in a different area, a task that involves learning the relationships among materials as a paper is created that may refer to its sources without resembling them.

Moreover, a given task can be interpreted as requiring an easy method, a difficult method, or any of a hundred intermediate methods. In this context, Flower has observed, "The different ways in which students [represent] a 'standard' reading-to-write task to themselves lead to markedly different goals and strategies as well as different organizing plans" ("Role" iii). To write a synthesis, Shirley may or may not need to quote, summarize, or select material from her sources; to evaluate the sources for bias, accuracy, or completeness; to develop original ideas; or to persuade a reader. How well she performs any of these tasks—and whether she thinks to perform these tasks—depends on how she reads the texts and on how she interprets the assignment. Shirley's representation of the task, which in this case was easier than her teacher had in mind, depends on the goals that she sets for herself. The goals that she sets depend on her awareness of the possibilities and her confidence in her writing skills.

Feeling unhappy about her grade, Shirley consulted her friend Alice. Alice, who is an expert, looked at the task in a completely different way and used strategies for thinking about it that were quite different from Shirley's.

"Who were your sources?" asked Alice. "Winston Churchill, right? A French couple and a few others. And they didn't agree about the details, such as the sizes of the armies. Didn't you wonder why?"

"No," said Shirley. "I thought the history books would know the truth. When they disagreed, I figured that they were wrong on those points. I didn't want to have anything in my paper that was wrong."

"But Shirley," said Alice, "you could have thought about why a book entitled *A History of France* might present a different view of the battle than a book subtitled *A History of British Progress*. You could have asked if the English and French writers wanted to make a point about the history of their countries and looked to see if the factual differences suggested anything. You could even have talked about Shakespeare's *Henry V*, which I know you've read—about how he presents the battle, or about how the King Henry in the play differs from the Henrys in your other books. You would have had an angle, a problem. Dr. Boyer would have loved it."

Alice's representation of the task would have required Shirley to formally select and evaluate her material and to use it as proof in an original argument. Alice was suggesting that Shirley invent an original problem and purpose for her paper and create an original structure for her argument. Alice's task is much more sophisticated than Shirley's. Shirley replied, "That would take me a year to do! Besides, Henry was a real person. I don't want to make up things about him."

"Well," said Alice, "You're dealing with facts, so there aren't too many choices. If you want to say something original you either have to talk about the sources or talk about the material. What could you say about the material? Your paper told about all the reasons King Henry wasn't expected to win the battle. Could you have argued that he should have lost because he took too many chances?"

"Gee," said Shirley, "That's awesome. I wish I'd thought of it."

This version of the task would allow Shirley to keep the narrative structure of her paper but would give her an original argument and purpose. To write the argument, Shirley would have only to rephrase the events of the story to take an opposite approach from that of her English sources, emphasizing what she perceived as Henry's mistakes and inserting comments to explain why his decisions were mistakes—an easy argument to write. She could also, if she wished, write a conclusion that criticized the cheerleading tone of her British sources.

As this anecdote makes clear, a given topic can be treated in more or less sophisticated ways—and sophisticated goals, such as inventing an original purpose and evaluating sources, can be achieved in relatively simple versions of a task. Students have many options as to how they can fulfill even a specific task (cf. Jeffery). Even children can decide whether to process a text deeply or not, and purpose in reading affects processing and monitoring of comprehension (Brown). Pichert has shown that reading purpose affects judgments about what is important or unimportant in a narrative text, and other research tells us that attitudes toward the author and content of a text affect comprehension (Asch; Hinze; Shedd; Goldman).

One implication of this story is that the instructor gave a weak assignment and an ineffective critique of the draft (her only comment referred to Shirley's footnoting technique; cf. Appendix A). The available research suggests that if Dr. Boyer had set Shirley a specific rhetorical problem such as having her report on her material to the class and then testing them on it, and if she had commented on the content of Shirley's paper during the drafts, Shirley might well have come up with a paper that did more than repeat its source material (Nelson and Hayes). My teaching experience supports this research finding. If Dr. Boyer had told Shirley from the outset that she was expected to say something original and that she should examine her sources as she read them for discrepant facts, conflicts, or other interesting material, Shirley might have tried to write an original argument (Kantz, "Originality"). And if Dr. Boyer had suggested that Shirley use her notes to comment on her sources and make plans for using the notes, Shirley might have written a better paper than she did (Kantz, "Relationship").

Even if given specific directions to create an original argument, Shirley might have had difficulty with the task. Her difficulty could come from any of three causes: 1) Many students like Shirley misunderstand sources because they read them as stories. 2) Many students expect their sources to tell the truth; hence, they equate persuasive writing in this context with making things up. 3) Many students do not understand that facts are a kind of claim and are often used persuasively in so-called objective writing to create an impression. Students need to read source texts as arguments and to think about the rhetorical contexts in which they were written rather than to read them merely as a set of facts to be learned. Writing an original persuasive argument based on sources requires students to apply material to a problem or to use it to answer a question, rather than simply to repeat it or evaluate it. These three problems deserve a separate discussion.

Because historical texts often have a chronological structure, students believe that historians tell stories and that renarrating the battle cast them as a historian. Because her sources emphasized the completeness of the victory/defeat and its decisive importance in the history of warfare, Shirley thought that making these same points in her paper completed her job. Her job as a reader was thus to learn the story, i.e., so that she could pass a test on it (cf. Vipond and Hunt's argument that generic expectations affect reading behavior. Vipond and Hunt would describe Shirley's reading as story-driven rather than point-driven). Students commonly misread texts as narratives. When students refer to a textbook as "the story," they are telling us that they read for plot and character, regardless of whether their texts are organized as narratives. One reason Shirley loves history is that when she reads it she can combine her story-reading strategies with her studying strategies. Students like Shirley may need to learn to apply basic organizing patterns, such as cause-effect and general-to-specific, to their texts. If, however, Dr. Boyer asks Shirley to respond to her sources in a way that is not compatible with Shirley's understanding of what such sources do, Shirley will have trouble doing the assignment. Professors may have to do some preparatory teaching about why certain kinds of texts have certain characteristics and what kinds of problems writers must solve as they design text for a particular audience. They may even have to teach a model for the kind of writing they expect.

The writing version of Shirley's problem, which Flower calls "writer-based prose," occurs when Shirley organizes what should be an expository analysis as a narrative, especially when she writes a narrative about how she did her research. Students frequently use time-based organizing patterns, regardless of the task, even when such patterns conflict with what they are trying to say and even when they know how to use more sophisticated strategies. Apparently such common narrative transitional devices such as "the first point" and "the next point" offer a reassuringly familiar pattern for organizing unfamiliar material. The common strategy of beginning paragraphs with such phrases as "my first source," meaning that it was the first source that the writer found in the library or the first one read, appears to combine a story-of-my-research structure with a knowledge-telling strategy

(Bereiter and Scardamalia, *Psychology*). Even when students understand that the assignment asks for more than the fill-in-the-blanks, show-me-you've-read-the-material approach described by Schwegler and Shamoon, they cling to narrative structuring devices. A rank ordering of sources, as with Mary's analysis of the football game coverage with the sources listed in an order of ascending disapproval, represents a step away from storytelling and toward synthesizing because it embodies a persuasive evaluation.

In addition to reading texts as stories, students expect factual texts to tell them "the truth" because they have learned to see texts statically, as descriptions of truths, instead of as arguments. Shirley did not understand that nonfiction texts exist as arguments in rhetorical contexts. "After all," she reasoned, "how can one argue about the date of a battle or the sizes of armies?" Churchill, however, described the battle in much more detail than Shirley's other sources, apparently because he wished to persuade his readers to take pride in England's tradition of military achievement. Guizot and Guizot de Witt, on the other hand, said very little about the battle (beyond describing it as "a monotonous and lamentable repetition of the disasters of Crecy and Poitiers" [397]) because they saw the British invasion as a sneaky way to take advantage of a feud among the various branches of the French royal family. Shirley's story/study skills might not have allowed her to recognize such arguments, especially because Dr. Boyer did not teach her to look for them.

When I have asked students to choose a topic and find three or more sources on it that disagree, I am repeatedly asked, "How can sources disagree in different ways? After all, there's only pro and con." Students expect textbooks and other authoritative sources either to tell them the truth (i.e., facts) or to express an opinion with which they may agree or disagree. Mary's treatment of the football coverage reflects this belief, as does Charlie's surprise when he found that even his most comprehensive sources on the Kent State killings omitted certain facts, such as interviews with National Guardsmen. Students' desire for truth leads them to use a collating approach whenever possible, as Shirley did (cf. Appendix A), because students believe that the truth will include all of the facts and will reconcile all conflicts. (This belief may be another manifestation of the knowledge-telling strategy [Bereiter and Scardamalia, *Psychology*] in which students write down everything they can think of about a topic.) When conflicts cannot be reconciled and the topic does not admit a pro or con stance, students may not know what to say. They may omit the material altogether, include it without comment, as Shirley did, or jumble it together without any plan for building an argument.

The skills that Shirley has practiced for most of her academic career—finding the main idea and learning content—allow her to agree or disagree. She needs a technique for reading texts in ways that give her something more to say, a technique for constructing more complex representations of texts that allow room for more sophisticated writing goals. She also needs strategies for analyzing her reading that allow her to build original arguments.

One way to help students like Shirley is to teach the concept of rhetorical situation. A convenient tool for thinking about this concept is Kinneavy's triangular diagram of the rhetorical situation. Kinneavy, analyzing Aristotle's description of rhetoric, posits that every communicative situation has three parts: a speaker/writer (the Encoder), an audience (the Decoder), and a topic (Reality) (19). Although all discourse involves all three aspects of communication, a given type of discourse may pertain more to a particular point of the triangle than to the others, e.g., a diary entry may exist primarily to express the thoughts of the writer (the Encoder); an advertisement may exist primarily to persuade a reader (the Decoder). Following Kinneavy, I posit particular goals for each corner of the triangle. Thus, the primary goal of a writer doing writer-based discourse such as a diary might be originality and self-expression; primary goals for reader-based discourse such as advertising might be persuasion; primary goals for topic-based discourse such as a researched essay might be accuracy, completeness, and mastery of subject matter. Since all three aspects of the rhetorical situation are present and active in any communicative situation, a primarily referential text such as Churchill's *The Birth of Britain* may have a persuasive purpose and may depend for some of its credibility on readers' familiarity with the author. The term "rhetorical reading," then (cf. Haas and Flower), means teaching students to read a text as a message sent by someone to somebody for a reason. Shirley, Mary, and Charlie are probably practiced users of rhetorical persuasion in non-academic contexts. They may never have learned to apply this thinking in a conscious and deliberate way to academic tasks (cf. Kroll).

The concept of rhetorical situation offers insight into the nature of students' representations of a writing task. The operative goals in Shirley's and Alice's approaches to the term paper look quite different when mapped onto the points on the triangle. If we think of Shirley and Alice as Encoders, the topic as Reality, and Dr. Boyer as the Decoder, we can see that for Shirley, being an Encoder means trying to be credible; her relationship to the topic (Reality) involves a goal of using all of the subject matter; and her relationship to the Decoder involves an implied goal of telling a complete story to a reader whom Shirley thinks of as an examiner—to use the classic phrase from the famous book by Britton et al.—i.e., a reader who wants to know if Shirley can pass an exam on the subject of the Battle of Agincourt. For Alice, however, being an Encoder means having a goal of saying something new; the topic (Reality) is a resource to be used; and the Decoder is someone who must be persuaded that Alice's ideas have merit. Varying task representations do not change the dimensions of the rhetorical situation: the Encoder, Decoder, and Reality are always present. But the way a writer represents the task to herself does affect the ways that she thinks about those dimensions—and whether she thinks about them at all.

In the context of a research assignment, rhetorical skills can be used to read the sources as well as to design the paper. Although teachers have probably always known that expert readers use such strategies, the concept of rhetorical reading is new to the literature. Haas and Flower have shown that expert readers use rhetorical strategies "to account for author's purpose, context, and effect on the audience . . . to recreate or infer the rhetorical situation of the text" (176; cf also Bazerman). These strategies, used in addition to formulating main points and paraphrasing content, helped the readers to understand a text more completely and more quickly than did readers who concentrated exclusively on content. As Haas and Flower point out, teaching students to read rhetorically is difficult. They suggest that appropriate pedagogy might include "direct instruction . . . modeling, and . . . encouraging students to become contributing and committed members of rhetorical communities" (182). One early step might be to teach students a set of heuristics based on the three aspects of the communicative triangle. Using such questions could help students set goals for their reading.

In this version of Kinneavy's triangle, the Encoder is the writer of the source text, the Decoder is the student reader, and Reality is the subject matter. Readers may consider only one point of the triangle at a time, asking such questions as "Who are you (i.e., the author/Encoder)?" or "What are the important features of this text?" They may consider two aspects of the rhetorical situation in a single question, e.g., "Am I in your intended (primary) audience?"; "What do I think about this topic?"; "What context affected your ideas and presentation?" Other questions would involve all three points of the triangle, e.g., "What are you saying to help me with the problem you assume I have?" or "What textual devices have you used to manipulate my response?" Asking such questions gives students a way of formulating goals relating to purpose as well as content.

If Shirley, for example, had asked a Decoder-to-Encoder question—such as "Am I in your intended audience?"—she might have realized that Churchill and the Guizots were writing for specific audiences. If she had asked a Decoder-to-Reality question—such as "What context affected your ideas and presentation?"— she might not have ignored Churchill's remark, "All these names [Amiens, Boves, Bethencourt] are well known to our generation" (403). As it was, she missed Churchill's signal that he was writing to survivors of the First World War, who had vainly hoped that it would be war to end all wars. If Shirley had used an Encoder-Decoder-Reality question—such as "What are you saying to help me with the problem you assume I have?"—she might have understood that the authors of her sources were writing to different readers for different reasons. This understanding might have given her something to say. When I gave Shirley's source texts to freshmen students, asked them to use the material in an original argument, and taught them this heuristic for rhetorical reading, I received, for example, papers that warned undergraduates about national pride as a source of authorial bias in history texts.

A factual topic such as the Battle of Agincourt presents special problems because of the seemingly intransigent nature of facts. Like many people, Shirley believes that you can either agree or disagree with issues and opinions, but you can only accept the so-called facts. She believes that facts are what you learn from textbooks, opinions are what you have about clothes, and arguments are what you have with your mother when you want to stay out late at night. Shirley is not in a position to disagree with the facts about the battle (e.g., "No, I think the French won"), and a rhetorical analysis may seem at first to offer minimal rewards (e.g., "According to the Arab, Jewish, and Chinese calendars the date was really . . .").

Alice, who thinks rhetorically, understands that both facts and opinions are essentially the same kind of statement: they are claims. Alice understands that the only essential difference between a fact and an opinion is how they are received by an audience. (This discussion is derived from Toulmin's model of an argument as consisting of claims proved with data and backed by ethical claims called warrants. According to Toulmin, any aspect of an argument may be questioned by the audience and must then be supported with further argument.) In a rhetorical argument, a fact is a claim that an audience will accept as being true without requiring proof, although they may ask for an explanation. An opinion is a claim that an audience will not accept as true without proof, and which, after the proof is given, the audience may well decide has only a limited truth, i.e., it's true in this case but not in other cases. An audience may also decide that even though a fact is unassailable, the interpretation or use of the fact is open to debate.

For example, Shirley's sources gave different numbers for the size of the British army at Agincourt; these numbers, which must have been estimates, were claims masquerading as facts. Shirley did not understand this. She thought that disagreement signified error, whereas it probably signified rhetorical purpose. The probable reason that the Guizots give a relatively large estimate for the English army and do not mention the size of the French army is so that their French readers would find the British victory easier to accept. Likewise, Churchill's relatively small estimate for the size of the English army and his high estimate for the French army magnify the brilliance of the English victory. Before Shirley could create an argument about the Battle of Agincourt, she needed to understand that, even in her history textbooks, the so-called facts are claims that may or may not be supported, claims made by writers who work in a certain political climate for a particular audience. She may, of course, never learn this truth unless Dr. Boyer teaches her rhetorical theory and uses the research paper as a chance for Shirley to practice rhetorical problem-solving.

For most of her academic life, Shirley has done school tasks that require her to find main ideas and important facts; success in these tasks usually hinges on agreeing with the teacher about what the text says. Such study skills form an essential basis for doing reading-to-write tasks. Obviously a student can only use sources to build an argument if she can first read the sources accurately (cf. Brown and Palincsar; Luftig; Short and Ryan). However, synthesizing tasks often require that readers not accept the authors' ideas. Baker and Brown have pointed out that people misread texts when they blindly accept an author's ideas instead of considering a divergent interpretation. Yet if we want students to learn to build original arguments from texts, we must teach them the skills needed to create divergent interpretations. We must teach them to think about facts and opinions as claims that are made by writers to particular readers for particular reasons in particular historical contexts.

Reading sources rhetorically gives students a powerful tool for creating a persuasive analysis. Although no research exists as yet to suggest that teaching students to read rhetorically will improve their writing, I have seen its effect in successive drafts of students' papers. As mentioned earlier, thetorical reading allowed a student to move from simply summarizing and evaluating her sources on local coverage of the championship football game to constructing a rationale for articles that covered the fans rather than the game. Rhetorical analysis enabled another student to move from summarizing his sources to understanding why each report about the Kent State shootings necessarily expressed a bias of some kind.

As these examples suggest, however, rhetorical reading is not a magical technique for producing sophisticated arguments. Even when students read their sources rhetorically, they tend merely to report the results of this analysis in their essays. Such writing appears to be a college-level version of the knowledge-telling strategy described by Bereiter and Scardamalia *(Psychology)* and may be, as they suggest, the product of years of exposure to pedagogical practices that enshrine the acquisition and expression information without a context or purpose.

To move students beyond merely reporting the content and rhetorical orientation of their source texts, I have taught them the concept of the rhetorical gap and some simple heuristic questions for thinking about gaps. Gaps were first described by Iser as unsaid material that a reader must supply to/infer from a text. McCormick expanded the concept to include gaps between the text and the reader; such gaps could involve discrepancies of values, social conventions, language, or any other matter that readers must consider. If we apply the concept of gaps to Kinneavy's triangle, we see that in reading, for example, a gap may occur between the Encoder-Decoder corners when the reader is not a member of the author's intended audience. Shirley fell into such a gap. Another gap can occur between the Decoder-Reality corners when a reader disagrees with or does not understand the text. A third gap can occur between the Encoder-Reality points of the triangle if the writer has misrepresented or misunderstood the material. The benefit of teaching this concept is that when a student thinks about a writer's rhetorical stance, she may ask "Why does he think that way?" When a student encounters a gap, she may ask, "What effect does it have on the success of this communication?" The answers to both questions give students original material for their papers.

Shirley, for example, did not know that Churchill began writing *The Birth of Britain* during the 1930s, when Hitler was rearming Germany and when the British government and most of Churchill's readers ardently favored disarmament. Had she understood the rhetorical orientation of the book, which was published eleven years after the end of World War II, she might have argued that Churchill's evocation of past military glories would have been inflammatory in the 1930s but was highly acceptable twenty years later. A gap between the reader and the text (Decoder-Reality) might stimulate a reader to investigate whether or not she is the only person having this problem; a gap between other readers and the sources may motivate an adaptation or explanation of the material to a particular audience. Shirley might have adapted the Guizots' perspective on the French civil war for American readers. A gap between the author and the material (Encoder-Reality) might motivate a refutation.

To discover gaps, students may need to learn heuristics for setting rhetorical writing goals. That is they may need to learn to think of the paper, not as a rehash of the available material, but as an opportunity to teach someone, to solve someone's problem, or to answer someone's question. The most salient questions for reading source texts may be "Who are you (the original audience of Decoders)?"; "What is your question or problem with this topic?"; and "How have I (the Encoder) used these materials to answer your question or solve your problem?" More simply, these questions may be learned as "Why," "How," and "So what?" When Shirley learns to read sources as telling not the eternal truth but a truth to a particular audience and when she learns to think of texts as existing to solve problems, she will find it easier to think of things to say.

For example, a sophomore at a private university was struggling with an assignment that required her to analyze an issue and express an opinion on it, using two conflicting source texts, an interview, and personal material as sources.

Using rhetorical reading strategies, this girl discovered a gap between Alfred Marbaise, a high school principal who advocates mandatory drug testing of all high school students, and students like those he would be testing:

> *Marbaise, who was a lieutenant in the U.S. Marines over thirty years ago . . . makes it very obvious that he cannot and will not tolerate any form of drug abuse in his school. For example, in paragraph seven he claims, "When students become involved in illegal activity, whether they realize it or not, they are violating other students . . . then I become very, very concerned . . . and I will not tolerate that."*

> *Because Marbaise has not been in school for nearly forty years himself, he does not take into consideration the reasons why kids actually use drugs. Today the social environment is so drastically different that Marbaise cannot understand a kid's morality, and that is why he writes from such a fatherly but distant point of view.*

The second paragraph answers the So what? question, i.e., "Why does it matter that Marbaise seems by his age and background to be fatherly and distant?" Unless the writer/reader thinks to ask this question, she will have difficulty writing a coherent evaluation of Marbaise's argument.

The relative success of some students in finding original things to say about their topics can help us to understand the perennial problem of plagiarism. Some plagiarism derives, I think, from a weak, non-rhetorical task representation. If students believe they are supposed to reproduce source material in their papers, or if they know they are supposed to say something original but have no rhetorical problem to solve and no knowledge of how to find problems that they can discuss in their sources, it becomes difficult for them to avoid plagiarizing. The common student decision to buy a paper when writing the assignment seems a meaningless fill-in-the-blanks activity (cf. Schwegler and Shamoon) becomes easily understandable. Because rhetorical reading leads to discoveries about the text, students who use it may take more interest in their research papers.

Let us now assume that Shirley understands the importance of creating an original argument, knows how to read analytically, and has found things to say about the Battle of Agincourt. Are her troubles over? Will she now create that A paper that she yearns to write? Probably not. Despite her best intentions, Shirley will probably write another narrative/paraphrase of her sources. Why? Because by now, the assignment asks her to do far more than she can handle in a single draft. Shirley's task representation is now so rich, her set of goals so many, that she may be unable to juggle them all simultaneously. Moreover, the rhetorical reading technique requires students to discover content worth writing about and a rhetorical purpose for writing; the uncertainty of managing such a discovery task when a grade is at stake may be too much for Shirley.

Difficult tasks may be difficult in either (or both of) two ways. First, they may require students to do a familiar subtask, such as reading sources, at a higher level of difficulty, e.g., longer sources, more sources, a more difficult topic. Second, they may require students to do new subtasks, such as building notes into an original argument. Such tasks may require task management skills, especially planning, that students have never developed and do not know how to attempt.

The insecurity that results from trying a complex new task in a high-stakes situation is increased when students are asked to discover a problem worth writing about because such tasks send students out on a treasure hunt with no guarantee that the treasure exists, that they will recognize it when they find it, or that when they find it they will be able to build it into a coherent argument. The paper on Marbaise quoted above earned a grade of D because the writer could not use her rhetorical insights to build an argument presented in a logical order. Although she asked the logical question about the implications of Marbaise's persona, she did not follow through by evaluating the gaps in his perspective that might affect the probable success of his program.

A skillful student using the summarize-the-main-ideas approach can set her writing goals and even plan (i.e., outline) a paper before she reads the sources. The rhetorical reading strategy, by contrast, requires writers to discover what is worth writing about and to decide how to say it as or after they read their sources. The strategy requires writers to change their content goals and to adjust their writing plans as their understanding of the topic develops. It requires writers, in Flower's term, to "construct" their purposes for writing as well as the content for their paper (for a description of constructive planning, see Flower, Schriver, Carey, Haas, and Hayes). In Flower's words, writers who construct a purpose, as opposed to writers who bring a predetermined purpose to a task, "create a web of purposes . . . set goals, toss up possibilities . . . create a multidimensional network of information . . . a web of purpose . . . a bubbling stew of various mental representations" (531–32). The complex indeterminacy of such a task may pose an intimidating challenge to students who have spent their lives summarizing main ideas and reporting facts.

Shirley may respond to the challenge by concentrating her energies on a familiar subtask, e.g., repeating material about the Battle of Agincourt, at the expense of struggling with an unfamiliar subtask such as creating an original argument. She may even deliberately simplify the task by representing it to herself as calling only for something that she knows how to do, expecting that Dr. Boyer will accept the paper as close enough to the original instructions. My students do this frequently. When students decide to write a report of their reading, they can at least be certain that they will find material to write about.

Because of the limits of attentional memory, not to mention those caused by inexperience, writers can handle only so many task demands at a time. Thus, papers produced by seemingly inadequate task representations may well be essentially rough drafts. What looks like a bad paper may well be a preliminary step, a way of meeting certain task demands in order to create a basis for thinking about new ones. My students consistently report that they need to marshal all of their ideas and text knowledge and get that material down on the page (i.e., tell their knowledge) before they can think about developing an argument (i.e., transform their knowledge). If Shirley's problem is that she has shelved certain task demands in favor of others, Dr. Boyer needs only to point out what Shirley should do to bring the paper into conformity with the assignment and offer Shirley a chance to revise.

The problems of cognitive overload and inexperience in handling complex writing tasks can create a tremendous hurdle for students because so many of them believe that they should be able to write their paper in a single draft. Some students think that if they can't do the paper in one draft that means that something is wrong with them as writers, or with the assignment, or with us for giving the assignment. Often, such students will react to their drafts with anger and despair, throwing away perfectly usable rough drafts and then coming to us and saying that they can't do the assignment.

The student's first draft about drug testing told her knowledge about her sources' opinions on mandatory drug testing. Her second draft contained the rhetorical analysis quoted above, but presented the material in a scrambled order and did not build the analysis into an argument. Only in a third draft was this student able to make her point:

> *Not once does Marbaise consider any of the psychological reasons why kids turn away from reality. He fails to realize that drug testing will not answer their questions, ease their frustrations, or respond to their cries for attention, but will merely further alienate himself and other authorities from helping kids deal with their real problems.*

This comment represents Terri's answer to the heuristic "So what? Why does the source's position matter?" If we pace our assignments to allow for our students' thoughts to develop, we can do a great deal to build their confidence in their writing (Terri raised her D + to an A). If we treat the researched essay as a sequence of assignments instead of as a one-shot paper with a single due date, we can teach our students to build on their drafts, to use what they can do easily as a bridge to what we want them to learn to do. In this way, we can improve our students' writing habits. More importantly, however, we can help our students to see themselves as capable writers and as active, able, problemsolvers. Most importantly, we can use the sequence of drafts to demand that our students demonstrate increasingly sophisticated kinds of analytic and rhetorical proficiency.

Rhetorical reading and writing heuristics can help students to represent tasks in rich and interesting ways. They can help students to set up complex goal structures (Bereiter and Scardamalia, "Conversation"). They offer students many ways to think about their reading and writing texts. These tools, in other words, encourage students to work creatively.

And after all, creativity is what research should be about. If Shirley writes a creative paper, she has found a constructive solution that is new to her and which other people can use, a solution to a problem that she and other people share. Creativity is an inherently rhetorical quality. If we think of it as thought leading to solutions to problems and of problems as embodied in questions that people ask about situations, the researched essay offers infinite possibilities. Viewed in this way, a creative idea answers a question that the audience or any single reader wants answered. The question could be, "Why did Henry V win the Battle of Agincourt?" or, "How can student readers protect themselves against nationalistic bias when they study history?" or any of a thousand other questions. If we teach our Shirleys to see themselves as scholars who work to find answers to problem questions, and if we teach them to set reading and writing goals for themselves that will allow them to think constructively, we will be doing the most exciting work that teachers can do, nurturing creativity.

Appendix A: Page 1 of Shirley's Paper

The battle of Agincourt ranks as one of England's greatest military triumphs. It was the most brilliant victory of the Middle Ages, bar none. It was fought on October 25, 1414, against the French near the French village of Agincourt.

Henry V had claimed the crown of France and had invaded France with an army estimated at anywhere from 10,000[1] to 45,000 men.[2] During the siege of Marfleur dysentery had taken 1/3 of them[3], his food supplies had been depleted[4], and the fall rains had begun. In addition the French had assembled a huge army and were marching toward him. Henry decided to march to Calais, where his ships were to await him[5]. He intended to cross the River Somme at the ford of Blanchetaque[6], but, falsely informed that the ford was guarded, he was forced to follow the flooded Somme up toward its source. The French army was shadowing him on his right. Remembering the slaughters of Crecy and <u>Poictiers</u>, the French constable, Charles d'Albret, hesitated to fight[8], but when Henry forded the Somme just above Amiens[9] and was just

1. Carl Stephinson, *Medieval History*, p. 529.

2. Guizot, Monsieur and Guizot, Madame. *World's Best Histories-France, Vol II,* p. 211.

3. Cyrid E. Robinson. *England-A History of British Progress*, p. 145.

4. *Ibid.*

5. Winston Churchill. *A History of the English-Speaking Peoples. Volume 1: Birth of Britain*, p. 403.

6. *Ibid.*

7. *Ibid.*

8. Robinson, p. 145.

9. Churchill. p. 403.

Works Cited

Asch, Solomon. *Social Psychology*. New York: Prentice, 1952.

Atlas, Marshall. *Expert-Novice Differences in the Writing Process*. Paper presented at the American Educational search Association, 1979. ERIC ED 107 769.

Baker, Louise, and Ann L. Brown. "Metacognitive Skills and Reading." *Handbook of Reading Research*. Eds. P. D Person, Rebecca Barr, Michael L. Kamil, and Peter Mosenthal. New York: Longman, 1984.

Bazerman, Charles. "Physicists Reading Physics: Schema-Laden Purposes and Purpose-Laden Schema." *Written Communication* 2.1 (1985): 3–24.

Bereiter, Carl, and Marlene Scardamalia. "From Conversation to Composition: The Role of Instruction in a Developmetal Process." *Advances in Instructional Psychology*. Ed. R. Glaser. Vol. 2. Hillsdale, NJ: Lawrence Erlbaum Associates, 1982. 1–64.

———. *The Psychology of Written Composition*. Hillsdale, NJ: Lawrence Erlbaum Associates, 1987.

Briscoe, Terri. "To test or not to test." Unpublished essay. Texas Christian University, 1989.

Britton, James, Tony Burgess, Nancy Martin, Alex McLeod, and Harold Rosen. *The Development of Writing Abilities (11–18)*. Houndmills Basingstoke Hampshire: Macmillan Education Ltd., 1975.

Brown, Ann L. "Theories of Memory and the Problem of Development: Activity, Growth, and Knowledge." *Levels of Processing in Memory*. Eds. Laird S. Cermak and Fergus I. M. Craik. Hillsdale, NJ: Laurence Erlbaum Associares, 1979, 225–258.

———, Joseph C. Campione, and L. R. Barclay. *Training Self-Checking Routines for Estimating Test Readiness: Generalizations from List Learning to Prose Recall*. Unpublished manuscript. University of Illinois, 1978.

——— and Jeanne Day. "Macrorules for Summarizing Texts: The Development of Expertise." *Journal of verbal Learning and Verbal Behavior* 22.1 (1983): 1–14.

——— and Annmarie S. Palincsar. *Reciprocal Teaching of Comprehension Strategies: A Natural History of One Program for Enhancing Learning*. Technical Report #334. Urbana, IL: Center for the Study of Reading, 1985.

Churchill, Winston S. *The Birth of Britain*. New York: Dodd, 1956. Vol. 1 of *A History of the English-Speaking Peoples*. 4 vols. 1956–58.

Flower, Linda. "The Construction of Purpose in Writing and Reading." *College English* 50.5 (1988): 528–550.

———. *The Role of Task Representation in Reading to Write*. Berkeley, CA: Center for the Study of Writing, U of California at Berkeley and Carnegie Mellon. Technical Report, 1987.

———. "Writer-Based Prose: A Cognitive Basis for Problems in Writing." *College English* 41 (1979): 19–37.

Flower, Linda, Karen Schriver, Linda Carey, Christina Haas, and John R. Hayes. *Planning in Writing: A Theory of the Cognitive Process*. Berkeley, CA: Center for the Study of Writing, U of California at Berkeley and Carnegie Mellon. Technical Report, 1988.

Ford, James E., and Dennis R. Perry. "Research Paper Instruction in the Undergraduate Writing Program." *College English* 44 (1982): 825–31.

Ford, James E., Sharla Rees, and David L. Ward. *Teaching the Research Paper: Comprehensive Bibliography of Periodical Sources*, 1980. ERIC ED 197 363.

Goldman, Susan R. "Knowledge Systems for Realistic Goals." *Discourse Processes* 5 (1982): 279–303.

Guizot and Guizot de Witt. *The History of France from Earliest Times to 1848*. Trans. R. Black. Vol. 2. Philadelphia: John Wanamaker (n.d.).

Haas, Christina, and Linda Flower. "Rhetorical Reading Strategies and the Construction of Meaning." *College Composition and Communication* 39 (1988): 167–84.

Hayes, John R., D. A. Waterman, and C. S. Robinson. "Identifying the Relevant Aspects of a Problem Text." *Cognitive Science* 1 (1977): 297–313.

Hinze, Helen K. "The Individual's Word Associations and His Interpretation of Prose Paragraphs." *Journal of General Psychology* 64 (1961): 193–203.

Iser, Wolfgang. *The act of reading: A theory of aesthetic response*. Baltimore: The Johns Hopkins UP, 1978.

Jeffery, Christopher. "Teachers' and Students' Perceptions of the Writing Process." *Research in the Teaching of English* 15 (1981): 215–28.

Kantz, Margaret. *Originality and Completeness: What Do We Value in Papers Written from Sources?* Conference on College Composition and Communication. St. Louis, MO, 1988.

———. *The Relationship Between Reading and Planning Strategies and Success in Synthesizing: It's What You Do with Them that Counts.* Technical report in preparation. Pittsburgh: Center for the Study of Writing, 1988.

Kennedy, Mary Louise. "The Composing Process of College Students Writing from Sources." *Written Communication* 2.4 (1985): 434–56.

Kinneavy, James L. *A Theory of Discourse.* New York: Norton, 1971.

Kroll, Barry M. "Audience Adaptation in Children's Persuasive Letters." *Written Communication* 1.4 (1984): 407–28.

Langer, Judith. "Where Problems Start: The Effects of Available Information on Responses to School Writing Tasks." *Contexts for Learning to Write: Studies of Secondary School Instruction.* Ed. Arthur Applebee. Norwood, NJ: ABLEX Publishing Corporation, 1984. 135–48.

Luftig, Richard L. "Abstractive Memory, the Central-Incidental Hypothesis, and the Use of Structural Importance in Text: Control Processes or Structural Features?" *Reading Research Quarterly* 14.1 (1983): 28–37.

Marbaise, Alfred. "Treating a Disease." *Current Issues and Enduring Questions.* Eds. Sylvan Barnet and Hugo Bedau. New York: St. Martin's, 1987. 126–27.

McCormick, Kathleen. "Theory in the Reader: Bleich, Holland, and Beyond." *College English* 47.8 (1985): 836–50.

McGarry, Daniel D. *Medieval History and Civilization.* New York: Macmillan, 1976.

Nelson, Jennie, and John R. Hayes. *The Effects of Classroom Contexts on Students' Responses to Writing from Sources: Regurgitating Information or Triggering Insights.* Berkeley, CA: Center for the Study of Writing, U of California at Berkeley and Carnegie Mellon. Technical Report, 1988.

Pichert, James W. "Sensitivity to Importance as a Predictor of Reading Comprehension." *Perspectives on Reading Research and Instruction.* Eds. Michael A. Kamil and Alden J. Moe. Washington, D.C.: National Reading Conference, 1980. 42–46.

Robinson, Cyril E. *England: A History of British Progress from the Early Ages to the Present Day.* New York: Thom Y. Crowell Company, 1928.

Schwegler, Robert A., and Linda K. Shamoon. "The Aims and Process of the Research Paper." *College English* (1982): 817–24.

Shedd, Patricia T. "The Relationship between Attitude of the Reader Towards Women's Changing Role and R sponse to Literature Which Illuminates Women's Role." *Diss.* Syracuse U, 1975. ERIC ED 142 956.

Short, Elizabeth Jane, and Ellen Bouchard Ryan. "Metacognitive Differences between Skilled and Less Skilled Readers: Remediating Deficits through Story Grammar and Attribution Training." *Journal of Education Psychology* 76 (1984): 225–35.

Spivey, Nancy Nelson. *Discourse Synthesis: Constructing Texts in Reading and Writing.* Diss. U Texas, 1983. Newar DE: International Reading Association, 1984.

Toulmin, Steven E. *The Uses of Argument.* Cambridge: Cambridge UP, 1969.

Vipond, Douglas, and Russell Hunt. "Point-Driven Understanding: Pragmatic and Congnitive Dimensions of Lite ary Reading." *Poetics* 13, (1984): 261–77.

Winograd, Peter. "Strategic Difficulties in Summarizing Texts." *Reading Research Quarterly* 19 (1984): 404–25.

29

Kickin' Reality, Kickin' Ballistics

Robin D. G. Kelly

"Gangsta Rap" and Postindustrial Los Angeles

In ways that we do not easily or willingly define, the gangster speaks for us, expressing that part of the American psyche which rejects the qualities and the demands of modern life, which rejects "American-ism" itself.

—Robert Warshow, *"The Gangster as a Tragic Hero"*[1]

Oppressed peoples cannot avoid admiring their own nihilists, who are the ones dramatically saying "No!" and reminding others that there are worse things than death.

—Eugene Genovese, *Roll, Jordan, Roll*[2]

From Robin D. G. Kelley's *Race Rebels: Culture, Politics, and the Black Working Class* The Free Press, NY, NY: 1994

*fore*WORD: *South Central Los Angeles, April 29, 1992*

Believe it or not, I began working on this chapter well over a year before the Los Angeles Rebellion of 1992, and at least two or three months before Rodney King was turned into a martyr by several police officers and a video camera.[3] Of course, the rebellion both enriched and complicated my efforts to make sense of gangsta rap in late twentieth-century Los Angeles. West Coast gangsta-flavored hip hop—especially in its formative stage—was, in some ways, a foreboding of the insurrection. The previous two years of "research" I spent rocking, bopping, and wincing to gangsta narratives of everyday life were (if I may sample Mike Davis) very much like "excavating the future in Los Angeles." Ice T, truly the "OG" (Original Gangster) of L.A. gangsta rap, summed it up best in a recent *Rolling Stone* interview:

> *When rap came out of L.A., what you heard initially was my voice yelling about South Central. People thought, "That shit's crazy," and ignored it. Then NWA [the rap group Niggas With Attitude] came and yelled, Ice Cube yelled about it. People said, "Oh, that's just kids making a buck." They didn't realize how many niggas with attitude there are out on the street. Now you see them.[4]*

Indeed, though the media believes that the riots began with the shock of the beating of Rodney King, neither the hip hop community nor residents of South Central Los Angeles were really surprised by the videotape. Countless numbers of black Angelenos had experienced or witnessed this sort of terror before. When L.A. rapper Ice Cube was asked about the King incident on MTV, he responded simply, "It's been happening to us for years. It's just we didn't have a camcorder every time it happened." (Subsequently, Cube recorded "Who Got the Camera," a hilarious track in which he asks the police brutalizing him to hit him once more in order to get the event on film.)[5]

Few black Angelenos could forget the 1979 killing of Eula Mae Love, a five-feet four-inch, thirty-nine-year-old widow who was shot a dozen times by two LAPD officers. Police were called after she tried to stop a gas maintenance man from turning off her gas. When they arrived she was armed with a kitchen knife, but the only thing she stabbed was a tree in her yard. Nor could anyone ignore the fifteen deaths caused by LAPD chokeholds in the early eighties, or Chief Darryl Gates's infamous explanation: "We may be finding that in some blacks when [the choke-hold] is applied the veins or arteries do not open up as fast as they do on normal people." And then there were the numerous lesser-known incidents for which no officers were punished. Virtually every South Central resident has experienced routine stops, if not outright harassment, and thousands of African American and Latino youth have had their names and addresses logged in the LAPD antigang task force data base—ironically, called a "rap sheet"—whether they were gang members or not.[6]

The L.A. rebellion merely underscores the fact that a good deal of gangsta rap is (aside from often very funky music to drive to) a window into, and critique of, the criminalization of black youth. Of course, this is not unique to gangsta rap; all kinds of "B-boys" and "B-girls"—rappers, graffiti artists, break dancers—have been dealing with and challenging police repression, the media's criminalization of inner-city youths, and the "just-us" system from the get-go. Like the economy and the city itself, the criminal justice system changed just when hip hop was born. Prisons were no longer just places to discipline; they became dumping grounds to corral bodies labeled a menace to society. Policing in the late twentieth century was designed not to stop or reduce crime in inner-city communities but to manage it.[7] Economic restructuring resulting in massive unemployment has created criminals out of black youth, which is what gangsta rappers acknowledge. But rather than apologize or preach, most attempt to rationalize and explain. Virtually all gangsta rappers write lyrics attacking law enforcement agencies, their denial of unfettered access to public space, and the media's complicity in equating black youth with criminals. Yet, the rappers' own stereotypes of the ghetto as "war zone" and the black youth as "criminal," as well as their adolescent expressions of masculinity and sexuality, in turn structure and constrain their efforts to create a counternarrative of life in the inner city.

Indeed, its masculinist emphasis and pimp-inspired vitriol toward women are central to gangsta rap. While its misogynistic narratives are not supposed to be descriptions of everyday reality, they are offensive and chilling nonetheless. Of course, it can be argued that much of this adolescent misogyny is characteristic of most male youth cultures, since male status is defined in part through heterosexual conquest and domination over women. Part of what distinguishes gangsta rap from "locker room" braggadocio is that it is circulated on compact discs, digital tapes, and radio airwaves. But the story is so much more complicated than this. In order to make sense of the pervasiveness and appeal of the genre's misogyny, I also explore the traditions of sexism in black vernacular culture as well as the specific socioeconomic conditions in which young, urban African American males must negotiate their masculine identities.

Lest we get too sociological here, we must bear in mind that hip hop, irrespective of its particular "flavor," is music. Few doubt it has a message, whether they interpret it as straight-up nihilism or the words of "primitive rebels." Not many pay attention to rap as art—the musical art of, for example, mixing "break beats" (the part of a song where the drums, bass, or guitar are isolated and extended via two turntables or electronic mixers); the verbal art of appropriating old-school "hustler's toasts"; or the art simply trying to be funny. Although what follows admittedly emphasizes lyrics, it also tries to deal with form, style, and aesthetics. As Tricia Rose puts it, "Without historical contextualization, aesthetics are naturalized, and certain cultural practices are made to appear essential to a given group of people. On the other hand, without aesthetic considerations, Black cultural practices are reduced to extensions of sociohistorical circumstances."[8]

Heeding Rose's call for a more multilayered interpretation of cultural forms that takes account of context *and* aesthetics, politics *and* pleasure, I will explore the politics of gangsta rap—its lyrics, music, styles, roots, contradictions, and consistencies—and the place where it seems to have maintained its deepest roots: Los Angeles and its black environs. To do this right we need a historical perspective. We need to go back . . . way back, to the dayz of the O[riginal] G[angster]s. This, then, is a tale of very recent and slightly less recent urban race rebels, a tale that cannot be totally separated from black workers' sabotage in the Jim Crow South or young black passengers' "acting up" on streetcars in wartime Birmingham. Still, these more recent tales of rebellion, which highlight the problems of gangsta rappers against a background of racial "progress," reveal that the black working class of the late twentieth-century city faces a fundamentally different reality—the postindustrial city.

OGs in Postindustrial Los Angeles: Evolution of a Style

L.A. might be the self-proclaimed home of gangsta rap, but black Angelenos didn't put the gangsta into hip hop. Gangsta lyrics and style were part of the whole hip hop scene from its origins in the South Bronx during the mid-1970s. In Charlie Ahearn's classic 1982 film *Wild Style* about the early hip hop scene in New York, the rap duo Double Trouble stepped on stage decked out in white "pimp-style" suits, matching hats, and guns galore. Others in the film are "strapped" (armed) as well, waving real guns as part of the act. The scene seems so contemporary, and yet it was shot over a decade before the media paid attention to such rap songs as Onyx's "Throw Ya Guns in the Air."[9]

But to find the roots of gangsta rap's violent images, explicit language, and outright irreverence, we need to go back even further. Back before Lightin' Rod (aka Jalal Uridin of the Last Poets) performed toasts (narrative poetry from the black oral tradition) over live music on a popular album called *Hustlers' Convention* in 1973; before Lloyd Price recorded the classic black baaadman narrative, "Stagger Lee," in 1958; even before Screamin' Jay Hawkins recorded his explicitly sexual comedy "rap" "Alligator Wine." Indeed, in 1938 folklorist Alan Lomax recorded Jelly Roll Morton performing a number of profane and violent songs out of the black vernacular, including "The Murder Ballad" and "Make Me a Pallet on the Floor." Morton's lyrics rival the worst of today's gangsta rappers: "Come here you sweet bitch, give me that pussy, let me get in your drawers/I'm gonna make you think you fuckin' with Santa Claus." In other words, we need to go back to the blues, to the baaadman tales of the late nineteenth century, and to the age-old tradition of "signifying" if we want to discover the roots of the "gangsta" aesthetic in hip hop. Irreverence has been a central component of black expressive vernacular culture, which is why violence and sex have been as important to toasting and signifying as playfulness with language. Many of these narratives are about power. Both the baaadman and the trickster embody a challenge to virtually *all* authority (which makes sense to people for whom justice is a rare thing), creates an imaginary upside-down world where the oppressed are the powerful, and it reveals to listeners the pleasures and price of reckless abandon. And in a world where male public powerlessness is often turned inward on women and children, misogyny and stories of sexual conflict are very old examples of the "price" of being baaad.[10]

Nevertheless, while gangsta rap's roots are very old, it does have an identifiable style of its own, and in some respects it is a particular product of the mid-1980s. The inspiration for the specific style we now call gangsta rap seems to have come from Philadelphia's Schooly D, who made *Smoke Some Kill,* and the Bronx-based rapper KRS 1 and Scott La Rock of Boogie Down Productions, who released *Criminal Minded.* Although both albums appeared in 1987, these rappers had been developing an East Coast gangsta style for some time. Ice T, who started out with the technopop wave associated with Radio and Uncle Jam's Army (recording his first single, "The Coldest Rap," in 1981), moved gangsta rap to the West Coast when he recorded "6 in the Mornin' " in 1986. Less than a year later, he released his debut album, *Rhyme Pays*.[11]

Ice T was not only the first West Coast gangsta-style rapper on wax, but he was himself an experienced OG whose narratives were occasionally semi-autobiographical or drawn from things he had witnessed or heard on the street. A native of New Jersey who moved to Los Angeles as a child, "T" (Tracy Marrow) joined a gang while at Crenshaw High School and began a very short career as a criminal. He eventually graduated from Crenshaw, attended a junior college, and, with practically no job prospects, turned to the armed services. After four years in the service, he pursued his high school dream to become a rapper and starred in a documentary film called "Breaking and Entering," which captured the West Coast break dance scene. When Hollywood made a fictionalized version of the film called "Breakin'," Ice T also made an appearance. Although Ice T's early lyrics ranged from humorous boasts and tales of crime and violence to outright misogyny, they were clearly as much fact as fiction. In "Squeeze the Trigger" he leads off with a brief autobiographical, composite sketch of his gangsta background, insisting all along that he is merely a product of a callous, brutal society.[12]

Even before *Rhyme Pays* hit the record stores (though banned on the radio because of its explicit lyrics), an underground hip hop community was forming in Compton, a predominantly black and Latino city south of Los Angeles, that would play a pivotal role in the early history of gangsta rap. Among the participants was Eric Wright—better known as Eazy E—who subsequently launched an independent label known as Ruthless Records. He eventually teamed up with Dr. Dre and Yella, both of whom had left the rap group World Class Wreckin Cru, and Ice Cube, who was formerly a member of a group called The CIA. Together they formed Niggas With Attitude and moved gangsta rap to another level. Between 1987 and 1988, Ruthless produced a string of records, beginning with their twelve-inch *NWA and the Posse,* Eazy E's solo album, *Eazy Duz It,* and the album which put NWA on the map, *Straight Outta Compton*.[13] Dr. Dre's brilliance as a producer—his introduction of hard, menacing beats, sparse drum tracks, and heavy bass with slower tempos—and Ice Cube's genius as a lyricist, made NWA one of the most compelling groups on the hip hop scene in years.

A distinctive West Coast style of gangsta rap, known for its rich descriptive storytelling laid over heavy funk samples[14] from the likes of George Clinton and the whole Parliament-Funkadelic family, Sly Stone, Rick James, Ohio Players, Average White Band, Cameo, Zapp and, of course, the Godfather himself—James Brown—evolved and proliferated rapidly soon after the appearance of Ice T and NWA. The frequent use of Parliament-Funkadelic samples led one critic to dub the music "G-Funk (gangsta attitude over P-Funk beats)."[15] Within three years, dozens of Los Angeles-based groups came onto the scene, many produced by either Eazy E's Ruthless Records, Ice T and Afrika Islam's Rhyme Syndicate Productions, Ice Cube's post-NWA project, Street Knowledge Productions, or Dr. Dre's Deathrow Records. The list of West Coast gangsta rappers includes Above the Law, Mob Style, Compton's Most Wanted, King Tee, The Rhyme Syndicate, Snoop Doggy Dogg, (Lady of) Rage, Poison Clan, Capital Punishment Organization (CPO), the predominantly Samoan Boo-Yaa Tribe, the DOC, DJ Quick, AMG, Hi-C, Low Profile, Nu Niggaz on the Block, South Central Cartel, Compton Cartel, 2nd II

None, W.C. and the MAAD (Minority Alliance of Anti-Discrimination) Circle, Cypress Hill, and Chicano rappers like Kid Frost and Proper Dos.

Although they shared much with the larger hip hop community, gangsta rappers drew both praise and ire from their colleagues. Indeed, gangsta rap has generated more debate both within and without the hip hop world than any other genre.[16] Unfortunately, much of this debate, especially in the media, has only disseminated misinformation. Thus, it is important to clarify what gangsta rap is *not*. First, gangsta rappers have never merely celebrated gang violence, nor have they taken a partisan position in favor of one gang over another. Gang bangin' (gang participation) itself has never even been a central theme in the music. Many of the violent lyrics are not intended to be literal. Rather, they are boasting raps in which the imagery of gang bangin' is used metaphorically to challenge competitors on the microphone—an element common to all hard-core hip hop. The mic becomes a Tech-9 or AK-47, imagined drive-bys occur from the stage, flowing lyrics become hollow-point shells. Classic examples are Ice Cube's "Jackin' for Beats," a humorous song that describes sampling other artists and producers as outright armed robbery, and Ice T's "Pulse of the Rhyme" or "Grand Larceny" (which brags about stealing a show), Capital Punishment Organization's aptly titled warning to other perpetrating rappers, "Homicide," NWA's "Real Niggaz," Dr. Dre's "Lyrical Gangbang," Ice Cube's, "Now I Gotta Wet'cha," Compton's Most Wanted's "Wanted" and "Straight Check N' Em." Sometimes, as in the case of Ice T's "I'm Your Pusher," an antidrug song that boasts of pushing "dope beats and lyrics/no beepers needed," gangsta rap lyrics have been misinterpreted by journalists and talk show hosts as advocating criminality and violence.[17]

This is not to say that all descriptions of violence are simply metaphors. Exaggerated and invented boasts of criminal acts should sometimes be regarded as part of a larger set of signifying practices. Performances like The Rhyme Syndicate's "My Word Is Bond" or J.D.'s storytelling between songs on Ice Cube's *AmeriKKKa's Most Wanted* are supposed to be humorous and, to a certain extent, unbelievable. Growing out of a much older set of cultural practices, these masculinist narratives are essentially verbal duels over who is the "baddest motherfucker around." They are not meant as literal descriptions of violence and aggression, but connote the playful use of language itself. So when J.D. boasts about how he used to "jack them motherfuckers for them Nissan trucks," the story is less about stealing per se than about the way in which he describes his bodaciousness.[18]

When gangsta rappers do write lyrics intended to convey a sense of social realism, their work loosely resembles a sort of street ethnography of racist institutions and social practices, but told more often than not in the first person. Whether gangsta rappers step into the character of a gang banger, hustler, or ordinary working person—that is, products and residents of the " 'hood"—the important thing to remember is that they are stepping into character; it is for descriptive purposes rather than advocacy. In some ways, these descriptive narratives, under the guise of objective "street journalism," are no less polemical (hence political) than nineteenth-century slave narratives in defense of abolition. When Ice Cube was still with NWA he explained, "We call ourselves underground street reporters. We just tell it how we see it, nothing more, nothing less."[19]

It would be naive to claim that descriptive lyrics, as an echo of the city, do not, in turn, magnify what they describe—but to say so is a far cry from claiming that the purpose of rap is to advocate violence. And, of course, rappers' reality is hardly "objective" in the sense of being detached; their standpoint is that of the ghetto dweller, the criminal, the victim of police repression, the teenage father, the crack slanger, the gang banger, and the female dominator. Much like the old "baaad-man" narratives that have played an important role in black vernacular folklore, the characters they create, at first glance, appear to be apolitical individuals only out for themselves; and like the protagonist in Melvin Van Peebles's cinematic classic, *Sweet Sweetback's Baaadass Song,* they are reluctant to trust anyone. It is hard not to miss the influences of urban toasts and "pimp narratives," which became popular during the late 1960s and early 1970s. In many instances the characters are almost identical, and on occasion rap artists pay tribute to black vernacular oral poetry by lyrically "sampling" these early pimp narratives.[20]

For other consumers of gangsta rap, such as middle-class white males, the genre unintentionally serves the same role as blaxploitation films of the 1970s or, for that matter, gangster films of any generation. It attracts listeners for whom the "ghetto" is a place of adventure, unbridled violence, erotic fantasy, and/or an imaginary alternative to suburban boredom. White music critic John Leland once praised NWA because they "dealt in evil as fantasy: killing cops, smoking hos, filling quiet nights with a flurry of senseless buckshot." This kind of voyeurism partly explains NWA's huge white following and why their album, *Efil4zaggin,* shot to the top of the charts as soon as it was released. As one critic put it, "In reality, NWA have more in common with a Charles Bronson movie than a PBS documentary on the plight of the inner-cities." And why should it be otherwise? After all, NWA members have even admitted that some of their recent songs were not representations of reality "in the hood" but inspired by popular films like *Innocent Man* starring Tom Selleck and *Tango and Cash* starring Sylvester Stallone and Kurt Russell.[21]

While I'm fully aware that some rappers are merely "studio gangstas," and that the *primary* purpose of this music is to produce "funky dope rhymes" for our listening pleasure, we cannot ignore the fact that West Coast gangsta rap originated in, and continues to maintain ties to, the streets of L.A.'s black working-class communities. The generation that came of age in the 1980s was the product of devastating structural changes in the urban economy that date back at least to the late 1960s. While the city as a whole experienced unprecedented growth, the communities of Watts and Compton faced increased economic displacement, factory closures, and an unprecedented deepening of poverty. The uneven development of L.A.'s postindustrial economy meant an expansion of high-tech firms like Aerospace and Lockheed, and the disappearance of rubber and steel manufacturing firms, many of which were located in or near Compton and Watts. Deindustrialization, in other words, led to the establishment of high-tech firms in less populated regions like Silicon Valley and Orange County. Developers and local governments helped the suburbanization process while simultaneously cutting back expenditures for parks, recreation, and affordable housing in inner-city communities. Thus since 1980 economic conditions in Watts deteriorated on a greater scale than in any other L.A. community, and by some estimates Watts is in worse shape now than in 1965. A 1982 report from the California Legislature revealed that South

Central neighborhoods experienced a 50 percent rise in unemployment while purchasing power dropped by one-third. The median income for South Central L.A.'s residents was a paltry $5,900–$2,500 below the median income for the black population a few years earlier.

Youth were the hardest hit. For all of Los Angeles County, the unemployment rate of black youth remained at about 45 percent, but in areas with concentrated poverty the rate was even higher. As the composition of L.A.'s urban poor becomes increasingly younger, programs for inner-city youth are being wiped out at an alarming rate. Both the Neighborhood Youth Corps and the Comprehensive Employment and Training Act (CETA) have been dismantled, and the Jobs Corps and Los Angeles Summer Job Program have been cut back substantially.[22]

Thus, on the eve of crack cocaine's arrival on the urban landscape, the decline in employment opportunities and growing immizeration of black youth in L.A. led to a substantial rise in property crimes committed by juveniles and young adults. Even NWA recalls the precrack illicit economy in a song titled "The Dayz of Wayback," in which Dr. Dre and M. C. Ren wax nostalgic about the early to mid-1980s, when criminal activity consisted primarily of small-time muggings and robberies.[23] Because of its unusually high crime rate, L.A. had by that time gained the dubious distinction of having the largest urban prison population in the country. When the crack economy made its presence felt in inner-city black communities, violence intensified as various gangs and groups of peddlers battled for control over markets. In spite of the violence and financial vulnerability that went along with peddling crack, for many black youngsters it was the most viable economic option.[24]

While the rise in crime and the ascendance of the crack economy might have put money into some people's pockets, for the majority it meant greater police repression. Watts, Compton, Northwest Pasadena, Carson, North Long Beach, and several other black working-class communities were turned into war zones during the mid- to late 1980s. Police helicopters, complex electronic surveillance, even small tanks armed with battering rams became part of this increasingly militarized urban landscape. During this same period, housing projects, such as Imperial Courts, were renovated along the lines of minimum security prisons and equipped with fortified fencing and an LAPD substation. Imperial Court residents were now required to carry identity cards and visitors were routinely searched. As popular media coverage of the inner city associated drugs and violence with black youth, young African Americans by virtue of being residents in South Central L.A. and Compton were subject to police harassment and, in some cases, feared by older residents.[25]

All of these problems generated penetrating critiques by gangsta rappers. M. C. Ren, for example, blamed "the people who are holding the dollars in the city" for the expansion of gang violence and crime, arguing that if black youth had decent jobs, they would not need to participate in the illicit economy. "It's their fault simply because they refused to employ black people. How would you feel if you went for job after job and each time, for no good reason, you're turned down?"[26] Ice T blames capitalism entirely, which he defines as much more than alienating wage labor; the marketplace itself as well as a variety of social institutions are intended to exercise social control over African Americans. "Capitalism says you must have an upper class, a middle class, and a lower class. . . . Now the only way to guarantee a lower class, is to keep y'all uneducated and as high as possible."[27] According to Ice T, the ghetto is, at worst, the product of deliberately oppressive policies, at best, the result of racist neglect. Nowhere is this clearer than in his song "Escape from the Killing Fields," which uses the title of a recent film about the conflict in Cambodia as a metaphor for the warlike conditions in today's ghettos.[28]

Gangsta rappers construct a variety of first-person narratives to illustrate how social and economic realities in late capitalist L.A. affect young black men. Although the use of first-person narratives is rooted in a long tradition of black aesthetic practices,[29] the use of "I" to signify both personal and collective experiences also enables gangsta rappers to navigate a complicated course between what social scientists call "structure" and "agency." In gangsta rap there is almost always a relationship between the conditions in which these characters live and the decisions they make. Some gangsta rappers—Ice Cube in particular—are especially brilliant at showing how, if I may paraphrase Marx, young urban black men make their own history but not under circumstances of their own choosing.

"Broke Niggas Make the Best Crooks"[30]

The press is used to make the victim look like the criminal and make the criminal look like the victim.

       —Malcolm X, "Not Just an American Problem"[31]

In an era when popular media, conservative policy specialists, and some social scientists are claiming that the increase in street crime can be explained by some pathological culture of violence bereft of the moderating influences of a black middle class (who only recently fled to the suburbs), L.A.'s gangsta rappers keep returning to the idea that joblessness and crime are directly related.[32] Consider W.C. and the MAAD Circle's manifesto on the roots of inner-city crime. Its title, "If You Don't Work, U Don't Eat," appropriates Bobby Byrd's late 1960s' hit song of the same title (it, too, is sampled), and replicates a very popular Old Left adage. Describing the song in a recent interview, W.C. explained the context in which it was conceived: "I've got to feed a family. Because I don't have [job] skills I have no alternative but to turn this way. My little girl don't take no for an answer, my little boy don't take no for an answer, my woman's not going to take no for an answer, so I gotta go out and make my money."[33] In the song, members from his own crew as well as guest artists (M. C. Eiht from Compton's Most Wanted [CMW] and J.D. from Ice Cube's posse, Da Lench Mob) each give their own personal perspective on how they (or their character) became criminals. For MAAD Circle rapper Coolio, crime is clearly a means of survival, though he is fully cognizant that each job he pulls might lead to death or incarceration.[34] M. C. Eiht (pronounced "eight") of CMW openly declares that crime is his way of resisting wage labor ("I ain't punchin' a clock"), but admits with some remorse that his victims are usually regular black folk in the hood. Unless conditions change, he insists, neighborhood crime will continue to be a way of life.[35]

Ice Cube's "A Bird in the Hand," from his controversial album *Death Certificate,* is about the making of a young drug peddler. In this narrative, Cube plays a working-class black man just out of high school who can't afford college and is consistently turned down for medium-wage service-sector jobs. Because he is also a father trying to provide financial support for his girlfriend and their baby, he decides to take the only "slave" (job) available—at McDonald's. As the bass line is thumpin' over well-placed samples of screaming babies in the background, Ice Cube looks for another way out. It does not take much reflection for him to realize that the drug dealers are the only people in his neighborhood making decent money. Although his immediate material conditions improve, he now must face constant hounding from police and the mass media: "Now you put the feds against me/ Cause I couldn't follow the plan of the presidency/ I'm never gettin' love again/ But blacks are too fuckin' broke to be Republican." In the end, the blame for the rapid expansion of crack is placed squarely on the Bush administration. "Sorry, but this is our only room to walk/ Cause we don't want to drug push/ But a bird in the hand, is worth more than a Bush."[36]

The characters in gangsta narratives defy our attempts to define them as Robin Hoods or "criminal-criminals."[37] The very same voices we hear "jackin' " (robbing) other brothers and sisters occasionally call on male gangsters to turn their talents against the state. In "Get up off that Funk," W.C. and the MAAD Circle take a sort of Robin Hood stand, declaring that their own agenda includes jackin' the powerful and distributing the wealth. Rapping over a heavy bass and trap drum, reminiscent of the hardcore "go-go" music one hears in the darker side of the nation's capital, W.C. describes the Minority Alliance of Anti-Discrimination as an organization intent on stealing from the rich to give "to the poor folks in the slums."[38]

Ice Cube takes the Robin Hood metaphor a step further, calling for the "ultimate drive-by" to be aimed at the U.S. government. In a recent interview, he even suggested that gang bangers "are our warriors. . . . It's just they're fighting the wrong gang." The gang they ought to be fighting, he tells us, is "the government of the United States."[39] "I Wanna Kill Sam" on his album *Death Certificate* is his declaration of gang warfare on America. It begins with Cube loading up his "gat" in anticipation of taking out the elusive Uncle Sam. Following a brief interlude— a fictional public service announcement on behalf of the Armed Services—Cube gives us his own version of American history in which the slave trade, forced labor in the era of freedom, and army recruitment are all collapsed into a single narrative of racist repression and exploitation. He then connects the "pasts" to the present, suggesting that while the same old racism still lingers, the victims are unwilling to accept the terms of order. Instead of retreats and nonviolent protests, there will be straight jackin', gangsta style. Da Lench Mob's "Guerrillas in tha Midst" takes its title from an infamous LAPD term describing African Americans in the vicinity, which itself puns on the popular film set in Africa titled *Gorillas in the Mist*. But for Da Lench Mob, the "gorillas" are America's nightmare, organized and armed gangstas ready for the Big Payback.[40]

Of course, the idea of street gangs like the Crips and Bloods becoming a revolutionary guerrilla army seems ludicrous, especially given the role street gangs have assumed as protectors of the illicit economy. Consider the words of a Chicano gang member from Los Angeles: "I act like they do in the big time, no different. There ain't no corporation that acts with morals and that ethics shit and I ain't about to either. As they say, if it's good for General Motors, it's good enough for me."[41] Hardly the stuff one would expect from an inner-city rebel. Nevertheless, we need to keep in mind that the hip hop generation consumed movies like *The Spook Who Sat by the Door,* a film version of Sam Greenlee's novel about a former black CIA agent who uses his training to turn gang members into a revolutionary army. *The Autobiography of Malcolm X* convinced unknown numbers of kids that even second-rate gangsters can become political radicals. It's possible that a few black Angelenos absorbed some OG oral history about the gang roots of the Black Panther Party. L.A. Panther leaders Bunchy Carter and John Huggins were former members of the Slausons gang, and their fellow banger, Brother Crook (aka Ron Wilkins), founded the Community Alert Patrol to challenge police brutality in the late 1960s. And the postrebellion role of gang leaders in drafting and proposing the first viable plan of action to rebuild South Central Los Angeles cannot be overlooked. Indeed, much like today, both the presence of the Nation of Islam and the rise in police brutality played pivotal roles in politicizing individual gang members.[42]

By treating crime as a mode of survival and as a form of rebellion, gangsta rappers partly serve to idealize criminal activity. However, they also use the same narrative strategies—the use of first-person autobiographical accounts or the ostensibly more objective "street journalism"—to criticize inner-city crime and violence. Songs like Ice T's "Pain," "6 in the Mornin,' " "Colors," "New Jack Hustler," and "High Rollers"; Ice Cube's "Dead Homiez" and "Color Blind"; NWA's "Alwayz into Somethin' "; Cypress Hill's "Hand on the Pump" and "Hole in the Head"; and the gangsta groups that participated in making "We're All in the Same Gang" express clear messages that gang banging and jackin' for a living usually ends in death or incarceration—that is, if you're caught.[43] CPO's "The Wall" (as well as "The Movement," and sections from "Gangsta Melody"), performed by their quick-tongued lead lyricist Lil Nation, rail against drive-by shootings, the rising rate of black-on-black homicide, and brothers who try to escape reality by "Cold drinkin' 8-ball." Lil Nation even breaks with the majority of his fellow gangsta rappers by announcing that black youth today need more religion, a better set of values, and a radical social movement.[44]

Most gangsta rappers, however, are not so quick to criticize violence, arguing that it is the way of the street. This reticence is certainly evident in Ice Cube's advice that "if you is or ain't a gang banger/ keep one in the chamber" as well as his tongue-in-cheek call to replace guard dogs with guns ("A Man's Best Friend"). Even his anti-gang song, "Color Blind," implies that inner-city residents should be armed and ready in the event of a shoot-out or attempted robbery. Likewise, MAAD Circle rappers Coolio and W.C. emphasize the need for protection. Although they both agree that gang banging will ultimately lead to death or prison, they also realize that "rolling with a crew" serves the same purpose as carrying a gun. As Coolio points out, "They say on the radio and TV that you have a choice, but it's bullshit. If you're getting your ass whipped everyday, you've got to have some protection."[45]

The gendering of crime also helps explain why gangsta rappers are reluctant to denounce violence, why the criminals in their narratives are almost always men, and why, in part, violence against women appears consistently in the music of many gangsta groups. As criminologist James Messerschmidt reminds us, "Throughout our society . . . violence is associated with power and males, and for some youth this association is reinforced as part of family life. As a result, most young males come to identify the connection between masculinity-power-aggression-violence as part of their own developing male identities." Being a man, therefore, means not "taking any shit" from anyone, which is why the characters in gangsta rap prefer to use a gat rather than flee the scene, and why drive-by shootings are often incited by public humiliations. Second, although it might be argued that men dominate these narratives because they construct them, it is also true that the preponderance of street crime is committed by marginalized males. The matter is far too complicated to discuss in detail here, but several scholars attribute these patterns to higher rates of male unemployment, greater freedom from the restraints of the household compared to females (i.e., more opportunities to engage in criminal activity), and a patriarchal culture that makes earning power a measure of manhood.[46]

The misogyny of gangsta rap is deeply ingrained. Most gangsta rappers take violence against women for granted. It is primarily the dark, nasty side of *male-on-male* street violence that they attempt to illustrate. Sir Jinx's use of documentary-style recordings of simulated drive-by's and fights that escalate into gun battles are intended to deromanticize gang violence.[47] A much more clear-cut example is CMW's "Drive By Miss Daisy," a powerful, complex depiction of the ways in which ordinary bystanders can become victims of intergang warfare. The story begins with a young man assigned to assassinate a rival gang-banger who had just killed his homie. Afraid and intimidated, he decides to get drunk before calling his posse together for the drive-by. When they finally pull up in front of the house, he is apparently unaware that the boy's mother is in the kitchen cooking dinner. Just before he pulls the trigger his conscience intervenes for a second and he questions the morality of his actions. But because of gang loyalty, he does the deed just the same.

What makes the song so compelling is its music. Although CMW had already established a reputation among gangsta rappers for employing more laid-back jazz and quiet storm tracks than hardcore funk, their choice of music in "Drive By" was clearly intended to heighten the intensity rather than provide an understated backdrop for their lead rapper. Thus we hear straight-ahead modal jazz circa 1960s—heavy ride and crash cymbals and acoustic bass beneath the laid-back and strangely cartoonish, high-pitched voice of M. C. Eiht. The two instrumental interludes are even more powerful. The bass and cymbal combination is violently invaded by an acoustic piano playing strong, dissonant block chords very much in the vein of Don Pullen or Stanley Cowell. Mixed in are the sounds of automatic weapons, a looped sample of blood-curdling screams that has the effect of creating an echo without reverberation, and samples of would-be assassins hollering "you die motherfucker." This disturbing cacophony of sounds all at once captures the fragility of human life, the chaos of violent death, and the intensity of emotions young murderers and their victims must feel.[48]

Ice Cube's "Dead Homiez" uses a graveyard to reflect on the tragedy of inner-city homicide. An able storyteller, he is especially effective at painting a detailed picture of his homie's funeral, interrupting periodically with loving as well as frustrating memories of his dead friend. No matter how many forty-ounce bottles of malt liquor he downs, his friend's death continues to haunt him: "Still hear the screams from his mother/as my nigger lay dead in the gutter." The anger, pain, confusion, and fear of those left behind are all inscribed in the ritual of mourning.[49]

Drug dealers have been a common target of gangsta rap from the beginning. One of NWA's very first releases, "Dope Man," offers some brutal insights into the effects of the rising crack cocaine economy. Screamed over electronic drum tracks and a Middle Eastern-sounding reed instrument, Dr. Dre first declares that "If you smoke 'caine you a stupid motherfucker" and then goes on to describe some nameless "crackhead" whose habit forced him into a life of crime.[50] CPO's "The Movement" and "The Wall" wage frontal attacks on all pushers, whom he accuses of committing genocide against black people; he advocates a social movement to wipe them out, since law enforcement is half-hearted and the justice system both inept and corrupt.[51]

Because most gangsta rappers simultaneously try to explain why people turn to drug dealing and other assorted crimes, and vehemently attack drug dealers for the damage they do to poor black communities, they have often been accused of being inconsistent, contradictory, or even schizophrenic. For example, on the same album with "A Bird in the Hand," Ice Cube includes an uncompromising attack on drug dealers, calling them "killers" and insisting that they exploit black people "like the caucasians did."[52] That Cube finds nothing redeeming in the activities of crack peddlers underscores the point that his descriptions are not intended as advocacy. His effort to explain why the drug trade is so appealing to some inner-city residents is not an uncritical acceptance of it. Indeed, "My Summer Vacation," a third song on his *Death Certificate* album about the crack economy, not only reveals the immense violence that goes along with carving out new markets, but borrows from typical images of legitimate entrepreneurship to argue that legal and illicit capitalism are two sides of the same coin—both are ruthless, exploitative, and often produce violence. The point is certainly not to glorify violence. Similarly, Ice T, in "New Jack Hustler," not only suffers from a "capitalist migraine" but asks if the luxury he enjoys as a big-time drug dealer is "a nightmare, or the American dream?" His implication is clear, for this particular enterprise leads to death, destruction, and violence rather than accumulation and development.[53]

Let me not overstate my case, for these economic critiques resist labels. The recasting of capitalism as gangsterism is not simply intended to legitimate the illicit economy or de-legitimate capitalist exploitation. Gangsta rappers discuss capitalism in varying contexts, and to portray them as uniformly or consistently anti-capitalist would certainly misrepresent them. All groups emphasize getting paid and, in real life, the more successful artists invest in their own production companies. They understand better than their audiences that music is a business and rapping is a job. At the same time, being paid for their work does not mean they accept the current economic arrangements or think their music lacks integrity. On the contrary, for many black and Latino working-class youth who turned to hip hop music, rapping, deejaying, or producing is a means to avoid low-wage labor or, possibly, incarceration. As Cube said of his own crew, "You can either sell dope or get your ass a job/ I'd rather roll with the Lench Mob."[54]

Their ambivalence toward capitalism notwithstanding, gangsta rappers are consistent about tracing criminal behavior and vicious individualism to mainstream American culture. Contrary to the new "culture of poverty" theorists who claim that the lifestyles of the so-called black "underclass" constitute a significant deviation from mainstream values, most gangsta rappers insist that the characters they rap about epitomize what America has been and continues to be. In challenging the equation of criminality with some sort of "underclass" culture, Ice T retorts, "America stole from the Indians, sure and prove/What's that? A straight up nigga move!" Similarly, in "AmeriKKKa's Most Wanted," Ice Cube considers crime as American as apple pie: "It's the American way/ I'm a G-A-N-G-S-T-A." He even takes a swipe at the purest of American popular heroes, Superman. The man who stands for Truth, Justice, and the American Way is appropriated and then inverted as Public Enemy Number 1. From Ice Cube's perspective, Superman is a hero because the Americanism he represents is nothing but gangsterism. Donning the cape himself, Cube declares, "I'm not a rebel or a renegade on a quest, I'm a Nigga with an 'S'/So in case you get the kryptonite/I'm gonna rip tonight cause I'm scaring ya/ Wanted by America."[55]

These artists are even less ambiguous when applying the gangster metaphor to the people and institutions that control their lives—especially politicians, the state, and police departments. Ice T's "Street Killer," for example, is a brief monologue that sounds like the boasts of a heartless gangbanger but turns out to be a cop. In a recent interview, Coolio and W.C. of the MAAD Circle reverse the dominant discourse about criminals, insisting that the powerful, not powerless, ghetto dwellers, are the real gangsters:

COOLIO: Who's the real gangsta, the brotha with the khakis on, the brotha with the Levis on or the muthafucka in the suit? Who's the real gangsta?

W.C.:   Well, the suit is running the world, that's the real gangsta right there.[56]

Dozens of rap artists, both inside and outside L.A., indict "America" for stealing land, facilitating the drug trade either through inaction or active participation of the CIA and friendly dictators, and waging large-scale "drive-by shootings" against little countries such as Panama and Iraq. In the aftermath of the L.A. uprising, while politicians and media spokespersons called black participants "criminals" and "animals," Ice Cube reminded whoever would listen that, "The looting . . . in South-Central was nothing like the looting done by the savings and loans." Cube's video for "Who's the Mack," which reveals a photo of George Bush playing golf over the caption "President Mack" and a graffiti American flag with skull and crossbones replacing the stars, further underscored the argument that violence and gangsterism are best exemplified by the state, not young inner-city residents.[57]

Police repression remains gangsta rap's primary target. We must bear in mind that this subgenre was born amidst the militarization of Compton, Watts, and other black communities like Southgate, Carson, Northwest Pasadena, Paramount, and North Long Beach, which became the battlefields of the so-called "war on drugs" in L.A. The recasting of South Central as an American war zone was brought to us on NBC Nightly News, in Dan Rather's special report "48 Hours: On Gang Street," and in Hollywood films like *Colors* and *Boyz in the Hood*. *Straight Outta Compton*, for example, was released about the time Chief Darryl Gates implemented "Operation HAMMER," when almost 1,500 black youth in South Central were picked up for merely "looking suspicious." While most were charged with minor offenses like curfew and traffic violations, some were not charged at all but simply had their names and addresses logged in the LAPD anti-gang task force data base.[58] In this context NWA released their now classic anthem, "F———Tha Police." Opening with a mock trial in which NWA is the judge and jury and the police are the defendants, each member of the group offers his own testimony. After promising to tell "the whole truth and nothing but the truth," Ice Cube takes the stand and explodes with an indictment against racism, repression, and the common practice of criminalizing all black youth. NWA emphasizes the fact that police repression is no longer a simple matter of white racists with a badge, for black cops are just as bad, if not worse, than white cops.[59]

L.A. rappers have since expanded their critique of the relationship between police repression and their own political and economic powerlessness. Ice Cube's solo effort, NWA's most recent album, and groups like Compton's Most Wanted ("They Still Gafflin"), Cypress Hill ("Pigs" and "How I Could Just Kill a Man"), Kid Frost ("I Got Pulled Over" and "Penitentiary") to name but a few, try to place their descriptions of police repression within a broader context of social control.[60] "One Time's" or "Five-O's," as the police are called in L.A., are portrayed as part of a larger system of racist and class domination that includes black officers. For W.C. and the MAAD Circle, policing as a form of racial and class oppression is part of a longer historical tradition etched in the collective memory of African Americans. "Behind Closed Doors" begins with lead rapper W.C. writing a letter of complaint to the chief of police describing an incident in which he was beaten and subsequently shot by officers with no provocation. In just a few lines, W.C. links antebellum slavery and depression-era fascism to the more recent police beating of Rodney King.[61]

Mirroring much current political discourse in urban black America, some gangsta rappers implicitly or explicitly suggest that police repression is a genocidal war against black men.[62] "Real Niggaz Don't Die," which samples the Last Poets' live performance of "Die Nigger," and Ice Cube's "Endangered Species (Tales from the Darkside)" construct black males as the prey of vicious, racist police officers. Cube's lyrics underscore the point that the role of law enforcement is to protect the status quo and keep black folks in check:

Every cop killer goes ignored,
They just send another nigger to the morgue.
A point scored. They could give a fuck about us.
They'd rather catch us with guns and white powder.

They'll kill ten of me to get the job correct
To serve, protect, and break a nigga's neck[63]

In the title track of *AmeriKKKa's Most Wanted,* in which Ice Cube assumes the role of an inner-city criminal who ventures into the suburbs, he closes the song having learned a valuable lesson about community differences in policing: "I think back when I was robbing my own kind/The police didn't pay it no mind/But when I started robbing the white folks/Now I'm in the pen with the soap on the rope."

"Behind Closed Doors" by W.C. and the MAAD Circle speaks to the less dramatic incidents of police repression that frequently have greater resonance among black youth. In one of the stories, Circle rapper Coolio is a recently discharged ex-convict working hard to survive legitimately, until he is stopped and harassed for no apparent reason by "the same crooked cop from a long time ago/ Who planted an ounce in my homie's El Camino." He and the cop exchange blows, but instead of taking him into custody the officer and his partner decide to drop him off in hostile gang territory in order to incite violence. Coolio's narrative is more than plausible: among the tactics adopted by Chief Darryl Gates in his antigang sweeps was to draw out gang bangers by "leaving suspects on enemy turfs, writing over Crip graffiti with Blood colors (or vice versa) and spreading incendiary rumors."[64]

Even more common to the collective experience of young black residents of L.A.'s inner city was the police policy of identifying presumably suspicious characters on the basis of clothing styles. Indeed, officers who were part of the Gang Related Active Trafficker Suppression program were told to "interrogate anyone who they suspect is a gang member, basing their assumptions on their dress or their use of gang hand signals."[65] Opposition to this kind of marking, along the lines of a battle for the right to free expression and unfettered mobility in public spaces, has been a central subtheme in gangsta rap's discursive war of position against police repression. In CMW's cut "Still Gafflin," lead rapper M. C. Eiht complains that the police are "on my dick trying to jack me/ I guess because I sport a hat and the khakis." Perhaps the sharpest critique is W.C. and the MAAD Circle's "Dress Code." Directed at ordinary white citizens, club owners, as well as police officers, the Circle tell stories of being stereotyped as common criminals or gang bangers by complete strangers, all of whom presume that "If you dress like me, you gotta run with a crew." Clothing also signifies status, as is evident in the way W.C. is treated when he tries to get into a club: "Got a wear a silk shirt/ just to dance to a funky song." Nevertheless, he and his crew not only refuse to apologize for their appearance, insisting all along that young working-class black men have the right to dress as they please without being treated with fear or contempt, but W.C. also attributes his style to his class position. Because he "can't afford to shop at Macy's or Penney's . . . its off to the swap meet for a fresh pair of dicky's [khaki pants]."[66]

Of course, style politics are much more complicated. Even the most impoverished black youth do not choose styles solely on the basis of what is affordable. Young men wear the starter jackets, hoodies, L.A. Raiders caps, baggy khaki pants, and occasionally gold chains not only because they are in style, but because it enables them to create their own identity—one that defines them as rebels. While clothes are not intrinsically rebellious, young people give them what Dick Hebdige identifies as " 'secret' meanings: meanings which express, in code, a form of resistance to the order which guarantees their continued subordination."[67] It is naive to believe, for example, that black youth merely sport Raiders paraphernalia because they are all hardcore fans. Besides, as soon as NWA and more recent L.A. groups came on the scene sporting Raiders caps, the style became even more directly associated with the gangsta rappers than with the team itself, and the police regarded the caps, beanies, hoods, and starter jackets as gang attire.

What we need always to keep in mind is the degree of self-consciousness with which black urban youth—most of whom neither are gang members nor engage in violent crime—insist on wearing the styles that tend to draw police attention. By associating certain black youth styles with criminality, violence, and (indirectly) police repression, the dominant media unintentionally popularize these styles among young men who reinterpret these images as acts of rebellion or outright racist terror.[68] The styles also suggest an implicit acceptance of an "outlaw" status that capitalist transformation and the militarization of black Los Angeles have brought about. Hence the adoption and recasting of "G" as a friendly form of address used by young African American men and, to a lesser degree, women. While the origins of "G" apparently go back to the Five-Percent Nation (a fairly unorthodox Black Muslim youth group) on the East Coast where it was an abbreviation for "God," among youth in California and elsewhere it currently stands for "gangsta."[69] Finally, my own discussions with black youth in L.A. reveal that the black and silver Los Angeles Kings caps, associated with artists like King Tee, NWA, and other gangsta groups, have become even more popular following the King beating and the subsequent uprising—and hockey clearly has nothing to do with it. These caps signify very powerfully that all young African Americans are potential "L.A. [Rodney] Kings."[70]

In the streets of Los Angeles, as well as in other cities across the country, hip hop's challenge to police brutality sometimes moves beyond the discursive arena. Their music and expressive styles have literally become weapons in a battle over the right to occupy public space. Frequently employing high-decibel car stereos and boom boxes, black youth not only "pump up the volume" for their own listening pleasure, but also as part of an indirect, ad hoc war of position. The "noise" constitutes a form of cultural resistance that should not be ignored, especially when we add those resistive lyrics about destroying the state or retaliating against the police. Imagine a convertible Impala or a Suzuki pulling up alongside a "black and white," pumping the revenge fantasy segment of Ice Cube's "The Wrong Nigga to F——Wit" which promises to break Chief Darryl Gates's "spine like a jelly fish" or Cypress Hill vowing to turn "pigs" into "sausage."[71] Hip hop producers have increased the stakes by pioneering technologies that extend and "fatten" the bass in order to improve clarity at higher volume (appropriately called "jeep beats"). We cannot easily dismiss Ice Cube when he declares, "I'm the one with a trunk of funk/ and 'Fuck the Police' in the tape deck."[72]

For gangsta rappers, and black urban youth more generally, the police are a small part of an oppressive criminal justice system. The fact that, in 1989, 23 percent of black males ages twenty to twenty-nine were either behind bars or on legal probation or parole, has been a central political issue in the hip hop community. The combination of rising crime rates and longer sentencing has led to a rapid increase in the black prison population in the United States, and there is substantial evidence that racial bias is partly responsible; studies have shown, for example, that black men convicted of the same crime as whites receive longer sentences on average. The racial inequities were even more pronounced for juvenile offenders; during the last two decades, whereas most African American juveniles ended up in prisonlike public detention centers, white youths were more likely to end up in private institutions (halfway houses, shelters, group homes, etc.) that encouraged rehabilitation, skill development, and family interaction.[73]

With rising rates of incarceration for young black males, life behind bars has become a major theme in gangsta narratives. Through thick descriptions of prison life and samples of the actual voices of convicts (e.g., Ice T's "The Tower," W.C. and the MAAD Circle's "Out on a Furlough," and Kid Frost's "The Penitentiary") gangsta rappers come close to providing what Michel Foucault calls a "counter-discourse of prisoners." As Foucault explains, "when prisoners began to speak, they possessed an individual theory of prisons, the penal system, and justice. It is this form of discourse which ultimately matters, a discourse against power, the counter-discourse of prisoners and those we call delinquents—and not a theory *about* delinquency."[74] Most rappers—especially gangsta rappers—treat prisons as virtual fascist institutions. At the end of his *OG* album, Ice T suggests that prisons constitute a form of modern-day bondage. "They say slavery has been abolished except for the convicted felon." Moreover, mirroring the sentiments of a significant segment of the black community, several rappers suggest that the high incarceration rate of black males is part of a conspiracy. In "The Nigga Ya Love to Hate," Ice Cube asks aloud, "why [are] there more niggas in the pen than in college?"[75] He even suggests in "The Product" that prison is the inevitable outcome for young black men who fail or refuse to conform to the dominant culture. Inmates, he argues, are "products" of joblessness, police repression, and an inferior and racist educational system.[76]

Gangsta rappers tend toward a kind of "scared straight" approach to describing actual prison life. But unlike, say, the "Lifer's Group," their descriptions of prison are not intended merely to deter black youth from crime, for that would imply an acceptance of prisons as primarily institutions to punish and reform "criminals." Instead, their descriptions of prison life essentially reverse the popular image of black prisoners as "Willie Horton" and paint a richer portrait of inmates as real human beings trying to survive under inhuman conditions. While they do not ignore the physical and sexual violence[77] between prisoners, they do suggest that prison conditions are at the root of such behavior. Again, we return to "The Product":

> Livin' in a concrete ho house,
> Where all the products go, no doubt.
> Yo, momma, I got to do eleven,
> Livin' in a five by seven.
> Dear babe, your man's gettin worn out
> Seeing young boys gettin' their assholes torn out.
>
> It's driving me batty,
> Cause my little boy is missing daddy.
> I'm ashamed but the fact is,
> I wish pops let me off on the mattress [i.e., wishes he was never conceived.]
> Or should I just hang from the top bunk?
> But that's going out like a punk.
> My life is fucked. But it ain't my fault
> Cause I'm a motherfuckin' product.

Ice T's "The Tower" suggests that violence between inmates, especially racial conflict, is permitted if not instigated by guards and administrators as a means of controlling "the yard." The song consists of several first-person anecdotes rapped over a haunting synthesized cello track and punctuated by "audio verité" samples of presumably authentic prisoners telling their own stories of violence in the pen.

By focusing on prison architecture rather than the inmates themselves, the video for "The Tower" emphasizes how the structural and spatial arrangements themselves reproduce the prisoners' powerlessness. After each verse, Ice T asks "who had the power?/ The whites, the blacks, or just the gun tower?"[78]

The criminalization, surveillance, incarceration, and immizeration of black youth in the postindustrial city have been the central theme in gangsta rap, and at the same time, sadly, constitute the primary experiences from which their identities are constructed. Whereas Afrocentric rappers build an imagined community by invoking images of ancient African civilizations, gangsta rappers are more prone to follow Eric B. and Rakim's dictum, "It ain't where you're from, it's where you're at." When they are not describing prison or death, they describe daily life in the "ghetto"—an overcrowded world of deteriorating tenement apartments or tiny cement block, prisonlike "projects," streets filthy from the lack of city services, liquor stores and billboards selling malt liquor and cigarettes. The construction of the "ghetto" as a living nightmare and "gangstas" as products of that nightmare has given rise to what I call a new "Ghettocentric" identity in which the specific class, race, and gendered experiences in late capitalist urban centers coalesce to create a new identity—"Nigga."

Niggas in Post-Civil Rights America

I'm a nigger, not a colored man or a black
or a Negro or an Afro-American—I'm all that
Yes, I was born in America too.
But does South Central look like America to you?

—Ice T, "Straight Up Nigga"[79]

Perhaps the most soulful word in the world is "nigger."

—Claude Brown, "The Language of Soul"[80]

Gangsta rappers have drawn a lot of fire for their persistent use of "Nigga." Even the *New York Times* and popular magazines like *Emerge* have entered the debate, carrying articles about the growing popularity of the "N" word among young people. Rap artists are accused of inculcating self-hatred and playing into white racism. Yet those who insist that the use of "Nigga" in rap demonstrates self-hatred and ignorance of African American history do not generally impose the same race-conscious litmus test to black folklore, oral histories, ordinary vernacular speech, or other cultural traditions where "nigger" is used as a neutral or even friendly appellation. In these latter circumstances, "nigger" was/is uttered and interpreted among black folk within a specific, clearly defined context, tone, and set of "codes" rooted in black vernacular language. As anthropologist Claudia Mitchell-Kernan explained, "the use of 'nigger' with other black English markers has the effect of 'smiling when you say that.' The use of standard English with 'nigger,' in the words of an informant, is 'the wrong tone of voice' and may be taken as abusive." Very few African Americans would point to such dialogues as examples of "self-hatred." This is what Ice Cube was trying to get at in an interview: "Look, when we call each other nigger it means no harm, in fact, in Compton, it's a friendly word. But if a white person uses it, it's something different, it's a racist word."[81]

To comprehend the politics of Ghettocentricity, we must understand the myriad ways in which the most Ghettocentric segments of the West Coast hip hop community have employed the term "Nigga." Gangsta rappers, in particular, are struggling to ascribe new, potentially empowering meanings to the word. Indeed, the increasingly common practice of spelling it "N-i-g-g-a" suggests a revisioning. For example, Bay Area rapper and former Digital Underground member, 2Pac (Tupac Shakur), insists in his first album that Nigga stands for "Never Ignorant, Getting Goals Accomplished."[82] More common, however, is the use of "Nigga" to describe a condition rather than skin color or culture. Above all, Nigga speaks to a collective identity shaped by class consciousness, the character of inner-city space, police repression, poverty, and the constant threat of intraracial violence. Part of NWA's "Niggaz4Life," for instance, uses "Nigga" almost as a synonym for oppressed.[83]

In other words, Nigga is not merely *another* word for black. Products of the postindustrial ghetto, the characters in gangsta rap constantly remind listeners that they are still second-class citizens—"Niggaz"—whose collective experiences suggest that nothing has changed *for them* as opposed to the black middle class. In fact, Nigga is frequently employed to distinguish urban black working-class males from the black bourgeoisie and African Americans in positions of institutional authority. Their point is simple: the experiences of young black men in the inner city are not universal to all black people, and, in fact, they recognize that some African Americans play a role in perpetuating their oppression. To be a "real nigga" is to be a product of the ghetto. By linking their identity to the " 'hood" instead of simply skin color, gangsta rappers implicitly acknowledge the limitations of racial politics, including black middle-class reformism as well as black nationalism. Again, this is not new. "Nigger" as a signifier of class and race oppression has been a common part of black rural and working-class language throughout the twentieth century, if not longer. In fact, because of its power to distinguish the black urban poor from upwardly mobile middle-class blacks, "Nigger" made a huge comeback at the height of the Black Power movement. Robert DeCoy's infamous book, *The Nigger Bible*, published in 1967, distinguishes "Nigger" from "Negroes"—the latter a derogatory term for sellouts. DeCoy defined "Negro" as a "vulgar but accepted description of the Nigrite or Nigger. Referring to an American Nigger of decency and status. A White-Nigger. Or a brainwashed Black who would be Caucasian if possible . . ." And one Los Angeles-based black nationalist artist's collective, the Ashanti Art Service, launched a journal called *Nigger Uprising* in 1968.[84]

Perhaps not since the days of blues singer "Leadbelly" has the word "bourgeois" been so commonly used by black musicians. It has become common lingo among hip hop artists to refer to black-owned radio stations and, more generally, middle-class African Americans who exhibit disgust or indifference toward young, working-class blacks. For Ice T, living in the lap of luxury is not what renders the black bourgeoisie bankrupt, but rather their inability to understand the world of the ghetto, black youth culture, and rap music. In an interview a few years back he explained, "I don't think the negative propaganda about rap comes from the true black community—it comes from the bourgeois black community, which I hate. Those are the blacks who have an attitude that because I wear a hat and a gold chain, I'm a nigger and they're better than me." More recently, on his album *The Iceberg/Freedom of Speech . . . Just Watch What You Say,* he expressed similar sentiments: "I'm trying to save my community, but these bourgeois blacks keep on doggin' me. . . . You just a bunch of punk, bourgeois black suckers."[85] W.C. and the MAAD Circle level an even more sustained attack on those they call "bourgeois Negroes." Proclaiming that the Circle's sympathies lie with "poor folks in the slums," W.C. writes off suburban middle-class African Americans as turncoats and cowards.[86]

And to be fair, not only is there increasing intraracial class segregation with the suburbanization of the black middle class, but wealthy African Americans are often guilty of the kind of social labeling associated with white suburbanites and police. One need only visit predominantly black public spaces with considerable cross-class mixing (e.g., L.A.'s venerable Fox Hills Mall) to notice the considerable disdain many middle-class African Americans exhibit toward youth who are dressed a certain way or elect to walk in groups. Moreover, having come of age under a black mayor, black police officers, and a city council and legislature with a small but significant black presence, L.A. gangsta rappers blame black politicians and authority figures as much as their white counterparts for the conditions that prevail in poor communities.[87]

L.A. gangsta rappers are frequent critics of black nationalists as well. They contend that the nationalists' focus on Africa—both past and present—obscures the daily battles poor black folk have to wage in contemporary America. In what proved to be a highly controversial statement, Eazy E declared: "Fuck that black power shit: we don't give a fuck. Free South Africa: we don't give a fuck. I bet there ain't nobody in South Africa wearing a button saying 'Free Compton' or 'Free California.' "[88] Ice Cube poses the same issue in "Endangered Species (Tales from the Darkside)," but in a less dismissive and more meaningful manner:

> You want to free Africa,
> I'll stare at ya'
> Cause we ain't got it too good in America.
> I can't fuck with 'em overseas
> My homeboy died over kee's [kilos of cocaine][89]

To say that gangsta rappers are *anti*nationalist overstates the case. Groups like CPO and, more recently, Ice Cube express some explicitly nationalist positions, though L.A. groups have shown less inclination than their East Coast counterparts to openly support the Nation of Islam or the Five-Percent Nation. West Coast gangsta groups tend to be more wary of nationalism given the real divisions that exist among African Americans, the Afrocentric celebration of a past which, to them, has no direct bearing on the present, and the hypocrisy and inconsistency exhibited by individual black nationalists. The last point is the subject of W.C. and the MAAD Circle's "Caught N' a Fad," wherein they tell the story of a hustler who joined the Nation and wore African garb because it was in style but never changed his ways. He was "popping that 'too black, too strong/ But he was the first to get the dice game going on." Likewise, in "The Nigga Ya Love to Hate" Ice Cube takes a swipe at the Afrocentrists who speak of returning to Africa: "All those motherfuckers who say they're too black/ Put 'em overseas, they be beggin' to come back."[90]

For all of its rebelliousness, Ghettocentricity, like Afrocentricity, draws its arsenal from the dominant ideology. As products of sustained violence, the characters in gangsta rap are constantly prepared to retaliate with violence, whether it's against a cop or another brother; those unwilling are considered "cowards," "punks," or as Ice T would say, "bitches." In other words, "real Niggaz" are not only victims of race and class domination but agents—dangerous agents, nightmarish caricatures of the worst of the dispossessed. What is most striking about gangsta rappers' construction of "Nigga" as the embodiment of violence is the extent to which this highly masculinist imagery draws from existing stereotypes. Once again, we find black youth subculture reconstructing dominant representations of who they are in order to "remake" their image in popular discourse.[91] Negative stereotypes of black men as violent, pathological, and lazy are recontextualized: criminal acts are turned into brilliant capers and a way to *avoid* work; white fears of black male violence become evidence of black power; fearlessness is treated as a measure of masculinity. A large part of Eazy E's repertoire has him proving his manhood and authenticity as a "real nigga" by bustin' caps on anyone who stands in his way.[92]

Following a long tradition of black humor, both Ice T and Eazy E appropriate and recast stereotypes of black men as hypersexual beings with large penises. Eazy explains that one of the reasons why he calls *himself* a "Nigga" is because he "can reach in my draws and pull out a bigger dick." Ice T, who refers to himself as a "White woman's dream/ Big dick straight up Nigger," combines several stereotypes in the following passage:

> I'm loud and proud,
> Well endowed with the big beef.
> Out on the corner,
> I hang out like a horse thief.
> So you can call me dumb or crazy,
> Ignorant, stupid, inferior, or lazy,
> Silly or foolish,
> But I'm badder and bigger,
> And most of all
> I'm a straight up Nigga.[93]

While the meanings of these appropriations and reversals of racial stereotypes constantly shift with different contexts, in many cases they ultimately reinforce dominant images of African Americans. Moreover, the kinds of stereotypes they choose to appropriate—hypermasculinity, sexual power, and violence as a "natural" response—not only reproduce male domination over women, but often do so in an especially brutal manner.

"Pimpin' Ain't Easy": Women in the Male Gangsta Imagination

> *To me, all bitches are the same: money-hungry, scandalous, groupie hos that's always riding on a nigger's dick, always in a nigger's pocket.*
>
> —Eazy E, *"One Less Bitch"*[94]

While young African American males are both products of and sometimes active participants in the creation of a new masculinist, antifeminist cultural current, we cannot be too quick to interpret sexist and misogynist lyrics as a peculiarly modern product. African American vernacular culture has a very long and ignoble tradition of sexism evidenced in daily language and other more formal variants such as "the dozens," "toasts," and the age-old "baaadman narratives." A word like "bitch," for example, was not suddenly imported into African American male vocabulary by rap music. In the late 1950s, it was such a common reference to women that folklorist Roger Abrahams, in his study of black oral culture in Philadelphia, added it to his glossary of terms as "Any woman. As used here, usually without usual pejorative connotations."[95] While his claim that the term was usually not pejorative is highly suspect, the pervasiveness of the term is clearly longstanding. Some of the toasts that are at least a few decades old are more venomous than much of what we find today in Hip Hop. In 1966, Bruce Jackson recorded a toast titled "The Lame and the Whore" in which a veteran pimp teaches a "weak" mack daddy how to treat his women:

> Say, you got to rule that bitch,
> you got to school that bitch,
> you got to teach her the Golden Rule,
> you got to stomp that bitch,
> you got to tromp that bitch,
> and use her like you would a tool.
> You got to drive that bitch
> and got to ride that bitch
> like you would a motherfucken mule.
>
> Then take the bitch out on the highway and drag her
> until she's damn near dead.
> Then take your pistol and shoot her
> right through her motherfucken head.[96]

Aside from narratives that have been recovered by historians and folklorists, I personally remember having learned by heart "Imp the Skimp, the Tennis Shoe Pimp," a long first-person narrative in which we bragged incessantly of being "the baby maker/ the booty taker." "Imp" became part of my verbal repertoire around 1971; I was nine years old. Unlike rap music, however, our sexist and misogynist street rhymes were never discussed on Ted Koppel's *Nightline* because they never made it to wax; they remained where our mamas said they should—in the streets.[97]

But the story is a bit more complicated than black youth recording and distributing an oral tradition of "hustler poetry." During the late 1960s and early 1970s, as America became an increasingly "sexualized society," we witnessed an explosion of recorded sexually explicit comedy routines by black comics like Rudy Ray Moore, Redd Foxx, and Richard Pryor, as well as the publication and popularization of so-called genuine "pimp narratives." The *Pimp*, not just any "baaadman," became an emblematic figure of the period, elevated to the status of hero and invoked by Hollywood as well as in the writings of black nationalist militants like H. Rap Brown, Eldridge Cleaver, Bobby Seale, and Huey P. Newton. Aside from film and popular literature, the Pimp appeared in a proliferation of sensationalist autobiographies, scholarly ethnographies, and "urban folklore" collections of incarcerated hustlers.[98]

Old school rappers like Ice T and Philly's Schooly D were strongly influenced by some of these published reminiscences of hustlers. Ice T recalls, "I used to read books by Iceberg Slim. . . . He would talk in rhyme—hustler-like stuff—and I would memorize lines." The classic recording of *Hustlers' Convention* in 1973 by an ex-prisoner who would eventually help found the Last Poets, and the celebrated status of the pimp in blaxploitation films also had a profound impact on gangsta rap.[99] In fact, the word "gangsta" is frequently used interchangeably with terms like "Pimp," "Mack Daddy," "Daddy Mack," and "Hustler." One can hear the influence of the pimp narratives and black comedians on several Ice T cuts, especially "Somebody's Gotta Do It [Pimpin' Ain't Easy]," "I Love Ladies," and "Sex," which were recorded on his first album, *Rhyme Pays*. Boasting about his ability to please women sexually, the number of women he sleeps with, and the money he is making in the process, these kinds of rhymes are not descriptions of social reality but recorded versions of what anthropologist Ulf Hannerz calls "streetcorner myth-making" or what hip hop critic Dan Charnas simply calls "bullshit, schoolboy humor."[100]

The critical question, it seems to me, is why has the pimp returned to an exalted status in black male popular culture in the 1990s? Or more broadly, why has the pimp figured so prominently in the late 1960s/early 1970s and the late 1980s/early 1990s, periods of rising black nationalism and male backlash? I have to believe that the celebration of the pimp in popular culture during the Black Power era is in part a response to the image of black female dominance created by the Moynihan report. Perhaps young black men identified with the pimp because he represented the ultimate dominator, turning matriarchy on its head. Perhaps the valorization of the pimp was just another example of black militants celebrating a "lumpen" lifestyle.

As for the present, the pimp may have made such a strong return via gangsta rap because the dominant discourse—from conservatives to African American nationalists—demands the restoration of the patriarchal family. But why do gangsta rappers (not unlike other male hip hop performers) exhibit a profound fear of black female sexuality, which manifests itself as open distrust or, in some cases, an aggressive hatred, of women?[101]

Given the central place that misogyny occupies in the gangsta/baaadman aesthetic, it would be hard to trust a straight sociological answer to this question. Furthermore, I do not believe rap music can or ever intended to represent the true and complex character of male/female relations among black urban youth. Too many critics have taken the easy way out by reading rap lyrics literally rather than developing a nuanced understanding of actual social relations among young people, in all of their diversity and complexity. And there is no reason in the world to believe that any music constitutes a mirror of social relations that can be generalized for entire groups of people.

Nevertheless, I do think that there is a specific social context that provides some insights into the *popularity* of gangsta rap and the particular forms its misogyny takes. For example, although the "traditional" family itself might be fading, neither the ideology of male dominance nor the kinds of economic negotiations that have always been a part of intrafamily conflict have disappeared. As is evident in both contemporary popular culture and current policy debates, the last decade or so has witnessed a reassertion of masculinity and the increasing commodification of sexual relations. Moreover, gangsta rappers, the mass media, and mainstream black leadership commonly cast the problems of the inner city as a problem of black males, even if their interpretations differ. Some intellectuals and politicians propose saving the "underclass" by eliminating welfare, retraining young black men in all-male schools, and reinstituting the nuclear family, implying, of course, that the cause of the current crisis lies not in economic decline but in the collapse of the male-headed family.[102]

But apparently it is not just men who are to blame: young working-class African American women are often portrayed as welfare queens making babies merely to stay on public assistance, or "gold diggers" who use their sexuality to take black men's meager earnings. Of course, this image is hardly new. But it has become an increasingly prominent theme in hip hop over the last ten years or so. In a "tongue-in-cheek" verbal duel with female rapper Yo Yo, Ice Cube offers some lyrics that are partly meant in jest but nonetheless reflect the thinking of many of his black male compatriots: "I hear females always talking 'bout women's lib/Then get your own crib, and stay there/Instead of having more babies for the welfare/Cause if you don't I'll label you a gold digger."[103]

Part of the attack has to do with what these rappers feel are overly high expectations of black men held by young black women. Thinking back to their pre-celebrity days when they were reportedly jobless or worked for minimum wages, a number of male rappers criticize women who wanted to go out only with men who were stable or fairly well-off financially. Given the lack of employment opportunities available to young black women, and the still dominant notion that males ought to be the primary wage earners, these expectations could hardly be considered unreasonable. Yet, in interviews and in their music, most gangsta rappers label such women "bitches," "hos," or "skeezers." W.C. of the MAAD Circle, who is unique for avoiding these epithets on his debut album, tries to be slightly more conscientious by blaming "society" for inculcating women with materialistic values. Nevertheless, he throws up a weak argument for the use of the term "bitch": "Well, society has us all believing that if you don't fit up to their standard, then you're not shit. . . . If you have that attitude, then W.C. is calling you a bitch. But I'll never call a *woman* a bitch, because a real woman doesn't think with that mentality. This society has us believing that if you don't drive a brand new car, if you drive a bucket, you're not shit."[104]

While W.C. reveals one dimension of the pain poverty causes, his response is nonetheless a weak attempt to shift the issue. Distinguishing "bad" women from "good" women (or, in W.C.'s case, "real" women) still justifies violence against women by devaluing them, like most gangsta rap.[105] The most obvious examples can be found on NWA's recent album *Efil4zaggin*. Songs like "One Less Bitch" and the audio-verité recording "To Kill a Hooker" justify outright brutality and murder by using labels intended to strip women of any humanity. Hardly the stuff of everyday life in the ghetto, these draconian fantasy performances are more akin to "snuff films" than the kind of ethnographic observations NWA claim as their raw material. And like violent pornography, NWA's misogynist narratives are essentially about the degradation and complete domination of women. On the one hand, like the vast array of cultural images, they reinforce existing forms of patriarchal power; on the other hand, they construct male fantasy scenes of uncontested domination. They are never resisted or held accountable for acts of violence against women. In "One Less Bitch," Dr. Dre assumes the role of a pimp who discovers that his prostitute is trying to "steal" from him by retaining some of the money she earned. Reminiscent of "The Lame and the Whore" (or a "snuff film"—take your pick), Dre orchestrates what is best described as a lynching:

> I tied her to the bed, I was thinking the worst
> But, yo, I had to let my niggers fuck her first
> Yea, loaded up the .44
> Yo, then I straight smoked the ho.

Each story of mayhem and murder is broken up with a chorus of the entire NWA crew chanting: "One Less, one less, one less bitch you gotta worry about."

Economic conflict and a reassertion of male dominance in response to shifting gender and family relations still does not fully explain misogyny. Another part of the answer can be found in Tricia Rose's provocative and compelling argument that misogynist lyrics in rap reflect black male fears of black women's sexuality. Unlike male utopian spaces like "playboy clubs" where women are paid to be packaged fantasies, young inner-city black men have to deal with black women with real voices, demands, expectations, and complaints—women with agency. In the everyday lives of young black men, sexuality is always a process of negotiation. Rose suggests that "many men are hostile toward women because the fulfillment of male heterosexual desire is significantly checked by women's capacity for sexual rejection and/or manipulation of men." Manipulation, in this context, refers to the perceived power of black women to obtain money and goods in exchange for sex.[106]

Pregnancy is one way women allegedly extract attention and financial support, as is depicted in Ice Cube's "You Can't Fade Me." The narrative opens with Cube's character, who is on the corner drinking with his homies, discovering that he might have fathered a child by a young woman with whom he had a one-night stand. His initial impulse, not surprisingly, is to blame *her* rather than take responsibility. As the story progresses he recounts that one fateful night in stark, unflattering terms stripped completely of sensuality or pleasure. Because he saw her as physically unattractive he felt compelled to sneak around in order to have sex with her while preserving his reputation. When they finally found a safe place to have intercourse—in the backseat of his "homie's Impala"—both the sex and the end of their "date" were anticlimactic:

> I dropped her off man, and I'm knowing,
> That I'm a hate myself in the morning.
> I got drunk to help me forget,
> Another day, another hit, shit, I'm getting faded.

But once he returns to the present and she's about to have the child, the character Cube plays turns all of his anger and frustration upon her, threatening to beat her down and perform an abortion himself. In the end, the baby turns out not to be his, but the whole ordeal illustrates the possible consequences of his actions, even if the character Cube plays failed to learn anything from it. Sex as an act of conquest can also degrade men. Moreover, the end result of sexual conquest might be pregnancy, leading to the very thing the "playboy" ethic tries to avoid: commitment. In short, like all forms of power, male domination not only produces its own limits but it is constantly contested.

While songs like "You Can't Fade Me" are decidedly sexist, Ice Cube was among the first L.A. gangsta rappers to incorporate women's voices that contested his own lyrics. On *AmeriKKKa's Most Wanted,* for example, we not only hear a young woman's voice disrupt "The Nigga You Love to Hate" with vehement protests over the use of the word "bitch," but Ice Cube invited Yo Yo, an extraordinary female rapper concerned with building a progressive movement of black women, to engage him in a verbal "battle of the sexes." "It's a Man's World" is the classic "dis" tune, a duet rooted in the "dozens" tradition and thus intended to be humorous. But it also reminds us that the discursive space in which young black men assert their masculinity and dominance over women is always highly contested terrain. After the song opens with literally dozens of sampled voices saying "bitch"—ranging from Richard Pryor, Eazy E, and controversial comedian Andrew "Dice" Clay—the machine-gunlike assault of sexist epithets closes with a lone male voice who responds, "don't talk about my mamma!" Ice Cube launches into what is ostensibly supposed to be monologue about what women are "good for," when suddenly Yo Yo seems to come out of nowhere and interrupts with, "What the hell you think you're talkin' about?" Because her initial intervention takes place away from the microphone in a sort of echo mode, her interruption is presented as an unexpected penetration into all-male space, reminding the "brothas" just how vulnerable "the circle" is to female invasion and disruption. From that point on, Yo Yo criticizes Cube's ability to rap, questions his manhood, and even makes fun of the size of his penis.[107]

Finally, I must caution against interpreting the misogyny in gangsta rap as merely a reflection of daily gender conflicts and negotiations among inner-city black youth. In many instances, their narratives are based on their lived experiences as *performers* whose status as cultural icons gives them an enormous amount of sexual power and freedom. The long version of Ice Cube's "Get Off My Dick Nigger—and Tell Yo' B—to Come Here," which is primarily an attack on male "groupies," simultaneously celebrates his new status and ridicules starstruck teenage women who ultimately become the prey of male performers. In a line that falls somewhere between masculinist boast and paternal warning, Cube tells these women "See for a fact, I do damage/ They think I'm a star, so I take advantage."[108] Several songs on NWA's *Efil4zaggin* assert both the newfound power the group holds over impressionable and sexually curious young female fans and the brutality that can result from such power. One of the more vicious segments in "She Swallowed It" is the story of a woman who "did the whole crew." As NWA tried to make the difficult shift from "street niggas" to fame and fortune, it became increasingly clear that they not only saw their newfound power as boundless but had no qualms about practicing what they "preach." Dr. Dre's assault on Dee Barnes, the host of the video show *Pump It Up* and member of the rap duo Body and Soul, is a case in point, as is Tupac Shakur's recent arrest for sexually assaulting a young woman whom he and his friends had imprisoned in a hotel room.[109]

Are there any potential cracks or ruptures in the gangsta rappers' constructions of women or in their efforts to reassert male power through violence and sexual domination? Occasionally there are, especially when rappers focus their attention on bad fathering and family violence. Indeed, Ice T's "The House" demands an end to violence against children within the family context, and W.C. and the MAAD Circle critiques domestic violence against women. The medium-tempo, hauntingly funky "Fuck My Daddy" shows the flip side of the world NWA raps about:

> I'm giving peace to moms
> Cause moms was the strongest.
>
> Dad was a wino, as sick as a psycho.
> I used to hide under the covers with my eyes closed.
> Crying and hoping tonight that daddy didn't trip,
> Cause mama already needs stitches in her top lip.
>
> I used to pray and hope that daddy would die,
> Cause over nothing mama suffered from a swole up black eye.
> And at the end of my prayers cry myself to sleep.
> All I could think about was "Fuck my daddy."[110]

While W.C.'s lyrics mark a significant break from earlier gangsta groups, by focusing on his own mother as victim he does not directly challenge the dichotomy between "good" and "bad" women.[111] Moreover, neither of these examples challenges male domination, and reflections on lived experience alone are unlikely to convince most young men—gangsta rapper or not—that the overthrow of patriarchy should be part of an emancipatory agenda. However, the introduction of new *discourses* can play an important role in shaping the politics of rap music, and has. Not only have black women rappers played a crucial role in reshaping the attitudes toward women among a substantial segment of the hip hop community, they are also largely responsible for raising the issue of sexism within rap. Insofar as recording technology has conveyed the voices of ghetto youth (or those who claim the "authenticity" of ghetto living) to a national audience, it has brought rappers face-to-face with other critical communities, including feminists, left-wing radicals, suburban white youth, and Christian fundamentalists. The heated debates surrounding rap music have found their way into mainstream media where rap is generally either misunderstood or gangsta rap is regarded as real descriptions of daily life in the "ghetto." More significantly, the mass media attack on sexism in hip hop has obscured or ignored the degree to which rappers merely represent an extreme version of sexism that pervades daily life, across race and class. The devaluation of women goes on constantly, in television and film, in the labor market, in the courts, in educational and religious institutions, in suburban tract homes and gentrified high-class row houses, even in the way children are raised. Sexism is very much a part of "mainstream" American culture, and yet it is very difficult to generate a national dialogue about how pervasive it is in our society without eliciting diatribes about "political correctness" or the hypersensitivity of females. The Anita Hill/Clarence Thomas hearings are a case in point. The attacks on rap music also imply that misogyny is the unique property of young black males. While black male sexism should certainly not be ignored, the particular class and racial cast these criticisms take ultimately diverts attention form the general sexism in American culture. Hence, black youths' use of the term "bitch" gets more publicity than male bias on the bench in rape cases or gender discrimination in wages.

On the other hand, although the dialogue itself is limited, public discussions about rap's sexism have disrupted or challenged the narrow and localized assumptions of young black males. In other words, if rap had never become a commodity but remained forever in the streets and house parties of urban America, derogatory terms like "bitch" and misogyny within black communities would probably not have been so widely debated with such force. By turning what is frequently "street talk" into a national discussion that crosses gender, class, and racial boundaries, new discourses have the potential of at least challenging misogyny and possibly enabling black youth to perhaps see the limitations of the ideology of male dominance.

afterWORD: A Genre Spent?

> I don't like the trend toward so many gangster records in rap, but I am an art dealer and that's what is selling now.
>
> —Russell Simmons, CEO of Rush Communications[112]

> After the National Guard leaves, there's still gonna be angry, psycho motherfuckers out there.
>
> —B-Real of Cypress Hill[113]

Who is Snoop Doggy Dogg? He's the latest superstar addition to Dr. Dre's stable on Deathrow Records, a gangsta rapper from Long Beach with the coolest, slickest "Calabama"[114] voice I've ever heard. You know his name because his recent arrest for the fatal shooting of a young black man became national news. While his picture never made the post office, Snoop's face graced the cover of *Newsweek* and almost every major music magazine, and gained notoriety on a variety of television news programs. That Snoop's murder charges coincided with the release of his debut CD/album did not seem to hurt record sales one bit. On the contrary, the shooting simply confirmed his claims to be a "real" gangsta, to have committed more "dirt" than the next man. The hype around the man is clearly responsible for pushing *Doggy Style* to the top of the charts *before* it was released. Most of his lyrics represent nothing but senseless, banal nihilism. The misogyny is so dense that it sounds more like little kids discovering nasty words for the first time than some male pathos. It is pure profanity bereft of the rich storytelling and use of metaphor and simile that have been cornerstones of rap music since its origins.

Snoop Doggy Dogg is just the tip of the iceberg. Former NWA member Eazy E (aka Eric Wright) has either turned conservative or (more likely) found a new gimmick to sell records. Recently he donated money to the Republican Party and publicly defended one of the police officers accused of beating Rodney King. Not your typical gangsta posture. Furthermore, the current war between Dr. Dre and Eazy E has reduced gangsta rap to a battle over who has done the most dirt. According to Eazy, Dr. Dre and his new partners on Deathrow Records are just "studio gangstas" because they've committed little or no crimes.

While I still contend that most of the early gangsta rappers did not set out to glamorize crime, by the summer of 1993 gangsta rap had been reduced to "nihilism for nihilism's sake." For a moment, the hardest-core, most fantastic, misogynist, and nihilistic music outsold almost everything on the rap scene, burying the most politically correct. In some respects, this development should not be surprising. Hard-core gangsta rap has become so formulaic that capturing even a modicum of reality no longer seems to be a priority. Ironically, the massive popularity of gangsta rap coincided with a fairly substantial increase in white suburban consumers of rap. This is in spite of the post–L.A. rebellion political climate, when many commentators and cultural critics had hopes for a progressive turn in Ghettocentric music, and a militant backlash against gangsta rap specifically, and hip hop more generally (led mainly by middle-class male spokespersons like the Reverend Calvin Butts of Abyssinian Baptist Church in New York, African American feminist groups, and some black workingclass communities concerned about violence in their midst). And, as I pointed out elsewhere in this chapter, some of the most vociferous critics of gangsta rap come from within the hip hop community itself.[115]

As I close this chapter, with just two weeks left in 1993, one cannot help but notice how rap music generally, and gangsta rap in particular, has become the scapegoat for some very serious problems facing urban America. Besieged communities who are truly drowning in poverty and violence, it seems, are reaching out for a straw. Spokespersons for these antirap movements invoke a mythic past in which middle-class values supposedly ruled. They point to a "golden age" of good behavior, when the young respected their elders, worked hard, did not live their lives for leisure, took education seriously, and respected their neighbor's property. But this has been the claim of every generation of black intellectuals and self-appointed leaders since the end of Reconstruction (see chapter 2). The critique of the middle class that was so powerful in some glimmers of early gangsta rap is now silenced, as is the critique of what the economy has done to people. The door is open, more so than ever, for more all-male schools, heavier discipline, more policing, censorship, dress codes—what amounts to an all-out war on African American youth. On the other hand, the money is still flowing for gangsta rappers, many of whom now live in the hills overlooking the ghetto. The tragedy of all this is that the gangsta rappers have gotten harder and harder, kicking more ballistics than "reality"; critics and opponents have become harder and more sweeping in their criticism, dismissing not only the gangsta stuff but the entire body of rap; and the very conditions they are concerned about remain the same.

Gangsta rap might be on its last legs, a completely spent genre that now exists in a cul-de-sac of posturing, adolescent misogyny and blood-and-guts narratives. But it would be a mistake to dismiss gangsta rap and other genres of hip hop as useless creations of the marketplace. If we want to know the political climate among urban youth, we should still listen to the music and, most importantly, to the young people who fill the deadened, congested spaces of the city with these sonic forces. And as we all probably realize, the world from which this music emerged, and to which it partially speaks, inevitably faces the further deterioration of already unlivable neighborhoods, more street crime, and increased police repression. To take their voices seriously, however, is not to suggest that they are progressive or correct, or that every word, gesture, or beat is dripping with social significance. More often than not, "G-boys" are simply out to get paid, making funky jeep music, practicing the ancient art of playing the dozens, trying to be funny, and giving the people what they want. And when they are addressing the problems of inner-city communities we have to keep in mind that their sharpest critiques of capitalist America are derived from the same social and economic contexts that led a lot of homies to distrust black women and each other. Nevertheless, if we learned anything from that fateful night of April 29, it is that, whether we like the message or not, we must read the graffiti on the walls and, as Ice T puts it, "check the pulse of the rhyme flow."

Kickin' Reality, Kickin' Ballistics (The "Race Rebel" Remix Version)

. . . A nice, neat ending to be sure, but I can't go out like that. To write about the "politics" of gangsta rap is only part of the story. Let's face it: listening to gangsta rap, or any hardcore hip hop, is not exactly like reading an alternative version of the Times *(New York or L.A.). Hip hop is first and foremost music, "noize" produced and purchased to drive to, rock to, chill to, drink to, and occasionally dance to. To the hardcore, how many people get fucked up in a song is less important than an MC's verbal facility on the mic, the creative and often hilarious use of puns, metaphors, similes, not to mention the ability to kick some serious slang and some serious ass on the microphone. A dope MC leaves a trail of victims to rot in body bags, perpetrators who had the audacity to front like they could flow. This is why I insisted from the get-go that gangsterism is integral to all hardcore hip hop, from EPMD to MC Lyte, from Big Daddy Kane to Nice n' Smooth, just as gangstas have been integral to all African American and, for that matter, black Atlantic oral traditions. Moreover, as microphone fiend Rakim might put it, hip hop ain't hip hop if you can't "move the crowd." In my book, the most politically correct rapper will never get my hard-earned duckets if they ain't kickin' some boomin' drum tracks, a phat bass line, a few well-placed JB-style guitar riffs, and some stupid, nasty turntable action. If it claims to be hip hop, it has to have, as Pete Rock says, "the breaks . . . the funky breaks . . . the funky breaks."*

I wrote this little refrain not to contradict my analysis but to go out with a dose of reality while giving a shout out to the hardcore. For all the implicit and explicit politics of rap lyrics, hip hop must be understood as a sonic force more than anything else. You simply can't just read about it; it has to be heard, volume pumping, bass in full effect, index finger in reach of the rewind button when a compelling sample, break beat, or lyric catches your attention. This is why, for all my left-wing politics, when you see me driving by in my Subaru wagon, windows wide open, digging in the seams with the gangsta lean, rearview mirror trembling from the sonic forces, I'll probably be rockin' to the likes of King Tee, Dr. Dre, Pete Rock and C. L. Smooth, Das EFX, The Pharcyde, Cypress Hill, Boss, Lords of the Underground, MC Lyte, Ice T, The Coup, Jeru da Damaja, Son of Bazerk, Gangstarr, and, yes, Ice Cube. Keep the crossover and save the "PC" morality rap for those who act like they don't *know. I'm still rollin' with Da Lench Mob, kickin' it with the Rhyme Syndicate, hanging out in the Basement with Pete Rock and the rest, and, like Das EFX, I'm coming straight from the Sewer . . .*

I'm out. . . . Peace.

Notes

1. Quoted in Robert Warshow, *The Immediate Experience: Movies, Comics, Theatre and Other Aspects of Popular Culture* (New York: Atheneum, 1970), 130.

2. Eugene Genovese, *Roll, Jordan, Roll: The World the Slaves Made* (New York: Pantheon Books, 1974), 629.

3. For those who might have forgotten, several thousand people seized the streets on April 29, 1992, in part to protest the acquittal of the four officers who brutally beat a black motorist named Rodney King thirteen months earlier. For more on the L.A. rebellion, see especially Mike Davis, "In L.A., Burning All Illusions," *Nation* 254, no. 21 (June 1, 1992), 743–46; *L.A. Weekly,* 14, no. 23 (May 8–14, 1992); Los Angeles Times, *Understanding the Riots: Los Angeles Before and After the Rodney King Case* (Los Angeles: Los Angeles Times, 1992); Robert Gooding-Williams, ed., *Reading Rodney King, Reading Urban Uprising* (New York: Routledge, 1993).

4. Alan Light, "L.A. Rappers Speak Out," *Rolling Stone* 633 (June 25, 1992), 21; see also Light's "Rappers Sounded Warning," *Rolling Stone* 634/35 (July 9–23, 1992), 15–17, which appeared a month after my own article, "Straight from Underground," *Nation* 254, no. 22 (June 8, 1992), 793–96.

5. MTV News interview, May 3, 1992; Ice Cube, *The Predator* (Priority Records, 1992).

6. Quote from Kofi Buenor Hadjor, *Days of Rage: . . . Behind the Los Angeles Riots* (unpublished manuscript, 1992, in author's possession). I'm grateful to Ula Taylor and Kofi Hadjor for making this manuscript available to me. It is an incredible exploration of the roots and consequences of the L.A. Rebellion. The best sources on recent police brutality cases in Los Angeles are The Independent Commission on the Los Angeles Police Department, *Report of the Independent Commission on the Los Angeles Police Department* (Los Angeles: The Commission, 1991) [hereafter *The Christopher Report*]; Mike Davis, *City of Quartz: Excavating the Future in Los Angeles* (London: Verso, 1990), 267–92; see also Douglas G. Glasgow, *The Black Underclass: Poverty, Unemployment, and Entrapment of Ghetto Youth* (New York: Random House, 1981), 101; M. W. Meyer, "Police Shootings at Minorities: The Case of Los Angeles," *Annals* 452 (1980), 98–110; and for other local and national examples, one might consult, S. Harring, T. Platt, R. Speiglman, and P. Takagi, "The Management of Police Killings," *Crime and Social Justice* 8 (1977), 34–43; P. Takagi, "A Garrison State in 'Democratic Society,' " *Crime and Social Justice* (Spring–Summer 1978), 2–25; Community Relations Service, *The Police Use of Deadly Force: What Police and the Community Can Do About It* (Washington, D.C.: Department of Justice, Community Relations Service, 1977); Jerry G. Watts, "It Just Ain't Righteous: On Witnessing Black Crooks and White

Cops," *Dissent* 90 (1983), 347–53; Bruce Pierce, "Blacks and Law Enforcement: Towards Police Brutality Reduction," *Black Scholar* 17 (1986), 49–54; A. L. Kobler, "Figures (and Perhaps Some Facts) on Police Killing of Civilians in the United States, 1965–1969," *Journal of Social Issues* 31 (1975), 163–91; J. J. Fyfe, "Blind Justice: Police Shootings in Memphis." *Journal of Criminal Law and Criminology* 73 (1982) 707–22; Bernard D. Headley, " 'Black on Black' Crime: The Myth and the Reality," *Crime and Social Justice* 20 (1983), 52–53.

7. For this analysis, which runs throughout much of the chapter, I am indebted to my conversations with Charles Bright and to reading John Irwin, *The Jail: Managing the Underclass in American Society* (Berkeley and Los Angeles: University of California Press, 1985); Diana R. Gordon, *The Justice Juggernaut: Fighting Street Crime, Controlling Citizens* (New Brunswick, N.J.: Rutgers University Press, 1990); Michel Foucault, *Discipline and Punish: The Birth of the Prison,* trans. Alan Sheridan (New York: Pantheon Books, 1977), esp. pp. 195–228.

8. Tricia Rose, "Black Texts/Black Contexts," in *Black Popular Culture,* ed. Gina Dent (Seattle: Bay Press, 1992).

9. Charlie Ahearn, *Wild Style* (film) (1982).

10. David Toop, *Rap Attack 2* (London: Serpent's Tail, 1991), 40; the Morton lyrics are quoted from the "Rockbeat" column in the *Village Voice,* 39, no. 4 (January 25, 1994), 76; on the baaadman narratives, see John W. Roberts, *From Trickster to Badman: The Black Folk Hero in Slavery and Freedom* (Philadelphia: University Pennsylvania Press, 1989), 171–215; and on signifying, see Henry Louis Gates, Jr., *The Signifying Monkey: A Theory of African-American Literary Criticism* (New York: Oxford University Press, 1988), especially 64–88; Claudia Mitchell-Kernan, "Signifying, Loud-talking, and Marking," in *Rappin and Stylin' Out: Communication in Urban Black America,* ed. Thomas Kochman (Urbana: University of Illinois Press, 1972); Bruce Jackson, *"Get Your Ass in the Water and Swim Like Me": Narrative Poetry from Black Oral Tradition* (Cambridge, Mass.: Harvard University Press, 1974); Lawrence W. Levine, *Black Culture and Black Consciousness: Afro-American Folk Thought from Slavery to Freedom* (New York: Oxford University Press, 1977), 407–20.

11. Darryl James, "Ice-T the Ex-Gangster," *Rappin'* (January 1991), 37; Havelock Nelson and Michael A. Gonzales, *Bring the Noise: A Guide to Rap Music and Hip Hop Culture* (New York: Harmony Books, 1991), 30–31. When this book went to press, Brian Cross's incredible book on the L.A. hip hop scene, *It's Not about a Salary . . . Rap, Race and Resistance in Los Angeles* (London: Verso, 1993), had just come out. Unfortunately, I did not have a chance to incorporate his insights or his interviews with L.A. rappers into this chapter, aside from a few small corrections. It doesn't matter, however, since the material essentially reinforces my interpretation. Nevertheless, I would suggest that all serious readers and hip hop fans check out Cross's book.

12. James, "Ice-T the Ex-Gangster," 37; "T for Two," *Details* (July 1991), 51–55; Alan Light, "Rapper Ice-T Busts a Movie," *Rolling Stone* (May 16,

1991), 85; Mills, "The Gangsta Rapper," 32; Cross, *It's Not About a Salary,* 24; Ice T, *Rhyme Pays* (Sire Records, 1987).

13. Mills, "The Gangsta Rapper," 32; Frank Owen, "Hanging Tough," *Spin* 6, no. 1 (April 1990), 34; Nelson and Gonzales, *Bring the Noise,* 80–81, 165–67; NWA, *Straight Outta Compton* (Ruthless Records, 1988).

14. Sampling refers to the practice of incorporating portions of other records, or different sounds, into a hip hop recording. Digital samplers are usually used, which enable producers to isolate specific sounds and manipulate them (change the register, the tempo, etc.).

15. "1993 Summer Jeep Slammers," *Source* (July 1993), 76. There are some exceptions, the most obvious being Compton's Most Wanted which is more inclined toward jazz and quiet storm tracks (see especially, CMW, *Straight Check N' Em* (Orpheus Records, 1991). Nevertheless, funk dominates West Coast gangsta rap, and the introduction of reggae and jazz, unlike the East Coast, has been slow coming.

16. The larger hip hop community has maintained an ambivalent, and occasionally critical, stance toward most gangsta rappers. See, for instance, the criticisms of Kool Moe Dee, YZ, and others in "Droppin' Science," *Spin* 5, no. 5 (August 1989), 49–50; The J, "If you don't know your Culture, You don't Know Nothin'!: YZ Claims He's 'Thinking of a Master Plan' for Black Awareness," *Rap Pages* (December 1991), 64; "Views on Gangsta-ism," *Source* (December 1990), 36, 39, 40; as well as critical perspectives in the music itself, e.g., Del the Funkee Homosapien, "Hoodz Come in Dozens," *I Wish My Brother George Was Here* (Priority Records, 1991); Public Enemy, "No Nigga," *Apocalypse '91* (Def Jam, 1991); Arrested Development, "People Everyday," and "Give a Man A Fish," *3 Years, 5 Months and 2 Days in the Life Of . . .* (Chrysalis Records, 1992); The Disposable Heroes of Hipoprisy, especially "Famous and Dandy (Like Amos N' Andy)," *Hypocrisy is the Greatest Luxury* (Island Records, 1992); The Coup, *Kill My Landlord* (Wild Pitch Records, 1993).

17. Ice T, *OG: Original Gangster* (Sire Records, 1991); Ice Cube, *Kill at Will* (Priority Records, 1992); Ice Cube, *The Predator* (Priority Records, 1992); Ice T, *Power* (Warner Bros., 1988); CPO, *To Hell and Black* (Capitol Records, 1990); NWA, *100 Miles and Runnin'* (Ruthless, 1990); Dr. Dre, *The Chronic* (Interscope Records, 1992); CMW, *Straight Check N' Em* (Orpheus Records, 1991). How Ice T's lyrics from "I'm Your Pusher" were misinterpreted was discussed on the *MacNeil-Lehrer Newshour* on a special segment on rap music.

18. Ice T [and the Rhyme Syndicate], "My Word is Bond," *The Iceberg/Freedom of Speech . . . Just Watch What You Say* (Sire Records, 1989); Ice Cube, "J.D.'s Gafflin'," *AmeriKKKa's Most Wanted* (Priority Records, 1990). West Coast rappers also create humorous countercritiques of gangsterism; the most penetrating is perhaps Del tha Funkee Homosapien's hilarious, "Hoodz Come in Dozens," *I Wish My Brother George Was Here* (Priority Records, 1991).

19. Cube quote, David Mills, "The Gangsta Rapper: Violent Hero or Negative Role Model?" *Source* (December 1990), 39; see also Dan Charnas, "A

Gangsta's World View," *Source* (Summer 1990), 21–22; "Niggers With Attitude," *Melody Maker* 65, no. 44 (November 4, 1989), 33; and the Geto Boys' Bushwick Bill's explanation in J. Sultan, "The Geto Boys," *Source* (December 1990), 33.

20. Digital Underground's, "Good Thing We're Rappin'," *Sons of the P* (Tommy Boy, 1991) is nothing if not a tribute to the pimp narratives. One hears elements of classic toasts, including "The Pimp," "Dogass Pimp," "Pimping Sam," "Wicked Nell," "The Lame and the Whore," and perhaps others. Even the meter is very much in the toasting tradition. (For transcriptions of these toasts, see Bruce Jackson, *"Get Your Ass in the Water and Swim Like Me"*, 106–30.) Similar examples which resemble the more comical pimp narratives include Ice Cube, "I'm Only Out for One Thing," *AmeriKKKa's Most Wanted* (Priority, 1990) and Son of Bazerk, "Sex, Sex, and more Sex," *Son of Bazerk* (MCA, 1991).

21. See John Leland, "Rap: Can It Survive Self-Importance?" *Details* (July 1991), 108; Owen, "Hanging Tough," 34; James Bernard, "NWA [Interview]," *Source* (December 1990), 34. In fact, Ice Cube left NWA in part because they were not "political" enough. Though most accounts indicate that financial disputes between Cube and manager Jerry Heller caused the split, in at least one interview he implied that politics had something to do with it as well. As early as *Straight Outta Compton,* Cube wanted to include more like songs "F[2mthe Police," and when the FBI sent a warning to them because of their inflammatory lyrics, Cube planned to put out a twelve-minute remix in response. Of course, neither happened. It finally became clear to Cube that he could not remain in NWA after Jerry Heller kept them from appearing on Jesse Jackson's weekly TV show. Darryl James, "Ice Cube Leaves NWA to Become Amerikkka's Most Wanted," *Rappin'* (January 1991), 20.

22. Davis, *City of Quartz,* 304–7; Edward Soja, *Postmodern Geographies: The Reassertion of Space in Critical Social Theory* (London: Verso, 1989), 197, 201.

23. NWA, *Efil4zaggin* (Priority Records, 1991).

24. The idea that unemployed black youth turn to crime because it is more rewarding than minimum-wage, service-oriented work has been explored by a number of social scientists. See, for example, Richard B. Freeman, "The Relation of Criminal Activity to Black Youth Employment," in Margaret C. Simms and Samuel L. Myers, Jr., eds., *The Economics of Race and Crime* (New Brunswick, N.J.: Transaction Books, 1988), 99–107; Llad Phillips and Harold Votey, Jr., "Rational Choice Models of Crimes by Youth," in ibid., pp. 129–187; Llad Phillips, H. L. Votey, Jr., and D. Maxwell, "Crime, Youth, and the Labor Market," *Journal of Political Economy* 80 (1972), 491–504; Philip Moss and Chris Tilly, *Why Black Men Are Doing Worse in the Labor Market: A Review of Supply-Side and Demand-Side Explanations* (New York: Social Science Research Council Committee for Research on the Underclass, Working Paper, 1991), 90–93. For a discussion of the role of gangs in the illicit economy, see Martin Sanchez Jankowski, *Islands in the Street: Gangs and American Urban*

Society (Berkeley and Los Angeles: University of California Press, 1991), 119–31. Despite the general perception that dealers make an enormous amount of money, at least one study suggests that the average crack peddler only makes about $700 per month. See Peter Reuter, Robert Mac-Coun, and Patrick Murphy, *Money from Crime: A Study of the Economics of Drug Dealing in Washington, D.C.* (Santa Monica, Calif.: Rand, Drug Policy Research Center, 1990); Davis, *City of Quartz,* 322.

25. For discussions of the ways in which the mass media depict black youth gangs, violence, and the crack economy in inner-city neighborhoods, see Jankowski, *Islands in the Street,* 284–302; Jimmie L. Reeves and Richard Campbell, *Cracked Coverage: Television News, The Anti-cocaine Crusade, and The Reagan Legacy* (Durham, N.C.: Duke University Press, 1994); Herman Gray, "Race Relations as News: Content Analysis," *American Behavioral Scientist* 30, no. 4 (March–April 1987), 381–96; Craig Reinarman and Harry G. Levine, "The Crack Attack: Politics and Media in America's Latest Drug Scare," in *Images of Issues: Typifying Contemporary Social Problems,* ed. Joel Best (New York: Aldine de Gruyter, 1989), 115–35; Clarence Lusane, *Pipe Dream Blues: Racism and the War on Drugs* (Boston: South End Press, 1991).

26. "Niggers With Attitude," *Melody Maker* 65, no. 44 (November 4, 1989), 33.

27. James, "Ice T the Ex-Gangster," 38. Of course, the last part of Ice T's pronouncements echoes a range of conspiracy theories that continue to float among communities under siege, and even found a voice in Furious Styles, a lead character in John Singleton's *Boyz N the Hood.* But T's assertion cannot be dismissed so easily, since there are more liquor stores per capita and per square mile in low-income inner-city neighborhoods than anywhere else in the United States. See George A. Hacker, *Marketing Booze to Blacks* (Washington, D.C.: Center for Science in the Public Interest, 1987); Manning Marable, *How Capitalism Underdeveloped Black America: Problems in Race, Political Economy, and Society* (Boston: South End Press, 1983).

28. Ice T, *OG: Original Gangster* (Sire Records, 1991)

29. Bill Moyers interview with Bernice Johnson Reagon, PBS; Abrahams, *Deep Down in the Jungle,* 58–59; Mark Zanger, "The Intelligent Forty-year-old's Guide to Rap," *Boston Review* (December 1991), 34.

30. *AmeriKKKa's Most Wanted.*

31. Bruce Perry, ed., *Malcolm X: The Last Speeches* (New York: Pathfinder Press, 1989), 161.

32. This argument has been made by numerous scholars. For a sampling, see Ken Auletta, *The Underclass* (New York: Random House, 1982), 90–108 passim.; Charles Murray, *Losing Ground: American Social Policy, 1950–1980* (New York: Basic Books, 1984); see also Roger Lane's more historical but equally flawed treatment in *Roots of Violence in Black Philadelphia, 1860–1900* (Cambridge, Mass.: Harvard University Press, 1986). Williams Julius Wilson, *The Truly Disadvantaged: The Inner City, the Underclass, and Public Policy* (Chicago: University of Chicago Press, 1987), 30–32, 37–38, makes a different argument, suggesting that social

dislocation is the ultimate cause of criminal behavior, which in turn becomes one out of a set of pathologies brought about by persistent poverty. Nevertheless, there is a large body of research that suggests poverty and joblessness are directly related to crime. In addition to sources cited in note 27, see Steven Box, *Recession, Crime and Punishment* (Totowa, N.J.: Barnes and Noble Books, 1987); D. Glaser and K. Rice, "Crime, Age, and Employment," *American Sociological Review* 24 (1959), 679–86; Jason Ditton, *Part-Time Crime: An Ethnography of Fiddling and Pilferage* (London: Macmillan, 1977); Richard C. Hollinger and J. P. Clark, *Theft by Employees* (Lexington, 1983); A. J. Reiss and A. L. Rhodes, "The Distribution of Juvenile Delinquency in the Social Class Structure," *American Sociological Review* 26 (1961), 720–43; Elliot Currie, *Confronting Crime: An American Challenge* (New York: Pantheon Books, 1985), 146; E. Green, "Race, Social Status, and Criminal Arrest," *American Sociological Review* 35 (1970), 476–90; R. W. Beasley and G. Antunes, "The Etiology of Urban Crime: An Ecological Analysis," *Criminology* 11 (1974), 439–61; J. R. Blau and P. M. Blau, "The Cost of Inequality: Metropolitan Structure and Violent Crime," *American Sociological Review* 47 (1982), 114–29; James W. Messerschmidt, *Capitalism, Patriarchy and Crime* (Totowa, N.J.: Rowman and Littlefield, 1986), 54–58; I. Jankovic, "Labor Market and Imprisonment," *Crime and Social Justice* 8 (1977), 17–31; D. Humphries and D. Wallace, "Capitalist Accumulation and Urban Crime, 1950–1971," *Social Problems* 28 (1980), 179–93; A. D. Calvin, "Unemployment among Black Youths, Demographics, and Crime," *Crime and Delinquency* 27 (1981), 9–41.

33. D. Dub, "We're Not Glamorizin'—But We're Factualizin,' " *Rap Pages* 1, no. 2 (December 1991), 55–56. For Bobby Byrd, however, a job is not something one pulls, but something one has. His lyrics are clearly about wage labor: "You got to have a job/ Put meat on the table/ You got to have a job/ to keep the family stable." (Quoted in Michael Haralambos, *Soul Music: The Birth of a Sound in America* [New York: De Capo, 1974], 115.)

34. W.C. and the MAAD Circle, *Ain't A Damn Thang Changed* (Priority, 1991).

35. Ibid.

36. Ice Cube, *Death Certificate* (Priority, 1991).

37. The phrase "criminal-criminals" is taken from Peter Linebaugh's amazing book, *The London Hanged: Crime and Civil Society in the Eighteenth Century* (London: Allen Lane, The Penguin Press, 1991). Of London's working-class criminals, he writes: "If we categorize them too quickly as social criminals taking from the rich, or criminal-criminals stealing from the poor, in the process of making these judgements we cloud our attentiveness to theirs" (p. xxiii).

38. *Ain't A Damn Thang Changed.*

39. James Bernard, "Ice Cube: Building a Nation," *Source* 27 (December 1991), 34.

40. Da Lench Mob, *Guerrillas in Tha Mist* (Priority, 1992).

41. Quoted in Jankowski, *Islands in the Street,* 103.

42. Davis, *City of Quartz,* 297; Los Angeles *Times,* May 25, 1992; Alexander Cockburn, "Beat the Devil," *Nation* 254, no. 21 (June 1, 1992), 738–39.

43. Ice T, "Pain" and "6 in the Mornin," *Rhyme Pays,* "High Rollers," *Power,* "New Jack Hustler," *OG: Original Gangster,* Ice Cube, "Dead Homiez" *Kill at Will,* "Color Blind," *Death Certificate,* NWA, "Alwayz into Somethin," *Efil4zaggin;* Cypress Hill, *Cypress Hill* (Columbia, 1991).

44. Capitol Punishment Organization, *To Hell and Black* (Capitol Records, 1990). It might be worth noting that even a group as hard as Da Lench Mob suggests that black urban youth should become more religious.

45. D. Dub, "We're Not Glamorizin,' " 57.

46. Messerschmidt, *Capitalism, Patriarchy and Crime,* 58–60, quote p. 59; Tony Platt, " 'Street' Crime: A View from the Left," *Crime and Social Justice* 9 (Spring–Summer 1978), 26–34; Walter J. Ong, *Fighting for Life: Contest, Sexuality, and Consciousness* (Ithaca, N.Y.: Cornell University Press, 1981), 68–69; R. W. Connell, *Gender and Power: Society, the Person, and Sexual Politics* (Stanford, Calif.: Stanford University Press, 1987), 57–58, 85–86; R. E. Dobash and R. P. Dobash, *Violence against Wives: A Case against Patriarchy* (New York: The Free Press, 1979); Barbara Ehrenreich, *Hearts of Men: American Dreams and the Flight from Commitment* (Garden City, N.Y.: Anchor Press, 1983), 7–11. One very obvious example of gangsta rappers measuring one's masculinity by his ability and willingness to fight is Ice T's "Bitches 2" from *OG: Original Gangster.* One woman's gangsta group whose music talks about women engaging in drive-by shootings and taking out police in a flurry of buckshot is the New York-based Bytches With Problems. See their "We're Coming Back Strapped" and "Wanted," *The Bytches* (Def Jam, 1991)

47. See "The Drive By," *AmeriKKKa's Most Wanted* and *Kill at Will.*

48. Compton's Most Wanted, *Straight Check N' Em* (Sony, 1991). In a recent article in the *Source,* hip hop critic Reginald C. Dennis, who also shares these gangsta rappers' sensitivity to both the logic of crime and its detrimental effects, has even made a plea for criminals to be socially responsible when engaging in violence: "If you have chosen the lifestyle of the 'gangsta' you can still contribute to the cause by making sure the blood of innocents is not randomly spilled because of your irresponsibility. Do what you gotta do, but keep it limited to your social circle. If you must be criminal minded be professional and responsible—don't drag children and other innocents down with you. . . . In this way we can attempt to find some common ground between the criminal and the activist, and in diverse ways, work towards the same goal." ("After all . . . We are the ones who are Dying: Inner City Crime," *Source* 18 [February 1991], 34.)

49. Ice Cube, *Kill at Will.*

50. NWA, *NWA and the Posse* (Ruthless Records, 1988).

51. From "The Wall," *To Hell and Black.*

52. *Death Certificate* (Priority, 1991).

53. Ice T, "New Jack Hustler," *OG: Original Gangster.*

54. Ice Cube, "Rollin' Wit the Lench Mob," *AmeriKKKa's Most Wanted.*

55. Ice T, *OG: Original Gangster;* Ice Cube, *AmeriKKKa's Most Wanted.*

56. D. Dub, "We're Not Glamorizin,' " 56–57.

57. Quoted in Robert Hilburn, "The Rap Is: Justice," *Los Angeles Times,* May 31, 1992; Ice Cube, "Who's the Mack," MTV video; see also "Niggers With Attitude," *Melody Maker* 65, no. 44 (November 4, 1989), 34. Of course, the complicity of the U.S. government in the distribution of drugs into the black community is not a new theme, nor is it unique to hip hop. See Sir Mix-a-Lot, "National Anthem," lyrics reprinted in Lawrence A. Stanley, ed., *Rap: The Lyrics* (New York: Penguin Books, 1992), 294; 2 Black, 2 Strong MMG, "War on Drugs," *Doin' Hard Time on Planet Earth* (Relativity Records, 1991); Geto Boys, "City under Siege," *The Geto Boys* (Def American Records, 1989).

58. Davis, *City of Quartz,* 268; Jankowski, *Islands in the Street,* 252, 254; also see Glasgow, *The Black Underclass,* 100–101.

59. NWA, "F——Tha Police," *Straight Outta Compton;* Owen, "Hanging Tough," 34.

60. CMW, *Straight Check N 'Em;* Cypress Hill, *Cypress Hill;* Kid Frost, *East Side Story* (Virgin Records, 1992).

61. George Lipsitz, *Time Passages: Collective Memory and American Popular Culture* (Minneapolis: University of Minnesota Press, 1990), 5; W.C. and the MAAD Circle, *Ain't A Damn Thang Changed.*

62. Although young black women also occupied public space, were victims of police marking, and experienced outright brutality, L.A. gangsta rappers have been silent on the policing of women. Combined with a dominant black political ideology that has framed the issues solely in terms of the problems of black males, the refusal to acknowledge black women's experiences with state-sanctioned violence has effectively rendered them invisible in the whole discourse about police brutality in the aftermath of Rodney King. Even black female rappers have ignored the issue of state-sanctioned violence against women—one exception being "Wanted" by the New York-based rap group, Bytches With Problems. "Wanted" not only reminds listeners that women are victims of police harassment, but briefly adds the dimension of sexual abuse in their descriptions of day-to-day repression. (BWP, *The Bytches* [Def Jam, 1991].) While it is true that the percentage of black male victims of police repression is much, much higher than that of females, we cannot ignore the fact that the most important police homicide and brutality cases over the past decade have had black female victims: Eula Love and Eleanor Bumpurs, to name a few. Unfortunately, scholarship on policing is equally male-focused and thus complicit in rendering black women's experiences invisible. One recent exception is Ruth Chigwada's study of black women in Britain, "The Policing of Black Women," in *Out of Order? Policing Black People,* eds. Ellis Cashmore and Eugene McLaughlin (London: Routledge, 1991), 134–50.

63. *AmeriKKKa's Most Wanted;* also re-mixed on *Kill at Will.*

64. Davis, *City of Quartz,* 274.

65. Ibid., 272. Of course, L.A. is not unique in this respect. See, for example, Box, *Recession, Crime and Punishment,* 46–47; Lee P. Brown, "Bridges

over Troubled Waters: A Perspective on Policing in the Black Community," in *Black Perspectives on Crime and the Criminal Justice System,* ed. Robert L. Woodson (Boston: G. K. Hall, 1977), 87–88; Elijah Anderson, *Streetwise: Race, Class, and Change in an Urban Community* (Chicago: University of Chicago Press, 1990), 194–96.

66. "Dress Code," *Ain't A Damn Thang Changed.*

67. Dick Hebdige, *Subculture: The Meaning of Style* (London: Methuen, 1979), 18.

68. This interpretation is derived from a reading of Stuart Hall, "Culture, Media, and the 'Ideological Effect,' " in James Curran, Michael Gurevitch, and Janet Woolacott, eds., *Mass Communication and Society* (Beverly Hills: Sage Publications, 1979), 315–48.

69. From its founding in the mid-1960s, the Five-Percenters believe that every person is God. Less commonly, "G" is used as a shorthand term for "money," which is also used as a form of address. Although my point that this terminology cuts across gender lines is drawn from very unscientific participant observation, one might listen to the music of Yo Yo, M. C. Lyte, or Queen Latifah for their employment of "G" as a form of address.

70. Again, we must be careful not to presume that these styles are merely the authentic expressions of poor black urban youth. Many middle-class suburban black kids and many more white kids—males and females—can be found sporting the "G" style on college and high school campuses, malls, and playgrounds throughout the country. What this means deserves an essay in itself.

71. Ice Cube, *Death Certificate;* Cypress Hill, "Pigs," *Cypress Hill.*

72. Ice Cube, "The Wrong Nigga to F——Wit," *Death Certificate,* and "Endangered Species (Tales from the Darkside)," *AmeriKKKa's Most Wanted.*

73. Marc Mauer, *Young Black Men and the Criminal Justice System: A Growing National Problem* (Washington, D.C.: The Sentencing Project, 1990), 1–11; John Irwin, *The Jail;* Gordon, *The Justice Juggernaut;* Messerschmidt, *Capitalism, Patriarchy and Crime,* 52–53; Jefferey Reiman, *The Rich Get Richer and the Poor Get Prison,* 2nd ed. (New York: Wiley, 1984); R. Sheldon, *Criminal Justice in America: A Sociological Approach* (Boston: Little, Brown, 1982), 39–50; Brown, "Bridges over Troubled Waters," 87–88; Alfred N. Garwood, *Black Americans: A Statistical Sourcebook* 3rd ed. Rev. (Palo Alto, Calif.: Information Publishers, 1993), 210–13. Statistics aside, many rappers take up the subject of incarceration because they know people who are "locked down," and in some instances, a few rap artists have actually served time in the penitentiary. Some examples include MAAD Circle rapper Coolio, East Coast rappers Intelligent Hoodlum (Percy Chapman), K-Solo, and the currently incarcerated Lifer's Group.

74. Michel Foucault, "Intellectuals and Power," *Language, Counter-memory, Practice: Selected Essays and Interviews by Michel Foucault,* trans. Donald F. Bouchard and Sherry Simon (Ithaca, N.Y.: Cornell Univ. Press, 1977), 209.

75. Ice T, "You Shoulda Killed Me Last Year," *OG: Original Gangster;* Ice Cube, "The Nigga Ya Love to Hate," *AmeriKKKa's Most Wanted;* other examples include 2Pac, "Trapped," *2Pacalypse Now;* Public Enemy, "Black Steel in the Hour of Chaos," *It Takes a Nation of Millions to Hold Us Back* (Def Jam, 1988); MMG, 2 Black, 2 Strong, "Up in the Mountains," *Doin' Hard Time on Planet Earth* (Relativity, 1991). Popular texts which suggest that incarceration reflects part of a conspiracy include Jawanza Kunjufu, *Countering the Conspiracy to Destroy Black Boys* (Chicago: African American Images, 1985–86), 3 vols.; Baba Zak A. Kondo, *For Homeboys Only: Arming and Strengthening Young Brothers for Black Manhood* (Washington, D.C.: Nubia Press, 1991). Although women's voices are absent in these narratives about incarceration, we should keep in mind that 96 percent of the nation's prison population is male. (Franklin E. Zimring and Gordon Hawkins, *The Scale of Imprisonment* [Chicago: University of Chicago Press, 1991], 73.)

76. *Kill at Will* (Priority Records, 1990). A similar point is made in W.C. and the MAAD Circle's "Out on a Furlough," *Ain't A Damn Thang Changed.*

77. Clearly, the roots of homophobia among African American males lay elsewhere, but it is interesting to note how frequently homosexuality is talked about in terms of prison rape. This pervasive image must shape the particular character of homophobia in African American urban communities.

78. *OG: Original Gangster.*

79. Ibid.

80. Claude Brown, "The Language of Soul," *Esquire Magazine* 69 (April 1968), 88.

81. Claudia Mitchell-Kernan, "Signifying, Loud-talking, and Marking," 328; and for numerous examples from folklore, see Levine, *Black Culture;* Roberts, *From Trickster to Badman,* 174–215 passim.; "Niggers With Attitude," *Melody Maker* 65, no. 44 (November 4, 1989), 33. As Ice Cube slowly moves away from gangsta rap, influenced largely by the Nation of Islam, his views on the use of the word seem to have undergone a substantial shift. In a recent interview, he told hip hop journalist James Bernard, "The reason I say 'nigger' is because we are still 'niggers' cuz we got this white man in our heads. Until we get him out our heads, that's when we become Black men [*sic*] and that's when I'll stop using the word." (James Bernard, "Ice Cube: Building a Nation," *Source* 27 [December, 1991], 32.) Although most cultural nationalist groups critique or avoid the term "Nigga" altogether, X-Clan apparently embraces the phrase as an ironic, often humorous comment on white fears of black militancy. See especially their most recent album, *Xodus: The New Testament* (Polygram Records, 1992).

82. 2Pac, *2pacalypse Now* (Interscope, 1991).

83. NWA, *Efil4zaggin.*

84. Robert H. DeCoy, *The Nigger Bible* (Los Angeles: Holloway House Publishing Co., 1967), 33; William L. Van Deburg, *New Day in Babylon: The Black Power Movement and American Culture, 1965–1975* (Chicago:

University of Chicago Press, 1992), 218; *Nigger Uprising* (Los Angeles: Ashanti Art Service, 1968). There are dozens of examples. We might point to the light-skinned character in the film version of "The Spook Who Sat by the Door" who claimed his authenticity by calling himself a "Nigger," or Cecil Brown's reference to James Brown's music as "Nigger feeling" in his brilliant essay, "James Brown, Hoodoo, and Black Culture," *Black Review* (1971), 182. We might also consider the prize-winning and celebrated narrative compiled by Theodore Rosengarten, *All God's Dangers: The Life of Nate Shaw* (New York: Avon, 1974). When Shaw (whose real name was Ned Cobb) used the word "nigger" as a form of self-designation, it signified more than color. In making distinctions between "niggers" and "better class Negroes," he represented the impoverished, the exploited, the working person.

85. Quoted in Michael Eric Dyson, "The Culture of Hip Hop," *Zeta Magazine* (June 1989), 46; Ice T, *The Iceberg/Freedom of Speech . . . Just Watch What You Say;* see also Ice T, "Radio Suckers," *Power* (Sire Records, 1988), "This One's For Me," *The Iceberg/Freedom of Speech . . . Just Watch What You Say;* Ice Cube, "Turn off the Radio," *AmeriKKKa's Most Wanted.*

86. *Ain't A Damn Thang Changed.*

87. On the complicity of black politicians, see Davis, *City of Quartz,* 290–92.

88. Owen, "Hanging Tough," 34. A comparable line can be found in M. C. Ren's contribution to "Niggaz 4 Life," *Efil4zaggin.*

89. Ice Cube, "Endangered Species (Tales from the Darkside)," *AmeriKKKa's Most Wanted.*

90. W.C. and the MAAD Circle, *Ain't a Damn Thang Changed;* Ice Cube, "The Nigga Ya Love to Hate," *AmeriKKKa's Most Wanted.*

91. Hebdige, *Subculture,* 86.

92. Examples can be found in most gangsta rap, but see especially *Eazy-Duz-It* (Ruthless, 1988); *Straight Outta Compton; 100 Miles and Running;* "Niggaz 4 Life," *Efil4zaggin.*

93. NWA, "Niggaz 4 Life," *Efil4zaggin;* Ice T, "Straight Up Nigga," *OG: Original Gangster.* The black male celebration of stereotypes of black sexuality is common in much black humor. Lawrence Levine writes, "Black humor reflected an awareness that the pervasive stereotype of Negroes as oversexed, hyper-virile, and uninhibitedly promiscuous was not purely a negative image; that it contained envy as well as disdain, that it was a projection of desire as well as fear." *Black Culture,* 338.

94. *Efil4zaggin.*

95. Roger Abrahams, *Deep Down in the Jungle: Negro Narrative Folklore from the Streets of Philadelphia,* rev. ed., (Chicago: Aldine, 1970, orig. 1963), 258.

96. Jackson, *"Get Your Ass in the Water and Swim Like Me,"* 129; see also several other toasts in Jackson's collection as well as Dennis Wepman, Ronald B. Newman, and Murray Binderman, *The Life: The Lore and Folk Poetry of the Black Hustler* (Philadelphia: University of Pennsylvania Press, 1976).

97. Henry Louis Gates, Jr., "Two Live Crew De-Coded," *New York Times,* June 19, 1990; on urban toasts and "baaadman" narratives, see especially Jackson, *"Get Your Ass in the Water and Swim Like Me"*; Levine, *Black Culture,* 407–20; Roberts, *From Trickster to Badman,* 171–215; Abrahams, *Deep Down in the Jungle*; Anthony Reynolds, "Urban Negro Toasts: A Hustler's View from Los Angeles," *Western Folklore* 33 (October 1974), 267–300; Wepman, Newman, and Binderman, *The Life.*

98. "Sexualized Society" is borrowed from John D'Emilio and Estelle Freedman, *Intimate Matters: A History of Sexuality in America* (New York: Harper and Row, 1988), 326–30. The more popular pimp narratives include Iceberg Slim [Robert Beck], *Pimp: The Story of My Life* (Los Angeles: Holloway House, 1969); Christina Milner and Richard Milner, *Black Players: The Secret World of Black Pimps* (New York: Little, Brown, 1972). On the pimp in popular film, see Donald Bogle, *Toms, Coons, Mulattoes, Mammies and Bucks: An Interpretive History of Blacks in American Films,* new ed. (New York: Continuum, 1989), 234–42; Daniel Leab, *From Sambo to Superspade: The Black Experience in Motion Pictures* (Boston: Houghton Mifflin, 1975); David E. James, "Chained to Devilpictures: Cinema and Black Liberation in the Sixties," in *The Year Left 2: Toward a Rainbow Socialism—Essays on Race, Ethnicity, Class and Gender,* ed. Mike Davis et al., (London: Verso 1987), 125–38. Black nationalist narratives that tend to celebrate or romanticize the pimp in African American communities include H. Rap Brown, *Die, Nigger, Die* (New York: Dial Press, 1969); Bobby Seale, *Seize the Time* (New York: Random House, 1970); and *Lonely Rage* (New York: Times Books, 1978) in which Seale himself takes on the characteristics of a pimp; Huey P. Newton, *Revolutionary Suicide* (New York: Harcourt Brace Jovanovich, 1973); Eldridge Cleaver, *Soul on Ice* (New York: McGraw-Hill, 1968).

99. Ice T quoted in Nelson and Gonzales, *Bring the Noise,* 110;

100. Ulf Hannerz, *Soulside: Inquiries into Ghetto Culture and Community* (New York: Columbia University Press, 1969), 105–7; Charnas, "A Gangsta's World View," 22.

101. In the following discussion I limit my critique of sexism to L.A. gangsta rap and thus do not deal with better-know controversies (e.g., the Two Live Crew obscenity trial). For general treatments, see especially, Tricia Rose, "Never Trust a Big Butt and a Smile," *Camera Obscura* 23 (1991), 109–31; Kimberle Crenshaw, "Beyond Racism and Misogyny: Black Feminism and 2 Live Crew," *Boston Review* 16, no. 6 (December 1991), 6, 33; Michelle Wallace, "When Black Feminism Faces the Music and the Music Is Rap," *New York Times,* July 29, 1990; Michael Eric Dyson, "As Complex as They Wanna Be: 2 Live Crew," *Zeta Magazine* (January 1991), 76–78; Paulla Ebron, "Rapping between Men: Performing Gender," *Radical America* 23, no. 4 (June 1991), 23–27.

102. For example, see *Los Angeles Times,* August 22, 1991; Jewell T. Gibbs, *Young, Black and Male in America: An Endangered Species* (Dover, Mass.: Auburn House, 1988); interview with Harry Edwards, *San*

Francisco Focus (March, 1984), 100; Murray, *Losing Ground;* Lawrence Mead, *Beyond Entitlement: The Social Obligation of Citizenship* (New York: Free Press, 1985); and for a liberal approach which also suggests that family structure is partly to blame for persistent poverty, see Eleanor Holmes Norton, "Restoring the Traditional Black Family," *New York Times Magazine* (June 2, 1985).

103. "It's a Man's World," *AmeriKKKa's Most Wanted.*

104. D. Dub, "We're Not Glamorizin' " 57; Ice Cube made a similar point in Bernard, "Ice Cube: Building a Nation," 32.

105. Messerschmidt, *Capitalism, Patriarchy and Crime,* 134.

106. Rose, "Never Trust a Big Butt and a Smile," 115. A clear example is Ice T, "I Love Ladies," from his *Rhyme Pays* album.

107. "It's a Man's World (Featuring Yo Yo)," *AmeriKKKa's Most Wanted.* I am grateful to Tricia Rose for her insights into the ways in which Yo Yo's intervention disrupts Cube's masculinist discourse. (Conversation with Tricia Rose, December 26, 1991.) See also Yo Yo's other lyrical challenges to sexism on *Make Way for the Motherlode* (Profile, 1991). It should be noted that some of the most antisexist lyrics on Yo Yo's album were written by Ice Cube.

108. *Kill at Will* (Priority, 1991); a shorter version appeared first on *AmeriKKKa's Most Wanted.*

109. Alan Light, "Beating Up the Charts," *Rolling Stone* (August 8, 1991), 66; Calvin Sims, "Gangster Rappers: The Lives, the Lyrics," *New York Times,* November 28, 1993.

110. *Ain't a Damn Thang Changed.*

111. "The House," *OG: Original Gangster;* "Fuck My Daddy," *Ain't a Damn Thang Changed.* Bay Area gangsta rapper 2PAC has dealt critically with issues such as incest ("Brenda Has a Baby") and the rape of young women by their stepfathers ("Part-Time Mutha"). See *2Pacalypse Now.*

112. Quoted in Sims, "Gangsta Rappers."

113. Light, "L.A. Rappers Speak Out," 21.

114. I credit the music critic Toure with that term; at least that's where I got it from. It's hard to describe, other than a kind of West Coast "twang," a Texas-meets-California accent.

115. Brent Staples, "The Politics of Gangster Rap; A Music Celebrating Murder and Misogyny," *New York Times,* August 27, 1993; Michel Marriot, "Harsh Rap Lyrics Provoke Black Backlash," *New York Times,* August 15, 1993; Sims, "Gangster Rappers: The Lives, the Lyrics"; Donna Britt, "A One-Word Assault on Women," *Washington Post,* November 30, 1993; Scott Armstrong, "Backlash Is Brewing over 'Gangsta Rap' Lyrics as Public Says 'Enough,' " *Christian Science Monitor,* December 13, 1993; Michael Farquhar, "Gangsta Rap Ripped by Protesters: Black Women's Group Arrested at D.C. Store," *Washington Post,* December 22, 1993.

30

Girl

JAMAICA KINCAID

Wash the white clothes on Monday and put them on the stone heap; wash the color clothes on Tuesday and put them on the clothesline to dry; don't walk barehead in the hot sun; cook pumpkin fritters in very hot sweet oil; soak your little cloths right after you take them off; when buying cotton to make yourself a nice blouse, be sure that it doesn't have gum on it, because that way it won't hold up well after a wash; soak salt fish overnight before you cook it; is it true that you sing benna in Sunday school?; always eat your food in such a way that it won't turn someone else's stomach; on Sundays try to walk like a lady and not like the slut you are so bent on becoming; don't sing benna in Sunday school; you mustn't speak to wharf-rat boys, not even to give directions; don't eat fruits on the street—flies will follow you; *but I don't sing benna on Sundays at all and never in Sunday school*; this is how to sew on a button; this is how to make a buttonhole for the button you have just sewed on; this is how to hem a dress when you see the hem coming down and so to prevent yourself from looking like the slut I know you are so bent on becoming; this is how you iron your father's khaki shirt so that it doesn't have a crease; this is how you iron your father's khaki pants so that they don't have a crease; this is how you grow okra—far from the house, because okra tree harbors red ants; when you are growing dasheen, make sure it gets plenty of water or else it makes your throat itch when you are eating it; this is how you sweep a corner; this is how you sweep a whole house; this is how you sweep a yard; this is how you smile to someone you don't like too much; this is how you smile to someone you don't like at all; this is how you smile to someone you like completely; this is how you set a table for tea; this is how you set a table for dinner; this is how you set a table for dinner with an important guest; this is how you set a table for lunch; this is how you set a table for breakfast; this is how to behave in the presence of men who don't know you very well, and this way they won't recognize immediately the slut I have warned you against becoming; be sure to wash every day, even if it is with your own spit; don't squat down to play marbles—you are not a boy, you know; don't pick people's flowers—you might catch something; don't throw stones at blackbirds, because it might not be a blackbird at all; this is how to make a bread pudding; this is how to make doukona; this is how to make pepper pot; this is how to make a good medicine for a cold; this is how to make a good medicine to throw away a child before it even becomes a child; this is how to catch a fish; this is how to throw back a fish you don't like, and that way something bad won't fall on you; this is how to bully a man; this is how a man bullies you; this is how to love a man, and if this doesn't work there are other ways, and if they don't work don't feel too bad about giving up; this is how to spit up in the air if you feel like it, and this is how to move quick so that it doesn't fall on you; this is how to make ends meet; always squeeze bread to make sure it's fresh; *but what if the baker won't let me feel the bread?*; you mean to say that after all you are really going to be the kind of woman who the baker won't let near the bread?

—1983

31

Language

AMITAVA KUMAR

Everytime I think I have forgotten,
I think I have lost the mother tongue,
it blossoms out of my mouth.
Days I try to think in English:

I look up,
paylo kallo kagdo
oodto oodto jai, huhvay jzaday pohchay
ainee chanchma kaeek chay
the crow has something in his beak.
Sujata Bhatt

Name

Place of Birth

Date of Birth

Profession

Nationality

Sex

Identifying Marks

My passport provides no information about my language. It simply presumes I have one.

If the immigration officer asks me a question—his voice, if he's speaking English, deliberately slow, and louder than usual—I do not, of course, expect him to be terribly concerned about the nature of language and its entanglement with the very roots of my being. And yet it is in language that all immigrants are defined and in which we all struggle for an identity. That is how I understand the postcolonial writer's declaration about the use of a language like English that came to us from the colonizer:

> *Those of us who do use English do so in spite of our ambiguity towards it, or perhaps because of that, perhaps because we can find in that linguistic struggle a reflection of other struggles taking place in the real world, struggles between the cultures within ourselves and the influences at work upon our societies. To conquer English may be to complete the process of making ourselves free.*

I also do not expect the immigration officer to be very aware of the fact that it is in that country called language that immigrants are reviled. I'd like to know what his thoughts were when he first heard the Guns N' Roses song:

> *Immigrants*
> *and faggots*
> *They make no sense to me*
> *They come to our country—*
> *And think they'll do as they please*
> *Like start some mini-Iran*
> *Or spread some fuckin' disease.*

It is between different words that immigrants must choose to suggest who they are. And if these words, and their meanings, belong to others, then it is in a broken language that we must find refuge. Consider this example.

I took this photograph while standing outside an Arab grocery store in Brooklyn. While pressing the shutter I was aware of another grocery store, in the film

Falling Down, where the following exchange took place between a white American male, played by Michael Douglas, and a Korean grocer:

MR. LEE: Drink eighty-five cent. You pay or go.

FOSTER: This "fie," I don't understand a "fie." There's a "v" in the word. It's "fie-vah." You don't got "v's" in China?

MR. LEE: Not Chinese. I'm Korean.

FOSTER: Whatever. You come to my country, you take my money, you don't even have the grace to learn my language?

What Foster doesn't realize is that not only is it not his country alone, it is also not his language anymore. (That should be obvious to the ordinary American viewer, except that it *wasn't* obvious to every one. And it isn't.) But what I'm interested in asking is this: what is it that Mr. Lee is saying?

In saying "Not Chinese. I'm Korean," Mr. Lee is talking about difference. He is trying to tell another story. His story. Except that Foster won't listen. He is more interested in taking apart Mr. Lee's store with a baseball bat—the same way that, as Rita Chaudhry Sethi reminds us, others destroyed Japanese cars before Vincent Chin died. Vincent Chin was a young Chinese American who was murdered, also with a baseball bat, by two white autoworkers in Detroit. Chin was called a "Jap" and told "It's because of you motherfuckers that we're out of work." When I say Mr. Lee is talking about differences, I don't simply mean the difference between someone who is Chinese and someone else who is Korean. Instead, by difference I mean a sense of where it is a person is coming from. Both in terms of a location in place and in history.

Vincent Chin was an American of Chinese origin. The year he was killed marked the hundred-year anniversary of the Chinese Exclusion Act; in the year 1882, lynch mobs had murdered Chinese workers who were working on the West Coast.

Chin's murderers, Ronald Ebens and Michael Nitz, were autoworkers in Detroit, the city that entered the annals of early U.S. industrialism through its success in manufacturing cars. Ebens and Nitz did not know the difference between a worker and a capitalist. They were kept ignorant of the world of transnational capitalism, their very own world in which "General Motors owns 34 percent of Isuzu (which builds the Buick Opel), Ford 25 percent of Mazda (which makes transmissions for the Escort), and Chrysler 15 percent of Mitsubishi (which produces the Colt and the Charger)." Chin's killers did not spend a single night in prison and were fined $3,780 each. A Chinese American protesting the scant sentence is reported to have said, "Three thousand dollars can't even buy a good used car these days."

What does the word "Jap" mean? What is the difference between a Japanese and a Chinese American? What is the difference between a Chinese American and a used car? How does language mean and why does it matter?

As the Swiss linguist Ferdinand de Saussure argued very early in this century, language is a system of signs. And any sign consists of a signifier (the sound or written form) and a signified (the concept). As the two parts of the sign are linked or inseparable (the word "camera," for instance, accompanies the concept "camera" and remains quite distinct in our minds from the concept "car"), what is prompted is the illusion that language is transparent. The relationship between the signifier and the signified, and hence language itself, is assumed to be natural.

When we use the word "alien" it seems to stick rather unproblematically and unquestioningly to something or someone, and it is only by a conscious, critical act that we think of something different. Several years ago, in a public speech, Reverend Jesse Jackson seemed to be questioning the fixed and arbitrary assumptions in the dominant ideology when he reminded his audience that undocumented Mexicans were not aliens, they were *migrant workers*.

E.T., Jackson said emphatically, was an *alien*.

That is also the point made, albeit with more special effects than political ones, by the opening sequence of the film *Men in Black*.

The empty legs of the trousers hung up to dry in my birthplace, Ara, can be seen as just that, empty, lacking the fullness of meaning. But the image of the trousers— or the *signifier*—can also, however, be imaginatively joined to the concept of the bourgeoisie—or the *signified*—in whose service the half-clad washermen, not to mention the washerwoman with her back turned to us, labor in the river. These men who are poor do not wear the trousers they wash. The critical reader can fill the empty legs of these trousers with another meaning, the meaning born of a class and caste analysis of contemporary Indian society.

If you have been patient with my exposition so far, we might ask the same question of the object called the passport. How do we understand it as a term of language?

Let me, somewhat polemically, establish its meaning precisely by foregrounding a difference. For those who live in affluent countries, the passport is of use for international travel in connection with business or vacations. In poorer nations of the world, its necessity is tied to the need for finding employment, mainly in the West.

Once the process of acquiring a passport is over, you are reminded by friends and relatives that the real hurdle is getting the visa to enter that country that has now become this real place in your dreams. The passport is without any value if it does not have the visa. In other words, it is meaningless as a passport.

Abraham Verghese, writing in the *New Yorker*, had this report from the U.S. consulate in his home city of Madras, India:

> *One morning, the visa officer turned down six consecutive doctors and told the seventh, who happened to be a friend of mine, and whom I'll call Vadivel, "Spare me the crap about coming back with specialized knowledge to serve your country. Why do you really want to go?" Vadivel, who had held on to his American dream for so long that he could speak with the passion of a visionary, said, "Sir, craving your indulgence, I want to train in a decent, ten-story hospital where the lifts are actually working. I want to pass board-certification exams by my own merit and not through pull or bribes. I want to become a wonderful doctor, practice real medicine, pay taxes, make a good living, drive a big car on decent roads, and eventually live in the Ansel Adams section of New Mexico and never come back to this wretched town, where the doctors are as numerous as fleas and practice is cutthroat, and where the air outside is not even fit to breathe." The consul gave him a visa. The eighth applicant, forewarned, tried the same tactic but was turned down.*

If, on the one hand, the meanings of words like passport and visa are tied to dreams and fantasies, they are also, on the other, inextricably woven into the fabric of power and social prejudice. Americans learned recently of what one commentator called the "State Department visa 'profiles' of foreign applicants based on skin color, ethnicity, looks, speech—and remarkably enough—fashion sense." A Federal District Court judge had questioned the legality of State Department manuals that, apart from encouraging "special handling" of blacks, Arabs, and others, provide a list of abbreviations to help sort applicants: "RK=rich kid, LP=looks poor, TP=talks poor, LR=looks rough, TC=take care." In the case in which the judge had provided his ruling, among the evidence submitted were rejected applications with notations like "slimy looking," "Wears jacket on shoulders w/earring" and "No way . . . poor, poor, poor."

A fictional tale that takes place against the background of the humiliating drama of getting a visa is Salman Rushdie's marvelous short story "Good Advice Is Rarer than Rubies." It is also a tale about an old man's falling in love with a young woman who is a stranger. The beautiful Miss Rehana, whose "eyes were large and black and bright enough not to need the help of antimony," arrives at the gates of the British Consulate to apply for a visa. As we learn later in the story, she is about to go to what she calls "Bradford, London" to join a man who she had been engaged to as a child. She is approached outside the gates by Muhammad Ali who specialized in wheedling money from unsuspecting, illiterate women who had no skills in the language of the state.

The old man is struck by Miss Rehana's singular charm. "Her innocence made him shiver with fear for her." He is bewitched by her beauty, and he finds himself moving beyond the set speech in which he would warn applicants of the kinds of questions the British authorities would ask. "Muhammad Ali spoke brutally, on purpose, to lessen the shock she would feel when it, or something like it, actually happened."

"The oldest fools are bewitched by the youngest girls," writes Rushdie. And Muhammad Ali offers Miss Rehana, almost helplessly, a forged British passport, gratis.

But Miss Rehana does not accept Muhammad Ali's gift; it is only his advice she wants, for, as she says, "good advice is rarer than rubies." As she turns away from him, Muhammad Ali says to Miss Rehana, "Bibi, I am a poor fellow, and I have offered this prize because you are so beautiful. Do not spit on my generosity. Take the thing. Or else, don't take, go home, forget England, only do not go into that building and lose your dignity."

I do not think that what would cause Miss Rehana to lose her dignity is only the violence of a particular inquiry by immigration agents, say about her virginity, a subject of inquiry vehemently protested in the 1980s; instead, it is also the violence of the immense erasure of differences, historical particularities, and the individual humanity that is at the heart of Muhammad Ali's fears for her.

You start with an inquiry into the meaning of a word and you enter a world of difference. What are the answers to the question of an Indian woman's identity? Similar to the point about difference raised in the context of the Korean grocer, Mr. Lee, this question, too, finds an answer only in the form of more questions—at least in this brief fragment from an epic poem "Aay Wha' Kinda Indian Arr U?" written by a Sri Lankan-Canadian poet, Krisantha Sri Bhaggiyadatta:

> am i the Indian wearing salwar or a sari, a turban or a pottu
>   on the subway platform at 10 p.m.
> am i the mother awaiting the scalpel-wielding
>   C-section surgeon at Scarborough hospital?
> am i the baby who puts off being born
>   from June to October to February to June
>   awaiting a Jullundur Spring
> am i the self-sacrificing monogamous Sita
>   or am i the strong-willed and passionate
>   revengeful polyandrous Draupadi
>   (& her five Pandavas),

> *or am i the "we shoulda met earlier" Usha of Urvashi*
> *am i the Indian who must submit to virginity tests*
> *from immigration's con/insultants?*
> *am i the sponsored Indian whose husband owns her*
> *for ten years or else . . .*
> *thanks again, to the immigration department's*
> *department of familiar values*
> *am i the Indian who is kept 5 oceans apart from her lover?*
> *am i the Indian hiding in a women's shelter*
> *from her "til death do us apart" husband. . . .*

The question asked by the poet are important not only because they are so heterogeneous. They also hold a special appeal for their ability to returns us to language as the terrain on which difference is constructed or resisted. That is what I see, for example, in the poet's novel splitting of the word "con/insultants." Or in this anthropological account from 1924 about an early Sikh migrant in the U.S., which is cited by the Asian American scholar Ronald Takaki: "In one of the camps [for migrant workers in California], an Asian Indian told a visiting lady: 'We eat no meat, that is, no beef—the cow is sacred.' 'But you drink milk?' she snapped skeptically. 'And your cow gives you the milk!' 'Yes,' he countered, 'we drink our mother's milk also, but we do not eat her!'"

When you turn to me in the bus or the plane and talk to me—*if* you talk to me— you might comment, trying to be kind, "Your English is very good."

If I am feeling relaxed, and the burden of the permanent chip on my shoulder seems light, I will smile and say, "Thank you" (I never add, "So is yours"). Perhaps I will say, "Unfortunately, the credit goes to imperialism. The British, you know . . . " (Once, a fellow traveler widened her eyes and asked, "The British still rule over *India*?").

It was the British who, in the first half of the nineteenth century, under the imperative of Lord Macaulay, introduced the systematic teaching of English in India in order to produce a class of clerks. In Rushdie's novel *The Moor's Last Sigh*, a painter by the name of Vasco Miranda drunkenly upbraids the upper-class Indians as "Bleddy Macaulay's Minutemen. . . . Bunch of English-Medium misfits, the lot of you. . . . Even your bleddy dreams grow from foreign roots." Much later in the novel, the protagonist, Moor Zogoiby, reflects on Macaulay's legacy as he is leaving for the last time the city of his birth, Bombay:

> To form a class, *Macaulay wrote in the 1835 Minute on Education,* . . . of persons, Indian in blood and colour, but English in opinions, in morals, and in intellect. *And why, pray? O, to be* interpreters between us and millions whom we govern. *How grateful such a class of persons should, and must, be! For in India the dialects were* poor and rude, and a single shelf of a good European library was worth the whole native literature. *History, science, medicine, astronomy, geography, religion were likewise derided.* Would disgrace an English farrier . . . would move laughter in girls at an English boarding-school.

This historical reverie is an occasion for Zogoiby to declare retrospective judgment on the drunken Miranda, to assure the reader and posterity that "We were not, had never been, that class. The best, and worst, were in us, and fought in us, as they fought in the land at large. In some of us, the worst triumphed; but still we could say—and truthfully—that we had loved the best."

But what is it that was judged the best—in English?

The answer to that question can be sought in the pages of another Third-World writer, Michelle Cliff, who in writing about a Jamaican childhood describes how the schoolteacher's manual, shipped year after year from the London offices, directed the teacher

> *to see that all in the school memorized the "Daffodils" poem by William Wordsworth. . . . The manual also contained a pullout drawing of a daffodil, which the pupils were "encouraged to examine" as they recited the verse. [Cliff rightly adds,] No doubt the same manuals were shipped to villages in Nigeria, schools in Hong Kong, even settlements in Northwest Territory—anywhere that "the sun never set". . . . Probably there were a million children who could recite "Daffodils," and a million more who had actually never seen the flower, only the drawing, and so did not know why the poet had been stunned.*

I was one of those children, though I cannot remember being shown even a drawing of the flower! And this in an independent nation, still unable to shrug off, when it comes to education in English, its colonial heritage. I can, therefore, understand the critique of that education lying at the heart of the Jamaican cultural theorist Stuart Hall's observation: "When I first got to England in 1951, I looked out and there were Wordsworth's daffodils. Of course, what else would you expect to find? That's what I knew about. That is what trees and flowers meant. *I didn't know the names of the flowers I had left behind in Jamaica.*" In some ways, admittedly, we cannot speak of the postcolonial experience as only limited to the idea of the absent daffodil. A more adequate representation of that experience would encompass, at the same time, that moment when the Indian child thinks of the daffodil as a bright marigold—or when, as in Cliff's novel, a student in the Caribbean colors it "a deep red like a hibiscus. The red of a flame." In that instant, which I can only call one of creative appropriation, language does not remain an instrument of cultural domination. It is transformed, knowingly or unknowingly, into a weapon of protest.

But let me return to that particular moment when, as his plane banks over the smoky landscape of Bombay, Moor Zogoiby finds himself thinking of the doings of the Indian elite in the past ("In some of us, the worst triumphed; but still we could say—and truthfully—that we had loved the best"). His thought can also be seen as a protest. His Bombay was a Bombay that is no longer. For his Bombay was, as he says, "a city of mixed-up, mongrel joy." That vision of the city is in direct conflict with the Bombay, or Mumbai as it has now been renamed, of the right-wing, Hindu rule of the Shiv Sena in Maharashtra. The Shiv Sena's vision of Mumbai is essentially a purist one. It is intolerant of those that fall outside its own, arbitrary, even atavistic, frame of reference. What Zogoiby seems to be savoring in his past, as he leaves his city behind him with no companion other than a stuffed mutt by the name of Jawaharlal, is the kind of modern liberal-democratic vision we associate with an earlier India led by Nehru. "Unlike many other nationalists who had come to a sense of their Indianness through the detour of the West," Sunil Khilnani points out, "there is no trace in Nehru of that inwardly turned rage of an Aurobindo or Vivekananda, political intellectuals who strove to purge themselves of what they came to regard as a defiling encounter with the modern West—an encounter that had first planted in them the urge to be Indian." Against the memory of Jawaharlal Nehru, the mongrel visionary, we have the reality of the Shiv Sena supremo, Bal Thackeray, who lists Hitler among his models.

And yet there is one detail that deserves commentary. The Shiv Sena leader's own name owes its origins to his Hindu father's admiration for the English novelist William Makepeace Thackeray. I recall that detail not in order to point out that the Shiv Sena leader is hypocritical—though he might be that, and he can certainly be accused of much else—but to point out that, in the postcolonial condition, contradictions are inescapable.

To begin to *see* the contradictions is to become aware of history and, therefore, of another relation that this history has with the present. And to think of these contradictions *as inescapable* is to abandon a naive and dangerous view of history that inevitably harbors in its heart murderous longing.

Let's take the fairly banal example of the name of the street on which I passed most of my youth in India. My parents' house in Patna was on a street that is still called "Hardinge Road" by the city's mail carriers, the riksha pullers, and a wide variety of the city's citizenry. The road was named by the British after Charles Hardinge, the viceroy in India around 1914. In the 1980s, forty years after independence, the provincial government renamed the street "1942 Kranti Marg" (literally, 1942 Revolution Street). This was in honor of the high school students who, while participating in the 1942 Quit India movement, had fallen to British guns. For as long as I can remember, their historic statues have stood at the mouth of the street.

For me, this renaming wasn't without significance: it attached me to a history of nationalist struggle and its local roots. It made more real and meaningfully concrete what otherwise remain grand and empty proclamations of patriotism. However, at the same time, while indeed calling that street "1942 Kranti Marg," I cannot ever forget that there are in use in that town, and in the country as a whole, other names that are, if not English, at least *in English*. To deny that would be once again to deny our history. It would be to succumb, perhaps as hypocritically as the Shiv Sena chief does, to a purism that, at least in his case, has no role other than sanctifying the persecution of those that are relegated to the role of Others in his history. They are the Muslims, the untouchables, Communists, progressive women . . .

Which is not to say that any defense of the use of English should be uncritical. In a fine, witty novel, *English, August,* written by Upamanyu Chatterjee, the narrator's amusement at the use of English in small-town India is designed to mock the pretensions and the complacencies of the petty bourgeoisie. The narrator, while certainly very much an elitist, does not remove himself from the circle of critique. Take his own name, for example. He was named Agastya after a famous sage in the Hindu vedas. While in school, he told his friends he had wished he was a part of Westernized "Anglo-India, that he had Keith or Alan for a name, that he spoke English with their accent." From that day, he had been given among other names—which included "last Englishman" or just "English"—the name that stuck, "August." In the novel, even while baring his own repressed Anglo-envy or expressing his enjoyment at the spicy masala mix of his tongue, August does not fail to lampoon the affectations of his friend, a member of the metropolitan Americanized bourgeoisie in India:

> *"Amazing mix, the English we speak. Hazaar fucked. Urdu and American," Agastya laughed, "a thousand fucked, really fucked. I'm sure nowhere else could languages be mixed and spoken with such ease." The slurred sounds of the comfortable tiredness of intoxication, "'You look hazaar fucked, Marmaduke dear.' 'Yes Dorothea, I'm afraid I do feel hazaar fucked'—see, doesn't work. And our accents are Indian, but we prefer August to Agastya. When I say our accents, I, of course, exclude yours, which is unique in its fucked mongrelness—you even say 'Have a nice day' to those horny women at your telephones when you pass by with your briefcase, and when you agree with your horrendous boss, which is all the time, you say 'yeah, great' and 'uh-uh.'"*

The one named August is "hazaar fucked," the other, if I may hazard a guess, "plainly fucked." It is for the latter, from the position, perhaps of the former, that I had coined an (im)proper name, a name for a dog that is, and yet isn't, a cousin to the mongrel we encountered beside Zogoiby's legs:

LORD MACAULAY'S TAIL

TheEnglishlanguage was the second name
of Lord Macaulay's pet dog.
So we became its tail.

The mistake was
that we believed this tail
actually wagged the dog.

Now the condition is such
that on that side the teeth of the dog might well be
devouring someone

but on this side
we keep wagging the tail vigorously.

Those of Lord Macaulay's breed occupy the missionary position in relation to Indian education in the English medium. They are the ones who receive their training in convents from Christian priests described by the writer Shashi Tharoor as those "who serve their foreign Lord by teaching the children of the Indian lordly." Those priests might not be the ones, however, who teach in schools with names like Bright Future English School—a name noticed by Pankaj Mishra during his travels through small towns in India, narrated in his book *Butter Chicken in **Ludhiana**.*

Or even in institutions with names more like St. Joseph's Cross School—a name that, with the word "cross," has connotations not only of Christ but also of an unstable hybridity or mixing. The name draws Mishra on this speculative path:

> *St. Joseph's Cross School? Even the name sounded dubious. I couldn't recall a school with that name in Meerut. It was probably very recent, cleverly exploitative of the Indian regard, not entirely misplaced, for Christian schools and English-medium education. Scores of such schools, more than half of them fraudulent, had come up all over small-town India, some with incomplete buildings that frequently collapsed and left in their stead a turbid dust of recriminations and denials hanging over buried bodies.*

In this contemporary rewriting of the colonial project of missionary education, new fraudulent acts forge the consciousness of small-town India in the name of older, more legitimized, acts of moral uplift and business as usual. Mishra imagines only the pile of collapsing rubble on children's bodies, but in the decades that followed Indian independence there were many deaths as a part of what was called "language riots." In the demand of various groups for separate states under the federal Indian government, one bone of contention quite often was the existence of "English-medium" schools. If India was now free, did we need to have schools that prided themselves on teaching only English?

Among my earliest memories of going to school is of a rainy day when I was perhaps five. The car taking us to school suddenly stopped. Men, shouting slogans and waving their arms, smeared the license plate with tar. The driver turned the car around and brought my sisters and me back home. We were off from school; and, though not entirely unshaken by the event, I remember being very happy at the prospect of playing with paper boats.

Those men, although I did not know at that time, were part of the "Hindi Only" movement that considered the use of English in India a throwback to the imperialist era of the British. In *Midnight's Children* Rushdie's hero, the boy Saleem Sinai, finds himself crashing on his bicycle into one of the protest marches. The narrative is unable to hide the fact that grave issues of class identity gave intensity to what would be described as a merely cultural demand for a "linguistic state":

> *Hands grabbing handlebars as I slow down in the impassioned throng. Smiles filled with good teeth surround me. They are not friendly smiles. "Look look, a little laad-sahib comes down to join us from the big rich hill!" In Marathi which I hardly understand, it's my worst subject at school, and the smiles asking, "You want to join S.M.S. [Samyukta Maharashtra Samiti, or United Maharashtra Party], little princeling?" And I, just knowing what's being said, but dazed into telling the truth, shake my head No. And the smiles, "Oho! The young nawab does not like our tongue! What does he like?"*

Sinai, in Rushdie's novel, makes his escape from his predicament by giving to the crowd a nonsense rhyme in Gujarati, the language of the crowd's opponents.

> *Soo ché? Saru ché!*
> *Danda lé ké maru ché!*

A nonsense rhyme—"How are you? I am well! / I'll take a stick and thrash you to hell!"—and cleverly designed to mock the rhythms of Gujarati, it gets adopted as a slogan, a war cry, an insult. Soon the first language riot is under way, leaving fifteen killed and over three hundred wounded.

When I was a schoolboy and confronted by the faces outside the windows of the car taking us to school, I was unable, lacking the prescience of Saleem Sinai, to read in those faces, in their words and gestures, the signs of social disenfranchisement and anger. Nor was I involved with those people in exchanges that would impress me with premonitory messages about the power of words. But a somewhat jagged line joins that event with the more immediate reality in which I find myself: an immigrant speaking a language that, even when it is the one that my listeners speak, still *sounds* different from theirs. As I stand in front of a classroom filled with English-speaking, mostly white-skinned, students—we could be engaged in a discussion about a writer, the sounds of whose name are utterly alien and distant not only to to my illiterate grandparents but also, it sometimes seems, to my own lips—I might be composing my own nonsense rhyme to give those I see ringed around me.

> *I leave the door open*
> *when I teach. And turn back*
> *to spell on the board the word*
> *they said they "didn't get."*
> *"Oh that!" they say, moving*
> *quickly to the next point. Sometimes*
> *I apologize. They understand*
> *I don't have to. "No big deal."*
> *"Doesn't bother me." We agree*
> *to hide our embarrassment.*
> *And put everything within*
> *quotes (like "they" and "I")*
> *to keep things manageable.*
> *I turn from the board: black*
> *wall with weak ribs of chalk.*
> *My voice rises, fills the room*
> *and moves out of the door.*
> *It dances in the corridor, tripping*
> *with its foreign accent*
> *those calmly walking past.*

I took this photograph very close to the U.S.-Mexico border, somewhere between San Diego and Tijuana. There was a tear in the fence; I climbed under it and came up close to the highway to get a better shot. When I went back to the place in the fence, I was startled out of my skin by a Border Patrol van that was very slowly driving past. The officer did not see me, however, and I was soon back in the bar next to my motel.

While sipping my beer, I imagined a conversation with the border patrol officer who had only narrowly missed catching me.

OFFICER: I saw you photographing that sign. That was good, an excellent idea. What do you think about the sign though?

ME: Mmm. I don't know. It's just that—this is the first time I saw that sign. In my country, we have family-planning signs with figures like that. Father, mother, kid. The Health Ministry has a slogan painted it, One or Two kids. Then Stop.

OFFICER: That's very interesting. This is what I like about multiculturalism. You get to learn about cultural difference.

ME: You really think so? Yes, that's great. What can I learn from *this* sign?

OFFICER: Well, you've gotta get into the semiotics of it, you know what I'm saying?

ME: Uh-huh.

OFFICER: I'll be damned if language is transparent. That's the bottom line here. Just look at that sign—in English it's Caution, but in Spanish, it's *Prohibido*. You don't think those two words mean the same thing, do you?

ME: I don't know. I don't know Spanish.

OFFICER: Okay, well, I'll be patient with you. The sign in English is for folks who drive. They're being cautioned. Now, the sign in Spanish—

ME: Yes, yes, I see what you're driving at! The *Prohibido* sign is for the Spanish speaker—

OFFICER: There you go! Bingo! Bull's eye! They don't have the word *Caución* there. It's plain Prohibited: pure and simple. The picture, the image—it splits, right before your eyes!

ME: The scales have fallen . . .

OFFICER: Well, but you gotta stay alert. 'Cause culture is a moving thing, meaning change. Or sometimes, just get plain run over. All the time.

ME:	Yes, yes.
OFFICER:	What work do you do?
ME:	I teach English.
OFFICER:	No kidding! See, this is America! You teaching *English* to our kids, I love it. Say, did you ever watch *Saturday Night Live* when it first came on?
ME:	No, I don't think so.
OFFICER:	Michael O'Donoghue played a language instructor. He was teaching this confused immigrant played by John Belushi. You know the sentence that O'Donoghue used to introduce the language?
ME:	What was it?
OFFICER:	I will feed your fingers to the wolverines.

We could have gone on, the officer and I. If we were swapping stories today, I'd have mentioned the news report that the telephone company Sprint, in its billing letter in Spanish, threatens customers with phone cutoff unless their check is received by the end of the month. According to the news report, the Anti-Defamation League and the National Council of La Raza have filed complaints. Why? Because the billing letter in English is somewhat differently worded: "As a customer you are Sprint's number one priority. We . . . look forward to serving your communication needs for many years to come."

And, if the officer had had more time, we might have arrived at an understanding that language, especially English, has been used as a racial weapon in immigration.

To cite a historical example: in 1896 a colonial official argued against the restrictions imposed on the entry of Indians in South Africa, adding that this would be "most painful" for Queen Victoria to approve. At the same time, he sanctioned a European literacy test that would automatically exclude Indians while preserving the facade of racial equality.

Almost a hundred years later a Texas judge ordered the mother of a five-year-old to stop speaking in Spanish to her child. Judge Samuel Kiser reminded the mother that her daughter was a "full-blooded American." "Now, get this straight. You start speaking English to this child because if she doesn't do good in school, then I can remove her because it's not in her best interest to be ignorant. The child will only hear English."

Who is permitted to proceed beyond the gates into the mansion of full citizenship? And on what terms? These are the questions that the episode in the Texas courthouse raises. Apart from the issue of gross paternalism and an entirely injudicious jingoism, what comes into play here is the class bias in North American society that promotes bilingualism in the upper class but frowns on it when it becomes an aspect of lower-class life.

More revealing of the ties between language and U.S. immigration is the following newspaper report: "School and city officials expressed outrage this week over the Border Patrol's arrest of three Hispanic students outside an English as Second Language class."

For the Chicano poet Alfred Arteaga, the above story about arrest and deportation has a double irony: "irony, not only that 'officials expressed outrage' at so typical an INS action, but irony also, that the story made it into print in the first place." Arteaga knows too well that what Chicanos say and do in their own language is rarely found worthy of printing.

I think it is equally significant to remark on the fact that the officers who conducted the arrest were patrolling the borders of the dominant language to pick up the illegals. They are ably assisted by the likes of the California state assemblyman William J. Knight, who distributed among his fellow legislators a poem, "I Love America." That poem begins with the words "I come for visit, get treated regal, / So I stay, who care illegal." This little ditty makes its way through the slime of a racist fantasy. Its landscape is filled with greedy swindlers and dishonest migrant workers. The breeding subhumans speak in a broken syntax and mispronounce the name Chevy, the heartbeat of America, as (call the National Guard, please!) Chebby. The poem ends with a call that emanates like a howl from the guts of the Ku Klux Klan:

> *We think America damn good place,*
> *Too damn good for white man's race.*
> *If they no like us, they can go,*
> *Got lots of room in Mexico.*

If the immigration officer were to ask me about my language, what would I say? That any precious life-giving sense of language loses all form in this arid landscape of Buchanan-speak? Perhaps. That any answer I could possibly give is nothing more defined than a blur moving on the infrared scopes of those guarding the borders of fixed identity.

Homi Bhabha writes: "The enchantment of art lies in looking in a glass darkly—a wall, stone, a screen, paper, canvas, steel—that turns suddenly into the almost unbearable lightness of being." But where is this buoyancy, the refulgence, the mix of new life and new art? As the case of Fauziya Kasinga reminds us—the young woman who fled Togo to avoid genital mutilation and was held for long in detention by the U.S. Immigration authorities—grim reality so often persists in its unenchanting rudeness.

In such conditions to speak is only to declare any speech a station of loss.

> *I brought two bags from home, but there was a third that I left behind.*
> *In this new country, apart from the struggles that made me a stranger,*
> *were your needs, of the ones who bid me goodbye, those I left behind.*
> *Among the papers I collected, you had put a small bag of sweets, I left*
> *behind.*
>
> *There were divisions at home, there were other possibilities; there*
> *were communities in my town, there were communities where I came;*
> *I found a job, called it a struggle for survival, everything else I left*
> *behind. I didn't want to forget my traditions, the tradition of forget-*
> *ting I left behind.*
>
> *Bags, passport, my shoes crossed the yellow lines, something was left*
> *behind.*

> *Here I am, a sum of different parts; travel agents everywhere are selling ads for the parts that were left behind.*

And yet, while speaking of the patrolling of the borders of dominant identity, I must note the presence of one who is still eluding arrest: a border-artist/poet-performer/hoarder-of-hyphens/warrior-for-Gringostroika. Officer, meet Guillermo Gómez-Peña. You have been looking for him not only because Gómez-Peña declares "I speak in English therefore you listen/I speak in English therefore I hate you." But also because, like a "Pablo Neruda gone punk," this "border brujo" threatens mainstream America with the swaggering banditry of language, demanding as ransom a pure reality-reversal:

> *What if the U.S. was Mexico?*
> *What if 200,000 Anglo-Saxicans*
> *Were to cross the border each month*
> *to work as gardeners, waiters*
> *3rd chair musicians, movie extras*
> *bouncers, babysitters, chauffeurs*
> *syndicated cartoons, feather-weight boxers, fruit-pickers*
> *and anonymous poets?*
> *What if they were called Waspanos*
> *Waspitos, Wasperos or Waspbacks?*
> *What if literature was life, eh?*

32

Persimmons

LI-YOUNG LEE

In sixth grade Mrs. Walker
slapped the back of my head
and made me stand in the corner
for not knowing the difference
between *persimmon* and *precision*.
How to choose.

persimmons. This is precision.
Ripe ones are soft and brown-spotted.
Sniff the bottoms. The sweet one
will be fragrant. How to eat:
put the knife away, lay down newspaper.
Peel the skin tenderly, not to tear the meat.
Chew the skin, suck it,
and swallow. Now, eat
the meat of the fruit,
so sweet,
all of it, to the heart.

Donna undresses, her stomach is white.
In the yard, dewy and shivering

with crickets, we lie naked,
face-up, face-down.
I teach her Chinese.
Crickets: *chiu chiu.* Dew: I've forgotten.
Naked: I've forgotten.
Ni, wo: you and me.
I part her legs,
remember to tell her
she is beautiful as the moon.

Other words
that got me into trouble were
fight and *fright, wren* and *yarn.*
Fight was what I did when I was frightened,
fright was what I felt when I was fighting.
Wrens are small, plain birds,
yarn is what one knits with.
Wrens are soft as yarn.
My mother made birds out of yarn.
I loved to watch her tie the stuff;
a bird, a rabbit, a wee man.

Mrs. Walker brought a persimmon to class
and cut it up
so everyone could taste
a *Chinese apple.* Knowing
it wasn't ripe or sweet, I didn't eat
but watched the other faces.

My mother said every persimmon has a sun
inside, something golden, glowing,
warm as my face.

Once, in the cellar, I found two wrapped in newspaper,
forgotten and not yet ripe.
I took them and set both on my bedroom windowsill,
where each morning a cardinal
sang, *The sun, the sun.*

Finally understanding
he was going blind,
my father sat up all one night
waiting for a song, a ghost.
I gave him the persimmons,
swelled, heavy as sadness,
and sweet as love.

This year, in the muddy lighting
of my parents' cellar, I rummage, looking
for something I lost.
My father sits on the tired, wooden stairs,
black cane between his knees,
hand over hand, gripping the handle.
He's so happy that I've come home.
I ask how his eyes are, a stupid question.
All gone, he answers.

Under some blankets, I find a box.
Inside the box I find three scrolls.
I sit beside him and untie
three paintings by my father:
Hibiscus leaf and a white flower.
Two cats preening.
Two persimmons, so full they want to drop from the cloth.

He raises both hands to touch the cloth,
asks, *Which is this?*

This is persimmons, Father.

Oh, the feel of the wolftail on the silk,
the strength, the tense
precision in the wrist.
I painted them hundreds of times
eyes closed. These I painted blind.
Some things never leave a person:
scent of the hair of one you love,
the texture of persimmons,
in your palm, the ripe weight.
                              –1986

33

Rhetorical Sovereignty: What Do American Indians Want from Writing?

Scott Richard Lyons

Now, brothers and sisters . . . the white man has his ways. Oh gracious me, he has his ways. He talks about the Word. He talks through it and around it. He builds upon it with syllables, with prefixes and suffixes and hyphens and accents. He adds and subtracts and divides and multiplies the Word. And in all of this he subtracts the Truth. And, brothers and sisters, you have come to live in the white man's world. Now the white man deals in words, and he deals easily, with grace and sleight of hand. And in his presence, here on his own ground, you are as children, mere babes in the woods.

—N. Scott Momaday (*House*, 93–94)

CCC 51:3/ Kehrug 2000
College Composition & Communication

A student asked, "Can Essential Nature be destroyed?"
Coyote said, "Yes, it can."
The student asked, "How can Essential Nature be destroyed?"
Coyote said, "With an eraser."

—Robert Aitken

In *My People the Sioux,* Luther Standing Bear recounts the moment when he and other children arrived at the Carlisle Indian School and received for the first time the European implements of writing. "Although we were yet wearing our Indian clothes," Standing Bear writes, "we were marched into a school room, where we were each given a pencil and slate. We were seated at single desks. We soon discovered that the pencils made marks on the slate" (*Sioux* 136). Pulling their blankets over their heads to conceal both slate and the marks they would make upon them, a child's act of modesty, the children's first impulse was to draw scenes from their recently departed home life—"a man on a pony chasing a buffalo, or a boy shooting birds in a tree, or it might be one of our Indian games"—and when finished, "we dropped our blankets down on the seat and marched up to the teacher with our slates to show what we had drawn" (*Sioux* 136). Picture these children withdrawing into their blankets with a curious new technology, concealing their texts from each other and the teacher until just the right moment, then emerging from their blankets proud and eager to share the fruits of their labor. They were, at least until this point, the same children, and the marks they made were earnest representations of their lives. Shortly thereafter, however, this same technology would be used to change them:

> One day when we came to school there was a lot of writing on one of the blackboards. We did not know what it meant, but our interpreter came into the room and said, 'Do you see all these marks on the blackboard? Well, each word is a white man's name. They are going to give each one of you one of these names by which you will hereafter be known.' None of the names were read or explained to us, so of course we did not know the sound or meaning of any of them. (*Sioux* 136–37)

These arbitrary, meaningless names were selected by students who were given a pointer by the teacher; the chosen name was then written on cloth and sewed on the back of each student's shirt. Standing Bear recalls how the first boy to choose a name looked back at the others "as much as to say . . . 'Is it right for me to take a white man's name?' " (*Sioux* 137). But Standing Bear himself "took the pointer and acted as if I were about to touch an enemy" (*Sioux* 137), counting coup on the text, so to speak, and probably eliciting laughter in support of his mock bravery from the other kids. "Soon we all had names of white men sewed on our backs" (*Sioux* 137).

That laughter, which is not in Standing Bear's book but remains my guess, my desire, would nonetheless be short-lived, as is known by anyone familiar with the boarding school story. As David Wallace Adams tells it in *Education for Extinction,* this tale "constitutes yet another deplorable episode in the long and tragic history of Indian-white relations"—specifically, the development of education designed to promote "the eradication of all traces of tribal identity and culture, replacing them with the commonplace knowledge and values of white civilization" (336, 335). This forced replacement of one identity for another, a cultural violence enabled in part through acts of physical violence, was in so many ways located at the scene of writing. More horrific than most scenes of writing, however, the boarding school stands out as the ultimate symbol of white domination, even genocide, through assimilation in the American Indian experience. And although Standing Bear and others would recall multiple forms of Indian resistance, from torching schools to running away to counting coup on the Western text, the duplicitous interrelationships between writing, violence, and colonization developed during the nineteenth-century—not only in the boarding schools but at the signings of hundreds of treaties, most of which were dishonored by whites—would set into motion a persistent distrust of the written word in English, one that resonates in homes and schools and courts of law still today. If our respect for the Word remains resolute, our faith in the written word is compromised at best.

What do Indians want from writing? Certainly something other than the names of white men sewn to our backs. And for its part, resistance to assimilation through the acts of writing should entail something more than counting coup on the text (or for that matter, torching the school). I suggest that our highest hopes for literacy at this point rest upon a vision we might name *rhetorical sovereignty*. Sovereignty, of course, has long been a contested term in Native discourse, and its shifting meanings over time attest to an ongoing struggle between Americans and the hundreds of Indian nations that occupy this land. Our claims to sovereignty entail much more than arguments for tax-exempt status or the right to build and operate casinos; they are nothing less than our attempt to survive and flourish as a people. Sovereignty is the guiding story in our pursuit of self-determination, the general strategy by which we aim to best recover our losses from the ravages of colonization: our lands, our languages, our cultures, our self-respect. For indigenous people everywhere, sovereignty is an ideal principle, the beacon by which we seek the paths to agency and power and community renewal. Attacks on sovereignty are attacks on what it enables us to pursue; the pursuit of sovereignty is an attempt to revive not our past, but our possibilities. Rhetorical sovereignty is the inherent right and ability of *peoples* to determine their own communicative needs and desires in this pursuit, to decide for themselves the goals, modes, styles, and languages of public discourse. Placing the scene of writing squarely back into the particular contingency of the Indian rhetorical situation, rhetorical sovereignty requires of writing teachers more than a renewed commitment to listening and learning; it also requires a radical rethinking of how and what we teach as the written word at all levels of schooling, from preschool to graduate curricula and beyond. In what follows, I hope to sketch out some preliminary notes toward the praxis that is rhetorical sovereignty. I begin with a discussion of the concept of sovereignty, followed by a dialogue between the fields of composition and rhetoric and Native American studies, concluding with some very general recommendations for expanding our canons and curricula. My argument is motivated in part by my sense of being haunted by that little boy's backward glance to those other Indian children: *Is it right for me to take a white man's name?*

Sovereignty is (also) rhetorical

Sovereignty, as I generally use and understand the term, denotes the right of a people to conduct its own affairs, in its own place, in its own way. The concept of sovereignty originated in feudal Europe, and as a term it arrived to the English language by way of France; *souverain* signified a ruler accountable to no one save himself or God (Duchacek 47). Early modern European monarchs employed the language of sovereignty to secure their grip on state power in the face of a threatening nobility and papacy. A declaration of one's right to rule, a monarch's claim to sovereignty "stood as a ringing assertion of absolute political authority at home, one that could imply designs on territory abroad" (Fowler and Bunck 5). As modern nations and states underwent their various forms of development, the concept was consistently deployed to address not only domestic authority at home but a state's relative independence from *and among* other states; thus, sovereignty came to mean something systemic and relational. A sovereign's power was generally a force understood in relation to other sovereigns in the emerging international scene; hence, "a sovereign was to respect the sovereignty of its peers" (Fowler and Bunck 6). As political institutions continued to develop under modernity, the meanings of sovereignty changed with them, signifying such matters as the right to make and enforce laws, notions of political legitimacy and international recognition, and national self-determination. While the meanings of sovereignty have shifted and continue to shift over time, the concept has nonetheless carried with it a sense of locatable and recognizable power. In fact, the location of power has depended upon the crucial act of recognition—and vice versa.

From the early moments of first contact on this continent, the construction of Indian and non-Indian senses of sovereignty was a contested and contradictory process. It was also a rhetorical one. Although there is no possible way to describe its many and complicated logics in necessary detail here, we can see that for at least two centuries following Columbus, "European states were compelled to recognize and engage Indian nations as political actors in their diplomatic activities" (Berman 128). They did this in large part through making treaties with Indian nations, a process that created a relationship between groups of "an international rather than internal character," even in sites of severe colonizing activity (Berman 129). This acknowledged sense of Indian national sovereignty was so strong among European states that it actually became a means of legitimizing European claims to new world resources; a territorial dispute between the English and the Dutch, say, might be settled by one side producing a treaty with the sovereign nation who actually owned the land (Berman 132). After the American revolution, the United States maintained the practice of treaty-making with Indian nations begun by European powers, and "from the beginning of its political existence, recognized a measure of autonomy in the Indian bands and tribes" (Prucha, *Treaties* 2). During the years 1778–1868, the U.S. signed and ratified some 367 treaties with Indian nations, all of which presumed a sense of sovereignty on the part of Indian groups. About two-thirds of those treaties were land deals, and as Prucha points out, "cession of Indian lands . . . was an indication of Indian sovereignty over those lands, and the recognition by the United States of Indian ownership to the lands remaining strengthened the concept" (*Treaties* 4). You can't give up what you don't own, after all; nor can you buy what's already yours.

However, the Americans would gradually assume a dominant stance in Indian-white relations, leading to an erosion of Native sovereignty that Prucha credits to overwhelming American military strength, growing Indian economic dependence on white goods, and treaty provisions that left stipulations to be carried out by Congress (Prucha, *Treaties* 6–7). After the American revolution, it wasn't long before the nation-to-nation stance Indians and their interlocutors had operated from was simultaneously attacked and affirmed in a couple of landmark U.S. Supreme Court cases concerning the Cherokee of Georgia facing removal in the early nineteenth century. In *Cherokee Nation v. Georgia* (1831), Chief Justice John Marshall's famous pronouncement of the Cherokees as a "domestic dependent nation" constituted the United States' first major, unilateral reinterpretation of Indian sovereignty, one further tinkered with a year later by the same court in *Worcester v. Georgia* (1832). In the former opinion, Marshall deemed the Cherokees limited in their claim to sovereignty, seeing them as a nation not-quite-foreign, but suggested nonetheless that the Cherokees still formed "a distinct political society, separated by others, capable of managing its own affairs and governing itself" (Prucha, *Documents* 58). This somewhat glaring contradiction was explained in the latter decision, where Marshall opined that "Indian nations had always been considered as distinct, independent political communities, retaining their original natural rights, as the undisputed possessors of the soil, from time immemorial, *with the single exception* imposed by irresistible power" (Prucha, *Documents* 60; emphasis mine). In other words, while recognizing Indian sovereignty in terms we can fairly describe as eternal and absolute, the Supreme Court's decisions on the Cherokee cases ultimately caved in to what would become a persistent, uniquely American, and wholly imperialist notion of recognition-from-above. The United States could limit Cherokee sovereignty simply because it could, and it could because it is the United States. American exceptionalism won the day, thanks to its "irresistible power," and while U.S. plenary power wouldn't become fully articulated in a legal sense until *United States v. Kagama* in 1886, it found its rhetorical groundwork laid solidly in the Cherokee cases of the 1830s.

In a sense, these cases exemplify what we might call rhetorical imperialism: the ability of dominant powers to assert control of others by setting the terms of debate. These terms are often definitional—that is, they *identify* the parties discussed by describing them in certain ways. Take, for example, Marshall's rather self-reflective analysis of the language of sovereignty in his *Worcester v. Georgia* opinion:

> . . . *'treaty' and 'nation' are words of our own language, selected in our diplomatic and legislative proceedings . . . having each a definite and well-understood meaning. We have applied them to Indians, as we have applied them to the other nations of the earth. They are applied to all in the same sense. (Prucha, Documents 60)*

In short, Indians are defined here as fellow nations requiring treaties. Yet in *Cherokee Nation v. Georgia*, Marshall wrote that "the term foreign nation" *wasn't* quite applicable to Indian nations, suggesting instead that the Cherokee Nation's "relation to the United States resembles that of a ward to his guardian." This was because Indians—"savages" newly arrived on "civilization's" fresh path—were "in a state of pupilage" (Prucha, *Documents* 59). More than an agonistic legal contest over sovereign rights, the language of this decision shows Indian people being completely redefined by their interlocutors: a ward or pupil—that is, a child—is quite a different animal than a fellow nation in the community of sovereigns. As the exercise of rhetorical imperialism, Marshall's metaphors effectively paved the way for the United States to assume a position of political *paternalism* over Indian nations that has thrived up to this very day—chalk one up for the "Great White Father." The lesson here seems obvious: namely, he who sets the terms sets the limits. And likewise the rewriting of Indian sovereignty would continue over time. As Prucha points out, the word "tribe" increasingly came to replace "nation" in treaties, substituting one highly ideological European word for another, and with the Abolition of Treaty-Making Act of 1871, a powerful little rider tacked on to an Indian appropriations bill that formally ended the practice of treaty-making, "treaties" henceforth came to be called "agreements" by the authoring Americans (Prucha, *Treaties* 4, 211–13). From "sovereign" to "ward," from "nation" to "tribe," and from "treaty" to "agreement," the erosion of Indian national sovereignty can be credited in part to a rhetorically imperialist use of writing by white powers, and from that point on, much of the discourse on tribal sovereignty has nit-picked, albeit powerfully, around terms and definitions.

None of this stopped Indian exercises of sovereignty—it just threw things into different modes and sites of contest, for instance, that of language and representation. Not to downplay the tremendous cost to Indian people these struggles for sovereignty have entailed, but I want to point out that the dominant stance achieved by the Americans must continue to be seen as merely that—dominant, not omnipotent—which is far from saying all things are said and done. Indian nations still possess, and are still recognized to possess, varying and constantly shifting degrees of sovereignty. While hegemonic versions of the American Indian story implying the obverse continue to be told in schools, scholarship, and popular culture—generally in the past tense—discourses of resistance and renewal have never ceased in Indian country, and these marginalized narratives of the continuing struggle for Indian sovereignty are making themselves more and more visible in public representations and talk. It's worthwhile to note how so much of this struggle, from treaties to court cases to the growing popularity of Native American literature—has taken place at what we might call the colonized scene of writing: a site of contact-zone rhetoric in its fullest sense. One way of approaching this site is to find in American legal, political, and cultural written discourses recurrent, yet ambivalent, assaults on Native sovereignty answered by recurrent, yet subordinate, defenses and redefinitions of the same by Indians. These textual exchanges are eminently rhetorical: arguments motivated by highly ideological conflations and intertwinings of motives, beliefs, and assumptions that do not lend themselves to a sense of consensually-derived conclusions. One reason for this is certainly due to power imbalances between whites and Indians, but another seems owing to truly salient differences in cultural understandings of what it means to be political human beings. That is, I want to suggest that the rhetorics of sovereignty advanced by both Indian and non-Indian people often claim to be talking about the same thing, when actually they differ considerably.

For example, for Western powers after the Enlightenment, the meaning of sovereignty became contingent upon freshly-formed conceptions of the modern nation-state and new bourgeois ideologies of the individual. The former was a legal-political understanding of the right to popular self-governance freed from the shackles of older forms of monarchical sovereignty, the latter a new subjectivity enjoyed and defended by the bourgeoisie. Both were generated from a desire to develop and protect the idea of private property. In this context, for a thinker like Kant, sovereignty became essentially procedural, the exercise of reason and public critique generated by the bourgeoisie who as "the people" construct the nation-state through the act of making coercive laws, and subsequently as "sovereign" coerce through them as a *nation* and are coerced by them as *individuals* ("Metaphysics" 142). Sovereignty for Kant was a largely technical process of communicative rationality ultimately designed to benefit and control solitary monads; hence, the nation-state became something of an instrument. Sovereignty rested primarily with the "public," itself constituted by the communicating mass of wholly "private" individuals acting out of self-interest (Kant, "Enlightenment" 55–7; see also Habermas). The dialectic of private and public constituted the business of the nation-state, even while resting upon a series of exclusions (for example, of gender, race, and class) that belied its utopian claims to equality, as public sphere theorists have demonstrated (see Fraser; Ryan). But ultimately, for the young United States of the Enlightenment, sovereignty was exercised through the communicative procedures developed and maintained by individuals who, through reason, would form the public and run the nation-state (Eley).

By contrast, Indians who entered into treaties as nations are better understood as representing themselves as a *people:*

> *The idea of the people is primarily a religious conception, and with most American Indian tribes it begins somewhere in the primordial mists. In that time the people were gathered together but did not yet see themselves as a distinct people. A holy man had a dream or a vision; quasi-mythological figures of cosmic importance revealed themselves, or in some other manner the people were instructed. They were given ceremonies and rituals that enabled them to find their place on the continent. (Deloria and Lytle 8)*

A people is a group of human beings united together by history, language, culture, or some combination therein—a community joined in union for a common purpose: the survival and flourishing of the people itself. It has always been from an understanding of themselves as a people that Indian groups have constructed themselves as a nation. In *The Power of Identity,* Manuel Castells defines nations as "cultural communes constructed in people's minds and collective memory by the sharing of history and political projects," adding a political dimension to a sense of peoplehood (51). In his analysis, nations, with or without states, tend to be organized around the sensual cultural material of peoples—for example, language—and the First Nations were and are no exception (Castells 31). "Indians had a good idea of nationhood," Deloria and Lytle write, defining the exercise of nationhood as "decision-making that is free and uninhibited within the community" and suggesting it was always conducted out of regard for the survival and flourishing of the people (8, 13). In that sense, the making of political decisions by Indian people hasn't been the work of a nation-state so much as that of a *nation-people*. The sovereignty of individuals and the privileging of procedure are less important in the logic of a nation-people, which takes as its supreme charge the sovereignty of the group through a privileging of its traditions and culture and continuity.

One example of a nation-people might be found in the system of Cherokee towns prior to their formal and essentially forced incorporation as a nation-state in the early nineteenth century, itself a desperate political maneuver in the face of impending removal. Some sixty in all, traditional Cherokee towns in Georgia were generally decentralized but loosely linked through language and kinship, each village ultimately retaining its own sense of independence (Champagne 25). As both people and nation, "the Cherokees found unity in an overarching principle that governed their behavior in both domestic and foreign affairs." Namely, "Cherokees believed that human beings had the responsibility for maintaining cosmic order by respecting categories and maintaining boundaries" (Perdue 56). These categories and boundaries were often derived from mythological understandings of their culture but were also open to democratic contest in council houses (Champagne 29). This was no nation of individuals, nor one reducible to procedure; rather, the Cherokees found their national identity and interests in the concept of the people. Reason, deployed regularly and at will in council-house decision making, did not militate against their understandings of themselves as a group; nor was reason contingent upon a sense of privacy. Rather, reason and rationality were deployed always with an idealistic eye toward the betterment of the people, including but not limited to the individuals which constituted it, through the practices of tradition and culture.

Another, more cosmopolitan example of a nation-people is the Haudenosaunee, or Iroquois League, which was actually a consciously constructed confederation of *different* peoples based upon the principle of peaceful coexistence. As Onandaga leader and professor Oren Lyons tells it, "Haudenosaunee political organization demonstrated that a form of participatory democracy was possible on a fairly large geographic scale," and what's striking in his account is how democratic procedures were constructed into a "primordial" myth that spoke to and of multiple cultures (32). Linked by the story of the Peacemaker and the practice of respectful communication, the Haudenosaunee were—and remain—a *multicultural* nation-people (34–42). "Since the beginning of our memory," Lyons writes, "this distinctiveness has been seen as a foundation for mutual respect; and we have therefore always honored the fundamental right of peoples and their societies to be different" (42). Here, too, the traditions of the people coexisted with the exercise of a communal, communicative rationality:

> *Indian decision-making processes at the local level required the free*
> *input of information and advice for these processes to work at all.*
> *Any proposal brought to the Haudenosaunee was carried to each of*
> *the nations, where it was discussed either in clan or general meetings;*

> *the sentiments of the nation were then carried by the principal chiefs*
> *to the confederate council . . . and the chiefs had the authority to*
> *negotiate details of a proposed agreement according to their own judg-*
> *ment and in line with political reality. (Lyons 32)*

Thus conceived, Haudenosaunee sovereignty is probably best understood as the right of a people to exist and enter into agreements with other peoples for the sole purpose of promoting, not suppressing, local cultures and traditions, even while united by a common political project—in this case, the noble goal of peace between peoples.

In the context of the colonized scene of writing, the distinction between a nation-state and a nation-people might get at the root of why Indians and non-Indians tend to view things like treaties so differently even today. "In almost every treaty," Deloria and Lytle write, "the concern of the Indians was the preservation of the people": that is, the successful perpetuation of life, land rights, community, and cultural practice (8). Sovereignty in this regard is concerned not only with political procedures or individual rights but with a whole way of life. Non-Indian reductions of Indian claims to sovereignty as arguments for "self-governance"—that is, for a degree of local financial and political control modeled after western governmental systems—obscures this holistic people-oriented emphasis. "Self-government is not an Indian idea," write Deloria and Lytle. "It originates in the minds of non-Indians who have reduced the traditional ways to dust" (15). Self-governance is certainly the work of a state but not necessarily that of a people; a people requires something more. However, while self-governance alone may not constitute the whole part and parcel of sovereignty, it nonetheless remains a crucial component. "I believe that the future of our nations is singularly dependent upon our ability to self-govern," writes Robert B. Porter. "If we can do this, then all of our other problems—the loss of language and culture, the need for economic stability, and the preservation of tribal sovereignty—can then be addressed and, hopefully, resolved" (73). What we might need, then, is an understanding of the twin pillars of sovereignty: the power to self-govern and the affirmation of peoplehood. For without self-governance, especially in America, the people fragment into a destructive and chaotic individualism, and without the people, there is no one left to govern and simply nothing left to protect.

And so it has been with both self-governance and the people in mind that Indians have been advancing new rhetorics of sovereignty—both to themselves and to outside powers—and some of these have found their way into the academy. In *We Talk, You Listen,* Deloria explicitly addresses the concept in a chapter entitled "Power, Sovereignty, and Freedom." Suggesting that "few members of racial minority groups have realized that inherent in their peculiar experience on this continent is hidden the basic recognition of their power and sovereignty," Deloria argues for action at the group level to replace legal claims for self-determination "since power cannot be given and accepted" (115); rather, it must be first asserted and then recognized. As Robert Warrior points out, Deloria's is a "process-centered definition of sovereignty," one contingent upon the renewal of groups at the community level (91). From this reading of Deloria, Warrior has advanced his own concept of "intellectual sovereignty," a process devoted to community renewal through the paying of attention to the American Indian intellectual tradition, one he lays out in the form of a materialist history (1–3). While I question the end game of a project promoting Indian intellectuals studying Indian intellectuals, Warrior's work still has much to offer in a mainstream academic culture still obsessed with canonicity. Warrior has been praised for this work by Elizabeth Cook-Lynn, who finds most other critics, including some Natives, afraid to take on the nationalist implications of sovereignty in their critical theory and work (90–91). Cook-Lynn also criticizes mainstream multiculturalism, which she argues "has not and will not cast much light on the centuries-long struggle for sovereignty faced by the people" because it remains "in conflict with the concept of American Indian sovereignty, since it emphasizes matters of spirituality and culture" divorced from national recognition (91). Mainstream multiculturalism is not sovereignty *per se* because it abstracts its sense of culture from the people and from the land, and while it may indeed affirm the rightful and creative existence of Indian cultures and peoples among others, it tends not to discuss that other pillar of sovereignty: self-government. Mainstream multiculturalism may focus on the *people* but typically not the *nation* and thus isn't necessarily the practice or honoring of Indian sovereignty.

In all three of these thinkers, the rhetoric of sovereignty takes on a decidedly nationalistic cast, but while they all advocate focusing on action at the community level, none of them can adequately be described as purely separatist. Rather, in explicit opposition to this, Warrior calls for Indians to "withdraw without becoming separatists, being willing to reach out for the contradictions within our experience and open ourselves to the pain and the joy of others" (124). Rather than representing an enclave, sovereignty here is the ability to assert oneself renewed—in the presence of others. It is a people's right to rebuild, its demand to exist and present its gifts to the world. Also key to these thinkers' rhetorics of sovereignty is an adamant refusal to disassociate culture, identity, and power from the *land,* and it is precisely this commitment to place that makes the concept of rhetorical sovereignty an empowering device for all forms of community. While most Indians have a special relationship with the land in the form of an actual land base (reservations), this relationship is made truly meaningful by a consistent cultural refusal to interact with that land as private property or purely exploitable resource. Land, culture, and community are inseparable in Indian country, which might explain Native resistance to such policies as the Dawes Allotment Act of a century ago, which tried to transform Indians into bourgeois whites by making them property-holding farmers. This cultural resistance has consistently been made in objection to the way such policies divide Indian communities and disrupt traditional culture with radically individualist ideologies, and whenever I see community activists of whatever stripe—Black, Hmong, working-class, etc.—making arguments on behalf of "our community" in the face of apparently naked economic self-interest, I think those, too, are claims to sovereignty made by different groups. But most important, as voices of the people, scholars like Deloria, Warrior, and Cook-Lynn are asserting themselves as members of sovereign Indian nations, deploying power and seeking recognition at the colonized scene of writing.

I have gone on (and perhaps on and on) about the concept of sovereignty because I think it is not well understood by most non-Indian scholars and teachers. I also think the idea has something to offer the discourses of multiculturalism and critical race theory, or to anyone who sides with the oppressed or who works for community renewal, because of its applicability to the many contested sites (and actual places) of power in multiple senses: legal, cultural, intellectual, material, and so on. Sovereignty is a concept that has a history of contest, shifting meanings, and culturally-specific rhetorics. A reclamation of sovereignty by any group remains, as Deloria argues above, a recognition of that group's power—a recognition made by both self and other. It is not something "new" or, worse, something "given" by dominant groups, and for the sake of the people, we might all do well to contemplate what that might mean.

Rhetorical sovereignty at the C & R ranch

All of which brings me back to where I started: what do American Indians want from writing? At stake in this discussion are the peoples defined by the writing itself; thus one important tenet of rhetorical sovereignty would be to allow Indians to have some say about the nature of their textual representations. The best way to honor this creed would be to have Indian people themselves do the writing, but it might also be recognized that some representations are better than others, whoever the author. On that note, a quick perusal through the composition and rhetoric literature of the past few years shows a growing interest in American Indians and a general concern for including Native knowledges and voices in classrooms and curricula that should be commended. But some of this work hinders rhetorical sovereignty by presenting readers with Indian stereotypes, cultural appropriation, and a virtual absence of discourse on sovereignty and the status of Indian nations—that is, with a kind of rhetorical imperialism. Sometimes this writing has been done with all the best of intentions, but on that note it might be good to recall that Chief Justice Marshall, the original architect of limited sovereignty for Indians, was generally considered a very pro-Indian thinker in his day—to Indian-hating President Andrew Jackson's continual dismay—even as Marshall was busy composing the foundational documents for American imperialist control over tribes. So without getting into where good intentions sometimes lead, let me say for now that some of our most prominent work on Indians is not yet part of the solution.

Take, for example, the recent publication of George Kennedy's *Comparative Rhetoric: An Historical and Cross-Cultural Introduction*. Kennedy, who has taught me so much in his books about classical Greek and Roman rhetoric and who I continue to honor as a great scholar of those subjects, has now seen fit to locate rhetoric in nature and to place its history on a developmental, essentially evolutionary, model, the entire scheme of which seems to be based upon Western stereotypes of the Other. Divided into two sections, the oral and the literate, the study begins with an investigation of the rhetoric of animals, including bird calls, and works its way "up" through the language of "oral" indigenous people, then through the literacy of Egyptians, Chinese, Indians (from India) to its grand finale in the civilizations of Greece and Rome. In that order, African Americans are not even mentioned, which Kermit Campbell might have criticized more strongly in his mainly positive review of the "pioneering" work (174). It's worth noting that this evolutionary study actually works backwards in time; most of Kennedy's examples of "North American Indian Rhetoric" (Chapter 5), for example, are taken from the nineteenth century, a particularly devastating yet rhetorically profuse time for most Native people. Why Kennedy didn't acknowledge the overwhelming proliferation of *writing* by Native people during that century—not the least of which can be found in the many tribal newspapers of those years, for instance, in the bilingual *Cherokee Phoenix* of the 1820s—probably owes itself to the deeply ingrained stereotypes of Indians as 1) essentially oral creatures, and 2) existing only in an imagined savage past. Both of those persistent stereotypes are examined together in *Forked Tongues: Speech, Writing, and Representation in North American Indian Texts* by David Murray, who points out that in communicative exchanges between Indians and whites, "the cultural translation is all one-way, and the penalty to the subordinate group for not adapting to the demands of the dominant group is to cease to exist" (6). Thus, the logic Kennedy employs in his study might lead some to the conclusion that a writing Indian is no Indian at all.

In addition to the effect of making questions of sovereignty a moot point, Kennedy's erasure of real Indians serves other agendas as well. Finding in "early human language" a "connecting link" between the rhetoric of animals and that of oral (but not literate) humans, Kennedy has basically provided a theory of the Missing Link located within the speech of the people (2). The result is a quiet assumption that Indians are something less than human, if something more than animals. I don't know how else to take his comparison of red deer stags and "Eskimos" (by which I think he means Inuit):

> *In a previous chapter I described the rhetoric of red deer stags in seeking rights to mate with females—vocal encounters, stalking, and fights with their horns if one animal does not give way. A similar sequence has characterized Eskimo quarrels over women: insults, threatening gestures, and fights in the form of butting or wrestling contests. (77)*

And here I thought all that butting and wrestling was something we did for fun. What Inuit *women* might have to say about this characterization of their dating life notwithstanding, I have to ask if this is really where we want to go in the study of comparative rhetorics. Cultural evolutionism, a nineteenth-century phenomenon associated with early anthropologists like Lewis Henry Morgan (who studied "the vanishing Indian"), has long been used to justify an ideology of savagery-barbarism-civilization, which in turn has always operated to the detriment of Indian peoples (see Berkhofer, 49–61). To locate Indian rhetoric at an early point on the Great Chain of Speaking not only ignores *this* kind of speech for a claim about *that* kind, the results of which may be dehumanizing, but by implication also suggests that today's Indian peoples are probably not real anymore. I suppose Kennedy wanted to find oral eloquence and the like among Indian cultures, but through his desire, and his acceptance and perpetuation of stereotypes, he seems to have lost sight of actually existing indigenous people and has uncharacteristically misplaced rhetoric.

The oral-literate binary—which I apparently (and mistakenly) had thought dismantled by now—also lurks ominously in Bruce Ballenger's "Methods of Memory: On Native American Storytelling." Ballenger appropriates what he calls an " 'Indian way' of remembering" to make sense of his own life and writing, "methods" he locates in Native oral traditions (790; 792–3). Of course, his access to this oral tradition is enabled completely through the reading of Native *writers,* but never mind: the point of the article, it seems to me, is to grab and make use of what even Ballenger admits does not belong to him with the express purpose of "creat[ing] the 'whole story' of myself" (795). In other words, the "Indian way" serves as a kind of supplemental technology to aid and abet the construction of Ballenger's self as a sovereign, unique individual: a highly literate white man with all the benefits and privileges therein. "It is always the 'I'—not the 'we'—that concerns me most," Ballenger writes, adding that what distinguishes him from real Indians is his motivation for "self-expression" (795). Not unlike, Tonto, then, the Indian is there for the taking as a kind of helper and teacher in the white man's quest to Know Thyself. Since Ballenger's essay on Native American story-telling isn't about Native Americans at all, but rather about what Ballenger apparently feels free to *take* from Natives, we must find in this writing the logic of cultural imperialism. Wendy Rose has argued that by "appropriating indigenous cultures and distoring them for its own purposes . . . the dominant society can neatly eclipse every aspect of contemporary native reality, from land rights to issues of religious freedom" (404). Indeed, Ballenger's own expansive familiarity with Indian writers did not lead him to discuss any of the issues facing the people today (and which are often represented in the novels he reads); on the contrary, he seems to accept things as they are. One particularly troubling moment for me was his discussion of place in Native literature; after making the solid claim that Indians "tend to see the land as something with a presence"—fair enough—Ballenger goes on to recall his times on the shores of Lake Michigan, formerly and in some cases still Anishinabe country, remembered by him "with a kind of reverence" as, in his word, "unpeopled" (798). The actual history of peopling and unpeopling on those shores would be a worthwhile thing to investigate.

Ballenger's essay is perhaps a sensitive one to criticize because it is interspersed with some painful recollections of his childhood. But I have some painful recollections of my own, as many Native people do. Right now I'm thinking of my two young Ojibwe cousins who committed suicide in the same year—one in his early twenties, the other barely approaching his teens—two deaths that might be attributed to a kind of self-hatred experienced by many Indian youths today who find themselves trapped in colonial wreckage: poverty, violence, a racist dominant culture that hates and excludes them. Consider the findings of a recent study on American Indian crime produced by the Justice Department which found that "American Indians are victims of violent crime at a rate of more than double that of the rest of the population" ("American"). In seven out of ten of those episodes, the offender is non-Indian. The report also stated that the number of American Indians per capita in state and federal prisons is some thirty-eight percent above the national average; the rate in local jails is four times the national average. The arrest rate for alcohol-related offenses is more than twice the rate for the total population ("American"). Or consider the fact that "Native people endure the poorest quality of life in this country," because of which "1,000 more Native men, women, and children die each year than would be expected if they were living in the same conditions as white America." (This, remember, out of a total population of only 1.5 million.) "If these same conditions existed throughout the total population of our country, 150,000 more American people would die *each year*" (Charleston 17; emphasis in original). Nobody ever wants to appropriate stuff like that.

Rhetorical sovereignty, however, compels us to face it. It is always the "we"— not the "I"—that concerns me most, and my particular motivation is the pursuit of social justice. Or let's simply call it sanity in an age of unchecked American imperialism, rampant consumer capitalism on an unprecedented global scale, haphazard and unsustainable depletions and abuses of natural resources, naked European and American aggression around the globe, racism, sexism, homophobia, and the ever-widening gap between rich and poor in America and everywhere. In contexts such as these, there are very good reasons to fight for indigenous rights. Indigenous people, who in some senses are now forming a global movement (seen, for example, in growing international indigenous support for the Zapatista movement in Chiapas), may constitute the world's most adamant refusal of current expansions of global capitalism and imperialism that plague so many and benefit so few. As groups like Greenpeace have argued:

> Native people's homelands encompass many of the planet's last tracts of wilderness—ecosystems that shelter millions of endangered species, buffer the global climate, and regulate hydrological cycles. . . . Even without considering questions of human rights and the intrinsic value of cultures, indigenous survival is a matter of crucial importance. We in the world's dominant cultures simply can not sustain the Earth's ecological health without the help of the world's endangered cultures. (qtd. in Owens 233)

However, the people themselves are among those endangered species. Brazil alone has lost something like 90 tribes this century, and over half of all remaining 6,000 indigenous languages worldwide will become extinct in the next (Owens 233). Unless the people can prevent that from happening.

Composition and rhetoric certainly isn't going to stop it, although we can do some things that might have us play a more meaningful role—which brings me back yet again to the question: what do Indians want from writing? So far, I hope to have identified a few things Indians generally do *not* want from writing: stereotypes, cultural appropriation, exclusion, ignorance, irrelevance, rhetorical imperialism. The people want sovereignty, and in the context of the colonized scene of writing, rhetorical sovereignty. As the inherent right and ability of peoples to determine their own communicative needs and desires in the pursuit of self-determination, rhetorical sovereignty requires above all the presence of an Indian voice, speaking or writing in an ongoing context of colonization and setting at least some of the terms of debate. Ideally, that voice would often employ a Native language. "Language, in particular, helps to decolonize the mind," writes the Hawaiian nationalist Haunani-Kay Trask. "Thinking in one's own cultural referents leads to conceptualizing in one's own world view which, in turn, leads to disagreement with and eventual opposition to the dominant ideology" (54). The crucial subject of Native language in literacy research cannot be taken up here, except perhaps to say *nindozhibü'igemin*. But while it's hard to predict what that Indian voice would say in our many and varied classrooms—most of them Indian-free, some located at tribal colleges, others constituting dynamic contact-zones of their own—I can point to scholarly work in a couple of sites that might help us orient our commitment to rhetorical sovereignty and imagine new practices.

One location of rhetorical sovereignty that should be of interest to rhetoricians is the Tribal Law and Government Center, based at the University of Kansas Law School and directed by Seneca legal scholar (and former Attorney General of the Seneca Nation) Robert B. Porter. Focusing its energies on the study and development of tribal law (which is not the same thing as federal Indian law but rather the law of sovereign Indian nations), the Center sponsors the Indian Law Institute each summer for tribal officials, a yearly conference, and a specialization in tribal law within the law program. Of particular interest for our purposes, the Center has been sponsoring annual rearguments of some of the most powerful federal legal decisions in the history of Indian sovereignty, for example, *Cherokee Nation v. Georgia* and *Lone Wolf v. Hitchcock*. Under the auspices of the "Supreme Court of the American Indian Nations," these retrials are conducted by a distinguished array of Indian and non-Indian lawyers and judges, and the briefs they produce are published alongside the original opinions and briefs and are available for study and teaching (Ayana, Guhin, Yazzie). Critical pedagogues, contact-zone theorists, and post/anti-colonial rhetoricians might take note of these powerful Indian countersentences to colonialism; after all, these reargued indigenous reponses to legal and political history constitute an ongoing and dynamic practice of rhetorical sovereignty, and we could teach them.

Another key site of rhetorical sovereignty is the report produced by the Indian Nations At Risk Task Force (INARTF), "Toward True Native Education: A Treaty of 1992," which was commissioned by the Department of Education in 1990. INARTF was a 14-member committee established by U.S. Secretary of Education Lauro Cavazos and directed by Choctaw education professor, G. Mike Charleston. With two exceptions it was an Indian committee, and the document they produced is a classic example of the exercise of rhetorical sovereignty. First, as its title suggests, the report announces itself as a *treaty*, one designed to put an end to the "secret war" (also referred to as a "cold war") waged against indigenous peoples (Charleston 15–16). Distinguishing the metaphor of war from other more dominant ones in liberal and educational discourse—for example, the idea of an Indian "plight" and the notion of a "tug-of-war" between cultures—the report justifies the war metaphor on two accounts. First, this "war is over the continued existence of tribal societies of American Indians and Alaska Natives"; that is, at issue isn't so much the curing of Indian ills or celebration of diversity but rather a recognition of Indian sovereignty. Second, war is *stopped* by treaties between mutually recognized sovereign entities (16). The "Treaty of 1992," then, offers an educational theory inseparable from a recognition of sovereignty and a plea to stop the violence as well. Arguing that "school has become the weapon of choice for non-Native societies" to attack tribal sovereignty in all of its manifestations, the report distinguishes three types of Indian education. *Pseudo Native education* is "a process that diligently attempts to teach Native students the standard American curriculum needed to assimilate into American society" (19–20). *Quasi Native education* is "an education that sincerely attempts to make American education more culturally relevant and supportive of Native students and Native communities" through the teaching of Native cultural trinkets like "legends, history, and Native words" (27). *True Native education* rejects any "division between school climate and culture and . . . community climate and culture," replacing hierarchical models of curricula and pedagogy with a concerted community effort, envisioned by the committee as a circle (40, 31). What true Native education calls for in the final analysis is nothing less than the formal institutionalization of rhetorical sovereignty.

This rethought education remains insistent upon dialogue, land, and the continuation of the people, so we should all consider the implications of another metaphor in the INARTF report: the "new Ghost Dance." Invoking the first Ghost Dance movement of a century ago, a prophetic religious movement praying for the return of Indian power (answered by whites with the brutal slaughter of Chief Big Foot's band of Lakota at the Wounded Knee massacre of 1890), the Treaty of 1992 insists that the "new Ghost Dance calls Native *and* non-Native people to join together and take action." For non-Native participants, the new Ghost Dance "requires a major change in their behaviors, attitudes, and values"; for Natives, much of the work will be decolonization of the mind and self (28). Educators "need to teach the reasons for the hundreds of treaties and agreements between the various tribes and the United States" and promote "a basic understanding, respect, and appreciation for American Indian and Alaskan Native cultures" to all students (29). Altogether, this approach would work for "a revival of tribal life and the return of harmony among all relations of creation" (28). I can think of no better document than this to help us begin the work of rhetorical sovereignty in our field and start answering the question of what Indians want from writing. The metaphors of the INARTF report—treaty, war, Ghost Dance—are carefully chosen signifiers that aim to cast into full relief the fault lines of Indian-white interaction in America, and the report should be read as an extended hand, not a fist, in the very serious pursuit of a people's sovereignty. How will we respond?

I suggest we begin by prioritizing the study of American Indian rhetoric—and the rhetoric of the Indian—in our graduate curricula and writing programs, focusing on the history of both secret and not-so-secret wars in the contact-zone. We should be teaching the treaties and federal Indian laws as rhetorical texts themselves, situating our work within both historical and contemporary contexts. We should also study the ideologies of Indianness and Manifest Destiny that have governed it all. No student should encounter a Native American text without having learned something about Indian peoples' historical and ongoing struggles for sovereignty, and teachers of Native students in particular should create a space for those kinds of discussions. This work would continually examine one's relationship to Indian sovereignty, as well as expand our canons and current knowledge in ways that would hopefully make them more relevant to and reflective of actual populations on this land. On that note, I also think this site should be read and taught not in separation from other groups, but alongside the histories, rhetorics, and struggles of African-Americans and other "racial" or ethnic groups, women, sexual minorities, the disabled, and still others, locating history and writing instruction in the powerful context of American rhetorical struggle.

Ideally, this work should focus on local and community levels in hopes of lending support to the work already being done there. "There" is sometimes difficult to locate, I realize, but every university and school exists in a place, on a land, with a history and a community of struggle: every place has its peoples. For example, the Cincinnati-Tristate region where I went to graduate school, and which sometimes struck me as the most Indian-free zone I had ever seen, actually boasts a Native population of 2,365 people ("American"). Who are they, what is their history, and what are they facing now? Some of them are certainly homeless, and so their history might be read in the context of a current struggle. In that place, on that land, members of the local arts community have proposed moving the Drop-Inn Center, the area's largest homeless shelter, away from a gentrifying neighborhood so arts patrons won't have to look at the poor and despondent on their way to the concert (Knight 1). Considering geographer Neil Smith's contention that gentrifying inner-city neighborhoods like this one (Over-the-Rhine) constitute "the new frontier"—the site of increasing white "settlement" to the displacement of the "savages" who live there—it's perfectly reasonable to conclude that the Cincinnati controversy is nothing less than another debate over *removal*. What could be more teachable than this in the pursuit of sovereignty?

Ethnographers and service-learning theorists have already begun the valuable work of theorizing community-based pedagogy, but my hopes are also pinned on classroom theories oriented toward the formation of *publics*. Susan Wells has provided our best thinking so far toward these ends, arguing for and theorizing writing instruction geared toward "public literate action" (334). Wells would rethink publicly-oriented writing classrooms in four different ways: 1) as a version of the public sphere, 2) as a site for the study of public discourse, 3) as a place to produce student writing that might actually enter public space, and 4) as a location for the examination of how academic discourses and disciplinary knowledges intervene in the public (338–39). Read alongside the INARTF recommendations in the context of rhetorical sovereignty, her proposals sound vital to me, for sovereignty has always been on some level a public pursuit of recognition. A focus on American Indian publics is especially appropriate now in the fresh wake of two rather substantial Indian victories in the public, both of which have everything to do with literacy and rhetoric; reading and writing and arguing. The first is the April 1999 Supreme Court upholding of the 1837 Chippewa Treaty in Minnesota that guarantees my own people the right to hunt and fish on ceded lands (*Minnesota v. Mille Lacs Band*). The second is the federal Trademark Trial and Appeal Board's disrecognition of the Washington Redskins trademark, a move that could cost that organization millions of dollars in lost (because unprotected) revenues and, hence, provides a financial incentive to change the name (Rich 3). These victories were won by Native people who learned how to fight battles in both court and the culture-at-large, who knew how to read and write the legal system, interrogate and challenge cultural semiotics, generate public opinion, form publics, and create solidarity with others. That behind each of these victories were contests over the acts of reading and writing is obvious; what needs to be underscored is that both are also victories of rhetorical sovereignty. Both initiatives arose from the grassroots, each in their own way fought over questions of land and identity, and the ultimate outcome of both was an honoring of "a whole way of life," another productive step in the perpetuation of the people. Shouldn't the teaching of (American Indian) rhetoric be geared toward these kinds of outcomes?

That's what I want from writing. My particular desire asks a lot, I know, from teachers and students and readers and writers and texts. It wants to read history through a contemporary lens and continually beckon forth the public. It asks everyone, especially teachers, to think carefully about their positions, locations, and alignments: the differences and connections between sovereignty and solidarity. It wishes to reinscribe the land and reread the people; it cries for revision. However, without some turn in the current assault on affirmative action, I suspect all talk on rhetorical sovereignty will likely happen away from the university. Luther Standing Bear, writing in the 1930s, knew as much in his push for rhetorical sovereignty in American schools. "The Indian," he wrote, "should become his own historian, giving his account of the race—fewer and fewer accounts of the wars and more of statecraft, legends, languages, oratory, and philosophical conceptions" (*Eagle* 254). What did Standing Bear, formerly that little boy who once counted coup on the classroom text, want from writing? "No longer should the Indian be dehumanized in order to make material for lurid and cheap fiction to embellish street-stands," he *wrote*. "Rather, a fair and correct history of the native American should be incorporated in the curriculum of the public school" (*Eagle* 254).

Is it right for me to take a white man's name? The answer, it would seem, has always been no. But that refusal has never meant giving up or going away; rather, a No over there can sometimes enable Yes over here. The ability to speak both—indeed, to speak at all—is the right and the theory and the practice and the poetry of rhetorical sovereignty. *Ningiigid, nindinawe:* I speak, I speak like the people with whom I live.

Works Cited

Adams, David Wallace. *Education for Extinction: American Indians and the Boarding School Experience, 1875–1928.* Lawrence: U of Kansas P, 1995.

Aitken, Robert. "Essential Nature." *Coyote's Journal.* Eds. James Koller, "Gogisgi" Carroll Arnett, Steve Nemirow, and Peter Blue Cloud. Berkeley: Wingbow, 1982. 47.

"American Indians' Victim Rate Double Norm." *Cincinnati Enquirer* 15 Feb. 1999: A3.

Ayana, James. "Brief of Lone Wolf, Principal Chief of the Kiowas, to the Supreme Court of the American Indian Nations." *The Kansas Journal of Law and Public Policy* 7.1 (Winter 1997): 117–45.

Ballenger, Bruce. "Methods of Memory: On Native American Storytelling." *College English* 59 (1997): 789–800.

Berkhofer, Robert F., Jr. *The White Man's Indian: Images of the American Indian from Columbus to the Present.* New York: Vintage, 1978.

Berman, Howard R. "Perspectives on American Indian Sovereignty and International Law, 1600–1776." *Exiled in the Land of the Free: Democracy, Indian Nations, and the U.S. Constitution.* Eds. Chief Oren Lyons and John Mohawk. Santa Fe: Clear Light Publishers, 1992. 125–88.

Calhoun, Craig, ed. *Habermas and the Public Sphere.* Cambridge: MIT P, 1994.

Campbell, Kermit. "Rev. of *Comparative Rhetoric: An Historical and Cross-Cultural Introduction,* by George A. Kennedy." *Rhetoric Review* 17 (1998): 170–74.

Castells, Manuel. *The Power of Identity.* Oxford: Blackwell, 1997.

Champagne, Duane. *Social Order and Political Change: Constitutional Governments among the Cherokee, the Choctaw, the Chickasaw, and the Creek.* Stanford: Stanford UP, 1992.

Charleston, G. Mike. "Toward True Native Education: A Treaty of 1992. Final Report of the Indian Nations At Risk Task Force." *Journal of American Indian Education* 33.2 (1994): 7–56.

Cherokee Nation v. Georgia, 30 U.S. 1. U.S. Supreme Court. 1831.

Cook-Lynn, Elizabeth. "The American Indian Fiction Writers: Cosmopolitanism, Nationalism, the Third World, and First Nation Sovereignty." *Why I Can't Read Wallace Stegner and Other Essays: A Tribal Voice.* Madison: U of Wisconsin P, 1996. 78–98.

Deloria, Vine, Jr. *We Talk, You Listen: New Tribes, New Turf.* New York: Macmillan, 1970.

Deloria, Vine, Jr., and Clifford M. Lytle. *The Nations Within: The Past and Future of American Indian Sovereignty.* Austin: U of Texas P, 1984.

Duchacek, Ivo D. *Nations and Men: International Politics Today.* New York: Holt, Rinehart and Winston, 1966.

Eley, Geoff. "Nations, Publics, and Political Cultures: Placing Habermas in the Nineteenth Century." Calhoun 289–339.

Fowler, Michael Ross, and Julie Marie Bunck. *Law, Power, and the Sovereign State: The Evolution and Application of the Concept of Sovereignty.* University Park: Pennsylvania State UP, 1995.

Fraser, Nancy. "Rethinking the Public Sphere: A Contribution to the Critique of Actually Existing Democracy." Calhoun 109–42.

Guhin, John P. "Brief of Ethan A. Hitchcock, Secretary of the Interior, to the Supreme Court of the American Indian Nations." *The Kansas Journal of Law and Public Policy* 7.1 (Winter 1997): 146–69.

Habermas, Jurgen. *The Structural Transformation of the Public Sphere: An Inquiry into a Category of Bourgeois Society.* Trans. Thomas Burger. Cambridge: MIT P, 1989.

Kant, Immanuel. "An Answer to the Question: 'What is Enlightenment?' " *Political Writings.* 2nd Eng. ed. Ed. Hans Reiss. Trans. H. B. Nisbet. Cambridge: Cambridge UP, 1991. 54–60.

——. *"The Metaphysics of Morals:* Introduction to the Theory of Right." *Political Writings.* 2nd Eng. ed. Ed. Hans Reiss. Trans. H. B. Nisbet. Cambridge: Cambridge UP, 1991. 131–75.

Kennedy, George A. *Comparative Rhetoric: An Historical and Cross-Cultural Introduction.* New York: Oxford UP, 1998.

Knight, Susan. "New Arts Center Proposal Pits the Rich against the Poor." *Streetvibes, The Tri-State's Homeless Grapevine.* March 1999:1–3.

Lone Wolf v. Hitchcock. 187 U.S. 553. U.S. Supreme Court. 1903.

Lyons, Oren. "The American Indian in the Past." *Exiled in the Land of the Free: Democracy, Indian Nations, and the U.S. Constitution.* Eds. Chief Oren Lyons and John Mohawk. Santa Fe: Clear Light Publishers, 1992. 13–42.

Minnesota v. Mille Lacs Band of Chippewa Indians, 97 U.S. 1337. U.S. Supreme Court. 1999.

Momaday, N. Scott. *House Made of Dawn.* New York: Harper, 1989.

Murray, David. *Forked Tongues: Speech, Writing, and Representation in North American Indian Texts.* Bloomington: Indian UP, 1991.

Owens, Louis. *Mixedblood Messages: Literature, Film, Family, Place.* Norman: U of Oklahoma P, 1998.

Perdue, Theda. *The Cherokee Removal: A Brief History with Documents.* New York: Bedford, 1995.

Porter, Robert B. "Strengthening Tribal Sovereignty through Government Reform: What Are the Issues?" *The Kansas Journal of Law and Public Policy* 7.1 (Winter 1997): 72–105.

Prucha, Francis Paul. *American Indian Treaties: The History of a Political Anomaly.* Berkeley: U of California P, 1994.

——, ed. *Documents of United States Indian Policy.* 2nd ed. Lincoln: U of Nebraska P, 1990.

Rich, Sue. " 'Redskins' and 'Indian Red' No More." *The Circle: Native American News and Arts.* Apr. 1999: 3.

Rose, Wendy. "The Great Pretenders: Further Reflections on Whiteshamanism." *The State of Native America: Genocide, Colonization, Resistance.* Ed. M. Annette Jaimes. Boston: South End, 1992. 403–22.

Ryan, Mary. "Gender and Public Access: Women's Politics in Nineteenth-Century America." Calhoun 259–88.

Smith, Neil. *The New Urban Frontier: Gentrification and the Revanchist City.* New York: Routledge, 1996.

Standing Bear, Luther. *Land of the Spotted Eagle.* Boston: Houghton Mifflin, 1933.

——. *My People the Sioux.* Lincoln: U of Nebraska P, 1975.

Trask, Haunani-Kay. *From a Native Daughter: Colonialism and Sovereignty in Hawai'i.* Monroe, GA: Common Courage, 1993.

Warrior, Robert Allen. *Tribal Secrets: Recovering American Indian Intellectual Traditions.* Minneapolis: U of Minnesota P, 1995.

Wells, Susan. "Rogue Cops and Health Care: What Do We Want from Public Writing?" *College Composition and Communication* 47 (1996): 325–41.

Worcester v. Georgia, 31 U.S. 515, 562. U.S. Supreme Court. 1832.

Yazzie, Robert. "Opinion: Cherokee Nation v. Georgia." *The Kansas Journal of Law and Public Policy* 7.1 (Winter 1997): 159–73.

34

The Ins, Outs, and In-Betweens of Multigenre Writing

NANCY MACK

Like many teachers I have been working my way toward multigenre projects by adding visuals and creative formats to my writing assignments. I have been greatly assisted in my progress over the years by Tom Romano's books about teaching writing—*Clearing the Way; Writing with Passion;* and *Blending Genre, Altering Style*—which in themselves represent one teacher's professional development. After recently collecting a batch of stellar multigenre projects, I was so pleased that I took them to a faculty meeting and subversively arranged them on the center table in the hopes that their merit alone would convince my colleagues of the value of this type of assignment. Several of my colleagues generously took the time after the meeting to look through the projects and celebrate their excellence. Sharing my students' writing is a wonderful way to let my work as an educator speak for my methodology, but I owe myself and my colleagues a more thoughtful analysis of the academic virtues of multigenre projects.

My strongest motivation for studying multigenre writing is the compelling responses of my students who have authored writing projects that have awed me with their power and elegance. I am moved to think of my students' writing as more than reports or papers. They are works of art, not simply because of their visual or poetic inclusions, but because of their aesthetic meaningfulness. For support of my point about aesthetics, I turn to the work of Mikhail Bakhtin, a Russian literary critic, whose scholarship masterfully presents a similar case for accepting the dialogic language of the novel as art. Yet as I do so, I fully realize that some would not accept the mixed quality of these multigenre projects as academic writing. Perhaps the most persuasive argument that I can marshal to convince others of the usefulness of the multigenre assignment is that this type of writing requires much more in the way of academic skills than the minimal requisites of the traditional monogenre research paper. Combining these two perspectives, to foster writing as both an art and a skill, demonstrates how multigenre writing can be utilized to teach critical analysis, documentation of sources, and aesthetic unity.

Before examining multigenre writing in more depth, I need to respond to the myth of the traditional college research paper format. The most authoritative voice that I can invoke on this matter is that of composition scholar and journal editor, Richard Larson. In his article, "The 'Research Paper' in the Writing Course: A Non-Form of Writing," he explains that universities house a plethora of conflicting disciplines, all of which have competing notions of what academic research requires. I would add to Larson's critique that in any one area of study such as polymer engineering, market research, or geriatric sociology, what qualifies as research itself has probably changed significantly in the last twenty-five years and will continue to change, perhaps even more rapidly in the future. Understandably, high school teachers and general education professors harbor the unrealistic desire that one report format could be decided upon that would satisfy all of the disciplines and all of the courses at the university. If we had such an all-purpose, standardized format, writing would be far easier to teach and produce. The research report might even become a template or an icon on a word processing program that a student could simply click to set the format before beginning to write. Regretably, asking academics in any discipline to agree on something as limited as one brand of documentation style—MLA, APA, CSE, Chicago, etc.—could result in a duel to the death. Even within the discipline of English studies, linguists, literary critics, ethnographic researchers, English as a second language scholars, and professional writers all need diverse systems to cite their particular sources of information. In much the same way as the research paper myth, standards and proficiency initiatives push for the minimum in competencies and skills. Naming one written format as universal is not only fallacious but functions in practice to misrepresent academic research itself as little more than summarizing multiple textual sources on the same topic without any critical or creative interpretation. Having been both a secondary teacher and a university professor, I can say that asking students to imitate a dumbed-down, artificial research paper format most often results in boring, plagiarized papers. These drawbacks are part of the reason why I created a multigenre research assignment that I believe provides a more academically challenging learning experience for my students. Likewise, I have learned a great deal about teaching writing from this experience. Although the incidents and examples cited here are about college students, the lessons about how students and teachers learn from one another are more universal.

My Classroom Context

In a new course about writing workshop pedagogy, I planned for Integrated Language Arts majors to experience multigenre research writing in the middle part of a ten-week course. Our textbooks were Atwell's *In the Middle*, Romano's *Writing with Passion*, and Weaver's *Teaching Grammar in Context*. For the first two and a half weeks of the course, students wrote and published a portfolio of poetry, and during the last three weeks we focused on the teaching of grammar through writing projects. Students also kept reading journals and were e-pals with high school students. When I first introduced the idea of multigenre writing, none of the students had ever heard of such an assignment before, and some even complained that they were reluctant to participate in a less than traditional assignment. The topic of folklore was presented, using some of the introductory ideas from Simmons's *Student Worlds, Student Words*, and students completed several brainstorming sheets about family stories, folk group identities, and community history. Students were given an overview of the project that required both primary research from first person interviews and secondary research from books, newspapers, and Web sources. After initial exploratory interviews with informants, most students found a central story that they wanted to tell about a relative, group, or town. Students chose the following topics:

- family love stories
- a relative's experiences with racism
- the death of a great-uncle in WWII
- a remembrance of a mother's life
- three generations of mechanics
- a scout troop's bad weather camping trip
- the founder of a local church
- a difficult genealogy search
- two generations of teenage rebellion
- the role of dance in a couple's relationship
- a great-grandmother's strength through faith
- a family's pattern of affection and indifference
- a high school drama club
- a town's reactions to a prison riot
- a family farm's history
- a losing high school football team

At first I asked for the projects to include three genres but quickly expanded this requirement to five genres when I realized how much effort students wanted to invest in this project. I did mini-lessons on

- interviewing and note taking
- examining other students' multigenre projects
- sharing possible genres and unusual publishing formats
- finding historical and analytical sources

- selecting a theme and focusing on one event
- incorporating contextual details and multiple perspectives
- writing in another person's voice
- writing about a photograph
- troubleshooting problems
- documenting primary and secondary sources
- drafting a letter of introduction to the reader
- creating a bibliography and footnotes

Critical Analysis

I stressed early in the term that the academic discipline of folklore presumes that all cultures are worthy of study, analysis, and respect. I stressed critical analysis through two types of minilessons, researching historical contexts and including multiple perspectives of the same event, encouraging students to find places in their writing to add rich, contextual details about economics, politics, and cultural norms. In class discussions we considered how the mindset of the time period made it difficult for individuals to escape the pressures of predefined roles or cultural stereotypes. Jeff empathetically analyzed his mother's problems as a young wife in the late sixties and early seventies:

> My mother had grown up being a submissive woman, taught by a now-antiquated American logic—and my grandmother—to suppress her voice in favor of a man's. . . . The need of my mother for a strong husband and the need of my father for an obedient wife met like the pieces of a jigsaw puzzle. The pair, one might say, just fell into place.

Jeff used a historic discussion of the gender roles to foreground his memoir about his mother's sacrifices:

> When times were especially hard, and my father was at his worst, our mother had to walk from our house to a nearby strip mall in order to sell her class ring. It was precious to her, identical to her two best friends' rings, but she was willing to sacrifice anything for her children.

> Those images of my mother—her weakness and her strength, her humiliation in marriage and her pride in calling us her children—have flooded my senses with emotion in the days since she has been gone. Standing in the hallway outside my parent's bedroom or driving past the jewelry store that bought my mother's ring years ago grounds me, humbles me with identity. I am reminded of the turmoil my mother survived, the struggle that has bound us—my sister, my mother, and I—closer than any other family I know. I am reminded that I am a son, that I will one day be a father, that I am hers.

Jeff powerfully rewrote his mother's published obituary to include information that was not mentioned in the original newspaper article; both obituaries, the actual and the revised one, were placed side by side to emphasize the revision. Jeff's added details demonstrated many types of analysis: historic, gendered, economic, personal, and ironic. Students made a concerted effort to demonstrate in their writing that they understood the time period and the social forces that framed the stories that they wished to understand and honor.

I introduced another type of critical analysis with a minilesson that had students experiment with differences in perspective. After a few minutes brainstorming details about a particular person's habits and values, students enjoyed writing in the voice of a character from their folklore story. Most of the projects included multiple first person perspectives. I was impressed with how writing from multiple perspectives precipitated more complexity and conflict in students' representations of a selected event. A few students even made the resolution of ideological conflicts the focus of one of their final pieces. Rachel's family folklore project dramatized an act of discrimination against a relative. To represent conflicting beliefs about racism, Rachel wrote from six different perspectives and utilized the genres of a diary entry, a morning conversation, a one act play, a stream of consciousness monologue, an excerpt from an interview, and a eulogy from another character's perspective explaining how the main character's beliefs about race had changed over time to include family members from different races:

> *But Dad wasn't perfect. He had his faults like everyone else. He once told all of his kids that we shouldn't date "outside our kind." But I don't think Dad was truly prejudiced. I believe his intolerance was the result of a negative experience in his youth. He was targeted because of his "background" and I believe he wanted his kids to be safe by staying close to family and our culture. . . . We saw a change in Dad, he kind of softened a bit as he got older. Race and color didn't matter to him anymore. . . . He showed us all that it is possible to change our attitudes, and I hope we all will remember his life and learn a lesson from it.*

As a writer, Rachel's task was quite difficult. Originally, she focused only on a lunch counter incident in which the central character suffers racial bigotry, but she later decided to make the problem of racism more complicated by alluding to this character's own biases about race. Critically reflecting upon her ethical obligations to her family members and readers, Rachel chose to add the eulogy to clarify that time and family events had changed the main character's racial biases. Since a multigenre project can include fiction and nonfiction, authors must decide when it is ethical to fictionalize events in order to add another perspective.

As students generated multiple pieces for their projects, conflicts arose among differing perspectives of the same event that would not have occurred had I assigned a more traditional, monogenre format. Multigenre writing has the potential to make use of the dialogic quality of language. In his scholarly writing, Bakhtin often appropriates words and phrases in unusual ways to represent his unique concepts. A first impression of his use of "dialogic" might be that this term literally describes a dialogue that occurs among characters; however, Bakhtin extends this concept to include a social dialogue that exists implicitly within a single word. Accordingly, Bakhtin explains how language carries historic meanings that can potentially provoke dialogues across generations in which the author feels obligated to speak an "answer-word" to future generations:

> *The word in living conversation is directly, blatantly, oriented toward a future answer-word: it provokes an answer, anticipates it and structures itself in the answer's direction. Forming itself in an atmosphere of the already spoken, the word is at the same time determined by that which has not yet been said but which is needed and in fact anticipated by the answering word.* (Dialogic Imagination 280)

Writing about the past put students in the ethical position of interpreting the past for future generations. Rachel and other students authored multigenre projects that revealed a responsive dialogue among their different pieces of writing and across generations through a sophisticated use of multiple types of language. Bakhtin describes this hybrid quality of language as "heteroglossia," a useful tool for the writer since within any language there is a social stratification of diverse classes, generations, professions, epochs, politics, etc. I had not expected that the contextual and dialogic qualities of multigenre writing would elicit such intricate texts from my students. Their folklore research projects were so much more than a bunch of family stories or town legends. When I share copies of the projects of my former students with the new students next term, I will emphasize how the historic details and the multiple perspectives added layers of analysis to the representation of a single event.

Documentation

The contextual and dialogic quality of these multigenre projects commanded an equally complex process for referencing primary and secondary sources, fact and fiction, and authorial intent, which provoked students to reconsider their responsibilities as writers. I began the process by stressing that the oral interviews were serious data that must be documented just like books or Web sites. Students took notes or transcribed tapes for all of their interviews and cataloged each one in their bibliographies. Of the three or more interviews, two were to be with the same person on different dates in order to generate reflective, follow-up questions. I provided an interview release form for students to make informants aware of their rights and cautioned students to retell the stories of others respectfully. I checked interview notes and secondary research notes daily to be sure that students were not putting these tasks off until the last minute.

At first students had difficulty coming up with secondary sources. We discussed various types of contextual historical information that could be researched. Excitement erupted when Holly found a 1944 *Saga* magazine article to use as a model for her WWII story, and Kimberly found a database with information about Big Bands and the jargon associated with swing dancing. Analytical information was harder for students to locate. After a few suggestions, they eventually found articles by experts in related fields such as counseling, communications, management, sociology, and psychology. One student thought that it would be clever to involve Freud as a guest in a fictitious talk show. Originally, I feared that this student had no knowledge about Freud, but the student's writing evidenced a familiarity with the concepts of *ego* and *id* from readings for a psychology course. Suddenly their readings in other courses became relevant to their work in English class. Certainly these projects could have been completed without historical and analytical sources; hence, I called attention to the practices of fiction writers who spend a great deal of time in libraries researching information that makes their historical or murder mystery novels more realistic.

Due to the modernization of documentation systems such as MLA's internal citations, the use of footnotes has become somewhat *passé*. Footnotes are still utilized for content information, although some professional journals discourage authors from using them, and, if used, they are placed at the end of the article or chapter. I can remember the days before computers when students were taught the complicated process of placing footnotes at the bottom of the page on which the information was cited. Since most college and high school courses are no longer demanding them, I contemplated that requiring footnotes might be a nice opportunity to impress my colleagues by increasing the ante on academic skills. Actually, my insistence on footnotes for this paper was less a matter of feigning the appearance of rigorous standards and more a matter of necessity. The need for diverse genres prompted students to produce pieces that were imitations of newspapers, letters, textbooks, magazines, marriage certificates, etc. Some included copies of real documents, since I certainly didn't want students to incorporate rare family artifacts into their projects. Without footnotes it became almost impossible for me to tell which documents were copies and which ones were fakes. This ethical dilemma came up spontaneously in class just days before the projects were due. Footnotes were inserted in order to document which parts of the information given were factual and how primary and secondary sources were used. For example, Kimberly did her project about six generations of family love stories. The first story was the oldest and the one about which Kimberly had the least primary information. She knew that her relative was a millwright in northern Ohio in the late 1800s, and his wife was the former cook for the lumber camp, so she generated two fictitious pages of an Ohio history textbook. In addition to her excellent computer skills, Kimberly tore the edges of the pages to make them look like they were literally ripped out of a textbook and then mounted them in a large scrapbook along with her other pieces. Her footnote explains:

> *The facts surrounding Cal and Emma were used as much as possible for the piece. Little is known about their first encounters as they died in the late 1940s, with their daughter Lavada being the only child left to tell the story; however, the historical context for the time frame when they met is easily researched on the Web. Ironically enough, this abundance of information gave me the idea to do a textbook style story with my grandparents' story in an interview page of this text. The facts from Cal and Emma's life are paraphrased from Lavada's interview (Lavada 2, 8–9); the facts embedded in the textbook are paraphrased from various lumber camp Web sites (Huronia, LUMBER, Museum of Logging); the introduction is*

quoted from the era's widespread legend of Paul Bunyan (Folklore Class, Paul Bunyan).

In some cases, the students wanted to fool the reader but only temporarily, for effect. Footnotes were needed to provide spaces where students could explain their ethical intentions for composing a particular type of document. Many students created pieces with dual perspectives when they wrote letters, diary entries, eulogies, obituaries, and commendations in another character's voice. Bakhtin analyzes the writer's ability to create prose that is double-voiced: "It serves two speakers at the same time and expresses simultaneously two different intentions: The direct intention of the character who is speaking, and the refracted intention of the author" (*Dialogic Imagination* 324). Bakhtin writes extensively about several types of double-voiced discourse as an internal dialogue between various perspectives.

As I reread the footnotes written by my students for this article, I noticed that many used them to provide additional commentary about their pieces, with some even dialoging more directly with the piece. Rachel, whose project about racial discrimination was considered earlier, included a copy of the poem "Taking It Back" by Dixie Salazar prior to her own pieces of writing. Rachel employed footnotes so she could converse with specific lines in this poem. In direct response to the opening lines of the poem

> *Like Fugitives, or outlaws*
> *on the lam, we moved away,*
> *changed the spelling*
> *of our last name,*

Rachel's footnote stated:

> *My family never changed the spelling of our last names like Dixie Salazar's family does in the poem "Taking It Back"; however the pronunciation of the Spanish names became "Anglicized." My mother's maiden name is Tellez. (The correct pronunciation is Tey-ez, but they pronounce it Tell-ez. My father's last name is Lerma, which has a trickier pronunciation; the letter r should be softly rolled, but it isn't.) While this may not seem like a big deal to some people, I believe it is important because a name is the biggest identifier of who you are. I can relate to this poem because our family names were "assimilated" to become more acceptable to the rest of society. (Which in our case was Northwestern Ohio.)*

Frankly, I had not suggested the use of footnotes for commentary about a published author's writing, but Rachel impressed me with the many ways that she found to incorporate her research about racial identity into her project. In the future, I intend to give more guidance to students about what type of information to include in footnotes, but generally I was pleased with the constructive ways in which they used footnotes not only to document their use of research, but to explain how they had authored an ethical dialogue between fact and fiction.

Coherence and Aesthetic Unity

Years of teaching had prepared me to anticipate certain problems with this type of assignment, but I had not adequately thought through how difficult it would be for students to hold together several different pieces of writing on the same topic. A few students ended up with a hodgepodge of interchangeable parts that had no particular order and did not lead progressively from beginning to end. Other students solved their problems with coherence in interesting ways. Shauna, who did her report on three generations of mechanics in her family, articulated how she solved this problem in a class discussion, which happened too late for others to rework their projects. Shauna became a character in her own project by devising a larger story about helping a relative move, which established the conflict of whether to throw out a box of old family papers. The gambit of unpacking the box became a framework for several chapters about the family members that recounted Shauna's growing awareness of the pride that these men had in their knowledge about cars and planes. From this class of students, I have learned how various types of transitional devices such as chronology, narrative frame, thematic quotations, repetition of characters, and timelines can assist the multigenre writer, and I will certainly integrate these strategies into future mini-lessons.

Introductory and concluding documents did help to improve the projects' coherence and unity. I suggested introductory letters to the class after we read an example multigenre project from *Blending Genres*. The most effective letters were productive places for students to reflect upon how they selected their topic and what insights were gained from the research process. Since some of the genres were hard to identify at first, I will in the future assign a table of contents, listing titles of each selection and identifying the genre and page number. I will also emphasize the usefulness of a concluding piece that turns the reader's attention to the future or puts the whole experience into perspective through analysis or resolution/irres-olution of conflicting perspectives.

Coherence and unity are highly valued traits of published texts. I am reminded of how many works of fiction require the reader to make sense from multiple gen-res and perspectives such as *Canterbury Tales, A Midsummer Night's Dream, Crime and Punishment, Ulysses, The Great Gatsby, The Martian Chronicles, Nothing but the Truth, Tears of a Tiger,* etc. Similarly, my limited experience viewing Web pages has made me more critical of how Web designers combine competing information and hyperlinks to promote or in some cases deceive the viewer. Understandably, the tension that holds diverse elements together is a far more demanding skill than requiring that students prepare an outline of major and minor supports for a topic that they have researched. Multigenre projects place the burden on the student to author a coherent, unified whole out of dissimilar pieces of writing.

In the most interesting examples of published writing, coherence and unity are not determined by the dictates of the format but by the significance of the content. Thus, coherence has more to do with meaningfulness than mechanical requirements. Ironically, the teacher can construct an assignment in such a way as to cause students to have coherence problems. Indeed, it may be harder to make a piece of writing coherent that has several isolated requirements—whether

---

A Multigenre Paper

- requires that diverse types of writing be generated for a theme
- permits meaning to dictate form instead of vice versa
- presents multiple, conflicting perspectives of one event or topic
- stimulates critical analysis and higher level thinking skills
- provides a rich context for an event or topic
- integrates factual information into a meaningful text versus copying or simple recall
- can incorporate interviews, oral history, folklore, and ethnographic research
- demonstrates a sophisticated knowledge of various types and uses of language
- creates coherence among the parts of a problem to be solved
- requires a bibliography, footnotes, and careful documentation of sources
- is almost impossible to plagiarize
- permits the author to highlight personal interests and special expertise
- can make full use of computers and multimedia
- imitates the format of modern novels and innovative business reports
- results in an aesthetically attractive product
- demands careful reading and response

---

these requirements are mono- or multigenre in nature—but what ultimately motivates the writer to struggle to create a meaningful whole is the personal significance of the text.

Bakhtin discusses problems with unity in the first line of one of his earliest works: "A whole is called 'mechanical' when its constituent elements are united only in space and time by some external connection and are not imbued with the internal unity of meaning" (*Art and Answerability* 1). Bakhtin's philosophical view of aesthetic unity takes meaning into account. He explains that a dynamic, organic unity between art and life is an intentional construction by the author, an "architectonic"; however, this unity becomes meaningful only when art and life become answerable to one another. "Answerability" is an aesthetic responsibility for which Bakhtin believes that the author must take the blame for creating an organic unity between art and life.

My interpretation of Bakhtin's point is that, for writing to reach the level of art, it must bring the writer integrity by expressing a momentary answer for the unique experiences that are meaningful in the artist's life. By making their writing answerable for their life experiences, these students created art: Jeff honored his mother's strength, Rachel dramatized the complexity of racism, Kimberly celebrated love stories, Shauna lauded the labor of men from her family, and there were several other students whose projects were aesthetically meaningful. For the few days that I had them, I shared these projects with my friends and colleagues, who were moved by the students' powerful uses of language. Many students told me that they proudly shared their writing with family and friends. Art that is answerable seeks to continue its dialogue with others.

Far too many writing assignments answer only the need to generate a grade or check off an accomplished skill. Of course, the multigenre project has all the potential to become the traditional research paper of the future. Not all of my students' projects were of an amazingly high caliber; a few were perfunctory efforts done only to pass the course. The pitfall comes from focusing on form rather than content, not from the merit of a particular format. Answerability may sound like a nebulous goal for students' writing assignments, but I worry that when we leave meaning out of the picture and teach form as a universal construct, we make writing into a mechanical, mindless task. For me, multigenre assignments have instructional validity only when they produce meaningful texts.

Since no assignment or format will unilaterally guarantee meaningful writing, the teacher can only hope to create assignments that make it more likely that students will risk inserting meaningfulness into their writing. From my teaching experiences, I know that assignments must be innovative and interesting enough so that they appear unlike the old drudgery of hackneyed assignments. The format must be open and attractive to invite the possibility of doing something engaging rather than merely pursuing the trivial school game. Topics for writing should make use of the unique knowledge and skills that students already have, connecting school work in a respectful way to things that they value in their personal lives. The completed assignment should be personally significant and full of power and integrity for the author so that the writing itself demands to be heard by a real audience.

Perhaps it is easier to study what goes wrong with teaching than to study why a particular strategy or assignment works well. Classroom mistakes demand that we pay attention and, if at all possible, repair our mistakes by the next class period, whereas successes do not force us to consider what can be learned when students write well and enjoy themselves in the process. Teachers are criticized for being more interested in what works than in matters of theory and analysis. Maybe what works in the classroom is an enactment of personal theorizing that must be articulated and examined in more depth for continued professional development. The question that will lead us forward to better theories and practices is, Why does this work?

After three decades as a teacher, I have decided to assign only writing projects that I can't wait to read. Life is too short and too messy to teach phony formulas, and students are too wonderful and insightful to be trivialized by pointless assignments. Writing should be full of meaning and joyous to share. Likewise, the assignments that I author for my students are my own moment of personal integrity, my answerability for my career as a teacher of writing. Multigenre writing has worked in my classroom because students have been able to use this assignment to write artfully and skillfully about things that matter in their lives.

Works Cited

Bakhtin, Mikhail M. *Art and Answerability*, Austin: The University of Texas Press, 1990.

——. *The Dialogic Imagination*. Austin: The University of Texas Press, 1981.

Larson, Richard. "The 'Research Paper' in the Writing Course: A Non-Form of

Writing." *The Writing Teacher's Sourcebook*. New York: Oxford UP, 1994. 180–85.

Romano, Tom. *Blending Genre, Alternate Style*. Portsmouth, NH: Boynton/Cook, 2000.

———. *Clearing the Way: Working with Teenage Writers*. Portsmouth, NH: Heinemann, 1987.

———. *Writing with Passion: Life Stories, Multiple Genres*. Portsmouth, NH: Boynton/Cook, 1995.

Salazar, Dixie. "Taking It Back." *Unsettling America*. Eds. Maria Mazziotti Gillan and Jennifer Gillan. New York: Viking, 1994. 149–51.

Simmons, Elizabeth Radin. *Student Worlds, Student Words: Teaching Writing through Folklore*. Portsmouth, NH: Boynton/Cook, 1990.

35

Introduction to the Great Wells of Democracy: The Meaning of Race in American Life

MANNING MARABLE

What We Talk About When We Talk About Race

It is an historical fact that privileged groups seldom give up their privileges voluntarily. Individuals may see the moral light and voluntarily give up their unjust posture; but, as Reinhold Niebuhr has reminded us, groups tend to be more immoral than individuals.

—Martin Luther King, Jr.
"Letter from Birmingham Jail," April 16, 1963

When I was twelve years old, growing up in an African-American community in Dayton, Ohio, something happened at our church one Sunday afternoon that I've never forgotten. My family and I attended St. Margaret's Episcopal Church, which had a congregation that was almost completely black. Occasionally after mass, we'd go downstairs to the church basement and have Sunday dinner for the members of the congregation. On this particular afternoon, the church had organized a raffle. Each ticket cost fifty cents, and the first prize was a $100 U.S. savings bond.

From Manning Marable's *The Great Wells of Democracy: The Meaning of Race in American Life* Basic Civitas, NY: 2003

My allowance at the time was about one dollar and fifty cents per week. I calculated that I could afford to buy one raffle ticket. Before dinner was served, everybody gathered for the drawing. Much to my amazement, I had purchased the winning ticket.

As I walked forward to receive my savings bond, church members and family friends stood up to applaud. One elderly, somewhat heavyset church lady with a beautiful broad smile hugged me and proudly pinched my cheeks. She exclaimed, "Son, this must be your lucky day!"

There are moments like that in everyone's life. Like when you're standing at a city crosswalk and, looking down, see a crumpled twenty-dollar bill on the pavement. The event is unexpected, something that is unusual. I don't know what happened to that savings bond; it's probably somewhere in my mom's basement back in Dayton. But that doesn't diminish how I felt that special day when I was twelve.

Four decades have passed since then. I usually speak about once or twice each week, and I travel more than 120 days every year. Because of deregulation and the new post-9/11 security regulations, air travel for most Americans is nothing less than a kind of torture: long lines, surly ticket agents, uncomfortable seats, terrible meals, and constant delays. Sometimes I can observe the corporate executives sitting up in first class. They're usually chilled out. They seem pampered, well fed, and on especially long flights, generally intoxicated. Then I realize the obvious. For them, almost every day is their lucky day. These are the material benefits of whiteness and upper-class privilege in twenty-first-century America.

Sociologists often use a concept called "life chances." These are things that are likely to happen to you simply because you are identified with a particular group. If you're black or Latino in a racist society, where whiteness is defined as the social norm, you are statistically far more likely to experience certain unfortunate and sometimes even life-threatening events—not based on your behavior, but merely because of your identification with an oppressed social category. The Marxist philosopher Louis Althusser once described this process as "overdetermination." You become a social actor in the real world not on the basis of any objective criteria, but by the stereotypes imposed on you externally by others. The boundaries of one's skin become the crude starting point for negotiating access to power and resources within a society constructed around racial hierarchies. And after a period of several centuries, a mountain of accumulated disadvantage has been erected, a vast monument to the pursuit of inequality and injustice that to most black Americans is the hallmark of our "democracy."

Sitting back into my uncomfortable coach middle seat, I looked again at the first-class section. I then recalled the plot of comedian Bill Murray's movie *Groundhog Day* (1993). In the film, Murray plays an obnoxious weatherman who becomes trapped in a small Pennsylvania town on February 2, Groundhog Day. Despite every effort, he finds that he can't escape. The day repeats itself over and over again. The real world is similar, I thought: People wake up to the same racial discrimination or white upper-class privilege day after day. Affluent whites usually experience a lucky day and, with some minor variations, enjoy that same day repeatedly. The structure of white privilege sets certain parameters of existence that guarantee a succession of lucky days.

Then I began to have second thoughts. Are the overweight white guys in the first-class section *personally* responsible for an entire race being placed permanently back in coach, figuratively speaking? I recalled that Connecticut senator and former Democratic vice presidential candidate Joe Lieberman had traveled south in 1964 to participate in the "Mississippi Freedom Summer," organizing and registering African-American voters. And after all, more than 3 million white people did vote for Jesse Jackson in 1988. Some whites even endorsed Louis Farrakhan's 1995 "Million Man March."

But sympathy for the oppressed is not the same as having a shared or linked fate. We can only truly understand someone else's pain when we step outside the protected confines of our lives to take risks. The political culture of whiteness is conformity. Let's accept the way things are—because things aren't too bad. Power translates itself into "merit." Privileged access and opportunity create spaces for comfortable lives.

Conversely, the structural limitations and restrictions on black life have been continuous in this country. The effects can be seen in many realms, especially in the arts. Racism has produced aesthetically some of this country's most powerful music: for example, the blues. The politics behind this art form, simply put, are based on the harsh reality of having a "bad day" over and over again.

To take this example further, why were the blues produced by oppressed black sharecroppers in the Mississippi Delta, but not by the privileged families of George W. Bush and Dick Cheney? According to 2002 estimates, President Bush's personal assets are between $11.1 million and $21.6 million; Vice President Cheney's total assets are between $19.3 million and $81.8 million. Perhaps we might understand why Bush and Cheney don't sing the blues by reconsidering the real life chances of most African Americans who live under a system most of us call "democracy."

African Americans and Latinos constitute 25 percent of the U.S. population but represent nearly 60 percent of the 2 million Americans currently in prison. Statistically, blacks account for only 14 percent of all illegal drug users. Yet we make up over one-third of all drug arrests and 55 percent of all drug convictions. Are blacks just unlucky in the courts, or is something else at work here?

If it's bad luck, it must start before birth. White Americans in 1995 had an infant mortality rate of 6.3 deaths per 1,000 live births. The African-American infant mortality rate that same year was 15.1 deaths per 1,000 live births—a higher rate than in such places as Taiwan, Portugal, Cuba, Chile, or Bulgaria. Are black babies just unlucky, or are their deaths an inevitable consequence of inadequate health care, poor housing, and the destructive impacts of poverty, unemployment, and the extreme stresses of everyday life for pregnant black women?

The stresses are financial as well as emotional and physical. In several recent studies, major insurance companies were found to charge black homeowners significantly higher rates than whites to insure homes of identical value. Supermarket chains routinely charge higher prices for most groceries in minority urban neighborhoods than in predominantly white, upper-class suburbs. Are African-American consumers in the marketplace just unlucky, or is it the logical result of "equity inequity," the racial profiling of credit and capital investment in our communities? "Bad luck" clearly has nothing to do with the unequal outcomes that construct the normal conditions of our existence. If President George W. Bush and his buddies in the first-class seats who voted for him experienced what we see and feel in our daily lives—omnipresent racial inequality in the courts, in health care, education, employment, and many other areas—they might have invented the blues, too.

The two distinct sections of the airplane also symbolized for me the two strikingly different narratives that have evolved about the character of U.S. democracy and the nature of our social contract, the written and unwritten rules governing relations between the American people and their leaders that theoretically protects their collective interests. For most white Americans, especially those in the first-class seats, U.S. democracy is best represented by enduring values such as personal liberty, individualism, and the ownership of private property. For most of us African Americans and other marginalized minorities, the central goals of the Black Freedom Movement have always been equality—the eradication of all structural barriers to full citizenship and full participation in all aspects of public life and economic relations—and self-determination—the ability to decide, on our own terms, what our future as a community with a unique history and culture might be.

"Freedom" to white Americans principally has meant the absence of legal restrictions on individual activity and enterprise. By contrast, black Americans have always perceived "freedom" in collective terms, as something achievable by group action and capacity-building. "Equality" to African Americans has meant the elimination of all social deficits between blacks and whites—that is, the eradication of cultural and social stereotypes and patterns of social isolation and group exclusion generated by white structural racism over several centuries.

The airplane metaphor is somewhat useful in understanding the problems of race, gender, and class, but in other ways it is limited. The vast majority of the passengers in the coach section are also white, middle-class males. Perhaps one-quarter of the passengers are women. There are several Asian Americans, one or two Latinos, and maybe three other African Americans sitting side by side in two separate rows. As part of the middle class, we have the means and the resources to fly to our destination in relative comfort. But the vast majority of the African-American population, and a significant number of women and other racialized minorities, never board the plane at all. Their physical and social mobility is severely and deliberately restricted. During the era of Jim Crow segregation, the "white" and "colored" signs were the demarcation of society's racial fault line, and black "travelers" were restricted by the boundaries of color. Today, the segregationist signs have been taken down, but the ugly patterns of racialized inequality and white privilege persist in most respects. Through extraordinary efforts, those who never had access to the airplane fought and sacrificed to get some of us on board. Our tickets were purchased at an exorbitant price. Yet those of us fortunate enough to gain that access should recognize that the monopoly of power that severely restricts the mobility of our own community is still in place.

Think for a moment about the individuals in the first-class section. Relative to nearly everybody else, they have a privileged lifestyle. They have set up trust funds for their children, and they take advantage of elitist policies such as "legacies" to guarantee that their descendants will have access to the best university education. They lobby vigorously for the elimination of the inheritance tax to preserve the accumulation of their wealth over several generations. For the most part, they control the national discourse about politics and public policy, and they largely determine the outcomes of national elections. But despite their privileges and power, they nevertheless do not own the plane. They are favored customers, privileged "frequent flyers," but not the owners. They don't control the airplane's schedule or the direction the flight is taking. In fact, those who own the airliner are rarely on it, because they have their own private jets. In the 1990s, 90 percent of the total income gain of the upper one-fifth of U.S. households went to the top 1 percent. As Kevin Phillips observed, "Attention should focus on the top one-tenth of 1 percent, because these are the raw capitalists and money-handlers, not the high-salaried doctors, lawyers and Cadillac dealers." About 250,000 Americans have annual incomes above $1 million. As Phillips noted, "The 30 largest U.S. family and individual fortunes in 1999 were roughly *ten times* as big as the 30 largest had been in 1982, an increase greater than any comparable period during the 19th century."

We are living in a period when the concentration of wealth and economic power is unprecedented in human history. Wal-Mart, which in 1979 had $1 billion in sales for an entire year, now sometimes generates that amount in a single day worldwide. In 2001, Wal-Mart netted $219.81 billion in revenue, outdistancing the second-largest corporation, Exxon-Mobil, which had 2001 revenues of $191.58 billion. General Motors, which held the top spot for fifteen years until 2000, had $177.26 billion in revenues. Enron, the nation's largest energy corporation, which filed for bankruptcy in December 2001, nevertheless reported 2001 earnings of $130.9 billion. For many of the hundreds of thousands of Americans, regardless of race, who lost all or part of their pensions and life savings from the Enron fiasco, it may be difficult to reconcile such vast inequalities generated by this concentration of wealth within a political system that still claims to be a democracy. The racialized inequality that African Americans have brutally experienced and deeply feel is only one important dimension to the larger problem of inequality that is structured across the entire American social order.

The profound differences between the two narratives about the meaning of the American project are often reflected in our conflicts over historical symbols. For example, several years ago, the New Orleans School Board announced the renaming of one of its oldest elementary schools. What was previously George Washington Elementary had become the Dr. Charles Drew Elementary School. The name change was initiated and enthusiastically supported by the school's students, teachers, and parents. The school's African-American History Club had proposed the name to commemorate a famous black surgeon who had established research procedures for processing and storing blood plasma. Drew had been the leading organizer of blood-bank programs during World War II and was responsible for saving millions of lives.

When it became public knowledge that the first U.S. president had been symbolically "dumped" in favor of a black man, many local whites were outraged. But the white "Founding Fathers" aren't the only ones at the center of the school-naming controversies in New Orleans. Over the past 100 years, New Orleans public schools have been named for a series of white racists, slaveholders, and former Confederate army officers. A short list includes: John McDonogh, a wealthy Louisiana slaveholder who freed many of his slaves only on the condition that they would return to Africa; Henry W. Allen, a sugarcane planter and Confederate general; Confederate army commander Robert E. Lee; and Confederate president Jefferson Davis. Some people who have supported racial name changes have argued that the overwhelmingly black student population of the New Orleans public school system should be presented with positive role models from their own history and culture. Certainly this is a valid point. By cultivating greater awareness and appreciation among African-American young people about their heritage, they may acquire valuable lessons about black achievement against the odds.

But perhaps the greatest beneficiaries in the changing of public honorific names are white Americans. "Whiteness" imposes blinders that shut off the full spectrum of social reality, the shared experiences of people from different racialized backgrounds in the making of a common history. The symbolic act of naming makes a public statement about our relationship to the past and about the principles and values that should be preserved.

The larger political issue that lies just behind the debate over names is far more disturbing. The United States, from its origins to the present, has consistently lied to itself about what it actually is. We claimed to be a "democracy" in the early nineteenth century, even while denying voting rights to the majority of citizens. We claim "equal protection under the law" while millions of black, brown, and poor people have been and continue to be unjustly treated in our courts and prisons. Our economic system favors the privileged few, while allocating greater poverty and unemployment along the unequal boundaries of race.

There have always been Americans who have challenged the political hypocrisy of this nation. They have been black, brown, and white. In the 1960s, they were activists in civil rights, in the antiwar movement against U.S. involvement in Vietnam, in women's rights, and in the welfare-rights movement. In the nineteenth century, they were the abolitionists who fought to outlaw human bondage. They are the "Other America," those who dreamed of a truly democratic, pluralistic society. Their names—such as W.E.B. Du Bois, Cesar Chavez, Fannie Lou Hamer, Ida B. Wells-Barnett, Eugene V. Debs, William Lloyd Garrison, Joe Hill, and Paul Robeson—represent an alternative perspective on what America has been and what it could become. Our debate over history therefore is a debate about the future of the country itself.

I

"E Pluribus Unum": Out of many, one. Americans have been taught to believe that they have always been champions of religious, ethnic, and cultural pluralism. "Diversity" has become our multicultural mantra about America's past as well as its future. Offices of student life and student activities groups throughout the United States now fund thousands of celebrations promoting diversity, from the annual birthday events honoring Dr. Martin Luther King, Jr., to Cinco de Mayo, from programs for lesbian, gay, bisexual, and transgender awareness to those honoring the heritage of American Indians. Administrators in the private sector now routinely talk about "managing diversity," of creating workplace environments in which "difference" is not coded into institutional hierarchies. Yet there's a crucial difference between the recognition of "difference" and the acknowledgment that the reality of difference has produced unequal outcomes and divergent life chances for citizens within the same society. As Ron Wakabayashi, the executive director of the Los Angeles County Commission on Human Relations, has observed: "Politicians like to say that diversity is our greatest strength. That is b.s. Diversity simply *is*. The core question is how do we extract its assets while minimizing its liabilities."

Instead of "celebrating diversity," we must theorize it, interrogate it, and actively seek the parallels and discontinuities in the histories of the people who over many centuries have come to call themselves "Americans." Instead of talking abstractly about race, we should be theorizing about the social processes of racialization, of how certain groups in U.S. society have been relegated to an oppressed status, by the weight of law, social policy, and economic exploitation. This process of subordination has never been exclusively or solely grounded in a simplistic black-white paradigm. Although slavery and Jim Crow segregation were decisive in framing the U.S. social hierarchy, with whiteness defined at the top and blackness at the bottom, people of African descent have never experienced racialization by themselves.

As ethnic studies scholars such as Gary Okihiro and Ronald Takaki have observed, the 1790 Naturalization Act defined citizenship only for immigrants who were "free white persons." Asian immigrants who were born outside the United States were largely excluded from citizenship until 1952. U.S. courts constantly redefined the rules determining who was "white" and who was not. For example, Armenians were originally classed as "Asians" and thus were nonwhite, but they legally became "whites" by a 1909 court decision. Syrians were "white" in court decisions in 1909 and 1910; they became "nonwhite" in 1913, and became "white" again in 1915. Asian Indians were legally white in 1910, but they were classified as nonwhite after 1923. Historians such as David Roediger and Noel Ignatiev have illustrated how a series of ethnic minorities, such as the Irish and Ashkenazi Jews, experienced fierce racialization and discrimination but over several generations managed to scale the hierarchy of whiteness.

What many white Americans still refuse to consider is that their numerical majority in the United States is rapidly eroding. By approximately 2016, the population category defined by the U.S. Census Bureau as "non-Hispanic whites" will peak in size, and then it will gradually decline. As Asian Americans, Caribbean people, Latin Americans, Arab Americans, and other nationalities enter the national dialogue about democracy, we will inextricably move away from history's old honorific icons toward new names and symbols of political accomplishment. American democracy is still an unfinished project. Navigating within that new diversity will not be easy. One central reason is that oppression in the United States—or anywhere else, for that matter—has been constructed around interlocking systems of prejudice, power, and white heterosexual male privilege in which the vast majority of the population has been defined outside the acceptable boundaries of the mainstream.

There was, of course, the hierarchy of race: the social construction of whiteness as a category of privilege, the racial stereotyping of the vast majority of non-Europeans, the genocidal elimination of most American Indians, and the enslavement of people of African descent. But there was also a hierarchy of gender oppression or patriarchy: the beliefs of heterosexist male authority and domination, and female inferiority and subordination; the absence for centuries of voting rights and property rights for women; the deliberate uses of violence, such as rape, sexual harassment, and physical intimidation, to preserve patriarchal power.

The hierarchy of heterosexism and homophobia relied on beliefs and practices that reinforced heterosexual superiority and power and promoted institutional discrimination and subordination against lesbian, gay, bisexual, and transgendered people. It permitted the systematic use of violence of different types and degrees to intimidate and control people based on their sexual orientation. And there was the hierarchy of class: the unequal distribution of the bulk of all private property, productive resources, factories, banks, and financial institutions into the hands of a small minority of the population, with the great majority forced to live and exist only by its labor power; the development of an ideology of class privilege that masquerades by calling itself "merit"; and, increasingly, the monopolization and exploitation of global resources and transnational corporations to manufacture and preserve the privileges of class.

The key to properly understanding and theorizing what "racialization" has meant in our historical past and still means today was first conceptualized by legal scholar Cheryl Harris: "Whiteness as Property." To be white is not essentially a biological or genetically based, fixed social category; it is the social expression of power and privilege, the consequences of discriminatory policies in the past, and the practices of inequality that exist today. Thus we will never dismantle structural racism as a system unless we are also willing to address the transformation of the American social structure and the full democratization of our political and economic institutions.

The dynamics of socioeconomic and political marginalization and of social isolation and exclusion inevitably impact the behavior of any oppressed group. Oppressed people are constantly forced to define themselves, largely unthinkingly, by the crude boundaries of the formal, legal categories that have been imposed on them. Any people dwelling at the bottom of a social hierarchy will see themselves as the "Other," as individuals outside of society's social contract, as subordinated, marginalized, fixed minorities. Frequently, oppressed people have used these categories, and even terms of insult and stigmatization, such as "nigger" or "queer," as a site for resistance and counter-hegemonic struggle.

The difficulty inherent in this kind of oppositional politics is twofold. First, it tends to anchor individuals to narrowly defined, one-dimensional identities that are often the "inventions" of others. For example, how did African people become known as "black" or, in Spanish, "Negro"? Europeans launching the slave trade across the Atlantic 400 years ago created the terminology as a way of categorizing the people of an entire continent with tremendous variations in language, religion, ethnicity, kinship patterns, and cultural traditions. Blackness, or the state of being black, was completely artificial; no people in Africa prior to the transatlantic slave trade and European colonialism called themselves "black." Blackness only exists as a social construct in relation to something else. That "something else" became known as whiteness. Blackness as a category relegates other identities—ethnicity, sexual orientation, gender, class affiliation, religious traditions, kinship affiliations—to a secondary or even nonexistent status.

In other words, those who control or dominate hierarchies, whether by ownership of the means of production or by domination of the state, have a vested interest in manufacturing and reproducing categories of difference. An excellent recent example of this occurred in the United States in 1971, when the U.S. Census Bureau "invented" the category "Hispanic." The term was imposed on a population of 16 million people reflecting divergent and even contradictory nationalities, racialized ethnicities, cultural traditions, and political loyalties: black Panamanians of Jamaican or Trinidadian descent, who speak Spanish; Argentines of Italian or German descent; anti-Castro, white, upper-class Cubans in Miami's Dade County; impoverished Mexican-American farm workers in California's Central Valley; and black Dominican service and blue-collar workers in New York City's Washington Heights. Yet when states or hierarchies name the "Other," the act of naming creates its own materiality for the oppressed. Government resources, economic empowerment zones, and affirmative-action scholarships are in part determined by who is classified as Hispanic, and who is not. Identities may be situational, but when the power and resources of the state are used to categorize groups under a "one-size-fits-all" designation, the life chances of individuals who are defined within these categories are largely set and determined by others.

II

In post–civil rights era America, most white commentators on issues of race emphasize the necessity for all of us to become "color blind." That is, we should be "blind" to any imputed differences that tend to divide people by skin color or phenotype, by physical appearance, or by genetic background. The political version of this argument is that any special measures that created privileged classes based on racial categories are inherently unfair and discriminatory.

The color-blind thesis almost always is accompanied by an appeal to "forgive and forget." The logic of this argument goes as follows: Black Americans were certainly terribly oppressed during slavery and Jim Crow segregation. But no white Americans alive today owned slaves. There's been much social progress in recent years, thanks to the constructive cooperation between the races. It's time for us to move beyond ancient grievances and racial bitterness, toward taking greater personal responsibility for our own lives. All of us bear part of the blame for the burden of prejudice—that is, the minorities themselves are partly responsible for getting themselves into their current predicament.

With certain variations, this basic argument is repeated over and over again in the white media by white political leaders and institutions about the dynamics of race. Their thesis is that African Americans must stop being so "sensitive" and "defensive" about the problems of their people and communities. Whites have nothing to apologize for, and African Americans have little really to complain about.

In popular films and culture, the message is largely the same. At the beginning of *Die Hard with a Vengeance* (1995), a white actor, Bruce Willis, stands in Harlem, just off Amsterdam Avenue, wearing a huge sign that reads: "I Hate Niggers." A cluster of justifiably outraged young black men surrounds the undercover white cop. Yet the film, remarkably, portrays not the white cop, but the African-American males, as emotional, dangerous, unstable, and threatening. In the award-winning film *Pulp Fiction* (1994), a white criminal played by John Travolta "accidentally" blows off the head of a young black man when his gun discharges. Covered with blood and gore, the white killer and his black partner (Samuel L. Jackson) take refuge in the suburban home of a white criminal associate (Quentin Tarantino). The suburban mobster is outraged that this "dead nigger" has been dragged into his home. Yet to display that he could not really be a racist, the film then cuts away to show that this bigot is married to an African-American woman. The fact that he has a sexual relationship with a black woman is supposed to clear up any misunderstandings about his repeated stream of utterances about "dead niggers"!

The white corporate-oriented media loves to publicize stories about "black bigotry." Several years ago, for instance, when the Oakland, California, board of education suggested that African-American young people may learn best in an environment that validates the language they actually speak ("ebonics") in their neighborhoods and in daily interactions with friends, blacks everywhere were attacked for "rejecting" standard English, as if none of us speak it. When African-American students now demand black studies courses, or advocate campus housing emphasizing Caribbean, African, and black American cultural traditions and identity, they are subjected to ridicule as proponents of "self-segregation."

We will never uproot racism by pretending that everyone shares an equal and common responsibility for society's patterns of discrimination and inequality. Black people were never "equal partners" in the construction of slavery, Jim Crow segregation, and ghettoization. We weren't individually or collectively consulted when our criminal-justice system imprisoned one-third of our young men, or when we continue to be burdened with twice the unemployment rate of whites. To be "color blind" in a virulently racist society is to be blind to the history and reality of oppression. To forget the past and to refuse to acknowledge the color-coded hierarchies that constitute our parallel racial universes is to evade any responsibility for racial peace in the future.

Perhaps the greatest lie in the arsenal of the "color-blind" proponents of racism is the assertion that black people can be understood only as part of the larger narrative of standard American history. That is to say that "black history" is somehow inferior to or at odds with "American history." To be part of the national project, culturally and ideologically, means that we must surrender and abandon those lessons we've learned in our struggles along the way.

While it is certainly true that black Americans are survivors of a very destructive historical process from slavery, Jim Crow segregation, and ghettoization, we know within ourselves that we have never stood silently by, succumbing to the forces of white oppression. Any understanding of black history illustrates that we have consistently fought to maintain a unique set of cultural values that have shaped and continue to define our core identities as a people. We have, in effect, always been not only the makers of "our" history but also central to the construction and evolution of the larger American experience.

What are the cultural reservoirs that create the psychological, emotional, and cultural foundation of the strength and vision that the adventure of blackness in American life has produced? Even in the shadows of slavery, we found our humanity in the gift of song. Our music tells us much about who we are, how we have worked, how we have loved, where we've been, and where we're going. From the blues of the Mississippi Delta, to the soaring sounds of bebop in Harlem in the

1940s, to the provocative rhythms of today's hip hop, black music reflects the pulse and sensibility of blackness.

Black history and culture reveal the gift of grace, the fluidity of motion and beauty that an oppressed people have claimed as their own. It is constantly recreated in many ways: from the artistry of dance to the spectacular athleticism of Michael Jordan. Grace is the ability to redefine the boundaries of possibility. We as a people were not supposed to survive the ordeal of oppression and Jim Crow segregation, yet our very existence speaks to the creative power of our collective imagination. That power is reflected in our language, the rhythm of gospel, and the power of black preachers on Sunday morning in our churches. That power is found in the creative energy of our poets and playwrights. The gift of grace can be heard in the writings of Toni Morrison, James Baldwin, Amiri Baraka, and Alice Walker.

The experience of work has always been the foundation of black strength and capacity-building throughout history. Slavery was the only moment in American history when people of African descent experienced full employment: Everybody worked. If financial gain was commensurate with hard work, African Americans would undoubtedly be among the wealthiest people on earth. Yet despite our economic marginalization, despite the historic pattern of receiving barely 60 cents for every dollar of wages that comparable white work commands, we nevertheless have found real meaning in the world of work. Black labor, more than any other, is responsible for establishing much of the foundations of the economic productivity of this country. Black working-class women and men have for generations been at the forefront of the trade-union movement and collective efforts to improve the quality of life and the conditions of work for all Americans.

And then there is the historical strength of family and community, kinship and neighbors within the black experience. An oppressed people cannot survive unless there is close cooperation and mutual support by and for each other. The reservoir of strength within the black family has been anchored in our recognition that kinship is collective, not nuclear, in structure.

Throughout black history, along with the strength of family there has been the strength of our faith. During slavery, a prayer was in many ways an act of resistance. When we sang "Steal Away to Jesus," our eyes looked to the North Star, to the faraway promised land of freedom. Today that faith still resounds as the cultural heart of black community life in thousands of towns and cities across the country. From the courage of Dr. Martin Luther King, Jr., to the contemporary activism of a Jesse Jackson or an Al Sharpton, black faith has been most powerful as a historical force when spirituality reinforces fundamental social change.

It is only through the telling of our stories about the destructive dynamics of racialization that many white Americans will be able finally to come to terms with the social costs of "whiteness," for themselves, their children, and for the larger society. No genuine dialogue about race is possible when millions of whites are taught to believe that blacks have been marginal to the construction of American society, or that the "race problem" has now been solved.

No meaningful dialogue can take place when some whites still think about race as a "zero-sum game," where any economic or political advances by racial minorities must come at their expense. I believe that the only way for us to move toward a nonracist society is for white Americans to acknowledge that the struggles and sacrifices that blacks have made to destroy structural racism in all of its forms throughout history have directly contributed to enriching and expanding the meaning of democracy not just for ourselves, but for everyone within our society. As Martin Luther King, Jr., observed in the "Letter from Birmingham Jail," the "real heroes" of American democracy are those who actively challenged the immorality and injustices of racial inequality:

> *One day the South will recognize its real heroes. They will be the James Merediths, with the noble sense of purpose that enables them to face jeering, and hostile mobs, and with the agonizing loneliness that characterizes the life of the pioneer. They will be old, oppressed, battered Negro women, symbolized in a seventy-two-year-old woman in Montgomery, Alabama, who rose up with a sense of dignity and with her people decided not to ride segregated buses, and who responded with ungrammatical profundity to one who inquired about her weariness: "My feets is tired, but my soul is at rest." They will be the young high school and college students, the young ministers of the gospel and a host of their elders, courageously and nonviolently sitting in at lunch counters and willingly going to jail for conscience' sake. One day the South will know that when these disinherited children of God sat down at lunch counters, they were in reality standing up for what is best in the American dream and for the most sacred values in our Judeo-Christian heritage, thereby bringing our nation back to those great wells of democracy which were dug deep by the founding fathers in their formulation of the Constitution and the Declaration of Independence.*

Notes

1 *"Groups tend to be more immoral than individuals"*: Martin Luther King, Jr., "Letter from Birmingham Jail," in *Why We Can't Wait* (New York: Harper & Row, 1964).

4 *Under a system most of us call "democracy"*: See "The State of the Estate Tax," *Washington Post*, June 6, 2002.

7 *"Doctors, lawyers and Cadillac dealers"*: Kevin Phillips, "Dynasties! How Their Wealth and Power Threaten Democracy," *The Nation*, July 8, 2002, pp. 11–14.

7 *"Greater than any comparable period during the 19th century"*: Kevin Phillips, "The New Face of Another Gilded Age," *Washington Post*, May 26, 2002.

7 *Inequality that is structured across the entire American social order*: See Matt Moore, "Wal-Mart Passes Exxon to Top Fortune 500 List," *Washington Post*, April 1, 2002.

10 *Classified as nonwhite after 1923*: See Gary Okihiro, "Cheap Talk, er, Dialogue," *Souls*, vol. 1, no. 3 (Summer 1999), pp. 52–58; and Ronald Takaki, *A Different Mirror: A History of Multicultural America* (Boston: Little, Brown, 1993).

36

Criticism in the Zines

Vernacular Theory and Popular Culture

THOMAS MCLAUGHLIN

Mass-marketed popular culture has provoked in our time a huge and varied critical commentary. From *People* magazine and *Entertainment Tonight* to the moral outrage of the religious right and the cultural politics of academic critical theory, the latest Madonna video and the verbal violence of gangsta rap and the semiotics of late night television are subject to immediate interpretive attention. Commentary on popular culture has become simultaneously an integral part of the popular media, shaping audience response to current offerings, and the most vivid opportunity in our culture for critics to observe, analyze, and unmask the operations of ideology. Popular culture is spoken of by those who want to reinforce and refine its central role in our subjectivity and by those who resist by analysis its psychic and social dominance. All of the commentary produced by the industry and much of the analysis produced by cultural critics work on the assumption—one cynically and the other in near despair—that the fans, those who are subject to the power of the media, are malleable, unable to understand let alone resist that domination. But there is also a huge and varied fan commentary on popular culture. It happens in very informal situations—across the lunch counter or the xerox machine—in the casual conversations made possible by common pop culture tastes, but it also happens in a more formal and critical mode in what fans call "zines," amateur magazines written and edited and published by the fans themselves. Zines tend to focus on one particular fan obsession—*Star*

From *Street Smarts and Critical Theory: Listening to the Vernacular* Thomas McLaughlin Madison: U of Wisconsin Press 1996

Trek, or industrial music, or *The Brady Bunch,* or exploitation films—and they give fans of specific pop culture texts the opportunity to speak out of their own expertise, often in ways that resist the dominant messages of mass culture.

Cultural critics who reject the image of the fan as ideological dupe have seen in the zines evidence of what Michel de Certeau calls "poaching," a set of interpretive practices by which pop culture's subjects read against the grain, imposing on popular texts the meanings that they need rather than those the industry intends. Zine writers tend to approach texts with a skeptical and rebellious attitude, with an irony that allows them to enjoy a mainstream media text but still refashion it to their own ends. I want to maintain in this essay that they go further than that, that in the zines we can find the fans seeing through the ideological operation itself, practicing a vernacular cultural criticism. The zines are a space in which fundamental theoretical questioning of cultural systems manages—now and again, and against the wishes of popular culture itself—to occur.

A zine is a magazine produced by amateurs on the fringe of journalism and the publishing industry. Zines are related to but distinct from "fan magazines," which are produced by the entertainment business *for* fans, and from newsletters, which are produced by ongoing organizations. Zines are almost always produced by a few people loosely organized around some issue or pop cultural style or by one individual with an attitude that he or she is determined to share. Some zines think of themselves as part of a "samizdat" movement, operating outside official culture, on the fringe of the law (almost all zines operate on a cash basis), and at an acute angle to popular culture. These magazines have existed since the underground of the sixties at least, but with the personal computer revolution of the eighties, zines have proliferated. Some estimates go as high as 20,000 zines in America, on such topics as pop music, television, politics, women's issues, film, gay issues, sports, and fashion. There are Grateful Dead zines, punk zines, drag queen zines, *Brady Bunch* zines, exploitation movie zines, local music zines in cities across the country, rap and hip-hop zines, *90210* zines, etc. There are also thousands of political zines, most of them arguing for large and complex conspiracy theories.

I cannot claim in this essay to have mastered this gigantic field. To do justice to the history and the variety of zines would require a book-length study.[1] I have focused my attention on zines that deal with popular culture and on a few explicitly political zines that comment on pop culture as well as on many other subjects. This is, however, not a narrow focus. The number of pop culture zines is impossible to tell. They proliferate in local circumstances, in subcultural groups, many of them accessible to only a few personal friends and their connections. There are also a huge number of electronic zines that exist only in cyberspace, and I have not included them at all. My interpretation of the zine phenomenon is based on an aleatory search. I found references to zines in *Factsheet 5,* a zine about the zines, and I bought zines at *See Hear,* a music-oriented book and magazine store in New York. I wrote away for zines that were reviewed in other zines. This process did not result in a representative sample—I feel certain that no such sam-

---

[1]The best introduction to the world of zines is Mike Gunderloy's *The World of Zines: A Guide to the Independent Magazine Revolution* (Penguin, 1992).

ple could be assembled, since the field is so fluid and idiosyncratic. But this is the kind of acquisition process that any zine reader would follow. Zines announce their interests and attitudes very clearly, and fans graze through them until they find a match. Zines review other zines, and readers are led easily to zines that interest them.

Zines provide fans with the opportunity to articulate and circulate their own sense of popular culture, to make what feels like a desperate attempt to figure out how it works—how the business of it is conducted, how its texts are constructed, how it is marketed and distributed, how it affects its fans. There is an urgency to these reflections, a sense of high stakes. A fan who reflects seriously on popular culture is operating outside the passive modes of thought that pop culture is an attempt to enforce. Zines are full of unauthorized textual pleasures, full of what de Certeau calls "poaching," making texts mean what the reader needs them to mean, in the face of what their producers intended. Zines are high-attitude productions; each zine *takes an attitude* rather than passively consuming pop texts, and each attitude taken has the urgency of resistance. Zines also have the urgency of personal engagement. Writers and editors of zines are not detached from the phenomena they describe. How a band's career develops is central to the personal concerns—indeed the personal identity—of the zine writer covering the band. Zines live in the culture they describe. They make no pretense of anthropological detachment or interpretive distance. Zine writers and publishers *are* the fans on whom ideological effects are plotted. They *are* the social subjects that academic writers on popular culture theorize about. What we will find in zines is popular culture subjected to a popularly produced, resistant discourse of analysis and theory.

Zines have already attracted commentary and analysis from academic cultural critics. The most detailed and extensive analysis occurs in Henry Jenkins' *Textual Poachers: Television Fans and Participatory Culture.* As his title suggests, Jenkins depicts fans as de Certeau's "poachers," mobile and clever nomads on the cultural landscape. Jenkins is particularly interested in the creative works of fans. Zines often feature stories or scripts written by fans in the spirit of the mass media texts to which the zine is dedicated. *Star Trek* is the most important of these; there are *Star Trek* magazines, books, music, conventions, videos, films, and costumes, all the works of enthusiastic amateurs who want to be a part of the *Star Trek* universe.[2] Jenkins' book opens up a vision of a vast fan culture: creative and critical practices that spin off the objects of the fans' affection. That is, the fan as poacher does not simply produce a replica of the original text; rather, he or she develops an independent sense of the true spirit of the text and creates within that spirit, even if—as is often the case—the fan is convinced that the producers of the series have lost that spirit over time.

Jenkins is also interested in the fan as critic. He defines fandom as "an institution of theory and criticism, a semistructured space where competing interpretations and evaluations of common texts are proposed, debated, and negotiated and where readers speculate about the nature of the mass media and their own relationship to it" (86). Jenkins most frequently talks about zine criticism as an eval-

---

[2]See also Patricia Frazier and Diana L. Veith, "Romantic Myth, Transcendence, and *Star Trek* Zines" in *Erotic Universe: Sexuality and Fantastic Literature,* edited by Daniel Palumbo (Greenwood, 1986).

uative procedure in which theoretical questions exert an implicit force. I want, in this essay, to take a more extensive look at the overtly interpretive and theoretical activity that fans produce in the zines. I will be asking what issues worry zine writers when they consider popular culture, what kinds of questions they ask as critics in order to make their own sense of the text, and what kinds of theoretical insights these questions might lead to.

Almost every cultural critic who comments on fan activity cites Michel de Certeau's *The Practice of Everyday Life*. De Certeau's vision of contemporary culture depicts the individual as the subject of systematic "strategies" deployed by powerful cultural institutions. He accepts a Foucaultian awareness of cultural power, but unlike many Foucaultians, he does not end in cultural despair at the sheer extensivity of cultural manipulation. Rather, he emphasizes the "tactics" by which everyday citizens of modern societies resist and reappropriate a culture produced by corporate power. What de Certeau says of the act of reading typifies his vision of all contemporary subjectivity: "readers are travellers; they move across lands belonging to someone else, like nomads poaching their way across fields they did not write, despoiling the wealth of Egypt to enjoy it themselves" (174). Mass media texts are "strategies" designed to shape the consciousness of the mass audience, to encourage acceptance of current political and economic power by naturalizing its ideology. But fans take up pop texts, recombine them as they see fit, operate upon them as active readers with their own agenda, resisting the intended ideological effects. Because this reading practice often leaves no written trace of itself, de Certeau says that "the story of man's travels through his own texts remains in large measure unknown" (170). Strategies, that is, are easier to detect than tactics, and so we tend to notice the power of the media and to overlook the power of the fan.

Cultural critics who have written about fans in general and zines in particular point to zines as one of the places where that fan power is visible. Janice Radway, for example, argues in her essay "Reception Study: Ethnography and the Problem of Dispersed Audiences and Nomadic Subjects" that the contemporary popular culture fan should no longer be thought of in terms of "audience," a concept that implies the passive position of the addressee, but rather as an "active, producing cultural worker who fashions narratives, stories, objects and practices from myriad bits and pieces of prior cultural production" (362). This image of the fan provides the foundation for studies like David Jary, John Horne, and Tom Bucke's "Football 'fanzines' and football culture: a case of successful 'cultural contestation,' " in which they argue that the zines produced by British football fans are social spaces in which mainstream values are contested, not just reproduced, and in which the corporate control of sport gives way to resistant popular self-expression. The fans assert their own claim to the game, over against its owners, agents, and moneymen. One can see the same spirit in the work of John Fiske in *Television Culture*, which questions the dominant image of the mesmerized couch potato, in Radway's work on readers of romance novels, and in Ien Ang's *Watching Dallas*; all share a respectful

attitude toward fans as resistant readers. Lawrence Grossberg's "Is There a Fan in the House: The Affective Sensibility of Fandom" reminds us that such resistance is never totally successful. Grossberg argues that "even if it is true that audiences are always active, it does not follow that they are ever in control" (53–54). Fans always operate inside the strategies embodied in mass media texts, but they also "consume, interpret and use texts" in ways that those strategies cannot completely predict. Cultural critics who have looked at zines tend to see zine writers and publishers as among the most active and resistant of fans, as what Grossberg calls "elite fans." Young feminists writing about *The Brady Bunch*, gay writers fascinated by Madonna, *Star Trek* fans who identify with the outlaw Klingons are all clearly resistant readers, refusing to follow the directions that the pop texts provide.

My argument is that zines allow fans to go one step further; that is, they provide fans with the opportunity to acquire such expertise in reading a particular set of texts that they begin to *see through* the strategies, to understand the operations of the pop culture system itself. They become vernacular theorists, subjects who take up the work of dismantling the ideology they encounter in pop culture. I realize that the role of pop culture fan does not imply in the public imagination the active, questioning consciousness necessary for theoretical activity. Rather, the role of fan suggests irrationality, obsessive devotion, openness to manipulation, passivity in the face of media overkill—the subject as duped image consumer. A "fan" would seem to have none of the critical resources necessary to theorize his or her own systematic domination, especially in America, where "media literacy" education is still marginalized and mocked. But I would suggest that the role of the fan—particularly the "elite fan"—in media culture does make such theoretical reflection possible though not easy to come by.

First of all there is a widespread fan awareness that all media culture is produced by corporate power for economic purposes. Baseball fans, for example, took a lesson in the business of baseball during the long and bitter strike. Their love of the game now battles against a cynical awareness that team loyalty matters little to players or owners, as compared with the economic interests involved in the game. Not even the most naive fan can now think of baseball in idyllic or idealistic terms. Elvis fans know what Colonel Tom Parker helped Elvis become. Punk fans know how fast their music got coopted. Blues fans know what the business did to the geniuses who created the music. Film fans know that the art of the deal has eclipsed the art of film. These knowledges create a division in the fan. Enthusiasm battles irony. Pleasure is tinged with bitterness. The ostensible purpose of popular texts—fan pleasure—is seen to be an economic strategy. That knowledge in some cases leads to a theoretical questioning of the premises of popular culture itself. As I will argue later, the zines are obsessed with the *business*, in spite of the fact that "fans" are supposed to be obsessed with the product.

Fans are also quick to see and criticize the hype that surrounds pop culture. They realize that images can be manipulated and that public response can be artificially constructed. There is routine fan condemnation of the "crap" that the culture industries create, even though there may be a fierce loyalty to a *particular* style or star. More ironic fans may recognize the low quality of a popular TV show but still enjoy it as camp or kitsch. Fans of alternate media, on the other hand, roundly reject mainstream media texts and scorn the publicity apparatus that sustains them. In these various perceptions of the difference between what the media claim for themselves and what they deliver, there is the potential for theoretical consciousness. Fans often have intense loves but also intense hates, and it isn't far from such hatred of particular texts to suspicion of the system that produces them.

There is also a pervasive fan cynicism about the representation of reality in the media. Pop culture consumers talk every day about how politicians can manipulate the media, and how TV news distorts experience and omits alternative perspectives. Theories of media conspiracy abound. Who killed JFK? What happened at Roswell, New Mexico, or Waco, Texas? Wily pop subjects would never look to the mainstream media for answers to such questions. This critical awareness does not deny the power of media strategies to construct postmodern subjectivity, but it does mean that this power succeeds in spite of its subjects' critical consciousness. Seeing through media games does not by any means guarantee breaking free of them. But it is a habit of being for many fans, and it makes their vernacular theorizing possible. Zines are one of the cultural spaces in which fans can raise such questions.

I believe that these ways of thinking are common in pop culture fans, and particularly in the "elite fans" who tend to be the publishers, editors, and writers of zines. Elite fans become in effect scholars of their idols. Many Grateful Dead fans keep and constantly update playlists from all the concerts they have attended or can find out about. Fans of exploitation films can sometimes identify and discuss the work of important art directors in the genre. Jazz fans can name the session players on all of Miles Davis' albums. Because of this fanatical knowledge, elite fans can come to theoretical questions in ways similar to those of academic cultural critics: they engage in interpretive and evaluative disputes, they make subtle generic and stylistic distinctions, they possess an insider knowledge that gives biographical and cultural context to the texts they are engaged with. The evidence of the zines is that in this effort at interpretation, distinction, and contextualization, fans often raise fundamental questions about the premises that guide their critical practice.

Vernacular cultural theory lacks the systematics of academic theory; it occurs in flashes, in local circumstances, rather than in sustained analysis. Take as an example this brief article from *The ROC* (199?), a zine produced by a loose anticensorship alliance. A fan named Mark Mahaffey tells the story of a recent concert by the late G. G. Allin and a group called Plastic Man at the Penguin Pub in Youngstown, Ohio. These two hardcore bands play ultraloud, postpunk assault music. G. G. Allin, who has since died of a drug overdose, was an extremist performance artist, violent and self-destructive. What makes this story interesting is that Mahaffey reflects on his experience and recognizes with some irony that the violence and "confussion" he describes were FUN! At this moment in the story Mahaffey tries to put his experience into an intellectual and social context. G. G. Allin screams out, the storyteller says, against "an unjust and corrupt society," symbolized by the police use of attack dogs, an act that poisons the relationship between man and nature. G. G. Allin gets connected to *A Clockwork Orange* because both are examples of rage against social power, against systems of restraint and order. This is a story of violence in the streets and violence in the arts, refusals to accept socially enforced limits. But the scene plays more like a festival, a rowdy carnival, than like an insurrection, an act of transformative rage. Both G. G. Allin's act and the semiriot out in the streets are fun, and even the cops and the security guys are part of the fun, defining the limits past which we will go, adding to the energy charge that makes this an occasion.

The spin that Mahaffey puts on the story, the interpretation that he offers, is a staple of adolescence, the familiar theme of art and youth in rebellion against authority, but that's not to say it's simpleminded. The placement of this story inside this politically minded zine suggests that the interpretation is thoughtful, not automatic. *The ROC* speaks out against all the intricate forms of censorship of rock music. Its enemies are Tipper Gore and Donald Wildmon. It calls for absolute freedom of speech, and it pushes that argument hard by focusing its attention on bands that would offend almost *anyone*. The zine reports on censorship efforts around the country, and it does so in enough detail to guarantee that the adolescent shibboleth of "authority" takes on the specificity and extensivity of a Foucaultian disciplinary system. In Texas a murder suspect defends himself by claiming that listening to metal music made him do it. In New York the mayor speaks out against rap music. Music stores refuse to sell albums with warning labels to minors. Tapes get confiscated at customs. Arenas refuse to let *The ROC* set up informational booths. The zine constructs a picture of a society intent on patrolling and enforcing the boundaries of expression. *The ROC* gives us a perhaps paranoid, perhaps prophetic vision of society as spiritual prison, guarded when necessary by men with guns and dogs.

The ROC, like many zines, is an act of love, a huge task taken on for no money out of an extreme commitment to an attitude, a way of thinking, a theory of how popular culture works. I would not claim that the theory in this case is particularly subtle or original, but in little fragments like Mahaffey's story we see a flash of theoretical insight, a moment when the consensus interpretation (violence is bad, art is uplifting) is rejected in favor of an oppositional reading (violence is fun, art can be psychotic). We can find these flashes of theory throughout the zine world. The zines present to us popular culture's resistant theory of itself, one that holds up to a fragmented and weird popular culture a fragmented and weird representation of itself.

Another moment of vernacular theory can be seen in this angry and sardonic message from one of the editors of *Attitude Problem,* a "Multipurpose Nonconformist Rag" out of Prescott, Arizona. I quote this in full because it seems to me to provide a canny insight into the role of popular culture texts in the fantasy life of media subjects. The anger of the piece comes out of Bandhu's realization that *his own* text can be commandeered by an audience other than the one he imagined. What baby boomers do to *Attitude Problem* is an example of what the audience of pop culture texts in general do, which is to incorporate texts into their own psychic scenarios, to elaborate fantasy identifications with media figures. Postmodern subjectivity is precisely the result of such fantasy work, and Bandhu has the wit to understand the political impact of media subjectivity, which is to divorce the subject from the local social world, to provide an imaginary safe haven for the imaginary hip subject. Bandhu does not place the boomers inside this larger construct; he's too full of generational anger at sellout former freaks to see them in terms of pop audiences in general, but his moral outrage and sense of victimization do allow him to see that audiences have large psychic consequences at stake in their encounter with popular culture.

I am of course exactly the reader he detests. I am cruising the zines for my own purposes. I am not a part of the generation to which zines are addressed. I am part of the institution of cultural criticism, bringing to the practice of vernacular criticism the terms and concepts of academic discourse. There is therefore the danger that I am both misrepresenting and domesticating this vernacular discourse. But I am at least taking the zines seriously as outlets for theoretical practice. My tactic in this essay is to examine the explicit and implicit theoretical work done in the zines, work that makes a distinctive contribution to understanding popular culture because it comes from a perspective that academic cultural theory cannot adopt. Zine theory has the advantage of operating within the culture it describes, with an intimacy and specificity not possible for the academic observer, who may like me be a consumer of popular culture but whose institutional position makes the encounter with vernacular culture problematic. The zines are an example of a vast cultural practice that includes academic theory but also much more, the theoretical work that goes on in everyday life.

Some zines are explicitly theoretical, directed at big cultural or political questions, either because they are affiliated with some movement that has a theoretical edge to it, or because they come out of an avant-garde tradition that rejects the narrowness and dullness of mainstream values and beliefs, or because they are promoting a pop phenomenon so far out of the mainstream that they have to apologize for it by presenting a theoretical explanation of its premises and values.

An example of the first type is *No Longer Silent,* a zine "dedicated to exposing the coerciveness, injustice, and hypocrisy inherent in all authoritarian/hierarchical structures; inspiring and celebrating the growth of personal freedom as well as the claiming of individual responsibility; and creating a tangible, community based anarchism in our own lives." *No Longer Silent* has a strong political philosophy behind it, originating in an anarchist tradition that is not entirely vernacular. Its editor, Eliza Blackweb, is clearly familiar with canonical texts of political theory and philosophy, but the inspiration for the magazine comes from the informal network of local anarchist groups that supply her with articles, correspondence, ideas, and feedback. Issue number 4/5 of the zine includes an extensive review of a book on samizdat printing techniques, suggesting that the zine thinks of itself as part of a marginalized but insurgent movement that radically questions mainstream values. The issue also features explicitly theoretical reflections like "Revolutionary Self-Theory," a text produced and edited by many radical hands in many radical rags over the last fifteen years. The article argues that genuine selfhood can be achieved only by escaping preexisting theories and engaging in the process of cobbling together one's own vision of society, self, and politics out of the bits and pieces of theory that seem personally useful. This image of the lonely thinker, the *bricoleur* attempting to understand culture and society without benefit of—in fact skeptical of—any coherent system of thought could serve as an emblem for the zine enterprise and for the vernacular theorist in general.

No Longer Silent takes on issues that have concerned more academic theorists of popular culture. For example, the editor includes an essay called "Anarchist Separatism" that argues that the masses cannot be transformed and so anarchists should work toward setting up their own, self-sufficient communities in which anarchist principles can prevail. The author of the article, "Desperate Chris," argues vociferously that the masses have *chosen* their stupidity, their failure to see through socially imposed rules and propaganda. His argument runs that no even minimally intelligent person could be tricked by such inane media messages, and the compliant masses must therefore choose their ignorance because it is safe and simple. At this point in the essay the editor inserts herself in brackets, making the argument that those who control capital spend lots of money and energy *keeping* the masses stupid through a pop culture/propaganda system. The writer's position, with its existentialist, personal responsibility ethic, is one not often taken in contemporary theory debates, but the editor's rejoinder should sound familiar to anyone who has read academic theory. *No Longer Silent* is published as a theoretical project, an unmasking of cultural power and a call to reject and resist it. This is theory in a vernacular mode for a nonacademic audience, and it provides those who live exclusively in popular culture with an opportunity to reflect on the determinants of their experience.

Not surprisingly, the feminist movement has also inspired zines in which theoretical questions get raised explicitly. One of the most interesting is *Chickfactor*, a funny zine full of young feminist energy and style. In some ways this is a typical pop music zine, full of interviews with bands, ads for records and stores, and reviews of arcane records in the indie-pop style the editors prefer. But there is a pervasive feminist edge to the writing and the interviews. In an interview with musician Liz Phair, *Chickfactor* asks, "Is 'open season' a feminist song?" and Phair answers with great vernacular energy: "Feminism in my life isn't relegated to books or discussions, it's all mixed in. That's one of the beauties of being older rather than younger, your whole life fuses, your thoughts are combined, everything overarches everything and there's all these connecting ideas that were disjointed before . . . now feminism is the way I sit, it's the way I perk up when I can tell that no one's paying attention to what I say. How I live, how I breathe." Phair's comments speak to a desire to escape the fragmentation of contemporary culture by connecting a political and theoretical commitment—in this case feminism—to everyday life. This commitment also allows Phair to understand the role gender plays in how pop culture texts are processed by fans. When she is asked about whether critics and fans perceive her songs as "male bashing," she answers by criticizing the critics for assuming that all her songs reflect her personal life: "People take things so literally and so at face value that I used to bitch about not getting the credit for the creativity I possess. It doesn't just fly out of me, I really work hard on this stuff, I think about it a lot. I put a lot of energy into creating it. It isn't like 'oh, wow, she just kinda has a facility for it, it just kinda pops out of her,' and I think that's a really sexist thing to say. If it were a man saying the same things, people would assume that there was intent behind it, that it was constructed, and that he was conscious of his construction. . . ." *Chickfactor*, in its almost self-deprecatingly pop style, manages to get its readers in contact with an angry and affirmative feminism of the daily. As Phair says about her music, feminism pervades every move in this zine without compromising its light style or its focus on cool music and the fun of the club scene. Theory here is never thought of as such; it appears almost casually, and it achieves its effects more successfully just for that reason.

Another ideologically motivated zine is *Aladdin's Window: The Vision of Awakened Men*. This zine sets out to counter on every point the ideological tenets of feminism. In its vision men are the victims of feminism, which posits the moral superiority of women, ignores the violence that men suffer, fetishizes the woman's body by obsessing about rape, exaggerates men's economic superiority, denies divorced men visitation rights, etc. Almost all of the articles in the zine are attacks on feminism. There are only a few items that deal affirmatively with men's issues, which offer some vision of what men's lives should be. *Aladdin's Window* addresses basic questions of gender identity and power relations in a way that any reader can understand, and it taps into male backlash rage in a lively vernacular style. The tone of the writing is often self-pitying. These cultural conservatives seem a caricature of right-wing caricatures of identity politics—they present men as *victims* of a feminist movement that seems omnipotent. Any feminist would wish the movement had such power. But to the writers and editors of *Aladdin's Window*, feminist discourse has become the dominant in our society, and their job is to unmask its distortions of the lives of men. They see themselves as questioning orthodoxy, overturning the dominant ideology, resisting mainstream ideological power. They are doing the vernacular cultural theory of the antifeminist right.

The energy behind zine theory often comes from zines' connections with identity politics and subcultural insurgence. Zines help to create and sustain communities. They allow a community to articulate its own critical perspective, to "poach" on corporate-produced culture in ways that define what it means to be in the subculture. The editors and writers of a zine like *Dead Jackie Susann Quarterly*, a lesbian pop culture zine, clearly put Jackie Susann and her novels and a wide variety of other pop culture texts to uses different from those their marketers had in mind. The main interest of this zine is mainstream TV, a space that would seem to exclude the lesbian sensibility of the zine. *DJSQ* issue 2 exhibits in almost every item the many ways in which lesbian fans have reread TV from the perspectives made possible by being a member of the lesbian community. There is for example a homage to Sara Gilbert, who plays Darlene, the middle child on *Roseanne*. The character isn't lesbian, but she appeals "to our most lofty ideals of what every one of us wishes we were once like, smart, sarcastic, and principled at the tender age of sixteen as well as our most base desires by bringing out the chickenhawk in us all." The joy of lesbian desire reframes the TV text and reads *across* its consensus meaning. There is also a funny and malicious fantasy about a lost episode of *The Brady Bunch* in which all the characters encounter exotic sexuality in Las Vegas; a vignette entitled "The Stepford Queers," in which the writer imagines a town where all the lesbians are comfortable, narrow-minded Republicans; a porno-romance story of Hillary Clinton, Donna Shalala, and Janet Reno out on the town at lesbian bars; a guide to (very mainstream) makeout music for lesbian lovers; and a story about the first out lesbian MTV-VJ.

The pop culture texts serve as occasions for fantasy and for a forceful assertion of rights to cultural space, a refusal to be left out of everyday culture, and a radical claim to read it as the community sees fit. Lawrence Grossberg, Lisa Lewis, John Fiske, and other cultural theorists have commented on this function of zines.[3]

---

[3]See also Gabriel Gomez, "Spew 2 You Too: Gay Fanzines Convene," in *After-image* 19 (April 1992).

Zines allow disenfranchised voices to reach out to members of their communities and to the more amorphous community of zine readers.

Zines also play a complicated role in establishing and maintaining alternative youth communities that are organized around pop cultural style rather than established identity groups. In a culture in which membership in such groups has achieved a certain counter-cultural cachet, suburban white kids often search for a sense of identity and community in a particular style of dissent—in alternative music especially. Bands create followings, and if a particular band or style of music survives and remains vital long enough, that following can become a loose community, a group that provides individuals within it a sense of belonging and cultural placement. *Industrial Nation* is such a zine: it provides for fans of industrial music reviews of recent records, essays and pictorials on the styles of clothing and body decoration (tattoos, pierced and scarified bodies) that go with the music, correspondence among fans, lists of upcoming concerts, ads for stores that sell the records and the clothes, cafés and bars where members of the community hang out together. The same function is fulfilled by rap and metal zines and by local alternative music zines like *Jersey Beat* and *Texas Beat*.

Within these communities, zines set the tone of critical discussion. When a new band or a new style emerges, the zine writers give fans a vocabulary that makes sense of the new. Zines establish vernacular interpretive communities. Stanley Fish's term is particularly apt in this context, since the effort to establish a critical vocabulary is not just a function of existing communities, but one of the practices by which alternative communities are constituted. Zines play an important theoretical role in defining communities of dissent that make it possible for pop culture subjects to understand their own experience and to analyze the dominant culture.

Some zines deal with explicitly theoretical questions because they participate in or affiliate with an avant-garde aesthetic that takes as its goal the rejection of bourgeois values and the distortion of everyday reality. This affiliation is visible in many zines in their use of modern and postmodern visual design. The print and graphic styles of zines vary widely. Some are slick and professional, almost indistinguishable visually from mass market magazines. Some are print-heavy, double columned, resembling academic journals except with fancy covers. Some are full of a computer-generated multitude of print styles and graphic decorations. But most work in a collage aesthetic, breaking up the page with blocks of print, diagonal typesetting, shocking photographs and drawings, cartoons, handwritten comments, and nonlinear presentation. The effect is visual overload and a denaturalization of the reading experience. Multiple sources of sensation and information compete on the page for the reader's attention. Clearly this style derives from the avant-garde visual tradition of this century, which often employs these distortional techniques in order to signal a refusal of traditional values and beliefs. And such a refusal provides an atmosphere inside which more explicit theoretical insight and questioning are encouraged.

One zine that clearly thinks of itself as part of this tradition is *Your Flesh*, which combines an interest in extreme alternative music and shocking graphics with a cultural historian's attempt to explore the origins of today's popular culture in earlier twentieth-century avant-gardes. Thus we get in a recent issue a reference to John Cage as the unacknowledged father of noise rock groups like Sonic Youth; an article on Dadaist Tristan Tzara as a precursor of postpunk nihilism; a discussion of discipline and punishment by the vocalist of a band called Janitor Joe; an interview with deviant musician and film-maker Monte Cazazza that puts him in the context of "Dada, the French literature of transgression (Bataille, Lautreamont), Burroughs and Blake." *Your Flesh* combines shocking visual style and subject matter with an intellectual atmosphere that assumes an awareness of serious art and the possibility of theoretical questioning. This zine is one of the pieces of evidence that suggest some zine producers are postundergraduates who have heard something about academic cultural theory and want to pursue some of its concerns in a vernacular mode.

Another is *Ben Is Dead*, a zine situated at the place where the cybernetic, the psychedelic, and the pornographic intersect. Like many zines, *Ben Is Dead* is aware of how far outside the mainstream it is. Its audience consists of those who live inside the world of information and communications technology but refuse to accept the corporate rules that govern that world and in fact see in it a mode of resistance and transcendence. Its cyberpunk mentality is a critique of the potential for frightening mental control in the corporate information society and a commitment to modes of consciousness outlawed by that society even if they are made possible by its technology. An interview with media analyst Douglas Rushkoff introduces the term "media virus." A "media virus" (on the model of a "computer virus") is a calculated media event that sneaks a progressive or extremist message into the mainstream media. An example of a "media virus" would be Ice T's "Cop Killer," a song that gained notoriety because it combined a black street sensibility with a hardcore rock sound that appealed to hard-rocking white kids. The song was condemned by all the mainstream media, but it also gained Ice T a forum he would not otherwise have had—on *Entertainment Tonight* and *Today* and in the *New York Times*—so that he could extend and refine his still scary message for a wider audience. Clearly *Ben Is Dead* thinks of itself and all zines as potential media viruses, breeding grounds for subversive ideas that might infiltrate the mainstream and allow people to see their society and culture in another light. *Ben Is Dead* reports on all kinds of DIY (do it yourself) media, from street postering to zine editing to computer hacking. Here is a passage from an interview with Mark Fraunfelder, editor of the zine *bOING bOING:* "I was also interested in how technology was getting cheap enough so that it could get into the hands of hippies, weirdos, artists, and people who normally didn't have access to computers." In the weirdness of this alternative culture is a potential for ideological questioning. When you exist so far outside the corporate-sponsored culture, even if for hedonistic rather than political reasons, you have the opportunity to question its principles, to produce a world of discourse not totally governed by the rules in force.

I would like to turn now to the critical concerns and theoretical issues that are raised most frequently in the zines. There is a great deal of what could be called practical cultural criticism: reviews of records, concerts, films, videos, other zines. There are career retrospectives, essays on shifts in an artist's career, interviews that ask the artists to interpret their work, reflections on changes in audience taste, editorials about the relationship between artistic expression and social control, examinations of the history of pop culture and its political impact, etc. The vernacular style should not blind us to the seriousness of the critical endeavor here or to its procedural similarity to academic critical discourse. Zine criticism is a slightly more formal version of the lively critical discourse that happens around the lunch table at work as people talk about *Seinfeld* or Clint Eastwood, that gets whispered in school as kids tell each other about the trash books they're reading out of the teacher's ken, that kids in the park pass around about what's in and what's out and why, that shoppers exchange bitterly when they find out an ad was a lie, that youth groups in churches perform when they discuss pornography and violence on TV. The culture of everyday life is a critical culture, and the zines get that culture into print. And it is in these critical projects that zine writers find themselves on occasion up against theoretical questions. Especially in zines not affiliated with a political or subcultural movement that fosters theoretical insight, theory emerges out of practical criticism, out of local interpretive imperatives, questions that come up.

Zine critics often deal with questions of influence and history. Music zines are constantly engaged in the process of introducing new bands to their readers. Every zine has a particular style of music as its focus, and new bands constantly appear by the hundreds in each style. So the task is difficult. *No one* has heard of all these bands. In the effort to describe the new, zine writers make use of two key strategies: genealogy and classification. A new band can be described by how it derives from an already existing band. Irish bands, for example, are presented in the lineage of U2. A million bands are postpunk, deriving from the Slits, the Sex Pistols, the Ramones, etc. This strategy of description is tied into a complex attitude toward influence. A new band can derive from but cannot repeat an older band. There is in the zines a strong awareness of the anxiety of influence. A band can be true to the spirit of a powerful predecessor, but it must make a new sound, have a voice of its own. The alternative scene has been around long enough so that many of the imaginable styles of dissidence have already been used up. Doing something new is difficult in alternative culture. There are all these ghosts, all of them preserved on CD or tape. In this context the worst put-down is to say that a band just repeats an earlier band. This is to say that the band has no creativity and is not *of the moment*.

The other important strategy for description is microspecific genre classification. This new band plays *this precise kind* of music, or a combination of *these kinds*. It's not just metal but hardcore, not just hardcore but straightedge. These categories are crucial because they don't just describe a kind of music, they describe a discernible lifestyle—a micropolitics, a style of fashion, a place to go, a socio-economic category. It is here that the identity politics function of the zines works itself out. This is how the readers of the zines find themselves, in these razor-fine distinctions, invisible to anyone outside the subculture. But again these subcategories can be turned against a band if it fits the category too snugly. The ethos of testing the envelope is in place, even if the envelopes are very small. The definitions and limits of classification are constantly debated, just as they are in academic criticism.

Considering their connections to current concerns and their short half-life, it may be surprising to hear that many zines are obsessed with history. Zine interviews and band profiles often try to put current albums in the context of the band's past. Sophomore efforts, for example, are endlessly compared with first albums. Movements from indie to major are scrutinized carefully. New albums are criticized because they repeat past works too closely, or because they change too much, betraying the legacy of the band. Zines are also interested in the personal and professional history of the musicians in the band. Who did they play for and with in the past? How did they get involved with the current group? Has their music changed over time? This is very short-scale history, of course, but the questions that the zines ask are propelled by serious historical anxiety. Fans live in a terrain of shifting fads and short-lived styles. The zines give them at least a small sense of continuity and development. The current scene does not come out of nowhere; it can be traced down from earlier struggles, and it emerges out of the involvement of specific individuals with complex private and professional lives. Zines thus depend on a kind of biographical-historical criticism in which the text must be understood inside a micro-historical framework.

Some zines also engage in what could be called historical scholarship. They publish discographies and filmographies, concert histories and playlists. Such items appeal to the fan as collector or as vernacular curator. As Lisa Lewis says, fans need inside information to distinguish themselves from casual listeners, and they "appoint themselves historians of the resulting textual accumulation" (158). *Psychotronic Video* is a prime example. This zine focuses on sleazy subgenre films that mainstream film history rarely mentions—fifties nudie films, seventies blaxploitation films, drive-in horror films, ultraviolent films, slasher films—the dark and marginal element of the film business. But for all of its vigorous bad taste and offensive material, *Psychotronic Video* treats these films in a serious and scholarly way. Its audience is clearly the collector—reviews give straight-forward plot summaries, sometimes of amazingly perverse stories, that provide a prospective collector with a good clue about whether the film would interest him. *Psychotronic Video* also publishes accounts of careers of art directors, stuntmen, special effects experts, and marginal actors. The layout is lurid and jokey, but the articles are serious and knowledgeable studies of genre history.

Scholars have noted that the social category of "fan" is class-specific and demeaning (Jenson 18–19). An avid follower of opera is an aficionado, a curator of political memorabilia is a serious historian whose works might appear in a scholarly journal. A "fan" who gathers expertise about early punk music or *Star Trek* scripts is often thought to be wasting time with debased materials and can be understood only in terms of obsession and personal emptiness. I agree that zine writers and especially publishers are obsessed. Why else would they expend so much effort on work that will not be rewarded monetarily or by social status? But is their commitment so different from that of the academic scholar? Certainly working on the correspondence of Victorian poets seems no less bizarre to the general public than collecting the manuscripts of early punk rockers. And if there is a bit more social status to it, there is still little direct economic return. Zine scholarship, like academic scholarship, is motivated by a desire to master the details of a complex and valued phenomenon. It provides the fans at least a bit of historical context for the present.

There is also a complex historical hermeneutic practiced by zines that deal ironically with pop culture TV icons like *The Brady Bunch* and *Star Trek*. These series are seen simultaneously as embarrassing but sentimental products of their own historical context, kitschy elements of sixties and seventies culture, and as texts open to nineties reconstruction in terms of contemporary political and cultural concerns. Thus *Star Trek* can be rewritten from an openly gay/lesbian perspective, and *The Brady Bunch* can be rewritten from a nineties postmodern dysfunctional family perspective. The readers of these TV texts are clearly in the here and now, and the shows are clearly in the there and then, but a creative rewriting is still possible. Popular culture is constantly recycled: older shows are available on cable right next to the newest commodity. This adjacency at once highlights the pastness of the old texts and places them firmly in a present that reads them with its own interests. In all these ways zines characterize the popular culture past as a force that shapes the present and as a residue of texts that can be reshaped by the present.

The theoretical question that comes up most frequently within all these forms of zine criticism is, how does alternative culture get produced in a corporate economy? The zines are obsessed with the *business* of popular culture. Interviewers in music zines want to know how the band got its record contract, how they dealt with their producer, how they have been able to hold on to their artistic integrity, why past projects succeeded or failed, what future projects they plan, what kind of audience they aim for, how they feel about more mainstream bands. In very recent times this concern has become more complicated. In the eighties there was a clear distinction between major labels (corporate owned) and independent or alternative labels that would take the risk of the cutting edge. But now because of what is called "the Nirvana effect," major labels are signing very new and challenging bands, so that the term "alternative music" now makes sense only as a marketing strategy, and the "alternative culture" that surrounds the music and includes the zines has been incorporated within the marketing strategies of corporate popular culture. This development is not always characterized negatively in the zines—after all, the major labels make high-quality production possible, and want new bands to experiment. But there is a clear discomfort with the business in zine writing. Corporate pop culture is exactly what the alienated kids don't want, and a band's entry into it is a cause for concern for their very souls.

This skeptical and even disdainful attitude toward the corporate music business is complicated by the fact that zines are themselves a marginal but real part of the business. They carry ads, review albums, promote live shows, all of which helps create a market for their own musical genres. Zines create communities and identity groups, but they also create market segments that record companies, promoters, and retailers can reach through the zines. Some zines accept no advertising, but their function is still to alert the market to new commodities. It is exactly this ambiguity about the role of zines that leads their writers and editors to obsess about bands' economic lives. They are looking to the bands for solutions to the question of how to do what you want with your life, make money at it, and still hold onto your soul. For the fans, bands act out a solution to a key dilemma of nineties youth—knowing as I do how corrupt and dull are corporate economics and mainstream culture, how can I find my place in them without giving up the lifestyle I'm committed to? In zine criticism, corporate control endangers authentic expression, and music is above all about expression, an authentic, romantic cry of the heart. Once you are in the business, you become more concerned with audience and market share than with expressing your own feelings and visions. And since everyone is in the business, these questions become acute.

This issue comes up incessantly in zine interviews. Has the band stayed faithful to their true insight, or are they accommodating the desires of the producers and marketers? The answers to this question are varied. Some bands assert that their personal impulse has been left alone, that the labels have recognized it is in their best interests to allow a band to follow its own instincts because the band is likely to be closer to the kids than the label executives are. In this scenario the corporate world is not the enemy; it has its own agenda, but it still allows authentic personal expression. Other bands tell the story of dramatic conflict between the homogenizing corporation and the existential outlaw band. In this scenario authenticity is personal, and its enemies are the social and economic structures that vie for control of our lives. What seems significant to me is that both of these stories get told in the zines. That is, there is no single answer to the question of how selfhood and socioeconomic structures are related. That relationship has to be negotiated case by case. Sometimes you can clear out a space for yourself and make use of the corporate world to *expand* that space. In other instances the corporate world will crush your spirit, reduce your authentic expression into pure product, the next fashionable commodity. It is this sense that the story is open-ended that makes the question important to the zines, especially because the zines also see themselves as sites for authentic expression and for independent critical thinking. Zine writers and publishers have chosen to stay out of mainstream publishing precisely so that they can have editorial freedom. When the zines have to decide do we take ads? do we make money? do we get slick? do we use a national distributor?—all those daily questions of survival—they look to the bands as models, and they see that . . . it all depends. It's all up for negotiation. Selfhood is negotiated, and it takes a canny sense of the market and of your own identity to do so. These questions about the business come out of the daily work of reviewing and commenting on pop cultural texts. They open up for examination a set of corporate operations that seek to remain invisible so that they can deliver the audience without drawing attention to themselves.

To return to de Certeau's terms, zines are engaged not only in "poaching," in the development of tactics that resist the strategies of power, but also in the task of theory—questioning and challenging the strategies themselves. Zines exist precisely because their publishers and editors and writers understand that mainstream pop culture serves the strategic purposes of corporate power. Zines are one of the places where such power can be evaded, since there is no compelling profit motive, and where it can be examined from a distance. Zines are attracted to the cultural fringe, where corporate power is diluted, or to creative tactics for rewriting and recoding mainstream pop. Both of these moves connect to the ordinary fan's understanding of the fact that pop culture is a business, and that it thrives because it serves corporate interests. It is the daily concern of the zines to monitor cooptation, to unmask marketing hype, to decry sellouts, to ridicule mainstream clichés—in other words, to reveal the strategies by which power shapes culture and to understand the personal dilemmas faced by individual subjects attempting to survive and resist those strategies. In their critique of the business of popular culture, the zines perform an important theoretical task in a vernacular mode. They succeed, I think, in increasing the opportunities for cultural subjects to question the strategies that shape them and thus to inform their own "tactics" with a canny sense of how power operates.

When zine practical criticism engages with strictly aesthetic issues, it is always within this tactical context. The dominant theoretical question about style and artistic practice that the zines raise is whether the band practices musical craft or acts out of raw intuition. On the one side there is the ability to create song structure, to play creative solos, to display *chops*, and on the other there is energy, noise, punk rawness, the aesthetic of the intense. This is of course an ancient opposition in thinking about the arts, cast in various eras as reason versus intuition, classicism versus romanticism, or craft versus inspiration. Zines are not unanimous on this question. Even in zines that specialize in extreme thrash speed noise music, you will hear bands talk about how they are getting more interested in song structure as a function of growing musicianship. And even very adept bands will talk about tapping into the raw power of rock and roll. Song structure and skill are often associated with selling out to the business, but not if the song feels like the authentic expression of the band's state of mind. Noise is often associated with the authentic, but it has become a genre of its own that can be aped as a trend rather than embraced as a destiny. Zines are alert to the speed with which the revolutionary can become generic. And many bands want to be allowed to experiment in both directions and to combine the strengths of both approaches.

But zines certainly tend toward the raw rather than the cooked. To be a part of the alternative community, the zine has to sponsor bands (or films, or TV show, or ways of reading them) that defy the rules of mass culture, which values the finished, the expert product. The aesthetic of the zines tends toward roughened art forms that appeal to communities of dissent and resistance. Political and social dissidence takes as one of its visible signs an allegiance to forms of art that can't be processed using the mindset and values of the culture that it rejects. In a move reminiscent of Russian formalism, the zines approach the roughened form of alternative art as a way to achieve cultural awakening. Expertise and polish create art that is easily processed and thus doesn't draw attention to itself as a strategy of cultural power. Roughened form is a tactic of perception that draws attention to the conventions it rejects. The arts that zines value tend to disorient the mind and assault the body. When reviewers talk about live concerts, there is always talk about their visceral response to the music. There is ecstasy, there is arousal, there is ringing in the ears, a body that the music moves. Reviewers often have less to say about the music itself than about the body of the listener. And in the zines that feeling is characterized as an unauthorized bodily response, not anticipated by cultural strategies, that holds together the community—a community of ecstatic outsiders.

Thus we could say that in general zines promote art with a rough edge to it as a tactical response to mass cultural strategies. But they also honor other arrangements that bands, artists, and fans can negotiate. The camp reading of bad pop culture and the canny use of conventional forms are also honorable settlements with power. Zines are clear on the fact that the strategies of power will never disappear and must always be resisted. They call for and enact de Certeau's "poaching," in that they routinely reread mass-produced texts for the purposes of marginalized communities. But they also produce sophisticated questioning of the strategies themselves, of the power that flows through popular culture. This happens in the zines, I believe, in part because the zines are so dedicated to the phenomena they cover that the apologetic effort inevitably leads to theoretical questioning. Pop culture subjects who are expert enough to write in a zine are canny enough to see that pop culture is about a lot more than mindless entertainment. Its political and cultural role is not hidden or subliminal. It is relatively easy to become a resistant reader of popular culture texts, which lack the prestige of literature and require no humility in the reader. Even Beavis and Butthead could be thought of as resistant readers of MTV. And it is not a long step from resistant reading to skeptical questioning of premises, that is, to a vernacular cultural criticism.

Zine writers and editors may legitimately be thought of as "elite fans," fans who have accumulated textual and historical expertise that places them above the average couch potato, but the theoretical activity we have seen in the zines is also common, though harder to document, in the fan experience in general. Academic cultural theory is of course an even more formalized and systematic element in the same continuum; it is not essentially different from vernacular theorizing. And if it is true that fan theorizing cannot overthrow power but only try to understand it and bring it to light, and that power will always devise strategies that legitimate it, academic theory should be cautioned rather than feel superior. For all the powerful demystifications and deconstructions achieved by academic cultural theory in the last twenty years, I see no diminishment of ideological power, no radical transformation of cultural practices. Theory cannot change culture on its own. It must be connected with communities of dissent, as are the theoretical approaches allied with identity politics, and as the zines are. I believe that the theory practiced in the zines has at least as much potential for real political impact as does academic theory. The zines have a larger audience and a more immediate and intimate connection with those they address. And their theorizing occurs in a vernacular mode that at once captures them to some degree within conventional systems of meaning and value but also allows them to encourage large numbers of pop culture subjects to question those very conventions. The loss of "purity" is clearly worth the gain in effectiveness.

Zine Addresses

Zines may have gone out of business or moved, but try these addresses for some interesting zines.

Attitude Problem
PO Box 2354
Prescott, AZ 86302

Ben Is Dead
PO Box 3166
Hollywood, CA 90026

Chickfactor
245 E. 19th St.
New York, NY 10003

Dead Jackie Susann Quarterly
496a Hudson St.
New York, NY 10009

Industrial Nation
114 1/2 College Street
Iowa City, IA 52240-4005

No Longer Silent
PO Box 3582
Tucson, AZ 85722

Psychotronic Video
3309 Rt. 97
Narrowsburg, NY 12754-6126

Your Flesh
PO Box 583264
Minneapolis, MN 55458-3264

Bibliography

Ang, Ien. *Watching Dallas: Soap Opera and the Melodramatic Imagination*. Trans. Della Couling. London: Methuen, 1985.

De Certeau, Michel. *The Practice of Everyday Life*. Trans. Steven. F. Rendell. Berkeley: University of California Press, 1984.

Fiske, John. *Television Culture*. London: Methuen, 1987.

Grossberg, Lawrence. "Is There a Fan in the House? The Affective Sensibility of Fandom." *The Adoring Audience: Fan Culture and Popular Media*, ed. Lisa A. Lewis. London: Routledge, 1992.

Jary, David, John Horne, and Tom Bucke. "Football 'Fanzines' and Football Culture: A Case of Successful 'Cultural Contestation.' " *Sociological Review* 39 (August 1991): 581–92.

Jenkins, Henry. *Textual Poachers: Television Fans and Participatory Culture*. New York and London: Routledge, 1992.

Jenson, Jolie. "Fandom as Pathology: The Consequences of Characterization." *The Adoring Audience: Fan Culture and Popular Media*, ed. Lisa A. Lewis. London: Routledge: 1992

Radway, Janice A. *Reading the Romance: Women, Patriarchy, and Popular Literature*. Chapel Hill: University of North Carolina Press, 1984.

Radway, Janice A. "Reception Study: Ethnography and the Problem of Dispersed Audiences and Nomadic Subjects." *Cultural Studies* 2 (1988): 359–76.

37

"Mommy, What Does 'Nigger' Mean?"

GLORIA NAYLOR

anguage is the subject. It is the written form with which I've managed to keep the wolf away from the door and, in diaries, to keep my sanity. In spite of this, I consider the written word inferior to the spoken, and much of the frustration experienced by novelists is the awareness that whatever we manage to capture in even the most transcendent passages falls far short of the richness of life. Dialogue achieves its power in the dynamics of a fleeting moment of sight, sound, smell and touch.

I'm not going to enter the debate here about whether it is language that shapes reality or vice versa. That battle is doomed to be waged whenever we seek intermittent reprieve from the chicken and egg dispute. I will simply take the position that the spoken word, like the written word, amounts to a nonsensical arrangement of sounds letters without a consensus that assigns "meaning." And building from the meanings of what we hear, we order reality. Words themselves are innocuous; it is the consensus that gives them true power.

I remember the first time I heard the word nigger. In my third grade class, our math tests were being passed down the rows, and as I handed the papers to a little boy in back of me, I remarked that once again he had received a much lower mark than I did. He snatched his test from me and spit out that word. Had he called me a nymphomaniac or a necrophiliac, I couldn't have been more puzzled. I didn't know what a nigger was, but I knew that whatever it meant, it was something he shouldn't have called me. This was verified when I raised my hand, and in a loud voice repeated what he had said and watched the teacher scold him for using a "bad" word. I was later to go home and ask the inevitable question that every black parent must face: "Mommy, what does 'nigger' mean?"

And what exactly did it mean? Thinking back, I realize that this could not have been the first time the word was used in my presence. I was part of a large extended family that had migrated from the rural South after World War II and formed a close-knit network that gravitated around my maternal grandparents. Their ground-floor apartment in one of the buildings they owned in Harlem was a weekend mecca for my immediate family, along with countless aunts, uncles and cousins who brought along assorted friends. It was a bustling and open house with assorted neighbors and tenants popping in and out to exchange bits of gossip, pick up an old quarrel or referee the ongoing checkers game in which my grandmother cheated shamelessly. They were all there to let down their hair and put up their feet after a week of labor in the factories, laundries and shipyards of New York.

Amid the clamor, which could reach deafening proportions—two or three conversations going on simultaneously, punctuated by the sound of a baby's crying somewhere in the back rooms or out on the street—there was still a rigid set of rules about what was said and how. Older children were sent out of the living room when it was time to get into the juicy details about "you-know-who" up on the third floor who had gone and gotten herself "p-r-e-g-n-a-n-t!" But my parents, knowing that I could spell well beyond my years, always demanded that I follow the others out to play. Beyond sexual misconduct and death, everything else was considered harmless for our young ears. And so among the anecdotes of the triumphs and disappointments in the various workings of their lives, the word nigger was used in my presence, but it was set within contexts and inflections that caused it to register in my mind as something else.

In the singular, the word was always applied to a man who had distinguished himself in some situation that brought their approval for his strength, intelligence or drive:

"Did Johnny really do that?"

"I'm telling you, that nigger pulled in $6,000 of overtime last year. Said he got enough for a down payment on a house."

When used with a possessive adjective by a woman—"my nigger"—it became a term of endearment for husband or boyfriend. But it could be more than just a term applied to a man. In their mouths it became the pure essence of manhood—a disembodied force that channeled their past history of struggle and present survival against the odds into a victorious statement of being: "Yeah, that old foreman found out quick enough—you don't mess with a nigger."

In the plural, it became a description of some group within the community that had overstepped the bounds of decency as my family defined it: Parents who neglected their children, a drunken couple who fought in public, people who simply refused to look for work, those with excessively dirty mouths or unkempt households were all "trifling niggers." This particular circle could forgive hard times, unemployment, the occasional bout of depression—they had gone through all of that themselves—but the unforgivable sin was lack of self-respect.

A woman could never be a "nigger" in the singular, with its connotation of confirming worth. The noun girl was its closest equivalent in that sense, but only when used in direct address and regardless of the gender doing the addressing. "Girl" was a token of respect for a woman. The one-syllable word was drawn out to sound like three in recognition of the extra ounce of wit, nerve or daring that the woman had shown in the situation under discussion.

"G-i-r-l, stop. You mean you said that to his face?"

But if the word was used in a third-person reference or shortened so that it almost snapped out of the mouth, it always involved some element of communal disapproval. And age became an important factor in these exchanges. It was only between individuals of the same generation, or from an older person to younger (but never the other way around), that "girl" would be considered a compliment.

I don't agree with the argument that use of the word nigger at this social stratum of the black community was an internalization of racism. The dynamics were the exact opposite: the people in my grandmother's living room took a word that whites used to signify worthlessness or degradation and rendered it impotent. Gathering there together, they transformed "nigger" to signify the varied and complex most beings they knew themselves to be. If the word was to disappear totally from the mouths of even the most of white society, no one in that room was naive enough to believe it would disappear from white minds. Meeting the word head-on, they proved it had absolutely nothing to do with the way they were determined to live their lives.

So there must have been dozens of times that the word "nigger" was spoken in front of me before reached the third grade. But I didn't "hear" it until it was said by a small pair of lips that had already learned it could be a way to humiliate me. That was the word I went home and asked my mother about. And since she knew that I had to grow up in America, she took me in her lap and explained.

38

I Go Back to May 1937

SHARON OLDS

I see them standing at the formal gates of their colleges,
I see my father strolling out
under the ochre sandstone arch, the
red tiles glinting like bent
plates of blood behind his head, I
see my mother with a few light books at her hip
standing at the pillar made of tiny bricks with the
wrought-iron gate still open behind her, its
sword-tips black in the May air,
they are about to graduate, they are about to get married,
they are kids, they are dumb, all they know is they are
innocent, they would never hurt anybody.
I want to go up to them and say Stop,
don't do it–she's the wrong woman,
he's the wrong man, you are going to do things
you cannot imagine you would ever do,
you are going to do bad things to children,
you are going to suffer in ways you never heard of,
you are going to want to die. I want to go
up to them there in the late May sunlight and say it,
her hungry pretty blank face turning to me,

her pitiful beautiful untouched body,
his arrogant handsome blind face turning to me,
his pitiful beautiful untouched body,
but I don't do it. I want to live. I
take them up like the male and female
paper dolls and bang them together
at the hips like chips of flint as if to
strike sparks from them, I say
Do what you are going to do, and I will tell about it.

39

Living Her Best Life

JENNIFER L. POZNER

When novelist James Boylan was a young boy, he played a game in which he pretended to be an astronaut crashing onto a "Girl Planet" that turned anyone who breathed its air into a girl—body, clothes, and all. As a teenager he covertly tried on his mother's and sister's dresses, thinking, "Why am I doing this? . . . Because I can't not." Yet no amount of play was enough to calm his anxiety. "I was filled with a yearning that could not be quelled by rayon," Boylan muses.

It would be four decades before James would find peace . . . as Jennifer. It is this struggle—and eventual triumph—that lies at the heart of *She's Not There*, a memoir of one man's heart-wrenching journey to become the woman she always knew herself to be. I first became aware of *She's Not There* when Jennifer Finney Boylan promoted it on two *Oprah Winfrey Show* episodes. As a man, Oprah's audience learned, James Finney Boylan had had an intelligent, loving wife, Grace Finney, two spunky children, and four critically acclaimed novels—*The Constellations*, *The Planets*, *Getting In*, and *Remind Me To Murder You Later*. He chaired the English department at Colby College, was considered the one teacher whose class students had to take before graduation, and played in a rock band. It was a good life, a life Jim was proud of, a life he was desperately afraid of losing—yet he was plagued by the knowledge that it was only "the second best life" he could lead. The knowledge "that I was in the wrong body, living the wrong life, was never out of my conscious mind," she writes.

Boylan struggled every day to be a man, hoping love would "cure" him of his desire to be female. At age 42 he lost the struggle. After what amounted to a mental breakdown, Jim realized he couldn't take one more step in male shoes, literally or figuratively. Though he wished to protect Grace from heartbreak, he finally had to reveal to her the reality he'd concealed his entire life: He was transgendered, that wasn't ever going to change, and he had no choice but to face it.

And that, Boylan told Oprah's viewers, is when James began the emotionally, physically, and interpersonally challenging process of becoming Jenny, the articulate, attractive, and dignified woman who sat before them in the studio. Boylan described the impact her transition had on her family, noting that their love has endured even if it has changed along with her gender—she and Grace have stayed married and are raising their children together, though they now live more as sisters than lovers. Defusing contentious questions from the talk TV queen (such as Oprah's accusatory, pulse-of-the-audience query, "What do you think, ladies? Is it selfish to just up and turn yourself into a woman, or what?") with humor, insight, and grace, Boylan struck me as perhaps the most effective spokesperson for transgender acceptance I'd ever seen in any mainstream media interview.

In *She's Not There* as well as in her subsequent media tour, Boylan presents a picture vastly different from the images broadcast media love to portray of angry, grieving wives and pathetic, selfish husbands. For example, just recently *Dateline NBC* spent a year following a woman named Joyce and her husband David, who was in the process of becoming Victoria. Reporter Dawn Fratangelo repeatedly badgered Joyce with variations on the question "Why go through all of this? Why stay?" When Joyce said their love would prevail, *Dateline* was skeptical: "It seemed too calm a response for something so drastic," Fratangelo narrated. The newsmagazine edited a year's worth of footage to highlight Joyce's pain and loss and to downplay the couple's commitment to one another. The implication was that their marriage was bound to disintegrate, despite having survived "so far."

Sadly, that sort of framework is more the rule than the exception when media take on transsexuality—which makes Jennifer Finney Boylan's contribution to our political climate particularly important. Since the publication of *She's Not There*, Boylan has made the media rounds, her savviness as an interviewee resulting in a relatively rare phenomenon: coverage of transgender issues that educates rather than exploits. The same week as *Dateline* sensationalized Joyce and Victoria's story, CBS's *48 Hours Investigates* ran a sensitive, illuminating, and empowering segment (at least by the standards of broadcast news) on Boylan, focusing not on Grace's pain but on Boylan's struggle from childhood until the present, the acceptance she has been shown by the Colby College community, and the reality that she and thousands of others who have had gender reassignment surgery live full lives as well-adjusted, responsible adults. "When people see me," she says at the close of the segment, "they see a good parent. And when you see our family, it doesn't seem like an unusual thing. You see four people who love each other."

In the hands of a less gifted writer, the story of a woman forced to spend 40 years of her life trapped in a body that did not match her spirit (Boylan calls it her "*being alive problem*") would have provoked nothing as much in the reader as the desire to crawl into bed, play a maudlin CD, and bemoan life's cruelty. Likewise, if told by a more self-aggrandizing and less self-critical author, Boylan's memoir could have come off simply as a feel-good motivational tale, a roadmap for those seeking to overcome unthinkable obstacles to claim the identity that would make them feel whole—but this would have offered only a one-dimensional look at a complicated, emotionally tumultuous subject. Instead, *She's Not There* is fearlessly honest, sometimes sad, and often inspiring.

As professor James Finney Boylan, Jennifer writes, "I used to stand at the lectern in my coat and tie, waving my glasses around, urging students to find the courage to become themselves. Then I'd go back to the office and lock the door and put my head down on the desk." *She's Not There* brings readers along with Boylan as she finds the strength to take her own advice. Throughout the book heartbreaking anecdotes are tempered with the easy wit of a comic novelist, as when Boylan describes the anguish she felt as a young man trying to cope with an unbearable difference between internal truth and external reality. "I combed out my hair and looked in the mirror and saw a perfectly normal-looking young woman. This is so wrong? I asked myself in the mirror. This is the cause of all the trouble?" Dreaming of "just starting life over as a woman" in a new town, she figured "I'd tell everyone I was Canadian. Then I lay on my back and sobbed. Nobody would ever believe I was Canadian."

She's Not There balances Boylan's buoyant sense of joy in her new body with a frank description of the emotional fallout her sex change has had on her wife Grace, as well as on her best friend, tough-guy author Richard Russo, whose afterword, "Imagining Jenny," explores how a bond based in large part on male camaraderie evolved into a unique friendship tested—but ultimately enriched—by the interplay between men and women. It's a tribute to Boylan's beautiful prose that readers empathize with the losses Grace has endured and the resistance Russo felt, yet applaud Boylan's victory over nature, social stigma, and personal fear. In the end, we understand that Boylan's sex change was not so much a choice as a necessity.

Gender Immigrant

JENNIFER L. POZNER

A conversation with Jennifer Finney Boylan

*L*ight on political theory but full of stories about the ways gender politics *trickle into our daily lives*, She's Not There, *which became a* New York Times *bestseller, is subversive, illuminating, poignant, and funny. The book's working title was "Gender Immigrant": Boylan has traveled from the culture of men to the culture of women and lived to tell the tale. What follows is an edited transcript of a conversation about the ways that gender is "done" in our society, whether trading a plate of ribs for a salad is the result of nature or nurture, and the joys— and unexpected cultural baggage—that come with being female in America.*

Jennifer Pozner: The subtitle of your book is *A Life in Two Genders*. Having lived most of your life as a man, what were your expectations about becoming female?

Jennifer Finney Boylan: It's important to understand that if you're a transsexual, you're not changing genders in order to get a better deal. Having lived in this culture and having been a professor for many years, I had a pretty clear sense of the realities of being female, but what I most wanted was a sense of peace. And that is absolutely what I've found now that my gender and my spirit match. As I go through the course of my day there are things that are aggravating about being a woman and many things that are wonderful—but I can wake up in the morning without having to wonder "what gender am I?" or worry about what to do about a struggle that to most other people is incomprehensible. That is the particular dilemma for transsexuals: The main thing that is required to understand the condition is imagination.

JP: During your transition, you noticed yourself gaining food issues and body image anxieties along with your new breasts and hips. You say the culture had its hooks in you to the point where you felt like you were oppressing yourself. A lot of women can relate to that feeling—but it must have been incredibly confusing to be dealing with issues at 42 that most girls started having to cope with at 11. Or, did being socialized with a male sense of confidence for four decades prepare you in any way to reject negative, external judgments?

JFB: Initially, I had to go through a second adolescence, and it was a time of real awkwardness and narcissism for me. Most post-operative transsexuals eventually become rather unexceptional men and women who go on with the business of their lives unnoticed. People don't look at them and say "Hey, wow, there's one of those transsexuals I've heard so much about." We think, "There's a mother, an English teacher, a musician." You asked whether 40 years of maleness in any way prepared me for this. I was not socialized as a woman and didn't suffer firsthand the slings and arrows that women have to experience. Those 40 years did give me a certain strength and patience, and I needed that to endure the indignity and awkwardness of changing-genders. It's possible in a strange, ironic way that the male life I lived gave me the courage to surrender it.

Being trangendered is not about masculinity and femininity, it's about maleness and femaleness. I'm female now, which is to say I have a female body, but I'm feminine in some ways and not in others. I have the right to decide on any given day, just as all women do, where I fall along the femininity spectrum—with Dolly Parton on one end and Janet Reno on the other.

JP: When most of us talk about "finding our voice," we mean it metaphorically. You had to find a literal, physical voice appropriate for your new body. You place an emphasis in the book on the language of gender—how men typically speak with authority yet women often speak with a questioning lilt, as in "Hello, my name is Michelle?" For years, you told your female students to state their names because "Your identity is not a question." Yet, you say that you found yourself introducing yourself as "Jenny Boylan?" What was behind that change: How much of it was about wanting to fit in, how much about unconsciously adapting to female socialization, and how much, if any, was about trying to get used to this new identity as Jenny, after struggling with the identity of Jim for decades?

JFB: Early on I took voice lessons, and learning that feminine inflection was one of the primary things I was "instructed" to perform. But it annoyed me, and in the end, I gave up most of the so-called "feminine" inflections and adopted a more androgynous voice, which feels natural to me.

I think the feminine inflection of voice rising at the end of sentences is a particularly adolescent inflection, and grown women are less likely to do it—which makes sense, since adults are more confident than teenagers. I've also occasionally heard it in the voices of young men. But think about the way you'd ask, on the phone, "Is Mr. Smith there?" You'd ask it as a question, I'd wager. A man is more likely to state it. "Yes, is Mr. Smith there." It's an order, not a request. My guess is that there's a whole lot of socially charged information in that inflection.

We all want to fit in, and I wanted to fit in, too. So I think both consciously and unconsciously I found myself adopting certain social behaviors we associate with women. But isn't that the difference between being an adult and being a teenager—finding the courage to be ourselves, rather than bending under the pressure of our peers, or society?

JP: There's a way most people "do" gender—we mimic what we're taught: shave our legs, apply eye-shadow, flick the blush brush. Then there's the way you had to do gender: As a man, you started out wearing your mother's and girlfriends' clothing, and eventually underwent therapy and hormone treatment and surgery to become female. Now that you're a woman, do you find that you spend more or less time "doing" gender?

JFB: You could argue that *all* gender is "done." The question is, how consciously? That's the definition of what we go through as adolescents, a time when, through trial and error, we're doing not only gender but our whole character. Trying on our whole persona, finding which songs, fashions, and interests feel comfortable, what creates the effect we desire. We call ourselves adults when all that stuff becomes less conscious. I would say that at some point most of our behavior is performative.

I shave my legs now, and what's interesting is that back in the old days when I was a guy, I felt that this was something very powerful I was doing. I'd sit there thinking. "I am crossing a divide here, I'm being daring, feminine, powerful." And now I think of it only as something tedious, annoying, and inevitable.

JP: You have this great joke in the book about the effects of estrogen pills and testosterone suppressors: "One pill makes you want to talk about relationships and eat salad. The other pill makes you dislike the Three Stooges." Part of the reason it's funny is because it gets at deeply held notions about nature versus nurture. From your unique experience, how much of male/female behavior do you believe is innate, and how much is socialization?

JFB: I'm nervous about declaring "The Truth" about nature versus nurture even from my own perspective. I am a story-teller, not a sociologist.

Here's what we know: There is a physical, neurological genesis for transsexuality. To get technical on you, the bed nucleus of the stria terminalis of the hypothalamus is 40 percent larger in women and in male-to-female transsexuals than it is in non-transgendered people born male. It's not caused by hormone use, it doesn't have anything to do with being gay, lesbian, or straight. It's there your whole life. That's real.

Now that I've said all that, I'm going to contradict myself. People in the "genderqueer" community are saying a very different thing. They say it is our duty or at least our prerogative to mess with accepted notions of gender, to turn every assumption upside down. They're particularly suspicious of some kind of hypothalamus litmus test to judge whether you're "really" transgendered or not. They say it's wrong to imply that there's just one thing that makes us this way.

JP: That sounds similar to the debate in the gay community about whether finding a "gay gene" would help end discrimination by showing people it's not a "chosen lifestyle," or whether it would give fundamentalists a way to isolate the "cause" of homosexuality in order to "cure" it.

JFB: From the research I've seen, the biological components of transsexuality seem to be a lot clearer than those involved in the genesis of homosexuality. But even if people could choose to prevent transsexuality, I hope they would not. As difficult and painful as it was, in many ways I consider myself to be very lucky. It is a great gift, this ability to see into two worlds.

Nurture, nature—the short answer is that a lot more is nature than any of us would like to think. We live in a patriarchal culture that we have to resist. I agree with that. But, hormones and genetics help to make us what we are. This makes us uncomfortable because it seems to take away our free will. It doesn't do us much good to cover our eyes to facts, and one of the facts I know is that hormones do matter.

But when I found myself worrying about my weight and ordering salad—that had nothing to do with biology and everything to do with culture. So, I made damn sure to stop acting like an idiot and eat the baby back ribs if I wanted them. In some ways, some things have become more complicated than they used to be. I don't have a constant internal battle about gender anymore, but I do have to make a conscious decision to have the ribs for lunch in a situation when people are going to notice and perhaps disapprove.

JP: You've said your students no longer see you as an authority figure because you're female.

JFB: In class, I was apparently more of an authority figure as a man. Students would write down what I'd say. Now I find they often sit there with their books closed, during the same lecture in which they used to take notes. They are more likely to challenge me now, to question my knowledge. There are advantages to this; in that it's easier to get a discussion going, but it also irks me because I want to be an authority figure sometimes. I reject the cliché that women always have to be empathic and sensitive and specialize in "talking about our feelings." I'm glad if students feel more comfortable with me now, but who knows? This may only be because I'm more comfortable with myself.

JP: One thing that comes across in your book is the sense of surprise you felt during your transition when bartenders started trying to offer Jenny sports insights Jim already knew, car dealers tried to hustle you, and neighbors addressed you as "just" Jim's sister. Was it really that surprising to you?

JFB: When I went to New York for the first time as Jenny, the level of harassment just walking down the street was amazing. I'm a professor of culture studies, and I've been a guy, and I have two eyes. What was the big surprise? It was everything that I knew to be true, but it was happening to me, not someone else; Faced with that aggressive attention, I felt scared, singled out, vulnerable, and angry. But here's the kicker—there was some part of me that thought, "Well, looking good today, Jenny Boylan." There's just enough adolescent in me to look to men for validation.

I'm in bars sometimes with my band. This guy came up to me last week and his first question was, "Can I French kiss you?" Just like that I shrugged and said, "Well, no!" And my friends asked me, "Why didn't you say 'Go screw yourself?'" You know, I don't have a long history with that. There is nothing in a man's experience that is like that.

JP: In one of the most powerful scenes in your book you describe a guy in a bar who stared at you all night, followed you into the parking lot, and tried to attack you. That scenario would be familiar to far too many women. You fought him off, got to your car, and escaped. You called it "immersion learning," and gave readers a glimpse into your mind after the encounter: What did I do to him, why does he hate me so much?"

JFB: I was terrified. I hadn't done anything other than to be attractive to him and then to say no, and suddenly I was an object of fury, lust, and loathing. I was on the receiving end of a hatred I'd never imagined before. It's no surprise to me that such moments exist for women, but it had never happened to me. I was never particularly physically intimidating as a man, but I wonder, if I had not had those years of male assurance, when he came at me would I have shoved him away, would I have fought? Or would I have already surrendered, just hoping to get through the situation without being killed? Sometimes I think it was because I still had enough male history in me that my first instinct was self-preservation.

JP: Drawing distinctions between sexual orientation and gender identity, you write that the main thing gays and lesbians have in common with transsexuals is "that we get beaten up by the same people." As a woman and as a transgendered person, how do you cope with being at risk in public space?

JFB: What do you do, both as a woman and as a visible transgendered person, if you want to live your life? You swim against the tide until you get tired, and then you swim with the tide until you get your courage back. I pass pretty well, so some of the violence that is reserved for people who are visibly transgendered is not shown me. In general people leave me alone. Rural Maine, where we live, is a wonderful place. Yankees generally respect each other's privacy. I have not been on the receiving end of much cruelty or stupidity yet—most of the burden I've had to shoulder is the result of being female in this culture, not because I'm transgendered.

JP: As a media critic I remember watching you on Oprah's show and getting frustrated at how often you and other transgendered guests were asked to repeat the same fundamentals ad nauseum—that being transgendered does not equal being gay, does not mean you're a drag queen, is not about clothes. I was struck by how viscerally angry the audience was when families were involved—they cheered when Oprah asked if it wouldn't have been better for you to stay miserable since now, your wife is miserable. How did you feel about that question, and about media coverage in general?

JFB: There's this assumption that people in so-called Middle America won't understand. But if people in rural Maine get this, people can get it anywhere. When I came out almost everybody knew what transsexuality was. I wasn't the first transgendered person they knew of. Yet the media is stuck in this idea of novelty. There's been no shortage of shows about transgendered people, but they tend to always be the same. I've done a lot of TV, and yet I constantly seem to be echoing the same interview I saw on TV with some other host, with some other transsexual, 15 or 20 years ago.

Reporters want to print a story around the heartbreak caused to the family. That's one of the reasons my wife, Grace, has not participated in any media stuff. When people see me in an interview, they see a woman who found the courage to become herself, but that isn't as interesting to media as stories about depressing, broken families. Even the title of Oprah's show was "The Husband Who Became a Woman." From the outset they define me as a man who betrayed people and broke everyone's hearts.

There's an old saying in creative writing: Show, don't tell. There are so few good examples of transsexual people living their lives with dignity, self-respect, and a sense of humor. All I really had to do on *Oprah* was sit there in my Ellen Tracy suit and smile. That did more good in terms of making people understand than all the lectures I can give. When people see me, they encounter a well-adjusted, nice, funny, middle-class English teacher. The funniest thing someone said was, "The weirdest thing about you, Jenny, is that you're so normal! You're like somebody I might actually know!" People tell me, "I didn't understand before, but now I get it." That's a pretty good day's work.

One thing about transsexuality, it takes a lot of explaining. It's not a great topic for short TV segments. At least on *Oprah* I got a whole hour to myself, and then I was a panelist when she did a second show. That's an eternity compared to the *Today Show*, where I had 6.5 minutes. And one of the minutes is always devoted to, "So, are you gay?" while another is always, "How sad is this for your poor wife?" The thing I hate about these short little shows is that they don't give me room to be funny. I don't get to be myself. I feel like I'm doing a book report: "How I Changed Genders on My Summer Vacation." It's very hard to have an intelligent discussion in these forums, because it's always okay to make fun of transsexuals—we're seen as pathetic and freakish.

JP: Media must have a harder time plunking you into their pre-written "family heartbreak" stories, since you and Grace have stayed together.

JFB: That's the thing people are most uncomfortable with—they're telling me, in effect, what people have told women for decades: I won't be a "real woman" until I find a nice man and marry him. Even people who have dealt with my transition in a very sophisticated way are uncomfortable with the fact that we are two women living together and legally married.

Somebody said to Grace, "Don't you understand? You need to get a divorce and move on with your life." And Grace—this is how phenomenal she is—Grace said, "No, *you* don't understand—this *is* my life."

JP: You seem to have gone to great lengths to make sure everyone around you was okay with your transition, not only your close family and friends but also Colby campus administrators, faculty, and students, as well as any number of current and former acquaintances. And your book seemed to be written with that same care. Why has taking care of other people's adjustment to your transition been so important to you?

JFB: I wanted to bring as many people along with me as possible. It's sadly true that most people, including liberal, compassionately minded people, don't understand transsexuality. They think it's some nutty lifestyle, or that it has something to do with being gay or lesbian or wanting to be "feminine." Alas, many people think that male-to-female transsexuals define themselves as women in terms of skirts and makeup and high heels and sponge cake.

Why was it so important to educate people? Because I wanted them to understand. Because I wanted people to recognize that in me, as a woman, they would find someone who is generally familiar to them, that as a woman my issues are pretty similar (although, admittedly not identical) to the issues of women-born women. It's also fair to say that some people will never get it. In which case, what can you do? You move on.

JP: You mentioned once that you don't want to be a "model transsexual." But your wit and your articulate style seem to have made you a bit of a media phenom. Are you actively involved with the transgender movement?

JFB: I am not involved in the transgender "movement," which is not a movement but a series of different groups of people doing different things. I've decided I can do the most good by concentrating on what I do well, which is telling stories, and just going about my life. It seems as if that has connected to people in some way, though, and maybe that is its own revolution.

I guess that for a little while I'm going to be a transgendered spokesmodel. There will be other people. I don't see myself being defined by this for the rest of my life. I'll write other books. I'll go back to fiction. But I'm glad to be in the public eye for the time being, because we need more good role models.

I'm tremendously proud of my book, because it did something I've always wanted to do in my writing, which is to stay in that zone between the tragic and the comic. This book has connected with a lot of people, and surprisingly so—my publisher, Random House, certainly didn't expect it. I like to think that this book connects with such a wide audience because the main question I'm asking is not, "How do you have a sex change?" but "How do you live an authentic life?" That's a question all people ask themselves, or should. The book isn't long on obscure gender theory or on gory details about the surgery. People don't necessarily want to know about that. They want to know about how they can be true to themselves, and what will the cost of that truth be to them and to the people they love. At the heart of the book are very mainstream questions: How do I tell the truth? How do I live my life with honor?

40

Gender Quiz

MINNIE BRUCE PRATT

quiz, n. [? suggested by L. quis, who, which, what, quid, how, why, wherefore]. 1. [Rare], a queer or eccentric person. 2. a practical joke; hoax. 3. a questioning, especially an informal oral or written examination to test one's knowledge.

Webster's New World Dictionary of the American Language

In 1975, when I first fell in love with another woman, and knew that was what I was doing, I was married to a man, had been for almost ten years, and I had two small sons. Everyone was shocked at the turn I was taking in my life, including me. Everyone—from the male lawyer who handled the divorce to my handful of lesbian friends—wanted to know: Had I ever had these feelings before? When had I realized I was "different"? When had I started to "change"? And the state of North Carolina, where I was living, certainly wanted to know: Did I understand that I could not be both a mother—a good woman—and also a lesbian—a perverted woman?

To answer their questions and my own, I did what perhaps every person who identifies as lesbian or gay does when we come out to ourselves. I looked back at my own life for the clues of memory to use as I struggled through a maze of questions: I didn't feel "different," but was I? (From who?) Had I changed? (From what?) Was I heterosexual in adolescence only to become lesbian in my late twenties? Was I lesbian always but coerced into heterosexuality? Was I a less authentic lesbian than my friends who had "always known" that they were sexually and affectionally attracted to other women? What kind of woman was a lesbian woman? Was I a "real" woman?

From Minnie Bruce Pratt's S/he Alyson Books, Los Angeles: 1995

What I found at the center of my exploration was my first friendship, when I was five and she was five, with a white girl who had lived next door to me, a tomboy. I had not talked to her since our high school graduation in our small Alabama town, but I knew from my mother that she had never married. I wondered at how intensely I remembered her. Then one evening, as I read my poetry in a Birmingham bookstore, she walked in, looking grown and fine in her cowboy boots, white shirt open at the collar, tailored slacks—looking like the butch dyke she had turned out to be. She was someone who had known me since I was small, but she was as shocked as everyone else that I had grown up to be a lesbian too.

When I found her, I found other questions that required me to turn back and look yet again: How was it possible that coming from the woman-hating, race-baiting, church town of our childhood, we had both grown up to live as lesbians? Why was she the first person I felt passionately about outside my family—someone who was not only a lesbian, but a butch lesbian? How had we recognized each other then, with no language for who we were? What mark had we each left on the other? And who *were* we to each other, at five years old? Were we "butch" and "femme"? Were we "boy" and "girl"? Why was I invisible in her memories, a "girl" but not a "lesbian"?

I turned and looked back again at the two of us, those two girls. I saw the kite string slack in my hand, the kite falling and crumpling, and how she reached out and pulled me forward into the wind with it. I said to her, "But after we were little, I never saw you. You were always playing with the boys. I was afraid of the boys." And she said, "But what you didn't know was that I was afraid of the girls." All through high school she fell miserably in love with straight girls who were aggressively femme, but at the senior prom she dated the captain of the football team. I sat sedate, awkward, and alone, in a strapless pink prom dress, full of anticipated power but unable to sail into a room of dancers who, like me, desired and despised the power of women.

Twenty years later these questions unwound before me: Was my femme style—the tilt of my head, my way of asking questions, the tone of my voice—related to my sexual desire? To my notion of myself as a woman? What did maleness and femaleness have to do with the identities of butch and femme we had grown up into? What did the gestures of masculinity and femininity have to do with us as women?

The next time I came home she arranged another reunion, a dinner with queer folks from our high school years. That night there were five, all of us white, a friendship network as segregated as our education, our never even getting to meet the Black students in the school on the other side of town. We hadn't known much about many of the lives hidden in our town, and now we gathered, ready to find out: Me and the woman who was my first friend, almost my first memory. And my best girlfriend from high school, who'd also grown up to be a lesbian and a mother. My first boyfriend, who'd turned out to be a gay man so sweet I remembered why I wanted to be his girl. And another gay man who still lived in our hometown. We gossiped about who we'd had crushes on, who we held hands with on the sly, who flirted back.

The list of people became staggeringly long, far beyond my idea of who might have been "lesbian" or "gay" in my tiny town of about two thousand. There was the girl classmate, long since married, who'd graduated and then had an affair with a woman gym teacher. And the girl classmate who had gone from one woman lover to another until her front door got broken down in the middle of the night. And the married Sunday School teacher whose daughter, later married, had had an affair with a girlfriend, who years later had had an affair with the teacher-mother. There were the boys who either did it with each other or watched the fucking that went on between them in a church, in a parsonage, with the preacher's son. There was the gay man who opened his door one night to find an envelope on his doorstep stuffed with photographs of a married male acquaintance, and a pleading invitation.

We told stories about taking the compulsory heterosexual quiz in high school, with its two ways to answer, its two ways to turn: straight or gay, heterosexual or queer. One choice would lead us out of the maze into adulthood, the other directly to hell. But it seemed that the public tally of our choices had almost no relation to our hidden lives, to whose hand was on whose ass, to the dream we buried, dead center, in our heart. The institution of heterosexuality certainly existed, but its daily practice—at least in my hometown in the deep South—suddenly seemed no more sturdy than the wedding pictures of man and wife printed on flimsy yellow paper in the local weekly.

Yet law and custom had usually been strong enough to make our public lives match the picture. The boundaries of heterosexuality strengthened other institutions—including those of race and class—whose limits were also unacknowledged. In the town newspaper I saw photographs of the sheriff and his deputies by the courthouse, pouring confiscated whiskey into the street gutters until the town reeked of moonshine. But there were no pictures of my girlfriend inside her house, on her hands and knees in the kitchen with a mother almost broken by poverty. No picture of her father jailed for trying to buy their way out by selling bootleg liquor. When my white father died in the county nursing home, the paper printed one version of his life, from semi-pro baseball to the lumber mill. No mention of him drinking the bootleg whiskey, no mention of his racist theories on who was taking over the world. The Black woman who raised me died across the hall from him in the home. There was nothing in the paper to say she had lived or died, or how many children she had mothered, nothing of her daughters or her grandchildren.

When I was engaged to be married to a man, the local paper published an announcement and a picture of me, groomed and womanly, ready to be a wife. Of those of us gathered at our queer reunion, there was no public record in our town— no note in the weekly chat column from Greenpond or Six Mile—of those we had loved faithfully for five years, ten years, the children we had familied. But in our bodies we knew that our way had not led to a dead end, a blank wall, a blank piece of paper. We had walked through into our own lives.

The last time I went home, I introduced my new love to my first girlfriend, and watched them greet each other warmly. After years of loving butch lesbians, I had taken as my mate a woman so stone in her masculinity that she could, and did, sometimes pass as a queer man. I had no language to talk about her or us together. I had to learn to say that I had fallen in love with a woman so *transgendered*, with such perceived contradictions between her birth sex and her gender expression, that someone at one end of a city block could call her "Ma'am" and someone at the other end would call her "Sir." I was learning that I was more complicated than I'd had any idea. I was beginning to pull the thread of who *I* was out of the tangle of words: *woman* and *lesbian, femme* and *female.*

That night I looked back at my first friend, a girl scalded by her mother's shame. The threats of walk-like-a-lady, of don't-be-so-loud-and-angry. (And hate yourself enough to almost go crazy.) I looked back at myself, the child flirting in photographs with angled head, sidelong glance. The child given an impossible choice by her teachers: Be smart or be a girl, be a girl or be strong. (And hate yourself enough to almost leave your body.) The two of us had sat at playtime in the dirt, barefoot, battling furiously hand-to-hand in the desire to defeat the other. How had we survived to meet again? Survived to grow up to be women for whom the word *woman* did not adequately describe the twists and turns our bodies, our lives, took through sex and gender?

No one had turned to us and held out a handful of questions: How many ways are there to have the *sex* of girl, boy, man, woman? How many ways are there have *gender*—from masculine to androgynous to feminine? Is there a connection between the *sexualities* of lesbian, bisexual, heterosexual, between desire and liberation? No one told us: The path divides, and divides again, in many directions. No one asked: How many ways can the *body's sex* vary by chromosomes, hormones, genitals? How many ways can *gender expression* multiply—between home and work, at the computer and when you kiss someone, in your dreams and when you walk down the street? No one asked us: What is your dream of who you want to be?

In 1975, when I first fell in love with another woman, and knew that was what I wanted, I had just begun to call myself a feminist. I was learning how many traps the female body could be caught in—sexual assault and rape, beatings in the home, our thoughts turned back in shame on our bodies. I learned how women's bodies could be used to reproduce children without our consent, to produce someone else's "pleasure" at our expense. Most importantly, I began to be able to explain many of the events of my own life that had been unintelligible to me.

I was able to recall and find a pattern in certain acts that had made no sense—like a sexually suggestive comment from a male co-worker—and acts that I hadn't understood as significant—such as the fact that a male job interviewer questioned me on my childcare arrangements. For the first time in my life, I understood myself as *woman*, the "opposite sex," a group of people subject to discrimination and oppression—and capable of resistance. I was able to locate my body and my life in the maze of history and power.

The oppression of women was a revelation to me; the liberation of women was my freedom. There was tremendous exhilaration in being part of a liberation movement, in gathering together with other women to explore how to get to freedom. In consciousness-raising circles, political action groups, cultural events, literary collectives—in all kinds of women's groups and spaces, we identified the ways oppression had fenced in our lives.

And we read the theories of women who had ideas about how to end the oppression of women as a sex. I found a few writers who examined the relation of capitalist economic development to women's oppression. But most of the theory available to me was a historical and monocultural. It emphasized that the solution was to eliminate differences between *women* and *men*. Some proposed abolishing distinctions in biological functioning—as in Shulamith Firestone's suggestion for artificial wombs to erase female biological functions that she believed were the basis of male and female, and of inequality. Others felt that the answer was to end modes of gender expression, patterns of femininity and masculinity. Carolyn Heilbrun advocated androgyny, the elimination of the polarities of "gender roles" that she considered the cause of power differences between men and women. Andrea Dworkin campaigned to alter the practice of sexual intercourse, to get rid of sexual images and acts she believed would perpetuate maleness and femaleness, and therefore domination and submission.

I found these theories persuasive. Maybe eliminating sex differences or transcending gender expression would end *woman* as a place of oppression. But, in fact, the theories didn't explain some important aspects of oppression against me as a woman in my daily life. I'd been pregnant with two children and given birth to them. The way the doctors treated me only made me ask, "If there were artificial wombs, whose hands would administer the technology, and for whose profits?" And those two children had been two boys, each of whom had possessed, by the time he was two or three, his own unique blend of masculine and feminine. Was it possible to train them into androgyny? Was this the skill they needed to take action against unjust power in the world? As for intercourse, this was where I had experienced the most pleasure in my relationship with a man; my husband had tried carefully to please me. I would have had more pleasure if my sexual play had not been damaged by fear about pregnancy—and by shame about what I could want as a woman. But my husband's penis was not dominating my life. Instead, I was concerned about the power of white men who interviewed me for possible jobs at large institutions, and then protected their economic position by never hiring me.

And, when I stood up to face the public opponents of my liberation as a woman, I got little help from the theories I was reading. When I debated right-wing women in my community in North Carolina, as they lambasted the Equal Rights Amendment, their tactics were based on baiting the women's movement precisely on the issue of elimination of sex and gender differences. They accused: Equal rights means unisex bathrooms. Equal rights means homosexual marriages. They meant: If you challenge gender boundaries, you will make women more vulnerable to abuse by eliminating gender protection. They meant: If you challenge gender boundaries, you will have men and women adopting the behavior of the opposite sex and getting pleasure from it.

I didn't know how to answer their raging remarks, accusations which were echoed throughout the United States as part of a concerted antifeminist campaign. Some of the first slogans I'd learned in the women's movement were "Biology is not destiny" and "Women are made, not born." I'd read feminist theory that analyzed how jobs and household chores and emotions were divided up between men and women according to sex. But I—and the primarily white middle-to-upper-class reform women's movement that backed the E.R.A.—did not have an analysis of sex, gender expression, and sexuality that was complex enough to respond to these right-wing attacks.

We could have said, in these debates, that the answer to violence against women was not the illusion of protection by limiting women's activity, but a movement in which women learned to fight back, with allies, to protect ourselves, and to move through the whole world safely. We could have answered that the split between *man* and *woman* was designed to keep one sex up and one sex down in an economic system where profiteers make money off a war between the sexes. We could have answered that *woman* was not the opposite of *man*, and that liberation meant crossing all arbitrary gender boundaries, to place ourselves anywhere we chose on the continuum of maleness and femaleness, in any aspect of our lives.

In some more private spaces within women's liberation, we did advance these arguments. But in hostile public space it was controversial to propose even the slightest changes in "normal" male and female behaviors. *That* was to question the foundation of "civilization." The reform wing of the women's movement was profoundly ambivalent about taking on lesbian and transgender issues publicly. It dealt with issues of race and class reluctantly and inconsistently, when at all. A victory for these reformers meant only a fractional expansion of the old public boundaries on what was acceptable behavior for "womanhood," on who was a "respectable" woman.

Some of these reformists accepted limits on what constituted womanhood because of uncritical allegiances to their own class and race positions. For others, this was a strategic decision; they believed a political definition of woman that deemphasized difference would secure more territory for more women in a hostile world. They hoped to establish a bulwark, and then a place that could be built on for greater liberation. In fact, the exclusion of women who blurred the edges of what was considered legitimate as *woman*—because of race or class or sexuality or gender presentation—made women's space smaller and more dangerous, made this aspect of the women's movement weaker and more limited in foundation.

In the end, I moved away from reform politics into cultural and political actions that embraced the complexities of *woman*. The group of women I began to work with was, at first, predominantly white, both working class and middle class, and lesbian. But we had been deeply influenced by the Black civil rights and liberation movements. We saw the freedom of all women as linked inextricably to the elimination of racism. In addition, we learned from the political and theoretical work of feminists and lesbians of color who showed us how to question—and place in an economic and historical context—the many categories of "difference," including those of race, sex, class, and sexuality.

But even as we traced how women's liberation could be extended through these connections, these untanglings and re-braidings, we still had not fully explored sex and gender. There were unanswered questions, and questions that were never raised, about "manhood" and "womanhood." We carried with us many of the negative assumptions and values that the larger culture had assigned to *woman, feminine, man, masculine*—ideas that served to limit women's behaviors and to prevent examination of how "masculinity" and "femininity" are not the basis of sex, race, and class oppression.

Often a lesbian considered "too butch" was assumed to be, at least in part, a male chauvinist. She might get thrown out of her lesbian collective for this, or refused admittance to a lesbian bar. Frequently a lesbian who was "too femme" was perceived as a woman who had not liberated her mind or her body. In ordinary arguments with a lesbian friend or lover, she could be dismissed—as I sometimes was—with, "You act just like a heterosexual woman." Yet during this same time, lesbians who were butch, femme, and all gender expressions in between were trying to decipher which of our behaviors still did reflect oppressive patterns learned in a woman-hating culture. These struggles were present in 1982, in New York City, when an alliance of women with a range of sexualities had planned "The Scholar and the Feminist" annual conference as a way to examine the complex intersections of pleasure and danger in women's sexuality and gender expression. They were condemned as "sexual deviants" and "sluts" by a group of women organizing against pornography, who identified themselves as "real feminists."

At about this time, I was teaching women's studies at a state university near Washington, D.C. One day in the classroom, we were discussing lesbian life in general, and butch/femme in particular. I was dressed casually, but in femme style. The white woman to my left was a muscular, big woman, with short hair and a black leather jacket; she drove a Harley to school every day. She said forcefully, "Butch and femme don't exist anymore." It was a moment typical, in many ways, of the lesbian-feminist space I lived inside during the 1980s. As women and as lesbians we wanted to step outside traps set for us as people sexed as *woman,* to evade negative values gendered to us. We didn't want to be women as defined by the larger culture, so we had to get rid of femininity. We didn't want to be oppressed by men, so we had to get rid of masculinity. And we wanted to end enforced desire, so we had to get rid of heterosexuality.

For some lesbians, one way out of these traps was to choose androgyny, or to practice a sexuality of "mutuality and equality"—an attempt to eliminate the variations of "man" and "woman" we saw in each other every day. Another way was to explain hostility toward "masculine" lesbians and "feminine" lesbians as arising from homophobia, rather than from prejudices about what kind of gender expression was appropriate for "respectable" women and "liberated" women. One answer for many was to deny the deep fear in the larger culture, and therefore within ourselves, about sex and gender fluidity.

The fear can take different forms. The classified sections of gay and lesbian newspapers still run personal ads that say "No butches, no drugs"—a statement equating gender defiance in a woman with self-destruction, a lesbian version of a gay man's "straight-appearing, no femmes" ad. Discussions of sexuality may exclude butch/butch and femme/femme pairings as too homoerotically queer. Some of us who talk of ourselves as butch or femme may reject identification with people like us who live at the extremes of gender. A coolly sophisticated lesbian at a dance may say, "I'm a femme, but I'm not like *her,*"—dismissing the woman she sees as "going too far" in her femininity.

We know, from being alive in the United States in the twentieth century, that there are severe punishments dealt to those who cross sex and gender boundaries, and terrible penalties visited on women who claim their womanhood independently. This is really no surprise, though, since the institutions of power are based, at least in part, on controlling difference—by sex, gender, and sexuality. No wonder we may feel there is safety in moderation, in assimilation, in a "normal" expression of sex and gender. But *moderation* means "to keep within bounds." Inside whose boundaries are we living?

And despite the punishments for boundary crossing, we continue to live, daily, with all our contradictory differences. Here I still stand, unmistakably "feminine" in style, and "womanly" in personal experience—and unacceptably "masculine" in political interests and in my dedication to writing a poetry that stretches beyond the woman's domain of home. Here I am, assigned a "female" sex on my birth certificate, but not considered womanly enough—because I am a lesbian—to retain custody of the children I delivered from my woman's body. As a white girl raised in a segregated culture, I was expected to be "ladylike"—sexually repressed but acquiescent to white men of my class—while other, darker women were damned as "promiscuous" so their bodies could be seized and exploited. I've worked outside the home for at least part of my living since I was a teenager—a fact deemed masculine by some. But my occupation now is that of teacher, work suitably feminine for a woman as long as I don't tell my students I'm a lesbian—a sexuality thought too aggressive and "masculine" to fit with my "femininity."

I am definitively lesbian to myself, but not in a way recognizable to a heterosexual world that assumes lesbians to be "mannish." Unless I announce myself to be lesbian, which I do often—in my classroom, at poetry readings, to curious taxi drivers—I am usually assumed to be straight. But unless I "butch up" my style, sometimes I am suspect inside my lesbian world as too feminine to be lesbian. And both inside and outside lesbian space, there is another assumption held by some: No "real" lesbian would be attracted to as much masculinity as I prefer in my lesbian lover.

How can I reconcile the contradictions of sex and gender, in my experience and my politics, in my body? We are all offered a chance to escape this puzzle at one time or another. We are offered the True or False correct answer. We are handed the questionnaire to fill out. But the boxes that we check, *M* or *F,* the categories *male* and *female,* do not contain the complexity of sex and gender for any of us.

The stories that follow are part of a new theory about that complexity which is appearing at the intersections: between the feminism of U.S. women's liberation; the writings of women of color nationally and internationally; the queer ideas of lesbian, gay, and bisexual liberation; and the emerging thought of transgender liberation—a movement that embraces drag queens and kings, transsexuals, crossdressers, he-shes and she-males, intersexed people, transgenderists, and people of ambiguous, androgynous, or contradictory sex and gender. These intersections make clear that every aspect of a person's gender expression and sex will not be consistently either masculine or feminine, man or woman. I find many layers of my own experience in this theory, and I find an exhilaration at the connections between myself and others as I see, with increasing clarity, how gender oppression and liberation affect everyone, how my struggle as a woman and a lesbian overlaps and joins with the struggles of other gender and sexually oppressed people. A friend of mine has said of this exhilaration: "It's like being released from a cage I didn't know I was in."

This is a theory that explores the infinities, the fluidities of sex and gender. The African-American woman eating sushi at the next table may be a woman lovely in her bones, gestures, tone of voice, but this does not mean that her genitals are female. If the handsome Filipino man in the upstairs apartment is straight-appearing, this does not mean his erotic preference is the "opposite sex." The white woman next to you at the doctor's office may have been born male, and have a complex history of hormones and surgery. Or she may have been born female and have a different but equally complex history of hormones and surgery. The person on the subway who you perceive as a white man in a business suit may have been born female, may consider herself a butch lesbian, or may identify himself as a gay man. The *M* and the *F* on the questionnaire are useless.

Now here I stand, far from where I was born, from the small segregated hospital in Alabama where a nurse checked *F* and *W* on my birth certificate. Far from my first tomboy girlfriend and the ways we played together, splashing barefoot in rainwater. Far from who I was as a wife and mother, almost twenty years ago, when I began to question the destiny I had been assigned as a woman. I have lived my life at the intersection of great waves of social change in the United States in the twentieth century: the Black civil rights and liberation movements, the women's liberation movement, the lesbian/gay/bisexual liberation movement, the transgender liberation movement. The theory developed by each has complicated our questions about the categories of race, sex, gender, sexuality, and class. And these theories have advanced our ability to struggle against oppressions that are imposed and justified using these categories. But we can not move theory into action unless we can find it in the eccentric and wandering ways of our daily life. I have written the stories that follow to give theory flesh and breath.

41

Looking for Nature at the Mall

A Field Guide to the Nature Company

JENNIFER PRICE

Entry

I don't recall the exact mall where I first encountered The Nature Company. It was around 1989, in the St. Louis Union Station, or perhaps the Bridgewater Commons in central New Jersey. Say it was a Saturday afternoon, and I was searching for the exit after three hours of shopping. I do remember that I stopped in my tracks, after which I slowly toured the entire store and bought something—but I do not remember what it was. "Customers often exclaim, 'Wow!' " The Nature Company's press release begins, and that accurately describes my reaction.

The history of the pink flamingo chronicles the baby boomers' attachments to a powerful definition of Nature as a nonhuman Place Apart. But if you want to see the uses, desires and convenience of these definitions powerfully at work in the 1980s and 1990s, there are few better places to go than your nearest nature store.

Since the early 1980s, the retail genre's meteoric success has paralleled exactly the well-off baby boomers' emergence as the consumer group with the most spending power. And it is exactly the yuppies—or "affluent middle-aged," as *Forbes* has ventured more sensitively—who have been enjoying these encounters with nature at the mall.

Why? The Nature Company pioneered the concept, and amid a spree of 1980s-zeitgeist enterprises, such as Sharper Image and The Banana Republic, has dominated the expanding subfield of companies—The Natural Selection, The Ecology House, Nature's Own Imagination and the company's most serious competitor, Natural Wonders—that specialize in geodes, bug T-shirts, bird sculptures and glow-in-the-dark stars. The Nature Company itself was founded in Berkeley in 1973 by a young couple, Tom and Priscilla Wrubel, who had met in the late 1960s in the Peace Corps. They gambled that a store "devoted to the observation, understanding and appreciation of the natural world" might fill a useful niche for a "population taking to the wilderness in record numbers," and for a generation of new parents, like themselves, who wanted to introduce children to the joys of nature. By 1983, they had four stores in the Bay Area. Seeking expansion capital, they sold their enterprise to the parent CML Group, which specialized in companies that might track the baby boomers' wealth into the 1990s, and which also has owned NordicTrack and Smith & Hawken—or in the not-so-sensitive words of *Business Week*, "a package of yuppie goodies unlike anybody else's." By 1994, The Nature Company ran 124 stores in the United States, 3 in Canada, 12 in Japan, and 7 in Australia. At the end of 1993, they posted net sales of $162 million. The baby boomers who set out hiking and backpacking in a generational drove in the 1960s clearly had taken to the malls as well.

Not without skepticism, however. "People come in and say, 'Ahhh!'" the Company's marketing director has said. But "wow" better describes my own reaction. It's subtler, more ambivalent. In 1989, a *New York Times* columnist wrote a glowing report after a first visit, to the Bridgewater Commons store, yet asked what is perhaps *the* nagging question: "Why, on earth, weren't the people in the store outside experiencing [nature] instead of . . . indoors buying it?" The Nature *Company*? In the Mall of America? The very name and habitat can provoke a post-1960s nature lover's deepest antimaterialist suspicions. I, too, have marveled at the wondrous array of bird feeders, kites, telescopes, fossils and jewelry, and at the trademark bins of wind-up dinosaurs, rubber animal noses and cow-moo noise boxes. As a birder and hiker, I have lingered by the shelves of videos and natural history books. "I bought a beautiful pair of gardening shears there," a friend explained, "but I feel somehow manipulated. It feels inauthentic"—but she loves the wildlife ties her brother gives her husband for Christmas. "It feels fake," another friend says—but she had just bought a spectacular geode there. If The Nature Company beckons irresistibly, to more than a few of its patrons it also feels vaguely troubling. And the real revelations of eighties nature stores, I'm convinced, and the persistent troubles with our definitions of Nature, rest squarely in that contradiction.

By the mid-1990s, The Nature Company's fortunes had started to slide, in part because its huge success spurred nature and nonnature stores alike to copy its innovations in design and wares. In 1996, CML sold the company to Discovery Communications, which would focus more squarely on adventure than nature. And the boomers' children have emerged to rival their parents as a powerful consumer demographic. But from 1983 to 1993—the very decade in which the baby boomers' social and economic power soared to match our desires—The Nature Company evolved to be an unusually powerful retail magnet for my generation and class. I myself have made frequent trips since my first visit—wherever it was. What has The Nature Company been selling us, exactly? Why have they sited most of their stores in upscale malls, within bowling distance of Emporio Armani? Why do people say "wow": why have many of us harbored such deep suspicions, and yet made The Nature Company a first stop for holiday shopping? And most of all, why has my adult generation of well-to-do baby boomers been looking for nature at the mall? Have we expected to find it there? And will we?

Natural Selection

What has The Nature Company been selling? Images of nature, pieces of nature, and tools for going out into nature. By 1994, the company was marketing over twelve thousand products. They have sold bird T-shirts, wind chimes, paperweights, bird feeders, wildflower seeds, field guides, videos, note cards, CDs, herb teas, bat shelters, rain gauges, field hats, Swiss army knives, Rainforest Crunch, plastic periscopes, amethyst geodes, stuffed tigers, Zuni fetishes, petrified wood, rock polishers, dinosaur everything, star charts and galaxy boxer shorts. At first glance, it seems that anything that has to do with the natural world must be here. But The Nature Company is not a biome. It is on average 2,900 square feet of retail space— a very small space for all of nature—and what lives here must sell. The company has, from the start, hewed to strict principles of natural selection. And the principles hew to the resonant, countermodern definition of Nature that the pink flamingo's history charts so well.

To see the definition clearly, it is easier to begin with what the company will *not* sell. What has it classified as not-Nature? The Nature Company refuses to market "trophy" items, which require the killing of animals: no butterflies, seashells or furs. No mounted heads. Under the Wrubels' regime, the company avoided products that anthropomorphize animals. The popular children's book *Goodnight*

Moon is still non grata, since the bunny wears pajamas and sleeps in a bed. Anthropomorphizers, as a species, were also unwelcome: you could discover almost no human images on the posters, and (until the Discovery takeover) very few human voices on the CDs. And no Enya, though often requested. Domestic animals have been in short supply. The company has selected nonhuman, wilder and unused forms of nature. When asked to sum up their inventory, Nature Company personnel have used the terms "authenticity," "uniqueness" and "quality." Also "whimsy"—but only authentic whimsy. The toy animals here do not smile or wag their tails. The dolphins and cicadas on the keychains have been accurate replicas. The bat puppets look like real bats, the piggy banks like real pigs and the angelfish bathtub toys like real angelfish. The wind-up dinosaurs in the stores' "ning-ning" bins (the Wrubels' children coined the term) still come in bright colors "in line with new scientific thought," and the inflatable emperor penguins are anatomically correct. Nature Company products have been humorous, but not kitschy, cliché or sentimental. They are inexpensive, but not cheap. You see real rocks, plastic grasshoppers, dolphin keychains and stone bird sculptures—but no I [heart] dolphins bumperstickers, plastic pink flamingos, real grasshoppers or plastic rocks.

Among all the items, the products that limn the definitions of Nature here most visibly are the ones that do not, if you think about it, look like nature as a separate place, or summon it to you or send you out into it. For example, The Nature Company has marketed handmade paper lamps and Amish oak-hickory rockers. And why Zuni fetishes? The company has enjoyed a brisk business in Native American crafts, and, until the CML sale, the few human voices on the CDs were ethnic or indigenous. "Each product," says the company's press kit, " . . . introduces customers to an aspect of the natural world"—so how do the Australian wool throw blankets connect you to nature? They don't, at least not directly. Zulu baskets satisfy the entrance criteria not because they are nature, but because like the brightly colored wind-up dinosaurs, they are "authentic" or "unique": many of us tend to invest rocks and Zulu handcrafts with the same meanings. Each item here, the company states more accurately in a handout for employees, "[relates] in some magical way to . . . natural phenomena." *Viento de los Andes*, a CD of Andean folk music, got in by meaningful association, since to so many baby boomers, both nature and indigenous cultures connote authenticity and simplicity in a modern era. And why ask for Enya, a New Age Irish singer, in a nature store? The piggy bank has to look like a real pig, but more important, it comes with "layers and layers of associations," including "French farmyards," "childhood dreams" and "the good old days." The Nature Company has billed itself as your direct connection to the natural world. But the stores connect us not so much to what nature is as to what Nature *means*: they tap the powerful, meaningful routes by which we use Nature to define who we are, and with which we have navigated late-twentieth-century American life.

At The Nature Company, you can really put Nature to work. If the stores have sold over twelve thousand products, they have hawked a small and well-chosen set of outsized meanings. The *Glacier Bay* CD invites shoppers to "escape" to one of the "Last Great Places"; and in 1994, you could buy a trip to "Alaska: the Last Great Adventure," as advertised in the catalog:

> *People in towns . . . dream of serene sanctuaries far away from fax*
> *machines. . . . This is where you pull out of the fast lane and change*
> *the course of your revved-up life. . . . Please see the order form.*

You can buy walking sticks, vests and backpacks here, too, to enjoy nonhuman
Nature as Wilderness—a distant and untamed realm, a solitary refuge from the
modern city, which is ideally as unpeopled (and as devoid of cows and cats) as
The Nature Company's poster collection. Nature as Adventure is vivified in the
subgenre of books (the book section has anchored the stores as a kind of philosophy section) that the head book buyer in 1987 classified as "tales of personal
adventure in a wild land." *Wolf: Spirit of the Wild. Forgotten Edens: Experienc-*
ing the Earth's Wild Places. A canvas hat from the Sierra Club John Muir collection will "give me the Simple Life." The Zuni fetishes, Zulu baskets and African
jewelry associate Nature nearly interchangeably with indigenous peoples. The
throw blankets "might have come from the cedar chest of your great-grandmother."
And the whole inventory constitutes a monument to an understanding of Nature
as a place for Leisure: the Nature Company Cap is "for days off . . . afoot and lighthearted down an open road." Leisure, Adventure, Simplicity, Uniqueness, Authenticity, the Primitive, the Past, the Autochthonous, Tranquility, Exoticism, Wildness,
Freedom. Here you can use the definition of Nature as a Place Apart to define,
critique or counteract the urbanism, anonymity, commercialism, technological control, complexity, white-collar work, artifice and alienations of the postwar era.
What is for sale here is exactly the established definition of Nature that well-to-do
baby boomers adapted for themselves in the 1960s, and marshaled as a chief
weapon to critique what troubled them about American society. On the first page
of *Walden*, Thoreau opposed Nature to "civilized life"—and you can buy the essay
here in a pocket size edition for hikers.

Nature is available for purchase above all as what is Real: what is enduring,
nonreplicated, non-mass culture, Authentic, non-Artificial and absolute. The
amethyst pieces "vary according to natural structure." The Polish folk-art candles
are "one-of-a-kind handmade." The Get Real generation have always used Nature
to combat their postwar anxieties about mass culture and high-tech society.

> *Jet has been fashioned into beads and amulets for 5,000 years and*
> *Native Americans have fashioned turquoise into . . . jewelry for cen-*
> *turies. Now Chilean artists combine the gems to create a . . . handmade*
> *necklace, bracelet and pair of earrings which follow the natural curve*
> *of the throat, wrist and ear. . . . Bracelet $95.00*

> *Our Dakota Earth Mailbox is a piece of history, made of reclaimed*
> *barnwood . . . to look like a rustic, wind-weathered birdhouse. Each*
> *one-of-a-kind piece . . . recalls a way of life amid hard Great Plains*
> *winters. . . . $49.95*

The fossils, "sculpted by nature . . . more than 350 million years ago," and "quar-
ried and polished by Moroccan crafts-people," are "handfinished." "Our Nature
Company Recordings" in the Last Great Places series, the company assured us in
a 1994 catalog, "blend the elemental harmonies of music and the earth." Nature

Company products, Priscilla Wrubel stated in the Fall 1994 catalog, are "tools"— and "human hands have guided tools since the Ice Age."

Of course, while baby boomers in the 1960s adapted the idea of Nature as a Place Apart to combat artifice, conformity and anonymity, in the 1980s—as we became affluent professionals and consumers—we began to use Nature less as a tool for battling the System than to get some temporary relief from it. CML's stated mission was to "enhance people's health, understanding of the natural world, and sense of well-being." Or in the slightly different words of an investment-analysis firm, CML marketed "products for stress relief." At The Nature Company, the "yuppie leisure market," in *Business Week*'s words, could enjoy Nature as a key therapeutic resource for what has become a virtual obsession with stress relief:

> *Pachelbel Canon in D Blended with the Eternal Sound of the Sea—*
> *Creates a tranquil atmosphere for quiet meditation. . . . CD $16.98.*

The *Cloud Forest* CD, in the 1994 catalog, "weave[s] a spell of peace." If you sited the birdbath fountain indoors, "the sound of running water [had] a calming, beautiful effect." And *Tranquility*, a video "moodtape" of sunrises, clouds and "peaceful ocean waves," "perfect for relaxing, entertaining, love-making" and designed to create a "soothing and harmonious atmosphere," was an especially safe bet to sell well. Of course, the yuppies have searched for stress relief, and harvested Nature for a psychic yield, not just to escape the system but to act more effectively within it. "Clearly," the investment-analysis firm remarked with enthusiasm, "anything which reduces stress increases time and energy, which are always valuable commodities."

Reality, stress relief, self-improvement and emotional healing: these had more generally emerged in force as chief New Age goals in the 1980s. The explosive New Age movement is multifaceted, but on average the pursuits have tended to exalt a search for a more Authentic self and more Authentic experience in a modern society that seems to fail to offer it. The well-off baby boomers had always advertised themselves as the Real generation. But New Age philosophies have tended to reorient the quest for Reality away from society and the self—that is, from changing both one's head and the system—toward the Self *in* Society. And New Age adherents have recruited the countermodern definition of Nature as an essential and authoritative tool. The Nature Company's mission statement says: "Authenticity and knowledge are balanced with sufficient humor to give our customers an experience which makes them *feel good* about themselves and the world in which they live." At The Nature Company, you can construct an authentic, Real Self in an un-Real society. The whale and eagle calls on the *Glacier Bay* CD "create moods and emotions within us." Environmental Sounds CDs "will open your mind and awaken your heart." Nature is the source of Real emotion, Real thinking, Real feeling. To appreciate Nature here is to be a more Real person. It is to be a *better* person and the right *sort* of person.

Who can use Nature as a route to the Real? The use of Nature to define a certain kind of person recalls the fifties suburban lawn owners, and the English landowners who lounged in Natural postures in their own vast and Natural landscapes. The Nature Company brand of Nature appreciation can work best if you have the means to shop here, and to travel to Glacier Bay and other far wildernesses on your vacation. Like others before us, affluent baby boomers have tended to invest a lot of human social authority in our encounters with nature. We graft meanings onto nature to make sense out of modern middle-class life, but also define ourselves by what we think nature means. What better resource, then, to use to educate the baby boomers' children? Nature is also the source of Real values. The company's large, highly publicized kids' section usefully teaches children about the nonhuman natural world—but you can also use it to teach them how be the right sort of person, and how to join the human company of the Real. As the Company's Summer 1994 catalog assures us, "Kids are the original naturalists."

If The Nature Company's trademark sense of humor, or "whimsy," caters to the baby boomers' evolving parental desires, it also appeals directly to a consumer generation who once vowed notoriously, in an enduring gesture of self-identity, to remain forever young. "Pretend it's for the kid," the company advertised its butterfly raise-and-release kit. Spy Scope: "if the kid in you isn't quite a serious grown-up yet." Rubber noses, wild-animal cookies, *Scaly & Slimy, Everyone Poops*, gecko ties, bird-droppings T-shirts, UnpredictaBalls! Whimsy is a tricky meaning here. Laughter in the American tradition of Nature has been notably scarce—which is why John Waters could use anti-Nature so easily to get laughs. Not too many jokes in Thoreau: Nature and Reality must not be trivialized, so The Nature Company walks a fine line here. But the 1960s children of Nature have also always been the ironic lovers of Artifice—the keepers of the pink flamingo. Whether partial to Nature or Artifice, we've committed to a boundary between the two. As a source of laughs, the angelfish bathtub toys that look like real angelfish encourage the children of baby boomers to be at once Real children and initiates into Artifice. Kites, bubble kits, bat puppets and paint-a-snakes encourage the parents to remain ironic, young and playful, and to stay trustworthy past the age of thirty.

The store sounds like fun. And it is. And The Nature Company has both catered and served as monument to the no-Artifice definition of Nature as a key to the identity of my generation and class. Why, then, have some of us felt so uneasy? Why have the stores sparked ambivalence? I finger everything in the ning-ning bins, but maintain a cool reserve. Why have the stores felt "fake," "inauthentic" or "manipulative" to at least some of its patrons?

To begin with, The Nature Company has not sold nature. It has not sold forests, deserts and wetlands. It has sold meanings. And in the pool of changing, countermodern meanings, the most powerful and overarching has always been that Nature is *not* a changing set of human meanings. Nature, unlike everything else, is unchanging. It is absolute. It is stable, secure, tangible, rocklike, self-evident, definable, Real. Of course, we know that nature means certain things to us, such as "solitude" and "authenticity." But the meanings seem universal, indelible and unchanging: they're indigenous to the rocks and trees themselves. And shouldn't the meanings of Nature be for everyone?

But if you take the complete set of meanings and stack and shelve them together in one room, they can start to look like a stack of meanings. The definitions of Nature may inhere deeply in a plastic pink flamingo, but they are harder to see in the plastic bird. And in your garden or on a camping trip, where you are surrounded by what is undeniably tangible and real about nature, the countermodern definition of Nature feels securely unconstructed. It is safer, really, to shop for your gardening tools at the hardware store: my friend testified that if she had bought her pruning shears at Ace Hardware, it would not have felt like an "inauthentic" experience, nor would she have felt "manipulated." But here, when you are surrounded by thousands of "nature-oriented" products that "relate in some magical way" to nature, definitions of Nature begin to look a lot like definitions. And in this upscale venue, just down the hall from Neiman Marcus and Victoria's Secret, *whose* meanings these are becomes an almost palpable question. Of course, few of us have walked into The Nature Company, looked around, and said, "Aha, so the meaning of nature is not so self-evident, universal, or absolute after all." Rather, the response, I think, has often been closer to "wow." Nature stores have invited us in, but have planted the vague uneasiness that the meaningful Nature that we look for here, as an unchangeable Place Apart, is not necessarily what nature *is*—and that the Nature here actually says less about nature than about ourselves.

The meanings of a pigeon ballotine, a tern on a hat, and a plastic flamingo betray the same disconnections. But at a nature store, the disconnections and the constructedness of Nature—generally more safely hidden—all threaten to surface. The Nature Company and the nature-store clones that followed have engaged in a tricky and very ambitious pursuit. They have marketed a commodity—middle- to upperclass meanings of nature—to a class of consumers who nourish serious doubts that the product exists. The Nature Company has tapped flawlessly into the market for anatomically correct inflatable penguins. The pioneer nature store has been an excellent place to go to encounter what Nature has meant to "affluent middle-aged" Americans in the 1980s and into the 1990s. But this retail genre inevitably has bred a degree of mistrust among its target clientele.

Habitat

Yet in the 1980s, backed by CML capital, The Nature Company set out to expand into shopping malls, of all places—and their competitors followed suit. Why sell Nature or anti-Artifice at a site that is famous as a black hole for Artifice? Why hawk Authenticity at a locale whose reputation for genericness is so notorious that we call every mall on the continent "the mall"? And why the glitziest sites and the mega-malls? It is not difficult to predict where to find a Nature Company. In Denver, the Cherry Creek Mall. In St. Louis, the Galleria and Union Station. In Los Angeles, the Century City Shopping Center and the Beverly Center in Beverly Hills. In Orange County, South Coast Plaza. The Mall of America has one.

The logic lies surely in how malls work, and in the intricacies of the *mall's* particular worlds of meaning—and how these worlds have intertwined with the meanings of Nature. Shopping malls: Americans have called them "gardens of delight," "worlds of artifice" and "palaces of consumption." And since the 1950s, when the first enclosed centers began to dot the suburban landscape, they've been targets of derision, or at least ambivalence. Between 1957 and the mid-1970s, developers built fourteen thousand shopping malls to cater to the postwar affluence and the expanding suburban populations. With large open spaces and deliberately modern in design, most of these malls looked essentially like broad indoor avenues, with a few plants, that connected the "magnet" department stores at either end.

In 1979, Joan Didion branded them "toy garden cities in which no one lives but everyone consumes." Malls have been accused, before and since, of being identityless, un-Real, devoid of character and, along with TV, a major culprit in the postwar homogenization of American culture. With interstate highways, they have homogenized the American landscape. Lost along the corridors of chain-outlet shoe stores, you could be anywhere. The mall, as Frank Lloyd Wright has said about the postwar sprawl generally, is every place and no place.

In the 1980s, mall developers hired architects cross-country to outfit these installations with more individuality. The new designers gave face-lifts to most of the larger malls built in the sixties and seventies, injected the new eighties megamalls with more character, and designed the malls to be more upscale on average—and these are exactly the malls The Nature Company moved into. Many malls now look like European villages or Mexican haciendas. The corridor spaces are more mazelike, irregular and niched. The designers favored tropical settings, especially—in no small part because plants such as figs and rhododendrons grow well in climate-controlled indoor spaces. In other words, the ungeneric malls of the 1980s, like the Foot Locker stores, are essentially replicants. They simulate and connote other places. (The Los Angeles malls tend to simulate Los Angeles, a city notorious as both a simulation of place and an outsize shopping mall.) The Italian piazza and Caribbean courtyard are places out of place. Architects have gathered together the *meanings* of more Real-seeming places than suburbs and malls, mixing and matching as if the globe were a giant salad bar. And the replicants say less about the real places than about what consumers want them to mean. The 1992 Mall of America, Minneapolis's mall for the twenty-first century, contains within its ninety-six acres an "East Broadway" avenue, a mock European railway station, a seven-acre theme park with a Minnesota woodland motif, and the Rainforest Cafe, with live animals, waterfalls, fog and a "star-filled" sky.

The Nature Company has been a one-store global assemblage itself: it sells posters, videos and calendars of Alaska, Tanzania and the Galapagos. And most of the nature here is simulated: the plastic whales and sculpted giraffes, the inflatable penguins, the spiders on the T-shirts. The Nature Company markets nature out of place. You can buy African malachite earrings patterned on Indonesian designs. Here you can connect to the world's wild things close to home, because the company has installed similar assemblages in malls in thirty-four states and two Canadian provinces, in Australia, and in the giant malls in Japan's underground railway stations. The stores at South Coast Plaza (store no. 7), the St. Louis Galleria (no. 60) and the Century City Shopping Center (no. 21) stock the same *Virtual Nature* videos and inflatable globes. On a 1994 visit to the store at the breezy Century City center in Los Angeles, where The Nature Company faces Rand-McNally, a "map and travel store," I could choose to eat at the Market food court next door, at Bueno Bueno, Gulen's Mediterranean Cuisine, DeMartino's Pizzeria, Raja, La Crepe or Kisho An. On the store's other flank sat El Portal Luggage, two doors down from Toys International and within sight of the United Colors of Benetton. The "now playing" CD combined Western instrumental forms with Baka Pygmy music from the border of Congo and Cameroon. I sifted through the zebra- and panda-footprint stamps, but bought the polar bear.

The Nature Company makes sense here. If I harbor doubts about the mall as a suitable habitat, The Nature Company feels intuitively well-sited. Why? Since the

The Nation's Malls

THE FASHION CENTRE
AT PENTAGON CITY
Arlington, VA

BRIDGEWATER COMMONS
Bridgewater, NJ

OWINGS MILLS TOWN CENTER
Owings Mills, MD

late-nineteenth-century adventures (and misadventures) with bird hats and wild pigeons, Americans' encounters with wild nature have become as thoroughly disconnected from place, but also as intensively simulated, as malls themselves. Economic globalization, and explosive postwar advances in manufacturing and communications technologies, have made my generation's adventures more consistently long distance, and far more mediated. Even postwar nature lovers—who hike and camp, and make vacation pilgrimages to wild places—encounter wild nature more often in the everyday urban and suburban haunts of living rooms, shopping malls, magazines and TVs. Most of our daily encounters with nature transpire quite separately from real pieces of nature rooted in specific places. We have become globe coasters all. *Where* have we been looking for nature most often since the 1980s? Not in the "where" where we generally think of nature as being. It is not surprising that one of the more successful Nature Company stores, while not in a mall, has been in the Pittsburgh Airport.

Just as with the pink flamingo, we've used Nature Company totems to tell meaningful stories about where we live and who we are—as all humans do in their encounters with nature—but these totems often tell us markedly little about the pieces of nature. And yet, The Nature Company's stated mission is to connect us to nature—not disconnect us. And to be sure, postmodern globe coasting works both ways. The products teach their owners potentially a great deal about distant places and animals. The toy plastic whale in the Ocean Authentics Collection, for example, can convey information about the blue whale, and about the circumpolar oceans the species inhabits. What it basically does, however, is to bring a miniature, essentially accurate image of a whale into one's life. What one does with it is up to its new owner. To a child in suburban Chicago, the palm-size whale might look like an endangered blue whale, the largest animal that ever lived. And it might look like Jonah, Shamu, Monstro, the hero in *Free Willy* or a friend or enemy of a Mighty Morphin Power Ranger. The distance from the Pacific makes the whale unusually open to interpretation.

And if The Nature Company connects us less to nature itself than to what Nature *means*, the modern unmoored-ness of meanings has not been flatly undesirable. As always, modern complexities of geography and economics conveniently encourage a consumer's desire to make a piece of nature—or Nature itself—mean whatever one wants it to. Far from the ocean, the plastic whale reduces more readily to a motif, a feeling, an association, a meaning. The company's best-selling *Glacier Bay* CD comes with a booklet that reads: "ALASKA— . . . a superlative for . . . unbounded wilderness"—or as the catalog blurb reads, "Escape to Glacier Bay's arctic cathedrals." The CD is "for relaxation," one sales clerk told me—so I bought it. The music has a New Age dreamlike quality. It's a quiet, flowing mélange of flute, cello, whales, eagles and waves, that sounds not unlike the flute, cello, frogs, wrens and flowing water on the Costa Rica *Cloud Forest* CD. It's self-advertised mood music, in which the humpback whale makes a cameo appearance. From a boat in the Bay itself, would Alaska be relaxing? Isn't the far North notorious as mosquito country? I've been to a rain forest: in Peru, at least, the jungle is not relaxing. It requires alertness; it has mildew. In suburban somewhere, however, after a stressful day at work, in counterpoint to noise, enclosure and schedules—even if one reads the notes on natural history in the booklets—Glacier

Bay and a Central American rain forest easily reduce to meaningful abstractions such as Wilderness, Relaxation and Tranquility: the call of the humpback whale promotes human peace of mind. Distant landscapes and wild animals become ever more shadowy realities. And what better place to sell these abstractions of Nature and the Last Places than in the placeless vacuum of the mall?

And yet, Place—along with Reality and an Absolute Force—is among the most powerful in the set of meanings that the affluent baby boomers have invested in Nature. Place has been one of The Nature Company's most appealing commodities. "The Last Great Places": Nature counters the pervasive, troubling placelessness of modern (and postmodern) life that the mall so definitively represents. In this fast-paced, ever-changing world, we count on nature not only to stay constant in meaning but to stay put.

Just as collecting the many meanings of Nature into one store can plant the suspicion that Nature *is* a set of meanings, does this assemblage of the world's places suggest the actual rootlessness of our encounters with nature? Again, the store nearly unmasks our definitions as definitions. Again, "wow." The Nature Company connects me to Nature and Place, but it can also instill a sneaking sensation of detachment. You can *almost* see the contradiction—that the ways I *think* I connect to nature are the ways I *want* to connect to nature but are not the ways I actually *do*.

At the nature store, the meetings of the worlds of meaning in the Mall and Nature get more ironic and complex. The mall architects in the 1980s, of course, had converted the sixties and seventies malls into Mexican haciendas and New England fishing villages exactly to assuage countermodern angst about malls and the meltdown of Place. Not surprisingly, they added liberal new quantities of Nature. Skylights, greenery, fountains: the St. Louis Galleria's "garden court" has topiary bird mobiles and a fountain that is eight stores long. The face-lifts were designed precisely to attract the baby boomers—the new chief commanders of disposable income—who objected to the generic, placeless aura of the malls they grew up on. Build a fountain, they will come: mall developers installed Nature like a sign to the affluent thirty-somethings, saying this place is a Real Place, and it's for you.

The Nature Company took the design strategy to its logical extreme. The dark-hued slate-block entrance, and the stream flowing through an open window display: the exterior quickly became famous for its ability to immobilize shoppers, as if they had stumbled onto a landmark in a maze. Into the early 1990s, especially (before the designers of malls and other stores caught up with them), the store stood out. It looked like a distinctive Place. Inside, in contrast to the open and brightly lit interiors of its neighbors, The Nature Company looked more like sun and shadows, and not cluttered but intricately niched. The Wrubels deliberately set out to replicate a "dappled forest." And browsing here feels a bit akin to taking a nature walk in that forest. The company's strategists have instructed store managers to set products low on the shelves, out of their boxes, inviting shoppers to touch, experience. Videos attract browsers to stop and watch. Open the mineral drawers, turn the posters, put a quarter in the Rainforest Meter, read a book on the couch in the book nook, all to the accompaniment of Baka Pygmy music or bird tweets: the stores have promoted a mall version of a Thoreauvian outing. In the 1980s mall, the store felt like a sylvan refuge—a quiet glade amid the bright lights and echoes. To anyone at all anxious about malls, it could feel like a relief. "I suppose I should state," the *New York Times* columnist claimed his countermall bona fides as he reported on his surprisingly enjoyable first run-in with The Nature Company at the sprawling Bridgewater Commons, "that shopping bores me and malls make me yearn for the relative tranquillity of a dentist's chair." The Nature Company has attracted nature lovers precisely by inhabiting a notoriously placeless site.

THE CHERRY CREEK MALL STORE *in Denver*

The upscale mall boasts at least one more advantage as a logical home for nature stores. As Tom Wrubel has pointed out (in a 1986 interview for the *San Francisco Chronicle*), "There's nothing we sell here that [people] really need." The *Tranquility* moodtape may be meaningful, but it's been an optional item in most people's lives. And the upscale mall itself specializes in the strategic marketing of things we don't really need. It can be hard to find something you *do* need. Why, for example, in the vast acreage of the mall, is it so difficult to find a bar of Dial soap? The motives behind mall design lie in the answers to questions so many of us have asked. Why are there so few entrances? Where is the one map? Why is it so hard to find the restrooms? Why can't I ever remember which floor The Gap is on? And why can't any of us remember where we parked the car? Nearly every square inch of the mall, from the locations of stores to the curves in the hallways, hews to a science the shopping-center industry has been refining since the 1950s, in which "discourage direct navigation" reigns as the supreme law. It has been statistically proven that the longer we stay, the more we buy. Hence, no Dial. No drugstores, Safeway or dry cleaners: necessities encourage beeline, goal-oriented, quick-exit shopping. "It's a hard place to run in to for a pair of stockings," as a friend of Joan Didion's remarked. The upscale mall draws in shoppers (or "invitees," as the trade literature refers to us) through a few well-spaced entrances and keeps us rambling around inside—the current average mall visit is three hours—to stimulate

Sign for nature-based combination-museum-zoo-and-theme-park
at Ontario Mills mall, Ontario, CA

the 45 percent of total purchases in the mall that we make on impulse. After one's first run-in with The Nature Company, like any other store it can be difficult to relocate. In the mall, looking for nature can become a very literal search.

For a company that markets moodtapes and plastic polar bears—who intentionally sets out to find these?—the mall therefore is an optimal site. The architecture of malls has careened more than a few invitees through the company's doors. Inside the store itself, if you careen into the field hats while searching for the Rainforest Crunch, you may be tempted to buy one. Have patience, though. You will find the candy eventually, next to a telescope, though en route you may decide to buy a wildflower T-shirt and a wind-up dinosaur. The company has deployed mall-design savvy. Even the catalog has no index, and has been organized as much by color as by item. The search for items can be an outdoor adventure. Friends report that although they played with the toys and watched the videos, they didn't buy much—except for fish magnets, and a geode and the wind chimes. The design is so successfully antimall that patrons might not even notice when they have purchased something unnecessary.

Yet, the same patrons feel somehow "manipulated." But has The Nature Company manipulated us more objectionably than The Gap or The Banana Republic? It should not surprise us that the company speaks two languages: the language of Nature, Reality and Place, and the language of profits. It has to. The mall has sales-per-square-foot requirements for its tenants. The store can *feel* more manipulative, I think—because it hawks Nature, not jeans. If the very meanings the company markets can make me uneasy about what nature the company sells, and how and where we really connect to nature, I am a little suspicious that they sell it at all.

The main reason, after all, that we've been looking for nature in the mall is that the mall is the place where you buy things. And it's the buying and selling, I'm convinced, that engenders the greatest uneasiness. Why have we been looking for nature with our credit cards? After the *New York Times* columnist left the Bridgewater Commons, and while searching for his car in the parking lot, he experienced a troubling set of second thoughts—but not because he had forgotten the computer paper he had driven to the mall to buy or because "we bought something we didn't need and didn't mind a bit." Rather, he voiced a deep anxiety that many of the company's affluent clientele have shared: "Is it possible that people in our culture have become so estranged from nature that their only avenue to it is consumerism?"

Ecology

Americans spend a tremendous amount of time buying things. The ways we use a world of *consumerism*, to make meanings and to navigate modern life, are what makes the malls work. Shopping ranks second only to TV-watching as a leisure-time pursuit—but not every American watches TV. Even those of us who aren't thrilled about shopping still make frequent shopping trips, and have filled our homes, offices and cars with necessities, luxuries, gadgets, equipment, art, décor and knickknacks. We fill our lives with an abundance of *things*. In the early 1800s, when Taste emerged so forcefully as a route to middle-class identity, Americans used an ever-expanding cornucopia of consumer items to define themselves. After 1900, as the national economy grew increasingly dependent on consumer spending, buying things evolved into an ever more important way of moving through the world. And in the affluent post–World War II era, the baby boomers grew up more instinctively consumeristic than any prior generation. In the global-market, high-tech late twentieth century, Americans make only a tiny percentage of the items we personally use—and in an urban society of comparative anonymity, we use the things we buy to create ourselves. The clothes, the sound systems, the books, computers, cars and bumperstickers: we use these not only as key tools to work and to have fun, but also to act, think and communicate. Gifts, too—and one could argue that an upscale mall is an outsize gift arcade—have become essential and abundant fuel for social relationships. We give gifts to mark important events, to reward and motivate, to tell stories about the places we travel. And shopping itself can be as much a social outing as a quest for goods. Buying something is at once an economic act, a social act and an act of creativity and imagination. And it's been shown that many Americans prefer shopping to sex.

Baby boomers have approached the natural world, like everything else, intuitively as consumers. It is perfectly logical—even inevitable—to articulate a vision of nature, to learn about nature, to share our enthusiasms through the common arts of shopping for things, buying them, using and displaying them and giving them to others. The bird feeder imports Nature into one's life. We make the Yosemite calendar a daily utterance about what Nature means: Majesty, Solitude, Adventure, Escape. The ready-to-install waterfall marks the owner as the kind of Real person who knows and values what Nature means. A Saturday-afternoon browse through geodes, bat puppets and rain forest posters can be a value-forming experience, and fun, too—and with a friend or partner, an affirmation of shared values. On a birthday, an inflatable emperor penguin—in 1994, The Nature Company's best-selling inflatable—binds an adult gift giver to a child, fosters shared meanings, purveys values about people and animals and places from one person to another. Within the economic logic and routes to meaning in the late-twentieth-century United States, The Nature Company has been an excellent place to reiterate, enjoy and share one's commitments to nature. It has made perfect sense to connect to nature on a trip to the mega-mall.

If a run-in with The Nature Company sets one's consumer instincts into motion, the store can also trigger a nature lover's anticonsumer instincts. Many of us use Nature, too, to define who we are and to navigate the world. Nature means a countermodern Force, an antidote to modern life—and critics and enthusiasts alike have so often pegged consumerism as the economic and cultural lifeblood of modern American society. Simple, primitive and Natural, Nature is a palliative for modern materialism. Like the *Times* columnist, many Nature Company patrons define Nature as something we should experience rather than consume, and the whole store flashes NATURE like a neon warning sign. "Thoreau was right," the company has advertised their Survival Tool, which has twelve tools in one: "Simplify, simplify." Doesn't that feel contradictory? If I define myself using the things I buy, I define myself also by what I think Nature means. At The Nature Company, I am an anticonsumer consumer.

Again, "wow," in all its ambivalent glory. The definition of Nature that The Nature Company sells tells me Nature is separate from consumerism. And the store telegraphs that an essential way I connect to nature, and make it meaningful, is via consumerism. The Nature Company is nothing if not self-contradictory and ironic. And no ironies get more complicated here than those swirling around consumerism. The company has countered anticonsumer instincts—"It looks so mercantile," Tom Wrubel said during the 1986 interview, as he took down a "cash only" sign in the San Jose store—in ways that are both well-intentioned and very strategic. Essentially, The Nature Company has positioned the store as a site for *better* consumerism. To begin with, it emphasizes "quality" consumer products—lifelike bronze frogs for $995, for example, rather than plastic lawn creatures—with a rhetoric that echoes Taste, and urges consumers to exercise restraint on quality, if not on quantity. The company makes concerted efforts, too—and publicizes them avidly—to sell recycled products, such as luminaria, "waste not" stationery and flying-animals wrapping paper. Riding the crest of Green Consumerism in the 1980s, The Nature Company has divided acts of consumption into good and bad. A customer can put a quarter in the Rainforest Meter and send her money off to a worthy cause. You can buy home recycling kits and books about tropical deforestation. A percentage of profits goes to the Nature Conservancy. Here, you can consume to preserve nature. At the same time, in the Mall of America or South Coast Plaza—a monument to overconsumption—it can be hard not to conceive of shopping as a quantity more than a quality experience. If there are hundreds of ways to shop for a better world, do we shop too much? And this, I'll venture, points to the most stubborn irony, and to the most troubling and deeply buried source for "wow." Every "nature-oriented" product—recycled, nonrecycled, "quality," nature-preserving, Nature Conservancy-supporting—has literally been manufactured *from* nature. An inflatable plastic penguin constitutes approximately the same natural resources and energy as the utterly non-grata plastic pink flamingo. Who thinks about that? Looking for the meanings of Glacier Bay from my living room, I so readily lose track of real facts about the actual Arctic landscape—yet doubly ironic, its oil might be in my stereo system, or in the CD itself. Who thinks of the whale calls on the *Glacier Bay* CD as Petroleum more than Freedom? Has The Nature Company connected people to nature? Absolutely: perhaps too much. And it would be impossible not to find nature at the mall: Nature provides the raw materials

the malls are made from. Here, the definition of Nature as a Place Apart—as separate from modern consumerism—not only tells us little about what nature is and where we actually connect to it. It also actively *hides* our connections, as the definition always has done. And can I really be a better consumer if I fail to identify my connections to nature?

The mall itself historically has been designed to disguise all these connections, natural and economic, to the world outside. Architects and managers deliberately sequester all traces of producing, sending and receiving: for example, they relegate business offices to the basement, and truck in goods in the early morning hours before the invitees arrive to shop. They have actively set out to erase connections—to encourage us to focus on the meanings we make, but not on our complicity in the economic networks through which people convert nature and human labor into the stuff and sustenance of everyday lives. As Leah Hager Cohen has written about our modern brand of fetishism: "The notion of connections seems charming, but not quite real." Retail stores, too, set out to create slices of magic that bear few traces of where products came from, other than "made in China," of how they got to suburban Chicago, or where your money will go after you trade it for a shirt. "Gardens of delight," "palaces of consumption." The Nature Company calls its stores a "magical space." The back rooms, however, are windowless spaces of steel and concrete stacked with boxes floor to ceiling. And while the nature store may be Oz, like the mall it is also a flow chart.

As the company has detailed its own workings in an informational sheet for the sales staff: "Although the public would hardly be aware of it, there is, in fact, an order to the magic in the form of eight professionally managed buying departments." The Nature Company has sold products from Brazil, China, Zaire, Portugal, Chile and the Philippines, among other countries. All the products are shipped to a distribution center in Kentucky, which in 1994 was reshipping them to 146 stores in 4 countries. Profits from these products have gone far too many places to map, but among other places: the eight buying departments; 850 sales employees (in 1994); a vice president of real estate development; a director of public relations, image and special events; a company naturalist; mall managers and leasing agents; advertising agencies; the CEO and the president of CML, who earned $1.38 million and $1.37 million, respectively, in fiscal year 1993; and among CML's stockholders, Reader's Digest, the Ford Foundation, my former phone company US West, and the Bank of Tokyo, IBM and GE.

"Commodity consumption," the historian Jean-Christophe Agnew has written, has not "enhanced our appreciation of the remote consequences of our acts or . . . clarified our responsibilities for them." During my research visits, I spent $180.18 at The Nature Company—mostly on gifts. The *Glacier Bay* CD (recorded in San Francisco, with notes printed in Canada), a polar bear stamp (made in China) and other items connect me to the working conditions and everyday lives of people worldwide who mine, plant, assemble and transport the company's materials and products. A hummingbird feeder on my back porch connects me to the CML Group chairman, who in the 1980s delved into his $1 million-plus salary to contribute to his friend George Bush's political campaigns. These items also connect me to nature—to the abundant pieces of nature worldwide that The Nature Company's operations touch on, and that stockholder companies mine with the profits. To shop at The Nature Company has been to plug into the flows of energy and resources, economic power and influence that have defined the American capitalist economy in the 1980s and 1990s. And one of the touchstones of this economy has been the ravenous global consumption of natural resources. Like any successful company, The Nature Company has expanded as rapidly as possible. In 1992, *Fortune* named CML one of the best hundred growth stocks—one of seven to make the list two years in a row—and *Money* named it one of the seven best growth buys. Perhaps the perfect metaphor for The Nature Company is a famous outdoor sculpture by Isamu Noguchi at South Coast Plaza, called "California Scenario"— a strikingly serene landscape of rock and cactus and water. If you turn around, you see its perfect reflection in the thirty-story glass walls of the Great Western Bank.

And who controls the bulk of this economic activity? The class of shoppers the stores have drawn—*whose* meaningful Nature the company has marketed—are exactly the affluent baby boomers who, coming into their economic power in the 1980s, now own and invest substantial capital and reap the material benefits. CML's target consumers, in the words of *Business Week*, are the "folks [with] lots of money to spend and a seemingly irrepressible urge to spend it": we have come to control, according to a 1988 *Forbes* profile of CML, "a great deal of the economy's discretionary income." If Americans in the late twentieth century are globe coasters all, the globe has increasingly belonged to my generation of higher-income baby boomers not only figuratively but literally. The *Glacier Bay* CD channels serenity into my leisure hours, and channels profits from Alaskan oil mining into my portfolio. As Susan Davis has concluded, of her own visits to Sea World, the kind of person who has appreciated Nature is likely to be the kind of person who has consumed more nature than most.

The very people who have used an idea of a Nature Out There to define who we are, and to navigate the hallmarks and confusions of postwar American life, are also the people who use nature the most. And evasions are themselves a way of navigating. We've used Nature to circumvent our own complicity in the serious modern problems we critique. And here, at last, are the ur-ironies that lie at the heart both of the new nature stores and of the affluent baby boomers' encounters with nature since the 1980s. The Nature Company has marketed twelve thousand products that, on one hand, have sustained an American middle- to upper-class definition of Nature that mitigates the materialism and artifice of modern capitalist society—and at the same time, have sustained, through the creation of artifice, the capitalist overconsumption of resources that underpins American middle- to upper-class life. The Nature Company constitutes a store-size contradiction between how we want to connect to nature and how we actually do, and between what we want Nature to be and what nature actually is. It is also a store-size monument to the convenience, however willful or half-conscious, of these contradictions.

Exit

It's exactly these contradictions that prompt me to say "wow." As the well-off baby boomers have acquired more economic power, the contradictions have become more powerful. And The Nature Company is a rare place where these contradictions *almost* speak to us. When I hike or cross-country ski, or go to the park or tend my garden, these ironies tend not to chase after me. But in a nature store, they practically catch up. I feel ambivalent about what nature these stores are hawking—and where they do it and whether they should do it at all—but mostly I am uneasy about myself, and my own attraction. I fear that my meanings for nature, all on sale here, contradict the actual whats, wheres and hows of my connections to the natural world. At the heart of my ambivalent "wow" lies not so much the nature store itself, but a vague, uneasy suspicion that the store is a logical place for me to be.

And I think "wow," as a one-word analysis, sums up my uneasiness about The Nature Company more effectively than "contradiction." "Wow" projects more of the desire, confusion, utter meaning and depth of feeling that *drive* the contradictions. "Wow" betrays a certain confusion of intention. It suggests a murkiness of desires. What do I really want? How do I really *want* to connect to nature? The contradictions make me uneasy because they threaten the definitions of Nature as a Place Apart that are so powerfully meaningful to me. But they are disturbing also because I *want* to connect to wild nature, and to understand it, and to not destroy it. I want to counter—not strengthen or indulge—my own complicity in economic excesses, in social inequities and in ecological devastations. Yet how much? Am I willing to yield these meanings? Do I really want to see humans and cows and cats on the posters here? Do I want my definitions of nature to help me track the routes by which I convert nature to useful artifice? In the early 1990s, The Nature Company itself installed "field stations" in some of its stores, and stocked them with maps and guides for nearby wild areas—but would shoppers want to see maps for where the water comes from and where the garbage goes? In the 1990s, I think, there are few better routes in American culture to examine these desires and intentions than through television.

Practical decisions about nature stores remain. Is The Nature Company really "a gracious balance between commerce and environmental consciousness"? Should I be using the sounds of Glacier Bay to relax? And should I buy the inflatable penguin for my nephew on his birthday? These turn out to be extraordinarily wide-ranging, conflicted questions. In the 1990s, the marketing of Nature continues to expand. Nature's Jewelry, The Natural Selection, Forever Green, Into the Woods, The Last Best Place, NorthStyle, Coldwater Creek, the Rainforest Company, Serengeti, the Endangered Species Store. American Wilderness Zoo and Aquariums are now appearing in malls cross-country. In 1996, the Mall of America posted a large sign: OCEAN UNDER CONSTRUCTION. The definition of Nature as a Place Apart seems only to continue to grow more compelling. The contradictions have gotten stronger. The questions get more expansive.

42

Artificial Assimilation

Representational Politics of the Gayby Boom

MARGARET PRICE

Five years ago, I wrote an indignant letter to the *New York Times Magazine* expressing my hope for some lesbian-parent visibility (they had just published a special issue on motherhood, and had failed to include any representations of queer moms). Well, be careful what you wish for.

Now queer parents[1] are all over the media: Custody disputes in Florida. Adoption documentaries on PBS and Cinemax. Smiling, sweaty dykes giving birth on *Friends* and *Queer As Folk*. And with the recent progress toward the legalization of gay marriage, we can expect even more queering of the crib in the months and years to come. This surge of attention to queer parents mirrors a rise in actual numbers. According to the nonprofit Adoption Family Center, in 1976 there were only about 500,000 biological children of gay and lesbian parents. As noted by Suzanne Johnson and Elizabeth O'Connor in *The Gay Baby Boom: The Psychology of Gay Parenthood*, as of 2002, as many as 14 million kids (biological, foster,

---

[1] By "queer parents" I mean parents who are queer, as opposed to parents of queer kids. Queer parents, as this article loosely defines them, are those whose sexuality or gender is bent in some way. This includes gays and lesbians, transpeople, bi- and pansexuals, queer parents who had kids while straight, and Marilyn Manson, who is not a parent, but we can always hope.

and adoptive) have at least one gay or lesbian parent.[2] As David Elliott of the National Gay and Lesbian Task Force said proudly in a 2001 *Washington Post* article headlined "Lesbians Find Haven in Suburbs," "We are indeed everywhere."

But who is this "we," and how are they represented? If you refer to the available media images of queer parents, what do you see? I've spent the last couple of months reading magazines, searching the web, talking to queer parents, and watching innumerable episodes of *Queer As Folk* on DVD. And from where I sit, it seems that queer parents—in both fictional and nonfictional representations—are an awfully *Brady*-like bunch.

They're predominantly white, middle- or upper-class, and partnered; moreover, they usually don't push boundaries of gender or sexuality. For example, "Lesbians Find Haven in Suburbs" eagerly documents all the ways in which lesbians are discovering their inner soccer moms: "They're active in the PTA of their daughter's school," reads the piece. "They drive a minivan and help at block parties. Neighborhood children flock to the huge trampoline in their backyard." Now, there's nothing diabolical about helping at block parties or having a trampoline, but the real point of the article seems to be to underscore what these moms are not doing: namely, shaking things up.

Queer parents tend to be portrayed in ways that play up their normativity. "We're just like you" is the rallying cry—or, depending upon who is producing the images, "They're just like us." Author and columnist Dan Savage, who adopted a son with his partner, Terry, has commented on the pressure that's placed on queer parents to seem as uncontroversial as possible. "Some [gays and lesbians] felt that Terry and I—young, urban types—weren't the 'right' kind of gay couple to be adopting," he explained in an online interview with ABC News. "They felt that, due to the political controversy surrounding gay men and lesbians adopting, that older, 'safer,' cozier gay couples should adopt." Although in that interview Savage didn't elaborate on what "safer" and "cozier" might mean, he does say more in his 1999 book, *The Kid*, which details his and Terry's experience. One objection came from a queer activist who argued, in Savage's words, that gay adoptive parents should be "men in their forties, together at least eight years, monogamous, professional, irreproachable, and unassailable." Dan and Terry failed to meet the specs of this hypervirtuous profile on a number of counts, particularly given Savage's career as a sex columnist. Writing about bondage and anal fisting, apparently, does not mix with parenting. Or isn't supposed to.

This is a conflict familiar to many groups battling for civil rights: Is the best strategy to assimilate with mainstream culture, or to try to radicalize it? Often, the urge is to downplay difference and therefore avoid conflict. But the fact is, queer parenting is itself a paradox. It's both conventional and radical, a gesture toward joining mainstream culture and a way to transform it. Johnny, who narrates the 2002 documentary *Daddy & Papa*, and who adopts two sons with his

---

[2]A couple disclaimers about these numbers: First of all, statistics overwhelmingly refer to parents who are "gay or lesbian," with virtually no numbers available on parents with other queer identities (e.g., bisexual or trans). Also, although the gayby boom is to some degree a real boom, it's worth noting that the rising numbers are also due to increasingly accurate data collection. But, however flawed its outlines, a new demographic is undeniably emerging.

partner, William, in the course of the film, sums up this perspective: "My most revolutionary act would be the most traditional thing in the world."

How does this paradox emerge in mainstream portrayals of queer parents? In a word, rarely. Most representations either explicitly or implicitly focus on the seemliness of their subjects. It's almost as if, having decided to focus on one freak factor (the queerness), those shaping the stories feel compelled to keep everything else (race, class, gender, family structure) as bland and unremarkable as possible.

The Unbearable Whiteness of Being a Queer Parent

QUEER PARENTS NOW HAVE THEIR VERY OWN GLOSSY magazine, *And Baby*, and the images on the pages of its May/June 2003 issue look like a family reunion in Iowa. On the contributors page, for instance, seven people are pictured, all of whom are white; in the table of contents, photos of no fewer than 17 people appear, only one of whom even *might* be a person of color. Television isn't much better: The parents in the Lifetime movie *What Makes a Family*, HBO's dyke drama *If These Walls Could Talk 2*, Showtime's *Queer As Folk*, the ubiquitous *Friends*, and the Cinemax documentary *He's Having a Baby* are, to a person, overwhelmingly Caucasian.

And the problem goes beyond quantity and into quality. Most portrayals of queer parents not only underrepresent parents of color, they downplay the ways that race can complicate the lives and choices of queer parents and their kids. This deficiency is unnervingly apparent throughout *He's Having a Baby*, which follows a white father, Jeff Danis, as he adopts a Vietnamese son. Danis decides early in the film that he wants to adopt a child from abroad, but fails to make even a peep about the issues inherent in cross-cultural and cross-racial adoption. Instead, his concerns are shown to be shallow to the point of absurdity. To wit: "The pictures of kids from China and Guatemala were very cute," Danis reports, "but the one from Cambodia, the kid wasn't that cute. So I'm like, Oh, god, what if I don't get a cute kid? He has to be a cute kid. Or at least kind of cute. He can't be ugly. I can't have an ugly kid." As far as I can tell, this is meant to be a flattering portrayal of Danis, but with biographers like that, who needs enemies?

The racial/cultural questions that come up over the course of *He's Having a Baby* are all but brushed off, and Danis's apparent ignorance of them is never questioned by the filmmakers. In a scene where he is deciding on a future son, Danis holds up two photos provided by the adoption agency and explains, "One is called Duong Dinh Tan, but I'm going to change his name to Bruce, or Harvey. And this one's name is Lam Xuan Chinh, who might be named Bob." (Ultimately, he and his partner go with the name Joe.) Of course, it's fine to rename your adoptive baby, but here it's done in a boorish, let's-get-that-scary-foreign-name-out-of-here kind of way. (In another scene, Danis takes a poll at his office to help him choose his kid, and when he asks office mates for a "celebrity look-alike" for one of the pictures, someone shouts out, "The Little Emperor!")

Fortunately, the documentary *Daddy & Papa*, which was shown both at the 2002 Sundance Film Festival and more recently on PBS, is an exception. It follows four families, each of which has one or two gay men as parents. Three of the families have adopted black children; of these three families, only one includes a nonwhite parent. (The fourth family is two white men who had a daughter through a white surrogate mother.) Instead of glossing over the issue as a common consequence of the foster care and adoption system (as, for instance, Rosie O'Donnell does when publicly discussing her adoptive children), *Daddy & Papa* takes a serious look at this phenomenon. One of the white parents, Kelly, notes that he deliberately adopted brothers so that his sons, who are black and Latino, would each have a family member of the same race. Another parent, William, who is biracial, comments on the politics of white parents adopting children of color: "I have mixed feelings about it. I think a lot of these [white] men believe that they can just raise African-American kids in a color-blind way, so that they don't really have to deal with race, and as long as there's love, it shouldn't matter. Well, that's bullshit. I mean, the reality is that their child is going to be treated differently." *Daddy & Papa* presents all four families in a highly positive light, but doesn't offer pat solutions or bromides.

An unnerving side effect of parents choosing children, whether they are flipping through catalogs of foster children or of potential sperm donors, is that the racist attitudes underlying so much mainstream discourse suddenly pop out. For example, there's the third segment of HBO's *If These Walls Could Talk* 2,[3] which stars Ellen DeGeneres and Sharon Stone as Kal and Fran, two Southern California dykes with a pronounced case of baby fever. The most bizarre moment in this short film comes when Fran proposes to Kal, "Maybe we should think about having an ethnic baby. Ethnic babies are so beautiful." Given the dafiness of this comment (all babies are "ethnic," folks), not to mention its conventional racist attitude that babies of color are somehow ornamental, it's hard to discern its purpose. Is it meant unproblematically? Or perhaps to show that queer adoptive parents are susceptible to the same foibles as straight ones? Hard to say; the issue is not discussed any further.

. . . And the Unbearable Wealth

ACCORDING TO MOST POP CULTURE REPRESENTATIONS, not only are queer parents overwhelmingly white, they're also extraordinarily well-off. One of the more egregious examples I've seen, among fictional representations, is *Walls* 2. Neither Fran nor Kal appears to be employed. However, they live in a large, well-appointed house, drive an SUV, and apparently have no concerns about undertaking a project whose dollar-suckage per month will run them somewhere between a car payment and a mortgage. Sitting in their kitchen next to a brushed-aluminum refrigerator, among yards of glowing blond-wood cabinetry, they get on the phone with a sperm bank. Kal's end of the conversation goes like this: "We want it. Yes. We want it. All of it! All of it! How much is it? Wow. Okay, whatever."

Just to put this dialogue in perspective, sperm banks charge between $150 and $300 for a single vial. Apparently, these dykes are in a position to order thousands of dollars' worth of jizz without thinking twice about it. *Walls* 2 concludes when

---

[3]The three segments that compose this film are separate stories. When I refer to *Walls* 2 from here on, I mean the third segment, which takes place in 2000

Kal and Fran discover that they are pregnant after their fourth attempt. They do a dance of victory together in their bathroom (which, in case you're interested, has hardwood floors, a sink shaped like a large calla lily, and walls of blue tile and textured concrete).

The narrative struggle focuses solely upon whether Fran and Kal are able—biologically—to get pregnant. Although they're shown making multiple attempts, expressing frustration at their lack of success, and finally stepping up their efforts by visiting a fertility specialist, all of this is untrammeled by financial constraints. Their upper-middle-class standing allows them—and, by extension, viewers—to ignore the problems that might arise in a more complex (i.e., less moneyed) scenario. Thus, the audience can cheer wholeheartedly for them without having to consider difficult questions such as: Do Fran and Kal have health insurance? Can one of them cover the other through domestic partnership? Does their policy have implicit penalties for using donor sperm (for instance, a required 12-month waiting period in which they must try to get pregnant before any coverage kicks in)? What options are open to the gals if they can't afford that nice fertility specialist—or the sperm sperm bank in the first place? How much does second-party adoption cost, and is it even legal in the state where they live? What safeguards can they put in place if Kal can't adopt Fran's baby, and how much would the legal fees for those safeguards run?

Admittedly, *Walls 2* would be as dull as dirt if it addressed every one of those questions. But the film avoids the topic of money to such an extreme that Fran and Kal seem to exist in a sunny, airbrushed paradise where tanks of frozen sperm, helpful medical professionals, and surgical procedures simply appear for the taking. And this omission, in turn, allows the heterosexist policies and laws that are built into our medical and legal systems to go unnoticed.

On the nonfiction side, *He's Having a Baby* once again disappoints. Potential dad Danis, who is "gay, nearing 50," is a Hollywood (do I sense a pattern?) talent agent who has discovered a sudden longing to have a child. The opening scenes of the film are taken up with luscious shots of his home, which includes an in-ground swimming pool, abstract sculptures, and enough square footage of hardwood floor to play roller hockey. Much of the film's action takes place in his BMW, from which he conducts impatient, agency conversations on the phone while driving from adoption interview to adoption interview. A later sequence shows his partner, Don, mulling over the idea of having a child. It's hard to tell whether the directors meant this montage cynically or not, but it's framed as a series of pensive shots of Don and Jeff on vacation, each with a subtitle to identify the posh locale: Saint Barts. Palm Springs. The Hamptons. Big Sur. When Danis eventually gets on the telephone to inform the adoption agency which of two Vietnamese orphans he wants, the conversation sounds disturbingly as if he is purchasing a piece of real estate: "I'm going to go for Lam Xuan Chinh. . . . Karen, thanks so much, I'll be back in touch with you real soon. Let's put a hold on Lam Xuan Chinh."

These representations of free-spending queer parents are problematic in that they simply don't mention the issue that is uppermost in so many parents' minds: How the fuck am I going to afford this? When parents get pregnant for free (i.e., sperm meets egg without any further complications), money tends to become an issue after conception. But for queers, money is often a barrier to getting sperm near egg in the first place. Inseminating with sperm from a sperm bank runs—depending on where you live and what kind of specimens you want—between $300 and $1,000 a month. This might be manageable if one could count on getting pregnant immediately, but the average number of tries before conception, using frozen sperm, is between 6 and 12.[4] Adoption is still pricier, usually costing between $10,000 and $20,000. And surrogacy costs the most of all, generally coming in at more than $30,000. Even if you're lucky enough to go the cheap route—that is, you possess a healthy reproductive system and a male friend who is willing to deliver his sperm into that system by some means or other—you're still looking at legal fees for a donor agreement and, if you're partnered, second-party adoption.

I can't find one example of queer parenting in the media in which the issue of money is addressed in any depth. There are occasional glancing references; for example, in *Daddy & Papa* it's mentioned that adopting hard-to-place foster children is less expensive than private adoption or trying to adopt a more "desirable" (i.e., young, white, healthy) baby. And in the Lifetime movie *What Makes a Family*, although there is no discussion between the two dykes of the cost of sperm-bank sperm, some attention is given to the financial strain that ensues after one parent becomes ill with systemic lupus. But the most common approach is simply to ignore money as a factor. Asked by an *Advocate* interviewer why more gay men don't have children, actor and parent B.D. Wong responds, "I guess a lot of gay people have issues with their parents, and that must color their ideas about whether they want to be parents or not." Well, sure—but could it also be, perhaps, that they don't have $10,000 lying around?

Queer Queers

DID YOU KNOW THAT TRANSPEOPLE HAVE BABIES? YOU wouldn't, if you got your information from television, films, and most print media. Generally, representations of queer parents show them to be extremely gender-determinate gay men or lesbian women, without a hint of genderfuck anywhere in the picture. Sometimes this phenomenon is jacked up to the level of unintentional self-parody, as with the super-femmey lesbian moms in *Friends* and *Queer As Folk*. More often, it's simply taken for granted.

Every once in a while, though, a queer queer shows up with a kid. One instance is the 2002 Norwegian documentary *Alt Om Min Far (All About My Father)*, which traces a series of conversations between Esben/Esther, a doctor who identifies as both a man and a women, and his/her son Even, the filmmaker, who struggles to reconcile his own view of his father with the out transperson who now confronts him. Another example comes from the *New York Times Magazine*, which in 2001 ran an article titled "When Debbie Met Christina, Who Then Became Chris," about a transman, Chris, and his partner, Debbie. When the article was published, the couple had a 4-year-old daughter and were expecting another child in a few months.

---

[4]Since there are few studies of queer parents, and those that exist often contradict one another, many of the numbers I've collected for this article are approximate. Medical facts have been checked with at least one OB/GYN.

Both *All About My Father* and "When Debbie Met Christina" pay substantial attention to the ways that genderqueer life is materially different from conventionally gendered life. While they don't paint being genderqueer as either tragic or bizarre, they do acknowledge that it's a different row to hoe, both as a person and as a parent. Esben/Esther and Even, for instance, are shown engaged in passionate debate about the ways that Esben/Esther's shifting gender identification has affected both their lives: Esben/Esther insists that his/her son accept him/her as he/she is now, and Even insists, just as firmly, that he cannot accept Esben/Esther as anything but a man and a father. Admirably, the film refuses to conclude their struggle with a pat resolution. Instead, it ends in a kind of stalemate, which is then further tempered by an outtake, shown with the credits, in which Even and Esben/Esther hug each other, and Even asks half-jokingly, "Are you all right?"

In "When Debbie Met Christina," the couple is described with care; the story doesn't simply check off a diversity box for the magazine (the article was part of a special issue called "Love in the 21st Century"), but constructs a full and complicated portrait of Debbie's and Chris's lives. For instance, author Sara Corbett notes that when Chris transitioned from female to male, Debbie's sexuality and identification were affected as well. "I really questioned who I was, suddenly, this lifelong lesbian living with a man," Debbie explains. And Corbett observes, astutely, that the "daily contradictions" of genderqueer life are faced by Debbie as well as Chris. As parents, Debbie and Chris build the genderqueer aspects of their lives into their raising of their daughter, Hannah. Corbett explains, for instance, that Debbie and Chris tend to "switch the genders of the characters in Hannah's children's books to keep things more fluid, more equitable—and as they like to see it, more true to life."

Both *All About My Father* and "When Debbie Met Christina" are sensitive portrayals of genderqueer parents, but both are third-person accounts, narrated in the first case by the genderqueer person's son and in the second case by a journalist. A first-person account comes courtesy of a 2000 *Village Voice* article, in which writer Patrick Califia describes his own queer family: "We are both transgendered men (female-to-male or FTM), and my boyfriend [Matt] is the mother of my child." Not only does he identify his family's queerness, but Califia spends considerable time exploring the implications of being the queer dads of a baby, one of whom gave birth to the child. One stereotype he refutes is the notion that queer dads will meet their fiercest opposition from straight people; in fact, Califia reports, his and Matt's straight acquaintances "have been pretty sweet." Their most hostile responses have been from FTMS they know. (Members of an online FTM group, for instance, "started calling Matt by his girl name, because real men don't get pregnant.") Other transpeople have been more supportive, however, Califia notes; in fact, many FIMS have contacted them to ask about the experience of getting pregnant and coparenting. Califia's article goes beyond "We're here, we're queer, we gave birth" and explores much deeper implications of identity that are shared not only by transgendered parents but by queer parents as a whole.

In a different article, originally published in the magazine *Skin Two*, Califia discusses BDSM,[5] another queer-parenting issue that doesn't get much play (so to speak). Outraged at the common assumption that people who are part of the leather community cannot also be responsible parents, Califia points out that this assumption relies upon a simplistic view of leatherpeople as "two-dimensional caricatures of vanilla people's erotic paranoia, emerging from our warrens only after dark, always clad in body-hugging fetish gear, having no real lives outside of public dungeon clubs and 'violent' pornography." As much as any parent, Califia argues he is perfectly capable of drawing appropriate boundaries between his sex life and his life as a parent. In fact, he maintains, his experience as a responsible member of the leather community is an asset, because it has required him to develop qualities such as empathy, patience, flexibility, and, above all, the ability to negotiate relationships in an open and ethical way. Califia's assertion that pervs can be parents—and good parents—is welcome and rare. However, because his article appeared in a fetish magazine, this point remains confined to a sort of journalistic ghetto, and does not emerge in mainstream representations of queer parents.

Most portrayals of queer parents keep sex out of the picture; when it does appear, it tends to be handled with extreme, well, normativity. The Fran-and-Kal segment of *Walls 2*, for example, shows them naked in bed, but the sexual activity resembles an animated Hallmark card, with golden light suffusing the scene as they kiss each other's smooth bodies and Dido croons "Thank You" in the background. Similarly prissy action occurs between Lindsay and Melanie, the dyke-mom couple on *Queer As Folk*. Occasionally they're naked in bed together, but, as with Fran and Kal, pretty much all that happens is in the realm of (not to put too fine a point on it) tongue-plus-nipple. This is partly to do with gender (girl-on-girl sex on television or in movies is often presented as cleaner, simpler, somehow *nicer* than boy-on-boy), but more to do with the fact that most portrayals of queer parents seem to fear allowing them any complexity as people, and that precludes showing them as individuals with active and varied sex lives. Most straight parents represented in the media don't appear to have active and varied sex lives, either, so I would guess this to be a final frontier of queer-parent representation.

Making the Baby

PERHAPS BECAUSE THE PRODUCTION OF OFFSPRING by queers so rarely involves sexual intercourse, media representations of queer parents seem positively obsessed by the issue of where the baby comes from. The swell of media attention accompanying the gayby boom focuses not on queer parents who already have children, or queer stepparents joining existing families, but queer people who are making or obtaining children (usually babies). In other words, what you will see on television, in film, and in print is the *procurement* of babies by queer parents. If you're a 37-year-old mother of two, you've just left your husband, and you're trying to coordinate babysitting schedules with dating your first girlfriend, not to mention the issue of coming out to your kids—well, there are plenty of you out there, but your story's not going to show up next week on *Queer As Folk*.

---

[5]BDSM is an acronym that refers to three pairings: bondage/discipline, dominance/submission, and sadism/masochism. People who practice some variation of BDSM are often said to be part of "the leather community," the phrase I'll use here.

So, for instance, on *QAF*, we have Lindsay, fresh from labor, being visited in the hospital by the donor dad. In *Walls 2*, we have Fran leaping around her house with a turkey baster while Kal visits the sperm bank to pick up the specimen. In *Daddy & Papa* and *He's Having a Baby*, we see gay men deciding to adopt, choosing names, meeting their kids for the first time, and learning their way around a Snugli. In his *Advocate* interview, B.D. Wong delivers the apotheosis of this attitude: "There are no accidental kids of gay parents. Every single gay parent passionately wanted to be a parent." Oh, really? Did you ask the single dyke on food stamps who has three kids from a former marriage? Or the gay man who just came out to his two teenage kids? Wong's comment assumes that gay parenting involves a predetermined order of events: First, be gay; second, decide to parent; third, become a parent. Scenarios in which the order of these steps may be shuffled are erased.

Not that people who come out after having children didn't want their kids, but let's remember, not all children of queer parents sprout magically in the petri dish. Some of them are already hanging around the house, asking, "What's rimming?" or squirming during the coming-out talk and then saying dismissively, "What*ever*, Mom, everyone at my school is bisexual." However, most stories about queer parenting center upon a single glimpse: the moment of becoming. It's as though the plot arc of TLC's *A Baby Story*—pregnancy, baby shower, birth, next episode—has taken over the queer-parenting narrative. Sometimes there are variations—in adoption stories, the peak moment is not birth but the first contact between parent and child—but the central focus remains the same.

A similar proclivity is demonstrated by the pictures of queer parents (sometimes author photos, sometimes cover art) on books such as Rachel Pepper's *The Ultimate Guide to Pregnancy for Lesbians*, Judy Dahl's *River of Promise: Two Women's Story of Love and Adoption*, and the aforementioned *The Gay Baby Boom*. In these pictures, parents are shown with their newly procured babies, which are cuddled lovingly against a cheek or held up like a prize. It's a money shot, with baby as climax.

So what's going on here? Why this obsession with getting the goods, and the simultaneous downplaying of living with the result? Again, it seems to stem from an impulse to make things as normal and as unqueer as possible. The parents in these portrayals mouth platitudes that align them with depressing heteronormative myths, such as the belief that a potential parent should feel empty and lonely without a child. "Without [parenthood]," mourns Jeff in *He's Having a Baby*, "I feel very empty. Without it, I feel very incomplete." The next shot shows him walking sadly on his treadmill, while in the background we hear the opening bars of "You're Nobody 'til Somebody Loves You." As the film goes on, Jeff's partner, Don, is shown to be reluctant to have children. However, he agrees to the adoption of little Joe (né Lam Xuan Chinh), and much of the latter half of the film is taken up with heartwarming scenes that show Don's conversion to delighted dad. Parenthood, according to this scenario, is not only something that all normal adults should desire; it's something that the appearance of a small, soft baby will magically make desired. This myth insults those (queer or straight) who choose not to have children; it also insults those who choose to have children for reasons other than to fill a yawning void in their lives.

But there's more going on. Joe becomes just another consumer acquisition to go with Jeff's treadmill, artworks, and potted palms; children in general become yet another means by which queers can be folded into a larger, homogeneous American culture—one in which there are differences, sure, but nothing that a little "tolerance" and a few "Celebrate Diversity!" bumper stickers can't overcome. If queers have Subarus, house payments, and daycare schedules to attend to, how threatening can they be?

Daddy & Papa offers an entertainingly self-aware account of William and Johnny's absorption into baby-related consumer culture when they attend a picnic for gay dads and their kids. "It's raaanch-style," William singsongs as they pull up to the suburban home where the picnic will take place. They park behind and take notice of a neat lineup of three Volvo station wagons. Johnny muses in voiceover: "Were we mimicking straight people, trying to prove that we could be good parents, too? Or was this just the life of a parent, gay or straight, doing our best for our kids?" Shortly thereafter, Johnny ruefully reports, he and William bought a Volvo station wagon. This segment is insightful in the way it both documents and comments upon the connections between babies and consumer goods. However, like most representations of queer parenting, it avoids the topic of babies *as* consumer goods, thus failing once again to answer the question of why it's more appealing to watch queers get their kids than to watch them living with their kids.

And is there one answer? It's hard to say for sure. But maintaining a focus on the acquisition of a baby allows the creators of and audience for TV shows, magazine articles, and books to maintain a tacit connection between consumer items and legitimate membership in society. If queers can pile up the possessions that signal capitalist citizenship—babies, houses, Volvos, even our very own "Rainbow" Visa card—then we can assure ourselves that we have indeed been given the proverbial place at the table.

Finally, there's one more issue tangled up with the repetitive theme of baby-making. Focusing on the moment of acquisition allows creators of queer-parenting stories to—you guessed it—keep things simple, and this simplicity allows normativity to prevail yet again. If the image of queer parents is kept to the relatively brief moments surrounding their acquisition of babies, then there are no messy consequences to consider. How does the first coming-out talk go (or is a coming-out talk even necessary)? What happens when the kids get harassed at school? In what ways do the kids rebel against their parents, or not, and how do parents' sexualities and genders play into these events? What might older kids of queer parents have to say about their lives? We rarely get to hear answers to such questions—though Even's side of the discussion in *All About My Father* is a welcome exception—because when queer parents appear in the media, their offspring are usually preverbal.

Straightness Becomes You

THIS PUSH TOWARD NORMATIVITY ISN'T SIMPLY something that is thrust upon queer parents by a homophobic media empire. In some cases, it's an impression that queer parents themselves seem eager to embrace. For instance, a 1996 *People* magazine article arguing that queer (excuse me, "gay or lesbian") families are "so different, so much the same" presents a gay father, Ron Frazier, who enthusiastically endorses *People*'s safety-in-sameness angle. "We weren't stereotypical gays," he explains. "So when people saw that we were just two ordinary men, they realized there was no cause for alarm."[6] Well, I can think of a few reasons to be alarmed by his remark. But no one on the Fraziers' block is, and I guess that makes the barbecues a lot more comfortable for everyone. *People* certainly isn't going to call our attention to the problems with this viewpoint; it's too busy assuring us that it "helped" (helped what?) that Heidi Frazier's dads "live their day-to-day lives in relative anonymity."

But the issue is more complex than simple avoidance. This *People* article points—albeit not very thoughtfully—to an ongoing problem faced by queer parents. Like oil and water, queerness and parenting seem to resist blending. "Becoming a parent was the straightest thing I ever did," a friend wrote me when she found out I was working on this article. As writer Mary Martone, a new queer mom, argues, "Babies make lesbians disappear." She describes herself as a "big, short-haired gal," but notes that the social stigma she usually encounters tends to evaporate when she's with her small daughter. She's often placed into some acceptable social narrative—for example, that she has a husband who happens to be somewhere else. The usual view of parents tends to adhere to the logical syllogism "If parent, then straight," as well as its corollary, "If queer, then not a parent."

Queer as well as mainstream cultures perpetuate the assumption that queerness and parenthood don't mix. In *Daddy & Papa*, when Johnny and William try to take their toddler, Zach, to Gay Day at the Great America theme park, they discover (after paying $20 for Zach's ticket) that all the rides for children have been closed for the day. Another of *Daddy & Papa*'s dads walks through his neighborhood in San Francisco's famously gay Castro district, saying ruefully, "We go to the park three or four nights a week, and I would say there's been twice in a year and a half that there's been other kids there." And the saddest part of the *People* article about Heidi Frazier's gay dads, for me, is the passage that recounts Ron and Tom's loss of their gay community:

> Though Frazier and McCulley have lost some of their gay friends because of their mutual commitment to parenthood, that doesn't seem to have bothered them much. Between dashing off for school functions, helping shuttle Heidi and her friends to choir practice and church affairs, they discovered that they had more in common with the straight families in their neighborhood. Parenthood trumped sexual preference as the governing social factor in their lives. "Now our friends are mostly heterosexual couples," says Frazier.

Regardless of how common this phenomenon is (many areas have relatively few other queer families to befriend), it's outrageous that this loss is marked not as an isolation that Ron and Tom must live with, but merely as something that "doesn't seem to have bothered them much."

Now, I'll be the first to say that hanging out with straight folks is not a horrible fate. But the point is that queer parents are being forced to make an either/or choice. "Being a parent has put me in between gay and straight communities,"

---

[6]The term "stereotypical" isn't elaborated on, but I assume it means "throwing large house parties with 'it's Raining Men' turned up to ear-shattering levels" or "wearing a feather boa to the Stop & Shop."

writes Patrick Califia. In queer spaces, he reports, people are often "hostile to children"; in straight spaces, people who see him and his partner parenting often "[invent] some reason to think we are not queer." Areas of overlap are difficult—often impossible—to find.

Media representations of queer parents create an inaccurate and damaging impression of normativity—white, middle- or upper-class, and so forth. Without a doubt, we need more varied representations in the future. But we should also pay attention to the grain of truth in such portrayals: that queer parents are simultaneously thrust inside and kept out of mainstream culture. The queer parents in TV shows, films, articles, and books that I admire are those who can acknowledge the paradoxes they live with, those who give me some insight into what life is like when such paradoxes must be negotiated every day. I laugh when Johnny and William shamefacedly include a shot of their new Volvo station wagon. I'm unable to side wholly with either Esben/Esther or Even, each of whom passionately defends a compelling position. And I feel relief when Dan Savage and Patrick Califia remind me that pervs are parents, too. These are the kinds of queer-parenting lives I want to see: messy, complicated, flawed. They don't simply announce that queers can be parents; they queer the institution of parenthood itself.

43

The 1963 Hip-Hop Machine: Hip-Hop Pedagogy as Composition

JEFF RICE

This essay proposes an alternative invention strategy for research-based argumentative writing. By investigating the coincidental usage of the term "whatever" in hip-hop, theory, and composition studies, the essay proposes a whatever-pedagogy identified as "hip-hop pedagogy," a writing practice that models itself after digital sampling's rhetorical strategy of juxtaposition.

I begin with an analogy: teaching research-based argumentation and critique in composition studies is like learning how to perform hip-hop music. My analogy's focus on argumentation does not exclude traditional methods of argumentative pedagogy based on models like Stephen Toulmin's complex hierarchies or the Aristotelian triad of deliberative (offering advice), forensic (taking a side in a debate, often a legal or controversial matter), and epideictic (a speech of praise or blame appealing to an already won-over audience) discourse. Instead, I pose the analogy as a first step towards developing alternative or additional ways to engage composition students with the argumentative essay. In choosing hip-hop as a model for the composition essay, I attempt to draw upon a dominant form of contemporary culture familiar to the majority of students I encounter in my classrooms. Does a relationship between hip-hop and composition pedagogy exist as my analogy proposes? Can there be such a thing as "hip-hop pedagogy" for the composition classroom?

My question begins with Houston Baker's work. In "Hybridity, the Rap Race, and Pedagogy for the 1990s," Baker proposes an English studies-based pedagogy centered around hip-hop. Describing his teaching experience at the college level, Baker finds hip-hop helpful in teaching the canon of literary studies to disinterested students. Baker shares an anecdote about teaching one such course, which involved showing students "how Henry V was a rapper—a cold dissing, def con man, tougher than leather and smoother than ice, an artisan of words" (227). The principle behind Baker's pedagogy is to provide students with familiar situations and language that allow for complex textual readings, situations that allow students to identify with the figures of American and European literature.

Baker's lesson compels me to explore my initial interest in hip-hop as a composition pedagogy. What I want to add to Baker's pedagogy, however, is an examination of the way hip-hop constructs discourse, the way it produces rhetorical meaning through its complex method of digital sampling, and how such a rhetoric functions within the scope of argumentation. Baker defines sampling as

> *taking a portion (phrase, riff, percussive vamp, etc.) of a known or unknown record (or a video game squawk, a touch-tone telephone medley, a verbal tag from Malcolm X or Martin Luther King) and combining it in the overall mix (The "sample" was called a "cut" in the earliest days). (221)*

Sampling is the hip-hop process of saving snippets of prerecorded music and sound into a computer memory. These sounds become cut from their original source and pasted into a new composition. In hip-hop, the "take *whatever* you find and use it" principle acts as the dominant force in sampling. Whatever is available to composers (samplers) often includes TV shows, political speeches, past musical recordings of a variety of genres, or any sound at all. Through the complex juxtaposition of these isolated sounds, samplers construct new forms of meaning. Some of the most complex and intriguing examples of the "whatever process" in digital sampling can be found in Public Enemy's *It Takes a Nation of Millions to Hold Us Back*, Digable Planets' *Reachin' (A New Refutation of Time and Space)*, Grandmaster Flash's "The Adventures of Grandmaster Flash on the Wheels of Steel," and the Beastie Boys' *Paul's Boutique*. "High Plains Drifter" from *Paul's Boutique*, for instance, juxtaposes the unlikely samples of The Eagle's "Those Shoes," The Fatback Band's "Put Your Love in My Tender Care," and The Ramones's "Suzie Is a Headbanger" with scattered cultural references to Hunter S. Thompson's *Fear and Loathing in Las Vegas*, Steve McQueen, *The Andy Griffith Show*, and off-track betting. What emerges from this mix is a writing both provocative and compelling. A song like "High Plains Drifter" reveals that ideas take shape out of the restless culture surrounding writings; in other words, discourse emerges from the cultural odds and ends we assemble. Hip-hop teaches that cultural research and awareness produce composite forms of writing.

The "whatever" principle of sampling extends into general discourse. *Whatever* is best understood as a popular, everyday term used heavily by youth culture when an experience or reaction can't be named. The response, "whatever," evokes not so much a lack of response but either a sense that something has eluded the meaning of the response or of defiance, dismissal, and opposition. The term carries over into hip-hop culture in methodology (sampling) and attitude, where *whatever* informs lyrical composition. As in rap star Redman's "Whateva Man," *whatever* means something indefinable, obscure, out of reach:

> *You ready to get down?*
> *Whateva man.*

"Whatever" as motivating principle within the sampling composition process overlaps Roland Barthes's efforts to understand alternative meanings in photographs. In *Camera Lucida*, Barthes settles on a dichotomy of image meanings—the informational content of the image and the elusive meaning, the detail that draws a viewer into the image on a personal level. Labeling these reading practices *studium* and *punctum* respectively, Barthes constructs an alternative reading practice in which an isolated detail of the image drives its reading. One image Barthes directs attention to is a 1963 Richard Avedon photograph, *William Casby, Born a Slave*. For Barthes, this image shocks; it strikes him with a sense of defiance. Barthes writes, "the essence of slavery is here laid bare: the mask is the meaning, insofar as it is absolutely pure" (34). Barthes's choice of Avedon's photograph stems from an unnamed detail within the image that provokes his interest. Working with this image, Barthes claims that the logic of photography as we currently know it, the referent of the image relating back to a real-life thing, no longer aids critical analysis. In electronic culture, something else remains after we have deducted and named an image's referent, something beyond initial meaning, something elusive. This something is the punctum. By shifting attention to the punctum, Barthes constructs an alternative critique of photography and its relationship to personal experience. Barthes's rationale involves finding the punctum, an isolation of "that accident which pricks me" (27) and which is "the anything *whatever*, the sophisticated acme of value" (34, emphasis added). In its English translation, Barthes' punctum transforms into whatever.

For Barthes, the whatever offers more than just indefinable reaction. Barthes's punctum (or whatever) initiates an attempt to develop an alternative critical practice. The whatever challenges conventional reading practices by cutting a detail from its original source and recontextualizing it within a different setting. Barthes's purpose is to use the detail as a way to critique cultural practices. The detail he extracts from *William Casby, Born a Slave* leads to a general critique of photography. "[The detail] would tell me what constituted that thread which drew me toward Photography" (73). The juxtaposition of Barthes's isolation of the detail with hip-hop's isolation of disparate sounds returns me to my earlier proposition for writing pedagogy. In contemporary digital culture, elusive meanings abound as the emerging, electronic tools of expression rapidly alter discourse in general. Print culture's linear, nonassociative methods of reasoning break down in an electronic realm where cutting and pasting guide communication. Gregory Ulmer makes a similar point in his definition of an emerging post-criticism, a collagist writing practice that models itself after poststructuralist writings and the avant-garde.

> *In criticism, as in literature, collage takes the form of citation, but citation carried to an extreme (in post-criticism), collage being the "limit-case" of citation, and grammatology being the theory of writing as citation. (Ulmer 89)*

For critique, Ulmer proposes a sampling practice of cut-and-paste citation. Ulmer samples Jacques Derrida, Michel Serres, and John Cage to construct his theory of critique as collage. In composition, Geoffrey Sirc extends such thinking as he considers the relationship between popular music (the punks) and composition studies in the mid-1970s. Sirc's project revolves around the idea of the temporal moment as heuristic. "Contemporary scholars of composition studies," Sirc writes, "might have a difficult time believing that CCC 1977–1979 happened at the same time as the Sex Pistols" ("Never Mind" 13). Sirc demonstrates the meaning of this overlap through a temporal juxtaposition of the Sex Pistols with composition studies; he utilizes punk music to reread composition's history and contemporary status.

> *I'd like now to replay sounds from that silenced era; reread the almost erased palimpsest of Punk, on which our field's official history has been overwritten; poke around in a cultural parallelism—popular music and composition theory ("Never Mind" 10)*

Following Sirc's work with punk music and Ulmer's definition of critique as sample, I introduce the model of digital sampling and hip-hop in order to rethink the argumentative essay. This model asks: how does one account for the ways isolated details prompt analytical gestures? Can one construct critique from a series of unrelated details? Can there be such a thing as a "whatever writing practice?"

The "Whatever Classroom"

In the university classroom, the phrase "whatever" often marks an indifferent or oppositional student reaction to course demand. Patricia Harkin notes that when a student is confronted with a contradiction, "she is less likely to contemplate the cognitive dissonance as a spur to invention and more likely simply to say 'whatever' " (Harkin 496). For Harkin, *whatever* creates "a problem for invention" within the student-research paper (Harkin 497). The typical student reply to instructor demand for analytical expansion, "whatever," challenges instructors to push students for more detailed responses. The university classroom often expects such responses to come in the form of the college essay, a paper-based interface inherited from the Ciceronian breakdown of invention (exposition, narrative, evidence, refutation of opposing opinions, and conclusion). Harkin rejects the whatever response as antithetical to any heuristic basis for student work. Instead of motivating students, Harkin argues, to take a word from their everyday language (whatever) and convert it into an invention strategy, a way to write, instructors should confront the whatever in order to overcome its classroom presence. Missing, then, from Harkin's reading of student responses is how the whatever can become a

guide for contemporary student research. In his exploration of a nonbinary discourse (the third sophistic), Victor Vitanza challenges Harkin to consider *whatever*
as heuristic.

> *Harkin has her greatest insight in her blindness: reinventing by way*
> *of "whatever." Yes! Whatever beings intuit that the principles of iden-*
> *tify, non-contradiction, and excluded-middle (all the principles of*
> *negation informing re/invention) are the very principles that exclude,*
> *that disallow the thing with all its properties, that disallow radical*
> *singularities, themselves as such, in community. ("Seeing in Third"*
> *173)*

Vitanza directs Harkin to his essay "From Heuristic to Aleatory Procedures;
or, Toward 'Writing the Accident,'" which outlines a whatever-based invention
strategy for rhetoric. This strategy allows chance and randomness a prominent
role in discursive constructions. My interest is in expanding Vitanza's critique by
generating such a practice for the writing classroom and by using sampling as the
model for such a practice. The coincidental overlap of Barthes's and hip-hop's
usage of the whatever leads me to look to both for instructions on how to create
this unnamed way of writing. For Barthes, the whatever (or punctum) is the isolated detail recontextualized. In digital sampling, the whatever offers an alternative research methodology for composition—the accumulation and appropriation
of citations recontextualized into a new work. While not all applications of sampling are the same, overall, sampling allows me to expand Baker's interest in hip-
hop by offering it as a model for a whatever-centered pedagogy. Such a pedagogy,
I propose, might redefine student relationships to the various genres and demands
of academic writing: the argumentative essay, the research paper, and the critical
analysis paper. In order to explain what such a pedagogy entails, I want to demonstrate a whatever method of writing that students can use for engaging in these
areas. Because both hip-hop and Barthes isolate moments from their original context, to create my demonstration of this method, I will use their work as a justification for proceeding. I, likewise, will isolate several moments, and I will do so by
specifically drawing upon the date 1963.

The rationale for choosing 1963 as an organizing principle stems from Barthes's
temporal choice of the Avedon photograph. In addition, the year 1963 maintains
importance to writing and cultural study for a number of reasons. Eric Havelock's
observation that 1963 produced an increased awareness in grammatology (the science and history of writing)[1] found the year to be a turning point in the study of
how writing shapes culture. In composition studies, the 1963 Los Angeles meeting of the field's most important yearly event, the Conference of College Composition and Communication (CCCC), led to what several composition theorists have
labeled the beginning of contemporary writing instruction.[2] Cultural studies can
also be traced to the time period surrounding 1963: the 1964 founding of the Center for Contemporary Cultural Studies at Birmingham, England (the origin of contemporary cultural studies), as well as Raymond Williams's 1962 *Communications*,
in which he argued that the analysis of mass media include "the institutions and
forms in which ideas, information, and attitudes are transmitted and received"
(17). Hip-hop belongs to one such popular cultural institution of mass media,

popular music. Following Williams's advice, I ask if this particular institution can serve the interests of writing and, more specifically, cultural study.

I also focus on 1963 by way of Cecil Williams and Allan Stevenson's 1963 composition handbook, *A Research Manual*. The authors suggest that, when doing research, students examining a text for the first time "sample some passages to see what experience, penetration, and logic the writer seems to be endowed with. Sampling will also help you determine whether a work is more on the periphery of a particular study than at the center" (Williams and Stevenson 30). The isolation of Williams and Stevenson's text, juxtaposed with these other 1963 temporal moments, instructs me to sample in order to do research. Therefore, my explanation of hip-hop pedagogy emerges from a series of sampled 1963 moments.[3] My purpose, then, is to demonstrate how composition students can research and form arguments through sampling.

Borrowing from the language of hip-hop, throughout the rest of this essay these samples are interspersed with cuts and breaks, mixes, and playbacks. The fragmented sections I work from follow a whatever logic; read in isolation, their meanings are elusive, possibly evoking the student-inspired response, "whatever." Moreover, they come from *whatever* I have discovered occurring in 1963. When viewed together, they offer the model for hip-hop pedagogy; in other words, I perform hip-hop pedagogy as a way of explaining how it functions. As I cut and paste these moments together, I hope to begin the process of hip-hop pedagogy as argumentation and cultural critique.[4]

Hip-hop pedagogy
The cut: Gordon Parks

Gordon Parks's 1963 photograph of Malcolm X, entitled *Malcolm X, Harlem*, exhibits the civil rights leader holding up a newspaper whose bold headline reads: "Seven Unarmed Negroes Shot in Cold Blood by Los Angeles Police." The photograph draws attention to two important issues for the post-World War II era: civil rights and information technology. In Parks's photograph, the two items juxtapose, revealing the subtle ways both inform one another. Parks's photo is a reminder of Gwendolyn Brooks's 1963 poem "Negro Hero": "But let us speak only of my success and the pictures in the Caucasian dailies" (Brooks 19). In 1963, print media, for the most part, belongs to a mostly white, dominant discourse, Directed by white boards of directors, major newspapers, for the most part, tended to treat civil rights issues from the perspective of white, not black, America. Unequal levels of production ownership tainted any reporting regarding key civil rights issues. Familiar today in the long-standing debate of the digital divide, access to information production and distribution proved elusive to an African American populace attempting to voice its opinions and frustrations. Writing in 1963, African American journalist Simeon Booker questioned overall African American access to the communication industry.

> *For too long, Negroes have known and grown to accept news managing of their affairs, attitudes and selection of leaders by most of the communications industry. And for too long, the industry has not*

> *recognized Negroes as even a part of the community, locally or nation-*
> *ally, except as an undersirable part. (143)*

Booker's complaint rewrites the Parks image. The degree of being "unarmed" as the headline indicates means more than gun power. The weapon power implicit here resides in information production. To be "shot" in cold blood means to be struck with both a weapon and to be captured within the boundaries of photography; one "shoots" an image. In this case, an African American photographer (Parks) attempts to capture the complexity of Malcolm X's action. In 1963 newspaper photographys, the photograph seems to ask, who shoots whom? Who controls the power of the image and its display? Does Malcolm X remain in power by holding the image? Is this a black-owned or white-owned paper? What is the relationship between information technology and how such technology is controlled?

Paste: Leonard Freed

In Leonard Freed's 1963 photograph *New York City*, an African American man also holds up a newspaper; the headline reads, "We Must Have Justice." Behind him, New York's commercial district comes alive with billboards advertising soda fountains and hot dogs. Around him, people make their way in and out of shops. The demand for justice ties racism to economics. The insertion of one African American man in a crowd of white shoppers is an effort to foreground these connections. The task, though, defies simplicity. Like Charles Mingus's "Freedom," a track not included on his 1963 record *Mingus, Mingus, Mingus* but later added to subsequent printings, African American representations in the arts sustain a continued discourse of social justice that often yields to frustration.

> *Freedom for your daddy*
> *Freedom for your mamma*
> *Freedom for your brothers and sisters*
> *But no freedom for me. (Mingus)*

Mingus's recording, like Parks's photograph, exhibits a disenchantment with the NAACP's slogan "Free by '63," whose purpose was to mark "the Centennial celebration of the signing of the Emancipation Proclamation" (Booker 29). Pasted together, both moments offer a joint critique of an early '60s civil rights rhetoric that centralizes the elusive meanings of freedom in American democracy. Who is free? Who receives justice? these works ask. Lacking a name for a culture whose attention fixates more on commercial consumption than on social justice, moments like Freed's photo and Mingus's music suggest an elusive "whatever" as response.

Cut: Romare Bearden

African American artist Romare Bearden's 1963 *Prevalence of Ritual Series* approaches such elusiveness through collage and nostalgia. In the works comprising the series, Bearden, the one-time realist painter, "had come back to the subject matter he started out with—Black American life as he remembered it in the South of his childhood in North Carolina, and in the North of his coming of age in Pittsburgh and Harlem and later in life the Caribbean island of St. Martin"

(Conwill 8). For Bearden, the rituals of religion and popular culture provided iconic markers of African American practices, practices that could be nostalgically represented within collage. Notably, Bearden's nostalgia for 1920s and 1930s black culture drew inspiration from the Civil Rights movement of 1963, particularly Martin Luther King. Jr.'s March on Washington and "I Have a Dream" speech. Works like *Cotton, The Dove,* and *Jazz* are cut and pasted displays of an African American presence no longer in existence; the nostalgia for the past (and all of its racial struggles) contrasts with the fight against contemporary, institutionalized racism and the exertion to join the developing information-driven economy.

Bearden's collages of the Old South, the Cotton Club, and inner city poverty of the 1920s and 30s appear out of place in contrast to the works' temporal civil rights movement. And yet, this sense of nostalgia marks a moment of temporal cultural critique defined by nostalgia. Bearden's lesson for a hip-hop pedagogy involves utilizing the past in new ways. *The Dove* (1964), for instance, pastes an assortment of cut-up African American faces and bodies over a Harlem stoop. They seem to be nowhere, yet everywhere at once. The markers of African American presence are felt in the images of cigarettes dangling out of empty spaces, masked faces, and solitary hands leaning idly out of windows. While *The Dove* treats African American inner-city life nostalgically (the communal feeling of living in a close area), it also offers the beginnings of a critical gesture intent on questioning the elusive meaning (Where do these people go? What do they do? Why are they idle? What has caused this?). Bearden's collage argues that an impoverished black underclass can search for meaning in carefully composed, visual juxtapositions when no other resolution seems apparent.

Paste: Mo Greens Please

The usage of juxtaposition for critical purposes also appears via the 1963 cover art of Blue Note Records. Blue Note, one of the most prolific producers of jazz in the post-war period, produced a number of record covers in 1963, distinct in their style: Freddie Roach's *Mo Greens Please*, Donald Byrd's *A New Perspective*, Jackie McLean's *One Step Beyond*, Hank Mobley's *No Room for Squares*, Blue Mitchell's *Step Lightly*, and Horace Silver's *Silver's Serenade*. Marked by geometric shapes and patterns, tilted angles, and sharp recolorations and shadings, these record covers, all designed by Reid Miles, revealed a new aesthetic for jazz and marketing, what Felix Cromey calls "an abstract design hinting at innovations, cool strides for cool notes, the symbolic implications of typeface and tones" (Marsh, Cromey, Callingham 7).

In particular, cover art like that of Roach's *Mo Greens Please* used information technology (the record) to emphasize African American pride, even if in somewhat stereotypical ways. *Mo Greens Please* features an African American man purchasing soul food at either a roadside cart or take-out window of a small restaurant. Soul food serves as a prominent iconic display of African American eating habits. Covers like Roach's stressed black pride and power (choices in what African Americans eat as opposed to what white-dominated advertising tells its audience to eat), topics that would eventually govern the themes of hip-hop albums recorded in the '80s and '90s by such groups as Public Enemy, A Tribe Called Quest, Digable Planets, and The Roots.

The design innovations Reid brought to Blue Note's record covers also situate the innovative move within African American musical production to sample themes related to both the immediate African American experience as well as generalized issues of self-reliance, civil rights, and equality. Blue Note's designs and sound fused with the emerging 1960s soul music produced in Detroit and Memphis, fashioning a new level of self-expression as critique. In jazz, this merger led to the formation of "soul jazz" or hard-bop, a movement critic Amiri Baraka felt relevant to the formation of a new African American identity in which political and social detachment (what Baraka called "cool") give way to a new system of value (soul). In his 1963 definition of the move from cool to soul, Baraka claims

> *The step from cool to soul is a form of social aggression. It is an attempt to place upon a meaningless social order, an order which would give value to terms of existence that were once considered not only valueless but shameful. Cool meant nonparticipation; soul means a "new" establishment. It is an attempt to reverse the social roles within the society by redefining the canons of value. (Blues People 219)*

The inclusion of soul into the composition process redirects canonical understandings of not only reading (or listening) practices but writing itself. A new sound demands a new writing form. The most sampled of all soul artists is James Brown, who as Mark Anthony Neal comments, introduced rhythms to "a younger, politically motivated, culturally assured audience raised on the music and production techniques of the Motown and Stax recording companies" (33). This political audience, Baraka's new establishment, forms the basis of contemporary hip-hop culture.

Paste: James Brown

In 1963, James Brown released *Live at the Apollo Vol. I*. Recorded the previous year at the famous Apollo theater in Harlem, Brown's album became the first soul record to significantly chart on the white-dominated Billboard sales charts. Brown's entrance into the segregated music divisions of popular music (rhythm and blues for African Americans, pop music for whites) marked the new establishment Baraka describes, the entrance of black music into the homes of white America. Live at the Apollo also created an iconic identification of African American cultural production through the crossover celebrity, one that would quickly identify black musical production with social concerns and values. Baraka writes:

> *James Brown's form and content identify an entire group of people in America. However these may be transmuted and reused, reappear in other areas, in other musics for different purposes in the society, the initial energy and image are about a specific grouping of people, Black People. (Black Music 185)*

With Brown, cultural transformation manifests by way of song writing. The early love songs on *Live at The Apollo* eventually become manifestos for black empowerment when juxtaposed with Brown's late-'60s work. *Live at The Apollo's* "Please, Please, Please" and "Try Me" read in the light of '60s Black Power become entreaties for equal rights and self-awareness. They become the building blocks of later hits like "Say It Loud—I'm Black and I'm Proud Pt. 1," "Soul Power," and "I Don't Want Nobody to Give Me Nothing (Open Up the Door I'll Get It Myself)." Brown's concerns with social power echo James Baldwin's 1963 *The Fire Next Time* in which he writes, "The only thing white people have that black people need, or should want, is power—and one holds power forever" (Baldwin 95–96). Brown's music is an early reminder of hip-hop's political beginnings, its attempts to decode power relations and ideology through an aggressive back beat configured by cut-and-pasted sound selections. Brown's interest in Black Power re-emerges in Ice-T's "Power," Salt N Pepa's "Solo Power (Syncopated Soul)," and Public Enemy's "Fight the Power." Public Enemy's song remains one of the best examples of hip-hop's interest in unequal power relations. Sampling Brown's "Funky President" and "Funky Drummer," the "I" of Bob Marley's "I Shot the Sheriff," and numerous other sources, Public Enemy shifts musical power from mainstream studio production to the compact digital sampler.

Brown, like many of the artists of Blue Note records, appealed to Djs experimenting with sampling practices in the 1970s, '80s, and '90s. Both Brown and Blue Note's artists addressed conflicts confronting various levels of social class. In addition, they provided a means for a future confrontation with discourse itself, supplying contemporary hip-hop with the basis of a new method of composition: empowerment through sampling.

Playback: The Writing Machine

In order to convert this material into a composition, I sample these cut-and-pasted moments into a hypothetical writing machine, a pedagogical digital sampler. The model for a pedagogical digital sampler comes from Suzanne McElfresh's definition of the electronic version:

> *A recording device that captures sound as digital information, which is then saved in computer memory instead of on magnetic tape, the sampler made it possible to create intricate soundscapes with virtually any source material, including already recorded music and live instruments. (170)*

The pedagogical sampler, with a computer or without a computer, allows cultural criticism to save isolated moments and then juxtapose them as a final product. The student writer looks at the various distinct moments she has collected and figures out how these moments together produce knowledge. Just as DJs often search for breaks and cuts in the music that reveal patterns, so, too, does the student writer look for a pattern as a way to unite these moments into a new alternative argument and critique.

My sampler shifts back and forth through the selections I have fed into it. The pattern I hear includes the ways information technology informs power relations at the levels of race and class. This issue is raised through image (Parks and Freed), sound (Blue Note and James Brown), and method (Bearden). The argument I perform here, therefore, emerges from the juxtaposition of all three areas.

Print literacy advocates the linear argument as the most appropriate way to establish critique. In the contemporary classroom, critique often follows Toulmin's model of argumentation as outlined in the widely adopted *Uses of Argument*. Toulmin's breakdown of the structure of the argument can be summed up as follows:

> *There must be an initial stage at which the charge or claim is clearly stated, a subsequent phase in which evidence is set out or testimony given in support of the charge or claim, leading on to the final stage at which a verdict is given, and the sentence or other judicial act issuing from the verdict is pronounced. (Toulmin 16)*

In the mix of the hip-hop pedagogy, sampling finds Toulmin's work in need of an update. Toulmin's dependence on the "charge" or "claim" as the principal force of argumentation appears out of place within the mix, in which the claim emerges as the result of whatever is played back in juxtaposition. In order to update argumentation for the electronic sphere, hip-hop pedagogy takes its cue from Leronne Bennett's 1963 reading of King's civil rights plan entitled "Project 'C'." Bennett writes:

> *Project "C" was the code name for a proposed series of demonstrations in Birmingham. And what did the "C" stand for? It was a shorthand symbol for a chillingly blunt concept: CONFRONTATION. A confrontation between Negroes and whites—not in the courts but on the steps of city hall, not at the conference table but in the streets, not by ones and twos but by hundreds and thousands. (4)*

Within my mix, the sampled passage from Bennett involves confronting the ways argumentation is formed in writing. Transformed from its 1960s racial purpose, Project "C" becomes a question of confronting the nature of Toulmin's "claim" in the mix. The desire to compose through confrontation appears as well in King's canonized 1963 "Letter from Birmingham Jail": "The purpose of our direct-action program is to create a situation so crisis-packed that it will inevitably open the door to negotiation" (King 767). King asked that his methods of confronting the dominant order be considered extremist. "The question is not whether we will be extremists, but what kind of extremists we will be" (King 773). In its conception of argumentation as confrontation, hip-hop pedagogy borrows King's extremism and joins it to another temporal extremist, William S. Burroughs, whose cut-up method proposed an extreme way of challenging institutionalized discourse: cutting up texts, speeches, slogans, etc., and pasting them back together in provocative ways. Burroughs argued for a confrontation with so-called "reality," the dominant ideology propagated in media formations and often taken for granted as natural. Writing in the time period surrounding 1963, Burroughs wrote that submission to reality without question was analogous to drug addiction:

> *The scanning pattern we accept as "reality" has been imposed by the controlling power on this planet, a power primarily oriented towards total control—In order to retain control they have moved to monopolize and deactivate the hallucinogen drugs by effecting noxious alternations on a molecular level. (53)*

If hip-hop pedagogy seeks to confront these types of power relations, it must alter the ways discourse is formed by student writers (and, hopefully, instructors as well). In this way, hip-hop pedagogy performs an extremist act by arguing that the "reality" of academic writing (the linear structure of thesis, support, conclusion) is in fact an ideological formation that can and should be challenged through the sample. Hip-hop pedagogy, therefore, borrows the student confrontational response to the traditional writing assignment by saying out loud. "whatever."

The Mix

In the mix (the writing I am performing), Allen Kaprow's 1962 Happening *Words* (originally performed at the Simolin Gallery in New York) is the space where my composition finally takes place. Falling within my 1963 series of samples, *Words* collected quotations from a variety of sources (comic books, political slogans, published writings) and hung them from the ceiling and the walls of an enclosed room. Viewers were encouraged to either add to the hanging and posted collections or rearrange the display. In the background, turntables played recordings of Kaprow's voice. The various selections and participant input created a collective-based space in which discourse surrounds viewers/readers rather than being concentrated on a single page. *Words* brought together the output of various media forms as collection. In this sense, communicating means collecting. *Words* also maintains a link to hip-hop; the expression "word" functions as a be-all answer to whatever-type questions, a way to deal with allusive meanings when no answer is forthcoming.

Words, then, serves as an early form of hip-hop pedagogy. Kaprow's collage of text, sound, and image set up a confrontation with the dominant art institution's preference for gallery space and museum shows. The "word" confrontation acts to motivate the sampling process, to push writers to engage with not only the language they use to construct discourse but also the mediums in which the discourse is conveyed. To think of the classroom and the academic essay as two mediums in need of confrontation is to create an analogy with Tricia Rose's definition of rap music. "Rap music is a contemporary stage for the theater of the powerless" (Rose 101). In this sense, students who are powerless (powerless to choose their own forms for writing, powerless to adapt the discourses they are most familiar with such as music, television, or film) become empowered at some level to reshape their relationship to literature, sports, music, politics, art, etc., through the sample. "Powerful, alternative formal possibilities are now key genres of public discourse," Geoffrey Sirc claims, "and kids understand them, and Composition Studies could care less" ("Virtual Urbanism" 14). Or to sample Public Enemy as a voice for the contemporary writing student: "Power and equality / and we're out to get it." ("Party").

Teaching the Whatever: Hip-Hop Pedagogy

I leave this composition as a mix to be played back by different students of contemporary culture, through different isolated moments, through a different whatever. My choice of 1963 acts merely as a model for further exploration; samples do not have to be temporal; they may come from specific spaces of public discourse, contemporary issues, or even physical spaces. And while many of the samples in my composition independently maintain a connection to African American culture, their thematic similarities don't override the disparate concerns of each piece (Mingus and Bearden work in distinctive, separate ways, for instance). For this demonstration, the commonality serves the specific purpose to identify the practice's potential. Student writing benefits from choosing contrasting samples and allowing the dissimilarities of the material to function as heuristic.

However the composition course poses the assignment (as temporal, spatial, or some other form), students gain insight into the writing process at levels they had not yet considered. Taking my performance of 1963 as one such example, the student engaged with a similar temporal project researches the year's moments in a variety of disciplines (film, politics, science, music, television, sports, etc.) and thus gains insight into the process of research. The student finds a common pattern or element that binds these moments and then understands how to form a claim out of research and investigation. The student juxtaposes these moments in one of a variety of ways and thus learns about organization. And through the process of juxtaposing the samples, the student locates her own position within the various cultural, ideological, economic, racial, gendered, etc., discussions consistently taking place around her. The student as sampler creates an argument.[5]

The ultimate test for such a project is to recognize that this process doesn't have to be done only with hip-hop music. The lesson of sampling can be extrapolated from this example in order to form various alternative methods of critique drawing from a variety of isolated details in order to allow pedagogy room for further development. The writing classroom, then, would shift critique from the standardized methodology inherited from figures like Toulmin and, instead, adopt the logic of hip-hop's composition innovators, figures like Grand Master Flash or the group Public Enemy. Doing so allows students to resist the imposed linear methods of critique in favor of practices already working within digital culture. Doing so repeats Digable Planets' message of whatever as resistance, repositioning the student writer's resistance (whatever) to the writing assignment in a productive manner:

> For this is the season of our self savior
> Like Ché Guevara, the guerilla
> Sparks the revolution black tactics, whatever. ("Agent 7")

One can speculate as to what extent this type of writing promotes not only a critical practice for how it synthesizes unlike material in order to construct an argument but also for how it registers our specific involvements in consumer culture. Because this practice models itself after a consumer product (popular music), we must also recognize that the cultural awareness sampling as critical practice brings to light is not a given in itself. The potential for critical understanding always contrasts with the potential for student cynicism (we know how the practice resists dominant thinking, but we still accept the dominant anyway), what Victor Vitanza has called a "false coconsciousness" often prevalent in cultural-studies-influenced classrooms ("The Wasteland Grows" 700). Hip-hop pedagogy is not meant as a given substitute for dominant thinking but, rather, as an alternative practice whose own application must be problematized even while students engage with it. Thus, I propose hip-hop pedagogy as the place to begin such questioning regarding our ability to resist dominant modes of thinking, to engage with consumerism while working against it, to spark the resistance, whatever.

Acknowledgments

I thank Geoffrey Sirc and Victor Vitanza for helpful comments and suggestions on earlier versions of this essay.

Notes

1. Because of space limitations, I mark these two observations with footnotes. See *The Muse Learns to Write* for Eric Havelock's observation of the near simultaneous publications on writing by Marshall McLuhan, Jack Goody and Ian Watt, and Claude Levi Strauss.

2. See Stephen North *The Making of Knowledge in Composition: Portrait of an Emerging Field*, Lester Faigley *Fragments of Rationality*, and Geoffrey Sirc's "English Composition As a Happening II, Part One."

3. Geoffrey Sirc has pointed out to me that Fluxus founder George Maciunas engaged with temporal dates for composing in the mid-1970s. His Biography Boxes contained "objects relating to the year of one's birth, perhaps a newspaper from the day one was born, things that were invented that year, etc" (Hendricks 322). See also Larry Miller's "Interview with George Maciunas" in *The Fluxus Reader*, edited by Ken Friedman. Maciunas states that 1963 was the first year he began making related boxes.

4. In addition to Victor Vitanza's response to Patricia Harkin, he also treats the whatever as the focus of an emerging identity. His work on this version of the whatever can be viewed online at <http://www.uta.edu/english/V/test/interface/v.1x.html> and <http://www.uta.edu/english/V/test:/agamben/>. While there exist distinct differences in the way we both use the term, Vitanza's work has greatly influenced my use of *whatever*.

5. Examples of student work that have performed temporal juxtapositions can be viewed online at <http://web.nwe.ufl.edu/~jrice/1629/2> and <http://web.nwe.ufl.edu/~jrice/1685/2>.

Works Cited

Baker, Houston. "Hybridity, the Rap Race, and Pedagogy for the 1990s." *Black Music Research Journal* 11 (2) Fall 1991.

Baldwin, James. *The Fire Next Time*. New York: The Modern Library, 1963.

Baraka, Amiri. *Black Music*. New York: W. Morrow, 1967.

———. *Blues People: Negro Music in White America*. New York: William Morrow and Co., 1963.

Barthes, Roland. *Camera Lucida*. New York: Hill and Wang, 1981.

Beastie Boys. *Paul's Boutique*. Capitol Records, 1989.

Bennett, Leronne, Jr. *The Black Mood and Other Essays*. New York: Barnes & Noble, 1964 (1963).

Booker, Simeon. *Black Man's America*. Englewood Cliffs, NJ: Prentice-Hall, 1964.

Brooks, Gwendolyn. "Negro Hero." *Selected Poems*. New York: Harper and Row, 1963.

Burroughs, William S. *The Nova Express*. New York: Grove, 1992 (1964).

Conwill, Kinshasha Holman. "Introduction." *Memory and Metaphor: The Art of Romare Bearden 1940–1987*. New York: Oxford UP. 1981.

Digable Planets. "Agent 7 Creamy Spy Theme: Dial 7 (Axioms of Creamy Spies)" EMD/Pendulum, 1994.

———. "Cool Like Dat." *Reachin' (A New Refutation of Time and Space)*. EMD/Pendulum, 1993.

Eshun, Kodowo. *More Brilliant Than the Sun:* Adventures in Sonic Fiction. London: Quartet, 1999.

Harkin, Patricia. "Rhetorics, Poetics, and Cultures As an Articulation Project." *JAC: A Journal of Composition Theory* 17.3 (1997): 494–97.

Hendricks, Jon. *Fluxus Codex*. New York: Harry N. Abrams, Inc., 1998.

Grandmaster Flash. "The Adventures of Grandmaster Flash on Wheels of Steel." *Grandmaster Flash Greatest Mixes*. Bangon, 1998.

King, Martin Luther, Jr. "Letter from Birmingham Jail." *The Little, Brown Reader*. Ed. Marcia Stubbs and Sylvan Barnet. New York: Harper Collins, 1996, 763–78.

McElfresh, Suzanne. "DJs Vs. Samplers." *The Vibe History of Hip-Hop*. Ed. Alan Light. New York: Three Rivers P, 1999.

Marsh, Graham, Felix Cromey. and Glyn Callingham. *Blue Note: The Album Cover Art*. San Francisco, CA: Chronicle Books, 1991.

Mingus, Charles. "Freedom." *Mingus, Mingus, Mingus*. Impulse! 1963.

Neal, Mark Anthony. *What the Music Said: Black Popular Music and Black Public Culture*. New York: Routledge, 1999.

Public Enemy. "Can I Get a Witness!" *It Takes a Nation of Millions to Hold Us Back*. UNI/DEFJAM, 1988.

———. "Party for Your Right to Fight." *It Takes a Nation of Millions to Hold Us Back*. UNI/DEFJAM, 1988.

Redman. "Whateva Man." *Muddy Waters*. UNI/DefJam, 1996.

Rose, Tricia. *Black Noise: Black Music and Black Culture in Contemporary America*. Hanover: Wesleyan UP, 1994.

Sirc, Geoffrey. "Never Mind the Tagmemics, Where's the Sex Pistols?" CCC 48.1 (Feb.) 1997.

———. "Virtual Urbanism." *Computers and Composition* 18(1) 2001: 11–19.

Toulmin. Stephen. *Uses of Argument*. Cambridge; Cambridge UP, 1958.

Ulmer, Gregory. "The Object of Post-Criticism." *The Anti-Aesthetic: Essays on Postmodern Culture*. Ed. Hal Foster. Seattle, WA: Bay Press, 1983.

Vitanza, Victor J. "From Heuristic to Aleatory Procedures; Or, Toward 'Writing the Accident'." *Inventing a Discipline: Rhetoric Scholarship in Honor of Richard E. Young*. Ed. Maureen Daly Goggin. Urbana, IL: NCTE, 2000.

———. "Seeing in Third Sophistic Ways." *Rhetoric and Composition As Intellectual Work*. Ed. Gary Olson. Carbondale: Southern Illinois UP, 2002.

———. " 'The Wasteland Grows': Or, What is 'Cultural Studies for Composition' and Why Must We Always Speak Good of It? ParaResponse to Julie Drew." *JAC: A Journal of Composition Theory* 19 (1999): 699–703.

Williams, Cecil B., and Allan Stevenson. *A Research Manual*. New York: Harper and Row, 1963.

Williams, Raymond. *Communications*. London: Chatto and Windus, 1966 (1962).

44

For Sweet Honey in the Rock

SONIA SANCHEZ

I'm gonna stay on the battlefield
I'm gonna stay on the battlefield
I'm gonna stay on the battlefield til I die.

I'm gonna stay on the battlefield
I'm gonna stay on the battlefield
I'm gonna stay on the battlefield til I die.

i had come into the city carrying life in my eyes
amid rumors of death,
calling out to everyone who would listen
it is time to move us all into another century
time for freedom and racial and sexual justice
time for women and children and men time for hands unbound
i had come into the city wearing peaceful breasts
and the spaces between us smiled
i had come into the city carrying life in my eyes.
i had come into the city carrying life in my eyes.

And they followed us in their cars with their computers
and their tongues crawled with caterpillars
and they bumped us off the road turned over our cars,
and they bombed our buildings killed our babies,
and they shot our doctors maintaining our bodies,
and their courts changed into confessionals
but we kept on organizing we kept on teaching believing
loving doing what was holy moving to a higher ground
even though our hands were full of slaughtered teeth
but we held out our eyes delirious with grace.
but we held out our eyes delirious with grace.

I'm gonna treat everybody right
I'm gonna treat everybody right
I'm gonna treat everybody right til I die.

I'm gonna treat everybody right
I'm gonna treat everybody right
I'm gonna treat everybody right til I die.

come. i say come, you sitting still in domestic bacteria
come. i say come, you standing still in double-breasted mornings
come. i say come, and return to the fight.
this fight for the earth
this fight for our children
this fight for our life
we need your hurricane voices
we need your sacred hands

i say, come, sister, brother to the battlefield
come into the rain forests
come into the hood
come into the barrio
come into the schools
come into the abortion clinics
come into the prisons
come and caress our spines

i say come, wrap your feet around justice
i say come, wrap your tongues around truth
i say come, wrap your hands with deeds and prayer
you brown ones
you yellow ones
you black ones
you gay ones
you white ones
you lesbian ones

Comecomecomecomecome to this battlefield
called life, called life, called life. . . .

I'm gonna stay on the battlefield
I'm gonna stay on the battlefield
I'm gonna stay on the battlefield til I die.

I'm gonna stay on the battlefield
I'm gonna stay on the battlefield
I'm gonna stay on the battlefield til I die.

45

The Veil

MARJANE SATRAPI

The Veil

THIS IS ME WHEN I WAS 10 YEARS OLD. THIS WAS IN 1980.

AND THIS IS A CLASS PHOTO. I'M SITTING ON THE FAR LEFT SO YOU DON'T SEE ME. FROM LEFT TO RIGHT: GOLNAZ, MAHSHID, NARINE, MINNA.

IN 1979 A REVOLUTION TOOK PLACE. IT WAS LATER CALLED "THE ISLAMIC REVOLUTION".

THEN CAME 1980: THE YEAR IT BECAME OBLIGATORY TO WEAR THE VEIL AT SCHOOL.

WEAR THIS!

WE DIDN'T REALLY LIKE TO WEAR THE VEIL, ESPECIALLY SINCE WE DIDN'T UNDERSTAND WHY WE HAD TO.

IT'S TOO HOT OUT!

EXECUTION IN THE NAME OF FREEDOM.

GIVE ME MY VEIL BACK!

YOU'LL HAVE TO LICK MY FEET!

OOH! I'M THE MONSTER OF DARKNESS.

GIDDYAP!

AND ALSO BECAUSE THE YEAR BEFORE, IN 1979, WE WERE IN A FRENCH NON-RELIGIOUS SCHOOL.

WHERE BOYS AND GIRLS WERE TOGETHER.

AND THEN SUDDENLY IN 1980...

ALL BILINGUAL SCHOOLS MUST BE CLOSED DOWN.

THEY ARE SYMBOLS OF CAPITALISM.

BRAVO!

WHAT WISDOM!

OF DECADENCE.

THIS IS CALLED A "CULTURAL REVOLUTION."

WE FOUND OURSELVES VEILED AND SEPARATED FROM OUR FRIENDS.

AND THAT WAS THAT...

EVERYWHERE IN THE STREETS THERE WERE DEMONSTRATIONS FOR AND AGAINST THE VEIL.

AT ONE OF THE DEMONSTRATIONS, A GERMAN JOURNALIST TOOK A PHOTO OF MY MOTHER.

I WAS REALLY PROUD OF HER. HER PHOTO WAS PUBLISHED IN ALL THE EUROPEAN NEWSPAPERS.

AND EVEN IN ONE MAGAZINE IN IRAN. MY MOTHER WAS REALLY SCARED.

HAVE YOU SEEN THIS?

DON'T WORRY, DARLING.

SHE DYED HER HAIR,

AND WORE DARK GLASSES FOR A LONG TIME.

I REALLY DIDN'T KNOW WHAT TO THINK ABOUT THE VEIL. DEEP DOWN I WAS VERY RELIGIOUS BUT AS A FAMILY WE WERE VERY MODERN AND AVANT-GARDE.

I WAS BORN WITH RELIGION.

AT THE AGE OF SIX I WAS ALREADY SURE I WAS THE LAST PROPHET. THIS WAS A FEW YEARS BEFORE THE REVOLUTION.

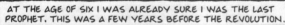

O' Celestial light!

BEFORE ME THERE HAD BEEN A FEW OTHERS.

A WOMAN?

I AM THE LAST PROPHET.

I WANTED TO BE A PROPHET...

BECAUSE OUR MAID DID NOT EAT WITH US.

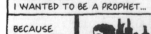

BECAUSE MY FATHER HAD A CADILLAC.

AND, ABOVE ALL, BECAUSE MY GRANDMOTHER'S KNEES ALWAYS ACHED.

COME HERE MARJI! HELP ME TO STAND UP.

DON'T WORRY. SOON YOU WON'T HAVE ANY MORE PAIN. YOU'LL SEE.

LIKE ALL MY PREDECESSORS I HAD MY HOLY BOOK.

THE FIRST THREE RULES CAME FROM ZARATHUSTRA. HE WAS THE FIRST PROPHET IN MY COUNTRY BEFORE THE ARAB INVASION.

YOU MUST BASE EVERYTHING ON THESE THREE RULES: BEHAVE WELL, SPEAK WELL, ACT WELL.

I ALSO WANTED US TO CELEBRATE THE TRADITIONAL ZARATHUSTRIAN HOLIDAYS. LIKE THE FIRE CEREMONY,

BEFORE THE PERSIAN NEW YEAR, NOROUZ, ON MARCH 21ST, THE FIRST DAY OF SPRING.

ONLY MY GRANDMOTHER KNEW ABOUT MY BOOK.

RULE NUMBER SIX: EVERYBODY SHOULD HAVE A CAR.

RULE NUMBER SEVEN: ALL MAIDS SHOULD EAT AT THE TABLE WITH THE OTHERS.

RULE NUMBER EIGHT: NO OLD PERSON SHOULD HAVE TO SUFFER.

IN THAT CASE, I'LL BE YOUR FIRST DISCIPLE.

REALLY?

BUT TELL ME HOW YOU'LL ARRANGE FOR OLD PEOPLE NOT TO SUFFER?

IT WILL SIMPLY BE FORBIDDEN.

EVERY NIGHT I HAD A BIG DISCUSSION WITH GOD.

GOD, GIVE ME SOME MORE TIME. I AM NOT QUITE READY YET.

YES YOU ARE, CELESTIAL LIGHT, YOU ARE MY CHOICE, MY LAST AND MY BEST CHOICE.

EXCEPT FOR MY GRANDMOTHER I WAS OBVIOUSLY THE ONLY ONE WHO BELIEVED IN MYSELF.

WHAT DO YOU WANT TO BE WHEN YOU GROW UP?

I'LL BE A PROPHET.

HAHA! HAHA! HAHA!

SHE'S CRAZY.

MY PARENTS WERE CALLED IN BY THE TEACHER.

YOUR CHILD IS DISTURBED. SHE WANTS TO BECOME A PROPHET.

WHAT ABOUT IT?

DOESN'T THIS WORRY YOU?

NO! NOT AT ALL!

?

581

46

Introduction to Geographies of Exclusion

DAVID SIBLEY

The human landscape can be read as a landscape of exclusion. This was clear to Engels in his observations on the industrial city, to Raymond Williams in his account of the landscapes of landed capital in eighteenth-century England in *The Country and the City*, and to Lewis Mumford, writing about Baroque cities in *The City in History*. Because power is expressed in the monopolization of space and the relegation of weaker groups in society to less desirable environments, any text on the social geography of advanced capitalism should be concerned with the question of exclusion. My purpose in writing this book, however, is not to provide a comprehensive account of exclusionary processes. There is already a substantial literature on the capitalist city which is, to some extent, concerned with exclusion, insofar as it is concerned with problems of access to urban resources, particularly housing, and associated spatial outcomes.[1] I would also leave off my agenda those programmes of exclusion which are starkly expressed in spatial terms and connect with clearly articulated ideologies, such as apartheid in. South Africa and the 'race' policies of Nazi Germany, although I would not wish to suggest that these cases of oppression could not be further illuminated by geographical analysis.[2]

While this may seem like a perverse avoidance of central theoretical issues and crucial social and political problems, my intention in this book is to foreground the more opaque instances of exclusion, opaque, that is, from a mainstream or majority perspective, the ones which do not make the news or are taken for granted as part of the routine of daily life. These exclusionary practices are important because they are less noticed and so the ways in which control is exercised in society are concealed. One cue for my analysis comes from Paul Rabinow,[3] who has suggested that 'we need to anthropologize the West'. Rabinow argues that we need to 'show how exotic [the West's] granted as universal (this includes epistemology and economics); [and] make them seem as historically peculiar as possible'. To me this implies that we need to recognize as problems those aspects of life of which you might be unaware, particularly if you happen to be white, adult, male, and middle class, but which contribute to the oppression of others. Human geography, in particular, should be concerned with raising consciousness of the domination of space in its critique of the hegemonic culture. This has been the objective of Marxist analysis in human geography, but as a totalizing discourse Marxism has inevitably been insensitive to difference, almost as insensitive as the dominant capitalist culture which is the subject of Marxist critique. To get beyond the myths which secure capitalist hegemony, to expose oppressive practices, it is necessary to examine the assumptions about inclusion and exclusion which are implicit in the design of spaces and places. The simple questions we should be asking are: who are places for, whom do they exclude, and how are these prohibitions maintained in practice? Apart from examining legal systems and the practices of social control agencies, explanations of exclusion require an account of barriers, prohibitions and constraints on activities from the point of view of the excluded. I would agree with Jane Flax, however, that there is no single oppressive reality, no single structure obscured by the images of the dominant culture, to uncover. She suggests that

> *Perhaps reality can have 'a' structure only from the falsely universalizing perspective of the dominant group. That is, only to the extent that one person or group can dominate the whole will reality appear to be governed by one set of rules or to be constituted by one privileged set of social relations.*

One part of the problem, then, is to identify forms of socio-spatial exclusion as they are experienced and articulated by the subject groups. These groups, however, may be seen as both dominant and subordinate, depending on the way in which they are categorized. Both men and women may experience exclusion as members of an oppressed minority group, for example, but men may be dominant in their relationship with women in a minority culture.[5] These different realities can be difficult to recognize, and the observer must appreciate that his or her own understanding of the socio-spatial worlds of others will inevitably be limited by his or her own background and perspectives. However, I still feel that it is possible, and certainly desirable, to represent other people's experience of socio-spatial exclusion while acknowledging that the question of positionality is one that has to be addressed.[6]

For the moment, rather than pursuing this argument in the abstract, I will comment on a few cases of exclusion which signal the specific kinds of socio-spatial issues which I will be considering in this book. The first concerns what is now a widely discussed problem, namely, the function of indoor shopping centres as social space.[7] These centres have become a significant mode of retail service provision in the developed capitalist economies, projected by both commercial and civic interests as progressive, and providing an improved environment for consumption and leisure for all the family. In the more extravagant developments, a fantasy world of imagined places is created, effectively removing consumption from associations with need. As Shields has observed in an account of the West Edmonton Mall in Canada, the model for several very large retailing developments in North America and Europe:

> *It fragments conventional geographical space and historical time with its wild combination of interior settings; evoking disparate times and places while it seeks to impose its own stable order on the ensemble. At the turn of a corner, one is in a simulated 'New Orleans'. Another corner – 'Paris'.*

In comparable British developments, including the Meadowhall Shopping Centre, near Sheffield, which similarly recreates the romance of Paris and Florence under one roof, and the Metro Centre in Gateshead, their exoticism has stimulated a new form of holiday experience. For some, a coach trip to the shopping centre has become a substitute for a day by the sea, in Blackpool, Scarborough or Skegness. Such places clearly do provide an attractive alternative to a traditional shopping street, polluted by vehicle exhausts and exposed to the weather (and they may be rather more appealing than a decaying seaside resort). Thus, a British television documentary on the Metro Centre in Gateshead focused in a positive way on the characteristic features of international consumption style and the consumers, all apparently white, middle-class nuclear families, the kind of public which populates architects' sketches. The documentary had a rather different sub-text, however. Out of sight in the control room, employees of the private security firm which polices the centre had their eyes fixed on closed-circuit television screens. They were looking for 'undesirables', mostly groups of teenage boys who did not fit the family image projected by the company. When they were located, security guards evicted them, not just from the building but from the precinct. Such actions point to the fact that shopping centres like this one constitute a kind of ambiguous, seemingly public but actually private space. There are implicit rules of inclusion and exclusion in a built form that contribute to the structuring of society and space in a way which some will find oppressive and others appealing. 'Being in the tightly policed, semi-private interior of a mall is quite different from being "on the street". "No loitering", as the signs in the mall say. Certain types of comportment are expected'.[8] In the shopping centre management's response to the presence of adolescents, maybe not consuming very much, in a place dedicated to consumption by the family, there is a connection between the function and design of the space as determined by commercial interests and design professionals, architects and planners, and the construction of one group of the population as 'deviant', out of place, and threatening the projected image of the development. Again, Shields notes that the shopping mall introduces 'an unheard of degree of surveillance, with almost Orwellian overtones, into daily life', and, in this controlled environment, teenagers who have few other places in which to congregate are one of the principal groups targeted by the security guards. Their presence necessarily constitutes deviance.[9] Comparing this with my own experience as a teenager in the 1950s, sitting for hours over a cup of coffee in an ABC café in a north London suburb, undisturbed by staff, it appears that the boundaries between the consuming and non-consuming public are strengthening, with non-consumption being constructed as a form of deviance at the same time as spaces of consumption eliminate public spaces in city centres.

This view gains some empirical support in a number of studies of teenage sub-cultures. For example, in a Home Office study of 'downtown drinkers' in the planned shopping precinct in Coventry,[10] the writer reported that:

> *Unruly groups of young people were seen as a problem by approxi-mately two out of three interviewees. As with litter, the problem is not just a local matter. Throughout the country, shopping centres often serve as convenient places for youth subcultures to meet – places to which there may be a lack of obvious alternatives. On the other hand, the mere sight of such groups, however rarely they actually infringe any laws, can be alarming to others. This is a delicate issue. [Attempts] to exclude youth groups from shopping centres are likely to bring fur-ther problems, and may also be quite unjust. Nevertheless, in Coven-try, perception of unruly groups of young people as a common problem was significantly associated with the fear of crime. This link was stronger than that between perceptions of litter and fear of crime but not as powerful as that between perceptions of public drinkers and fear of crime [my italics].*

This quotation, like the television documentary on the shopping centre, sug-gests that it is not adolescent males as a social category, or even 'unruly' groups of young people, *per se*, who are seen as threatening; rather, it is their presence in spaces which comprise part of 'normal family space' which renders them discrepant and threatening. Exclusion may be an unintended consequence of commerical development. Adolescents will be acutely aware of discrimination against them, while their exclusion is much less likely to impinge on the consciousness of con-forming adults.

In the interaction of people and the built environment, it is a truism that space is contested but relatively trivial conflicts can provide clues about power relations and the role of space in social control. This is demonstrated in a second example, dredged from memory, which concerns an incident in Philadelphia in the late 1960s. At this time, hippies were still a threatening species in Philadelphia, the category 'hippy' embracing just about any man with long hair or woman wearing beads. Rit-tenhouse Square, in the city centre, was popular with slightly non-conforming peo-ple at the weekend; in it was a low wall which was a convenient place to sit. One warm Sunday afternoon, there were a lot of people sitting on the wall, some play-ing acoustic guitars, but mostly just chatting and enjoying the sunshine. At some point, a park guard started to order people off the wall on the grounds that it was *not* a place to sit. The wall, he asserted, was there to separate the path from the grass. It was definitely not to sit on. Almost everyone acquiesced. This might have been because the park guard, who, like many agents of social control in the United States, was equipped with a revolver and a night-stick, appeared intimidating. It could also be the case that this group of middle-class American youth, having been brought up in conformist communities, were accustomed to accepting authority despite their trappings of non-conformity.

There are two aspects of this incident which are of more general significance. The first concerns ambiguity. To the park guard, the function of the wall was unambiguous. It was simply a boundary between one kind of space and another and, apparently, he could not conceive of alternative interpretations. His job was to police the wall, to ensure its sanctity and prevent its violation. It may be reading too much into the incident, but his behaviour appeared to fit a pattern noted in a number of studies of the authoritarian personality, following Adorno's early study of the psychology of authoritarianism.[11] Shils suggested that authoritarians were distrustful and suspicious, that they had on *intolerance of ambiguity*, and, thus, differentiated clearly between those on the outside, the 'other', and the relevant in-group.[12] Similarly, Rokeach[13] suggested that authoritarian individuals '[protected] inner weaknesses by a ready acceptance of the views of higher authorities and by forming unambiguous judgements which rigidly separate, into distinct categories, objects of approval and those of disapproval'.

The issue is not just about an unsuspecting park guard overloaded with theoretical meaning. Apart from the park guard's own perception of non-conformity, the social status of Rittenhouse Square also contributed to the representation of its hippy-ish occupants as conspicuously deviant. The square was surrounded by solid apartment buildings occupied by affluent middle-aged and elderly residents who saw the hippies as polluting 'their' space. In fact, the park guard admitted to me that he had been told to clear the square of young people because their presence offended the residents. The arbitrary use of power by the guard thus reflected a more fundamental aspect of power relations. The square as a contested public space exposed the conflictual nature of social relations and the design of the square itself assumed symbolic importance in this conflict. It should not be seen just as an arena where this particular power game was played, however, but as one instance of the interaction of space and people which forms part of the routines for the reproduction of power relations in an advanced capitalist society.[14]

The policing of Rittenhouse Square, a rather unsubtle example of social control, might be compared with many instances of exclusion where boundaries are drawn discretely between dominant and subordinate groups. Martin Walker notes the spread of the private pool club in the United States, an institution, like the whites-only golf club, which continues 'the discrete and self-deceiving way of modern American apartheid. It is now justified as a way to avoid the crowds, crime and drugs of the municipal pools, these being code words which are used to signify black people.'[15] Elsewhere, Mike Davis has captured the helplessness of the poor and homeless in the large North American city, faced with exclusionary developments by corporate capital.[16] Talking to a black, homeless man in downtown Los Angeles, Davis comments: 'In front of us, tens of thousands of poor people, homeless people; at back opulence, affluence, Bunker Hill, the new L.A.' He then asks: 'Could you walk up there?' and the man replies: 'If they were to catch me in that building, they would have so much security on my ass, I would probably be in jail in five minutes.' Again exclusion is felt acutely, but the homeless are rendered invisible to the affluent downtown workers by the spatial separations of city centre development which keep the underclass at a distance.

These examples give some indication of the concerns of this book, exclusions in social space which may be unnoticed features of urban life. It is the fact that exclusions take place routinely, without most people noticing, which is a particularly important aspect of the problem. In an attempt to make these practices more transparent what I try to do in the first part of the text is to define attitudes to others which inform exclusionary practices and to set the control problem in the broader context of the cultures of modern societies. I then try to show how the processes of control are manifested in the exclusion of those people who are judged to be deviant, imperfect or marginal. A study of exclusion, however, is necessarily concerned with inclusion, with the 'normal' as much as the 'deviant', the 'same' as well as the 'other', and with the credentials required to gain entry to the dominant groups in society. Thus, I focus on processes of boundary erection by groups in society who consider themselves to be normal or mainstream. The curious practices of this majority, the oddness of the ordinary which is examined microscopically by authors and playwrights from Jane Austen to Mike Leigh, have been neglected in social geography, and one of the purposes of this book is to rectify this omission.

My treatment of space and society is concerned particularly with symbol, ritual and myth, taking cues from social anthropology and psychoanalysis, subjects which have not been overly concerned with space but which provide many useful analogues for spatial problems. I would argue that many social problems can be profitably spatialized, but, at the same time, a human geography which attempts to assume a distinct identity within social science is necessarily impoverished. For example, it seems to me that the concern of social anthropology with representation, imagery and alternative world-views should also be central to human geography, hence 'geographies' in the title of the book. To uncover these diverse geographies, reflecting varied experiences and interpretations of space and place, involves drawing on a wide range of ideas located elsewhere in the social sciences and the humanities. A post-disciplinary perspective on social and spatial problems is preferable to viewing the world from within conventional subject boundaries.

In Part I, 1 first attempt to build up pictures of the rejecting and the rejected and then travel along several theoretical avenues in order to identify exclusionary processes affecting both groups and individuals. In addition to theories of socio-spatial structuring, this section makes reference to psychoanalytic theories of the self, which assumed greater importance as the writing progressed. This was partly because I was trying to familiarize myself with this literature while working on the text but also because some ideas from psychoanalysis seemed to connect with what were, for me, more familiar arguments about boundary formation developed in social anthropology and human geography. I would not claim that this account achieves any real synthesis, but it does suggest some connections between individual and group behaviour, and between environment and behaviour, which might be integral elements of the problem.

These theoretical arguments connect with instances of exclusion at different spatial scales, starting with the home and moving out to the nation-state and questions of geopolitics. Exclusion in the home, in the locality and at the national level are not discrete issues. A number of reciprocal relationships are examined and there is, inevitably, considerable cross-referencing in this part of the book. While there are common strands to the argument here, the problems considered are very different, ranging from conflicts within families and homes to international relations.

In Part II, I get away from the usual subjects of geographical analysis to consider academics as subjects, but what I claim in this section is that we can use the same arguments to explain the exclusion of knowledge as to explain the exclusion of discrepant others. I suggest that the production of knowledge involves both the exclusion of knowledge which is deemed dangerous and the exclusion of some categories of intellectual. The processes of social segregation observable in the modern city, for example, are mirrored in the segregation of knowledge producers. The defence of social space has its counterpart in the defence of regions of knowledge. This means that what constitutes knowledge, that is; those ideas which gain currency through books and periodicals, is conditioned by power relations which determine the boundaries of 'knowledge' and exclude dangerous or threatening ideas and authors. It follows that any prescriptions for a better integrated and more egalitarian society must also include proposals for change in the way academic knowledge is produced.

I do not attempt in this book to give an account of exclusion in advanced capitalist societies which covers all salient forms of difference. There would be a long list of these, including exclusion based on race, gender, sexuality, age, and mental and physical disability. What I hope to do, however, is to clarify some of the spatial and social boundary processes which separate some groups and individuals from society and render deviant those who are different. At the same time, I suggest that social scientists need to look more closely at their own practices and develop critiques of their work which parallel their analyses of the marginalized and oppressed.

Notes

1. Thus, much of David Harvey's work could be read as a (class-based) geography of exclusion. His essay 'Class structure and residential differentiation' (in *The Urban Experience*, Basil Blackwell, Oxford, 1989, pp. 109–124) is specifically concerned with closure and exclusion as they operate in the property market. In a similar theoretical vein, we could note Blair Badcock's *Unfairly Structured Cities*, Basil Blackwell, Oxford, 1984. Weberian closure theory is also concerned with exclusion — through the erection of barriers to entry into more privileged groups. Closure theory has been given a spatial dimension, particularly in Christopher Husband's work on racism. See his 'East End racism, 1900–1980', *The London Journal*, 8, 1982, 3–26.

2. Rössler's study of the connection between central place theory and the concept of *lebensraum* in Nazi Germany demonstrates that there is considerable scope for the kind of research on fascist and other authoritarian regimes which explores ideology, spatial theories and spatial practices (Mechtild Rössler, 'Applied geography and area research in Nazi society: central place theory and planning, 1933 to 1945', *Environment and Planning D: Society and Space*, 7 (4), 1989, 363–400).

3. Paul Rabinow, 'Representations are social facts: modernity and postmodernity in anthropology', in James Clifford and George Marcus

(eds), *Writing Culture*, University of California Press, Berkeley, 1986, 234–261. This echoes Robert Park's recommendation in his 1925 essay on the city:

Anthropology, the science of man, has been mainly concerned up to the present with the study of primitive peoples. But civilized man is quite as interesting an object of investigation and, at the same time, his life is more open to observation and study. Urban life and culture are more varied, subtle and complicated, but the fundamental motives in both instances are the same. The same patient methods of observation which anthropologists like Boas and Lowie have expended on the study of the life and manners of the North American Indian might be even more fruitfully employed in the investigation of the customs, beliefs, social practices and general conceptions of life prevalent in Little Italy or the lower North Side in Chicago or in recording the more sophisticated folkways of the inhabitants of Greenwich Village and the neighborhood of Washington Square, New York.

(Robert Park, The City, University of Chicago Press, Chicago, 1925, p. 2)

4. Cited by Linda Nicholson (Linda Nicholson (ed.), *Feminism/Postmodernism*, Routledge, London, 1990, p. 6).

5. In patriarchal Gypsy communities, for example, women suffer double exclusion, as women and as members of a marginalized minority.

6. However, agonizing over position leads to authors denying the possibility of writing with any authority about anybody other than their own social group, which may be quite narrowly defined. Given appropriate methods of investigation, I feel that some generalization about those with different world-views is possible and desirable, although there is always a risk of distortion and misrepresentation which can only be guarded against by repeated engagement with other groups.

7. Rob Shields's 1989 essay is one of the more thoughtful studies of shopping centres, but David Harvey also makes some relevant comments on the blurring of public and private space in the new arenas of consumption. See Rob Shields, 'Social spatialization and the built environment: the West Edmonton Mall', *Environment and Planning D: Society and Space*, 7, 1989, 147–164, and David Harvey, 'Postmodern morality plays', *Antipode*, 24, 1992, 300–326.

8. Shields, op. cit.

9. With a thorough application of surveillance technology, the shopping centre can become a panoptican mall', echoing Jeremy Bentham's design for a model prison. See Mike Davis, *City of Quartz*, Verso Press, London, 1990, pp. 240–244, on 'the mall-as-panoptican-prison' as it has been realized in inner-city Los Angeles.

10. M. Ramsay, *Downtown Drinkers: The perceptions and fears of the public in a city centre*, Crime Prevention Unit, Paper 19, Home Office, London, 1989.

11. Theodor Adorno, *et al., The Authoritarian Personality*, Norton, New York, 1982.

12. Edward Shils, 'Authoritarianism: "right" and "left' ", in R. Christie and M. Jahoda (eds), *Studies in the Scope and Method of the Authoritarian Personality*, Free Press, Glencoe, 1954.

13. Michael Rokeach, *The Open and Closed Mind*, Basic Books, New York, 1960.

14. David Harvey makes similar points about social relations in Tompkins Square Park, New York City, where 'On a good day, we could celebrate the scene within the park as a superb example of urban tolerance for difference', but 'on a bad day . . . so-called forces of law and order battle to evict the homeless, erect barriers between violently clashing factions. The park then becomes a locus of exploitation and oppression' (1992, op. cit.).

15. Martin Walker, *Guardian*, 26 May 1990.

16. *Rear Window*, Channel 4 TV, London, 1991. As Davis puts it, rather floridly: 'The Downtown hyperstructure – like some Buckminster Fuller post-Holocaust fantasy – is programmed to ensure a seamless continuum of middle-class work, consumption and recreation, without unwonted exposure to Downtown's working-class street environments' (op. cit., 1990, p. 231).

47

Broken Sentences: Women In Prison Tell Their Stories Straight

ANNA DEAVERE SMITH

FIFTH GRADE: A few weeks before my tenth birthday. Segregated school in Baltimore. My bedroom, where I studied. An O.K. place with a nice window that looked out over a graveyard, which was scary, but we played in the snow there, and I liked the sound of the trains that went by just beside it. My mother was pregnant, with what I prayed on my knees every night would be a girl. I had two brothers. They were disobedient, or so I thought. I was obedient. Or so I thought. But I was headed toward breaking the law. The laws of grammar. I can't imagine where this tendency came from. I had a very respectable mother. An educator. And my aunts and uncles and everyone else were respectable, too. My father? Well, come to think of it . . . He called tomatoes potatoes "just to make us think." He was a black version of Ionesco.

SENTENCES. Grammatical incarceration. My mother began to express a disapproval toward me which I hadn't experienced before. She had an uncompromising disdain for run-on sentences, and for incomplete ones. In school, too, there was a very serious tone about breaking the rules of grammar. And the same serious tone would be used a few years hence about ending up pregnant. In the Baltimore I knew, there was no discussion of drugs, or any apparent threat of them. If there had been, I'm sure the same serious tone would have been used.

THERE was a sudden release of pressure. A few of us were placed in the sixth grade before Christmas. We'd skipped a grade. I was relieved of a fear of failure that was increasing with every book report. The more I had to say, the more improper my grammar became. Thank God the test I had to take to skip the fifth grade had no writing. Just circle the proper answer. Just learn the rules and follow them. Now I had some peace. I did have to write in complete sentences, but I felt it would all be O.K. I could fake it. Nonetheless, I experienced a loss, and I associate the introduction of the perfect sentence with the end of my girlhood.

Truth be told, we all break the laws of grammar. We all have the potential to speak in broken, collaged, colluded, jumbled, run-on sentences. Truth be told, the sentence is sometimes no more and no less than a mask. I have been looking for sentences with enough breath to let the subtext live, in fact, where words don't kill the "truth."

What better place to find the broken sentences of my birthplace than a prison— a women's prison outside my home town? The Maryland Correctional Institution for Women, in Jessup, Maryland, detains many women from Baltimore and surrounding areas, like the Eastern Shore (which was referred to as "the country" when we were kids). There I listened to stories that account for life styles that I barely knew existed in my sheltered Baltimore life. Each time I heard the name of a street, autobiographical images were evoked, of walks with my grandmother, of rides with my father, or of simple journeys to do errands, or to go to another church, or to see a play at a school where my mother taught, sometimes in strange areas of town. Some of those streets never felt familiar or safe, but my father's car or my grandmother's gait made them safe. The stories I heard in the prison told me something about the subtext, the underbelly, of those streets. Times have changed here, in particular for women.

There are about four times more women at the Maryland Correctional Institution than there were twenty years ago, and the overwhelming majority are colored. On the first trip to the prison, I went to, of all things, a Girl Scout meeting. The Girl Scouts bring the daughters of inmates on a bus to the prison on some Saturdays. The mothers meet first as a group, and talk about "issue" having to do with mothering in these restrictive circumstances. There are two whites. The others were black. They ranged in age from their early twenties to mid-thirties. The mothers were coiffed and manicured, and dressed in "casual wear"—jeans, sportswear, etc. (Only the "new admits" wear uniforms—pink jump-suits—and none of them would be allowed in the Girl Scouts, which is a "program" and a privilege to be earned.)

Even in a Girl Scout meeting, there are very specific rules that must be followed. One girl and her mother were dismissed when the girl wore oversized boots to the meeting, which she exchanged with the mother's shoes so that the mother could wear the boots back to her wing. Everyone is suspect. A daughter, like her mother before her, could be a "mule" for drugs or other contraband. Certainly, among adults, contraband is brought into the prison in a variety of creative ways.

Drugs come packed in balloons, which are carried in a visitor's mouth and "passed" in a kiss. Perhaps the balloon is swallowed, and the recipient waits until she is able to defecate it out of her system, at which time she can distribute the drugs in the population. One woman told me that she had a friend who died when a balloon she swallowed "burst," and "exploded in her heart."

The members of the Girl Scouts are particularly careful to follow every procedure properly, because they so value the time with their daughters. A child, therefore, cannot bring a gift of any kind to her mother.

I present some of their stories here, excerpted, from tape-recorded interviews. If a word has been added for clarity, parentheses are used.

Serious/Wicked Women
Sherri Rideout

The Visiting Room: The room has several long institutional tables, and there are vending machines against two walls.

Sherri Rideout is tall, with pressed hair that swoops up to the side. She is, by her own definition, a compulsive thief. She comes back and forth to prison a lot. She is thirty-three. Her demeanor is pleasant and open, and she has a very apparent sense of humor. When I asked her to say something into the microphone to test the machine, she yelled, "I love ya!"

Now, I take this place seriously
even the last time when I left here
it wasn't as strict.
I left this place in '93
And two years later
My God.
This is serious here.
This is serious times.
The most serious part about it is
they have a lot a new officers
that more so are young
very young
and the younger generation to me
they can't tolerate a lot of things that
    older people can.
They just cuff you
put you over
and you goin' on lock.
Unh unh.
I'm getting too old.
I'm thirty-three.
My children are getting old.
They need me.
The women, the women in this place
    some of them are so evil and wicked.
Some of these women

You got people that's
took someone else's life
that's chopped their baby and fed it to
    their husband
all kinds of ludicrous things
that has taken place.
And you know
they can get in here and portray
to be this and that
but I'm thinking
well my God
if you did that to your own child
what would you do to me?
To kill your child
and to do all these things?
Unh unh.
Now, there's one girl here
that committed a violent offense
and she got eighteen years for this offense
and she
when her roommate
went to sleep
she took something and shoved it up
    her vagina
It's just, it's some wicked women here.
It really is.

Christmas
Vera Banton

Vera is in prison for murder. By her account, while protecting herself from Sam, her boyfriend, who was coming at her with a steak knife and threatening to kill her, she grabbed the knife, "tousled" with him, and the knife accidentally went into his chest. She got eighteen years. She told me that when she first met Sam he told her he was an angel, and she believed him, but as he abused her she saw he was the devil. "The devil," she told me, "come as an angel, too. He was in Heaven at one time. And he also walks this earth as an angel."

Vera told me that her Christmas package had come from her family, "but there was something wrong in it," so it was sent back. She said she had decided to praise the Lord until she was "all fulled up," instead of getting angry.

This is the most painful time of the
    year for me
cause I'm in prison
I'm in this environment
Away from my family
I have four kids
out there
that I have been away now for three
    years
and I miss
putting up a Christmas tree,
wrapping gifts,
going to the mall buying the gifts,
and just seeing they face,
when they open 'em up,
cookin' the dinner,
sittin' at the table,
we all saying our grace,
we all eat together,

we all go visit Grandma,
go over to Auntie house,
and just being with my kids,
I miss that.
I don't feel like Christmas!
And it's sad
because I have to go back in
past the Christmas tree
past the decorations
and go in the little room and lock in
and it hurts
'cause I didn't do those decorations
I didn't put that Christmas tree up
I didn't have my kids
running around
"Mommy"
now that I have grandkids out there
I'm not able to be with them.
Christmas.

A Mirror to Her Mouth
Paulette Jenkins

It was about 6 P.M. when I met Paulette Jenkins. It was dark outside. The visiting room was quiet. A stream of officers had just gone home. She is black, simply presented, with her hair pulled back, wearing a T-shirt. Most of her sentences end with an upward inflection, as if she knows but is still looking for something, looking for a possibility.

They were still afraid.
They were still confused.
He would beat them.
They were not his children.
I had three children before it was all
    over with
but at the time we all started out it was
    just
me
and my daughter
and then
I had another baby
by my husband
and I left my husband
and went with this man.
It was like jumping out of the pan and
    right into the fire?
And he would beat my children,
out of his own insecurities
or his own jealousness.
He beat my daughter
and he beat my son.
My daughter was nine
and my son was six.
The beatings escalated
and I began to cover it up.
This went on for
five,
seven years
and my daughter had got a beatin' and
    he had scald her foot.
I lied to Social Service and I told them
"This didn't happen. He didn't do it."
You know—
"It was an accident."
I had came home from work and she was
    there with her feet all blistered up
and she told me he made her stand in
    the bathtub with hot water.
It was the fact,
that I didn't believe her
and even if I did believe her—

it was the fact
I hesitated.
I refused to do anything about it.
That was the fact.
It didn't take the blisters down.
It didn't change the fact that I lied to
    Social Service.
I denied all help and assistance.
I pushed my family away, when the
    abuse got so intense
that I wouldn't go visit.
I ran out of excuses!
Of how we got black eyes.
And busted lips and bruises.
And he beat me, too.
But
it didn't change the fact,
that
It was a nightmare for my children.
It was a nightmare.
And I failed them.
Dramatically.
Because I allowed it to continue.
On.
And on.
And on.

That night that she got killed—
we had went out,
And to subside my fear of being petrified
I was shootin' drugs all day long—
and was still able to cook a dinner.
You know.
(*Louder, and more emphatic.*)
Still was able to keep the house clean.
Wash clothes.
Hang 'em on the line.
And be blasted!
Heroin,
marijuana,
alcohol.
Y'know.

And then I started writing prescriptions.
Y'know.
And I thought he was gonna get better.
And I thought I could fix this man!
And the intensity just grew,
and grew,
and grew,
until one night we came home . . .
from getting drugs,
and he
got angry with Myeshia,
and he started beating her,
he would use a belt,
'cause he had this warped
perverted thing,
that Myeshia
was having sex with her little brother
or that they were fondlin' each other.
And he beat her
and he put her in the bathtub
and I was in the bedroom.
But
before
all this happened,
four months before she died,
I thought I could really fix this man
and so I had a baby by him!
Insane?!
Thinking if I give him his own kid,
he'll leave mine alone.
But it didn't work—
I wound up with three children—
and it was a boy
four months old when I came to jail.
So,
the night that Myeshia died
I stayed in the bedroom with the baby.
And every time he would hit her
she would fall,
and she would hit her head on the tub.
I could hear it!
And it happened continuously,
repeatedly.
(*She whispers.*)
And I dared not to move.
I didn't move.
I didn't even go see what was happening.
I just set there and listened.
And then later—
he set her in the hallway
and told her to set there.

And she set there for 'bout
four or five hours
and then he told her to get up
(*She starts to cry, her voice is very soft*)
and when she got up
she said she couldn't see
(*She cries*)
her face was bruised
(*She is whispering*)
and she had a black eye.
All around her head was just swollen.
Her head looked like it was two sizes
of its own size.
I told him to let her go to sleep,
and he let her go to sleep.
(*She is whispering.*)
The next morning
she was dead.
He went and checked on her
for school.
And he got very excited.
He said,
"She won't breathe."
I knew immediately that she was dead.
(*She is crying.*)
So I went in
I didn't want to accept the fact that she
    was dead.
So I went and took a mirror to her
    mouth.
There was no—thing
coming out of her mouth,
nothing.
He said,
"We cannot let nobody know about
    this.
So you got to help me."
So I agreed.
I agreed.
(*She is crying.*)
We waited that whole day.
She stayed in that room that whole day.
With no medical attention.
I didn't dare tell anyone.
'Cause I had been keeping it a secret
    for years and years.
And this just seemed like secondhand
    to me.
To keep a secret.
That night,
we went to the mall

and we told the
security guards in the mall
that she had been missing
that we had, like, lost her.
You know, we fabricated the story
and I went along with it.
And we told them
what she had on.
That night.
We got her dressed.
In—the—exact—same—thing,
that we told the police that she had on.
And we got the baby.
And my other son.
And we drove
like out to
I-95,
I was so petrified
and so numb
All I could look,
was in the rearview mirror
and he just laid her on the shoulder
of the highway.
My own child

I let that happen to.
The six-year-old,
he
was scared.
He was scared.
It was like livin' in a haunted house
for years and years.
She got killed on the fourth of March,
and no later than the sixth
they had found her and it was over
  with.
We had told the media that she was
  missing
'cause he was like—
"Well, why don't you just go on and
  tell 'em that she's missing?"
I confessed to everything
I plead guilty.
I took twenty-five on a plea bargain.
He took
sixty on a plea bargain.
Myeshia's birthday was December
  the 6th.
She would have been nineteen.

A Sam Shepardesque "Fool for Love" Kind of Story
Sherri Rideout

And one time—
And he used to gamble—
Compulsive.
He was a compulsive gambler
and I was a compulsive thief—
And
Tell you what!
My baby
was in the baby crib
'bout two months old
and he had a gun in the baby thing
and I didn't know it was in the baby
  thing
and he came home
running
Dumped the baby over!
This is how crazy this man was!
Could have hurt the baby!
And took the gun out and ran out the
  door.
I been through something!

I been through something with that
  man.
And then one time
me and him was in a motel room?
And he accused me of talking to some
  guy?
And he said that he was gon kill me
I said "Go 'head!
Go—'head—and—kill—me!
Go 'head!
I ain't no good anyway!
I ain't no good!
You wanna kill something that ain't no
  good!
Go 'head and kill it!"
Then he didn't kill me.
Then.
We was at this other motel one time.
And it was snow on the ground.
It was snow on the ground.
We was in the motel room.

He talkin' about he seen me talking to
this guy.
He know the guy want me and all this
crazy stuff.
He told me,
"Come on
This is it!
This is it!
You gon die tonight."
He said, "I'm gon take me a shower
and after that you gon die."
I was strip naked in the motel room.
I ran out the motel room
butterball naked in the snow
with nothing on
to get away from this man.
He had a gun in there!
(*She is laughing.*)
He had a gun!
Oh, man!

Coming to jail
coming in these rooms
and telling people
about what
all he used to do to me
and how I used to let him get away
with it,
how he would be with all these women
and they said,
"Stop letting him run free in your own
head!"
And how he still was
trying to say things
and scare me in some ways.
Eight years
me and this man was together
'cause 15, 16, 17, 18, 19, 20, 21, 22,
23, 24
Nine years.

Integration

The broad part of the prison population is called "population." Those women who accumulate a certain number of "tickets" for disobeying rules are placed on "segregation." Claudia McClain and Tyboria Stones have both been confined to segregation for substantial periods of time.

Tyboria Stones

Tyboria is twenty-six and was charged with raping a woman. She says she didn't do it. ("Why would I want to go out and do something to an old woman like that? When I have a woman?") She is stocky and muscular, with hair trimmed very close on the sides, short and curly on top.

I was in a single room.
They said nobody couldn't be my
    roommate
and the officers making a big thing of it
saying we're gonna put a little boy in
    your room
we ain't puttin' a fem in your room.
A fem
a straight woman.
You know they talking
about a little
boy. . . .
They call us
little boys
'cause we dress like men.
Our hair be like men.

We wear men cologne.
And I think that's wrong.
Saying,
"Don't nobody wanta be Tyboria's
    roommate,"
you know . . .
They don't know nothing about it. . . .
And I had that
I don't care attitude
just keep getting tickets
and getting tickets
and it was like a lot of officers kept
    bothering me
officer throwing piss un'neath my door.
The officers don't want me in population.

Ping-Pong Table

Tyboria came with a history of violence from inside institutions as well as out on the street. She described a run-in with a warden at another facility.

The warden . . .
hit me upside the head,
'cause I wouldn't take off a stocking cap.
And I hit him back
and
I threw him on the Ping-Pong table
in the rec area
and I started chokin' him
punchin' him back

and we got to fightin'
and the backups came in and put shack-
    les on me
and cuffs
and he came in the isolation room
and tried to choke me
and they left me in there for two days
    with the
shackles on and the cuffs on from behind.

When I Was About Six or Seven

I asked her where she thinks her violence comes from.

I don't know why I was into a lot of
    violence
I don't know.
'Cause um
I have a nice mother.
I have a real respectful mother.

Q: What about your father?

My father was a very violent person.
My mother was telling me
he always stayed in jail
for assault and batteries.

He shot this woman
he shot her in her stuff
in her vagina
'cause he found her in bed
with another man.
He had left my mother.
It happened when I was about six or
seven.

Claudia McClain

Claudia came to the interview with a sense of purpose, sitting behind the micro-phone in a formal manner. She is twenty-one years old, and she looks tough, like a bullet. Her head is shaved nearly bald. From a distance she looks like a boy. This is by design.

On the streets, she lived, as she said, "on the edges." She was a drug dealer. She is in prison for shooting Diko, a friend who sold drugs for her, when they were both teenagers. By her account, he had thirteen hundred dollars of hers and refused to give it back. She says Diko drew out his gun and pulled the trigger, but nothing came out. In response, she shot him six times, twice in his head and "the rest" in his upper body.

I mean,
I don't care if Warden Carter reads
  about this—
I mean right is right
and wrong is wrong.
Segregation inmates . . .
You get handcuffed
and locked in a cage.
Like you're really an animal.
Since he (*Warden Carter*)
has been here
you get three showers (*a week*).
Now,
what if a woman is menustratin?
Three showers?
What is that?
And then if a shower happens to fall
  on a day of a holiday
you can't come and take a shower
You don't get rec and showers on a
  holiday.
They have so many holidays
while I was in segregation.
Holidays that didn't speak in the calendar.
If they walk in today and don't feel like
showerin' you

'cause today is Wednesday
and shower day
they say it's a holiday.
And you look on your calendar or holler
    out the window
'cause you see the general population
on a working schedule
and you ask them is it a holiday.
And they say no.
The officer say

it doesn't matter
I say it's a holiday.

It makes you feel unclean.
'Cause
small as the sink
is you not gonna get clean.
Just a little strip a water comes
it comes like this.

(*She demonstrates an arc, slowly, with her hand, making eye contact with me. Her look is stern.*)

Just Playin'

We got to arguin'
me and Diko
so he brought out a gun on me
and said,
"I ain't givin' you shit."
All I seen was a gun and I seen my life
    flash before me

but each day as I think more and more
    about the situation
you know I'm sayin?
Although he pulled the trigger
and nothing came out
maybe he knew it was blanks in there.
Maybe he was just playin'.

No Longer Lovers

I asked her who called the police on her.

Someone living upstairs on the third
    floor.
This female I used to socialize with
intimately
sexually.
We was no longer lovers though.
One day I come in
and seen her throw something
and my instincts was to see what it was
it was a spike (*a needle*)
and I don't subject myself to that.

I do not involve myself in drugs
I mean usin'.
I don't do drugs.
I don't do alcohol.
So.
I left.

Q: And she didn't like that.

CLAUDIA: I guess not.

Pretty Teeth

(*She sits closer to the microphone and increases her volume.*)

This is on the record!
We had one girl
she has abscesses and

infections in her mouth.
And this other girl here
she just caught hepatitis.

And you know hepatitis could go away
or you could live with that
for the rest of your life.

But see I have pretty teeth
so I don't have to worry.

*(She smiles, baring her teeth. They
are quite pretty.)*

The Tour of Segregation
Lieutenant Somerville-Jones

*The Lieutenant is an attractive black woman who "loves her job." She has been
at M.C.I.W. for nine years. Our first stop is the segregation wing. The officer on
duty is a large black woman with small black glasses. Her uniform is not clean. She
is wearing a small black knit ski cap. She is the keeper of the hall. The women are
locked into rooms with brown doors that are controlled electronically. There is a
small, thick glass window on each door. There is a slot the size of a small food tray
a little below waist high. If the slot is opened, the women talk can through it.
Otherwise, they communicate by yelling at the top of their lungs or screaming to
each other through the vents. The rooms have a toilet, a bed, and very little else.
The officer seems in good spirits, and so does Lieutenant Somerville-Jones. As the
women realize that she has entered, they start to scream. They all have requests.
One needs a cigarette, one needs to see the doctor, another has a grievance about
an officer, etc. I was surprised at how quickly the entire wing realized Lieutenant
was there. And I was stunned when they realized she had a visitor.*

*Lt. S.-J. and I stoop down to the slot in order to talk. The woman we talk to
is sitting with her face at the slot. She is light-skinned black woman. She begins to
talk as if she had a very important role in a play or pageant.*

I wan tell you . . .
What I want to say is

That things here
Bein' here at this institution
There's a lot of things
that's not supposed to be done!
Far as like
the way we are being treated here—
like animals!
We get treated like animals!
As for the uh
the hygienes
your hygienes . . .
I been on lock

for two years and ten
months
in segregation . . .
These—officers—
they—egg—us—on
they—lie—on—us . . .
And you don't get showers every day
  here
you get showers three times a week
on segregation.

Within These Fences
Terri

*Terri is the only white woman I interviewed. She preferred not to use her real
name. She is composed and well spoken, has sparkling blue eyes, and is immacu-
lately groomed. She has a life sentence.*

Every single morning
when I go to work,
you can see this fire in the sky,
and I think of my grandmother and my
    grandfather.
And also the birds!
When I hear the birds chirping
I think of my grandmother
who I always thought was an angel.

She would always feed the birds
from her balcony
throwing bread crumbs
so there are things
within these fences
that remind
me of good memories
and loved ones from the past.

Hoppers

You know the housing unit I live on is
    the pits
A
Wing
You have all the
maximum security inmates
and it's where you have all the ticket
    maxes
people that constantly stay in trouble
that are on and off of lock.
So they have all the misfits
and outcasts
that they can't control
They're just loud
They're obnoxious
and just downright disgusting
They're hoppers.
They're buck wild.
Sometimes I have to laugh at 'em.
There are people who have been here
    a long time
that have a lot of time
they aren't troublesome people
they don't get into trouble
they don't look for trouble
they don't follow trouble
and they stay out of trouble

I don't think it's fair that they keep
    them on A Wing
with all the misfits
and the ticket maxes
and all the trouble
I mean we
have to be here
and we're gonna be here for a while
for now we have to be here
and we have to make the best of a bad
    situation
I'm trying to live
as normal a life
as I can possibly live
by getting up every morning
and going to work
and just
and coming in and gettin' your shower
and maybe going to dinner and going
    to school
and then in hopes
of quiet time for an hour
and then getting up and doing it all
    over again
and I just think it's so unfair
that I have to be in an environment
    like that.

Officer on Duty

Warden Carter told me that in 1939, when the prison was built, it was racially segregated, and there "was a handful—maybe twenty" women. The officers were called matrons. There were no security fences until the late sixties.

Lt. S.-J. and I walked around the grounds (called the campus). It was snow-covered and looked exactly like a college, with red brick buildings spaced apart. She yelled out to another officer who had agreed to go pick up her mother, since she'd be staying late with me. That's exactly the Baltimore I remember, a community where folks did favors for one another all the time. Inside these fences, however, a favor for the inmates was loaded. And a favor between officers and inmates could be a disaster. Lt. S.-J. had a kind of confidence about her relationship with the women. I asked her what the crux of it was. "They know I'm fair," she said.

I learned from her that it is often unclear how long a "life sentence" actually is.

Six Numbers
Lt. Somerville-Jones

I can't
judge somebody else
that's what I had to learn
about working in a prison.
I had a problem dealing with the crimes
    that these people had committed.
I was bothered by child murderers.
But I had to do some soul-searching.
Our job is not to judge anybody.
No one can ever say what they won't do.
Because you don't know what a person
    goes through.
Everyone here has six numbers.
There's no big crime
and there's no little crime.
There's no black crime.
There's no white crime.
Not everybody in here is a criminal.
You have people here who have done
    some horrendous things
and they deserve to be here.
But
let's say
last night
when the weather was real bad.
And you go up here to 175.
And you look left and right.
You don't see anything.

You pull out.
You hit a car.
And you kill a little old lady.
You're coming to jail for vehicular
    manslaughter.
So does that make you a criminal?
You have a lot of tragedies here.
I mean
to me
all of 'em is tragedies
especially
the teen-agers.
I mean
high-school kids
who had lives
and now they have six numbers.
I'm a Baptist.
I believe in God
and I pray
I pray for the girls every night
on my knees.
Yes I do.
I ask Him to bless everybody
and
let So-and-So get through this time.
And what I want to know is,
how long is life? ◆

48

Black English/Ebonics: What It Be Like?

GENEVA SMITHERMAN

I looked at my hands, they looked new
I looked at my feet, and they did too
I got a new way of walkin, and a new way
*   of talkin.*

Traditional Black Gospel Song

The month after the Oakland school board passed its resolution, the term *Ebonics* turned twenty-four years old. Yeah, dass right, the name is over two decades old. It was coined by a group of Black scholars as a new way of talkin bout the language of African slave descendants. Like the message of that old Gospel tune, "Ebonics" was about transformation, about intellectuals among the Talented Tenth striking a blow for the linguistic liberation of our people. The guru in this group of scholars at that "Language and the Urban Child" conference, convened in St. Louis, Missouri, in January 1973, was the brilliant clinical psychologist, Dr. Robert L. Williams, now Professor Emeritus, Washington University. In the book of conference proceedings Williams published in 1975, he captures the thinking of that historical moment:

> *A significant incident occurred at the conference. The black conferees were so critical of the work on the subject done by white researchers, many of whom also happened to be present, that they decided to caucus among themselves and define black language from a black perspective. It was in this caucus that the term* Ebonics *was created. [The term refers to] linguistic and paralinguistic features which on a concentric continuum represent the communicative competence of the West African, Caribbean, and United States slave descendant of African origin. It includes the various idioms, patois, argots, ideolects, and social dialects of black people, especially those who have been forced to adapt to colonial circumstances. (1975, Preface, Introduction)*

For this group of scholars, the conceptual framework of "Ebonics" represented an avenue for decolonization of the African-American mind, a way to begin repairing the psycholinguistically maimed psyche of Blacks in America. As Paulo Freire (1985) would put it twelve years later, "language variations (female language, ethnic language, dialects) are intimately interconnected with, coincide with, and express identity. They help defend one's sense of identity and they are absolutely necessary in the process of struggling for liberation" (p. 186). Ebonics reaffirms the inter-relatedness of language and culture and links Africans in America with Africans around the globe.

Ebonics: neither "broken" English, nor "sloppy" speech, nor merely "slang," nor some bizarre lingo spoken only by baggy-pants-wearing Black kids. Rather, the variety of Ebonics spoken in the United States (hereafter USEB) is rooted in the Black American Oral Tradition and represents a synthesis of African (primarily West African) and European (primarily English) linguistic-cultural traditions. The linguistic shape of the words in USEB can readily be identified as Standard English, that is, the Language of Wider Communication here in the United States (hereafter LWC), but these words do not always have the same meaning in USEB as in LWC. Further, there are many words of direct African origin—for example, *okay, gorilla, cola, jazz*—that are now part of LWC (often without props to us African slave descendants). However, what gives Black Language (un-huh, dat ain no typo, I meant "language") its distinctiveness is the nuanced meanings of these English words, the pronunciations, the ways in which the words are combined to form grammatical statements, and the communicative practices of the USEB-speaking community. In short, USEB may be thought of as the Africanization of American English.

Patterns of Ebonics

In the next section, I discuss the following patterns of USEB: (1) aspectual *be*; (2) stressed *been*; (3) multiple negation; (4) adjacency/context in possessives; (5) postvocalic /r/ deletion; (6) copula absence; (7) camouflaged and other unique lexical forms.

Consider this statement, which comes from some Black women just kickin it in the beauty shop (gloss: conversational chit-chat at a hair salon): "The Brotha be lookin good; that's what got the Sista nose open!" In this statement, *Brotha* is USEB for an African-American man, *lookin good* refers to his style, his attractive appearance (not necessarily the same thing as physical beauty in USEB), *Sista* is USEB for an African-American woman, and her passionate love for the Brotha is conveyed by the phrase *nose open* (in USEB, the kind of passionate love that makes you vulnerable to exploitation). *Sista nose* is standard USEB grammar for denoting possession, indicated by adjacency/context (that is, rather than the LWC /'s, s'/). The use of *be* means that the quality of *lookin good* is not limited to the present moment but reflects the Brotha's past, present, and future essence. As in the case of Efik and other Niger-Congo languages, USEB has an aspectual verb system, conveyed by the use of the English verb *be* to denote iterativity (that is, a recurring or habitual state-of-affairs; contrast *He be lookin good* with *He lookin good*, which refers to the present moment only—not the kind of *lookin good* that opens the nose!). Note further that many Black writers and Rap artists employ the spellings "Brotha" and "Sista." Now, they ain just tryin to be cute. These orthographic representations are used to convey a phonological pattern derived from the influence of West African languages, many of which do not have an /r/ sound. Also in these language communities, kinship terms may be used when referring to African people, whether biologically related or not.

Of course there is overlap between USEB and colloquial, everyday American English—for example, use of "ain't," ending sentences with prepositions, double negatives. However, there are critical distinctions that separate linguistically competent USEB speakers from the wannabes. For example, the colloquial speaker says *gonna* or *goin to* for the LWC form *going to*. But the USEB speaker uses the nasalized vowel form, producing a sound close to, but not identical with, LWC *gone*, thus: "What she go (n) do now?," that is, in LWC, "What is she going to do now?" Another example is in negation patterns. While those obsessed with the "national mania for correctness" often rail against colloquial speakers' double negatives, USEB is distinctive not only for its negative inversion, but also for its *multiple* negatives, that is, three or more negatives formed from combinations of indefinite pronouns and/or adjectives. Check out this exclamation of complex negative inversion from a devout church-goer: "Don't nobody don't know God can't tell me nothin!," that is, in LWC, "A person who doesn't believe in God and isn't saved has no credibility with me."

As mentioned above, USEB words may look like mainstream American English, but the usage and meaning are different. This is the source of a good deal of miscommunication and misunderstanding between USEB and LWC speakers. In response to the question, "Is she married?," the USEB speaker may answer "She been married." If the speaker pronounces *been* without stress, it means the woman in question was once married but is now divorced. If the speaker pronounces *been* with stress, it means she married a long time ago and is still married. Another example is the use of LWC words that are "camouflaged" (Spears, 1982). For example, in the USEB statement, "She come tellin me I'n [didn't] know what I was talkin bout," the verb *come* does not denote motion as in LWC. Rather the meaning of *come* in this context is one of indignation, that is, in LWC, "She had the audacity to tell me that I didn't know what I was talking about. How dare she!" Yet another kind of cross communication example comes from semantic inversion. Due to crossover and the popular appeal of Michael Jackson, most people are aware that *bad* in USEB translates to *good* in LWC; however, lexical items that haven't enjoyed such a high degree of crossover are problematic in these crosscultural exchanges. For example, consider the following form of address common among many Black males; "Yo, Dog!" *Dog* is a linguistic symbol of male bonding, most likely derived from the African-American fraternity tradition of referring to pledges as *dogs. Yo, Dog!* was used by a Brotha on lock down (gloss: imprisoned) to address his European-American male psychiatrist as an expression of camaraderie. Turns out, though, that this white psychiatrist was not yet down (gloss: hip, understanding of the Black Cultural framework). He misinterpreted the Brotha's greeting and made an issue of the "insult."

The above are only some of the patterns in the grammatical, phonological, and semantic systems of USEB. To explore the full 360 degrees of USEB, we need to move on to styles of speaking. In fact, it is the area of communicative practices—rhetorical strategies and modes of discourse—that cuts across gender, generation, and class in the African-American community. USEB speech acts may be classified as follows: (1) Call-Response; (2) Tonal Semantics; (3) Narrativizing; (4) Proverb Use/Proverbializing; (5) Signification/Signifyin; (6) The Dozens/Snappin/Joanin. Discussion of two of these discourse modes follows.

Signification or, more commonly, *signifyin*, which can be rendered with or without the phonological and morphosyntactical patterns of USEB, is a form of ritualized insult in which a speaker puts down, talks about, needles—signifies on—other speakers. In this communicative practice, the speaker deploys exaggeration, irony, and indirection as a way of saying something on two different levels at once. It is often used to send a message of social critique, a bit of social commentary on the actions or statements of someone who is in need of a wake-up call. When signifyin is done with verbal dexterity, it avoids the creation of social distance between speaker and audience because the rich humor makes you laugh to keep from crying. Like Malcolm X who once began a speech with these words: "Mr. Moderator, Brother Lomax, Brothas and Sistas, friends and enemies." Now, you don't usually begin a speech by addressing your enemies. Thus, Malcolm's signifyin statement let his audience know that he knew inimical forces were in their midst. Or like one of the deacons at this Traditional Black Church, where the preacher would never deal with the problems and issues folk were facing on a daily basis. Rather, he was always preachin bout the pearly gates and how great thangs was gon be at dat home up in the sky. So one day this deacon said to the preacher, "Reb, you know, I got a home in Heaven, but I ain't homesick!"

Signifyin is engaged in by all age groups and by both males and females in the Black community. It has the following characteristics: (1) indirection, circumlocution; (2) metaphorical-imagistic (images rooted in the everyday real world); (3) humorous, ironic; (4) rhythmic fluency; (5) teachy, but not preachy; (6) directed at person(s) present in the speech situation (signifiers do not talk behind your back); (7) punning, play on words; (8) introduction of the semantically or logically unexpected.

Types of Signification

There are two types of Signification. One type is leveled at a person's mother (and occasionally at other relatives). Traditionally, this first type was referred to as "The

Dozens"/"playin The Dozens." The second type of signifyin is aimed at a person, action, or thing, either just for fun or for corrective criticism. Today, the two types of Signification are being conflated under a more general form of discourse, referred to as "snappin."

To fully appreciate the skill and complexity of Signification, we shall analyze in some detail a conversational excerpt involving two Sistas in a group of several at a wedding shower:

LINDA: Girl, what up with that head? [Referring to her friend's hairstyle.]

BETTY: Ask yo momma. [Laughter from all the Sistas on this conversational set.]

LINDA: Oh, so you going there, huh? Well, I *DID* ask my momma. And she said, "Cain't you see that Betty look like her momma spit her out?" [Laughter from all, including Betty.]

Betty and Linda signify on each other. Instead of answering Linda's question directly, Betty decides to inform Linda that the condition of her hairstyle is none of Linda's business by responding with "Ask yo momma." The usual expectation in a conversation is that a speaker's question will be answered honestly and sincerely; thus Betty's unexpected indirection produces laughter from the listeners.

Speech act theory indicates that communication succeeds or fails as a result of the illocutionary (that is, intended) and perlocutionary (that is, received) effects of a message. The surface meaning of "yo momma" for those outside the USEB speech community is simply "your mother/mom." However, within the Black speech community, the utterance immediately signals that an insult has been hurled. The intended and received meaning of *yo momma* is invective; the game of ritual insult begins with participants creating the most appropriate, humorous, spontaneous, creative, exaggerated/untrue retorts that they can come up with.

The source of the retort "Ask yo momma" probably stems from family patterns in which mothers are consulted ("asked") about all kinds of things, great or small. Fathers may even respond to their children's questions or requests by saying "Ask your mother." In USEB, the speaker does not intend the direct meaning, "You should go and ask your mother about this situation." Rather, given the conversational context, the speaker is indirectly saying "Let the game of The Dozens begin." Linda clearly recognizes the entry into this game as indicated by her response, "Oh, so you going there, huh?" Unskilled players, lacking a spontaneous, apposite, humorous retort, would have let the conversation end at this point. However, Linda shows adeptness in playing the game. She regroups momentarily ("Oh, so you going there, huh?") and fires back skillfully. In fact, she "caps" (gloss: wins) this exchange with a more clever retort. Although Betty's use of the intragroup expression, *ask yo momma*, is humorous and sets up a challenge, it is formulaic, simplistic, and stylized. In this instance, it cannot, and does not, beat: "Well, I *DID* ask my momma. And she said, 'Cain't you see that Betty look like her momma spit her out?' " (Troutman-Robinson and Smitherman, 1997).

Although Rev. Jesse Jackson and Sista Maya Angelou came out in the national news and dissed the Oakland school board's resolution, they are well versed in

USEB. Twenty years ago, in my first major work on USEB, *Talkin and Testifyin*, I quoted both at length and lauded them as linguistic role models, who are adept at capitalizing on the forms of Black Language to convey profound political messages. Like Jesse who is down wit Signification: "Pimp, punk, prostitute, preacher, Ph.D.—all the P's, you still in slavery!" Thus he conveys the message that all members of the African-American community, regardless of their social status, are marginalized and disempowered, by virtue of U.S. historically institutionalized racism and skin color bias. (Jesse also uses copula absence here—"you still in slavery"— which has not been found in any of the dialects of British English that came over on the *Mayflower*, but which is used widely in the languages of West Africa.)

The Dozens

As mentioned above, The Dozens is one of several significant speech acts in USEB. This ritualized game of insult has analogues in West African communicative practices (see Smitherman, 1995, and the several reference cited there). Also referred to as "snappin" by many members of the Hip Hop Nation, The Dozens is like "Yo momma so dumb she thought a quarterback was a refund!"

Sista Maya Angelou is so bad she don't play The Dozens, she play The Thirteens! She uses this USEB discourse mode to critique the actions of Blacks and whites. Here how she do it:

> *(The Thirteens Black):*
>
> *Your Momma took to shouting*
>
> *Your Poppa's gone to war,*
>
> *Your sister's in the streets*
>
> *Your brother's in the bar,*
>
> *The thirteens. Right On . . .*
>
> *And you, you make me sorry*
>
> *You out here by yourself,*
>
> *I'd call you something dirty,*
>
> *But there just ain't nothing left,*
>
> *cept*
>
> *The thirteens. Right On . . .*
>
> *(The Thirteens White):*
>
> *Your daughter wears a jock strap,*
>
> *Your son he wears a bra*
>
> *Your brother jonesed your cousin*
>
> *in the back seat of the car.*

The thirteens. Right On . . .

Your money thinks you're something

But if I'd learned to curse,

I'd tell you what your name is

But there just ain't nothing worse

than

The thirteens. Right On.

(Angelou, 1971)

African-French psychiatrist Frantz Fanon (1967) taught that "every dialect, every language, is a way of thinking. To speak means to assume a culture." To speak Ebonics is to assume the cultural legacy of U.S. slave descendants of African origin. To speak Ebonics is to assert the power of this tradition in the quest to resolve the unfinished business of being African in America. While years of massive research (done in the 1960s and early 1970s) on the language of this group (mostly by white scholars) did indeed debunk cognitive-linguistic deficiency theory, in its place arose social inadequacy theory. Although the language was shown to be systematic and rule-governed, since it is not accepted by the white mainstream, difference became deficit all over again, and in the process, Africans in America suffered further dislocation. To speak (of/on/about) Ebonics, to consciously employ this terminology and conceptual framework, as those Black scholars did back in 1973, and as the Oakland school board has done a generation later, is to be bout the business of relocating African Americans to subject position. Large and in charge, as the Hip Hoppers say, Ebonics, then and now, symbolizes a new way of talkin the walk about language and liberatory education for African Americans.

References

Angelou, M. (1971). *Just Give Me a Cool Drink of Water 'fore I Die.* New York: Random House.

Fanon, F. (1967). The Negro and Language. In *Black Skin, White Masks.* New York: Grove Press.

Freire, P. (1985). *The Politics of Education: Culture, Power, and Liberation* (D. Macedo, Trans.). Massachusetts: Bergin & Garvey Publishers, now an imprint of Greenwood Publishing Group, Westport, CT.

Smitherman, G. (1977, 1986). *Talkin and Testifyin: The Language of Black America.* Detroit: Wayne State University Press.

Smitherman, G. (1995). Introduction. In J. Percelay, S. Dweck, and M. Ivey, *Double Snaps.* New York: William Morrow.

Spears, A. K. (1982). The Black English Semi-Auxiliary Come. *Language 58*(4), 850–872.

Troutman-Robinson, D., & Smitherman, G. (1997). Discourse as Social Interaction. In T. A. van Dijk (Ed.), *Discourse, Ethnicity, Culture, and Racism.* (pp. 144–180). London: Sage Publications.

Williams, R. L. (Ed.). (1975). *Ebonics: The True Language of Black Folks.* St. Louis: Institute of Black Studies.

49

Tense Present: Democracy, English, and the Wars Over Usage

DAVID FOSTER WALLACE

"Save up to 50%—and More!" Between you and I. On accident. Somewhat of a Kustom Kar Kare Autowash. "The cause was due to numerous factors." "Orange Crush—A Taste That's All It's Own." "Vigorex: Helping men conquer sexual issues." "Equal numbers of both men and women oppose the amendment." Feedback. "As drinking water becomes more and more in short supply." "IMATION—Borne of 3M Innovation." Point in time. Time frame. "At this point in time, the individual in question was observed, and subsequently apprehended by authorities." Here for you, there for you. *Fail to comply with* for *violate*. Comprised of. From whence. *Quote* for *quotation*. *Nauseous* for *nauseated*. Besides the point. To mentor, to parent. To partner. To critique. *Indicated* for *said*. *Parameters* for *limits* and *options* for *choices* and *viable options* for *options* and *workable solution* for *solution*. In point of fact. Prior to this time. As of this point in the time frame. Serves to. Tends to be. *Convince* for *persuade*. *Append* for *attach*, *portion* for *part*. Commence, cease. Expedite. *Request* for *ask*. *Eventuate* for *happen*. Subsequent to this time. Productive. Facilitate. Aid in.

Utilize. Detrimental. Equates with. In regards to. Tragic, tragedy. *Grow* as transitive. *Keep* for *stay*. "To demonstrate the power of Epson's new Stylus Color Inkjet Printer with 1440 d.p.i., just listen:" Could care less, Issues, core issues. Fellow colleagues. Goal-orientated. Resources. Unproductive. Feelings. *Share* for *speak*. Nurture, empower, recover. *Valid* for *true*. Authentic. Productive, unproductive. "I choose to view my opponent's negative attacks as unproductive to the real issues facing the citizens of this campaign." Incumbent upon. Mandate. Plurality. *Per anum*. Conjunctive adverbs in general. Instantaneous. *Quality* as adj. Proactive. Proactive Mission-Statement. Positive feedback. A positive role-model. Compensation. Validation. As for example. True facts are often impactful. "Call now for your free gift!" I only wish. Not too good of a. Pay the consequences of. At this juncture. "Third-leading cause of death of both American men and women." To reference. To process. Process. The process of. The healing process. The grieving process. "Processing of feelings is a major component of the grieving process." Commensurant. "Till the stars fall from the sky/For you and I" Working together. Efficacious, effectual. Lifestyle. This phenomena, these criterion. Irregardless. *If* for *whether*. "Both sides are working together to achieve a workable consensus." Functional, dysfunctional. Family of origin. S. O. To nest. Relationship. Merge together. KEEP IN LANE. Whomever wants it. "My wife and myself wish to express our gratitude and thanks to you for being here to support us at this difficult time in our life." Eventuate. Diversity. Quality time. Values, family values. To conference. "French provincial twin bed with canape and box spring, $150." Take a wait-and-see attitude. Cum-N-Go Quik Mart. Travelodge. Self-confessed. Precise estimate. "Travel-times on the expressways are reflective of its still being bad out there." Budgetel. EZPAY. RENT2OWN. MENS' ROOM. LADY'S ROOM. *Individual* for *person*. *Whom* for *who*, *that* for *who*. "The accident equated to a lot of damage." lpsedixie. Falderol. " 'Waiting on' is a dialectical locution on the rise and splitting its meaning." Staunch the flow A.M. in the morning. *Forte* as "forté." Advisement. Most especially. Sum total. Final totals. Complete dearth. "You can donate your used car or truck in any condition." "DiBlasi's work shows how sex can bring people together and pull them apart." "Come in and take advantage of our knowledgeable staff." "We get the job done, not make excuses." "Chances of rain are prevalent." National Highway Traffic Safety Administration Rule and Regulation Amendment Task Force. *Further* for *farther*. "The Fred Pryor Seminar has opened my eyes to better time management techniques. Also it has given real life situations and how to deal with them effectively." Hands-on, can-do. "Each of the variants indicated in boldface type count as an entry." Visualization. "Insert and tighten metric calibrated hexscrews (K) into arc (C) comprised of intersecting vertical pieces (A) along transverse section of Structure. (see Diagram for #(3–4 inv.)" Creative, creativity. To message, to send a message, to bring our message to. To reach out to. Context. Straightlaced. A factor, a decisive factor. Myriads of decisive factors. "It is a federal requirement to comply with all safety regulations on this flight." In this context, of this context. On a __ly basis. From the standpoint of. Contextualization. Within the parameters of this context. Decontextualization. Defamiliarize. Orientated. "The artist's employment of a radical visual idiom serves to decontextualize both conventional modes of representation and the patriarchal contexts on which such traditional hegemonic notions as representation, tradition, and even conventional contextualization have come to be seen as depending for their privileged status as aestheto-interpretive mechanisms." I don't feel well and hope I recoup. "As parents, the responsibility of talking to your kids about drugs is up to you." Who would of thought? Last and final call. As to. Achieve. Achievement. Competitive. Challenge, challenged, challenges. Excellence. Pursuit of a standard of total excellence. An astute observance. *Misrepresent* for *lie*. A longstanding tradition of achievement in the arena of excellence. "All copier stores are not the same." Visible to the eye. *Which* for *that, I* for *me*. That which. In regards to. Data as singular, *media* as singular, *graffiti* as singular. *Remain* for *stay*. On-task. Escalate as transitive. Closure. Community. "Iran must realize that it cannot flaunt with impunity the expressed will and law of the world community." Community support. Community-based. Broad appeal. Rally support. Outpourings of support. "Tried to lay the cause at the feet of Congress." Epidemic proportions. Proportionate response. Feasibility. "This anguishing national ordeal." Bipartisan, nonpartisan. Widespread outbreaks. To appeal to. To impact. Author's Foreward. Hew and cry. From this aspect. Hayday. Appropriate, inappropriate. Contingency. Contingent upon. Every possible contingency. Audible to the ear. *As* for *since*. Palpably. "The enormity of his accomplishment." Frigid temperatures. Loud volume. Surrounded on all sides, my workable options are at this time few in number. Chaise lounge, nucular, deep-seeded, bedroom suit, reek havoc. Her ten-year rein atop the competition. The reason is because she still continues to hue to the basic fundamentals. Ouster. Lucrative salaries, expensive prices. *Forbear* for *forebear; forgo* for *forego*. Breech of conduct. Award for meretricious service. Substantiate, unsubstantiated, substantial. Reelected to another term. Fulsome praise. Service. Public service. "A tradition of servicing your needs." A commitment to accountability in a lifetime of public service. As best as we can. WAVE ALL INTEREST FOR 90 DAYS "But I also want to have—be the president that protects the rights of, of people to, to have arms. And that—so you don't go so far that the legitimate rights on some legislation are, are, you know, impinged on." "Dr. Charles Frieses'." Conflict. Conflict-resolution. The mutual advantage of both sides in this widespread conflict. "We will make a determination in terms of an appropriate response." Future plans. Don't go there! PLEASE WAIT HERE UNTIL NEXT AVAILABLE CLERK. I thought to myself. Fellow countrymen. "Your efforts to recover from the experience of growing up in an alcoholic family may be very difficult and threatening for your family to hear about and accept, especially if they are still in the midst of their own survival." *Misappropriate* for *steal*. Nortorious. I'll be there momentarily. At some later point in time. I'm not adverse to that. "Hello-o?" Have a good one. Luv Ya.:)

Discussed in this essay:

A Dictionary of Modern American Usage, by Bryan A. Garner. Oxford University Press, 1998. 723 pages. $35.

A Dictionary of Modern English Usage, by H. W Fowler. Oxford University Press, 1926. Rev. by Sir Ernest Gowers, 1965. 725 pages.

The Language Instinct: How the Mind Creates Language, by Steven Pinker. William Morrow and Company, 1994. 494 pages.

Webster's Dictionary of English Usage, E. W Gilman, ed. Merriam-Webster Inc., 1989. 978 pages.

Usage and Abusage: A Guide to Good English, by Eric Partridge. Hamish Hamilton, 1957. 392 pages.

Webster's Third New International Dictionary of the English Language, Philip Gove, ed. G. & C. Merriam Company, 1961. 2,662 pages.

> *Dilige et quod vis fac.*

> —*ST. AUGUSTINE*

Did you know that probing the seamy underbelly of U.S. lexicography reveals ideological strife and controversy and intrigue and nastiness and fervor on a nearly hanging-chad scale? For instance, did you know that some modern dictionaries are notoriously liberal and others notoriously conservative, and that certain conservative dictionaries were actually conceived and designed as corrective responses to the "corruption" and "permissiveness" of certain liberal dictionaries? That the oligarchic device of having a special "Distinguished Usage Panel ... of outstanding professional speakers and writers" is an attempted compromise between the forces of egalitarianism and traditionalism in English, but that most linguistic liberals dismiss the Usage Panel as mere sham-populism?

Did you know that U.S. lexicography even *had* a seamy underbelly?

The occasion for this article is Oxford University Press's semi-recent release of Bryan A. Garner's *A Dictionary of Modern American Usage.* The fact of the matter is that Garner's dictionary is extremely good, certainly the most comprehensive usage guide since E. W Gilman's *Webster's Dictionary of English Usage;* now a decade out of date.[1] Its format, like that of Gilman and the handful of other great American usage guides of the last century, includes entries on individual words and phrases and expostulative small-cap MINI-ESSAYS on any issue broad enough to warrant more general discussion. But the really distinctive and ingenious features of *A Dictionary of Modern American Usage* involve issues of rhetoric and ideology and style, and it is impossible to describe why these issues are important and why Garner's management of them borders on genius without talking about the

---

[1]With the advent of online databases, Garner has access to far more examples of actual usage than did Gilman, and he deploys them to great effect. (FYI, Oxford's 1996 *New Fowler's Modern English Usage* is also extremely comprehensive and good, but its emphasis is on British usage.)

[2]Sorry about this phrase; I hate this phrase, too. This happens to be one of those very rare times when "historical context" is the phrase to use and there is no equivalent phrase that isn't even worse. (I actually tried "lexico-temporal backdrop" in one of the middle drafts, which I think you'll agree is not preferable.)

INTERPOLATION

The above [para] is motivated by the fact that this reviewer almost always sneers and/or winces when he sees "historical context" deployed in a piece of writing and thus hopes to head off any potential sneers/winces from the reader here, especially in an article about felicitous usage.

historical context[2] in which *ADMAU* appears, and this context turns out to be a veritable hurricane of controversies involving everything from technical linguistics to public education to political ideology, and these controversies take a certain amount of time to unpack before their relation to what makes Garner's usage guide so eminently worth your hard-earned reference-book dollar can even be established; and in fact there's no way even to begin the whole harrowing polymeric discussion without taking a moment to establish and define the highly colloquial term *SNOOT*.

From one perspective, a certain irony attends the publication of any good new book on American usage. It is that the people who are going to be interested in such a book are also the people who are least going to need it, i.e., that offering counsel on the finer points of U.S. English is Preaching to the Choir. The relevant Choir here comprises that small percentage of American citizens who actually care about the current status of double modals and ergative verbs. The same sorts of people who watched *Story of English* on PBS (twice) and read W Safire's column with their half-caff every Sunday. The sorts of people who feel that special blend of wincing despair and sneering superiority when they see EXPRESS LANE—10 ITEMS OR LESS or hear *dialogue* used as a verb or realize that the founders of the Super 8 motel chain must surely have been ignorant of the meaning of *suppurate*. There are lots of epithets for people like this—Grammar Nazis, Usage Nerds, Syntax Snobs, the Language Police. The term I was raised with is *SNOOT*.[3] The word might be slightly self-mocking, but those other terms are outright dysphemisms. A SNOOT can be defined as somebody who knows what *dysphemism* means and doesn't mind letting you know it.

I submit that we SNOOTs are just about the last remaining kind of truly elitist nerd. There are, granted, plenty of nerd-species in today's America, and some of these are elitist within their own nerdy purview (e.g., the skinny, carbuncular, semi-autistic Computer Nerd moves instantly up on the totem pole of status when your screen freezes and now you need his help, and the bland condescension with which he performs the two occult keystrokes that unfreeze your screen is both elitist and situationally valid). But the SNOOT's purview is interhuman social life itself. You don't, after all (despite withering cultural pressure), have to use a computer, but you can't escape language: Language is everything and everywhere; it's what lets us have anything to do with one another; it's what separates us from the animals; Genesis 11:7–10 and so on. And we SNOOTs know when and how to hyphenate phrasal adjectives and to keep participles from dangling, and we know that we know, and we know how very few other Americans know this stuff or even care, and we judge them accordingly.

In ways that certain of us are uncomfortable about, SNOOTs' attitudes about contemporary usage resemble religious/political conservatives' attitudes about con-

---

[3]*SNOOT* (n) (*highly colloq*) is this reviewer's nuclear family's nickname *à clef* for a really extreme usage fanatic, the sort of person whose idea of Sunday fun is to look for mistakes in Safire's column's prose itself. This reviewer's family is roughly 70 percent SNOOT, which term itself derives from an acronym, with the big historical family joke being that whether S.N.O.O.T. stood for "*Sprachgefühl* Necessitates Our Ongoing Tendance" or "Syntax Nudniks of Our Time" depended on whether or not you were one.

temporary culture:[4] We combine a missionary zeal and a near-neural faith in our beliefs' importance with a curmudgeonly hell-in-a-handbasket despair at the way English is routinely manhandled and corrupted by supposedly educated people. The Evil is all around us: boners and clunkers and solecistic howlers and bursts of voguish linguistic methane that make any SNOOT's cheek twitch and forehead darken. A fellow SNOOT I know likes to say that listening to most people's English feels like watching somebody use a Stradivarius to pound nails. We[5] are the Few, the Proud, the Appalled at Everyone Else.

---

[4]This is true in my own case at any rate—plus also the "uncomfortable" part. I teach college English part-time—mostly Lit, not Comp. But I am also so pathologically anal about* usage that every semester the same thing happens: The minute I have read my students' first set of papers, we immediately abandon the regular Lit syllabus and have a three-week Emergency Remedial Usage Unit, during which my demeanor is basically that of somebody teaching HIV prevention to intravenous-drug users. When it emerges (as it does, every time) that 95 percent of these intelligent upscale college students have never been taught, e.g., what a clause is or why a misplaced *only* can make a sentence confusing, I all but pound my head on the blackboard: I exhort them to sue their hometown school boards. The kids end up scared, both of me and for me.

*Editor's Note: Author insisted this phrase replace "obsessed with" and took umbrage at the suggestion that this change clearly demonstrated the very quality he wished to denigrate.

[5]Please note that the strategically repeated 1-P pronoun is meant to iterate and emphasize that this reviewer is very much one too, a SNOOT, plus to connote the nuclear family mentioned supra. SNOOTitude runs in families. In, *ADMAU's* Preface, Bryan Garner mentions both his father and grandfather and actually uses the word *genetic*, and it's probably true: 95 percent of the SNOOTs I know have at least one parent who is, by profession or temperament or both, a SNOOT. In my own case, my mom is a Comp teacher and has written remedial usage books and is a SNOOT of the most rabid and intractable sort. At least part of the reason I am a SNOOT is that for years Mom brainwashed us in all sorts of subtle ways. Here's an example. Family suppers often involved a game: If one of us children made a usage error, Mom would pretend to have a coughing fit that would go on and on until the relevant child had identified the relevant error and corrected it. It was all very self-ironic and lighthearted; but still, looking back, it seems a bit excessive to pretend that your child is actually *denying you oxygen* by speaking incorrectly. But the really chilling thing is that I now sometimes find myself playing this same "game" with my own students, complete with pretend pertussion.

INTERPOLATION

As something I'm all but sure *Harper's* will excise, I'll also insert that we even had a lighthearted but retrospectively chilling little family *song* that Mom and we little SNOOTlets would sing in the car on long trips while Dad silently rolled his eyes and drove (you have to remember the title theme of *Underdog* in order to follow the song):

When idiots in this world appear
And fail to be concise or clear
And solecisms rend the ear
The cry goes up both far and near
For Blunder Dog
Blunder Dog
Blunder Dog
Blunder Dog
*[etc.]**

*(Since this'll almost surely get cut, I'll admit that, yes, I, as a kid, was the actual author of this song. But by this time I'd been thoroughly brainwashed. And just about the whole car sang along. It was sort of our family's version of "100 Bottles . . . Wall.")

Thesis Statement for Whole Article

Issues of tradition vs. egalitarianism in U.S. English are at root political issues and can be effectively addressed only in what this article hereby terms a "Democratic Spirit." A Democratic Spirit is one that combines rigor and humility. i.e., passionate conviction plus sedulous respect for the convictions of others. As any American knows, this is a very difficult spirit to cultivate and maintain, particularly when it comes to issues you feel strongly about. Equally tough is a D.S.'s criterion of 100 percent intellectual integrity—you have to be willing to look honestly at yourself and your motives for believing what you believe, and to do it more or less continually.

This kind of stuff is advanced U.S. citizenship. A true Democratic Spirit is up there with religious faith and emotional maturity and all those other top-of-the-Maslow-Pyramid-type qualities people spend their whole lives working on. A Democratic Spirit's constituent rigor and humility and honesty are in fact so hard to maintain on certain issues that it's almost irresistibly tempting to fall in with some established dogmatic camp and to follow that camp's line on the issue and to let your position harden within the camp and become inflexible and to believe that any other camp is either evil or insane and to spend all your time and energy trying to shout over them.

I submit, then, that it is indisputably easier to be dogmatic than Democratic, especially about issues that are both vexed and highly charged. I submit further that the issues surrounding "correctness" in contemporary American usage are both vexed and highly charged, and that the fundamental questions they involve are ones whose answers have to be "worked out" instead of simply found.

A distinctive feature of *ADMAU* is that its author is willing to acknowledge that a usage dictionary is not a bible or even a textbook but rather just the record of one smart person's attempts to work out answers to certain very difficult questions. This willingness appears to me to be informed by a Democratic Spirit. The big question is whether such a spirit compromises Garner's ability to present himself as a genuine "authority" on issues of usage. Assessing Garner's book, then, involves trying to trace out the very weird and complicated relationship between Authority and Democracy in what we as a culture have decided is English. That relationship is, as many educated Americans would say, still in process at this time.

A *Dictionary of Modern American Usage* has no Editorial Staff or Distinguished Panel. It's conceived, researched, and written *ab ovo usque ad mala* by Bryan Garner. This is an interesting guy. He's both a lawyer and a lexicographer (which seems a bit like being both a narcotics dealer and a DEA agent). His 1987 *A Dictionary of Modern Legal Usage* is already a minor classic; now, instead of practicing law anymore, he goes around conducting writing seminars for J.D.'s and doing prose-consulting for various judicial bodies. Garner's also the founder of something called the H. W Fowler Society,[6] a worldwide group of usage-Trekkies who like to send

---

[6]If Samuel Johnson is the Shakespeare of English usage, think of Henry Watson Fowler as the Eliot or Joyce. His 1926 *A Dictionary of Modern English Usage* is the granddaddy of modern usage guides, and its dust-dry wit and blushless imperiousness have been models for every subsequent classic in the field, from Eric Partridge's *Usage and Abusage* to Theodore Bernstein's *The Careful Writer* to Wilson Follett's *Modern American Usage* to Gilman's '89 *Webster's*.

one another linguistic boners clipped from different periodicals. You get the idea. This Garner is one serious and very hard-core SNOOT.

The lucid, engaging, and extremely sneaky Preface to *ADMAU* serves to confirm Garner's SNOOTitude in fact while undercutting it in tone. For one thing, whereas the traditional usage pundit cultivates a sort of remote and imperial persona—the kind who uses *one* or *we* to refer to himself—Garner gives us an almost Waltonishly endearing sketch of his own background:

> *I realized early—at the age of 15[7]—that my primary intellectual interest was the use of the English language. . . . It became an all-consuming passion. . . . I read everthing I could find on the subject. Then, on a wintry evening while visiting New Mexico at the age of 16, I discovered Eric Partridge's Usage and Abusage. I was enthralled. Never had I held a more exciting book. . . . Suffice it to say that by the time I was 18, I had committed to memory most of Fowler, Partridge, and their successors. . . .*

Although this reviewer regrets the biosketch's failure to mention the rather significant social costs of being an adolescent whose overriding passion is English usage,[8] the critical hat is off to yet another personable section of the Preface, one that Garner entitles "First Principles": "Before going any further, I should explain my approach. That's an unusual thing for the author of a usage dictionary to do—unprecedented, as far as I know. But a guide to good writing is only as good as the principles on which it's based. And users should be naturally interested in those principles. So, in the interests of full disclosure. . . ."[9]

The "unprecedented" and "full disclosure" here are actually good-natured digs at Garner's Fowlerite predecessors, and a subtle nod to one camp in the wars that have raged in both lexicography and education ever since the notoriously liberal *Webster's Third New International Dictionary* came out in 1961 and included such terms as *heighth* and *irregardless* without any monitory labels on them. You can think of *Webster's Third* as sort of the Fort Sumter of the contemporary Usage Wars. These Wars are both the context and the target of a very subtle rhetorical strategy in *A Dictionary of Modern American Usage*, and without talking about them it's impossible to explain why Garner's book is both so good and so sneaky.

---

[7](Garner prescribes spelling out only numbers under ten. I was taught that this rule applies just to Business Writing and that in all other modes you spell out one through nineteen and start using cardinals at 20.* *De gustibus non est disputandum.*)

*Editor's Note: The Harper's style manual prescribes spelling out all numbers up to 100.

[8]From personal experience, I can assure you that any kid like this is going to be at best marginalized and at worst savagely and repeatedly Wedgied.

[9]What follow in the Preface are ". . . the ten critical points that, after years of working on usage problems, I've settled on." These points are too involved to treat separately, but a couple of them are slippery in the extreme—e.g., "10. **Actual Usage.** In the end, the actual usage of educated speakers and writers is the overarching criterion for correctness," of which both "educated" and "actual" would require several pages of abstract clarification and qualification to shore up against Usage Wars—related attacks, but which Garner rather ingeniously elects to define and defend via their application in his dictionary itself.

We regular citizens tend to go to The Dictionary for authoritative guidance.[10] Rarely, however, do we ask ourselves who decides what gets in The Dictionary or what words or spellings or pronunciations get deemed "substandard" or "incorrect." Whence the authority of dictionary-makers to decide what's OK[11] and what isn't? Nobody elected them, after all. And simply appealing to precedent or tradition won't work, because what's considered correct changes over time. In the 1600s, for instance, the second-singular pronoun took a singular conjugation—"You is." Earlier still, the standard 2-S pronoun wasn't *you* but *thou*. Huge numbers of now acceptable words like *clever, fun, banter,* and *prestigious* entered English as what usage authorities considered errors or egregious slang. And not just usage conventions but English itself changes over time; if it didn't, we'd all still be talking like Chaucer. Who's to say which changes are natural and which are corruptions? And when Bryan Garner or E. Ward Gilman do in fact presume to say, why should we believe them?

These sorts of questions are not new, but they do now have a certain urgency. America is in the midst of a protracted Crisis of Authority in matters of language. In brief, the same sorts of political upheavals that produced everything from Kent State to Independent Counsels have produced an influential contra- SNOOT school for whom normative standards of English grammar and usage are functions of nothing but custom and superstition and the ovine docility of a populace that lets self-appointed language authorities boss them around. See for example MIT's Steven Pinker in a famous *New Republic* article—" Once introduced, a prescriptive rule is very hard to eradicate, no matter how ridiculous. Inside the writing establishment, the rules survive by the same dynamic that perpetuates ritual genital mutilations"—or, at a somewhat lower pitch, Bill Bryson in *Mother Tongue: English and How It Got That Way:*

> *Who sets down all those rules that we all know about from childhood—the idea that we must never end a sentence with a preposition or begin one with a conjunction, that we must use* each other *for two* things *and* one another *for more than two . . . ? The answer, surprisingly often, is that no one does, that when you look into the background of these "rules" there is often little basis for them.*

In *ADMAU*'s Preface, Garner himself addresses the Authority Question with a Trumanesque simplicity and candor that simultaneously disguise the author's cunning and exemplify it:

> *As you might already suspect, I don't shy away from making judgments. I can't imagine that most readers would want me to. Linguists don't like it, of course, because judgment involves subjectivity.[12] It*

---

[10]There's no better indication of The Dictionary's authority than that we use it to settle wagers. My own father is still to this day living down the outcome of a high-stakes bet on the correct spelling of *meringue,* a wager made on 14 September 1978.

[11]*Editor's Note:* The Harper's *style manual prescribes* okay.

[12]This is a clever half-truth. Linguists compose only one part of the anti-judgment camp, and their objections to usage judgments in volve way more than just "subjectivity."

*isn't scientific. But rhetoric and usage, in the view of most profes-
sional writers, aren't scientific endeavors. You don't want dispassionate
descriptions; you want sound guidance. And that requires judgment.*

Whole monographs could be written just on the masterful rhetoric of this passage.
Note for example the ingenious equivocation of judgment in "I don't shy away
from making judgments" vs. "And that requires judgment." Suffice it to say that
Garner is at all times *Keenly* aware of the Authority Crisis in modern usage; and
his response to this crisis is—in the best Democratic Spirit—rhetorical.
   So . . .

Corollary to Thesis Statement for Whole Article

The most salient and timely feature of Garner's book is that it's both lexicographical and rhetorical. Its main strategy involves what is known in classical rhetoric
as the Ethical Appeal. Here the adjective, derived from the Greek *ethos*, doesn't
mean quite what we usually mean by *ethical*. But there are affinities. What the
Ethical Appeal amounts to is a complex and sophisticated "Trust me." It's the
boldest, most ambitious, and also most distinctively American of rhetorical Appeals,
because it requires the rhetor to convince us not just of his intellectual acuity or technical competence but of his basic decency and fairness and sensitivity to the audience's own hopes and fears.[13]

   These are not qualities one associates with the traditional SNOOT usage-
authority, a figure who pretty much instantiates snobbishness and bow-tied anality, and one whose modern image is not improved by stuff like *American Heritage
Dictionary* Distinguished Usage Panelist Morris Bishop's "The arrant solecisms of
the ignoramus are here often omitted entirely, 'irregardless' of how he may feel
about this neglect" or critic John Simon's "The English language is being treated
nowadays exactly as slave traders once handled their merchandise. . . ." Compare
those lines' authorial personas with Garner's in, e.g., "English usage is so challenging that even experienced writers need guidance now and then."

   The thrust here is going to be that *A Dictionary of Modern American Usage*
earns Garner pretty much all the trust his Ethical Appeal asks us for. The book's
"feel-good" spirit (in the very best sense of "feel-good") marries rigor and humility in such a way as to allow Garner to be extremely prescriptive without any
appearance of evangelism or elitist put-down. This is an extraordinary accomplishment. Understanding why it's basically a *rhetorical* accomplishment, and why
this is both historically significant and (in this reviewer's opinion) politically redemptive, requires a more detailed look at the Usage Wars.

You'd sure know lexicography had an underbelly if you read the little introductory
essays in modern dictionaries—pieces like *Webster's DEU*'s "A Brief History of
English Usage" or *Webster's Third*'s "Linguistic Advances and Lexicography" or
AHD-3's "Usage in the American Heritage Dictionary: The Place of Criticism." But

---

[13]In this last respect, recall for example W. J. Clinton's famous "I feel your pain," which was a blatant if
not particularly masterful Ethical Appeal.

almost nobody ever bothers with these little intros, and it's not just their six-point type or the fact that dictionaries tend to be hard on the lap. It's that these intros aren't actually written for you or me or the average citizen who goes to The Dictionary just to see how to spell (for instance) *meringue*. They're written for other lexicographers and critics, and in fact they're not really introductory at all but polemical. They're salvos in the Usage Wars that have been under way ever since editor Philip Gove first sought to apply the value-neutral principles of structural linguistics to lexicography in *Webster's Third*. Gove's famous response to conservatives who howled[14], when *Webster's Third* endorsed *OK* and described *ain't* as "used orally in most parts of the U.S. by many cultivated speakers [*sic*]" was this: "A dictionary should have no traffic with . . . artificial notions of correctness or superiority. It should be descriptive and not prescriptive." These terms stuck and turned epithetic, and linguistic conservatives are now formally known as Prescriptivists and linguistic liberals as Descriptivists.

The former are far better known. When you read the columns of William Safire or Morton Freeman or books like Edwin Newman's *Strictly Speaking* or John Simon's *Paradigms Lost*, you're actually reading Popular Prescriptivism, a genre sideline of certain journalists (mostly older ones, the vast majority of whom actually do wear bow ties) whose bemused irony often masks a Colonel Blimp's rage at the way the beloved English of their youth is being trashed in the decadent present. The plutocratic tone and styptic wit of Safire and Newman and the best of the Prescriptivists is often modeled after the mandarin-Brit personas of Eric Partridge and H. W. Fowler, the same Twin Towers of scholarly Prescriptivism whom Garner talks about revering as a kid.[15]

Descriptivists, on the other hand, don't have weekly columns in the *Times*. These guys tend to be hard-core academics, mostly linguists or Comp theorists. Loosely organized under the banner of structural (or "descriptive") linguistics, they are doctrinaire positivists who have their intellectual roots in the work of Auguste Comte and Ferdinand de Saussure and their ideological roots firmly in the U.S. sixties. The brief explicit mention Garner's Preface gives this crew—

---

[14]Really, *howled*: blistering reviews and outraged editorials from across the country—from the *Times* and *The New Yorker* and good old *Life*, or q.v. this from the January '62 *Atlantic*: "We have seen a novel dictionary formula improvised, in great part, out of snap judgments and the sort of theoretical improvement that in practice impairs; and we have seen the gates propped wide open in enthusiastic hospitality to miscellaneous confusions and corruptions. In fine, the anxiously awaited work that was to have crowned cisatlantic linguistic scholarship with a particular glory turns out to be a scandal and a disaster."

[15]Note for example the mordant pith (and royal *we*) of this random snippet from Partridge's *Usage and Abusage*: anxious of. 'I am not hopeless of our future. But I am profoundly anxious of it', Beverley Nichols, *News of England*, 1938, which made us profoundly anxious *for* (or *about*)—not *of*—Mr Nichols's literary future.

Or see the near-Himalayan condescension of Fowler, here on some other people's use of words to mean things the words don't really mean:

slipshod extension . . . is especially likely to occur when some accident gives currency among the uneducated to words of learned origin, & the more if they are isolated or have few relatives in the vernacular. . . . The original meaning of *feasible* is simply doable (L *facare* do); but to the unlearned it is a mere token, of which he has to infer the value from the contexts in which he hears it used, because such relatives as it has in English—*feat, feature, faction*, &c.—either fail to show the obvious family likeness to which he is accustomed among families of indigenous words, or are (like *malfeasance*) outside his range.

> *Somewhere along the line, though, usage dictionaries got hijacked by the descriptive linguists,[16] who observe language scientifically. For the pure descriptivist, it's impermissible to say that one form of language is any better than another: as long as a native speaker says it, it's OK— and anyone who takes a contrary stand is a dunderhead. . . . Essentially, descriptivists and prescriptivists are approaching different problems. Descriptivists want to record language as it's actually used, and they perform a useful function—though their audience is generally limited to those willing to pore through vast tomes of dry-as-dust research.*

—is disingenuous in the extreme, especially the "approaching different problems" part, because it vastly underplays the Descriptivists' influence on U.S. culture. For one thing, Descriptivism so quickly and thoroughly took over English education in this country that just about everybody who started junior high after c. 1970 has been taught to write Descriptively—via "freewriting," "brainstorming," "journaling," a view of writing as self-exploratory and -expressive rather than as communicative, an abandonment of systematic grammar, usage, semantics, rhetoric, etymology. For another thing, the very language in which today's socialist, feminist, minority, gay, and environmentalist movements frame their sides of political debates is informed by the Descriptivist belief that traditional English is conceived and perpetuated by Privileged WASP Males[17] and is thus inherently capitalist, sexist, racist, xenophobic, homophobic, elitist: unfair. Think Ebonics. Think of the involved contortions people undergo to avoid *he* as a generic pronoun, or of the tense deliberate way white males now adjust their vocabularies around non-w.m.'s. Think of today's endless battles over just the *names* of things—"Affirmative Action" vs. "Reverse Discrimination," "Pro-Life" vs. "Pro-Choice," "Undercount" vs. "Vote Fraud," etc.

The Descriptivist revolution takes a little time to unpack, but it's worth it. The structural linguists' rejection of conventional usage rules depends on two main arguments. The first is academic and methodological. In this age of technology, Descriptivists contend, it's the Scientific Method—clinically objective, value-neutral, based on direct observation and demonstrable hypothesis—that should determine both the content of dictionaries and the standards of "correct" English. Because language is constantly evolving, such standards will always be fluid. Gove's now classic introduction to *Webster's Third* outlines this type of Descriptivism's five basic edicts: "1—Language changes constantly; 2—Change is normal; 3—Spoken language is the language; 4—Correctness rests upon usage; 5—All usage is relative."

These principles look *prima facie* OK—commonsensical and couched in the bland simple s.-v.-o. prose of dispassionate Science—but in fact they're vague and muddled and it takes about three seconds to think of reasonable replies to each one of them, viz.:

1—OK, but how much and how fast?

2—Same thing. Is Heraclitean flux as normal or desirable as gradual change? Do some changes actually serve the language's overall pizzazz

---

[16]Utter bushwa: As *ADMAU*'s body makes clear, Garner knows exactly when the Descriptivists started influencing language guides.

[17](which is fact is true)

better than others? And how many people have to deviate from how many conventions before we say the language has actually changed? Fifty percent? Ten percent?

3—This is an old claim, at least as old as Plato's *Phaedrus*. And it's specious. If Derrida and the infamous Deconstructionists have done nothing else, they've debunked the idea that speech is language's primary instantiation.[18] Plus consider the weird arrogance of Gove's (3) w/r/t correctness. Only the most mullahlike Prescriptivists care very much about spoken English; most Prescriptive usage guides concern Standard *Written* English.[19]

4—Fine, but whose usage? Gove's (4) begs the whole question. What he wants to imply here, I think, is a reversal of the traditional entailment-relation between abstract rules and concrete usage: Instead of usage ideally corresponding to a rigid set of regulations, the regulations ought to correspond to the way real people are actually using the language. Again, fine, but which people? Urban Latinos? Boston Brahmins? Rural Midwesterners? Appalachian Neogaelics?

5—*Huh?* If this means what it seems to mean, then it ends up biting Gove's whole argument in the ass. (5) appears to imply that the correct answer to the above "which people?" is: "All of them!" And it's easy to show why this will not stand up as a lexicographical principle. The most obvious problem with it is that not everything can go in The Dictionary. Why not? Because you can't observe every last bit of every last native speaker's "language behavior," and even if you could, the resultant dictionary would weigh 4 million pounds and have to be updated hourly.[20] The fact is that any lexicographer is going to have to make choices about what gets in and what doesn't. And these choices are based on . . . what? And now we're right back where we started.

It is true that, as a SNOOT, I am probably neurologically predisposed to look for flaws in Gove et al.'s methodological argument. But these flaws seem awfully easy to find. Probably the biggest one is that the Descriptivists' "scientific

---

[18](Q.v. "The Pharmakon" in Derrida's *La dissémination*—but you'd probably be better off just trusting me.)

[19]Standard Written English (SWE) is also sometimes called Standard English (SE) or Educated English, but the inditement-emphasis is the same.

SEMI-INTERPOLATION

Plus note that Garner's Preface explicitly names *ADMAU*'s intended audience as "writers and editors." And even ads for the dictionary in such organs as *The New York Review of Books* are built around the slogan "If you like to WRITE . . . Refer to us."*

*(Yr. SNOOT rev. cannot help observing, w/r/t these ads, that the opening t in **Refer** here should not be capitalized after a dependent clause + ellipses—*Quandoque bonus dormitat Homerus.*)

[20]True, some sort of 100 percent compendious real-time Mega-dictionary might be possible online, though it'd take a small army of lexical webmasters and a much larger army of *in situ* actual-use reporters and surveillance techs; plus it'd be GNP-level expensive.

lexicography"—under which, keep in mind, the ideal English dictionary is basically number-crunching; you somehow observe every linguistic act by every native/naturalized speaker of English and put the sum of all these acts between two covers and call it The Dictionary—involves an incredibly simplistic and outdated understanding of what *scientific* means. It requires a naive belief in scientific objectivity, for one thing. Even in the physical sciences, everything from quantum mechanics to Information Theory has shown that an act of observation is itself part of the phenomenon observed and is analytically inseparable from it.

If you remember your old college English classes, there's an analogy here that points up the trouble scholars get into when they confuse observation with interpretation. Recall the New Critics.[21] They believed that literary criticism was best conceived as a "scientific" endeavor: The critic was a neutral, careful, unbiased, highly trained observer whose job was to find and objectively describe meanings that were right there—literally inside—pieces of literature. Whether you know what happened to the New Criticism's reputation depends on whether you took college English after c. 1975; suffice it to say that its star has dimmed. The New Critics had the same basic problem as Gove's Methodological Descriptivists: They believed that *scientific* meant the same thing as *neutral* or *unbiased*. And that linguistic meanings could exist "objectively," separate from any interpretive act.

The point of the analogy is that claims to objectivity in language study are now the stuff of jokes and shudders. The epistemological assumptions that underlie Methodological Descriptivism have been thoroughly debunked and displaced—in Lit by the rise of post-structuralism, Reader-Response Criticism, and Jaussian Reception Theory; in linguistics by the rise of Pragmatics—and it's now pretty much universally accepted that (a) meaning is inseparable from some act of interpretation and (b) an act of interpretation is always somewhat biased, i.e., informed by the interpreter's particular ideology. And the consequence of (a) and (b) is that there's no way around it—decisions about what to put in The Dictionary and what to exclude are going to be based on a lexicographer's ideology. And every lexicographer's got one. To presume that dictionary-making can somehow avoid or transcend ideology is simply to subscribe to a particular ideology, one that might aptly be called Unbelievably Naive Positivism.

There's an even more important way Descriptivists are wrong in thinking that the Scientific Method is appropriate to the study of language:

Even if, as a thought experiment, we assume a kind of nineteenth-century scientific realism—in which, even though some scientists' interpretations of natural phenomena might be biased,[22] the natural phenomena themselves can be supposed to exist wholly independent of either observation or interpretation—no such realist supposition can be made about "language behavior," because this behavior is both *human* and fundamentally *normative*. To understand this, you have only to accept the proposition that language is by its very nature public—i.e., that there

---

[21]*New Criticism* refers to T. S. Eliot and I. A. Richards and F. R. Leavis and Cleanth Brooks and Wimsatt & Beardsley and the whole "close reading" school that dominated literary criticism from WWI well into the seventies.

[22]("EVIDENCE OF CANCER LINK REFUTED BY TOBACCO INSTITUTE RESEARCHERS")

can be no such thing as a Private Language[23]—and then to observe the way Methodological Descriptivists seem either ignorant of this fact or oblivious to its consequences, as in for example one Charles Fries's introduction to an epigone of *Webster's Third* called *The American College Dictionary*:

> *A dictionary can be an "authority" only in the sense in which a book of chemistry or of physics or of botany can be an "authority"—by the accuracy and the completeness of its record of the observed facts of the field examined, in accord with the latest principles and techniques of the particular science.*

This is so stupid it practically drools. An "authoritative" physics text presents the results of *physicists'* observations and *physicists'* theories about those observations. If a physics textbook operated on Descriptivist principles, the fact that

---

[23]This proposition is in fact true, as is interpolatively demonstrated below, and although the demonstration is extremely persuasive it is also, you can see from the size of this FN, lengthy and involved and rather, umm, dense, so that again you'd probably be better off simply granting the truth of the proposition and forging on with the main text.

INTERPOLATIVE DEMONSTRATION OF THE FACT THAT THERE IS NO SUCH THING AS A PRIVATE LANGUAGE

It's sometimes tempting to imagine that there can be such a thing as a Private Language. Many of us are prone to lay-philosophizing about the weird privacy of our own mental states, for example, and from the fact that when my knee hurts only I can feel it, it's tempting to conclude that for me the word *pain* has a very subjective internal meaning that only I can truly understand. This line of thinking is sort of like the adolescent pot-smoker's terror that his own inner experience is both private and unverifiable, a syndrome that is technically known as Cannabic Solipsism. Eating Chips Ahoy! and staring intently at the television's network PGA event, for instance, the adolescent pot-smoker is struck by the ghastly possibility that, e.g., what he sees as the color green and what other people call "the color green" may in fact not be the same color experiences at all: The fact that both he and someone else call Pebble Beach's fairways green and a stoplight's GO signal green appears to guarantee only that there is a similar consistency in their color experience of fairways and GO lights, not that the actual subjective quality of those color experiences is the same; it could be that what the ad. potsmoker experiences as green everyone else actually experiences as blue, and what we "mean" by the word *blue* is what he "means" by *green*, etc., etc., until the whole line of thinking gets so vexed and exhausting that the a.p.-s. ends up slumped crumb-strewn and paralyzed in his chair.

The point here is that the idea of a Private Language, like Private Colors and most of the other solipsistic conceits with which this particular reviewer has at various times been afflicted, is both deluded and demonstrably false.

In the case of Private Language, the delusion is usually based on the belief that a word such as *pain* has the meaning it does because it is somehow "connected" to a feeling in my knee. But as Mr. L. Wittgenstein's *Philosophical Investigations* proved in the 1950s, words actually have the meanings they do because of certain rules and verification tests that are imposed on us from outside our own subjectivities, viz., by the community in which we have to get along and communicate with other people. Wittgenstein's argument, which is admittedly very complex and gnomic and opaque, basically centers on the fact that a word like *pain* means what it does for me because of the way the community I'm part of has tacitly agreed to use *pain*.

If you're thinking that all this seems not only abstract but also pretty irrelevant to the Usage Wars or to anything you have any real interest in at all, you are very much mistaken. If words' meanings depend on transpersonal rules and these rules on community consensus, language is not only conceptually non-Private but also irreducibly *public, political,* and *ideological.* This means that questions about our national consensus on grammar and usage are actually bound up with every last social issue that millennial America's about—class, race, gender, morality, tolerance, pluralism, cohesion, equality, fairness, money: You name it.

'some Americans believe that electricity flows better downhill (based on the observed fact that power lines tend to run high above the homes they serve) would require the Electricity Flows Better Downhill Theory to be included as a "valid" theory in the textbook—just as, for Dr. Fries, if some Americans use *infer* for *imply*, the use becomes an ipso facto "valid" part of the language. Structural linguists like Gove and Fries are not, finally, scientists but census-takers who happen to misconstrue the importance of "observed facts." It isn't scientific phenomena they're tabulating but rather a set of human behaviors, and a lot of human behaviors are—to be blunt—moronic. Try, for instance, to imagine an "authoritative" ethics textbook whose principles were based on what most people actually do.

Norm-wise, let's keep in mind that language didn't come into being because our hairy ancestors were sitting around the veldt with nothing better to do. Language was invented to serve certain specific purposes:[24] "That mushroom is poisonous"; "Knock these two rocks together and you can start a fire"; "This shelter is mine!" And so on. Clearly, as linguistic communities evolve over time, they discover that some ways of using language are "better" than others—meaning better with respect to the community's purposes. If we assume that one such purpose might be communicating which kinds of food are safe to eat, then you can see how, for example, a misplaced modifier might violate an important norm:

"People who eat that kind of mushroom often get sick" confuses the recipient about whether he'll get sick only if he eats the mushroom frequently or whether he stands a good chance of getting sick the very first time he eats it. In other words, the community has a vested practical interest in excluding this kind of misplaced modifier from acceptable usage; and even if a certain percentage of tribesmen screw up and use them, this still doesn't make m.m.'s a good idea.

Maybe now the analogy between usage and ethics is clearer. Just because people sometimes lie, cheat on their taxes, or scream at their kids, this doesn't mean that they think those things are "good." The whole point of norms is to help us evaluate our actions (including utterances) according to what we as a community have decided our real interests and purposes are. Granted, this analysis is over-simplified; in practice it's incredibly hard to arrive at norms and to keep them at least minimally fair or sometimes even to agree on what they are (q.v. today's Culture Wars). But the Descriptivists' assumption that all usage norms are arbitrary and dispensable leads to—well, have a mushroom.

The connotations of *arbitrary* here are tricky, though, and this sort of segues into the second argument Descriptivists make. There is a sense in which specific linguistic conventions *are* arbitrary. For instance, there's no particular metaphysical reason why our word for a four-legged mammal that gives milk and goes Moo is *cow* and not, say, *prtlmpf*. The uptown phrase for this is "the arbitrariness of the linguistic sign," and it's used, along with certain principles of cognitive science and generative grammar, in a more philosophically sophisticated version of Descriptivism that holds the conventions of SWE to be more like the niceties of fashion than like actual norms. This "Philosophical Descriptivism" doesn't care much about dictionaries or method; its target is the standard SNOOT claim *supra*—that

---

[24]Norms, after all, are just practices people have agreed on as optimal ways of doing things for certain purposes. They're not laws but they're not laissez-faire, either.

prescriptive rules have their ultimate justification in the community's need to make its language meaningful.

The argument goes like this. An English sentence's being *meaningful* is not the same as its being *grammatical*. That is, such clearly ill-formed constructions as "Did you seen the car keys of me?" or "The show was looked by many people" are nevertheless comprehensible; the sentences do, more or less, communicate the information they're trying to get across. Add to this the fact that nobody who isn't damaged in some profound Oliver Sacksish way actually ever makes these sorts of very deep syntactic errors.[25] and you get the basic proposition of Noam Chomsky's generative linguistics, which is that there exists a Universal Grammar beneath and common to all languages, plus that there is probably an actual part of the human brain that's imprinted with this Universal Grammar the same way birds' brains are imprinted with Fly South and dogs' with Sniff Genitals. There's all kinds of compelling evidence and support for these ideas, not least of which are the advances that linguists and cognitive scientists and A.I. researchers have been able to make with them, and the theories have a lot of credibility, and they are adduced by the Philosophical Descriptivists to show that since the really *important* rules of language are at birth already hardwired into people's neocortex, SWE prescriptions against dangling participles or mixed metaphors are basically the linguistic equivalent of whalebone corsets and short forks for salad. As Descriptivist Steven Pinker puts it, "When a scientist considers all the high-tech mental machinery needed to order words into everyday sentences, prescriptive rules are, at best, inconsequential decorations."

This argument is not the barrel of drugged trout that Methodological Descriptivism was, but it's still vulnerable to some objections. The first one is easy. Even if it's true that we're all wired with a Universal Grammar, it simply doesn't follow that *all* prescriptive rules are superfluous. Some of these rules really do seem to serve clarity and precision. The injunction against two-way adverbs ("People who eat this often get sick") is an obvious example, as are rules about other kinds of misplaced modifiers ("There are many reasons why lawyers lie, some better than others") and about relative pronouns' proximity to the nouns they modify ("She's the mother of an infant daughter who works twelve hours a day").

Granted, the Philosophical Descriptivist can question just how absolutely necessary these rules are—it's quite likely that a recipient of clauses like the above could figure out what the sentences mean from the sentences on either side or from the "overall context" or whatever. A listener can usually figure out what I really mean when I misuse *infer* for *imply* or say *indicate* for *say*, too. But many of these solecisms require at least a couple extra nanoseconds of cognitive effort, a kind of rapid sift-and-discard process, before the recipient gets it. Extra work. It's debatable just how much extra work, but it seems indisputable that we put *some* extra neural burden on the recipient when we fail to follow certain conventions. W/r/t confusing clauses like the above, it simply seems more "considerate" to follow the

---

[25]In his *The Language Instinct: How the Mind Creates Language* (1994), Steven Pinker puts it this way: "No one, not even a valley girl, has to be told not to say *Apples the eat boy* or *The child seems sleeping* or *Who did you meet John and?* or the vast, vast majority of the millions of trillions of mathematically possible combinations of words."

rules of correct SWE . . . just as it's more "considerate" to de-slob your home before entertaining guests or to brush your teeth before picking up a date. Not just more considerate but more *respectful* somehow—both of your listener and of what you're trying to get across. As we sometimes also say about elements of fashion and etiquette, the way you use English "Makes a Statement" or "Sends a Message"—even though these Statements/Messages often have nothing to do with the actual information you're trying to transmit.

We've now sort of bled into a more serious rejoinder to Philosophical Descriptivism: From the fact that linguistic communication is not strictly dependent on usage and grammar it does not necessarily follow that the traditional rules of usage and grammar are nothing but "inconsequential decorations." Another way to state the objection is that just because something is "decorative" does not necessarily make it "inconsequential." Rhetorically, Pinker's flip dismissal is bad tactics, for it invites the very question it begs: inconsequential to *whom*?

Take, for example, the Descriptivist claim that so-called correct English usages such as *brought* rather than *brung*, and *felt* rather than *feeled* are arbitrary and restrictive and unfair and are supported only by custom and are (like irregular verbs in general) archaic and incommodious and an all-around pain in the ass. Let us concede for the moment that these objections are 100 percent reasonable. Then let's talk about pants. Trousers, slacks. I suggest to you that having the "correct" subthoracic clothing for U.S. males be pants instead of skirts is arbitrary (lots of other cultures let men wear skirts), restrictive and unfair (U.S. females get to wear pants), based solely on archaic custom (I think it's got something to do with certain traditions about gender and leg position, the same reasons girls' bikes don't have a crossbar), and in certain ways not only incommodious but illogical (skirts are more comfortable than pants; pants ride up; pants are hot; pants can squish the genitals and reduce fertility; over time pants chafe and erode irregular sections of men's leg hair and give older men hideous half-denuded legs, etc. etc.). Let us grant—as a thought experiment if nothing else—that these are all reasonable and compelling objections to pants as an androsartorial norm. Let us in fact in our minds and hearts say yes—*shout* yes—to the skirt, the kilr, the toga, the sarong, the jupe. Let us dream of or even in our spare time work toward an America whhere nobody lays any arbitrary sumptuary prescriptions on anyone else and we can all go around as comfortable and aerated and unchafed and unsquished and motile as we want.

And yet the fact remains that, in the broad cultural mainstream of millennial America, men do not wear skirts. If you, the reader, are a U.S. male, and even if you share my personal objections to pants and dream as I do of a cool and genitally unsquishy American Tomorrow, the odds are still 99.9 percent that in 100 percent of public situations you wear pants/slacks/shorts/trunks. More to the point, if you are a U.S. male and also have a U.S. male child, and if that child were to come to you one evening and announce his desire/intention to wear a skirt rather than pants to school the next day, I am 100 percent confident that you are going to discourage him from doing so. *Strongly* discourage him. you could be a Molotov-tossing anti-pants radical or a kilt manufacturer or Steven Pinker himself—you're going to stand over your kid and be prescriptive about an arbitrary, archaic, uncomfortable, and inconsequentially decorative piece of clothing. Why? Well, because in modern America any little boy who comes to school in a skirt (even, say, a modest all-season midi) is going to get stared at and shunned and beaten up and called a Total Geekoid by a whole lot of people whose approval and acceptance are important to him.[26] In our culture, in other words, a boy who wears a skirt is Making a Statement that is going to have all kinds of gruesome social and emotional consequences.

You see where this is going. I'm going to describe the intended point of the pants analogy in terms I'm sure are simplistic—doubtless there are whole books in Pragmatics or psycholinguistics or something devoted to unpacking this point. The weird thing is that I've seen neither Descriptivists nor SNOOTs deploy it in the Wars.[27]

When I say or write something, there are actually a whole lot of different things I am communicating. The propositional content (the actual information I'm trying to convey) is only one part of it. Another part is stuff about me, the communicator. Everyone knows this. It's a function of the fact that there are uncountably many well-formed ways to say the same basic thing, from e.g. "I was attacked by a bear!" to "Goddamn bear tried to kill me!" to "That ursine juggernaut bethought to sup upon my person!" and so on. And different levels of diction and formality are only the simplest kinds of distinction; things get way more complicated in the sorts of interpersonal communication where social relations and feelings and moods come into play. Here's a familiar sort of example. Suppose that you and I are acquaintances and we're in my apartment having a conversation and that at some point I want to terminate the conversation and not have you be in my apartment anymore. Very delicate social moment. Think of all the different ways I can try to handle it: "Wow, look at the time"; "Could we finish this up later?"; "Could you please leave now?"; "Go"; "Get out"; "Get the hell out of here"; "Didn't you say you had to be someplace?"; "Time for you to hit the dusty trail, my friend"; "Off you go then, love"; or that sly old telephone-conversation ender: "Well, I'm going to let you go now"; etc. And then think of all the different factors and implications of each option.

The point here is obvious. It concerns a phenomenon that SNOOTs blindly reinforce and that Descriptivists badly underestimate and that scary vocab-tape ads try to exploit. People really do "judge" one another according to their use of language. Constantly. Of course, people judge one another on the basis of all kinds of things—weight, scent, physiognomy, occupation, make of vehicle[28]—and, again, doubtless it's all terribly complicated and occupies whole battalions of sociolinguists. But it's clear that at least one component of all this interpersonal semantic judging involves *acceptance*, meaning not some touchy-feely emotional affirmation

---

[26]In the case of Steve Pinker Jr., those people are the boy's peers and teachers and crossing guards, etc. In the case of adult cross-dressers and drag queens who have jobs in the Straight World and wear pants to those jobs, it's coworkers and clients and penple on the subway. For the die-hard slob who nevertheless wears a coat and a tie to work, it's mostly his boss, who himself doesn't want his employee's clothes to send clients "the wrong message." But of course it's all basically the same thing.

[27]In fact, the only time one ever hears the issue made explicit is in radio ads for tapes that promise to improve people's vocabulary. These ads are extremely ominous and intimidating and always start out with "DID YOU KNOW PEOPLE JUDGE YOU BY THE WORDS YOU USE?"

[28](. . . not to mention color, gender, creed—you can see how fraught and charged all this is going to get)

but actual acceptance or rejection of somebody's bid to be regarded as a peer, a member of somebody else's collective or community or Group. Another way to come at this is to acknowledge something that in the Usage Wars gets mentioned only in very abstract terms: "Correct" English usage is, as a practical matter, a function of whom you're talking to and how you want that person to respond—not just to your utterance but also to *you*. In other words, a large part of the agenda of any communication is rhetorical and depends on what some rhet-scholars call "Audience" or "Discourse Community."[29] And the United States obviously has a huge number of such Discourse Communities, many of them regional and/or cultural dialects of English: Black English, Latino English, Rural Southern, Urban Southern, Standard Upper-Midwest, Maine Yankee, East-Texas Bayou, Boston Blue-Collar, on and on. Everybody knows this. What not everyone knows—especially not certain Prescriptivists—is that many of these non-SWE dialects have their own highly developed and internally consistent grammars, and that some of these dialects' usage norms actually make more linguistic/aesthetic sense than do their Standard counterparts (see INTERPOLATION). Plus, of course, there are innumerable sub- and subsubdialects based on all sorts of things that have nothing to do with locale or ethnicity—Medical-School English, Peorians-Who-Follow-Pro-Wrestling-Closely English, Twelve-Year-Old-Males-Whose-Worldview-Is-Deeply-Informed-By-*South-Park* English—and that are nearly incomprehensible to anyone who isn't inside their very tight and specific Discourse Community (which of course is part of their function[30]).

Interpolation: Example of Grammatical Advantages of a Non-Standard Dialect That This Reviewer Actually Knows About Firsthand

This rev. happens to have two native English dialects—the SWE of my hypereducated parents and the hard-earned Rural Midwestern of most of my peers. When I'm talking to R.M.'s, I usually use, for example, the construction "Where's it at?" instead of "Where is it?" Part of this is a naked desire to fit in and not get rejected as an egghead or fag (see *sub*). But another part is that I, SNOOT or no, believe that this and other R.M.isms are in certain ways superior to their Standard equivalents.

---

[29]*Discourse Community* is an example of that rare kind of academic jargon that's actually a valuable addition to SWE because it captures something at once very complex and very specific that no other English term quite can.[*]

[*](The above is an obvious attempt to preempt readerly sneers/winces at the term's continued deployment in this article.)

[30](Plus it's true that whether something gets called a "subdialect" or "jargon" seems to depend on how much it annoys people outside its Discourse Community. Garner himself has miniessays on AIRLINESE, COMPUTERESE, LEGALESE, and BUREAUCRATESE, and he more or less calls all of them jargon. There is no *ADMAU* miniessay on DIALECTS, but there is one on JARGON, in which such is Garner's self-restraint that you can almost hear his tendons straining, as in "[Jargon] arises from the urge to save time and space—and occasionally to conceal meaning from the uninitiated.") [1](a redundancy that's a bit arbitrary, since "Where's it *from*?" isn't redundant [mainly because *whence* has vanished into semiarchaism]).

For a dogmatic Prescriptivist, "Where's it at?"[31] is double-damned as a sentence that not only ends with a preposition but whose final preposition forms a redundancy with *where* that's similar to the redundancy in "the reason is because" (which latter usage I'll admit makes me dig my nails into my palms). Rejoinder: First off, the avoid-terminal-prepositions rule is the invention of one Fr. R. Lowth, an eighteenth-century British preacher and indurate pedant who did things like spend scores of pages arguing for *hath* over the trendy and degenerate *has*. The a.-t.-p. rule is antiquated and stupid and only the most ayatolloid SNOOT takes it seriously. Garner himself calls the rule "stuffy" and lists all kinds of useful constructions like, "the man you were listening to" that we'd have to discard or distort if we really enforced it.

Plus the apparent redundancy of "Where's it at?"[31] is offset by its metrical logic. What the *at* really does is license the contraction of *is* after the interrogative adverb. You can't say "Where's it?" So the choice is between "Where is it?" and "Where's it at?", and the latter, a strong anapest, is prettier and trips off the tongue better than "Where is it?", whose meter is either a clunky monosyllabic-foot + trochee or it's nothing at all.

This is probably the place for your SNOOT reviewer openly to concede that a certain number of traditional prescriptive rules really are stupid and that people who insist on them (like the legendary assistant to P.M. Margaret Thatcher who refused to read any memo with a split infinitive in it, or the jr.-high teacher I had who automatically graded you down if you started a sentence with *Hopefully*) are that very most pathetic and dangerous sort of SNOOT, the SNOOT Who Is Wrong. The injunction against split infinitives, for instance, is a consequence of the weird fact that English grammar is modeled on Latin even though Latin is a synthetic language and English is an analytic language.[32] Latin infinitives consist of one word and are impossible to as it were split, and the earliest English Prescriptivists—so enthralled with Latin that their English usage guides were actually written in Latin[33]—decided that English infinitives shouldn't be split either. Garner himself takes out after the s.i. rule in both SPLIT INFINITIVES and SUPERSTITIONS.[34] And *Hopefully* at the beginning of a sentence, as a certain cheeky eighth-grader once pointed out to his everlasting social cost, actually functions not as a misplaced modal auxiliary or as a manner adverb like *quickly* or *angrily* but as a "sentence adverb" that indicates the speaker's attitude about the state of affairs described

---

[31](a redundancy that's a bit arbitrary, since "Where's it *from*?" isn't redundant [mainly because *whence* has vanished into semiarchaism]).

[32]A synthetic language uses inflections to dictate syntax, whereas an analytic language uses word order. Latin, German, and Russian are synthetic; English and Chinese, analytic.

[33](Q.v. for example Sir Thomas Smith's cortext-withering *De Recta et Emendata Linguae Anglicae Scriptione Diologus* of 1568.)

[34]But note that he's sane about it. Some split infinitives really are clunky and hard to parse, especially when there are a whole bunch of words between *to* and the verb—"We will attempt to swiftly and to the best of our ability respond to these charges"—which Garner calls "wide splits" and sensibly discourages. His overall verdict on s.i.'s—which is that some are "perfectly proper" and some iffy and some just totally bad news, and that no one wide tidy dogmatic ukase can handle all s.i. cases, and thus that "knowing when to split an infinitive requires a good ear and a keen eye"—is a good example of the way Garner distinguishes sound and helpful Descriptivist objects from wacko or dogmatic objections and then incorporates the sound objections into a smarter and more flexible Prescriptivism.

by the sentence (examples of perfectly OK sentence adverbs are *Clearly, Basically, Luckily*), and only SNOOTs educated in the high-pedantic years up to 1960 blindly proscribe it or grade it down.

The cases of split infinitives and *Hopefully* are in fact often trotted out by dogmatic Descriptivists as evidence that all SWE usage rules are arbitrary and stupid (which is a bit like pointing to Pat Buchanan as evidence that all Republicans are maniacs). Garner rejects *Hopefully*'s knee-jerk proscription, too, albeit grudgingly, including the adverb in his miniessay on SKUNKED TERMS, which is his phrase for a usage that is "hotly disputed . . . any use of it is likely to distract some readers." (Garner also points out something I'd never quite realized, which is that *hopefully*, if misplaced/mispunctuated in the body of a sentence, can create some of the same two-way ambiguities as other adverbs, as in the clause "I will borrow your book and hopefully read it soon.")

Whether we're conscious of it or not, most of us are fluent in more than one major English dialect and in a large number of subdialects and are probably at least passable in countless others. Which dialect you choose to use depends, of course, on whom you're addressing. More to the point, I submit that the dialect you use depends mostly on what sort of Group your listener is part of and whether you wish to present yourself as a fellow member of that Group. An obvious example is that traditional upper-class English has certain dialectal differences from lower-class English and that schools used to have courses in Elocution whose whole point was to teach people how to speak in an upper-class way. But usage-as-inclusion is about much more than class. Here's another thought experiment: A bunch of U.S. teenagers in clothes that look far too large for them are sitting together in the local mall's Food Court, and a 53-year-old man with a combover and clothes that fit comes over to them and says that he was scoping them and thinks they're totally rad and/or phat and is it cool if he just kicks it and does the hang here with them. The kids' reaction is going to be either scorn or embarrassment for the guy—most likely a mix of both. Q: Why? Or imagine that two hard-core urban black guys are standing there talking and I, who am resoundingly and in all ways white, come up and greet them with "Yo" and call them "Brothers" and ask "s'up, s'goin on," pronouncing on with that NYCish oo-o diphthong that Young Urban Black English deploys for a standard o. Either these guys are going to be offended or they are going to be offended or they are going to think I am simply out of my mind. No other reaction is remotely foreseeable. Q: Why?

Why: A dialect of English is learned and used either because it's your native vernacular or because it's the dialect of a Group by which you wish (with some degree of plausibility) to be accepted. And although it is the major and arguably the most important one, SWE is only one dialect. And it is never, or at least hardly ever, anybody's only dialect. This is because there are—as you and I both know and yet no one in the Usage Wars ever seems to mention—situations in which faultlessly correct SWE is clearly not the appropriate dialect.

Childhood is full of such situations. This is one reason why SNOOTlets tend to have a very hard social time of it in school. A SNOOTlet is a little kid who's wildly, precociously fluent in SWE (he is often, recall, the offspring of SNOOTs). Just about every class has a SNOOTlet, so I know you've seen them—these are the sorts of six- to twelve-year-olds who use *whom* correctly and whose response to striking out in T-ball is to cry out "How incalculably dreadful!" etc. The elementary-school SNOOTlet is one of the earliest identifiable species of academic Geekoid and is duly despised by his peers and praised by his teachers. These teachers usually don't see the incredible amounts of punishment the SNOOTlet is receiving from his classmates, or if they do see it they blame the classmates and shake their heads sadly at the vicious and arbitrary cruelty of which children are capable.

But the other children's punishment of the SNOOTlet is not arbitrary at all. There are important things at stake. Little kids in school are learning about Group-inclusion and -exclusion and about the respective rewards and penalties of same and about the use of dialect and syntax and slang as signals of affinity and inclusion.[35] They're learning about Discourse Communities. Kids learn this stuff not in English or Social Studies but on the playground and at lunch and on the bus. When his peers are giving the SNOOTlet monstrous quadruple Wedgies or holding him down and taking turns spitting on him, there's serious learning going on . . . for everyone except the little SNOOT, who in fact is being punished for precisely his *failure* to learn. What neither he nor his teacher realizes is that the SNOOTlet is *deficient* in Language Arts. He has only one dialect. He cannot alter his vocabulary, usage, or grammar, cannot use slang or vulgarity; and it's these abilities that are really required for "peer rapport," which is just a fancy Elementary-Ed term for being accepted by the most important Group in the little kid's life.

This reviewer acknowledges that there seems to be some, umm, personal stuff getting dredged up and worked out here;[36] but the stuff is relevant. The point is that the little A+ SNOOTlet is actually in the same dialectal position as the class's "slow" kid who can't learn to stop using *ain't* or *bringed*. One is punished in class, the other on the playground, but both are deficient in the same linguistic skill—viz., the ability to move between various dialects and levels of "correctness," the ability to communicate one way with peers and another way with teachers and another with family and another with Little League coaches and so on. Most of these dialectal adjustments are made below the level of conscious awareness, and our ability to make them seems part psychological and part something else—perhaps something hardwired into the same motherboard as Universal Grammar—and in truth this ability is a far better indicator of a kid's "Verbal I.Q." than test scores or grades, since U.S. English classes do far more to retard dialectal talent than to cultivate it.

---

[35] The SNOOTlet is, as it happens, an indispensable part of other kids' playground education. The kids are learning that a Group's identity depends as much on exclusion as inclusion. They are, in other words, starting to learn about Us and Them, and about how an Us always needs a Them because being not-Them is essential to being Us. Because they're kids and it's school, the obvious Them is the teachers and all the values and appurtenances of the teacher world. This teacher-Them helps the kids see how to start to be an Us, but the SNOOTlet completes the puzzle by providing the as it were missing link: He is the Traitor, the Us who is in fact not Us but *Them.*

In sum, the SNOOTlet is teaching his peers that the criteria for membership in Us are not just age, station, inability to stay up past 9:00, etc.—that in fact Us is primarily a state of mind and a set of sensibilities. An ideology.

[36] (The skirt-in-school scenario was not personal stuff, FYI.)

Well-known fact: In neither K-12 nor college English are systematic SWE grammar and usage much taught anymore. It's been this way for more than 20 years. The phenomenon drives Prescriptivists nuts, and it's one of the big things they cite as evidence of America's gradual murder of English. Descriptivists and English-Ed specialists counter that grammar and usage have been abandoned because scientific research proved that studying SWE grammar and usage simply doesn't help make kids better writers. Each side in the debate tends to regard the other as mentally ill or/and blinded by political ideology. Neither camp appears ever to have considered whether maybe the way prescriptive SWE was traditionally taught had something to do with its inutility.

By *way* here I'm referring not so much to actual method as to spirit or attitude. Most traditional teachers of English grammar have, of course, been dogmatic SNOOTs, and like most dogmatists they've been incredibly stupid about the rhetoric they used and the Audience they were addressing.[37] I refer specifically to their assumption that SWE is the sole appropriate English dialect and that the only reasons anyone could fail to see this are ignorance or amentia or grave deficiencies in character. As rhetoric, this sort of attitude works only in sermons to the Choir, and as pedagogy it's just disastrous. The reality is that an average U.S. student is going to go to the trouble of mastering the difficult conventions of SWE only if he sees SWE's relevant Group or Discourse Community as one he'd like to be part of. And in the absence of any sort of argument for why the correct-SWE Group is a good or desirable one (an argument that, recall, the traditional teacher hasn't given, because he's such a dogmatic SNOOT he sees no need to), the student is going to be reduced to evaluating the desirability of the SWE Group based on the one obvious member of the Group he's encountered, namely the SNOOTy teacher himself.

I'm not suggesting here that an effective SWE pedagogy would require teachers to wear sunglasses and call students "Dude." What I am suggesting is that the rhetorical situation of an English class—a class composed wholly of young people whose Group identity is rooted in defiance of Adult-Establishment values, plus also composed partly of minorities whose primary dialects are different from SWE—requires the teacher to come up with overt, honest, compelling arguments for why SWE is a dialect worth learning.

These arguments are hard to make—not intellectually but emotionally, politically. Because they are baldly elitist.[38] The real truth, of course, is that SWE is the dialect of the American elite. That it was invented, codified, and promulgated by Privileged WASP Males and is perpetuated as "Standard" by same. That it is the shibboleth of the Establishment and an instrument of political power and class division and racial discrimination and all manner of social inequity. These are shall we say rather *delicate* subjects to bring up in an English class, especially in the service of a pro-SWE argument, and *extra*-especially if you yourself are both a Privileged WASP Male and the Teacher and thus pretty much a walking symbol of the Adult Establishment. This reviewer's opinion, though, is that both students and

---

[37]There are still some of these teachers around, at least here in the Midwest. You know the type: lipless, tweedy, cancrine—Old Maids of both genders. If you had one (as I did, 1976–77), you surely remember him.
[38](Or rather the arguments require us to acknowledge and talk about elitism, whereas a dogmatic SNOOT's pedagogy is merely elitism in action.)

SWE are better served if the teacher makes his premises explicit and his argument overt, presenting himself as an advocate of SWE's utility rather than as a prophet of its innate superiority.

Because this argument is both most delicate and (I believe) most important with respect to students of color, here is one version of a spiel I've given in private conference[39] with certain black students who were (a) bright and inquisitive and (b) deficient in what U.S. higher education considers written English facility:

> *I don't know whether anybody's told you this or not, but when you're in a college English class you're basically studying a foreign dialect. This dialect is called Standard Written English. From talking with you and reading your essays, I've concluded that your own primary dialect is [one of three variants of SBE common to our region]. Now, let me spell something out in my official Teacher-voice: The SBE you're fluent in is different from SWE in all kinds of important ways. Some of these differences are grammatical—for example, double negatives are OK in Standard Black English but not in SWE, and SBE and SWE conjugate certain verbs in totally different ways. Other differences have more to do with style—for instance, Standard Written English tends to use a lot more subordinate clauses in the early parts of sentences, and it sets off most of these early subordinates with commas, and, under SWE rules, writing that doesn't do this is "choppy." There are tons of differences like that. How much of this stuff do you already know? [STANDARD RESPONSE: some variation on "I know from the grades and comments on my papers that English profs don't think I'm a good writer.'] Well, I've got good news and bad news. There are some otherwise smart English profs who aren't very aware that there are real dialects of English other than SWE, so when they're reading your papers they'll put, like, "Incorrect conjugation" or "Comma needed" instead of "SWE conjugates this verb differently" or "SWE calls for a comma here." That's the good news—it's not that you're a bad writer, it's that you haven't learned the special rules of the dialect they want you to write in. Maybe that's not such good news, that they were grading you down for mistakes in a foreign language you didn't even know was a foreign language. That they won't let you write in SBE. Maybe it seems unfair. If it does, you're not going to like this news: I'm not going to let you write in SBE either. In my class, you have to learn and write in SWE. If you want to study your own dialect and its rules and history and how it's different from SWE, fine—there are some great books by scholars of Black English, and I'll help you find some and talk about them with you if you want. But that will be outside class. In class—in my English class—you will have to master and write in Standard Written English, which we might just as well call "Standard White English," because it was developed by white people and is used by white people, especially educated, powerful white people. [RESPONSES by this point vary too widely to standardize.] I'm respecting you enough here to give you what I believe*

---

[39](I'm not a total idiot.)

is the straight truth. In this country, SWE is perceived as the dialect of education and intelligence and power and prestige, and anybody of any race, ethnicity, religion, or gender who wants to succeed in American culture has got to be able to use SWE. This is How It Is. You can be glad about it or sad about it or deeply pissed off. You can believe it's racist and unjust and decide right here and now to spend every waking minute of your adult life arguing against it, and maybe you should, but I'll tell you something: If you ever want those arguments to get listened to and taken seriously, you're going to have to communicate them in SWE, because SWE is the dialect our country uses to talk to itself. African Americans who've become successful and important in U.S. culture know this; that's why King's and X's and Jackson's speeches are in SWE, and why Morrison's and Angelou's and Baldwin's and Wideman's and West's books are full of totally ass-kicking SWE, and why black judges and politicians and journalists and doctors and teachers communicate professionally in SWE. Some of these people grew up in homes and communities where SWE was the native dialect, and these black people had it much easier in school, but the ones who didn't grow up with SWE realized at some point that they had to learn it and become able to write in it, and so they did. And [INSERT NAME HERE], you're going to learn to use it, too, because I am going to make you.

I should note here that a couple of the students I've said this stuff to were offended—one lodged an Official Complaint—and that I have had more than one colleague profess to find my spiel "racially insensitive." Perhaps you do, too. My own humble opinion is that some of the cultural and political realities of American life are themselves racially insensitive and elitist and offensive and unfair, and that pussyfooting around these realities with euphemistic doublespeak is not only hypocritical but toxic to the project of ever actually changing them. Such pussyfooting has of course now achieved the status of a dialect—one powerful enough to have turned the normal politics of the Usage Wars sort of inside out.

I refer here to Politically Correct English (PCE), under whose conventions failing students become "high-potential" students and poor people "economically disadvantaged" and people in wheelchairs "differently abled" and a sentence like "White English and Black English are different and you better learn White English if you don't want to flunk" is not blunt but "insensitive." Although it's common to make jokes about PCE (referring to ugly people as "aesthetically challenged" and so on), be advised that Politically Correct English's various pre- and proscriptions are taken very seriously *indeed* by colleges and corporations and government agencies, whose own institutional dialects now evolve under the beady scrutiny of a whole new kind of Language Police.

From one perspective, the history of PCE evinces a kind of Lenin-to-Stalinesque irony. That is, the same ideological principles that informed the original Descriptivist revolution—namely, the sixties-era rejections of traditional authority and traditional inequality—have now actually produced a far more inflexible Prescriptivism, one unencumbered by tradition or complexity and backed by the threat of real-world sanctions (termination, litigation) for those fail to conform. This is sort of funny in a dark way, maybe, and most criticism of PCE seems to consist in making fun of its trendiness or vapidity. This reviewer's own opinion is that prescriptive PCE is not just silly but confused and dangerous.

Usage is always political, of course, but it's complexly political. With respect, for instance, to political change, usage conventions can function in two ways: On the one hand they can be a *reflection* of political change, and on the other they can be an *Instrument* of political change. These two functions are different and have to be kept straight. Confusing them—in particular, mistaking for political efficacy what is really just a language's political symbolism—enables the bizarre conviction that America ceases to be elitist or unfair simply because Americans stop using certain vocabulary that is historically associated with elitism and unfairness. This is PCE's central fallacy—that a society's mode of expression is productive of its attitudes rather than a product of those attitudes—and of course it's nothing but the obverse of the politically conservative SNOOT's delusion that social change can be retarded by restricting change in standard usage.[40]

Forget Stalinization or Logic 101-level equivocations, though. There's grosser irony about Politically Correct English. This is that PCE purports to be the dialect of progressive reform but is in fact—in its Orwellian substitution of the euphemisms of social equality for social equality itself—of vastly more help to conservatives and the U.S. status quo than traditional SNOOT prescriptions ever were. Were I, for instance, a political conservative who opposed taxation as a means of redistributing national wealth, I would be delighted to watch PCE progressives spend their time and energy arguing over whether a poor person should be described as "low-income" or "economically disadvantaged" or "pre-prosperous" rather than constructing effective public arguments for redistributive legislation or higher marginal tax rates on corporations. (Not to mention that strict codes of egalitarian euphemism serve to burke the sorts of painful, unpretty, and sometimes offensive discourse that in a pluralistic democracy leads to actual political change rather than symbolic political change. In other words, PCE functions as a form of censorship, and censorship always serves the status quo.)

As a practical matter, I strongly doubt whether a guy who has four small kids and makes $12,000 a year feels more empowered or less ill-used by a society that carefully refers to him as "economically disadvantaged" rather than "poor." Were I he, in fact, I'd probably find the PCE term insulting—not just because it's patronizing but because it's hypocritical and self-serving. Like many forms of Vogue Usage,[41] PCE functions primarily to signal and congratulate certain virtues in the speaker—scrupulous egalitarianism, concern for the dignity of all people,

---

[40]E.G., this is the reasoning behind many Pop Prescriptivists' complaint that shoddy usage signifies the Decline of Western Civilization.

[41]*A Dictionary of Modern American Usage* includes a miniessay on VOGUE WORDS, but it's a disappointing one in that Garner does little more than list VW's that bug him and say that "vogue words have such a grip on the popular mind that they come to be used in contexts in which they serve little purpose." This is one of the rare places in *ADMAU* where Garner is simply wrong. The real problem is that every sentence blends and balances at least two different communicative functions—one the transmission of raw info, the other the transmission of certain stuff about the speaker—and Vogue Usage throws this balance off. Garner's "serve little purpose" is exactly incorrect; vogue words serve too much the purpose of presenting the speaker in a certain light (even if this is merely as with-it or hip), and people's subliminal B.S.-antennae pick this imbalance up, and that's why even nonSNOOTs often find Vogue Usage irritating and creepy.

sophistication about the political implications of language—and so serves the self-ish interests of the PC far more than it serves any of the persons or groups renamed.

Interpolation on a Related Issue in the Face of Whose Ghastly Malignancy This Reviewer's Democratic Spirit Just Gives Out Altogether, Admittedly

This issue is Academic English, a cancer that has metastasized now to afflict both scholarly writing—

> *If such a sublime cyborg would insinuate the future as post-Fordist subject, his palpably masochistic locations as ecstatic agent of the sublime superstate need to be decoded as the "now all-but-unreadable DNA" of the fast industrializing Detroit, just as his Robocop-like strategy of carceral negotiation and street control remains the tirelessly American one of inflicting regeneration through violence upon the racially heteroglassic wilds and others of the inner city.[42]*

—and prose as mainstream as *The Village Voice's*:

> *At first encounter, the poems' distanced cerebral surfaces can be daunting, evading physical location or straightforward emotional arc. But this seeming remoteness quickly reveals a very real passion, centered in the speaker's struggle to define his evolving self-construction.*

Maybe it's a combination of my SNOOTitude and the fact that I end up having to read a lot of it for my job, but I'm afraid I regard Academic English not as a dialectal variation but as a grotesque debasement of SWE, and loathe it even more than the stilted incoherences of Presidential English ("This is the best and only way to uncover, destroy, and prevent Iraq from reengineering weapons of mass destruction") or the mangled pieties of BusinessSpeak ("Our Mission: to proactively search and provide the optimum networking skills and resources to meet the needs of your growing business"); and in support of this utter contempt and intolerance I cite no less an authority than Mr. G. Orwell, who 50 years ago had AE pegged as a "mixture of vagueness and sheer incompetence" in which "it is normal to come across long passages which are almost completely lacking in meaning."[43]

It probably isn't the whole explanation, but, as with the voguish hypocrisy of PCE, the obscurity and pretension of Academic English can be attributed in part to a disruption in the delicate rhetorical balance between language as a vector of meaning and language as a vector of the writer's own résumé. In other words, it

---

[42]FYI, this passage, which appears in *ADMAU*'s entry on OBSCURITY, is quoted from a 1997 *Sacramento Bee* article entitled "No Contest: English Professor Are Worst Writers on Campus."

[43]This was in his 1946 "Politics and the English Language," an essay that despite its date (and its title a basic redundancy) remains the definitive SNOOT statement on Academese. Orwell's famous AE translation of the gorgeous "I saw under the sun that the race is not to the swift" in Ecclesiastes as "Objective considerations of contemporary phenomena compel the conclusion that success or failure in competition activities exhibits no tendency to be commensurate with innate capacity, but that a considerable element of the unpredictable must invariably be taken into account" should be tattooed on the left wrist of every grad student in the anglophone world.

is when a scholar's vanity/insecurity leads him to write *primarily* to communicate and reinforce his own status as an Intellectual that his English is deformed by pleonasm and pretentious diction (whose function is to signal the writer's erudition) and by opaque abstraction (whose function is to keep anybody from pinning the writer down to a definite assertion that can maybe be refuted or shown to be silly). The latter characteristic, a level of obscurity that often makes it just about impossible to figure out what an AE sentence is really saying, so closely resembles political and corporate doublespeak ("revenue enhancement," "downsizing," "pre-owned," "proactive resource-allocation restructuring") that it's tempting to think AE's real purpose is concealment and its real motivation fear.

The insecurity that drives AE, PCE, and vocab-tape ads is far from groundless, though. These are tense linguistic times. Blame it on Heisenbergian Uncertainty or postmodern relativism or Image Over Substance or the ubiquity of advertising and P .R. or the rise of Identity Politics or whatever you will—we live in an era of terrible preoccupation with presentation and interpretation. In rhetorical terms, certain long-held distinctions between the Ethical Appeal, Logical Appeal (= an argument's plausibility or soundness), and Pathetic Appeal (= an argument's emotional impact) have now pretty much collapsed—or rather the different sorts of Appeals now affect and are affected by one another in ways that make it almost impossible to advance an argument on "reason" alone.

A vividly concrete illustration here concerns the Official Complaint a black undergraduate filed against this rev. after one of my little *in camera* spiels. The complainant was (I opine) wrong, but she was not crazy or stupid; and I was able later to see that I did bear some responsibility for the whole nasty administrative swivet. My culpability lay in gross rhetorical naïveté. I'd seen my speech's primary Appeal as Logical: The aim was to make a conspicuously blunt, honest argument for SWE's utility. It wasn't pretty, maybe, but it was true, plus so manifestly bullshit-free that I think I anticipated not just acquiescence but gratitude for my candor.[44] The problem I failed to see, of course, lay not with the argument per se but with the person making it—namely me, a Privileged WASP Male in a position of power, thus someone whose statements about the primacy and utility of the Privileged WASP Male dialect appeared not candid/hortatory/authoritative/ture but elitist/highhanded/authoritarian/racist. Rhetoric-wise, what happened was that I allowed the substance and style of my Logical Appeal to completely torpedo my Ethical Appeal: What the student heard was just another PWM rationalizing why his Group and his English were top dog and ought "logically" to stay that way (plus, worse, trying to use his academic power over her to coerce her assent[45]).

If for any reason you happen to find yourself sharing this particular student's perceptions and reaction,[46] I would ask that you bracket your feelings long enough to recognize that the PWM instructor's very modern rhetorical dilemma in that

---

[44]Please just don't even say it.

[45](She professed to have been especially traumatized by the climactic "I am going to make you," which in retrospect was indeed a mammoth rhetorical boner.)

[46](The Dept. head and Dean did not, as it happens, share her reaction . . . rhough it would be disingenuous not to tell you that they happened also to be PWM's, which fact did not go unremarked by the complainant, such that the whole proceeding got pretty darn tense, indeed, before it was all over.).

office was really no different from the dilemma faced by a male who makes a Pro-Life argument, or an atheist who argues against Creation Science, or a Caucasian who opposes Affirmative Action, or an African American who decries Racial Profiling, or anyone over eighteen who tries to make a case for raising the legal driving age to eighteen, etc. The dilemma has nothing to do with whether the arguments themselves are plausible or right or even sane, because the debate rarely gets that far—any opponent with sufficiently strong feelings or a dogmatic bent can discredit the arguments and pretty much foreclose all further discussion with a single, terribly familiar rejoinder: "Of course *you'd* say that"; "Easy for *you* to say"; "What right do *you* have . . .?"

Now (still bracketing) consider the situation of any reasonably intelligent and well-meaning SNOOT who sits down to prepare a prescriptive usage guide. It's the millennium, post-Everything: Whence the authority to make any sort of credible Appeal for SWE at all?

Article's Crux: Why Bryan A. Garner Is a Genius, Though of a Rather Particular Kind

It isn't that *A Dictionary of Modern American Usage* is perfect. It doesn't seem to cover *conversant in* vs. *conversant with*, for example, or *abstruse* vs. *obtuse*, or to have anything on *hereby* and *herewith* (which I tend to use interchangeably but always have the uneasy feeling I'm screwing up). Garner's got a good discussion of *used to* but nothing on *supposed to*. Nor does he give any examples to help explain irregular participles and transitivity ("The light shone" vs. "I shined the light," etc.), and these would seem to be more important than, say, the correct spelling of *huzzah* or the plural of *animalculum*, both of which get discussed. Plus there's the VOGUE WORDS snafu and the absence of a pronunciation entry on *trough*.[47] In other words, a SNOOT is going to be able to find stuff to quibble about in any usage dictionary, and *ADMAU* is no exception.

But it's still really, really good—and not just lexicographically but rhetorically, politically (if it even makes sense to distinguish these any more). As a collection of judgments, *ADMAU* is in no way Descriptivist, but Garner structures his judgments very carefully to avoid the elitism and anality of traditional SNOOTitude. He does not deploy irony or scorn or caustic wit, nor tropes or colloquialisms or contractions . . . or really any sort of verbal style at all. In fact, even though Garner talks openly about himself and uses the 1-S pronoun throughout the whole dictionary, his personality is oddly effaced, neutralized. It's like he's so bland he's barely there. E.g., as this reviewer was finishing the book's final entry,[48] it struck

---

[47]To be honest, I noticed this omission only because midway through working on this article I happened to use the word *trough* in front of the same SNOOT friend who likes to compare public English to violin-hammering, and he fell sideways out of his chair, and it emerged that I have somehow all my life misheard *trough* as ending with a *th* instead of an *f* and thus have publicly mispronounced it God knows how many scores of times, and I all but burned rubber getting home to see whether perhaps the error was so common and human and understandable that Garner himself had a good-natured entry on it, but no such luck, which in fairness I don't suppose I can really blame Garner for.

[48](on *zwieback* vs. *zweiback*).

me that I had no idea whether Bryan Garner was black or white, gay or straight, Democrat or Dittohead. What was even more striking was that I hadn't once wondered about any of this up to now; something about Garner's lexical persona kept me ever from asking where the guy was coming from or what particular agendas or ideologies were informing what he had admitted right up front were "value Judgments."

Bryan Garner is a genius because *A Dictionary of Modern American Usage* pretty much resolves the Usage Wars' Crisis of Authority. Garner manages to control the comprescence of rhetorical Appeals so cleverly that he appears able to transcend both Usage Wars camps and simply tell the truth, and in a way that does not torpedo his own credibility but actually enhances it. His argumentative strategy is totally brilliant and totally sneaky, and part of both qualities is that it usually doesn't seem like there's even an argument going on at all.

Garner recognizes something that neither of the dogmatic camps appears to get: Given 40 years of the Usage Wars, "authority" is no longer something a lexicographer can just presume *ex officio*. In fact, a large part of the project of any contemporary usage dictionary will consist in establishing this authority. If that seems rather obvious, be apprised that nobody before Garner seems to have figured it out—that the lexicographer's challenge now is to be not just accurate and comprehensive but *credible*. That in the absence of unquestioned Authority in language, the reader must now be moved or persuaded to *grant* a dictionary its authority, freely and for what appear to be good reasons.

Garner's *A Dictionary of Modern American Usage* is thus both a collection of information and a piece of Democratic rhetoric.[49] Its goal is to recast the Prescriptivist's persona: The author presents himself as an authority not in an *autocratic* sense but in a *technocratic* sense. And the technocrat is not only a thoroughly modern and palatable image of Authority but also immune to the charges of elitism/classism that have hobbled traditional Prescriptivism.

Of course, Garner really *is* a technocrat. He's a lawyer, recall, and in *ADMAU* he consciously projects a sort of wise juridical persona: knowledgeable, dispassionate, fair, with an almost Enlightenment-grade passion for reason. His judgments about usage tend to be rendered like legal opinions—exhaustive citation of precedent (other dictionaries' judgments, published examples of actual usage) combined with clear, logical reasoning that's always informed by the larger consensual purposes SWE is meant to serve.

Also thoroughgoingly technocratic is Garner's approach to the issue of whether anybody's even going to be interested in his 700 pages of fine-pointed counsel. Like any specialist, he simply presumes that there are practical reasons why some people choose to concern themselves with SWE usage; and his attitude about the fact that most Americans "could care less" isn't scorn or disapproval but the phlegmatic resignation of a doctor or lawyer who realizes that he can give good advice but can't make you take it:

---

[49](meaning *literally* Democratic—It Wants Your Vote)

> *The reality I care about most is that some people still want to use the language well.[50] They want to write effectively; they want to speak effectively. They want their language to be graceful at times and powerful at times. They want to understand how to use words well, how to manipulate sentences, and how to move about in the language without seeming to flail. They want good grammar, but they want more: they want rhetoric[51] in the traditional .sense. That is, they want to use the language deftly so that it's fit for their purposes.*

It's now possible to see that all the autobiographical stuff in *ADMAU's* Preface does more than just humanize Mr. Bryan A. Garner. It also serves to detail the early and enduring passion that helps make someone a credible technocrat—we tend to like and trust experts whose expertise is born of a real love for their specialty instead of just a desire to be expert at something. In fact, it turns out that *ADMAU's* Preface quietly and steadily invests Garner with every single qualification of modern technocratic Authority: passionate devotion, reason, and accountability (recall "in the interests of full disclosure, here are the ten critical points . . ."), experience ("that, after years of working on usage problems, I've settled on"), exhaustive and tech-savvy research ("For contemporary usage, the files of our greatest dictionary makers pale in comparison with the full-text search capabilities now provided by NEXIS and WESTLAW"), an even and judicious temperament (see e.g. this from HYPERCORRECTION: "Sometimes people strive to abide by the strictest etiquette, but in the process behave inappropriately"[52]), and the sort of humble integrity (for instance, including in one of the entries a past published usage-error of his own) that not only renders Garner likable but transmits the same kind of reverence for English that good jurists have for the law, both of which are bigger and more important than any one person.

Probably the most attractive thing about *ADMAU's* Ethical Appeal, though, is Garner's scrupulous consideration of the reader's concern about his (or her) *own* linguistic authority and rhetorical persona and ability to convince an Audience that he cares. Again and again, Garner frames his prescriptions in rhetorical terms, e.g.: "To the writer or speaker for whom credibility is important, it's a good idea to avoid distracting *any* readers or listeners." *A Dictionary of Modern American Usage's* real thesis, in other words, is that the purposes of the expert authority and the purposes of the lay reader are identical, and identically rhetorical—which I submit is about as Democratic these days as you're going to get.

---

[50]The last two words of this sentence, of course, are what the Usage Wars are about—whose "language" and whose "well"? The most remarkable thing about this sentence is that coming from Garner it doesn't sound naïve or obnoxious but just . . . reasonable.

[51]Did you think I was kidding?

[52](Here this reviewer's indwelling and ever-vigilant SNOOT can't help but question why Garner uses a comma before the junction in this sentence, since what follows the conjunction is neither an independent clause nor any kind of plausible plement for *strive to*. But respectful disagreement between people of goodwill is of course Democratically natural and he and, when you come right down to it, kind of fun.)

50

A Boy's Life

For Matthew Shepard's killers,
what does it take to pass as a man?

JoAnn Wypijewski

"When I think of how fragile men are," a dominatrix once said to me, "I feel so much pity. All that fear, all that self-mutilation, just to be 'men.' When I heard that those guys in Laramie took Matthew Shepard's shoes, I was so creeped out. I mean, shoes are so symbolic— 'walk a mile in my shoes' and all that, Why did they take his shoes?"

From the beginning there was something too awfully iconic about the case. Matthew Shepard—young, small, gay, a college boy in the cowboy town of Laramie, Wyoming, a kid who, his father says, didn't know how to make a fist until he was thirteen—lured out of a bar by two "rednecks" ("trailer trash," "drop-outs," every tabloid term has been applied), hijacked to a lonely spot outside of town, strung up like a scarecrow on a buck fence, bludgeoned beyond recognition, and left to die without his shoes, his ring, his wallet, or the $20 inside it. With that mix of real and fanciful detail, it has been called a trophy killing, a hate crime, a sac-

THE ROMANCE OF THE WEST
Photograph by G. Rancinan/Sygma

rifice. Press crews who had never before and have not since lingered over gruesome murders of homosexuals came out in force, reporting their brush with a bigotry so poisonous it could scarcely be imagined. County Attorney Cal Rerucha says death by injection is the just response. At the site where Shepard was murdered, in a field of prairie grass and sagebrush within eyeshot of suburban houses, a cross has been laid out in pink limestone rocks. In crotches of the killing fence, two stones have been placed; one bears the word "love"; the other, "forgive." The poignancy of those messages has been transmitted out and beyond via television; it is somewhat diminished if one knows that the stones were put there by a journalist, whose article about the murder for *Vanity Fair* was called "The Cruci-fixion of Matthew Shepard."

Torture is more easily imagined when masked in iconography but no better understood. Perhaps it all will become clear in October, when one of the accused, Aaron McKinney, goes on trial for kidnapping, aggravated robbery, and capital murder (his companion, Russell Henderson, pled guilty on April 5 and avoided death with two consecutive life terms), but it seems unlikely. "The story" passed into myth even before the trials had been set, and at this point fact, rumor, politics, protective cover, and jailhouse braggadocio are so entangled that the truth may be elusive even to the protagonists.

What is known, though somehow elided, is that in the most literal definition of the word, Matthew Shepard was not crucified. His hands were not outstretched, as has been suggested by all manner of media since October 7, 1998, when the twenty-one-year-old University of Wyoming student was discovered near death, but rather tied behind him as if in handcuffs, lashed to a pole four inches off the ground. His head propped on the lowest fence rail, his legs extending out to the east, he was lying almost flat on his back when Deputy Reggie Fluty of the Albany County Sheriff's Department found him at 6:22 P.M., eighteen hours, it's believed, after he was assaulted. It was Shepard's diminutive aspect—Fluty thought he was thirteen—and the horrid condition of his face and head, mangled by eighteen blows from a three-pound Smith & Wesson .357 magnum, that most compelled her attention.

Shepard had encountered McKinney and Henderson, both also twenty-one, at the Fireside Bar on October 6. They exchanged words that no one heard, then left the bar and got into a truck belonging to McKinney's father. There Shepard was robbed and hit repeatedly. Out by the fence came the fatal beating. Shepard must have been kicked too, because he was bruised between his legs and elsewhere. Amid the blows he cried, "Please don't." He was left alive but unconscious, as McKinney and Henderson headed for an address they'd got out of him. En route they ran into two local punks out puncturing tires, Emiliano Morales and Jeremy Herrera, and started a fight. McKinney cracked Morales's head open with the same gun he'd used on Shepard, coating the weapon with still more blood. Herrera then whacked McKinney's head with a stick. Police arrived, grabbed Henderson (he and McKinney had run in different directions), and found the truck, the gun, Shepard's shoes and credit card. Police wouldn't put the crimes together until later, so Henderson was cited for interference with a peace officer and released. Henderson then drove to Cheyenne with his girlfriend, Chasity Pasley, and McKinney's girlfriend, Kristen LeAnn Price (both later charged as accessories after the fact), to dispose of his bloody clothes. McKinney, dazed from the gash in his head, stayed home in bed, and Price hid Shepard's wallet in the dirty diaper of her and McKinney's infant son, Cameron. Six days later, on October 12, Shepard died.

THE PRESS DESCENDS ON LARAMIE
Photograph by Richard Alan Hannon

Those are the facts as disclosed by court records and McKinney's confession. (He has pleaded not guilty.) In response, the Equality State—which enfranchised women long before anyplace else, which struck sodomy laws from the books in 1977—has disowned McKinney and Henderson as monsters. So has the rest of the country.

And yet McKinney and Henderson appear to be young men of common prejudices, far more devastatingly human than is comfortable to consider. They acquired the gun a few days before the murder in a trade for $100 in methamphetamine—crank, speed, crystal meth—the drug of choice among white rural youth, cheaper than cocaine and more long-lasting, more relentless in its accelerating effects, more widely used in Wyoming, per capita, than in any state in the country. McKinney, says the friend who traded him for it, desired the gun for its badass beauty—eight-inch barrel, fine tooling, "the Dirty Harry thing." The trade occurred while these three fellows and their girlfriends were on a meth binge. Before it was over they would smoke or snort maybe $2,000 worth of the drug. By the time they met Matthew Shepard, says the friend, who saw them that day, McKinney and Henderson were on the fifth day of that binge. They had not slept, he says, since before October 2, payday, when the partying had begun.

Those unreported facts—to the extent that anything can be factually determined in Laramie these days, with everyone involved in the case under a gag order*—may tell more about the crime, more about the everyday life of hate and hurt and heterosexual culture than all the quasi-religious characterizations of Matthew's passion, death, and resurrection as patron saint of hate-crime legislation. It's just possible that Matthew Shepard didn't die because he was gay; he died because Aaron McKinney and Russell Henderson are straight.

The order prohibits lawyers; witnesses; local, state, and federal law-enforcement officers; et al. from discussing the case. McKinney's friend says he was visited by black-suited agents of the Alcohol, Tobacco and Firearms Department shortly after McKinney and Henderson were arrested, and told them this story. Before it passed into his hands, says McKinney's friend, the gun had been stolen, which is consistent with court records. Henderson's grandmother says she noticed nothing unusual about Russell when he visited her on October 5. McKinney's friend and the other drug users, ex-users, or dealers in Laramie spoke with me on condition of anonymity.

"If you're telling your feelings, you're kind a wuss." Brent Jones, a heterosexual who went to high school with McKinney and Henderson, was guiding me through the psychic terrain of a boy's life.

"So what do you do when things hurt?"

"That's why God created whiskey, don't you think? You get drunker than a pig and hope it drains away—or you go home and cry."

"Is that true for most guys, do you think?"

"Yeah, pretty much."

"So secretly you're all wusses, and you know you're wusses, but you can't let anyone know, even though you all know you know."

"You could say that."

"Can you talk to girls about this stuff?"

"Unless you know this is the one—like, you're going to get married, and then you're in so deep you can't help yourself—but if not, if you think she might break up with you, then no, because she might tell someone, and then it gets around, and then everyone thinks you're a wuss. And you don't want people to think you're a wuss, unless you are a wuss, and then you know you're a wuss, and then it doesn't matter."

Among the weighty files on the proceedings against McKinney and Henderson in the Albany County Courthouse is a curious reference. The state had charged, as an "aggravating factor" in the murder, that "the defendant[s] knew or should have known that the victim was suffering from a physical or mental disability." The court threw this out; Judge Jeffrey Donnell, who presided over Henderson's case, told me he assumed it referred to Shepard's size (five foot two, 105 pounds) but was legally irrelevant whatever its intent. In a sense, it is sociologically irrelevant as well whether the prosecution regarded Shepard as crippled more by sexuality or size, since by either measure he was, in the vernacular of Laramie's straight youth, a wuss.

Wussitude haunts a boy's every move. It must have haunted Aaron McKinney most of his life. McKinney, too, is a little thing—not as little as Shepard, but at about five foot six, 145 pounds, he doesn't cut a formidable figure. George Markle, who roomed with him after they both dropped out of high school, describes McKinney as having "tiny arms, a tiny, tiny chest, no definition in his body." He affected a gangsta style—droopy jeans, baggy shirt, Raiders jacket, gold chains, gold on all his fingers. He'd ape hip-hop street talk, but "he couldn't get it going if he tried." His nickname was Dopey, both for his oversized ears and for his reputation as a serious drug dealer and user. His shoulder bears a tattoo of the Disney character pouring a giant can of beer on his mother's grave, an appropriation of a common rapper's homage to a fallen brother: "Pour a forty ounce on my homey's grave."

The prosecution contends that Shepard was lured out of the bar as if on a sexual promise. County public defender Wyatt Skaggs says that neither Henderson nor McKinney ever asserted that they came on to Shepard. And in his confes-

RUSSELL HENDERSON AND AARON McKINNEY
Photograph by Ed Andrieski/AP/World Wide Photos

sion, McKinney said Shepard "did not hit on or make advances toward" him and Henderson, according to Sheriff's Detective Sgt. Rob De-Bree. Perhaps McKinney said something different when he came home that night and wept in the arms of Kristen Price, or perhaps, presuming homophobia to be an acceptable alibi, she thought she was helping him when she told the press that he and Henderson "just wanted to beat [Shepard] up bad enough to teach him a lesson not to come on to straight people." But once at the Albany County Detention Center, McKinney seemed to take up the pose of fag-basher as a point of pride. At least five prisoners awaiting trial or sentencing have asked their lawyers if the things he's said to them might be leveraged to their own advantage. "Being a verry [sic] drunk homofobick [sic] I flipped out and began to pistol whip the fag with my gun," McKinney wrote in a letter to another inmate's wife. He didn't mean to kill Shepard, he wrote; he was turning to leave him, tied to the fence but still conscious, when Matthew "mouthed off to the point that I became angry enough to strike him more with my gun." Even then, he insists, his attitude toward homosexuals is not particularly venomous and the murder was unintentional.

McKinney's mother was a nurse; she died as a result of a botched operation when Aaron was sixteen. Markle says there was a kind of shrine to her in his house, but Aaron rarely spoke of her, and then only superficially and only when

THE FIRESIDE BAR
Photograph by Richard Alan Hannon

he was high: "He was always happy then. Once, on mushrooms, he said that if he would slide backward down a hill, he could see his mom in heaven." According to probate records, McKinney got $98,268.02 in a settlement of the wrongful-death lawsuit his stepfather brought against the doctors and the hospital. "After he got the money, he had a lot of friends," Markle told me. He bought cars and cracked them up, bought drugs and became an instant figure in town. He was engaged at one point—"she got the drugs, he got the sex; I guess it worked out for a while"—until the girl found a more attractive connection. "He wasn't a babe magnet," Brent Jones says. He might make a good first impression—he's funny, I was told, though no one could quite explain how—but he couldn't keep that up. Women were *bitches* and *hos*, just like other men, who might also be called *fag*, *wuss*, *queer*, *sissie*, *girly man*, *woman*, the standard straight-boy arsenal, which McKinney employed indiscriminately, says Markle, "about as much as anybody— you know, joking around—he never mentioned anything about hating gays." He talked about marrying Price, who is eighteen, but, according to more than one person who was acquainted with them, he wasn't faithful and didn't seem even to like her much.

He loves his son, I'm told. And what else? Blank. What did he talk about? Blank. What did he fear? Blank. Who is he? None of the boys can really say. Interior life is unexplored territory, even when it's their own. Exterior life, well, "Actually, when he wasn't high he was kind of a geek," says a guy who's done drugs with him since high school. "He wasn't the sharpest tool in the shed. He always wanted to seem bigger, badder, and tougher than anybody," says Jones, a strongly built fellow who first noticed McKinney when the latter hit him from behind. "He usually didn't pick on anyone bigger than him. He could never do it alone, and he couldn't do it toe-to-toe." Markle says nothing much mattered to McKinney in picking a fight, except that if he started to lose, his friends would honor the rule they had among themselves and come in to save him.

A stock media image of McKinney and Henderson in this tragedy has them counting out quarters and dimes with dirty fingers to buy a pitcher of beer at the Fireside. It is meant to indicate their distance from Shepard, who had clean hands and paid for his Heinekens with bills, and to offer some class perspective on the cheap. *They were poor, they were losers, they lived in trailers, for God's sake!* McKinney, as it happens, didn't live in a trailer, though he had when he was younger—a nice double one with his stepfather, until recently program director at KRQU radio. His natural father is a long-haul truck driver whom he was heard to call "Daddy" only a few years ago, and in Aaron's childhood the family lived on Palomino Drive in the Imperial Heights subdivision. As teenagers he and his friends would drink and get high in the field behind it—"quite the hangout," according to Markle—where McKinney had played as a boy and where he would later leave Shepard to die.

Henderson spent most of his childhood in the warmly appointed ranch house where his grandmother runs a day care and to which his late grandfather would repair after work at the post office. At the time of the murder, Russell lived with Pasley, a UW art student, now serving fifteen to twenty-four months, in a trailer court no uglier than most in Laramie and with the same kinds of late-model cars, trucks, and four-wheel-drive vehicles parked outside, the same proportion of people pulling in and out wearing ties or nice coats or everyday workers' clothes, and probably the same type of modest but comfortable interiors as in the ones I visited. No matter, in the monumental condescension of the press, "trailer" always means failure, always connotes "trash," and, however much it's wrapped up in sociocul-turoeconomico froufrou, always insinuates the same thing: What can you expect from trash?

McKinney and Henderson were workers. At the end of the day they had dirty hands, just like countless working men who head to the bars at quitting time. Dirt is symbolic only if manual labor is, and manual laborers usually find their symbolism elsewhere. The pair had drunk two pitchers of beer at the Library bar before going to the Fireside; no one remembers anything about them at the Library, presumably because they paid in dollars. Maybe they resented a college boy's clean hands and patent-leather loafers and moneyed confidence; they wouldn't have been the only people in town who do, though acquaintances ascribe no such sentiments to them. UW is a state school, the only university in Wyoming. It stands aloof from the town, but no more than usual. Poll a classroom, and about a fifth of the students are from Laramie, and half say their parents are manual workers. Shepard, originally from Casper but schooled abroad because his father is in the oil business, didn't need a job; Pasley, like most students, did. There's nothing unique here about the injuries of class. In a month at Laramie Valley Roofing, McKinney and Henderson each would gross around $1,200, roughly $7.50 an hour. With rent payments of $370 and $340, respectively, they were like a lot of people in Laramie, where the median household income is $26,000, the average monthly rent is $439, and the average family works two jobs, maybe more.

It's said that McKinney squandered the entire hundred grand from his mother's settlement, and in his application for a public defender he listed $0 in assets. Before moving to his last address, he and his family briefly lived rent-free in a converted indoor stable with no shower, no stove, no refrigerator, and, in some rooms, a cloth ceiling and cloth walls. But everyone I spoke with who was openly familiar with him through drugs was skeptical about the poverty story. To finance his recreation, I was told by the guy tweaking with him in the days before the murder, McKinney would often be fronted an "eight ball" of meth (three grams, an eighth of an ounce, street price about $300; for him, wholesale, sometimes as low as $100), keep two grams for himself, double the amount of the remaining powder by cutting it with vitamin B, sell that, and have $200 and enough crank to keep two people awake for practically a week before he'd even paid a cent. At one point a few years ago, according to a friend now monitored by an ankle bracelet, McKinney was buying an eight ball every few days.

Maybe he miscalculated the costs of his binge in that first week in October. A few days before Shepard would be tied to the fence, McKinney and Henderson walked into the Mini-Mart where George Markle works, and, in an agitated state, McKinney shouted that Markle owed him $4,000 and that he needed it. Years earlier, Aaron had bought George a used Chevy S-10 low-rider truck. First it was called a gift, then a loan, then no one talked about it much, Markle says, and after the friendship broke, he didn't intend to pay anything back. That day in the Mini-Mart, Aaron threatened to kill George. He had threatened him once or twice before within the last few weeks, always with Henderson silently in tow. Markle told his boss, but neither of them thought too much of it. "I'm gonna kill you"—it was just Aaron pretending to be big and bad. It was the way he talked; like when he first came into the Mini-Mart and, seeing George, exclaimed, "Oh, look at that—it's my favorite little bitch, my favorite little whore."

> *"Things are good enough for me to stay for now," Elam Timothy, a writer, gardener, and handyman, was telling me just before we decided what his pseudonym would be. "I have a relationship, I'm out at work and to as many people as I care to be—but I'm not looking through rose-colored glasses. They're demonizing those boys so they don't have to look at themselves. Yes, this could have happened anywhere, but it didn't. Can we please look at it? That whole 'live and let live' myth. In my mind that boils down to one sentence: If I don't tell you I'm a fag, you won't beat the crap out of me."*
>
> *"Have you ever been hurt or threatened here?"*
>
> *"No."*
>
> *"Do you know anyone who has been?"*
>
> *"No, but I don't know many gay men either."*
>
> *"So what is it that's dangerous?"*

"What's scary is just hearing people use the word 'faggot' all the time. It makes me feel like a pig at a weenie roast. Danger isn't palpable, but I keep myself in safe pockets. I wouldn't expect to find safety in the Cowboy [bar], but Coal Creek [coffeehouse], yeah, that's safe."

MCKINNEY'S CONVERTED STABLE APARTMENT
Photograph by Ted Wood

Laramie was founded on sex and the railroad, in that order. Women created the region's first service industry, and soon after the town's establishment, in 1868, it was associated with some thirty saloons, gambling houses, and brothels. Before any of that, it was associated with death. Around 1817, a French Canadian trapper named Jacques LaRamie was working these parts with his mates. As the story goes, he was young and handsome, and in winter decided to take his beaver traps upstream on what is now either the Big or the Little Laramie River. In spring he failed to return, and Indians told his erstwhile companions that he'd been killed by other natives and stuffed under the ice of a beaver pond. His headstone thus became the plains, a mountain range, two rivers, a fort, a county, a railroad terminal, and, ultimately, the city.

From the foothills of the Laramie Range, the high prairie where the city is situated stretches out, scored by steel tracks and pocked by late-model houses defiant of the city's already shaggy boundaries. From the right vantage point those are obscured, and all that's in sight is the plain and, to the west, the Snowy Range and what, against reason, seems like infinity. People may swoon about Wyoming's mountains and river valleys, but the power is all in the wind, which has shaped the plains like a pair of enormous hands playing in a sandbox of soft soil and red clay, massaging the earth into fine overlapping layers and fluid hollows. Such subtlety is merely the profit of aeons. Over spring break a student from the university left his truck out in an open field while the winds blew thirty, forty miles an hour; within two weeks, the windward side of the truck had been sandblasted down to bare metal.

Laramie, a pleasant place of liberal inclination and some 27,000 people, is not a railroad town anymore. Freight lines rush through but are marginal to the city's economy. It's not a sex town either, though in the history-charmed buildings abutting the rail yard along 1st Street shopkeepers will happily show off narrow cubicles in an upstairs flat, or a slotted box in a side door, where nighttime ladies deposited their earnings under the madam's gaze and key, their work organized as on a sharecrop, with ledgered debt always exceeding income. Carol Bowers, an archivist at the university's American Heritage Center, recounts a history in which the town elders seesawed between plans for eradication and regulation, usually recognizing the superior benefits of the latter. (In one nineteenth-century city record, all but $20 out of $240 in fines and fees collected one month came from prostitutes.) So the women were harassed, corralled, controlled by periodic raids, punished for any venture into legitimate civic life by threats to their licenses—but tolerated. "The town didn't want them to go away," Bowers says. "The town wanted them to be invisible."

A hundred years later, sex is almost totally in the closet. Only the truck stops off I-80 are worked, by mobile squads of women or by men, who also work the rest stops. For every other unspoken desire there's The Fort, a rambling warehouse south of town that has survived Cal Rerucha's tireless efforts at suppression. There men, mostly men, stop in (all classes and tendencies, all night on weekends), nervous and chatty—about a practical joke or a bachelor party or the wife—before surveying the aisles, then scuttling to the checkout with a strap-on dildo or a Miss Perfection "port-a-pussy" or a sexual banquet of videos. A tall, lean man of the muscular outdoors type crouches before a display and comes away with the Sauna Action Pump, guaranteed to improve an erection beyond any natural capacity. Now and then one man is followed five minutes later by another, under the red light and into the video booths in back.

In the best of times, sex is playground to the imagination, the place where what is need not be what it seems, where strength and weakness swap clothes, and the thin cry, "This is who I am, this is who I dream of being—don't hurt me" seeks its voice. Laramie happens now to be associated with sex in the worst of times, sex boxed and squared in the unexamined terms of the "natural" course of things or the unexamined terms of "identity." Many in town are irritated by this association and by all the talk of hate since the murder attracted national attention. McKinney and Henderson, it's said, are "not Laramie." Before his death, Shepard was surely "not Laramie" either, if only because he took risks that other gay men in town might not have. Laramie, it's said, is not censorious about sex, homo or hetero—*We're just tight-lipped. We don't go there. We believe "live and let live"*—and it's certainly not hateful, just as most of the country is not, just as, perhaps, even McKinney and Henderson are not. If they all were, everything would be much simpler.

Hatred is like pornography—hard to define, but you know it when you see it. On the morning before Russell Henderson pleaded guilty, the Reverend Fred Phelps of Topeka, Kansas, brought his flock to the county courthouse with signs declaring GOD HATES FAGS, FAG GOD=RECTUM, PHIL 3:19, SAVE THE GERBILS. Phelps cited as his guide for most of this (the Bible has nothing to say about gerbils) such scriptural passages as Leviticus 18:22, "Thou shalt not lie with mankind, as with womankind: it is abomination." I asked if he also subscribes to Moses' suggestion a bit further on in Leviticus 20:13, "If a man also lie with mankind, as he lieth with a woman, . . . they shall surely be put to death." He said he thought all civil law should be based on biblical code, but "it's never going to happen. I'm a pragmatist, a visionary."

"So, if you could, though, you would execute homosexuals?"

"I wouldn't execute them. The government would execute them."

His only audience were police, press, and a ring of angels—counterprotesters dressed in white robes, their great wings sweeping up before his gaudy placards.

The next day the university's student newspaper covered the day's events, running in enlarged type the observation of freshman Kristen Allen that "they have no business using the Bible verses out of context. God hates the sin but loves the sinner." On campus, where Phelps later moved his protest, onlookers expressed disgust at his message and invoked "tolerance."

Before it came to signify the highest state to which straight society could aspire, tolerance was something one had for a bad job or a bad smell or a nightmare relative who visited once a year. In its new guise, tolerance means straight people know of gay men and women, but there is no recognizable gay life, no clubs except a tiny one on campus, no bars or restaurants or bookstores flying the rainbow flag. It means the university might institute a Matthew Shepard Chair in Civil Liberties but has no antidiscrimination policy that applies to homosexuals and no employee benefit policy that extends to domestic partners.* It means the public school curriculum does not say teachers must "avoid planning curriculum promoting perversion, homosexuality, contraception, promiscuity and abortion as healthy lifestyle choices"—the policy in Lincoln County, Wyoming—but it also does not include "homosexuality" among vocabulary terms for sex-ed classes at any grade level and mentions the word only once, for eighth grade, under "Topics to be Discussed . . . particularly as they relate to [sexually transmitted diseases]." It means a father tells his lesbian daughter, "If you have to do this you should do it in the closet," and the mother tells her, "Let's just pretend I don't know, okay?" It means her brother "tries to be as supportive as he can be—and he is—but if a man hit on him, he'd beat the shit out of him. He wouldn't beat up someone for another reason, and he thinks that's an accomplishment—and it is." It means Chasity Pasley's mother won her custody battle over the charge that as a lesbian she was unfit, but her children had to call her partner "Aunt." It means if you're gay and out and attend a company party with your boyfriend, the sense in the room is "We know you're gay and that's okay, but do you have to bring your boyfriend?" It means Fred Dahl, the straight head of UW's Survey Research Center, accepts the university's expression of outrage over Shepard's murder but tells a social work master's candidate named Shannon Bell that her project to poll Wyoming residents on their attitudes toward homosexuality might amount to harassment of straight people, and anyway, "one good rodeo season and Wyoming will be back to normal."

In a graduate-class discussion right after Shepard was found, the high-minded talk was all of tolerance as students challenged a woman who had said she abhorred violence but still . . . homosexuality, it's immoral. Amid the chatter, a cowboy who'd been silent said plainly, "The issue isn't tolerance. We don't need to learn tolerance; we need to learn love."

---

*UW president Philip Dubois told me that the university has such an antidiscrimination policy, but as of July 1999 sexual orientation was still not included as a protected category in the university's official Equal Employment Opportunity/Affirmative Action Statement approved by the trustees. Nor does it appear in the antidiscrimination provisions for student admissions. Only these formal statements of policy have the force of law, says the ACLU's Marv Johnson.

DOWNTOWN LARAMIE
Photograph by Ted Wood

There may be, as the song goes, a thin line between love and hate, but, how-ever many twists it takes, it is life's defining line. And people like Phelps are no more responsible for it than pop music is responsible for the murders at Columbine High School. What keeps that line so strong, like strands of the clothesline used to tie Matthew Shepard's wrists, are all the little things of a culture, mostly unnoticed and unremarked, like the way in which the simplest show of affection is a decision about safety, like the way in which a man entwined with a woman is the stuff of everyday commerce but a man expressing vulnerability is equivalent to a quaint notion of virginity—you save it for marriage.

> *"Masks are no longer as protective as they used to be," John Scagliotti, the maker of* Before *(and now* After*) Stonewall, was telling me. "If you're gay, no longer can you hide, because straight people watch TV, and they see how people hide. And also this has changed straight cul-ture, so all the little things you do might make you question whether you're straight, or straight enough. Your own suspicions are suspicious.*

> *"It gets even more complicated now that all these things that repre-sent maleness are very attractive to both gay and straight men. The*

downside of this, in a way, is that straight male bonding, and male bonding in general, especially in rural places, is going to be a very confused thing. Already at gyms, eighteen-year-olds don't take showers anymore—or if they do, they take all their things in with them, like modest little girls. You're confused, you're eighteen, and you really like this guy; he's your best buddy, and you'd rather spend all your time with him than with this girl. And you are straight, but now you're worried too."

The Henderson trial was to have begun on the first Tuesday after Easter. At the Harvest Foursquare full-gospel church that Sunday, people wore name tags and expressed a serene camaraderie. Then they sent the children downstairs to play while the "illustrated sermon"—a dramatization of Christ's Passion and death—took place. It was a stunning performance, beginning with the Jesus character racked with sorrow in the Garden of Gethsemane. The narrator said Jesus suffered like any man. Then he said, departing from the script, "Every time I see an image of a feminine Jesus, it makes my blood boil. Jesus wasn't a weakling. Jesus was a man. If Jesus was here today, he could take on any man in this room." Later, when the Jesus character was tied to a post, flogged by two men—soldiers who took "sensual pleasure" in every fall of the whip, the narrator said—"Jesus didn't cry out for mercy . . . Jesus was a man. Jesus was a man's man." The Jesus character writhed in agony. After he stumbled offstage with the cross, and the only sounds

THE REVEREND FRED PHELPS
Photograph by Kevin Moloney / Liaison Agency

were his moans amid the pounding of nails, the narrator described the tender caress of the hands now ripped by sharp iron. In the congregation, men as well as women were moved to weeping. By the end, they were all singing, swaying, proclaiming their weakness before the Lord.

Time was when "a man's man" could mean only one thing, and in the romance of the West, that meant cowboys. In reality, Laramie is as contradictory as anything liberated from caricature, but in symbolism its outward identity remains hitched to the cowboy. Wild Willie's Cowboy Bar anchors one corner downtown; a few feet away is The Rancher. Farther up the same street is the Ranger Lounge and Motel; down another, the legendary Buckhorn Bar, with its mirror scarred by a bullet hole, its motionless zoo of elk and deer and prong-horned antelope, bobcat and beaver and buffalo, a two-headed foal, a twinset of boar. Around the corner stands the Cowboy Saloon, with its tableau of locomotives and thundering horses, lightning storms and lassos, portraits of grand old men who'd graced the town in history (Buffalo Bill Cody) and in dreams (Clint Eastwood). A wall inside the courthouse bears a silhouette of a bronco buster, whose figure has also appeared on Wyoming license plates since 1936. The university's symbol is the rodeo rider; its sports teams, the Cowboys and Cowgirls; its paper, the *Branding Iron*; its mascot, Pistol Pete; and its recruiting slogan, "It's in our nature."

For the men of Laramie who didn't grow up on a ranch riding horses and roping cattle—that is, most of them—the cowboy cult appears to be as natural as the antlers affixed to a female elk's head hanging on a wall at the Buckhorn. It all seems to fit, until you look closer and realize that this buck is actually Bambi's mother butched up. For those who did grow up to be cowboys, the rituals and vestments may be just as they were for their fathers and grandfathers—like going to the dance hall on a Saturday night, scrubbed and polished and wearing one's best hat and boots—but the meanings have changed, or at least got more complicated. In a different setting, the waves of men kicking it up to "Cotton Eye Joe" at the Cowboy Saloon would be high camp, just as the beautiful, guileless cowboy explaining the rodeo to me, undulating in a pantomime of the art of bull riding, could as easily have been auditioning for a spot with The Village People.

Camp still flies under the radar of straight Laramie: heterosexuals didn't wink when the golden anniversary commemorative booklet of the university union featured a sailor flanked by two gamesome cowboys, circa the 1940s, with the caption "Come alongside cowboys . . . let me tell you a sea story . . ." But the rodeo rider doesn't need to *know* he's a gay icon for such things to tinge his identity, any more than he needs to know he's a Western icon. He grows up on a ranch but takes a degree in civil engineering, forsaking the land but not the culture. His children then trade in the heels and pointy toes for something else, or they affect the look but with a suspect authenticity. Their grandfathers' world is still theirs as well, but now only in nostalgia.

The cowboy was not part of Wyoming's conscious image until after he had ceased to exist in the form later to be romanticized. In 1889, the governor's appeals for statehood contained none of the heroic references advertised on the front of the Cowboy Saloon; instead, he imagined Wyoming as a magnet for industrial capital, a dream that would not be fully abandoned by state planners until 1997. As detailed by Frieda Knobloch, a UW professor of American Studies, the state's history in this regard can be read as a continual longing to be what it is not: anticipation that vast oil and mineral reserves would issue forth factory towns like those in the East; then advancement of the Wild West as a tourist attraction just as the enclosure of the open range was complete. Central to the latter project were artists from the East—Frederic Remington, Owen Wister—whose work was financed or seized upon by local promoters. By 1922 the governor was urging citizens to put on "four-gallon hats" for the benefit of Eastern experience-seekers at the state's Frontier Days celebration. In 1939, even as the Department of Commerce and Industry was lobbying investors with forecasts of a manufacturing dawn, its head man was again reminding locals to dress up as cowboys to "give our guests what they want."

Perhaps some in Laramie bridled so at the presence of the national press on the Shepard case not only out of their own defensiveness and justified outrage at reporters' arrogance—jamming the door when Henderson's grandmother declined to comment, blustering over being barred from the courtroom even though they never reserved seats, mistaking cottonwoods for oaks—but also because of some deep vibrations of that old tradition of outside gawking and self-exploitation. A heterosexual lawyer named Tony Lopez chatted with me for a long time but nevertheless let me know, "This is home, and you're an uninvited guest."

Now in front of the small ranches on the edge of Laramie, the third vehicle might be a school bus, which the rancher drives to make $300, $400 a month in the off-season. No small spread survives just on cattle; in fewer than ten years the price of a calf has fallen from well over a dollar to sixty cents a pound. The profit margin for these ranches, never fantastic, according to Brett Moline, the University Agricultural Cooperative Extension educator for Albany Country, is now "squeezed so tight one financial mistake can be enough to wipe you out." Most ranch owners are in their late fifties or early sixties; younger ones have either inherited the land or are carrying so much debt from buying that they won't be in business long. Without a lot of money to live on and huge assets all tied up in land, the only way to realize the value of what they have is to sell it—usually to housing developers or to out-of-state gentility, who might pay three times the land's worth to set up what Moline calls their "ranchette."

Wyoming, with 480,000 people, still has the lowest population density in the country, and where there's space there is a kind of freedom. The state has no income tax, no motorcycle-helmet law, no law against openly carrying a gun, no open-container law on the interstates (meaning you can drink without worry unless you're drunk); there's a seat-belt law, but it's not enforced (police take $5 off the fine for another violation—say, speeding—if you're buckled up); until last year children didn't have to go to school before the age of seven and didn't have to stay in school past the eighth grade; unless there's a weapon involved, Laramie police say they prefer wrestling a suspect to the ground to other kinds of force, and in ten years they have killed only one civilian.

"COME ALONGSIDE COWBOYS . . ."

"This is the last frontier," says Laramie police officer Mike Ernst, with a curl in his voice. After the university, the government is the biggest employer, and after the bars, the most striking commercial establishments are bookstores and restaurants and, near UW, the fast-food strip. On the fringes of town rise some enormous houses, and elsewhere some people have no running water or refrigeration, so the soup kitchen substitutes peanut butter for meat in takeaway lunches in summer. Most, though, live in bungalows in town, trailers and suburban houses a bit farther out. Except for Mountain Cement and the sawmills, there's little manufacturing work, mostly only retail and service jobs, maid work at the motels, short-order cooking and rig washing out at the truck stops, telemarketing for the hippie kids, and temp work from construction to computers, but none of that pays more than $8 an hour.

McKinney and Henderson were roofers. Construction has a short season in Wyoming, intensifying even normally intense work. An eight-hour day can stretch into ten or twelve hours of fitting a shingle, banging a hammer, fitting and banging and banging bent over, on a grade, on your knees—bang, bang, bang. "I hurt a lot every day. I'm only twenty-one," Brent Jones told me. "My back shouldn't hurt." Jones works for a competing roofing company. "It's not bad if you use a nail gun, but if you use a hammer—eight hours of that and you can't even turn a doorknob . . . You just work through the pain. Sometimes you take a bunch of Advil. You go to bed at night and just pray that when you wake up you don't hurt so much."

Sometimes you drink—"booze, the cause of an answer to all of life's problems," in Jones's crisp phrase. Drinking is a pleasure in its own way in Laramie and a curse in all of the usual ways. Officer Ernst said that if alcohol somehow disappeared, Laramie wouldn't need three quarters of its police force. *The Boomerang's* daily police blotter is dominated by DUI and "domestic disturbance" calls, and not by coincidence. News of murder is rare, but it's ugly. In the year before Matthew Shepard was killed, fifteen-year-old Daphne Sulk was found naked in the snow, dead from seventeen stab wounds; eight-year-old Kristin Lamb, while away visiting her grandparents in the town of Powell, was kidnapped, raped, and thrown into the garbage in a duffel bag. No one calls those hate crimes. Just as six years ago no one called it a hate crime when the body of a gay UW professor, Steve Heyman, was found dumped by the side of a road in Colorado. Law enforcement and university administrators alike simply forgot that murder. After hearing of Shepard's beating, State Senator Craig Thomas declared, "It's the most violent, barbaric thing I've ever heard of happening in Wyoming."

There are 14,869 women in Albany County, according to the 1990 census, and 1,059 extra men. Stefani Farris at the SAFE Project, a haven and advocacy center for people who've been abused or sexually assaulted, said she thought "people in this town would be spinning if they knew how many times women were beaten by a husband or boyfriend." The state recorded 163 incidents of domestic violence in the county in 1997, nine rapes, and ninety-nine aggravated assaults. In its 1997–98 report, though, SAFE

ON THE FRINGES OF LARAMIE
Photograph by Ted Wood

records 3,958 phone calls, almost all from women, reporting battering, stalking, sexual assault, and other physical or emotional hurts, almost all committed by men. It notes 1,569 face-to-face sessions; 1,118 individuals served; 164 individuals sheltered for 2,225 total days. SAFE can't spend much time analyzing perpetrators, Farris explained. "When you see that women are being battered, their children are being abused, their pets are being killed, you see a woman who comes in and we've seen three other women before come in who were in the same situation with the same guy—it's hard to have any sympathy for what the man went through."

The court remands some batterers to the ADAM Program at the Southeast Wyoming Mental Health Center for reeducation, but the project's director, Ed Majors, says that all he can deal with is behavior. "I can't find a dime for services, [so] the deep issues are still not addressed. If you eat chocolate and use Clearasil, you're still going to have problems."

Such as?

"When it's fear or hurt, which is typically the primary emotion at work, when you can't say, 'I'm scared shitless,' most hurt and fear will come out in the only vehicle men are allowed. It comes out crooked. It looks like anger, it's expressed as anger, but it isn't."

> *"Here's a joke for you," an amiable guy offered: "What do you get when you play a country song backward? You get your car back, you get your dog back, you get your house back, you get your wife back . . .*
>
> *"Here's another one: You can have sex with a sheep in Wyoming, just don't tie the shepherd to the fence . . . Oh, God, now you're gonna think I'm an inbred redneck asshole."*

There was no trial for Russell Henderson in the end, so what drama his story could arouse had to be fit into one early-April hearing. According to his testimony, Henderson had disagreed when McKinney suggested robbing Shepard, but when they all left the bar, McKinney said drive, and he drove. McKinney said go past Wal-Mart, and he proceeded; stop the car, and he stopped; get the rope, and he got it; tie his hands, and he tied them. Henderson never hit Shepard, he said. "I told him [McKinney] to stop hitting him, that I think he's had enough." McKinney, in this account, then hit Henderson, who retreated into the truck. Finally, again McKinney said drive, and Henderson drove.

Henderson offered nothing more. How is it that Shepard left the bar with them? Why did they beat him? Why were they going to 7th Street—supposedly to rob Shepard's house—when he lived on 12th? Why did they fight with Morales and Herrera? When Henderson and Pasley and Price drove to Cheyenne to throw away the bloody clothes, why didn't they take McKinney and little Cameron with them and keep on going? Such questions have to wait for McKinney.

At the hearing Henderson looked like a man numb from combat as Cal Rerucha and Wyatt Skaggs—men whose names appear on court documents involving Henderson since childhood—went through the legal motions, as Judy Shepard told the court of Matthew's sweetness and ambition, of his mounting achievements, of the horror of his last days, and the depth of her loss; as Henderson's grandmother, Lucy Thompson, the woman who raised him, told of his own sweetness and disappointments, of his expectations for his GEDs, of the inexplicability of his actions and the breadth of her grief. When Russell told the Shepards, "There is not a moment that goes by that I don't see what happened that night," he spoke as one does of a bad dream half-remembered, hopeless to resurrect the rest. When Mrs. Shepard told him, "At times, I don't think you're worthy of an acknowledgement of your existence," he did not flinch. In a proceeding marked by sobs and tears suppressed, the only figure who flinched less was Mr. Shepard.

Henderson was transferred to the Wyoming State Penitentiary: The word around town, originating with a prison guard, was that the inmates had held an auction, or perhaps it was a lottery, for his services and those of McKinney. Prosecutor Rerucha says he expects the only time Henderson will leave the pen is as a corpse for burial. Only death would have been a harsher sentence. The tumbrels are rolling for McKinney.

It should be easier for the state to cast McKinney's trial as a contest between good and evil: to caricature Shepard as a child-saint, because to think of him as a man evokes a sexual experience no one wants to know; and to caricature McKinney as a devil-man, because to think of him as Laramie's, or anyone's, child sits harder on the conscience. In this respect, Henderson's was the more difficult case, because from the beginning he emerged as that stock character in the country's rerun violent drama—a quiet boy, kept to himself, "the most American kid you can get," in the words of his landlord.

Judy Shepard told Vanity Fair, "I believe there are people who have no souls," and others have told me they believe some people are just "born bad," but Russell Henderson was born like any child of a young mother in bad trouble—premature, sickly, poisoned by the alcohol in her blood. Cindy Dixon was nineteen when she had Russell, and, as Wyatt Skaggs remembers, "she was the sweetest, most considerate, loving person when she wasn't drinking; when she was drinking, she was abusive, obnoxious, every single adjective you could think of for an intoxicated person." On January 3, 1999, at forty, she was found dead in the snow about eight and a half miles from town. Early reports had her somehow losing her way after leaving the bars on foot, in light clothing, on a night so frigid and blustery that Elam Timothy and his boyfriend turned back while driving on the road where she'd be found. The death was later determined a homicide: Dixon was bruised, her underwear torn, there was evidence of semen; and now a Florida man, Dennis Menefee, is on trial for her murder. Somehow the fact that Russell lost a mother—and Mrs. Thompson, a daughter—through another murder, a sex crime, never counted for much in all the stories about Laramie.

"I don't like my place in this town," Henderson said to an old girlfriend, Shaundra Arcuby, not long before Shepard's murder. "Part of it," she said, "had to do with his mom and what people said about her. The thing about this town is that who you are is kind of set in stone. It's not that easy to remake yourself."

Shaundra fell in love with Russell when they both were in high school (he a sophomore, she a senior) and worked at Taco Bell. She was confused about an old boyfriend, who was bullying her to get back with him. "Do what makes you happy," Russell said. "That was the winning point with me," she recalled. "Someone's giving me an ultimatum and someone's telling me to be happy—there was no

INSIDE THE FIRESIDE BAR
Photograph by Chris Anderson/Aurora

question what I'd choose." They'd hang out, watch movies; he always came to the door, spoke to her mom. He made her tapes—Pearl Jam, The Violent Femmes. They went to her prom; friends thought they'd get married. Then she dumped him: "I was the first female in my family to graduate high school and not be pregnant," she said. "I just couldn't think of marriage. It scared me, so I ran away." Not long after, she'd get married, disastrously, and then divorce.

Most of the guys who knew McKinney in high school didn't know Henderson—"he was a little too good." He collected comic books and baseball cards, loved scouting, even beyond making Eagle Scout. He pumped gas, fiddled with an old Corvair. He played soccer—the "fag sport," as it's known. He had fantasies of being a doctor but was headed for Wyoming Technical Institute for mechanics until he was told, days before he was to celebrate high school graduation, that he wouldn't get a diploma because he'd missed a paper. He was prayerful in the Mormon tradition. About homosexuality, Lucy Thompson says, he believed "everyone has a right to their own free agency." Until he was fifteen he helped Lucy with the dialysis machine that kept his beloved grandfather alive, and watched as his life drained away. Bill Thompson never let on how he suffered. Neither did Russell. "He never ever talked about the hurt that was inside him," Lucy told me. "He'd say, 'That's okay, Grandma; don't worry, Grandma.' " She told the court, "When my husband and his grandfather passed away, so did a part of Russell."

Brent Jones remembers Henderson as "kind of an asshole," less of a troublemaker than McKinney but "his elevator didn't go to the top floor either." He had some juvie trouble. A judge once told Cindy Dixon she'd have to choose between Russell and her boyfriend. She was not in good shape that day and said, "Oh, that's easy," with an approving gesture toward the boyfriend.

It's said that over the past forty years Lucy Thompson has raised half the kids in Laramie. She is a woman of profound serenity. Russell was in his grandparents' care from his birth to the age of five, when they thought he should be in the nuclear family. Cindy was married then, with two little girls. Three and a half years later the Thompsons again got custody. In the intervening period, Russell took a physical and emotional battering from his mother's partners. Years of police reports follow Cindy's own familiarity with violence. Once Russell told his grandparents about a harrowing beating he had watched his mother endure. Why didn't he call them? "When that happens, I just freeze, and when I do something about it, I just get retaliation," Lucy remembers him saying.

The standard description of Henderson is that "he was a follower." At work, though, he was the leader, says Joe Lemus of Laramie Valley Roofing. Both boys are nice, friendly people. Sure, they'd talk *fag, wuss, sissy*, Lemus says. "In grade school, you call people *fat, stupid*. When you get older, this is just what you say; it's like calling someone a *retard*." Everybody does it, even college kids (one of whom scratched KILL THEM under the title of the UW library's copy of *How to Make the World a Better Place for Gays and Lesbians*), even the straight-boy cub reporter at *The Boomerang* who helped cover the case before becoming an intern at *Rolling Stone*. According to police accounts, when McKinney and Henderson came upon Morales and Herrera, it was Henderson who called them "fucking bitches." "Why the fuck are you calling us bitches?" Morales answered, and McKinney hit him from behind. Police Commander David O'Malley testified that in questioning Henderson about the fight, Officer Flint Waters said if police found someone with a bullet they'd have more to talk to him about: "Mr. Henderson laughed and said, 'I guarantee that you wouldn't find anybody with a bullet in them.' "

Lemus says that in the period leading up to the murder Henderson was downhearted; Chasity had cheated on him. McKinney was excited; he'd just bought a gun. They were working between eight and eleven hours a day. Henderson had recently turned twenty-one and was eager to go to a bar. It was new for him, though I'm told he was not a stranger to drink and had his own sources for crank as well. When he was younger, a doctor had told him that because of the circumstances of his birth, alcohol (and presumably drugs) could affect him very badly. His grandfather asked Russell if he understood what that meant. "Deeper than you think," he answered, gesturing to his mother's photograph.

> *"Certain things make sense only if you're out of your mind," a knowing woman told me. "On meth, you would know what you were doing, but in that moment it doesn't matter. We used to have the rankest, most foul sex when we were on dope. Men don't get erections too well on speed, so already that's bad, but then there's the two-hour blow job, because when you start something, you just have to finish, only you can't finish because he won't get an erection and he won't have an orgasm, and you'd really like to stop, but you just can't."*

Maybe Wyatt Skaggs is right when he says "drugs were not involved in this case," or maybe he's just being lawyerly. Rumors abound about what set that night in motion—love triangles, revenge, a mob-style debt collection. Reality is usually less baroque. Matthew Shepard smoked pot and had at least tried methamphetamine; McKinney dealt drugs and used them with Henderson; they all had a mutual acquaintance who regularly carries a police scanner, whose feigned ignorance about drugs could be matched only by an extraterrestrial, and whom every drug user I met recognizes as a link in the trade. Those things are not rumors but maybe just coincidence. And maybe Skaggs is more right when he adds, "That's not to say [meth] couldn't have been used sometime before; you don't need to take it that night to feel the effects." McKinney and Henderson never were tested for drugs, but then police say that one of the beauties of meth for the user is that there's no sure test for it.

History is one long quest for relief through chemicals, more powerful substitutes for endorphins, released when you cry so hard you run out of tears. But it is difficult to imagine a more unappetizing recipe for relief than methamphetamine. It is made from ephedrine or pseudoephedrine, extracted from over-the-counter cold and asthma medicines, then cooked up with any of a variety of agents—lye, battery acid, iodine, lantern fuel, antifreeze. A former user says it tastes like fake crab "sea legs" marinated in cat piss, but its medicinal benefits, especially for its large constituency of construction workers, is that "nothing hurts anymore; you're wide awake; you seem to accomplish what you set out to accomplish. Only later do you understand that you've been up for two days"—and that, depending on how much you smoke or snort or shoot, euphoria morphs into hallucination, which morphs into paranoia, which morphs into God knows what.

According to the state's Methamphetamine Initiative, Wyoming's eighth-graders use meth at a higher rate than twelfth-graders nationwide, and among juvenile offenders in its correctional institutions in 1997 at least 50 percent had a history of meth use. Albany County is not one of the state's top three target zones, but drug sources in Laramie volunteer that meth is everywhere. Maybe McKinney is lying and maybe he's not when he says Shepard "mouthed off," prompting him to the fatal frenzy of violence, but one crank-head told me that he once almost wasted someone just for saying hi—"You're so paranoid, you think, 'Why is he saying hi?' Does he know something? Is he a cop?'" And maybe all the meth users I met were lying or wrong or putting me on in saying they immediately took the murder for a meth crime because it was all too stupid and, except for one heinous detail, all too recognizable.

None of this is a defense for what happened, but it all complicates the singular picture of hate crime. Why did they kill him? "That was the meth talking," I was told. But why did they pick on him to begin with? "Because he was a fag." So why do you think they didn't kill him because he was gay? "They were regular guys, and then they beat up the Mexicans." And, anyway, "what kind of a man beats the shit out of a wussy guy?"

Ask around for impressions of Matthew Shepard and you find as many characters as there are speakers: a charming boy, always smiling and happy; a suicidal depressive who mixed street drugs and alcohol with Effexor and Klonopin; a good listener who treated everyone with respect; "a pompous, arrogant little dick" who condescended to those who served him; a bright kid who wanted to change the world; a kid you'd swear was mentally defective; a generous person; a flasher of

EMILIANO MORALES
Photograph by Ed Andrieski/
AP/World Wide Photos

money; a good tipper; a lousy tipper; a sexual seeker; a naif; a man freaked by his HIV status or at peace with it; a "counterphobic" who courted risk rather than live in fear; a boy who, his father said, "liked to compete against himself," entering races he couldn't win and swimming contests he'd finish "dead last by the length of the pool" just to prove he could do it; a boy never quite sure of his father's approval; a gay man; a faggot; a human being. Any one of those Matthew Shepards could have been set up for death; the only constant is that he'd still be dead, and McKinney and Henderson would still be responsible. Gay men are killed horribly everywhere in this country, more than thirty just since Shepard—one of them, in Richmond, Virginia, beheaded. Gay and straight, male and female, some 40,000 individuals have been murdered since Shepard; the only constant is that they are dead, and that most of their killers are straight and most of them are men.

Among those who advocate hate-crime laws, it's always the sexuality of the victim that's front and center, not the sexuality of the criminal or the everyday, undifferentiated violence he took to extremity. Among the tolerance peddlers, it's always the "lifestyle" of the gay guy, never the "lifestyle" of the straight guy or the culture of compulsory heterosexuality. Even among those who argue that the victim's sexuality is irrelevant—that Shepard died just because a robbery went bad or just because McKinney and Henderson were crazy on crank—the suggestion is that the crime is somehow less awful once homophobia is removed, and what is brewing inside the boys bears less attention. "The news has already taken this up and blew it totally out of proportion because it involved a homosexual," McKinney's father told the press. Eighteen blows with a .357 magnum—murder happens.

A few years ago during an exercise at Laramie High School, students were asked to list the five best things about being a boy or a girl. The boys' list noted no breasts, no period, no pregnancy, and one other scourge of femininity that the guidance counselor who told me this story had been too stunned to remember. I was at the school, flipping through yearbooks, noticing that the class of '96, Henderson's class, had identified its number two "pet peeve" as "skinny wimps who complain about jocks." The previous day, Dylan Klebold and Eric Harris had killed their classmates in Littleton, Colorado, 140 miles away. Through that crime ran a thread from every high-profile school shooting over the past two years. Springfield, Pearl, Paducah, Jonesboro, Conyers—every one of those boy murderers or would-be murderers had been taunted as a wuss, a fag, a loser, or had been rejected by a girl, or was lonely and withdrawn, or had written harrowing stories of mayhem and slaying. Two of them had killed their pets. All of it, like the meanness of the jocks some of them despised, was regarded as just boy play—Oh, Fluffy's in the trash can? Boys will be boys. And by the logic of the culture, it was just boy play, like McKinney's brawling, like Henderson's admonition out by the fence, "I think he's had enough." Only when it turned to murder did it register, and for that there's punishment, prison, the death penalty, more violence.

For any of these boys—for any boy, for that matter—what does it take to pass as a man? At Henderson's hearing, Judy Shepard memorialized the number of languages Matthew spoke, the friends he'd had and books he'd read, the countries he'd traveled, the promise life held. As she spoke the courtroom heaved with her agony. But in the story writ large, it's almost as if Matthew's death counted for more than it might have if he had been just

THE FENCE
Photograph by Reuters / Gary Caskey / Archive Photos

a wuss, a fag, her son; if he had been found in a ramble, with his pants down, with a trick (as have so many murdered gay men, whose cases have never been exploited by presidents to win points or by big, polite gay groups to raise dollars); if he had been killed simply because he was tiny and weak; if anything about the murder or its aftermath had forced a consideration of sex and freedom, instead of only tolerance and hate.

Since Shepard's death, the talk is all of hate-crime laws. But as Rita Addessa of the Lesbian and Gay Task Force in Philadelphia, who nevertheless supports such laws, admits, they "will have no impact whatsoever on addressing the causes of anti-gay violence." They matter only to the dead or the maimed, for even if Wyoming were to become the twenty-third state with a hate-crime law including anti-gay violence, and even if a federal law were to pass, the little Matt and Matty Shepards of America would still grow up learning their place, because for them in all but eleven states discrimination is legal, and everywhere equality under the law is a myth. It's said that hate-crime laws symbolize a society's values. If that is true, it means gay people are recognized only in suffering, and straight people are off the hook. It means Shepard may stand for every homosexual, but McKinney and Henderson stand just for themselves. It means nothing for life and, because its only practical function is to stiffen penalties, everything for death.

In her interview with Vanity Fair, Judy Shepard said she thought that her son would probably approve of the death penalty if he could know this case, if it had been his friend and not himself beaten at the fence. And in her conclusion at the hearing, she told Henderson, "My hopes for you are simple. I hope you never experience a day or night without feeling the terror, the humiliation, the helplessness, the hopelessness my son felt that night." Not just that night. As a gay man in America, Shepard must have sensed all of those things just around the corner, and not just in violence, not just in blood. Looking back on Henderson's biography, and on McKinney's, I wonder if, in different measure, they aren't already too well acquainted with such things; if perhaps the injuries of terror and humiliation aren't already too well spread around in this season of punishment and revenge.

"If a guy at a bar made some kind of overture to you, what would you do?"

"It depends on who's around. If I'm with a girl, I'd be worried about what she thinks, because, as I said, everything a man does is in some

way connected to a woman, whether he wants to admit it or not. Do I look queer? Will she tell other girls?

"*If my friends were around and they'd laugh and shit, I might have to threaten him.*

"*If I'm alone and he just wants to buy me a beer, then okay, I'm straight, you're gay—hey, you can buy me a beer.*" ■